# VILLAGES OF BRITAIN

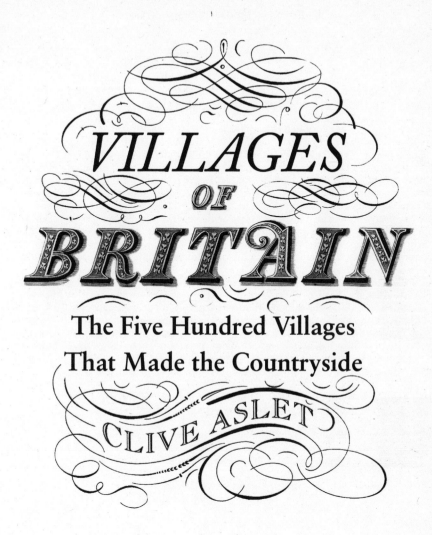

# VILLAGES OF BRITAIN

## The Five Hundred Villages
## That Made the Countryside

### CLIVE ASLET

BLOOMSBURY

LONDON · BERLIN · NEW YORK · SYDNEY

To Peter and Linda, Graham and Jean

First published in 2010

Plate section 1: p.1 © Sonia Halliday and Laura Lushington; p.2 © RIBA Library Drawings
Collection; p.3 (top) © Royal National Lifeboat Institution (RNLI); p.3 (bottom) © Corbis;
p.4 (top) © Clive Aslet; p.4 (bottom) © Mary Evans; p.5 (top) © Country Living Picture
Library; p.5 (bottom) © Corbis; p.6 © The Art Archive; p.7 (top) © Mary Evans; p.7 (bottom)
© Peter Nahum At The Leicester Galleries, London; p.8 (top) © Mary Evans; p.8 (bottom)
© Mary Evans; p.9 © Kobal Collection/Art Archive; p.10 © Mary Evans; p.11 (top) © British
Library; p.11 (bottom) © Alamy; p.12 © Alamy; p.13 (top) © Art Archive; p.13 (bottom) © Art
Archive; p.14 (top) © Clive Aslet; p.14 (bottom) © Bridgeman; p.15 (top) © Clive Aslet; p.15
(bottom) © Morley von Sternberg/RIBA Library Photographs Collection; p.16 © Mary Evans

Plate section 2: p.1 (top) © Art Archive; p.1 (bottom) © Art Archive; p.2 (top) ©
Clive Aslet; p.2 (bottom) © Bridgeman; p.3 © Paul Barker; p.4 (top) © V&A Images,
Victoria and Albert Museum; p.4 (bottom) © Alamy; p.5 © Alamy; p.6 (top) © Mary
Evans; p.6 (bottom) © Simon Ledingham www.visitcumbria.com; p.7 (top) © Alamy;
p.7 (bottom) © Ford & Etal Estates; p.8 © Paul Barker; p.9 (top) © Mary Evans; p.9
(bottom) © Mary Evans; p.10 (top) © Alamy; p.10 (bottom) © Alamy; p.11 © Alamy;
p.12 (top) © Alamy; p.12 (bottom) © Alamy; p.13 © Art Archive; p.14 (top) © Mary
Evans; pp.14–5 (bottom) © Corbis; p.15 (top) © Bridgeman; p.16 © Alamy

Bloomsbury Publishing Plc, 36 Soho Square, London W1D 3QY
Bloomsbury USA, 175 Fifth Avenue, New York, NY 10010

Bloomsbury Publishing, London, New York and Berlin

A CIP catalogue record for this book is available from the British Library

ISBN 978 0 7475 8872 6 (UK edition)
ISBN 978 1 60819 344 8 (US edition)

10 9 8 7 6 5 4 3 2 1

Illustrations by Jerry Hoare
Maps by Reginald Piggott
Design by Peter Dawson / Grade Design Consultants www.gradedesign.com
Typeset by Hewer Text UK Ltd, Edinburgh
Index by Sue Dugen

Printed in Great Britain by Clays Limited, St Ives plc

www.bloomsbury.com/cliveaslet
www.bloomsburyusa.com

# CONTENTS

# INTRODUCTION

This is a book about villages and their history: how they came into being, what shaped their development, who inhabited them. The story of the village is that of the countryside itself. I have chosen five hundred villages, each either remarkable in its own right or an example of a type. Each puts a single aspect of rural Britain under the spotlight: a country poet, a way of building, an agricultural innovation, a horrible death, a rare survival, a monument to an exceptional person or event. Pursuing the stories of these villages, and of the rocks and rivers and roads and railways that gave them shape, has taken me all around Great Britain, travelling not only from one end of the country to the other, but from the earliest times to the present.

'To the man or woman who is desirous of finding the best in this country I commend the English village,' the poet Edmund Blunden wrote shortly after the Second World War. I share his view, extending it to encompass the villages of Wales and Scotland, too. But the village Blunden knew was a different place from the village we know today – with its four-by-fours and satellite television, its prosperity and kerbstones – and far, far removed from the flyblown middens and polluted watercourses of the medieval village, many of whose inhabitants, short of stature, old by thirty, were often misshapen by disease.

There has been a tendency, particularly at times of national stress, to see villages as part of the old and immutable order of the countryside, a root going deep into the British soul: this was the case after the First World War, when some thinkers wanted to knit the damaged fabric of the world together by reconnecting with pre-industrial traditions. But the truth is that villages have always changed. They form, they grow, they morph, they shrink, they grow again. Sometimes they disappear, the only evidence of their existence being some overgrown foundations in a copse or bumps in a field, intelligible only to archaeologists. Some have been washed into the sea.

Many English villages began as dormitories. They put roofs over the heads of the families who toiled on the lord's fields and kept his sheep, managed his woods or dug his mines. It is rare to find the foundation of an old village documented. Few were formally planned, unless the lord had the ambition of founding a town. Some began life as a few huts in an unnoticed corner of a forest, whose squatter inhabitants managed to evade the eye of the authorities. These dwellings would have been insubstantial, but then so were most village houses in the Middle Ages: poorly built cabins with smoke from the central hearth escaping through the cracks, whose illiterate occupants probably spent as many daylight hours as they could outside.

Since these shacks were often rebuilt on the same sites, it is difficult for archaeologists to form a picture of how villages developed. Those that coalesced around a central core – often a green or a church – probably did so in response to farming practices. In the Dark Ages, the land was worked by farmers occupying scattered farmsteads. Then, in the tenth century, it would seem that the open field system began to develop. Areas of land were divided up among different families, each of whom cultivated a number of strips – some flat and fertile, some poor and hilly – while their animals grazed on difficult ground that was left as permanent pasture.

This kind of agriculture required a high degree of cooperation, with people ploughing and harvesting the same crops at the same time. The easiest thing was for farmers, smallholders and cottars (landless labourers) to live together in a village, trudging out from their vermin-infested dwellings, past vegetable patches, pigsties and orchards, to the patches of land on which they toiled. The spread of the open field system was accelerated by the Norman regime change, locking England into a feudal hierarchy, under which peasants were compelled to work the fields owned by the lord of the manor as well as their own.

Villages served different industries. On the coast, people fished; in other places – often remote and lonely moorland – they mined lead. Weaving at handlooms was a cottage occupation before the development of water-powered looms at the end of the eighteenth century. One of the few villages whose origins are documented – Bainbridge, in Wensleydale (see page 409) – was founded to house a dozen foresters. Iron-founding kept Sussex villages such as Burwash (see page 100) busy until the timber to make charcoal ran out and the industry moved North to mine iron ore and coal. They built boats on the river Wye (see Llandogo, page 488) and quarried stone at Collyweston in Northamptonshire (see page 312). Bedfordshire women made lace and straw hats (see Turvey, page 201). Coaching inns, such a spectacle in the age of Pickwick, came and went, as did canals. At Lambourn in Berkshire (see page 187), the training of thoroughbred racehorses still flourishes today.

Change took myriad forms. Medieval Caxton in Cambridgeshire (see page 221) moved to a new site to take advantage of the road that supplied passing trade. Landowners swept away villages that clustered at the skirts of their mansions and rebuilt them beyond the park gates. Or they won the lottery of life when their villages became absorbed into conurbations and land values went through the roof.

In short, villages did many things, but before 1800 most of them – like most of England itself – farmed. Until farming became mechanised after the Second World War, nearly all the inhabitants of a typical village derived their livelihoods from the land. If they did not themselves plough or herd animals or fell trees, they sold farm implements or shod horses, or made the farmer's corduroy trousers, or dealt in his grain. The coins that chinked into the tills of the shops, for bacon, boot polish and besoms, came from the pockets of farmers and farm labourers, or more likely the purses of their wives.

Only since 1950 has there taken place the total reversal by which farming now employs hardly anybody. The great village industries of today are tourism and retirement, with much of the village population commuting to jobs elsewhere. Villages that might have supported a dozen shops in the early twentieth century now have none; people drive to supermarkets to stock up on food and other goods. Dozens of pubs close every week. Those that survive are often of the gastro variety, beyond the pocket of ordinary locals. The village has once more transformed itself. That is nothing new.

Scotland and Wales have different traditions of rural settlement. Old villages in Scotland tend to be failed burghs, such as Rosemarkie in the Black Isle, north of Inverness (see page 621). Scotland barely had villages as they would be recognised in England before Lowland agriculture was 'improved' in the eighteenth century by enclosing commons, drilling seeds, planting turnips and attracting better tenants. Then landowners, such as John Cockburn of Ormiston, Lothian (see page 615), the Duke of Buccleuch at Newcastleton in the Borders (see page 610) and Sir Archibald Grant of Monymusk in Aberdeenshire (see page 608), saw the benefit of building villages, neatly ordered and calculated to increase industry and rents.

There were no villages at all in the Highlands until the Hanoverian government built roads to open them to the rest of Britain after the Jacobite rebellions. The traditional grouping was the clachan or fermtoun, where three or four families shared the tenancy of a farm; Auchindrain on the Duke of Argyll's estate, where the old way of life persisted into the 1960s, has been preserved as a museum (see page 530). Only the most meagre of livings could be eked from the Highlands. An early attempt to improve the economy was made by the British Fisheries Society, which built harbours such as Tobermory on Mull (see page 631).

The notorious Clearances drove Highland families out of their homes so that the land they occupied could be put down to sheep. The dispossessed might be set up – on inferior land – with crofts, which created dispersed settlements with no obvious centre; each house occupied its own smallholding, and the kirk may have stood on its own, away from habitation, in a place where families from all around could converge. Attempts were also made to encourage some Highlanders to take up a different life, in fishing villages such as Helmsdale in Sutherland (see page 586), albeit the landowners counted without the resistance of the people being resettled, who often would have preferred to stick with the ways they had known.

Much of Wales, a land of mountains and waterfalls, was as impenetrable as Scotland until Thomas Telford opened the road to Anglesey in the nineteenth century. The Romans reached Caerwent, in fertile Monmouthshire (see page 465), but penetrated Carmarthenshire only when gold from the mines at Pumpsaint (see page 503) was in prospect. The castles built or repaired by Edward I form an arc around Snowdonia.

Like Cornwall, Wales celebrated local saints and preserved ancient superstitions, before being shaken into a century of chapel building by the Great Awakening of the Methodist preachers. For once, John Wesley's powers of oratory failed to move, for the simple reason that English was a difficult language for many Welsh speakers; they trembled instead to the brimstone sermons of Daniel Rowland of Llangeitho in Ceredigion (see page 491), delivered in their native tongue.

The Calvinistic spirit entered the Welsh bloodstream and stayed there, Dylan Thomas evoking the 'Thou Shalt Not' texts on the walls in his fictional Llareggub (based on New Quay in Ceredigion, see page 500) in *Under Milk Wood*; to an outsider it seems to find a visual equivalent in the pinched terraces of the mining villages that are striated along the hillsides around Rhondda and Cwmbran, choral and close-knit. In the twentieth century, Wales's inaccessible centre may have drunk at pubs called the Drovers' Arms, remembering the cattle that would be iron-shod and driven, hundreds at a time, towards English markets (see Tregaron, page 509); but young people, wanting more excitement and money than was to be had from sheep farming on the hills, drifted away. Then the very quietness caught the eye of the Good Life generation, wanting to pursue its alternative lifestyles in privacy. Villages that had been at their last gasp inhaled deeply – in some cases, not only air.

If one of the graves in a country churchyard broke open and a Victorian villager, anywhere in Britain, rose from the dead, he would be struck by the affluence of the settlement he once knew. Cottages look much more robust, being properly maintained; no more damp or leaks. Piped water probably came in the decades before and after the Second World War, and there is now electric light. Gardens are full of flowers, not vegetables grown to feed the family.

Our ghost would find the village economy incomprehensible. In the south of England he would be unlikely to meet a farmer as he walked round a village. If his haunting took place during working hours, he might not find anyone at all. It comes as a shock to drive into Laxton in Nottinghamshire (see page 333), where, by a quirk of history, the open field system is still practised. There are fourteen working farms in the village. Only one 'stackyard', as farmyards are called there, has undergone conversion to a holiday let. Laxton is now unique. But as recently as the 1950s, every country village would have been full of farmers and farm machinery, carts and animals, bales and byres. Farmers were likely to run the village, too. Like the squire, the vicar and the policeman, who have also vanished as full-time presences, they served as figures of authority, who, going about, discouraged misbehaviour.

These days, most villages are empty during the day. If people work, they usually drive somewhere else to do so. In pretty villages, the rest of the population is retired, and house owners may only appear during weekends and school holidays. Villages used to work for their livings; now they are often in the position of courtesans, kept for their looks by people who turn to them for comfort and recreation. Thank leisure, thank retirement, thank the motor car – all unknown in earlier periods of village history.

If we are apt nowadays to picture villages in a time warp of upright bicycles and runner-bean poles, that is because their apparent cosiness forms a contrast to the grit of the inner city or the tedium of the commuter train. In a world of ugliness, villages are pretty to look at and interesting to explore. Here stands a medieval bridge with children shrimping underneath it, there a green, and, look, that building with benches outside it is, happily, a pub.

We cling to the idea that places are 'villagey' long after they have been absorbed into conurbations. Gatwick Airport contains a shopping village, however deep the ancient village of Gatwick, where John de Gatewyk held a manor in the thirteenth century and Victorian punters went racing, lies beneath the tarmac. London is often said to be a city of villages, creating the paradox of greens that are really greys, made up of paving stones and road surface without a blade of grass to be seen. True villages are small enough for neighbours to know one another, but large enough for the human resource to be fairly mixed, providing enough talent to run the pantomime or summer fete, the fire brigade that does not put out fires (as in Geddington, Northamptonshire, see page 324) or the guild that preserves a parlour bar (Leintwardine in Herefordshire, see page 334); it can be a creative dynamic.

But as anyone who has ever lived in a village knows, the reality does not always coincide with the image. Do not occupy a village house if you want privacy. From the moment you go outside your door, your life is conducted in public, nothing escaping scrutiny or comment. People who are used to city life might not notice whatever exuberance attends closing time at the pub. But newcomers can be distressed to find that villages may not be the havens of quiet they expect. Tractors rumble through them, trailers rattling; grain driers drone their way through damp harvests. The winter mist throbs to the sound of rotor blades as the Chinooks on a nearby RAF station are de-iced. As there is a time in life for gardening, so there is one for motorbikes and heavy metal. Different generations do not always see eye to eye.

On the whole, the village is a much more comfortable, better tempered and longer-lived place than it was when Richard Gough wrote the history of his Shropshire home, Myddle, around 1700 (see page 341). It is not perfect. Even paradise has snakes. But one of the wonders of villages is how generations of often anonymous people have worked, incrementally, to make them more convenient to live in, and more harmonious to the eye. Their labours have made my village odyssey a delight.

What is a village? It used to be a rural settlement capable of supporting daily life, material (shops, pub), spiritual (church) and hierarchical (policeman, squire); hamlets could not do this, being mere outliers or dependencies of other places. Now, however, there are countless villages that have no services at all, except those held in church once a fortnight by a vicar who shares the parish with eight others.

Size of population is surely a factor in the village persona, yet this is far from straightforward. A settlement of two thousand souls might seem like a town north of York, but it would, unquestionably, be a village in the Home Counties. It is easier to define a town than a village; towns have civic buildings and banks, fire stations and polyclinics, as well as a certain architectural presence. These qualities are important.

I have considered some villages with populations of several thousand to remain villages, albeit ones that may look like adolescents who have outgrown their clothes, because they lack the characteristics of a town.

Throughout the medieval, Tudor and Stuart periods, a would-be town needed a royal charter to allow it to hold a market. It was more valuable to the lord of the manor to have a bustling town on his land than a sleepy village. Ambitious lords would therefore acquire charters and found towns, in the hope that enterprising tenants would rent shops, market stalls and workshops. But they did not always take off. Some towns flourished for a period, then relapsed into village obscurity.

Lydford in Devon (see page 54) was an important place in the Saxon period: it had its own mint and two castles, one of which served as a prison into the seventeenth century. Such glories have long been forgotten, and little stirs there now. Fordwich in Kent (see page 115) had the right to put condemned criminals to death, by a specially grim means; it still has the town hall in which juries sat. But the river Stour, on which it depended, silted up, and it is now nothing more than a village. There are numerous other examples. Only a pedant would pretend that they are towns.

So, I have taken a broad idea of the village. My rule has been to include settlements that see themselves as villages; that is to say, where at least some of the people who live in them, or use them, will instinctively refer to them as a village rather than a town. I have not made a distinction between villages and hamlets, since that has become artificial. I do not pretend to infallibility. There will always be people who disagree, particularly in a land that rejoices in the quirks that result from a long history. Let them.

Two general themes have struck me during the writing of this book. First is the deep-grained conservatism of the countryside. Just as modern field boundaries may follow the lines of those established during the Iron Age, so it is not unusual for villages to be established in places with which humans have been associated for thousands of years. This does not imply absolute continuity: the Saxons who came and crouched amid the standing stones at Avebury in Wiltshire (see page 8) did not take over a pre-existing settlement – nobody had lived there for years. But when the Roman Empire collapsed, the Saxons and the people who came after them may well have taken over the same land divisions as those associated with Roman villas. They conformed to natural features and may have been marked by structures such as stone walls and ditches that would have been laborious to move. Perhaps they survive as parish boundaries today.

It would not be the only example of continuity. Even after successive farming revolutions, Honeychurch in Devon (see page 48) contains the same farms as those inspected by the clerks of the Domesday Book. While, throughout history, villages have formed to fulfil specific functions, and then decayed when those functions have ceased to exist, the pattern of settlement was often set long ago.

The second theme is the narrowness of village life before the motor car. Until the Second World War, most village people trudged through a weary existence, as cramped in its intellectual confines as in its geographical ones. They were often grindingly poor, destitution sometimes being treated with inhuman cruelty. Television adaptations of rural classics do not convey the misery of it: twenty-first-century actors have grown up well fed and healthy, unlike the country folk of William Cobbett's or Flora Thompson's day, many of them bent, their plodding gait formed by years of following the plough as children, each foot being lifted with difficulty from the clay. Coming home after twelve hours in the fields, men would have to go out again to tend the vegetable patch that provided much of their diet. They might have walked amid the abundance of a well-farmed countryside, but they rarely ate meat. Those who could leave often did so, and the gene pool diminished. In terms of health and prosperity, the twenty-first-century village is far superior to that of previous ages.

But the affluence of the modern age has also been accompanied by loss. Gone is the sense of rootedness and belonging that were the inheritance of men and women who rarely went more than a bicycle ride's distance from where they lived. Let us not sentimentalise. I remember exploring the Fens from 1970s Cambridge. They were notorious for the number of people who had never travelled beyond a bicycle ride's journey from their home, not to mention the rates of incest that were the corollary of such limitations. Nobody would want a return to that era. But communities are built on settled lives. When people are forever on the move, or rarely present, they have no shared history with their neighbours. They do not know where they are.

Which leads me to a prime reason for writing this book now: the village is at a cusp. Ever greater mobility was one of the outstanding features of the twentieth century, but it seems likely that the twenty-first will put limits on how much we move around. If the fossil fuels do not run out, they will become too expensive to use as liberally as we have been doing. Will they be replaced by alternative forms of energy? Possibly. But perhaps by the time electric cars and hydrogen fuel-cell technology become widely available, a different pattern of existence will have established itself. Broadband could enable many more people to work from wherever they choose to live. That place could be a village.

In 1770, Oliver Goldsmith wrote a poem called *The Deserted Village*. Perhaps we can look forward to the Repopulated Village, busy with people during the daytime, employed in well-paid, outward-looking jobs. It is noticeable that villages increasingly take communal action to save shops and pubs from closing or to provide services, such as fibre-optic cable. Is it possible to dream of a renaissance of village life that would come from residents working in or near the place where they live? If so, the community might not need to rally round to protect services, because enough people would use the shop for it to stay open by itself. Rather than being a stage set, empty until the return of commuters in the evening makes the curtain rise, the village would acquire that essential extra dimension: life.

# SOUTH-WEST ENGLAND

CORNWALL, DEVON, Somerset, Dorset, Wiltshire – each of these counties has its own identity, the buildings that stand on the surface of the land taking their character from the rocks that lie underneath. Two hundred and fifty million years ago, molten granite burst from the innards of the earth and gave Cornwall its backbone. Granite and slate, formed when mud from the sea floor was compressed and heated, make the Cornish village what it is: unyielding in the face of the elements, its homes as hard, externally, as the lives of the fishermen who lived in them.

Add some pots of geraniums and striped awnings and, behold, these tough little places, burrowed into the sides of their coves, become as pretty as Portscatho in regatta week (see page 63). Inland Cornwall never had this makeover, for the earth had also brought forth minerals, which have been mined and traded since ancient times. Holy springs – another gift of the earth – attracted saints.

In Devon, the only county to have two separate coastlines, Neolithic farmers cut down the trees that grew on Dartmoor around 4000BC (no mean feat using stone axes; they may have chopped through the surface root and then pulled the trees over using ropes of honeysuckle vine). They have been grazed by animals ever since, creating a uniquely British landscape, almost crowded with prehistoric remains. Devon villages are thatched, or were so originally. If stone could not be found, the walls of old houses were built of cob (see Down St Mary, page 32), a mixture of clay and straw and twigs and horse dung, surprisingly durable as long as water is kept off it.

Somerset has luxuriant pastures and the watery Levels, rugged hills and rounded hills, hills that stand alone and hills in ranges. There are beaches, too, along the Bristol Channel, and the wilds of Exmoor. So much variety makes it a picture of England in miniature, intimate and often changing, its villages pegged to their combes by the square towers of their churches.

In Dorset, we find limestone being ushered into England. It provides Britain's finest building stone, outcrops arcing up through Bath and the Cotswolds to the limestone pavements of Yorkshire. Thomas Hardy created a landscape of the imagination in his Wessex novels; the romance of history still rests on old manor houses, such as Hammoon (see page 41), and the curfew bell still sounds in Stoke Abbott (see page 75).

Wiltshire is the odd one out: open, and crossed by the great chalk escarpment that continues into the Chilterns and Norfolk. Chalk makes the clear streams in which watercress thrives, as well as trout. Flints occur in chalk, and Wiltshire builders sometimes used them to make squares on their facades, alternating with stone. The poet George Herbert lived in a flint-walled rectory at Bemerton (see page 12). Flints meant something different to the great archaeologist General Augustus Pitt-Rivers: he studied the prehistoric landscape of Cranborne Chase, creating a museum at Farnham in Dorset (see page 36), whose memory lives on in the name of the inn.

*Bristol*

Georgeham

EXMOOR

Barnstaple

Bideford

D E V

Clovelly

Morwenstow

Down St Mary

Honeychurch

Sampford
Courtenay

Okehampton

South
Tawton

Lydford

River Tamar

DARTMOOR

Launceston

Delabole

Altarnun

Blisland

Bodmin

C O R N W A L L

Plymouth

Modbury

Noss Mayo

Creed

St Agnes

Zennor

St Erth

Godolphin Cross

Portscatho

Penzance

St Michael's Mount

Falmouth

Mousehole

Helford

*E n g l i s h*

Lizard

| 0 | 10 | 20 | 30 miles |

| 0 | 10 | 20 | 30 | 40 | 50 km |

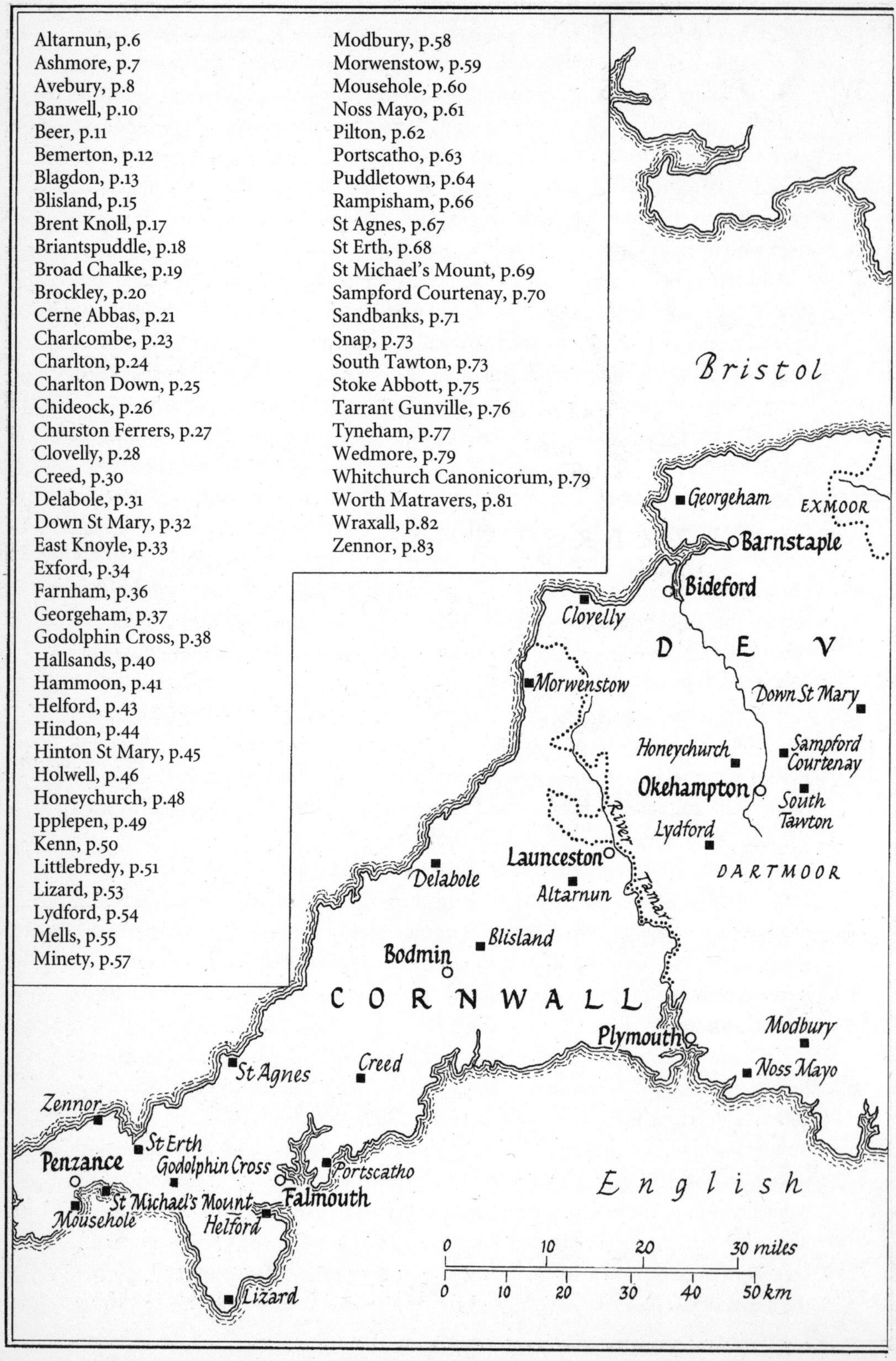

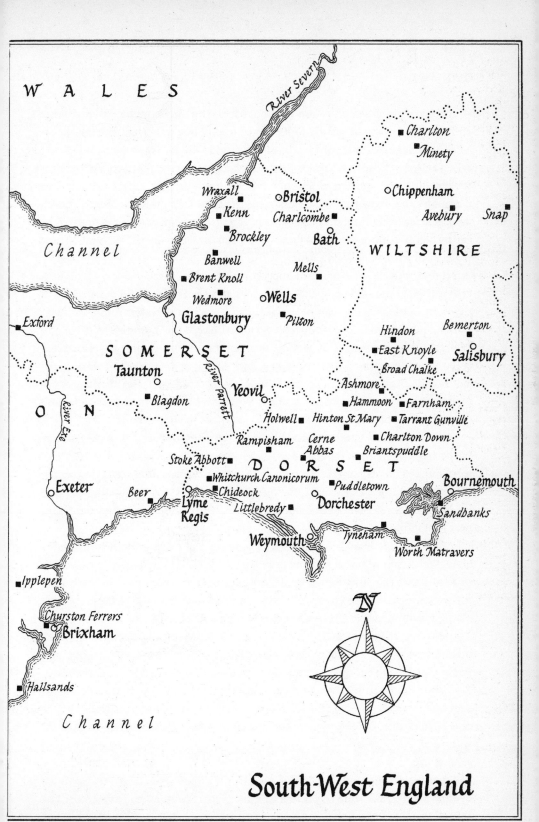

South-West England

# ALTARNUN
## CORNWALL

*Lady Nonna's miracle cure*

Witches can turn themselves into deer and hares. You might not have thought that either disguise was particularly well adapted to building work; nevertheless, it was a deer and a hare that, according to legend, carried the stones of the church being raised at West Carne to Altarnun. Night after night it happened, until the builders took the hint and transferred the church to Altarnun instead. This is a version of a common story, in which the Devil's agents frustrate the attempt to build a church at a particular site. Often that site has a pagan history, expressed by a stone circle, earthwork, barrow or fogou (an underground structure found in Cornwall). There was indeed a fogou at West Carne.

Yet Altarnun also had ancient associations. Near the church is a holy well. There are wells and springs with special properties all over England and particularly in the West Country. Some had prophetic qualities: a glut of water from a spring at Boughton in Northamptonshire foretold doom, as did the drying up of St Helen's Well at Rushton Spencer in Staffordshire. Several wells, when properly asked, could reveal the identity of a future husband. At North Kelsey in Lincolnshire the girl would approach the spring backwards, walk round it backwards three times then gaze into its depths to see his face. Whichever partner in a marriage drank first at the well of St Keyne in Cornwall would have the upper hand.

St Non's well at Altarnun was, like many others, supposed to have curative properties. Mad people could be made sane if they were hit on the chest and then dunked in its waters, a process known as 'bowssening'. Afterwards the sufferer would be carried into the church for prayers. No doubt the well was regarded as sacred before the coming of Christianity. Other churches were built next to standing stones.

St Non or Lady Nonna is supposed to have been St David's mother, an aristocratic Welsh nun who was seduced or raped by a Welsh prince and then gave birth to a baby that was surrounded by dazzling light. There is another St Non's well, with a statue and ruined chapel, at Caerfai in Pembrokeshire, where the event took place. It is thought that she herself came to Cornwall from Wales around 527.

The Celtic church lacked the hierarchical structure of the Church of Rome; missionaries were men or women who had attended centres of learning, and rather than being sent by the Pope, like St Augustine, operated off their own bats. They would walk from place to place, preaching and baptising in the open air at sites that were marked by a cross, lollipop-shaped and carved from the adamantine local granite, perhaps with a box of relics on top. They often chose to meld with local tradition by choosing places, such as Altarnun, that already received veneration.

Often the cross would become the centre of a monastic enclosure, occupied by holy people of austere life, living in huts. Churches emerged from these. The cross at Altarnun may date from the sixth century, conceivably St Non's time. In the fifteenth century, stones were taken from Bodmin Moor to build the present church. The tower reaches thirty-three metres. Inside, a remarkable series of bench ends was carved, according to inscription, by 'Robart Daye', showing both religious emblems and domestic scenes: a man with a cauldron, a bagpiper, a fiddler and a fool.

# ASHMORE
## DORSET
*Dancing round the village pond*

Any village with a half-decent claim to being coupled with the adjective 'idyllic' has a pond. In the Middle Ages and later, it would have been an essential part of the village economy, used to raise ducks and geese, water cattle and wash the wheels of carts; women who nagged their husbands might be dunked in the pond in an act of particular humiliation. By the time John Saunders wrote his novel *Martin Pole* in 1863, ponds were beginning to offend Victorian sensibilities, as places where horses cooled their legs and 'very young kittens, or very old cats' found their last resting place. But even a very 'commonplace piece of water' seemed to remember an earlier period, 'a time when, framed with its blue forget-me-nots, it was a fitting mirror to reflect heaven's face, in all its thousand and ever-beautiful changes'. This is perhaps

*Ashmore: that icon of village England, the pond.*

the aspect that most strikes the present age, aware of the importance that patches of water, surrounded by unsprayed and unkempt greenery, have for wildlife. Village ponds have taken on special importance following the huge loss of ponds to the countryside following field drainage in the late twentieth century.

The pond at Ashmore is understandably a source of pride. You wouldn't have thought there could be a pond here, given that this is the highest village in Dorset. Hop over a couple of stiles (or drive up the road) and be amazed: before you is the grand, little-populated sweep of Cranborne Chase, a landscape for which we must thank the billions upon billions of tiny sea creatures whose shells, floating to the seabed a hundred million years ago, made the billowing chalk hills (at a rate of one centimetre every hundred thousand years). Chalk makes thin soil; the fields, scattered with flints, soon dry out. Water is quite literally worshipped.

On Midsummer's Eve, the villagers of Ashmore perform the ancient ritual of Filly Loo, culminating in a dance in which they join hands as they circle the pond. Folk characters appear; a man comes down the road dressed as a tree (this is the Green Man, seen throughout England in church carving and pub signs). There is a horn dance by six men wearing antlers. These elements of the folk tradition occur in other places (Abbots Bromley in Staffordshire has a famous horn dance, for example), reflecting the ancient desire to conjure fertility out of the earth. The antiquity of Ashmore's Filly Loo (a West Country dialect expression for uproar) is not known, but it seems to have come down as an authentic echo of the pagan past.

The pond forms a neat circle, and the village has gathered itself round it. This is a monochrome sort of village, built from the materials that lay to hand: notably the greenish-grey stone called greensand, mixed with grey black flints (perhaps laid in bands) and a few orangey-red bricks. Most of the dwellings in the heart of the village are thatched. It is clearly a village that people have loved. The bus shelter is a splendid structure, hexagonal in form with an arcade of solid oak. Beside the pond, someone has put a limestone bench, beautifully carved with mottoes, such as 'Reflect A While' and 'Ancient aquifer'. It is not, however, an ancient aquifer that feeds the pond; this is a dew pond, filled with rainwater. Just now the tide is out: water has seeped away to the point that the ducks are beginning to look nervous. In 2008, the village began the task of raising £25,000 to put it right.

# AVEBURY
## WILTSHIRE

*In the footsteps of the ancient past*

The village of Avebury crouches amid the ancient stones that thread through and around it, much like the habitations that once clung to the monuments of Athens and Rome. Modern villagers, going about their daily life, tread the same ground as the people who used the henge many millennia ago – as do the visitors who come to admire the stones, or enjoy a drink at the Red Lion pub. Distant past and workaday present interlock. It is a conjunction to stop anyone in his or her tracks and inspire reflection.

The henge at Avebury was erected over a six-hundred-year period, beginning around 3000BC. It is an astonishing size – more than ten times that of Stonehenge – and bears witness to the extraordinary exuberance of monument-building that took place in Wiltshire during the Stone Age. A mile to the south stands Silbury Hill, the great dome of chalk that Neolithic people heaved, using antlers for tools, out of the ground beside what is now the A4. To the north-west of Avebury henge, Windmill Hill was banked up and inhabited during the fourth millennium BC; it became the site of some of the many burial mounds in the area, the most notable being the Long Barrows at East and West Kennet.

Used for millennia, Avebury henge had been abandoned by the Roman period. It was the Saxons who started to colonise it as a village. Now the village street, running from church to pub and beyond, rudely bisects the stone circle, itself being crossed by the B4003. Except for the church, partly chequered with flint, later builders preferred lighter and more perishable materials to stone; the thatched cottages and brick terraces look cosy but transient beside the bulging grey permanence of the monoliths.

To Alexander Keiller, born in 1889, the village was an intrusion. The heir to a marmalade fortune in Dundee, Keiller could indulge his interests and passions, which included skiing, racing cars, photography, witchcraft, criminology and sex. Archaeology came to fascinate him after the First World War. After visiting Avebury for the first time in 1924, he bought Windmill Hill to prevent Marconi from building an aerial mast on it. He began a series of excavations both at Windmill Hill and along the West Kennet Avenue, a line of standing stones that leads from the henge. From 1937, he began excavating the henge itself, uncovering stones that had been lost beneath the bracken and trees, and re-erecting them in their original holes. Taking a lease on Avebury Manor, he joined the ranks of the restorers who were transforming the manor houses of southern England into the visual equivalent of romantic poetry, releasing the spirits of history that had been locked up in them by insensitive alterations*.

As for the village, Keiller wanted none of it. Some houses he succeeded in demolishing, relocating their inhabitants to nearby Avebury Trusloe. Then came the Second World War; work stopped and was never resumed. Avebury the village survived to continue its whispered dialogue with Avebury Henge.

*See Hammoon, page 41; Hemingford Grey, page 244*

# BANWELL
SOMERSET                                      *Not Noah's Flood, but another one*

In 1824, George Henry Law, the Bishop of Bath and Wells, was in a state of excitement. A cave had been discovered at Banwell, on the edge of the Mendip hills. Its existence was previously unsuspected, and it was on his land. The cave contained an immense quantity of fossilised animal bones. To the Bishop, this was conclusive proof of the truth of Noah's Flood.

Then, the Mendips were still a mining area. Lead had been extracted since the Roman period, leaving the ground corrugated by the grooves left from surface works. In 1757, miners in search of calamine, an ore needed to make brass, broke into a cave at Banwell, where a spectacular display of stalactites had been formed. Dr Francis Randolph, the vicar of Banwell, realised its potential as a tourist attraction, by which he could raise money for a charity school. Accordingly he arranged that a more convenient entrance should be provided via another shaft. It was while digging this shaft that the bone cave was discovered.

Among the mud, sand and rocks on the floor were what a report in the *Philosophical Magazine* described as 'an enormous quantity of bones, horns, and teeth. The thickness of this mass has been ascertained, by a shaft sunk into it, to be in one place nearly forty feet.' Bones were soon being taken out for examination by the basket load. They were similar to bones that were found, commonly at the period, poking out of the hummocks of graveyards, although the fact that some of them came from a great and extinct species of bear declared them to be of 'antediluvian origin'. Arctic hare, reindeer, wolf, arctic fox, wolverine and bison were among the other species.

A local man called William Beard started guiding visitors around the cave, taking money on behalf of Dr Randolph. He organised the bones into neat piles. It developed into a full-time job; he acquired the semi-humorous title of Professor, and renamed his home Bone Cottage. The Bishop, meanwhile, was developing his grounds with follies, among them being a cottage orné and an observation tower that gives a panoramic view of the surrounding landscape; an Osteoicon was built for the display of the choicest bones. The Bishop was, of course, wrong in his assumption about the bones. The Natural History Museum dates them to the last ice age, around seventy thousand years ago. A flood probably explains how the bones got into the cave; they were washed there as the glaciers melted.

# BEER
## DEVON

Congregational chapels in fishing villages rarely hit great architectural heights, and that at Beer is no exception. 'Tall and flint-faced', as it is described in *The Buildings of England,* just about does it. But an unexpected treasure lies inside. This less-than-Ritzy building contains an important relic of cinema history: the earliest Wurtlitzer organ in the country.

The heyday of the Wurlitzer coincided with the golden age of the movies as a form of mass entertainment. Rising from beneath the floor at the beginning of the performance, the organist already at the keyboard conjuring sound pictures from the hidden pipes, the instrument became part of the *Gesamtkunstwerk* that was the cinema-going experience. It had been conceived, however, for the silent screen, by the Englishman Robert Hope-Jones. An amateur church organist, Hope-Jones, born in 1859, was a complicated man, secretive and possibly mendacious about his inventions, which had been greatly assisted by the knowledge he had gained as chief electrician with the Lancashire and Cheshire Telephone Company.

To begin with, he developed an electrical action for conventional organs, allowing the pipes to be at any distance from the keyboard. Seeing the need for an instrument to replace the pianos and string trios that had provided an acoustically unspectacular accompaniment to films since the dawn of cinema in the 1890s, he extended the range of sound possibilities. A new stop was the Diaphone, described in David Baker's *The Organ* as 'a reed stop of very pure tone', but so loud that it was also used to make foghorns. The Tremulant, imitating the vibrato of strings, was much used, as well as a range of special effects. The object was to create a 'unit orchestra', in which the whole gamut of orchestral sounds could be produced by a single performer. Hope-Jones crossed the Atlantic and started his own Hope-Jones Organ Company, but it failed and he took his own life in 1914. Not long before, his patents had been taken over by the Rudolph Wurlitzer Company in North Tonawanda, New York. The Mighty Wurlitzer, as the instrument was invariably known, was born.

The Beer Wurlitzer is not a particularly elaborate theatre organ, having been bought by Provincial Cinematograph Theatres in 1924. They installed it in the Picture House in Walsall rather than a big London cinema. But the vogue for Wurlitzers passed, and this one was rescued by a private enthusiast in 1955. In 1958, the Sweetland Organ Company of Bath moved it to Beer, alas without its percussion and special effects. 'But,' to quote the church's website, it 'is more than capable of giving a very good account of itself in the performance of light music, as well as accompanying the church services every week, as it has now done for fifty years.' Who knows? One day it may be restored to its original specification 'if space in the organ chamber permits'.

# BEMERTON

WILTSHIRE

*Teach me, my God and King*

It is easy to picture George Herbert, the metaphysical poet, in the rectory at Bemerton, opposite the modest church – and many people since Izaak Walton wrote the first 'Life' have done so. It could be misleading. Herbert spent only three years as a clergyman here before his death from consumption in 1633. Before that, he had shone in a brilliant academic career at Cambridge University, where he became public orator – a position that could have led to a starring role at court. Briefly he was an MP. Although Bemerton was, and still is, a little place, the living that Herbert occupied, thanks to the intervention of his distant cousin the Earl of Pembroke at nearby Wilton House, was Fugglestone with Bemerton, which took in part of Wilton, then a small town, and stands on the edge of Salisbury, of which it is now an outlier.

Nevertheless, it was at Bemerton that Herbert revised and shaped his prose book *The Country Parson* (or *A Priest to the Temple*) in which he set forth his ideal of

*Nicholas Ferrar of Little Gidding, Cambridgeshire (see page 252) and friend, the poet George Herbert, shown in a stained-glass window of 1934 in Bemerton church.*

the quiet, self-sacrificing life of a secluded divine. 'Country people,' he observed, 'live hardly.' The country parson was therefore to avoid being greedy; he was to avoid alehouses and drinking; his clothes should be sober and clean. He was to preach constantly: 'The pulpit is his joy and his throne.' Ideally he would be unmarried. This was not Herbert's own state, because he had married Jane Danvers, a cousin of his stepfather and apparently a buxom, clever lady, shortly before taking the living in 1630.

Country parsons with wives should expect three things of them: good teaching of the couple's children and maids; practical knowledge of homely medicine; and prudent housekeeping. He prescribed a parsonage that would have looked like some of the Dutch paintings of the time, with 'very plain' furniture, 'but clean, whole, and sweet; – as sweet as his garden can make; for he hath no money for such things, charity being his only perfume, which deserves cost when he can spare it. His fare is plain, and common, but wholesome. What he hath is little, but very good.' The parson was to be a supporter of 'old customs, if they be good and harmless', because 'country people are much addicted to them'.

One of his duties was to maintain his church. He had to make sure that it was sound and watertight, with windows, floor, seats, pulpit, desk and communion table in good repair, the whole place being 'swept and kept clean, without dust or cobwebs'. On feast days it should be decorated with green boughs and scented with incense. Before coming to Bemerton, Herbert had already been installed as prebendary of Leighton Ecclesia in Huntingdonshire; the expectations of him there were not onerous, since he was required only to preach an annual sermon and that could be done through a deputy, but he paid for the rebuilding of the church, fitted out with a pulpit and reading desk (of the same height to symbolise that the sermon was not mightier than the Word of God). He similarly restored the church and rectory at Bemerton. According to Walton, he had the poem 'To My Successor' written on a tablet and installed on a chimney mantle in the rectory:

> If thou chance for to find
> A new House to thy mind
> And built without thy Cost
> Be good to the Poor,
> As God gives thee store,
> And then, my Labour's not lost.

# BLAGDON
## SOMERSET

*Controversy over a bluestocking's school*

In the late eighteenth century, Hannah More was a celebrity. Her play *Percy* was received with rapturous applause in 1777. The literary world was small, and she knew most of it. 'Hush, hush; it is dangerous to say a word of poetry before her,' Dr Johnson said. 'It is talking the art of war before Hannibal.'

During the 1780s, however, she began her metamorphosis into Horace Walpole's 'Saint Hannah', increasingly drawn to evangelical religion, while at the same time disenchanted with London society. The daughter of a teacher in Bristol, she moved to Somerset, first to Cowslip Green and then to Barley Wood, where she built a cottage in 1801. To give herself a sense of purpose, she founded a series of charity schools, which would bring religion and some literacy to the 'poor barbarians' of the Mendips.

'Miss Hannah More, something must be done for Cheddar . . . If you will be at the trouble I will be at the expense.' The speaker was William Wilberforce, MP, evangelical and anti-slavery campaigner. Making a tour of Cheddar Gorge, his carriage packed with the necessaries of a good picnic, he had been appalled by the poor he had encountered, dwelling almost as cavemen. He dispensed money, for which their gratitude was pathetic, but continued to worry about their souls. This account was written by More's sister, Martha, whom she called Patty. While Hannah blew in with gusts of energy and grand ideas, Patty had the patience and quiet determination of a good teacher.

The Mendips did not provide promising raw material for scholarship. Gentry were few, and the farmers 'drunk every day, and plunged in such vices as make me begin to think London is a virtuous place'. The Church of England clergy took the tithes but 'neglected' their flock. Visiting poorer houses to drum up pupils, the Mores were dismayed to find only one Bible, which was used as a stand for a geranium pot.

The first school was opened at Cheddar in 1789, an inauspicious year for experiments, given events on the other side of the Channel. But it soon had three hundred pupils, who were taught to read the Bible and the catechism. During the next decade it would be followed by schools at Shipham, Rowberrow, Sandford, Banwell (see page 10), Congresbury, Yatton, Nailsea, Axbridge, Blagdon and Wedmore (see page 79).

The Mores have been accused of patronising their alumni, and attempting to impose alien cultural values on them – which rather ignores the children's freedom not to attend. Modern educationalists are more likely to note the project's fundamental conservatism: it was not expected that education would help the student to get on, other than by 'habits of industry and virtue'. Instead, expectations had to be managed so that the educated child would not later feel discontented with his or her lot.

The school at Blagdon ignited a national controversy when the schoolmaster was accused of holding Methodist meetings and extempore prayer sessions, an attack on the role of the established Church. The French Revolution had made any kind of radicalism suspect. The vehemence with which Hannah was denounced by High Churchmen was searing. She was forced to retreat to save her other charitable works; the school was closed. Nevertheless, Blagdon and the other schools, some of which continued into the twentieth century, drew attention to the need for education in poor communities; the Church of England's National Society for the Education of the Poor in the Principles of the Established Church, which took up the reins until the Education Act of 1870, was founded in 1811.

*See also Painswick, page 344*

# BLISLAND
## CORNWALL
*John Betjeman's favourite church*

Many Cornish villages are named after their patron saints, but not Blisland. Perhaps it is just as well; locally the saint in question was known as St Pratt. This was a corruption of St Protus, who, in the dedication of the church, is joined by his reputed brother, St Hyacinth, both of them having been martyred during the persecutions of Emperor Valerian in the third century. Blisland was supposed to have been called after the joyousness of the location, which may be fanciful but suggests how names (as Tristram Shandy's father maintained in Laurence Sterne's novel) can influence personality.

For Blisland is a serene and lovely place, its swelling green equipped with children's swings and overlooked by houses, built of the local moorland granite but, for once in Cornwall, on a comfortably prosperous scale. A notice for the village show has been drawing-pinned to a pole. Down the road, a frilled umbrella shelters a shelf, attached to a ferny bank, selling rhubarb and Swiss chard at a pound

*Shrine to home produce and honesty at Blisland.*

a bag. When the shop closed, villagers opened their own in a disused shipping container and ran it for seven years, until a wooden community centre of unexampled glory was built, with ground-source heating, photovoltaic panels and rainwater recycling to make it as green as a moorland tussock.

'It has not one ugly building in it,' John Betjeman remembered in *First and Last Loves* in 1952. He had first cycled there as a boy, from the family's holiday home by the sea. Straining up hills and careering 'heart-in-mouth' down into the next valley, he slowly left the stunted wind-blown trees of the coast and emerged into the richer landscape on the edge of Bodmin Moor. St Protus and St Hyacinth, carved with such labour out of the iron-hard stone, epitomised everything that he felt, throughout his life, a church should be. 'Sir Ninian Comper, that great church architect, says that a church should bring you to your knees when first you enter it. Such a church is Blisland.'

You reach it down the slope of the graveyard, past early Victorian slate headstones lettered as though they were circus posters, in a caprice of different fonts (did they inspire the neo-Victorian typography for Betjeman's Shell Guides?). Outwardly, beneath its square tower, the church spreads its skirts, with a couple of aisles lined up in parallel with the nave. It keeps itself low, crouching near to the ground, but need not worry about blowing away in the storms: some of the granite blocks from which it was built are as big as steamer trunks. Open the door and the interior has all the funny quirks that bespeak centuries of love and care; one of the nave columns leans so rakishly that it had to be propped up by a wooden beam in the fifteenth century. But, needing a beam, the congregation ensured that it was carved with mouldings and roses.

The ribs of the roofs, like upturned hulls of ships, were also carved. As for what Betjeman regarded as the pièce de résistance, let the Poet Laureate himself reveal it: 'Walls white, sun streams in through a clear west window and there – glory of glories! – right across the whole eastern end of the church is a richly painted screen and rood loft. It is of wood. The panels at its base are red and green. Wooden columns, highly coloured and twisted like barley sugar, burst into gilded tracery and fountain out to hold a panelled loft.'

'Incongruous', Pevsner sniffs, in his *Buildings of England* volume, of this contribution from the 1890s, when the little-known F. C. Eden restored the church. But the colour and gilding, the saints and theatre made a direct appeal to Betjeman's spirituality through his aesthetic sense. Struggling with faith, he wanted architecture to overpower his doubts and open, for the moment that he experienced it, a window onto eternity. Blisland did it for him.

# BRENT KNOLL
SOMERSET                                      *Geese hang the fox-in-a-mitre*

The only seating in an early medieval parish church was made of stone; congregations either stood or kneeled during worship, the only exceptions being made for
the old or infirm, who 'went to the wall', where they could find a hard bench. From
around 1300, counties that were rich in woodwork – principally East Anglia and
the West Country – began to introduce seating. It was a sign of affluence. Until
then, all parish occasions, including markets, took place in the open space of the
church nave. A church that was rich enough to install benches had also to build a
hall for other activities. Benches came to Brent Knoll in the fifteenth century.

Bench ends were often carved, as were misericords, the shelves on the underside
of tip-up seats in the choirs of monastic churches, on which monks could obtain
the 'mercy' (in Latin, *misericordia*) of support during the many services they were
obliged to attend. Both kinds of seat adornment are an insight into the medieval
mind, surviving from the times when every surface of the church (windows, walls,
rood screen, font cover, pulpit, chantries, tombs) was decorated to tell a story or
point a moral.

Misericords rarely depict religious scenes. Perhaps it would have been thought
sacrilegious to sit on a sacred image, or perhaps the position was so low in the
hierarchy of an intensely decorated church that carvers were allowed to let their
fancy dictate themes. About half of those that exist around Britain are decorated
with plants or leaves, the rest a variety of everyday scenes or fabulous creatures. On
benches, the most common ornament is a poppy head, a finial that might resemble a fleur-de-lys but had nothing to do with poppies, the term being derived from
the French *poupée*, a puppet or figurehead. The panels at the ends of the benches
might be carved with linenfold. Occasionally bench ends bear religious scenes or
symbols, and this is the case at Brent Knoll.

But there is a twist: three of the panels make it clear what the congregation
thought of the church hierarchy placed over them. They show a fox dressed as an
abbot. This in itself would have appealed to the medieval imagination, representing one of those inversions that could occur at any moment in a precarious and
unstable existence. Villagers knew all about foxes. There was, furthermore, a tradition of using them to make satirical fun of authority, as in the medieval *Roman de
Reynard* (adapted by Chaucer for his 'Nun's Priest's Tale'), where Reynard the fox
is brought before King Leo the Lion for trial, being freed on condition he goes on
a pilgrimage.

A worse fate is suffered by the Brent Knoll's fox in abbot's clothing. In the first
scene, he is shown holding a pastoral crook from which hangs a fleece – so much
for his care of the flock. At his feet are three pigs wearing monks' cowls, symbolising the greed of the monasteries. In a lower panel, two apes are roasting a pig on a
spit as an image of gluttony. The second scene shows the fox in irons. One of the

apes has ousted him, and is rousing some geese to rebellion. The story continues in the lower panel, where the fox is now in the stocks. In the third panel the fox is hanged, to the delight of two watchdogs, who bark in approval.

The Brent Knoll fox is generally identified with the Abbot of Glastonbury, although it is not clear quite why the villagers were so cross with him. We may not know the exact details of the case, but the message, half a millennium later, is unmistakable. Abbots stink.

# BRIANTSPUDDLE
DORSET                                        *Social engineering under thatch*

Sir Ernest Debenham was a remarkable patron. The grandson of the founder of the Debenhams department store and drapery business, he had been educated at Trinity College, Cambridge, before entering the family firm around 1900. In London, his progressive ideas about architecture were demonstrated by Halsey Ricardo, who created a colourful palace for him at 8 Addison Road, rich with opulent mosaics. In Dorset, where he began acquiring a large agricultural estate in 1914, the note was different: white walls and wavy thatch. Debenham again commissioned Halsey Ricardo, but here he wanted the enterprise to demonstrate the principles of self-sufficiency in a progressively scientific context. The hamlets of Briantspuddle and Affpuddle were transformed for the workers who would be so supported. They became a visionary combination: half local style, as beloved of the Arts and Crafts movement, half social engineering.

The estate had been formed in the 1680s, when William Frampton of Moreton bought three manors and consolidated them into one holding. Until the Debenham era, it had sustained a scant population living in a small number of cottages. By the time Debenham was able to start his contribution, the First World War had inter-vened. The first phase consisted of twelve cottages and a model farm, known as the Ring. Instead of the traditional cob or rammed earth technique used to construct the earlier dwellings, a cheaper, more industrial method was favoured: concrete blocks. They were covered with plaster, but the mechanical shape of the blocks is still apt to grin through – they are known to this day as Debenham block.

Nevertheless, the style was otherwise drawn from the locality, though perhaps heightened by Ricardo, who clearly enjoyed the sculptural possibilities of thatch (dormer windows were given peaked coverings resembling helmets). A number of thatched dairy buildings built to rationally circular plans (allowing lorries to turn) were built across Britain during the inter-war years, the Ovaltine Model Dairy at Abbots Langley in Hertfordshire (see page 164) being the most famous; Briantspuddle has one of the first.

'The first consideration when conditions became more normal [after the First World War] was the provision of suitable housing accommodation for the workers,' an estate brochure observed in 1929. In order to keep the workforce happy – and, by implication, productive – social facilities, such as the village hall, were built. Professor Boufleur, head of the Cirencester Agricultural College, advised on progressive agriculture. Milk was brought from the dairy farms around the estate to be tested, separated and bottled in the Ring. At a time when tuberculosis was still spread through dairy products, and before pasteurisation had become standard, Debenham led the way by installing a fully equipped laboratory to analyse the milk. Self-sufficiency also required the estate to generate its own power, which it did by means of two oil generators working eighteen hours a day. Water was pumped from a borehole.

In 1929, Debenham commissioned the radical sculptor Eric Gill* to construct a war memorial, in the shape of a wayside cross. Another took the form of a garden of peace at Affpuddle church. Nearby is the unpretentious tomb slab beneath which Debenham was buried after his death on Christmas Day, 1952. He had not realised his vision; Briantspuddle and Affpuddle could evolve towards self-sufficiency only with Debenham's backing, and that had to be drastically reduced during the Great Depression. It is now obvious that improvements in agricultural efficiency do not, by themselves, lead to the regeneration of communities, with more people being supported by the land. Recent experience shows that the reverse happened: mechanisation means that fewer people need to be employed on farms. The Ring has been converted to dwellings, with names such as the Old Dairy, Barn Court and the Old Stables.

*See Ditchling, page 107

# BROAD CHALKE
## WILTSHIRE
*Pure virtues of the nose-wrinkler*

Watercress beds used to be a relatively common sight in English villages, particularly in chalk counties, such as Hampshire and Wiltshire. They were a guarantee of purity, because watercress grows only in clear, bright water. Which is not to say that other things did not cohabit with the cress, including freshwater fish, such as chub and perch, and, less desirably, the liver fluke parasite, which does no good at all to your insides. The industry became regulated, which made village beds uneconomic; at Ewelme in Oxfordshire (see page 174), it has taken a local trust to restore them, after closure in the 1980s.

Watercress is still commercially grown at Broad Chalke. You can buy it from a shed with a fridge in it, putting fifty pence for a packet into a tube that goes into the interior of the shed if there is nobody there to take it. Watercress can also be seen in the stream at the beginning of the village, its dark green acting as a foil to the brilliant white of the egret that may be standing beside it. During spring, the watercress itself turns white with flower.

Watercress was known to the Greeks, who thought it made eaters strong and determined (as recommended by Aristophanes in *The Wasps*). It undoubtedly contains minerals (iodine, sulphur, iron) and high concentrations of vitamin C. From its smell and peppery taste, the Romans gave it the name of nasturtium, or nose-wrinkler. Doctors in the Middle Ages thought that the juice of the watercress, if rubbed on your head, would cure baldness.

Parboiled with beets, it became a condiment that could be served equally with meat or cheese. The Victorians saw it as a snack, to be eaten with bread at breakfast, or sold in the street in bunches to be consumed on the go. 'Fresh wo-orter-creases', was, according to Henry Mayhew in 1861, the 'first coster cry heard of a morning in the London streets'. Twenty years later, Richard Rowe, writing about London, found that watercress brought something of the country to town: 'In fine weather, in spite of the general squalor of the street-retailers, it is rather a pretty sight to see them flocking out of the great watercress market with their verdant basketfuls and armfuls, freshening their purchases under the sun-gilt water of the pump, splitting them up into bunches, and beautifying the same to the best of their ability to tempt purchasers.'

The first attempt at commercial cultivation in Britain had not been made until 1808. But the crop was established in time for the railway age to provide the transport that would take it fresh to urban markets. Chalke Valley Watercress at Broad Chalke was founded in 1880, and is now being run by the fifth generation of the original family. The site was chosen because of the spring water that rises there, having been filtered by the chalk hills, which give the village its name. The closure of branch railway lines and the arrival of exotic salad crops from overseas proved a challenge to many producers in the 1960s. At Broad Chalke, one modern development has helped the company fight back: gathered in the early morning when the beds are still steamy in the cool air, watercress is no longer picked by hand – a back-breaking business – but harvested by machine.

# BROCKLEY
SOMERSET                                                    *England's precious woodlands*

If you were setting yourself up in the Anglo-Saxon countryside, one of the most important considerations would have been timber. You needed it for fuel, and you built your house and barns from it; you shaped it into tables and benches, plates and spoons, spades and spears. Whippy young shoots could be woven into baskets, willows carved into clogs. Your pigs gobbled up the acorns that lay among the fallen leaves, and you yourself ate the wildlife you could catch, unless a lord had previously laid claim to it. The proximity of woodland was important.

There was not as much of it about as people used to think; by the time of the Domesday survey of 1086, the last vestiges of the primeval forest that once covered

Britain could be found only in steep, inhospitable places that were impossible to farm. Woods were named as carefully as settlements, and the existence and character of the one was often used to denominate the other. The Saxon word for a wood (or a clearing in a wood) was *leah*; it is one of the commonest elements in English place names.

There are physical descriptions, such as Bradley (broad wood) and Langley (long wood). Most types of trees are commemorated: the oak in Oakleigh and Oakley, the birch in Berkeley and Berkley, the box, elm and thorn in Boxley, Elmley and Thornley. We have lime woods (Lindley), willows (Willey) and yews (Uley). Thursley in Surrey (see page 145) and Thundersley in Essex were dedicated to the Saxon god of thunder, Thor. Animals lived in woods, and their presence is remembered in Foxley and Hartley, as well as Oxley, Cowley, Horsley and Lambley. Woolley remembers the wolves who once prowled.

Brockley had a wood full of badgers. The wolves have since gone, but Old Brock remains properly dug in in the West Country; in fact there are probably more badgers than at any other period of history (they would not have got on with the wolves.) There is still a Brockley wood clambering up the sides of Brockley Combe at Brockley (not so much a village as a name on the map) in Somerset, one of three or four Brockleys recognised by the Ordnance Survey, with others in Suffolk, Lewisham and Cumbria (Brockleymoor). It is typical of the thousands of woods that exist throughout the countryside, although it can boast that its wood is still turned into garden structures and fence posts, through the medium of Fountain Timber Products, which is based there.

In this Brockley wood is unusual. Medieval woods were regarded as a precious resource, which had to be managed through coppicing and pollarding, allowing young shoots to be harvested like a crop. A series of rights (firebote, which allowed villagers to collect firewood, ploughbote to make agricultural tools, housebote and so on) were patrolled by a manorial official known as the woodward. But with the appearance of other fuels and materials, together with factory production, we have ceased to treasure woods. Britain, as ever, is a paradox. It venerates ancient trees, the hollow oaks and millennia-old yews, of which we have more than any of our neighbouring countries, and yet we have one of the lowest rates of woodland cover in Europe. More leighs, please.

# CERNE ABBAS
## DORSET

*At the gates of the monastery*

How inconceivable it must have seemed to the inhabitants of Cerne Abbas in 1530 that within a decade the rich Abbey that gave its name to the village would become defunct, its abbot and monks expelled. The West Country was dominated by monasteries. Above Cerne, the club-wielding giant of prominent masculinity

– thought to represent Hercules in honour of the Emperor Commodus – which is etched onto Giant Hill demonstrates that people had been living here long before the monks came. But the Abbey was an ancient foundation, William of Malmesbury ascribing its origin to St Augustine himself. Like many early Christian sites, it had pagan associations: a 'silver well' attracted St Edwold, brother of King Edmund, to live beside it as a hermit in the ninth century. And the Abbey was rich: Henry VIII, who would abolish it in 1539, had himself given it land twenty-six years earlier. The village depended on the Abbey for its existence. It knew its place, clustering at the Abbey's skirts.

In its heyday, Cerne Abbey educated John Morton, Henry VII's chancellor (the inventor of Morton's Fork) and a cardinal. In 1535, its farms kept nearly six thousand sheep. But even before the Dissolution, complaints were being made by a disgruntled monk about the brothers' gross immorality (they were said to keep loose women in the cellars), not to mention neglect of duty. (A legend would grow up that the giant depicts the last Abbot, as a commentary on his lust.) It is therefore no surprise that he surrendered the Abbey without a fuss, retiring on a comfortable pension of £100 a year.

After 1539, short work was made of the Abbey buildings. Only the guest house and delicately carved Abbot's Porch (both in the grounds of Abbey House) and the Abbey Barn survive. The other structures were demolished soon after the departure of the monks by leaseholders who were after a quick buck. However, a trail of architectural fragments can be traced in the domestic buildings of the village: at the back of the New Inn, a piece of carving seems to have come from a canopy that once covered a shrine to St Catherine – it is possible to make out her wheel. Other pieces of sculpture and encaustic tiles used as decoration are supposed to exist in various places. It is notable that the Royal Oak claims to have been built in 1540.

While the villagers may have rejoiced in the windfall provided by so many good building materials, they did not grow rich from them. When a muster of able-bodied men capable of serving in the army was made in 1543, only sixty-five names could be recorded – down from nearly three hundred at the time of Domesday. John Norden, making a survey of Duchy of Cornwall lands in 1617, found many squatters living on the commons, and the 'ancient and spatious' Guildhall about to fall down. By the 1830s, it had become sufficiently active for a railway to be considered (it would, dreadfully, have tunnelled beneath Maiden Castle and Poundbury Camp). But instead main-line trains puffed into Dorchester (1847) and Sherborne (1860), leaving Cerne Abbas to its present giant and vanished monks.

# CHARLCOMBE
## SOMERSET
*Road safety for toads*

The year 2009 was a good one for toads in the village of Charlcombe. Nearly two thousand of them were put into buckets and carried across Charlcombe Lane, together with 570 frogs and a quantity of newts. Since 2003, normal traffic has been suspended on the road every February and March, in favour of the amphibians. Toad numbers across Britain have fallen since the 1970s, due to loss of habitat. Dense forestry plantations allow little room for toads; thousands of ponds and boggy places across Britain have been drained in the interests of farming. The human urge to tidy up its surroundings by building garden walls, as well as houses, has deprived the toad of free passage over what had previously been its terrain; untold numbers are squashed on roads.

Toads need fresh, clean water, preferably in large, deep ponds, to breed in; after they wake from hibernation, they try to return to the same sites each spring. That is the problem for the Charlcombe toads. Their path is blocked by a wall, along which they line up as they look for an opening; this leaves them vulnerable to predators, such as cats. Once they have found a gap, they have to cross the road. Even with the road closure, about 170 toads did not make it. Without the closure, far more would have died.

In folklore, the toad – 'ugly and venomous', as the Duke calls it in *As You Like It* – has enjoyed a mixed press. Wearing a toad's leg in a silk purse around your neck was supposed to ward off evil spirits. Dried toad was supposed to be one of the ingredients that formed an antidote to plague. Touching a toadstone, the precious jewel that toads were supposed to have inside their heads, was a sovereign remedy against snake bites. But the toad's curative properties were only a by-product of its generally evil persona. Macbeth's witches made sure that the first thing to go into their cauldron was toad.

Like cats and owls, toads were regarded as witches' familiars. They were thought to be extremely venomous. 'Never hung poison on a fouler toad,' Lady Anne says in *Richard III*. It is true that the toad's speckled brown skin (which in males changes colour almost to red in the mating season) is slightly poisonous, as a defence against other animals, but that was not what Shakespeare or his contemporaries had in mind. One might have expected country people, as most inhabitants of Shakespeare's England were, to have known more about creatures that they must have seen often. They would have viewed modern efforts to ensure toad welfare with the greatest suspicion.

Today, the toad is an indicator of environmental good health, because of its need for pure water. Squat and 'bunch-back'd' it may be, but the Common Toad, *Bufo bufo*, is a biodiversity action plan species, meaning that local authorities, such as Bath and North-East Somerset Council at Charlcombe, have to devise policies for its protection. Not everyone approves of closing a busy road that some drivers regard as an essential route to work or school. But the toads have attracted a loyal following of volunteers, who mount nocturnal patrols to help them on their way.

# CHARLTON
## WILTSHIRE                                    *Hard labour in rhyming couplets*

Every year a Duck Feast is held in the Charlton Cat pub. The Duck has, in this case, nothing to do with waterfowl, but refers to Stephen Duck, a poet who began life as a farm labourer and achieved such celebrity that Lord Palmerston, one of his patrons, provided the rent from a piece of land to hold an annual feast. (Alas, the income has now disappeared, according to the landlord of the Cat, although the feast continues – possibly 'the oldest of its kind in Europe'.) The first such 'handsome entertainment' (to quote a newspaper of the time) was held in 1734; Duck was then twenty-nine.

Duck was known as the thresher poet, after his first success, *The Thresher's Labour.* Written at the instigation of an early supporter, the Rev. Stanley, rector of nearby Pewsey, it is an accomplished work, by a man who, against the odds, had studied Milton, Dryden, *The Spectator* and Matthew Prior. There is an undercurrent of genuine feeling beneath its Augustan style; however elegantly written, this is a production from someone who knows the unremitting drudgery of harvesting, haymaking and threshing under a hot sun. Sweat, not a word much heard in eighteenth-century poetry, 'In briny Streams . . . descends apace, Drops from our Locks, or trickles down our Face.' Threshing 'sooty Pease', the workmen, stripped to the waist, go home so black that the children mistake them for bogeymen. One physically exhausting job succeeds another:

> Thus, as the Year's revolving Course goes round,
> No respite from our Labour can be found:
> Like Sysiphus, our Work is never done,
> Continually rolls back the restless Stone:
> Now growing Labours still succeed the past,
> And growing always new must always last.

For Duck there was an escape. The literary world feted him – a humble farm labourer, who transformed earthy occupations into the stuff of 'polite' poetry – as a prodigy. He was presented to Queen Caroline, who gave him an annuity, a house and a job as keeper of the Queen's Library in Merlin's Cave, a folly in Richmond Gardens. These were productive years, but the longer he stayed at Richmond, the further he got from the early experience of farm work that made his voice unique. After Queen Caroline's death in 1737, he had no patron. He took holy orders, became chaplain to a regiment of marines, and was appointed to a rectory in Surrey. He was diligent and popular, yet for reasons that are not clear – some maintain, probably wrongly, because of alienation from his Wiltshire roots – he drowned himself at Reading.

# CHARLTON DOWN
DORSET                                                    *What a madhouse*

Charlton Down has taken root within the carcass of a Victorian institution. Herrison Hospital, or the Dorset Lunatic Asylum, as it used to be known, was built in 1859–63 by H. E. Kendall Jr. Pevsner described it as 'notable mainly for its wild and ferocious polychromatic brickwork' – not, one might have thought, an architecturally calming environment for the inmates. But Kendall knew his job, having already designed several buildings of the same type, including the Essex County Asylum at Brentwood and the Sussex County Asylum at Haywards Heath. They were the expression of a more humane purpose than had been apparent before the Victorian age.

Lunacy appeared to rise throughout the nineteenth century, from two or three cases in every ten thousand in England and Wales at the beginning of the century to around thirteen per ten thousand when the Lunacy Act of 1845 was passed, to more than double that by the time of the next Act in 1890. This probably reflects the greater interest and compassion of the authorities. Earlier correctives had included the whip and the chain as well as the straitjacket. 'They said I was mad, and I said they were mad,' commented the seventeenth-century playwright Nathaniel Lee, 'damn them, they outvoted me.' He was consigned to Bethlem Hospital, or Bedlam, now famous for the callous manner in which lunatics were displayed to visiting gentlefolk as though they were menagerie animals.

Even so-called hospitals of this order were few in the Georgian period, most mad people being housed in their communities. The first county asylum opened in 1811, after the passing of the County Asylums Act. But few others followed, and the philanthropist Lord Shaftesbury headed the campaign for a new Lunacy Act, passed in 1845, which not only insisted on better provision of asylums but instituted the Commissioners in Lunacy to supervise their regime. Herrison Hospital was one of the fruits. Asylums were no longer to be classed with prisons but with residential buildings that provided comfort and care.

There were 315 patients at Herrison when the Commissioners visited in 1867. An effort was being made, according to the standards of the age, to be kindly, yet inevitably the stories among the records of the Dorset History Centre are poignant. Six-year-old Caroline Ellis was admitted in 1863, after having 'endeavoured about a fortnight ago to strangle her sister and very nearly succeeded'. She is described on her admission paper as a 'poor little half idiotic child [who] suffers from epilepsy. Is clean and tidy in her person.' In 1867, she became ill with protracted diarrhoea, was dosed with laudanum and 'other astringents' and died. Samuel Pitcher came to Herrison aged eight in 1864, 'a poor little half paralysed congenital idiot – very mischievous, destructive and dirty'. He was also violent, having thrown scissors and knives at his baby sibling. He showed some improvement, but died from influenza in 1869.

At its zenith, Herrison Hospital – extended several times – was its own world, with a church, sports facilities, allotments and a radio station on a four-hundred-acre site. But the 1970s and 1980s saw the rise of a new idea in mental health: patients could be reintegrated into the community, a policy that satisfied human rights campaigners and National Health Service accountants (the flaw being the inability of some sufferers to cope with life outside the institution, with the result that they slept rough). In 1992, Herrison Hospital closed. The three large blocks were converted into seventy apartments; the rest of the site was developed with cottages, terraces and five-bedroom houses, in a similar red brick to the original, by Bellway Homes.

# CHIDEOCK
## DORSET                                    *Smile, you're on camera*

In 1997, Chideock became the first village in Britain to be graced with two yellow speed cameras. Speed cameras had been introduced into the UK after the Road Traffic Act 1991 allowed courts to accept camera evidence. Cameras – generally made by Gatsometer B.V., a Dutch company founded by the rally driver Maurice Gatsonides, who invented the camera to measure his racing speed – were set up to deter speeding and the jumping of red traffic lights. Initially located in towns and cities, their spread across the kingdom was slow. By 1994, no more than thirty speed cameras had been installed, twenty-one of which were in West London. They were lucrative, making a return of more than twenty-five times the cost of installing them for every year after the first. However, the body responsible for putting them in (the police) did not receive the benefit of the fines, which went to the Exchequer. When arrangements were changed to allow local authorities to keep receipts, the rate of deployment got much quicker: four thousand five hundred safety cameras (mostly speed cameras) were operating by the Millennium. A decade later there are around six thousand.

Surrounded by the farmland of an Area of Outstanding Natural Beauty, Chideock is an apparently serene village with a violent past. In 1594, the Catholic priest John Cornelius, a member of Lady Arundell's household in Chideock Castle, was arrested with three others and then hanged, drawn and quartered. In 1685, the Chideock port (Seatown) was the scene of a landing by scouts from the Duke of Monmouth's army, who collected horses and men before the Duke himself disembarked onto the beach at Lyme Regis. Vengeance was soon wrought on those who took part in this disastrous rebellion. In the twenty-first century, conflict continues to haunt Chideock, because of the traffic. Through the middle of this otherwise delightful village runs the A35. The National Trust is lambasted by some for refusing to allow a bypass over the land that it owns; in other quarters, the speed cameras are no more popular.

In the second half of the twentieth century, rural Britain made a devil's bargain with the motor car. As branch lines closed and bus services failed to offer an adequate replacement, most people came to rely on it. But the car turned round and bit them for their dependency whenever fuel prices rose. With rural wages generally lower than those in cities, country folk felt the pain. A speeding fine from a Gatso at Chideock added another level of woe.

There is, however, another twist to the story. Alan Dawe, a Cornish lorry driver, appealed against a ticket he received for driving at a recorded speed of 41mph in a 30mph zone in 2005. His lawyer, Kenneth Rogers, argued that the restricted zone was measured from the junction of Seatown Road. While there is a road to Seatown, which leaves Chideock, it is called Duck Road. Since Seatown Road does not exist, the calculation could not be valid. Mr Dawe won the case. It opened the way for other drivers who had been illegally ticketed since 1997 to find redress. But there is still no sign of a bypass.

# CHURSTON FERRERS
## DEVON
*A rest for the little grey cells*

A mystery was afoot in Devon. It concerned a certain Mrs Mallowan. Outwardly she was the retiring wife of an archaeologist, with a house, Greenway, overlooking the river Dart. Mrs Mallowan loved houses, and had done since she had first begged for a second doll's house as a little girl (she got a cupboard, which was just as good). In Devon, her mind appeared to be focused on such harmless objects as the souvenir boxes and giant Derbyshire barge-ware teapots that she collected. She liked clothes: a wardrobe of her gowns and fur coats is still in the house. Yet she was so 'terribly shy' that she couldn't go to a party without 'gritting her teeth', or play the piano – though she performed to concert standard – without closing the door.

In the mid 1950s, fed up with looking at the insipid east window of the church at Churston Ferrers, she decided to make a thanks offering for a contented life by paying for a new one. She had strong views on the content: not the Crucifixion, but something redolent of the 'goodness of God . . . a happy window . . . for a simple country church with a rural population', as she put it. Mrs Mallowan had a strong vein of practical common sense.

But who was she? James Paterson, the principal of Bideford School of Art, who designed the window, found out only when his wife happened to hear it on the radio. In another world this retiring country lady was Agatha Christie, the most popular writer of whodunnits that has ever been. Her books have sold two billion copies around the world. At Greenway, now owned by the National Trust, guides say this record is surpassed only by Shakespeare, the Bible and the Koran.

Greenway was Christie's holiday home. She had been brought up on the outskirts of Torquay, in a large villa called Ashfield. It had been an idyllic childhood. Her father, Frederick Miller, was a conspicuously 'agreeable man', whose easy-going nature soothed his more volatile, clairvoyant wife, Clara. With a large private income, Frederick, an American, had no need to work. Unfortunately, like other agreeable men, he had lost most of his money by the time he died in 1901. Life for Agatha and her mother could continue only on a reduced scale. But there were books to read. Told that her voice was not strong enough to turn her into the opera singer she hoped to be, Agatha began to write books to pay the bills. The first, *The Mysterious Affair at Styles*, came out in 1920.

In 1938, she took the architect Guildford Bell, nephew of a friend, to visit Greenway, a largely Georgian building that Clara regarded as the most beautiful house on the Dart. She found it for sale, with thirty-three acres, for what seemed like the bargain price of six thousand pounds. Encouraged by her second husband, Max Mallowan, she bought it with her own money. Before long, war had come. A Messerschmitt appeared overhead, dropping bombs. The ferry boat, which crosses from a small quay to the village of Dittisham on the opposite bank, was machine-gunned, to the alarm of the nurse who was taking some children on it at the time. During the War, the house was requisitioned. Afterwards, with Christie being pursued for back taxes both in Britain and America, upkeep seemed practically impossible. The garden was turned into a trust, the house sold to Christie's daughter, Rosalind – both for tax reasons.

Somehow Christie continued to spend the summers there, warring with the head gardener, Frank Lavin, who nevertheless took all the prizes at the Brixham Flower Show, and supervising tennis, croquet, clock golf, boating expeditions, Dartmoor picnics, children and dogs. To the village, she was a country gentlewoman: the lady she had dreamt of being as a child. People were not supposed to know that she was also the imagination behind scores of gruesome murders; on the banks of the Dart, it would have made little difference if they had.

# CLOVELLY
DEVON                                        *Authors of the English Amalfi*

Clovelly in Devon would still be Clovelly if Charles Kingsley's father had not become rector in 1830; fishing, granite and whitewash had made it (as the travel writer H. V. Morton observed in the 1920s) the English Amalfi, 'rising sheer from the bay'. But the village might not have become such a cult if it had not formed one of the principal *mises en scène* of Kingsley's novel *Westward Ho!*, published in 1855.

*Clovelly, a Devon fishing village discovered by Victorian*
*writers and preserved as a holiday experience.*

In 1797, W. G. Maton had completely missed the charm, remarking, in his
*Observations . . . of the Western Counties of England*, that the farming was nothing special, 'nor is [Clovelly] novel or varied enough to be pleasing to the eye'.
Sensibility could fail, even in the Age of the Picturesque. But five years after the
appearance of *Westward Ho!*, Charles Dickens arrived, in company with Wilkie
Collins, and was sufficiently inspired to open 'A Message from the Sea', his
Christmas story for 1860, at Clovelly, 'built sheer up the face of a steep and lofty
cliff' with packhorses and donkeys toiling up the stepped, cobbled streets with
baskets of fish and coal from the boats. Clovelly's reputation was assured.

'The road to Clovelly was a flowery pathway,' the American James Mason Hoppin
gushed in 1867. The future President of the United States Woodrow Wilson was
enchanted when he arrived on a cycling tour in 1896. 'I can only suppose Clovelly
bewitched me,' he sighed. At the inn, they put him in a little house by himself; to
reach it, he had 'to climb through a little wonderfully tiled garden'. Wilson unintentionally paid a backhanded compliment when he described the village as though it

were stage scenery, 'a sort of devised street built at a cunningly constructed world's fair'. That was exactly what the then rector had begun to object to, deploring in the very year of Wilson's visit that the village 'positively suffers from excess of attention and [has] become the victim of publicity'. Clovelly had become somewhere to look at, rather than live in. It would be a fate shared by countless West Country villages, particularly on the coast, over the next hundred years.

In one respect, however, Clovelly was fortunate. The family that owned Clovelly Court – evoked, in its Elizabethan form, in *Westward Ho!*, although this house had burnt down, to be replaced by a late Georgian mansion – saw that it was special. Since it also owned the village, it was able to protect it from being swamped. As early as the 1920s, motor cars (which in those days could not manage the steep hill) were banned. Inevitably the process of renewing the fabric of the village was self-conscious, but the cottages and inn that were built in Tudor and Arts and Crafts styles are harmonious. Clovelly has become a work of art.

# CREED
CORNWALL                    *He went about doing good (and discovered titanium)*

William Gregor was an excellent man. Learned, kindly, unassuming, he became the rector of the parish of Creed in 1793. Thereafter, in the capitalised words of a memorial address to the Royal Geological Society of Cornwall in 1817, he 'WENT ABOUT DOING GOOD'. He had grown up in Cornwall. Born on Christmas Day 1761, he was the younger son of an old Cornish family, his father being a military man, his mother the sister of a baronet. He went to Cambridge, won a prize for Latin prose and gained a fellowship, but chose to give up the prospect of honours and high office in the Church to live near his brother, Francis Gregor, an MP for Cornwall. In the way of the eighteenth-century Church of England, the fact that his wife was related to the Bishop of Exeter put him in line for a parish. He was given one in Devon but swapped it for Creed: a scattered village whose houses are all but lost amid the lushness, where old people still proudly remember the tanners who made the leather for the shoes in which Roger Bannister broke the four-minute mile.

If this attractive clergyman had a fault it was chemistry. In his youth, it had proved a 'great nuisance' to the females of his family home, 'who were bothered by Master William's messes', a niece remembered. He continued his scientific interests when he grew up, together with painting, etching, playing Handel and Corelli on the piano and, more surprisingly for a man of the cloth, studying naval warfare (it was the age of Nelson). Geology was of practical importance in Cornwall; the minerals glinting on the surface of rocks might prove to be a valuable resource, capable of being mined.

Undaunted by his remote location or limited apparatus, Gregor began, in the words of the *Oxford Dictionary of National Biography*, 'to undertake original and, for the time, remarkably accurate analyses of Cornish minerals'. His reputation was such that, in 1791, someone sent him a sample of black sand taken from the leat of a mill in Manaccan, on the further side of Helford River. It took him twenty-one sometimes complicated experiments to construe it. Much of the sand was iron oxide, but he detected that the oxide of another, unknown metal was mixed in with it. He called it manaccanite, reporting his findings to the Royal Geological Society of Cornwall, of which he was a founding member, and publishing them in a German journal.

Six years later, the prominent German chemist Martin Heinrich Klaproth identified the same metal in another sample. We now know that it is the sixth most common of the earth's metals and the ninth most common element, present even in the human body. Lustrous and silver-coloured in its pure form, it occurs in compounds of minerals from which it is difficult to separate. Indeed, it is so tightly grappled to these compounds that Klaproth named it after the mythical Titans, who did battle with the gods. Klaproth, who did not know of Gregor's publication, generously gave Gregor credit for the discovery, but his more elegant name stuck. As Maurice Smelt observes in *101 Cornish Lives* (2003), Gregor's story in this respect is not unique, being paralleled in that of another Cornishman, also a Cambridge man, also brilliant, also modest, whose major discovery went similarly unobserved until a German had rediscovered it: John Couch Adams, who deduced the existence of the planet Neptune by mathematics in 1845.

# DELABOLE
CORNWALL                              *Disembowelling Mother Earth*

Slate is a great feature of Cornish building, used not just on the roofs of houses but on their walls: slate-hanging is part of the armoury against Atlantic gales. The quarry at Delabole has, for centuries, supplied most of it. Fine-grained, the slate is strong but light in weight; its colour of dark grey tinged with green complements the austerity of the Cornish palette, in which grey (local granite) and white (applied to the rendering that sometimes covers it) predominate. Its virtues were recognised by Victorian architects, who often specified it for structures in other parts of the country. And so the quarry, which had started as a scratch on the earth's surface, grew into a wen: a great open oval wound, one and a half kilometres around and a hundred and fifty metres deep, that never heals.

Before the coalfields were closed in the 1980s, southerners thought of pit regions, such as south Wales, Nottinghamshire and Co. Durham, as being lands of slag heaps. Most of those conical mountains of waste have been landscaped away. Delabole is still producing, piling up the parts of its geology that it cannot use. Every ten tons of slate that is quarried generates 250 tons of waste. This is the paradox of Cornwall: while the sea margin has been beautifully preserved as a place of secret coves, pretty fishing villages and wild flowers, inland Mother Earth has been, and continues to be, disembowelled.

It is easy to overlook the extent to which Man has worked the countryside (one could say humankind, but it is generally men who have done it). Countryside that has been scarred with mine workings, quarries and gravel pits tends not to be considered countryside, in the modern understanding of the word as somewhere pastoral and 'unspoilt'. Actually, the history of the land, all land, until the 1947 Town and Country Planning Act, is one of non-stop commercial exploitation, wherever people could see that it might pay.

Cornwall has been worked as hard as anywhere. China clay mines have created a moonscape around St Austell – English Heritage is now working on plans to convert it to heath and woodland – and the Eden Project occupies a disused china clay pit at Bodelva. There are no plans to reconfigure Delabole, which remains a working quarry owned by the Delabole Slate Company Ltd. It may be that the village no longer relies on it for employment: only five people are needed to quarry 120 tons of slate a day. But amelioration of the landscape would in itself present a ticklish dilemma: the quarry has its own drama as a landmark. Almost nothing in Britain, except arguably the river estuaries, could be considered a wilderness in the sense of a landscape untouched by human interference. Delabole is a man-made wilderness. Perhaps we shall grow to love it in time.

# DOWN ST MARY
DEVON                                                                *The cob revival*

In 1978, the village of Down St Mary got a new bus shelter. Nothing especially remarkable about that, except that it was thatched and built out of cob, making it the first cob structure of any significance to be constructed in Devon since the Second World War. Once, cob was the Devon building material par excellence. The red soil of the county was particularly well suited to it.

Cob is unbaked earth, rammed earth if you prefer, or clay lump, a.k.a. *pisé de terre.* Clom, clob and korb are other names that it goes by. Earth that has been sieved to a fine tilth is laid over straw; water is put on it to make it sticky, and more straw laid on top. The earth and the straw are trodden together, perhaps using cattle or horses; inevitably there is an admixture of dung. Other organic material, such as twigs, may be thrown into the mix. Lumps of the clay/straw mixture are then piled into a wall, one horizontal section at a time. Where the clay was not sufficiently sticky, wooden boards would be used to mould it into place, later being removed to reveal straight walls.

An enormous percentage of the world's population lives in earth buildings – perhaps as much as a third. It is estimated that there are twenty thousand cob houses in Devon. Before the nineteenth century, it could be found wherever stone, timber and other propitious building materials were scarce. (A correspondent to *Country Life* in 1914 wrote that most of Naseby in Northamptonshire [see page

343] had been built of mud before 1850, the method of construction being similar to that used in Nigeria for mud huts.)

But it was not altogether second best. Earth may seem to occupy a lowly place in the constructional hierarchy, but it has advantages. Visually, cob buildings, if unplastered, seem of a piece with the landscape; their walls have no knowledge of geometry, but appear to move in and out like a living creature. They will last, too, so long as they do not get wet. Water is the great destroyer of cob walling, turning it to mud. Knowing this, old builders would stand cob houses on a plinth of stone, then plaster and limewash the walls and have them overhung by deep eaves. By 1800, cob was being used for town houses with basements and attics, even if the walls of such buildings were (the Devon Historic Buildings Trust says) twenty feet thick.

In the Victorian period, the availability of industrially produced brick, transported around Britain by railway, pushed cob into the shade. Coxen, the cob house that the craftsman-architect Ernest Gimson, Jewson's mentor, built at Budleigh Salterton shortly before the First World War, was one of the last of its kind for sixty years. Clough Williams-Ellis, architect of Portmeirion (see page 502), made a brave case for *pisé de terre* to overcome the shortage of brick during the drive to construct a million homes after the First World War, but his arguments were not heard. Now, however, the craft – which is economic, low-energy and admirable in terms of recycling and thermal properties – has been revived by specialists, who are not only capable of repairing old buildings but creating new ones. The Down St Mary bus shelter is the first herald of a revival.

# EAST KNOYLE
## WILTSHIRE
*The rector in his chancel*

Sir Christopher Wren was born at East Knoyle, but not brought up here. His father, also Christopher, was East Knoyle's rector, a High Churchman, whose Laudian sympathies recommended him to Charles I: he rose to become chaplain in ordinary to Charles I, registrar of the Order of the Garter and dean of Windsor, acquiring the rich living of Great Haseley in Oxfordshire along the way.

In Wiltshire, the Wrens lived in the midst of Royalist families. As might be imagined, none of these factors recommended him to the Puritans at the start of the Civil War, and Dr Wren was accused of 'Delinquency'. It was an unjust charge, which may have resulted from too much activity on Dr Wren's part, rather than too little. During the thirty years that he ministered at East Knoyle, he rebuilt the church roof (like his son, he was 'well skilled in the mathematicks'). Around 1639, he also decorated the chancel with a scheme of plasterwork, which may have infuriated Low Church elements of the congregation.

As rector, Dr Wren had responsibility for the chancel of his church. This continued the medieval practice of separating the functions and responsibility of the chancel from the rest of the church building. The chancel was a place of holiness, where the sacred rites were performed. Since the Fourth Lateran Council had declared transubstantiation – the doctrine by which the bread and wine at communion are deemed to become Christ's body and blood – to be an article of faith in 1215, highly decorated rood screens had been erected to shield the holy mysteries from vulgar eyes. By law, the upkeep of the chancel fell to the rector. The parish, however, looked after the nave. Until pews came to be installed*, the space could be used for all manner of secular activities during the week – markets, meetings, even boozy 'ales' before the construction of the church house† – only reverting to its primary function as a place of worship on Sundays.

Dr Wren seems to have taken full advantage of his authority over the chancel by redecorating it. Since he had an ingenious mind, the precise meaning must have baffled the majority of his congregation; indeed the iconography is still impossible to unpick. But the general drift is clear. References to prayers rising like incense to heaven suggest that this High Churchman was having a dig at the Puritans. They got their own back by bursting into the church, seizing the doctor and hacking off part of his plasterwork. By this time, the future architect of St Paul's was already at Westminster School or living with his brother-in-law, an Oxfordshire rector and mathematician. Later, bits of the chancel ceiling simply fell down. Then a restoration of 1846 replaced the decorated chancel arch. What is left is an inscrutable curiosity. (Parishioners were luckier with the restoration of 1891, when the tower was in an alarming condition: the architect Philip Webb, founding secretary of the Society for the Protection of Ancient Buildings, who was building Clouds House for Percy Wyndham outside the village, carried out a sympathetic repair at modest cost, his own time being given for nothing.)

It is one of the quirks of the British system that chancel repairs are still part and parcel of being a rector (the word derives from the Latin for 'ruler', referring to the person who looks after church property in a parish; there are lay rectors as well as those in holy orders). Following the Dissolution of the Monasteries and the Enclosure Acts, which reorganised glebe lands, such responsibilities may have become attached to a property that has no modern connection with the church. Owners of Old Rectories beware.

*See Brent Knoll, page 17. †See South Tawton, page 73

# EXFORD
SOMERSET                                        *A community that lives for hunting*

'The uninformed traveller,' W. H. Hudson wrote in 1909, '. . . is surprised to find that the small village of Exford contains no fewer than half a dozen inns.' The reason, then as now, was not hard to find. It is a village that lives for and on stag hunting. 'Thither the hunters flock in August, and spend so much money during their brief season that the innkeepers grow rich and fat, and for the rest of the year can afford to doze peacefully behind their bars.' Hudson was not, perhaps, well informed about the dates of the stag-hunting season, which lasts from August until April. But he was right about the Devon and Somerset Staghounds that are kennelled here. You cannot sit on the green for long without hearing hooves ring out on the road surface; this is a place that prefers the horse to the car.

Stag hunting is one of the oldest sports; deer, unlike the fox, were regarded as a suitable quarry for kings and the high born. It was a passion of the Norman kings, who designated large areas of England as forests, where venison and its habitat would be preserved*. Because hunting took place on a horse, it had the benefit of honing a battlefield skill at a time when kings and great noblemen were expected to lead their armies in war. 'Venerie', by its proponents, was considered to be a 'profitable and godly' activity for 'the pleasure of all noblemen and gentlemen', according to George Gascoigne. But during Queen Elizabeth's reign, the royal forests lost their importance, and although James I was an obsessive hunter, the Stuarts were not sufficiently solvent to halt the decline.

Six hundred of Lord Middlesex's deer were massacred on his estate in the Severn valley at the outbreak of the Civil War in 1642, as a symbol of popular rebellion. With no incentive, or compulsion, to preserve England's deer herd, farmers killed the deer that they found eating their crops. The fox, previously regarded as vermin to be exterminated by fair means or foul, became a new quarry species. Deer hunting retreated to Exmoor and Dartmoor, which had never been royal forests. Even there it periodically died out.

By the time that stag hunting was revived in 1855, there were only seventy-five deer left. Hunting not only provided farmers with a reason for preserving the deer they would chase, but also a method of managing and improving the herd. It would be split up, so no one farmer suffered too great a burden; it would be culled to prevent inbreeding and contain the size. Evidently it proved effective, since in 1917 Lloyd George's administration paid for hunting to be re-established on the Quantock Hills to control the deer population, with the object of increasing agricultural production.

Like other rural villages, Exford was knocked by the farming depression of the 1990s and the foot-and-mouth disaster, which closed the countryside to visitors and stopped hunting, in 2001†. In 2004, its principal industry was targeted by the ban on hunting with hounds. Yet hunting continues, in modified form.

*See Rockingham, page 347. †See Heddon-on-the-Wall, page 423. See also Badminton, page 298; Caldbeck, page 379

# FARNHAM

DORSET                    *The potent conjunction of culture and a good tea*

Not much stirs on a Saturday morning before breakfast at Farnham. The golden leaves on the trees of Cranborne Chase hardly tremble, the pheasant on the roof ridge does not budge an inch (hardly surprising, since it is made of thatch). As yet, no children have come out to play on the swings and slides; frost dissolves undisturbed on the grass. With nobody to talk to, there is nothing for it but to consult the village noticeboard. Scraps of paper speak of yoga, parent-and-toddler groups and the accounts for bonfire night (alas, it made a loss). Breathe in deeply and take the essence of England into your lungs: the place seems to have splashed it on like cologne. This used to be Guy Ritchie and Madonna territory, when they lived at Ashcombe, down the road. In the heady days before the sub-prime crash, a hedge-fund manager bought Clarendon Park for a cool thirty-five million pounds.

But an altogether more exotic history can be disinterred without difficulty. One only has to look at the pub, The Museum. The character of the regulars has changed; the ninety-three-year-old whose photograph hangs over the place where he sat every evening until God called last orders worked in the woods around Farnham; there are not any jobs of that sort any more. The corrugated-iron extension tacked onto its side is now a restaurant (it used to be the village hall). It is not obviously museum-like. So why the name?

There was indeed a museum in the village until 1966, and an important one. It housed the second collection formed by General Augustus Pitt-Rivers, owner of the Rushmore estate on which Farnham stands. He had been born Augustus Fox, acquiring the additional name of Pitt-Rivers in 1880, when he inherited from his cousin, the 6th Baron Rivers; this made him a rich man. He was already a remarkable one. A soldier, he had been posted in the 1860s to Ireland, where he surveyed some prehistoric forts. This sparked an interest in archaeology and ethnography. He formulated the idea that objects could be placed in sequence according to the development of their design – a principle that revolutionised archaeology by providing a means by which artefacts could be dated.

From the 1850s, General Pitt-Rivers began to collect militaria, followed by ethnological pieces and antiquities. These objects were put on display in the South Kensington Museum, before being offered to the University of Oxford, fourteen thousand items going in 1884 to form the basis of the Pitt-Rivers Museum. Now that he was rich, however, he could start a completely new collection, housed in a building of nine rooms and galleries at Farnham. It sought to 'illustrate the arts and crafts of peasant communities', with peasant costumes, Breton peasant furniture, a library, locks and keys, finds from excavations that Pitt-Rivers had himself undertaken on Cranborne Chase, pottery, arts and crafts of prehistoric Europe and Asia, farm tools and ethnographic objects, notably weapons and ceremonial items.

Whereas the British Museum was, in the General's words, 'a Museum of Reference . . . or Research', his own museum at Farnham was 'an educational museum, in which the visitors may instruct themselves'. It sought to improve the mental range of working people, just as the Larmer Tree Gardens that he laid out in Cranborne Chase sought to entertain them. The two objectives were not incompatible: more people would visit the museum if they were enjoying themselves. To this end, the Museum Inn was an essential part of the project. In this he was once again pioneering. Culture and a good tea would prove a potent combination, to be richly exploited in the second half of the twentieth century by the National Trust.

# GEORGEHAM
DEVON                                         *In the country of the two rivers*

The author of the twentieth century's most famous nature book came from London. In 1914, Henry Williamson drove down on a motorbike to visit an aunt in the white-walled village of Georgeham. He walked, by his own account, twenty or twenty-five miles every day. Then came the First World War, during which he served as a machine gunner. Highly strung and romantic, he hated both the war and the system that had caused it.

Having read Richard Jefferies's *The Story of My Heart*, he determined to be a writer, and returned to Georgeham, where he lived alone at Skirr Cottage – named from the sound that owls made on the roof. He married, lived impecuniously, and kept a pet otter. His knowledge of otters and other wildlife was wrought into *Tarka the Otter*, telling of his 'joyful water life and death in the country of the two rivers'. It was sentimental, perhaps, but not idyllic; Tarka, the cub, has to survive on his own after being separated from his family and is finally killed by an otter hound.

After Skirr Cottage, Williamson moved a few yards to Crowbury Cottage (now marked by a plaque). In 1929, he left for Shallowford in Devon, and eight years later to Stiffkey in Norfolk*. He now had six children and, without any previous experience, wanted to farm. It was to be his contribution towards the new order that Oswald Mosley's British Union of Fascists seemed to promise; Williamson had already visited a Nazi rally at Nuremberg, where he had been impressed by the discipline and back-to-the-land ideals of the Hitler Youth Movement. In the trenches, he had been profoundly affected by the Christmas Day truce of 1914, and hoped that a spirit of shared cultural values could avoid the oncoming war. Fascism might reinvigorate what he saw as a dying civilisation.

Farming during an agricultural depression did nothing to cheer his view of the world. As he wrote in *The Story of a Norfolk Farm*: 'Rats, weeds, swamps, depressed markets, labourers on the dole, rotten cottages, polluted streams, political parties and class divisions controlled by the money-power, wealthy banking and insurance houses getting rid of their land-mortgages and investing their millions abroad (but not in the Empire), this was the real England of the period of this story of a Norfolk farm.' In 1940, Williamson was briefly interned. After the Second World War, he returned to Georgeham.

Williamson was not an easy neighbour. Women found him attractive, but his treatment of them earned him the nickname in some quarters of Tarka the Rotter. His habit of carrying the latest chapter of whichever of the fifty books he published in his pocket, ready to whip out and read at the least encouragement, was not always endearing. Reading to the author Negley Farson and his wife, Eve, in their house near Croyde, he found his attention being sought by their dachshund; without looking up, he lashed out with his toe and sent the animal flying across the room. He was banned from the house.

Williamson divorced in 1950, and remarried, although his choice did not fall on the daughter of the poet Edward Thomas, who had been his mistress, but on a pretty gym teacher. That marriage ended in 1962. Six years later he was the subject of a programme by BBC television. He spoke of his supersensory perception (his ability to notice things); his capacity for working, hardly moving, for thirty-six hours at a stretch, before the open hearth; and the Devon countryside. He owed, he said, 'everything' to it: 'I regained myself here.' In 1977, he was buried in Georgeham churchyard, beneath a headstone carved with an owl.

*See Stiffkey, page 268

# GODOLPHIN CROSS
CORNWALL              *The industry that built Cornwall . . . before it fell asleep*

You do not see the mines at Godolphin, on England's furthest western extremity. There is no Victorian pit shaft rising like a gloomy spirit exhaled by the invaded earth. The engine house and stack 'sank perpendicularly' into Simms Engine Shaft 'out of sight' when the works closed, according to the *West Briton*. That was in the mid nineteenth century. But for hundreds, indeed thousands of years before that, people had been poking into the ground in search of minerals. In the eighteenth century a cache of 'celts', a kind of bronze axe, was discovered in a shallow pit: evidence that mining took place here in 1200BC. Perhaps Godolphin was sending ingots of tin to be traded with Phoenicians such as Pytheas of Massilia (Marseilles), the account of whose journey of 325BC, summarised by the Greek historian Diodorus Siculus, provides the record of Britain in history.

The mine that was known, with grand simplicity, as the Great Work was opened in the late Middle Ages and it reigned supreme in Cornwall until at least the close of the seventeenth century. 'There are no greater Tynne works yn al Cornwal than be on Sir Wylliam Godolcan's Ground,' stated John Leland after visiting in about 1538. In 1584, another writer, John Norden, commented that the Great Work, or Godolphyn Ball, had been a mint for the Godolphin family, 'by reason of the riches which the same hill hath and doth yielde in Tynn works'. At least three hundred miners were employed; the annual profit was put at a thousand pounds.

As well as tin there was copper. The avidity with which these minerals were exploited can be seen in Godolphin House, begun as a castle in 1300 then rebuilt in the late fifteenth century and expanded into a house of two courtyards during the Tudor period. When Sir William Godolphin I panelled the dining room in 1537 he had to use imported wood: everything growing locally had been turned into charcoal for smelting. Sir William Godolphin II led a party of Cornish miners to undermine the walls of Boulogne when it was being besieged by Henry VIII.

By the 1630s, the mines were financing a lifestyle of serious pretension. This was when the house reached its apogee, in such a progressive style that Sir Francis Godolphin must have known Inigo Jones. Inspired by the Italian architect Scamozzi, the concept, whether drawn by a court architect such as Jones or by Sir Francis himself, is sophisticated. It seems then to have been taken to Cornwall and provincialised, with the addition of such notably unclassical details as a battlemented parapet. Nevertheless, the masons knew their granite: several different types are used in the entrance loggia.

Like so many Cornish gentlemen, Sir Francis was tenaciously attached to the past: he kept the old-fashioned Tudor doorway as the entry to his new house. Not surprisingly, this courtly sentimentalist fought for the King during the Civil War, and was ruined by doing so (he spent his last tin ingot escorting the future Charles II on his escape to the Isles of Scilly). Work on Godolphin stopped – so abruptly that graffiti left by the workmen beside one of the upstairs windows was never covered over. Among the different dates and initials one of 1634 can still be made out.

The family fortunes recovered under Sidney, 1st Earl of Godolphin, who became Queen Anne's lord high treasurer. It was his son, Francis, who imported the Godolphin Arabian, one of the three racehorses from which the Thoroughbred bloodline was formed. But Godolphin House received little attention. And then the minerals ran out, and Godolphin fell asleep, the Victorians only just succeeding to keep their eyes open sufficiently to build a church for the village in 1849–50. The National Trust, which now owns the house, is doing its best not to waken the silent place too abruptly. In this county of pixies, giants, ghosts and legends, it is only right there should be a sleeping beauty.

Fairies called knockers were supposed to live in the mines; they did not like whistling or the sign of the cross, but were otherwise benign, their knocking noises being the sign of a good lode. Perhaps if you listen carefully you may hear them still. They seem to have done at South Crofty: mining there is being revived.

# HALLSANDS
## DEVON

*Neptune takes his revenge*

One January night in 1917, the village of Hallsands was washed into the sea. For hundreds of years it had been making its living – not a great one – from fishing and crabbing. One hundred and twenty-eight people lived there: a tough lot, used to spartan conditions and the storms of Start Bay, on which Hallsands sat. There are happy pictures of Edwardian children in big sunhats sitting on stretches of a sea wall, the beach behind them a busy scene of rowing boats, crab pots and poles with fish drying, while a chicken pecks on the road.

The village itself had seemed secure enough. With the cliffs at their backs, the whitewashed cottages huddled on an apron of rock, protected by a sea wall, while the waves spent their energy crashing onto a great beach of pebbles. The wind roared, women might worry over men at sea, but the little parlours where the inhabitants would cook, eat and sit seemed snugly weatherproof. Until disaster struck.

It was not entirely an act of God. Man had taken a hand in it, too. In the last years of the nineteenth century, the Admiralty had decided to enlarge the Keyham dockyard at Devonport, a huge undertaking in which the principal building material would be concrete. Making the concrete required epic quantities of sand and gravel. The Board of Trade licensed a contractor to take it from Start Bay. When the residents of Hallsands saw the dredging ships at work – they had not been previously consulted – they complained, fearing disturbance to fishing grounds and the destruction of lobster pots. For this, they were allowed £125 a year in compensation.

It was not thought that extraction would threaten the coastline, because holes dug in the seabed would quickly fill up with sand from elsewhere. But by 1900, the parish council had noticed that the pebble shelf in front of the village had dropped. The foundations of the sea wall were exposed and it started to crumble. The fishermen eventually hauled in the buoys that marked the dredging site, causing a temporary halt to operations. They ceased altogether in 1901. By that time, however, 650,000 tons of sand and gravel had been removed from the seabed. The sea had been given a way in. The sea wall collapsed in 1903.

The end came on a night of exceptionally high tide. Evening had closed in early. Gale-force winds were tearing in, unusually, from the east, hurling waves across the diminished beach. The sea wall, though repaired, proved a puny defence. Water surged into the cottages, bursting open doors and smashing windows. The people of Hallsands gathered together what they could and hurried to the cliff tops. There they watched the destruction of their homes. By midnight, the sea had taken four of them. Next day, the high tide continued and so did the toll of dwellings, as one rugged cottage after another gave way and their debris was sucked and chewed upon by the waves. By the end of the day, only one house out of thirty was left habitable. The rest had been reduced to a mess of thatch and rubble, shells of houses with end walls torn down and their innards put on public display.

The gravel that the contractor had taken had been deposited at the end of the last ice age. The ruins that survive at Hallsands today are an object lesson in the need to tread cautiously when you disturb Neptune's kingdom.

# HAMMOON
## DORSET
*In and out of love with the manor house*

Manor house is an evocative idea to the English. The words conjure up a picturesque dream of roaring fires in whitewashed halls, of oak panelling and carved stonework glimpsed through the shadows, the glint of pewter, mysterious tapestries – a sense of architectural presence that remains approachable, antiquity not divorced from the comfort of a Knole sofa. Often built near the church, the manor house is part of the immemorial fabric of the countryside.

That is certainly true of Hammoon Manor. You approach the hamlet of Hammoon across a watery landscape, around which the river Stour seems to have thrown itself like a friendly arm – like other friendly arms, it doesn't always seem to know when it has become too familiar, during winter floods. The manor house sits modestly beside the lane to Manor Farm, without so much as a wrought-iron grille and gate piers to give it status (you reach the front door by a wooden farm gate).

*Manor houses, such as this one at Hammoon, seem to be an immemorial part of the countryside.*

This is one of the county's smallest manor houses, sheltering beneath a bulging roof of humble thatch that seems almost to breathe, like a Labrador asleep. Begun in the fifteenth century, it is built of creamy, lichen-covered stone, with mullion windows. Around 1600, the owner added a classical centrepiece, banded Tuscan columns below and curly Jacobean gable and finials above: it gives architectural piquancy to the composition. A sycamore tree inside the surrounding brick wall, so lichen-covered that it is almost the same colour as the wall, completes the picture.

The name itself is perfumed with mystery, as though some knight dragged part of Morocco back with him from a crusade. The truth, as so often, is less fanciful: it is simply a corruption of the name of the Norman owners – DeMohun. The manor was a basic unit in the Norman system of administration, a tool of land management and control. (Manors did not follow parish boundaries, nor did all manors have manor houses on them.) As feudalism declined, manor houses became gentry dwellings. Their high point came in the Tudor and Stuart periods, when city merchants wanted to put their profits into the best possible investment: land.

To the Georgians, the evocatively dark rooms of the manor house, lit by casement windows, seemed immensely old-fashioned. Those that weren't refaced or pulled down often fell into decay. In George Eliot's *Adam Bede*, set in 1799, the old manor house had become Manor Farm, 'a very fine old place', but with windows patched with board, a front door that was never opened and sacks of wool stored in the dining room. Other manor houses fared even worse, being left to collapse. Part of the problem was that the estates to which they belonged were not allowed to sell them.

A change in the law at the end of the nineteenth century coincided with a change in taste; to followers of William Morris, manor houses seemed the quintessence of Old England, ancient but not assertively grand. Many that we now regard as the most beautiful, often in Dorset, were restored at that date, by owners who loved the oak furniture and pewter that went with them. There was a degree of poetic fakery as panelled rooms and even whole structures were installed in new locations. As Jeremy Musson writes in *The English Manor House*, restored manor houses (Sutton Courtenay in Oxfordshire, Cothay in Somerset, Great Chalfield in Wiltshire, Athelhampton in Dorset) came to symbolise the house as a 'total work of art'. Hammoon, snuggling into the village without fuss, never rose to those heights of aesthetic completeness in the early twentieth century. Who knows if it will not in the future?

# HELFORD
CORNWALL *Second homes: right or wrong?*

Helford in Cornwall is a fishing village without a jetty to land the catch. Although more than a million pounds' worth of fish is caught each year by Helford-based ships, it has to be offloaded outside the harbour, onto dinghies, before being brought in. The houses on Helford's seafront are not owned by the fishermen they were built for. They are all second homes for people who live outside Cornwall, or holiday homes let to tourists.

Newcomers and visitors expect Helford, like other pretty villages, to be tranquil, forgetting it grew up in the first place to serve an industry. When Kerrier District Council approved an application to build a jetty in 2008, it received nearly two hundred letters of complaint, followed by a process of judicial review forced by a group of property owners. In 2009, the High Court in London overturned the planning consent, without leave to appeal. The fishermen feel bitter that their safety and livelihoods have been valued less highly than newcomers' peace and quiet.

The case illustrates the altered dynamics of many of Britain's most scenic villages. There is growing concern, anger in places, about the ability of second-homers to price locals out of the property market, leave their cottages empty for much of the year, then try to impose their own priorities on village life. An official report into the rural economy and affordable housing by the Liberal Democrat MP Matthew Taylor, presented to the government in 2008, called for homes in the most popular villages to be subject to a new form of planning regulation, which would require consent for less than full-time occupancy. In its response, the government rejected the idea, but as MP for a Cornish constituency, Mr Taylor appreciates the passions the subject arouses. There have been threats of violence from extreme anti-second-home groups on occasion.

But the forces at play are not always as straightforward as they seem. In 2004, the academic Michael John Ireland published a fine piece of social anthropology on the Lizard village of Sennen Cove. It disclosed a long-seated rivalry between the Covers – fishermen, supposedly inbred and prone to stutter, possibly descended from shipwrecked Spaniards – and the cannier Uphillers, or farmers, who still resented the raids that the Covers' donkeys once made on their turnip fields. Into this already fissiparous society came holidaymakers. Before the Second World War, they tended to be professional families who took rooms for six weeks at a time; they were regarded as shedding some lustre on the village and the families with which they lodged.

After the War, the social eligibility of the visitors appeared to fall. Self-catering became an alternative to bed and breakfast – preferable to some, because the host families had less contact with their guests. As well as new visitors, some families who used to be visitors, perhaps going back regularly ever since childhood, and perhaps the childhoods of their parents and grandparents, decided to stay. To people owning a second home, Sennen might represent, in the words of one, their 'spiritual home', better than the one outside London where they are constrained to live, now too noisy and crowded.

Two factors exacerbated the second-home issue. The first was the sale of council houses under the Thatcher government's right-to-buy initiative. This removed some social housing for rent from the market and branded the UK a 'property-owning democracy', where home ownership appeared to equate with capital growth. The second was the long bull market in domestic property, a nearly fifteen-year run that began around 1993. Merely visiting a place for a holiday was no longer enough. Cheap credit fuelled rising expectations, and more and more people found they could release equity from their first home to buy a second. The cost of pretty cottages went up accordingly, far beyond the reach of a local, possibly seasonal worker earning £15,000 a year. Second homes have become a shorthand for many ills, but they remain only the symptom of a problem, not its cause. The cause is the lack of high-paying jobs in remote villages. With broadband technology, can one hope that this will change?

# HINDON
## WILTSHIRE                                        *Coaching, in the glory days*

From the Regency until the 1840s, coaching inns were the great transport hubs of Victorian Britain. Coaches rattled down the newly improved turnpike roads at speeds of as much as twelve miles an hour, horns sounding, their appearance at the inn causing excitement and bustle, and tempting boys to jump (at some danger) onto the back for a free ride. Inns were essential to provide a change of horses. The larger ones had stables that could accommodate forty or fifty – the Bull and Mouth in the City of London had underground stabling for four hundred. They contained the offices where the tickets were sold and parcels dispatched. They also served food.

The idea grew up at the end of the nineteenth century that they were one of the glories of Old England, although contemporary experience tells a different tale. On busy routes, they developed the trick of bringing out food just before the coach was about to leave. 'You carved the wing of a fowl for the lady opposite . . . were proceeding to help yourself when – lo! That is the coachman . . . crying "All ready!" and [the innkeeper's] confidential waiter is collecting the three-and-sixpence – and you have not taken a mouthful.' As for the coach itself, it was remembered by one aristocratic enthusiast as 'not very pleasant to make one of four, the other three consisting of a stout farmer, rude both in health and manners, a fat nurse with a squalling child, and an elderly invalid who insisted on having both windows up'. But coaching revolutionised travel. In 1779, the Bath and Bristol New London Post Coach boasted that from Bristol it would reach London in eighteen hours.

Hindon was a coaching town on the London to Exeter run, and still possesses two inns – the Lamb and the Angel – out of the fourteen it had in the mid eighteenth century. It had grown out of a planned development by the Bishop of Winchester, who founded it in 1219. He hoped that his new settlement would serve as a market for the existing centres at Mere and Shaftesbury. It was laid out with burgage plots – long gardens stretching back from the main street – which would have been suitable for artisans and shopkeepers, rather than farmers.

By the mid thirteenth century, Hindon had a hundred and fifty houses, and thereafter it flourished, becoming an important corn market. Lord Clarendon met the Prince of Orange there in 1688; when the parson James Woodforde stayed in 1787, he found the Prime Minister William Pitt was at the same inn. Like countless other towns with thatched roofs, it suffered a calamitous fire, in Hindon's case after some sparks escaped from a forge in 1754. It was rebuilt, using Chilmark and Tisbury stone for the better houses. The makeover gave it an orderly, modern air, in readiness for the coaching age. The first mail coach stopped here in 1784. The Lamb was said to keep three hundred horses.

The population of the town peaked in 1831; then the Great Western Railway came. What the country gained in efficiency it lost in spectacle. No longer the danger that passengers travelling outside on the box would topple off in their sleep, perhaps killing themselves. No more piping hot brandy and water being served as the coach was due to leave, so the drinker could not take more than a sip, or the temptation to smuggle a roast fowl onto the coach (taking out food was strictly forbidden) because there had not been time to eat it inside. From 1879, train passengers could eat in the dining car.

# HINTON ST MARY
## DORSET
*Rome leaves a legacy*

Villa, village – the connection between the Roman countryside and our own is more than a matter of linguistics. A villa was a centre of administration, which was also home to a grand individual. The buildings must often have been taken over after the collapse of Roman government for local people to occupy; certainly the materials from which they were made were quarried for other purposes. You can often see traces of Roman tile in, for example, the towers of churches. Worn away, the remains of the domestic accommodation eventually disappeared beneath the soil. Of greater import was the unit of land that the villa oversaw. Successive regimes lived with what they had taken over; they were happy to take possession of a working countryside. In that way, although the rulers changed, the life of the peasants who tilled the soil continued much the same. It may be that the shape of the manors recorded in the Domesday Book ultimately derived from land divisions known to the Romans – and perhaps in existence before them. Villages formed themselves within these parcels of ownership, according to the lie of the land and farming needs.

Dorset is a county rich in villas, as many as eighteen having been discovered. One of them, at Hinton St Mary, contained, in a mosaic pavement, the earliest image of Christ to have been found in Britain. It dates from the mid to late fourth century, a couple of centuries before the first churches were built. Christ is depicted as though he was a high-status official, in a toga, his hair bobbed in Roman fashion, his cheeks rather chubby and clean shaven. Behind him is a Christian monogram, made from the Greek letters Chi and Rho, the first two letters of his name.

There are two floors at Hinton St Mary. Together with those at Frampton (now disappeared, but known from the comprehensive engravings made by Samuel Lysons in 1807) they form the masterpieces of the Durnovarian school of mosaicists, named after Durnovaria, as Dorchester was known. Mosaic-making had been practised in Britain since shortly after the Roman conquest, an early example – a geometrical pattern in black and white – surviving from the first phase of Fishbourne Palace, near Chichester. The most elaborate comes from the luxurious fourth-century villa at Woodchester in Gloucestershire, where at least twenty rooms had mosaics.

It has to be said that, despite the image of Christ, the Christian content at Hinton St Mary is rather small. Our Lord appears amid hunting scenes. The centrepiece of the other scheme is the Greek hero Bellerophon spearing the three-headed Chimera, while around him more stags are killed by hounds. But now that the Emperor Constantine had adopted Christianity, following a military victory in 312, it was as well to include the new God as the presiding deity of the home. The result forms the only representation of Christ to have been discovered on a mosaic floor anywhere in the Roman Empire.

The Hinton St Mary mosaics, with parts of the villa to which they belonged, lay under a field outside the village until they were literally unearthed in 1963. They are now in the British Museum.

# HOLWELL
## DORSET                                            *A rare postal treasure*

Are you a member of the Letter Box Study Group? If so, stop reading now; there is nothing that this entry can tell you. People outside that charmed circle may, however, not be in on the Holwell secret. This Dorset village, near Sherborne – not to be confused with the hamlet of the same name near Nunney in Somerset – boasts the oldest pillar box still in operation on the mainland of Britain. The qualification is important. The letter box was the idea of Anthony Trollope, now famed as a novelist but then working as a district surveyor for the Post Office, stationed in the Channel Islands. The penny black had been introduced in 1840, but no

*The oldest working letter box on the British mainland can
be found at Holwell: note the vertical slot.*

satisfactory system of collecting the letters. The French had got there: roadside boxes had existed in Paris since 1653. The very first pillar boxes – so called because of their classical form – appeared in 1852 in St Helier, Jersey; they were an instant success. One can still be seen, in the original position, in St Peter Port on Guernsey.

The first mainland box, since disappeared, was erected in Carlisle in 1853. It was to a different design from the Holwell box. In those experimental days, each district surveyor made his own arrangements. The Holwell box (or, strictly speaking, Barnes Cross box, since it sits in the southern half of the settlement) is octagonal, capped, with a vertical slit for the reception of letters (on the inner side was a swinging flap to keep out the rain) and, of course, Queen Victoria's initials embossed either side of a crown. It was made of iron and cast by John M. Butt and Company of Gloucester.

The post and the railways: together they made the hegemony of the Victorian age possible. Professional people, charged with the energy of the free market, could criss-cross Britain by train, dispatching sheaves of correspondence as they went. Most of them had few staff. They wrote using dip pens. Their writing, which poured out of them in torrents, was not always easy to read. But, thanks to three deliveries a day, they could communicate almost as freely as later generations did on the telephone. An answer by return sometimes arrived back the same day. Without the post, the Herculean labours of the architectural profession, for example, always on the move between commissions, meeting clients here and inspecting sites there, would hardly have been possible.

One of the principles on which the Post Office was established was that it would cover the whole country. In that respect, rural districts were just as well served as the metropolis. An efficient postal service opened up the countryside to the middle classes. It would hardly have been feasible for families to retire to Cornwall or the Norfolk coast for the summer without being able to stay in touch.

Nowadays, a similar role is provided by broadband, although it is not, as yet, a universal service. Meanwhile, post offices in rural locations close. There was, it might be suggested, a reason that postboxes were painted red. Post is the life blood of commerce, even today (just look at the number of trades, requiring delivery by post, transacted on eBay). Cut off the circulation, gangrene follows.

# HONEYCHURCH
DEVON                                        *Unchanged since the Domesday Book?*

Honeychurch is every bit as delightful as its mellifluous name. It is also a remarkable example of the continuity that, for a millennium, has been such a characteristic of the English countryside. In the tenth century, a church was founded here by a landowner called Huna, a Saxon, who endowed it with the tithes of his estate. In due course this landholding was detailed in the Domesday Book as Honechercha. It ran to some six hundred acres. There were five farms, one of them being the demesne farm (Middleton) worked directly by the lord, or rather his four slaves, the others run by villeins (Westacott, Slade, Bude and East Town). These farms have survived into the twenty-first century, the same size as they were one thousand years ago, joined only by a further farm created out of the former glebe lands that belonged to the church. The present parish is more or less coterminous with Huna's estate.

It was never a big place. The population of Honeychurch was around thirty in the eleventh century. It reached sixty-six in 1801, before falling back to less than a quarter of that number a century later. Honeychurch now sustains roughly the same level of population as it did at Domesday. Equally, the parish has never been rich, as can be seen in the church. Huna's church was completely rebuilt in the twelfth century; the bones of the little stone church survive, together with a twelfth-century font in the form of a tub.

This building was reworked in the fifteenth century, when it received a west tower and new windows. At the same time, the nave was kitted out with box pews, of rugged design. Little seems to have happened since, beyond the addition of a porch in the early sixteenth century. 'We push open the heavy door, and with it the centuries roll back,' the landscape historian W. G. Hoskins wrote in the 1950s. '. . . It is all so worn and uneven, not a straight line anywhere, soaked with so many centuries of Latin Mass spoken to a small gathering of Devonshire farmers and labourers and their households.' It is one of the simplest but most moving church interiors in Britain.

Being poor, Honeychurch was not a desirable living, and both the church and the parsonage – now Glebe Farm – were often in a tumbledown state. The walls were cob, the roof thatch. 'It is neither wainscoted nor ceiled,' the Rev. George Baron, rector, observed in 1727. As a consequence, he rarely went there, to judge from parishioners' complaints. The neglect would be all too often repeated during the next two hundred years. There was no squire to claim the Bishop of Exeter's attention. But neglect can be benign, and if the church authorities appear to have muddled the church dedication during the eighteenth century – they had it down as St James the Less, rather than the correct St Mary – Honeychurch was spared the sort of Victorian going-over that denatured many country churches. Who needs change?

# IPPLEPEN
DEVON                                                  *Home, please, Baskerville*

Which detective story has the most vivid sense of place? Even Dorothy L. Sayers's *The Nine Tailors*, set in the eerie Fens, must yield place to the most masterfully evocative tale of them all, *The Hound of the Baskervilles*. Arthur Conan Doyle heard about the Dartmoor hound legend, or a medley of hound legends, while recuperating from a fever caught in South Africa during the Boer War. He was staying at a hotel with Fletcher Robinson (sometimes, though not to Conan Doyle, known as Bobbles), whom he had met on the ship home. It was 1901, and Robinson had recently inherited a house at Ipplepen, nine miles from the moor. His father's coachman went by the suggestive name of Harry Baskerville.

Robinson's Park Hill House was an unremarkable villa on what is now the busy A381. During the course of his homework, Conan Doyle stayed there, at a hotel in Princetown and, like Sherlock Holmes, in a stone hut on the moor (although with Robinson for company). Baskerville Hall and the great Grimpen Mire are composites, but there are compelling precedents for other places. Nun's Cross Farm, shown as a primitive and cheerless building in contemporary photographs, was the model for Merripit House, home of Stapleton and his beautiful 'sister'. The house that Conan Doyle built for his family in Surrey – Undershaw, at Hindhead – seems to have contributed something; according to Philip Weller, author of *The Hound of the Baskervilles, Hunting the Dartmoor Legend* (2001), it was exceptionally gloomy.

Nothing was made of Park Hill House itself, nor of Ipplepen. It is too big to have inspired the 'small gray hamlet' of Grimpen, whose grocer doubled as the postmaster. Perhaps Conan Doyle came to the same verdict as the great landscape historian W. G. Hoskins, who dismissed Ipplepen as 'a grey and rather dismal village', with, by his time, 'much bad modern building', admitting only that the Perpendicular windows in the church are 'notably good'. Even Thimble Cottage – which sounds as if it ought to be inhabited by an apple-cheeked old lady who collects egg cups – has suffered a loss that is as common to elderly buildings as to elderly men. Its thatch has gone. So it is with most of the houses in Ipplepen, the present slate roofs looking sterner than the old tea cosies of thatch. If only Conan Doyle had known that the village lay in the hundred of Black Torrington: such a detail as that would surely have deserved weaving in.

# KENN
## SOMERSET                                    *Last hanging on the scene of crime*

In the summer of 1830, a procession of two hundred people left the county gaol at Ilchester in Somerset and set off towards Kenn, forty-two miles away. Their destination was a field – the Seven Acre Field, where, the previous October, three wheat ricks had stood. One night they had been burnt down. Now the arsonists – William Wall, John Rowley and Richard Clarke – were on their way to hang. It was to be the last execution to take place on the scene of crime in Britain.

Somerset, like most of rural England, was beset with petty crime. With labouring families woefully underfed, it is not surprising that potatoes were stolen (this was not a point of view generally shared by the magistrates). Even so, arson was regarded with particular hatred, because of its sneaking nature and spitefulness, from which the criminal did not benefit. Kenn was a village without the obvious figures of authority. The vicar had other fish to fry, and was in dispute with the local farmers over tithes – he had managed to increase them, pushing labourers' wages even lower. The payment of wages in the form of strong, home-brewed cider cannot have done anything for law and order.

Not much later, rick burning would be a form of protest employed in the Swing Riots*. Here, however, it was a personal act of revenge. Wall, a small farmer, ran an unlicensed cider house, and Benjamin Poole had informed against him. There is an obvious suspicion that Poole was motivated by the damage done to the trade at his brother's beer house. Thomas Hardy recorded the mechanics of the fire setting, as revealed in the trial, in his notebook: '[Wall's] wife melted brimstone in a spade; dipped 3 or 4 pieces of writing paper in it . . . got rags and made tinder, and went upstairs and fetched a flint, which Richard Clarke took with the matches. She asked if he wanted a steel – he s[ai]d he s[houl]d strike with his knife. They (4 men) then went out of the house – about 3 o'c. – towards the mows. Ten minutes later [the informant] saw 3 lights, on looking out. Sentenced to Death.'

The High Sheriff of Somerset decided on the place of execution. Presumably he wanted to make the punishment particularly poignant. As the Rev. John Leifchild, who was present, observed: 'What occasion had these men for deep sorrow and regret when brought for the last time to witness scenes familiar to them from their infancy – how often may they have paced this very spot in the innocence of child-hood!' Public hangings were not, by this time, the spectacle they had been in the eighteenth century. In London, last journeys had not been made to Tyburn since the place of execution had been switched to Newgate Gaol. But a crowd of four-teen thousand people turned up to watch the punishment, most of them country people like the condemned.

It did little to make Kenn a more peaceable place; violent reprisals were meted out on some of those who had taken part in the trial. Civilised opinion was appalled. The sentences handed out for machine breaking and rick burning in Kent at the beginning of the Swing Riots were lenient by comparison.

*See Lower Hardres, page 128

# LITTLEBREDY
DORSET                                    *Perfection of an estate village*

Bridehead: it is a romantic name, fragrant with the memory of *Brideshead Revisited*. But the Bridehead in Dorset, to which the village of Littlebredy belongs, has nothing to do with Madresfield Court in Worcestershire or Castle Howard in Yorkshire, the country houses on which Evelyn Waugh based the architectural element of his book. Nor does it have anything to do with marriage. Both names, Bride and Bredy, derive from a Celtic word meaning 'to boil', evoking the bubble of the spring that rises here. Bridehead is a lake, whose water, having served as a mirror to the Regency mansion house of Bridehead (deplored by Pevsner, but in a glorious setting), spills out over an artificial waterfall into a little stream of sparkling clarity that trips its way past the row of thatched cottages that stand beneath the church. Littlebredy is one of the last privately owned estate villages in Dorset. As a Tory, Waugh would have been pleased, Benjamin Disraeli even more so.

Littlebredy demonstrates an inescapable and, in this democratic age, unwel-come truth: the prettiest villages are often those owned by estates. The control exercised by family ownership is for the most part visually benign. It is difficult to think of many whose historical character has been traduced for ready money through inappropriate development. One would not dream of making a social case for the estate village: history is full of cases in which tenants have been treated appallingly, and others where well-intentioned paternalism has been resented. But on the whole, owners of landed estates have seen it as in their interest to preserve and enhance the appearance of villages.

Parsimony kept some of them safe from redevelopment during the dangerous years of the twentieth century. Agriculture – the traditional source of estate income – was at a low ebb during the first half of it. After the Second World War, when rents were protected but landowners still had to pay for repairs, consultants advised that villages should be sold, and the money reinvested in farm machinery. Thirty years later, this counsel did not look so wise; property prices had boomed, farm profits shrivelled. Landowners now had an incentive to look after their property assets.

Not all landed estates survive through the generations: like all other human endeavours, some fail, some are broken up by divorce, taxes, bad management and the end of primogeniture. But many estate-owning families want continuity. Believing – or at least hoping – that their heirs will still be in possession in a century's time, they can take a longer view of investment than most individuals or businesses. They also have a personal interest; they want their surroundings to look well.

At the western end of Littlebredy, a lodge and gate piers stand on the road to the village: pass us, they seem to be saying, and you enter somewhere special. The impression is confirmed by the bus shelter on the edge of the village green, an octagonal oak-framed structure with a shingle roof, although the school bus is now the only one that calls. Inside, an oak tablet records that the shelter was given to the people of Littlebredy to commemorate Philip and Margaret Williams's silver wedding anniversary in 1933. (Furniture maker turned banker Robert Williams – his bank eventually became Williams and Glyn's – bought the estate in 1797 and his family have been here ever since.)

From this plateau, a lane takes you down past the church, one of the few in Dorset to have a spire. Between gaps in the trees you glimpse roofs (thatched eaves rising like eyebrows over diamond-paned bedroom casements) and walls (dappled stone): they belong to the cottages in the valley, built by the first Robert Williams. Walk a little further and a notice invites visitors to pass into the parkland beside the lake. It may be that Sir Philip Williams, the seventh generation of his family to own Littlebredy, is there, too.

Through the estate office, Sir Philip keeps the place going – not just the fabric of the village, although that is important (the walled garden had become impenetrable until some keen gardeners took it on), but the soul. Prospective tenants are chosen with care. Willingness to support the church is an asset. A Social Club holds monthly events in the thatched Village Hall (once the schoolroom), and cricket is still played in the hauntingly lovely setting depicted by David Inshaw in his painting of 1975, *The Cricket Game*. Alterations to dwellings have to be approved by the estate, as well as the planning authorities. Weekenders are generally discouraged. Littlebredy is a lovely village and a community. Sir Philip conducts and the orchestra that surrounds him plays in tune.

# LIZARD

CORNWALL

*The hereditary privilege of crewing the lifeboat*

The Lizard lifeboatmen in Cornwall had to crawl and hang onto the handrail – and that was just to reach the lifeboat station. It was at the bottom of a deep cove, and the zigzagging staircase would be overwhelmed in high seas. The lifeboat's finest hour came on the night of 17 March 1907, when the White Star Liner *Suevic* became stranded on Maenheere Reef. All 524 people were taken safely to land – the biggest rescue in the history of the Royal National Lifeboat Institution.

The RNLI has its origins in the 1820s. Sir William Hillary was behind it: from a Quaker family in Wensleydale, he (unusually for a Quaker) raised a regiment, which he led to fight against the French. But losses on his West Indies investments meant that he withdrew from his country house in Essex to the Isle of Man. There he witnessed many shipwrecks, helping to save the crew of the government cutter *Vigilance* but being powerless to prevent the total loss of the naval brig *Racehorse*. 'Will Englishmen look quietly on and see hundreds of their fellow-creatures annually perish, when means of rescue, if supplied and properly used, are within reach?' he asked the nation in an appeal of 1823. The next year, the Royal National Institution for the Preservation of Life from Shipwreck (from 1854 the Royal National Lifeboat Institution) was founded.

Hillary would go out in the boats himself. He had plenty of opportunity. The wreck chart presented by the Board of Trade to Parliament would be studded with black dots throughout the Victorian period, each dot representing what the writer Alphonse Esquiros called 'a disaster, a tomb opened at the bottom of the abyss, frequently for hundreds of persons'. In a randomly selected year, 1863, the map was marked with 1,602 black dots. 'Who can be astonished at this?' Esquiros asked. 'The sea is the highway of the English.'

Cornwall has a particularly treacherous coast, rocks being piled up beneath the water to form treacherous hazards; some ships were so badly smashed to pieces during the nineteenth century that, with all the crew drowned, nobody could discover their names. At different times, lifeboats have been stationed at twenty-eight places around the county; now there are fourteen stations and twenty-one boats. The Lizard boat is no longer kept in Polpeor Cove; in 1961 it transferred to a new boathouse at Kilcobben Cove, and that station will soon be replaced if the RNLI's plans are approved. The new building will accommodate a larger Tamar-class lifeboat, as opposed to the old Tyne-class boat, *David Robinson*, that has done service for twenty years.

Even with new equipment, lifeboat crews are constantly in danger. In 1981, all eight of the Penlee lifeboat crew from Mousehole drowned when attempting to rescue sailors from the stricken coaster *Union Star*. Only volunteers do it. Newcomers may fund-raise, but they will not find places on the boat. The men (and now women) who sail in her come from families that have been seafarers – and probably lifeboatmen – for generations.

# LYDFORD
DEVON                                    *A big place in the tenth century*

Nothing much stirs in Lydford these days; even the sign to Silver Street cannot be bothered to stand up straight, having acquired a list to the left, as though it had overdone it in the Castle Inn. But the name of both Silver Street and the Castle are clues to the past. Lydford was sufficiently important in the tenth century to be one of forty places in England to have a mint. Not many Lydford pennies have come to light in the UK, but significant finds have been made in Scandinavia, having been taken there as part of the protection money, or Danegeld, paid to keep the Vikings from attacking Saxon land.

It was to keep the Vikings at bay that King Alfred ordained that a network of burghs, or fortified towns, should be established. Exeter was one of the four in Devon; Lydford another. Presumably an earlier settlement (since the church is dedicated to St Petroc, a Celtic saint), it was chosen because of its superb defensive position above Lydford Gorge. Parts of the banks that served as town walls still exist. It was also important commercially, as a centre of tin mining. They probably found silver together with the tin – hence the mint.

There are two castles at Lydford. The position is naturally defensive, a tongue of land bounded on one side by the steep and (formerly) impassable gorge of the river Lyd, and on the other by a ravine, at the bottom of which flows a tributary. The Normans rushed up the first castle in the 1080s, using a corner of the Saxon banks as part of the earthworks. Lydford would seem to have resisted Norman rule, since Domesday makes reference to forty houses having been destroyed since the Conqueror came to England.

Another castle, this time square and stone built, was raised in the twelfth century; it still stands on its mound. This was not, however, a military structure so much as a prison. It was where the Chief Warden of the Stannaries, whose jurisdiction covered the whole of the Devon tin-mining areas, dispensed justice. During Henry VIII's reign, the castle was described as 'one of the most heinous, contagious and detestable places in the realm'. Lydford Law preserved its exceptionally grim reputation into the seventeenth century, to judge from the verse written by William Browne:

> I oft' have heard of Lydford Law,
> How in the morn they hang and draw,
> And sit in judgment after;
> At first I wondered at it much,
> But since I find the matter such
> As it deserves no laughter.

When King John turned the whole of Devon into a royal hunting forest (later restricted, in return for a large payment, to Dartmoor), Lydford also became the capital of the Forest of Dartmoor. But this did not help it to develop in the long run. As a stronghold it was eclipsed by nearby Launceston, while Okehampton and Tavistock overtook it commercially. It mouldered. It is now a delight.

# MELLS
## SOMERSET
*Their name liveth for evermore*

'All their young men are killed,' lamented the architect Edwin Lutyens* to his wife, Lady Emily, in 1919. He was writing from Mells, home of Jack Horner (supposedly – although this is disputed – a descendant of the Little Jack Horner of the nursery rhyme, whose 'plum' had been lands acquired after the Dissolution of the Monasteries). Horner's wife, Frances, was sister-in-law to Sir Herbert Jekyll, brother of Lutyens's muse and collaborator, the garden designer Gertrude Jekyll, or Aunt Bumps, as he called her.

*Equestrian memorial to Edward Horner, who died of wounds in France in 1917, in Mells church.*

Lutyens had not done much at Mells Manor. But when Lady Horner gave the village its new water supply in memory of her son, Mark, who died in 1908, it was Lutyens who designed the associated stone shelter, a typically ingenious triangular structure, with carved lettering by Eric Gill†. He must have felt the losses at Mells deeply; it was natural that the Horners turned to him to commemorate the fallen.

Across Britain, there were only a few dozen Thankful Villages: communities to which all the men who had gone to fight in the First World War returned alive. As early as 1916, consideration was being given to the form in which the eight hundred thousand dead should be remembered. Lawrence Weaver, *Country Life*'s architectural editor, had been instrumental in founding the Civic Arts Association, to promote the best standards of appropriateness and design. 'The Association is first of all concerned to demand of our memorial art that it shall be common art in the sense of making a universal appeal to plain men and women,' he wrote in February 1916, 'that its making shall not be confused by fine phrases and talk of styles, but the natural expression of order and beauty.'

Weaver's hopes were largely fulfilled. Schools, colleges, industrial companies, offices, railway stations, regiments, trades, ports, town halls – all would want to commemorate their own. They were joined by thousands of villages up and down the land. The simplest of these rural memorials, inscribed with long rolls of local names, are often especially moving. At the other end of the scale, it is heart-stopping to see a great sculptural group, such as that made by Louis Deuchars for a scheme by Sir Robert Lorimer, which is silhouetted against the shore of Glenelg (see page 583), a scattering of hamlets at the ancient crossing from Skye.

It was not obvious what form a village memorial should take. Some voices argued for a feature of practical benefit to what were still sometimes needy communities. Village halls, cottage hospitals, bus shelters, park benches, bowling greens, relief funds and scholarships were among the options pursued. Lutyens's Cenotaph in Whitehall, the national focus of grief, makes no appeal to religion. But the over-whelmingly popular form was a cross: a permanent equivalent of the wayside shrines that had appeared during wartime, a seemingly spontaneous expression of the nation's unspoken beliefs.

At Mells, Lutyens spent a morning in August 1919 walking around the village with the Horners and local residents – 'a funny procession . . . Found a perfect site in the centre of the village'. The memorial takes the form of a tall Tuscan column, surmounted by a carved figure of St George slaying the dragon. It rises above a curved wall, into which two benches have been incorporated, for the laying of wreaths. Inside the church, Eric Gill carved into the bare stone of the tower wall a Latin inscription to Raymond Asquith, son of the prime minister, who had married the Horners' daughter Katharine; he had been killed on the Somme in 1916.

In the centre of the Horner chapel is an equestrian bronze by Alfred Munnings of a young cavalry officer, standing on a pedestal by Lutyens. It commemorates

Edward Horner, the last of the male line, whose body lies not in the church but where he fell in France. The War Office had decided that there should be equality in death; rich families could no more bring home the bodies of their menfolk than the families of ordinary Tommies.

*See Thursley, page 145. †See Ditchling, page 107*

# MINETY
## WILTSHIRE
*Travellers stop travelling*

During the August Bank Holiday weekend of 2003, a group of sixteen traveller families moved onto a field that they had bought outside Minety. Within days they had put up bungalows, laid roads and dug trenches for power and water supplies. They did this in the knowledge that they did not have planning permission, although they applied for permission to be granted retrospectively. North Wiltshire District Council (since subsumed into a new unitary authority) refused it, but the Deputy Prime Minister John Prescott gave them temporary permission to stay. In 2008, a government inspector ruled that that permission should be made indefinite. Minety (taking its name from the wild mint that grows on the riverbank) has become a cause célèbre. To country people who respect the law, which strictly controls where and what they can build, it is incomprehensible that travellers should be allowed to flout the rules with impunity. A new village has been born, and not everyone likes the look of the baby.

Gypsies have lived in Britain for centuries, generally being tolerated by rural communities. Their nomadic way of life is an essential part of their heritage, and it could be argued that this in turn makes it part of the communal heritage of Britain. Traditionally gypsies have moved between camp and camp, on sites that may or may not have been legal; but they never stayed long. This pattern has now changed. Travellers see the virtues of a permanent base, which brings better access to schools and doctors – gypsies are believed to have the worst health and educational status of any disadvantaged group in Britain. The sites made available by local authorities are not always in attractive locations.

These considerations cut little ice with the travellers' neighbours at Minety. Some of them have complained to the press that their teenage daughters have been subject to obscene abuse, of dead dogs being thrown into gardens, of signs imitating the pulling of a trigger on a gun being made at them when they pass. Others are reluctant to make their views known – objectors have been called racist. It is claimed that some houses have become more or less unsaleable.

Certainly travelling communities have found a way of working weak planning laws and the Human Rights Act to their advantage. The Minety case is only one of many sites around Britain where permanent settlements have sprung up overnight (they are indeed built through the night for the sake of speed), without regard for the cumbersome workings of democracy. They will usually stand every chance of staying for a decade or so, while the law works its labyrinthine course. They may remain, as seems likely to be the case at Minety, forever.

# MODBURY
## DEVON

*A prop for conversation*

One of the unsung delights of Modbury is its electricity junction box. I should say former junction box. Painted green, it was regarded as a thing of utility rather than loveliness by the electricity board, who took the obvious decision to remove it when it had ceased to serve any electrical purpose. They had, however, reckoned without the force of tradition in village and small-town life.

The breast-high box was just the right height for leaning on. During the fifty years that it had stood at the main crossroads of the town, it had become quite literally a prop for conversation (having a 'yar', as they call it down here), and it was felt that civic life would be diminished by its absence. When the electricity people came to remove the box, they found that some of the townsfolk had chained themselves to it. So they removed the apparatus inside and left the now-empty box, and there it still stands: a symbol of sociability and local initiative. How appropriate for a place whose name derives from the Saxon for meeting-place town, Moot Burgh.

You would not think this small town, rolling up- and downhill in a cheerful medley of coloured house fronts, would be a pioneering sort of place – sleepy is the adjective often applied to Devon. But Modbury (population sixteen hundred) gets things done. The saving of the junction box took place twenty years ago. On May Day 2007, the place went plastic-bag free – the first community in Europe to do so. The wildlife documentary maker Rebecca Hosking was behind the campaign. So appalled was she by the dying albatross chicks she had seen in the South Pacific – they had been mistakenly fed bits of plastic, fished from the sea by their parents – that she persuaded the town's traders to stop using plastic bags. Modbury now puts its sandwiches in brown paper bags, its clotted cream in cornstarch containers and its sausages in greaseproof paper. Its example is being copied all over the country.

But Modbury has always been feisty. Two battles were fought here during the Civil War, the rapid Royalist withdrawal during the second (they were heavily outnumbered) taking place via Runaway Lane. And with one of the kerbstones in Church Street having been made from a sixteenth-century fireplace, probably recycled from the old manor house, history is literally under your feet.

# MORWENSTOW

## CORNWALL

*An eccentric vicar invents Harvest Festival*

Harvest Festival is an institution of the Church of England that even non-church-goers are likely to recognise, perhaps having brought offerings of baked beans and toothpaste to the altar at primary school. But it occupies an equivocal place in the Christian calendar, having been invented, it would seem, by the colourful West Country vicar Robert Hawker of Morwenstow; he held the first service to give thanks for God's bounty in 1843. Morwenstow was, and is, a country parish; an act of thanksgiving seemed appropriate to those whose comfort (modest enough in some cases) depended on the results of their labours in the field. By the end of the century it had become a fixed point in the Church's year, cemented there not just by rural communities but by urban populations that wanted to feel a sense of communion with agriculture.

Hawker was a poet as well as a clergyman; at Oxford he won the Newdigate prize. (*The Song of the Western Men*, his best-known work, tells of the Cornish rising that followed the imprisonment of Sir Jonathan Trelawney, one of the Seven Bishops, in the Tower.) Although he had grown up in Plymouth (mostly in the house of his grandfather, Dr Robert Hawker, the vicar of Charles Church), Morwenstow must, before the railways came, have seemed exceptionally remote. At the age of nineteen, strapping and blue-eyed, he married a woman of some means, twenty-two years his senior. He was therefore comfortably off, and what had previously been high spirits – as a boy he had teased the people of Plymouth by impersonating a mermaid – turned to eccentricity (as it often did among the clergy of wild Cornish parishes). A handsome man, he liked to make an impression. Brown cassock would be set off by scarlet gauntlets, a fez-like hat and sea boots.

He was sufficiently highly regarded for Tennyson to have gone out of his way to visit him. 'Fine view of sea,' he wrote in a journal of 1848, 'coldest manner of Vicar till I told my name, then all heartiness.' (They walked on the cliffs together, talking shipwrecks.) But the view of the sea was not always so fine. One of Hawker's distressing duties was to bury the sailors whose bodies, in whole or in decomposed part, were washed up from wrecks on the coast, and this may have contributed to the unbalancing of his mind. He was greatly affected by the death of his wife, Charlotte, in 1863, when there was also a fire at the vicarage. Yet within a couple of years he had married a young governess, who gave him three children. This caused further agony as he realised he could not provide for them.

For all his problems, Hawker was generous-spirited and a conscientious shepherd of his flock. He restored the parish church, built a new bridge and school, and gave open-handedly, if capriciously, to the distressed. His poem *The Poor Man and his Parish Church* (1840) pleads for Christian charity to replace the sanctimoniousness of the workhouse, as instituted under the recent poor law.

O! for the poor man's church again!
With one roof over all,
Where the true hearts of Cornish men
Might beat beside the wall!

Harvest Festival was a gambit to attract more people to church; at a different season he supported carol singing. On his deathbed, Hawker astonished everyone except his wife by being received into the Roman Catholic Church – showman and devout Christian to the end.

# MOUSEHOLE
CORNWALL                    *The hardest building stone in Britain*

Cornwall is built of granite. Almost every pre-Victorian structure in the far west of the county has been constructed of this virtually indestructible stone, formed under immense heat and pressure below the earth's surface: a plague to the historian because old buildings wear so little that they are difficult to date. Cornish granite found its way to other parts of Britain. Its extreme durability made it a good choice for industrial buildings such as quays and bridges – Tower Bridge in London is built of it, not to mention the Victorian mine workings whose gaunt frames still punctuate the Cornish moors. We have granite to thank for our kerb-stones, our breakwaters, our lighthouses. Only in Cornwall, however, does this gritty, glittery rock make villages such as Mousehole a byword, in the tourist age, for everything that is charming. The dove-grey, sometimes white-painted walls are an essential part of its character.

But granite is difficult to work: before cutting machinery was improved in the nineteenth century, innumerable chisels must have been broken in the squaring of blocks. For that reason early builders tended to use blocks of bigger size, to reduce the amount of shaping required. The lower courses of a church such as Altarnun (see page 6) may include enormous boulders – moor stones, which occur naturally on the surface of the earth, and needed little more than to be heaved into position. This in itself cannot have been easy: granite is heavy. It is also difficult to carve with any refinement, not only being hard but too granular for delicate detail or undercutting. Leave urns and finials and shell hoods over doorways to the Cotswolds, where the stone carves like cheese when it is fresh. Cornwall is made of sterner stuff.

The fishermen of Mousehole and other villages used granite because they had nothing else: by the sixteenth century, Cornwall's trees had been cut down for charcoal to smelt tin, copper and iron*. The stone's unyielding character seems to suit the spirit of endurance that saw the villagers through their harsh lives. Nowadays, white walls combine well with pots of geraniums and blue awnings

– the architectural style of the Cornish Riviera, invented in the age of the train. But Mousehole is not just a white village: you can still enjoy the sight of granite au naturel, each dimple of the rough-hewn surface being a shadow and each point a speck of light when the sun is out. In cities, granite is cut smooth or polished to create a surface that may be ideal for repelling weather and pollution, but removes any surface variation, to deadening effect. But village builders struggled to cut their granite blocks square, much less polish them. Crusts of yellowish, pinkish lichen mottle the gritty face of the stone, spleenwort makes a home in cracks.

Not only is granite a Celtic stone – found (in Britain) in Scotland, Ireland and Cornwall – but the very word is Celtic. Dolly Pentreath could have told us that: the last person to speak Cornish as her native language, she died at St Paul, the village contiguous with Mousehole, in 1777. In 1860, a memorial cross was inserted into the lichen-blotched churchyard wall, a patchwork of greys and pinks and blacks, by Prince Louis Lucien Bonaparte 'in union with' the Rev. John Garrett, the vicar of St Paul. The monument is granite (of course), polished (alas) and as crisp today as when it was put there.

*See Godolphin Cross, page 38

# NOSS MAYO
DEVON                                              *A banker in the country*

When Lord Revelstoke bought Noss Mayo as part of the Membland estate in 1877, it needed taking in hand. 'The village seems to combine, in a remarkable degree, a moist and stagnant atmosphere, overcrowding of the houses, and the nuisances common to the inferior class of villages,' Dr William Guy had observed in *The Medical Times* in 1851. When a French vessel anchored in the river Yealm in 1849, the Noss fishermen were often on board; one of the things that they carried back to their village was cholera. Forty-eight people out of a population of three hundred perished – a terrible toll. Revelstoke, a Baring of Barings Bank – hard-working, self-satisfied and humourless – could not own such a place without setting it to rights.

Noss Mayo began life as La Nasse de Matthieu, the Yealm estuary being owned by the thirteenth-century Matthieu FitzHerbert: *la nasse* means net. At that time, it did not look out over the river, occupying a site on the other side of the promontory; its little church, dedicated to St Peter the Poor Fisherman, still exists above Stoke Bay. Like St Peter, Noss Mayo fished and it was poor. This place of worship was inadequate by Victorian standards, and inconvenient for a village that had shifted position to its present site: Revelstoke replaced it with a larger church, also dedicated to St Peter, above Noss Mayo.

Noss Mayo, which sounds like a sandwich, could well be considered one topographically, its filling being provided by Newton Creek. On the other side of the water is Newton Ferrers. The houses of both villages step gingerly down the steep hillsides, letting their occupants go before them by means of numerous little staircases engulfed in vegetation. Revelstoke emphasised the symmetry between the two settlements by borrowing the design of Newton's church of Holy Cross for his own. St Peter the Poor Fisherman, having fallen into ruin, has been rescued by local people with the support of the Churches Conservation Trust.

Revelstoke had the big house at Membland rebuilt by George Devey (it was demolished after the First World War) and generally brought the whole of his estate up to snuff, building farms and lodges, stables and steam laundries. His son Maurice Baring remembered that Noss Mayo saw the construction of many 'white-washed and straw thatched cottages and some new cottages of Devonshire stone'. A long carriage drive was laid so that he and his guests could admire both the scenery and his works, painted in the estate colour, which he liked to call 'Revelstoke blue'. Whatever Revelstoke's other failings – arrogance, complacency – he was not niggardly.

But alas, Ned Baring was riding for a fall. The bank overreached itself, there was reckless dealing in Argentina, and Barings would have crashed if the Bank of England had not bailed it out. Revelstoke was ruined; the household at Membland was broken up, the house put on the market. Most of Noss Mayo was sold during the First World War. It no longer has the character of an estate village. But Revelstoke ought to be remembered for one thing: he set Noss Mayo on a new path, broadening, as the twentieth century got into its stride, towards leisure. Beyond the vegetable patches and the derelict greenhouses bob the masts of the sailing boats. The harshness of the past is now remembered as an affectionate joke, expressed in the motto branded onto a wooden gate: 'Old Fishermen Never Die, They Just Smell That Way.'

# PILTON
## SOMERSET

*Rocking on*

For fifty-one weeks of the year, Pilton, with its population of a thousand, is a quiet Somerset village. Although twenty miles from the sea, it was originally – being on the edge of the watery Somerset Levels – a port: Pool Town. The Abbot of Glastonbury made sure there was someone there to look after his wine, on its journey to Glastonbury. After the Dissolution, when Abbot Whiting, his treasurer and another monk were hanged on Glastonbury Tor, the village sank into rural somnolence, until it was serenaded awake in 1970. Glastonbury reasserted its influence. That June, Michael Eavis, a local farmer, put on the first Glastonbury Festival.

It was a low-key affair to begin with. Inspired by American festivals of the 1960s, notably Woodstock, the Pilton Pop Festival, as it was first called, was an expression of the prevailing culture: fifteen hundred bearded, bandana-wearing hippies celebrated the twin ideals of free love and free music, in free-flowing clothes or, in some cases, no clothes at all.

Now, Glasto, as devotees know it, can claim to be the largest greenfield music and performing arts festival in the world. More than a hundred and seventy thousand people attend. Roads are closed, birdsong and the rumble of tractors are replaced by the sound of amplified music. Overnight, a town containing an equivalent population to that of Bath pops up (literally), as tents crowd onto the thousand-acre site – stretching over not just one farm, but five.

What began as a fringe event is now big business. It has to be. Thirty-seven thousand staff are required to lay it on. They provide three thousand toilets and more than seventeen thousand rubbish bins. If it rains – and there is a meteorological tradition that it should – the site returns to the waterlogged marsh that it would have been in the Middle Ages.

And then it is over. The festival-goers, many of whom belong to the generation that first came, return to their homes and often well-paid jobs, fortified for another year by their weekend of mud, music and togetherness. The grass grows back. Pilton goes back to sleep.

# PORTSCATHO
CORNWALL                                    *The boom-and-bust story of pilchards*

The village of Portscatho is *en fête*. The regatta committee is out, attaching bunting to pub signs and lamp posts. The sun is out, too, boats are bobbing in the harbour, there is hardly a man who does not wear shorts. This is a blue-and-white sort of place: white walls and blue everything else – woodwork, denim shirts, tubs of beach balls and (blue-handled) spades, glass craft objects, ancient pump, sea. The butcher has a red-and-white awning. It is quite a shock. You might have to sit down at The Boathouse restaurant – white weatherboarding, blue bargeboards – to recover.

A century ago, Portscatho was netting pilchards. The pilchard is a large sardine, about the same size as a herring but fatter and fuller of oil. Fish would appear in staggeringly vast shoals between July and September, turning the seas dark. They were caught in long seine nets, which were pulled around them in a circle until the water looked like boiling silver. It required a big capital outlay to buy the net and the three rowing boats that worked them – a six- or eight-oared seine boat, a follower or 'volyer' carrying the net to lift the fish from the water, and a fast 'lurker', from which the Master Seiner directed operations. Guided by shouts from the cliffs, the boats might land spectacular quantities of fish – four and a half million during the great catch of 1908, when the fishermen worked round the clock for several days.

On shore, the pilchards were taken to fish cellars, pressed under weights, smoked, salted or pickled, and sent, via some of the many Italian merchants along the coast, to the Mediterranean. The fish cellars were also expensive to maintain: since the fishermen were too independent to cooperate with one another, the trade was organised by pub landlords, who gave the fishermen easy credit until the next shoal was plundered. The poor got pilchard guts to eat; anything left manured the land.

It was a boom-and-bust occupation. In good years, the pilchards were almost overpoweringly abundant, and Portscatho had money in its pockets. The pilchard, wrote Alan Kittridge in *Cornwall's Maritime Heritage* (1989), 'was responsible for the development of virtually all of Cornwall's picturesque fishing villages and coves'. Since so many people depended on pilchards – not just the fishermen, but the boatbuilders, rope makers and the men who made nets, as well as the smiths, masons and carpenters who built the cellars – the government supported the export trade to the tune of 8s 6d per hogshead of fish. But the subsidy did not help during the blank seasons, when hardly a fish was netted. 'Few things are more precarious than the adventures in the pilchard fisheries,' observed Fortescue Hitchins and Samuel Drew in *The History of Cornwall* (1824).

The *coup de grâce* was Mussolini's invasion of Abyssinia, which abruptly put an end to the Italian trade in 1935. But the fishery had been in trouble before that. The great shoals had stopped coming. Nobody can say why, except that the pilchard was always an unpredictable fish. Recently, the pilchard has acquired a new life, at Newlyn, as the Cornish sardine, but Portscatho's fishing days are all but over. There is only one fishing boat in the harbour (it belongs to the harbour master) going out after crabs, lobsters, scallops, red mullet and sardines. The sea still yields a harvest, but the catch now is tourists. According to the local historian Hilary Thompson, as many as eighty-five per cent of the cottages in the old part of the village are now second homes.

# PUDDLETOWN
DORSET                                      *'Weatherbury was immutable'*

The Dorset County Museum in Dorchester contains a map annotated by Thomas Hardy. On it he marked the places in Dorset from which he drew the inspiration for his books. Puddletown, for example, became Weatherbury in *Far From the Madding Crowd* and other stories. There is no other English novelist whose works are so strongly identified with a single place and have conditioned many people's responses to it. Avid readers can relive the fiction by following the trails of its characters.

The literary critic William Archer made a walking tour in 1901, and described it to Hardy himself, during an interview for *The Pall Mall Magazine*. 'I climbed up to Shaston, in the tracks of Jude and Sue, went on to Sherton Abbas, and met Grace Melbury and Winterborne in Sheep Street: down through the country of the Woodlanders to Casterbridge: on to Budmouth, looking for (but not finding) Overcombe of The Trumpet-Major on the way.' At which Hardy said: 'You would have had to turn eastward from the main road.' Archer then recalled the place on the Isle of Purbeck (the Isle of Slingers, as Hardy had it) where Anne Garland watched HMS *Victory* fading from sight as she made her way to Trafalgar. Hardy: 'She did, you know – that was a true story.' Puddletown has not proved as 'immutable' as Hardy's Weatherbury, where the passage of four hundred years had produced little change. 'The citizen's Then is the rustic's Now,' Hardy wrote. 'In London, twenty or thirty years ago are old times; in Paris ten years, or five; in Weatherbury three or four score years were included in the mere present, and nothing less than a century set a mark on its face or tone.' Puddletown is a lot smarter than it was. The motor car has come, so have supermarkets, and nobody wears a smock. Still, Hardy would recognise the market square.

Not that Hardy's Wessex corresponds to the Ordnance Survey in every particular. It is a landscape of the imagination, a 'partly-real, partly-dream country', as Hardy phrased it. It was the place that he had known as a boy, and whose sights he replayed in his memory with the persistence that characterised his conversation, where the same themes kept recurring: 'ancient families, old choirs, his hostility to reviewers, architecture, Roman relics, Wessex folklore and dialect, animal welfare, and Napoleon. And of course hangings.' Hardy was a pessimist, preoccupied by time passing and the mutability of all human endeavour. His Wessex gets through life under louring skies.

This partly reflected the realities of existence for the rural poor. Dorset was a county of low wages, where half a dozen farm workers from Tolpuddle, in the same valley as Puddletown, had, within living memory, been banished for forming a union. In 1872, Puddletown could, to the outside world, display 'most of the essentials of Arcadian felicity', as the *Daily Telegraph* found when it visited. Small kindnesses – some straw for the pig here, a delivery of firewood there – made up for wages of nine shillings a week. But the newspaper wrinkled its nose at the attitudes of subservience that prevailed in a community where no one could forgo their pig straw or faggots of firewood.

Did Hardy set out to attack such wrongs? No. The journalist wears his agenda on his sleeve. The novelist keeps his under his hat.

# RAMPISHAM
## DORSET
*The great age of the rectory*

The rectory is almost as much of a village institution as the parish church itself. These days, it is a building type as much appreciated by affluent house-hunters as impecunious clergypersons, the Church of England having disposed of much of its housing stock in the bleak decades after the Second World War (with characteristically immaculate investment timing: property prices were about to soar). Still, the vicar's loss is the London professional's gain. The Old Rectory has become an icon of upper-middle-class life.

The Georgian period was not a great age of faith. As much as anything this was reflected in the state of country parsonages: so little had been spent on them that some were little better than hovels, or so their incumbents thought. It is quite clear that the oily Mr Elton lives in a very old-fashioned house by the standards of Emma Woodhouse in Jane Austen's *Emma*: one of the benefits of his worldly marriage is an improvement in his domestic circumstances. This situation gave clergymen, often the younger sons of gentry or even noble families, little incentive to live in the parishes they supposedly served. When pluralism (the holding of more than one benefice) came to be frowned upon, and vicars were forced to live in their parishes, the ramshackle cottages that their curates had previously put up with would no longer do. From 1776, legislation sponsored by the poor-law reformer Thomas Gilbert provided a mechanism to fund improvements – essentially, mortgages could be passed down from one vicar to another, extending the period of repayment. Little effort was made to take advantage of this system during the eighteenth century, but thereafter applications came in a rush.

Pugin Hall at Rampisham does not rejoice in being called an Old Rectory, yet that is what it is; the church authorities did not permit the use of any clerical term in the new name. It was built by the great A. W. N. Pugin in 1846–47. As a Catholic convert, Pugin worked little for the established church, and most of his domestic commissions were country houses for Catholic grandees. However, F. W. Rooke, the rector of Rampisham, was both a friend and an Anglo-Catholic (sufficiently High Church to be acceptable to Pugin's violently held principles). Typically, the previous parsonage had fallen into such disrepair that it was pulled down, some of the floorboards being reused in the new attic.

The house is similar to Pugin's own home at Ramsgate, Kent – The Grange, recently restored by The Landmark Trust. Unlike Pugin, a passionate sailor who used to supplement his income by claiming wrecks (having rescued their sailors) on stormy nights, Rooke had no need of a lookout tower, but in some ways Pugin Hall makes a more satisfactory composition. Inside, handsomely proportioned rooms are equipped with plain stone fireplaces and simple joinery. As at The Grange, Pugin ensured that servants were architecturally well-treated: the kitchen has a fine outlook and the attic fireplaces are as good as those on the principal floors.

The one failing of this rectory is that it was for some reason built a little distance from the church. In other villages, the classic grouping of parsonage and church symbolised the central role that the nineteenth-century vicar assumed in village life, the spacious nature of his dwelling demonstrating his claim to social as well as religious authority. Did Pugin Hall's more sequestered position reflect the increased need for privacy during the Victorian period?

# ST AGNES
## CORNWALL

*Inventing an immemorial tradition*

The giant, arms held up on sticks, totters. His blood has been pouring into a basin. When the basin fills, he will be able to claim the beautiful virgin – a saint to boot – who stands beside him, her great bulbous face registering no emotion. The basin has a hole in it, so it will never fill. Foolish giant. Giant collapses. Crowd cheers. The giant is carried back to a pick-up truck in the car park, to be stowed away until next year's pageant. The knight, another character in the story, is helped out of the elaborate hoops of her costume. A woman in a bowler hat waves a clarinet and the band starts playing. Both men and women wear black-and-red streaks of war paint on their cheekbones. 'I could tell you they were old Cornish tunes,' a musician laughs, with the disdain reserved for visitors and blow-ins, 'but they're not.'

*The Bolster Festival at St Agnes: a tradition of recent origin, evoking Cornwall's mythic past.*

This is the Bolster Festival. Bolster is the name of the giant, and he is a proper giant, too; the legend is immemorial. The re-enactment, using more than life-sized carnival figures, has become, in the words of one onlooker, 'a local tradition'. But it is not an old one. The first Bolster Festival was held twenty years ago. If not exactly an invention, it is certainly a creative reinterpretation of folklore, put on by the village of St Agnes (St Agnes is the saint) for its own satisfaction.

It may be that the Bolster giant dies on a miserable evening. And yet it can happen that you wake up on 1 May to a different Cornwall. Ferns unfurl their fronds, the primroses nestle like pats of butter in the hedgerows, tiny violets spangle the lawn. The sun shines, the sap rises, the world has been reborn. Has the ritual worked? Did the death of Bolster cause the transformation? I do not see why not.

# ST ERTH
CORNWALL                                    *Alight here for the Cornish Riviera*

In 1905, the Great Western Railway published *The Cornish Riviera*, a guide to the coast of Cornwall intended to popularise the train services that ran there. A poster promoted the joy of bathing in February, the climate of this far south-western tip of England being so balmy that almost anything was possible. Cornwall was established as a place apart from the rest of the country: warm, rich in wild flowers, its margin a picturesque fretwork of sandy coves. It was even, in its Celticness, faintly exotic. The modern idea of the place as the seaside destination par excellence was born.

What excitement there must have been as the train hissed to a halt beside the frilly canopies of St Erth station. It is the last stop before Penzance. You change here for the line curling northwards, past coves and never-ending beaches of white sand, to St Ives. Having started from London Paddington (platform 1) at 10.30 in the morning, families would have arrived at their holiday accommodation in time for tea. The GWR made their welcome at St Erth as attractive as it could, with palm trees on the station. Even now, a man in a fluorescent jacket can be seen tending the granite-edged flower-beds between trains.

Named after an obscure local saint, St Erth had been an industrial settlement, notable for its copper mills. Towards the end of the seventeenth century, it was one of the first sites in the country for a new kind of furnace, for iron smelting using coal. It also made some of its living from transport. The bridge over the river Hayle was first built in the fourteenth century, and while the advent of the earliest carriage, pulled by four black horses, in the eighteenth century 'caused no little ferment among the natives', according to a Victorian account, the village soon set itself up with coaching inns.

Tourism in the West Country began during the Napoleonic Wars. When travellers found that they could not go to the Continent, they discovered Penzance.

But until the coming of the railway, Cornwall had seemed too distant for casual visits. While Devon became the centre of the Regency holiday homes known as cottages ornés, Cornwall remained a county of tin mining, china clay and granite-built fishing villages, huddled wherever an inlet made a good harbour. When the record-breaking non-stop daily run from Paddington to Penzance (245.5 miles) was introduced in 1904 (later modified to stop at Truro and St Erth), the sort of upmarket holidaymakers it brought did not disturb Cornwall's natural calm. Seagulls, sea campion, tawny orange gorse and drifts of primrose, skylarks, more 'heather, kidney-vetch and squills' than could be found in 'gardened Surrey', a deep sense of romance and prehistory – these were what inspired the poet John Betjeman's* love affair with the place, which began in childhood before the First World War and lasted throughout his life.

There is an industrial estate at St Erth, in memory of its hard-working history, and not much else of note. It facilitates holidays, while belonging itself to that other Cornwall, the poor, bleak, post-industrial landscape of its innards. Holidaymakers hurry through the interior without seeing, their imaginations focused on their Cornwall: the pretty white fishing villages of the coast.

*See Blisland, page 15

# ST MICHAEL'S MOUNT
CORNWALL                                    *The first village mentioned in history*

Catch a glimpse of St Michael's Mount and the sight will flood you with romance. Just off the south-western edge of England, a castle grapples itself to the top of a granite rock; you can walk to it across the sands when the sea is out, but at high tide the place is cut off from the mainland, accessible only by boat. It looks as though it would have been a good place for holy men, wanting to shun the world, and there was indeed a monastery. Similarly, it has obvious advantages of defence.

But the Mount, as locals call it, may have entered history before either Christianity or castles reached Britain, for straightforward commercial reasons: it was a prehistoric trading centre to which skillfully worked tin was brought from Cornish mines to be sold to foreign merchants. It has been suggested that it was the island of Ictis mentioned by the Greek traveller Posidonius in the first century BC, whose account survives in a later copy by Diodorus: 'For, during the recess of the tide, the intervening space is left dry, and they carry over abundance of tin to this place in their carts.'

There must have been a settlement then, and one still exists: a row of granite cottages, looking solid enough to withstand even the battering that the Mount received during the tsunami that followed the second Lisbon earthquake in 1761, when the sea rose and fell violently for more than four hours in Mount's Bay. Within living memory it could boast three pubs and its own policeman (the presence of the one possibly influencing that of the other). You can still see the arm from which one of the pub signs hung when you step off the ferry, but communal life has for the most part retreated to the Johnny-come-lately settlement of Marazion, established originally as an overspill of the Mount.

When George Eliot visited Marazion in 1857, she found a 'pretty, clean village', but in previous centuries it had been a 'mercantile Town of great repute', according to the charter granted by Elizabeth I, a copy of which is in Marazion's one-room museum. Trading is embodied in the name, derived from the Cornish for 'little market'. An alternative name, which can lead to confusion, is Market Jew, from the Cornish *Marhas Yow*, meaning Thursday Market; the duality exists because Marazion grew from two hamlets. In fiercely Royalist Cornwall, Marazion was visited at least once by royalty: the young Charles II is thought to have stayed here in 1646 when making for the Isles of Scilly after the Battle of Naseby (see page 343).

Commerce is still busily pursued, though of a different order: money changes hands for nautically themed cushions, stripy T-shirts, model boats and draught excluders shaped like rows of beach huts. The Quaker Meeting House, which survives from 1688, suggests an early austerity; seaside jauntiness arrived, it seems, with the Regency. It is a pity about the hard-favoured Victorian church, but let us honour the architect for his local connections: James Piers St Aubyn was a cousin of Lord St Levan, occupant of the big house on St Michael's Mount.

# SAMPFORD COURTENAY
DEVON                                          *Devon defends the old ways*

Devon does not always take to innovation readily. William Harper found this when he adopted the new form of service, using the *Book of Common Prayer*, on Whit Sunday 1549. He was the priest of Sampford Courtenay, which is now, as it was then, a village of cob and thatch, the lofty grey tower of the church – made taller still by its pinnacles – rising above the green moorland that creeps up to the churchyard. The orange colours of the lichen, as W. G. Hoskins remarked, make the stone glow. But that was all the richness that villagers could find in their service, as Harper, seventy years old, entered without his customary vestments, holy water and bells. He said the liturgy in English rather than Latin.

When the villagers came to discuss things afterwards, they decided they preferred the ritual they had known all their lives. The next day, Whit Monday, was a holy day, with another service as well as the prospect of a church ale* in the newly built church house. As Harper was getting ready, William Underhill, a tailor, and William Segar, a well-to-do labourer, entered the vestry, insisting that he revert to the old ways. Perhaps because he sympathised, perhaps because he was old and had no choice, Harper complied.

Before long, Sampford Courtenay's act of defiance had reached the ears of two justices of the peace, who rode over to assert their authority. They arrived with their households, all armed, but could not prevail. And so they rode back again, and the people of Sampford Courtenay, joined now by those of other villages, scented victory. William Hellyons, a small farmer who must have been a Protestant zealot, decided to act where others had been timorous. His one-man stand was worse than futile. Arrested as he approached the village, he was taken to the rebel headquarters in the church house and marched up the external stairs (they are still there, although the rest of the exterior has changed).

Inside, the rebel leaders were sitting at the rough-hewn table. They were not intimidated by Hellyons; they had almost certainly been drinking. The scene was so heated that when Hellyons made his way back down the steps, a labourer hit him with a billhook. The crowd then hacked his body to pieces. After that, there was no going back. The year before, Cornwall had already rebelled, and it had risen again. They were marching through Devon. The men of Sampford Courtenay went to join them.

It took Lord Russell, sent by the government to restore order, several weeks to get on top of the crisis, and for the whole of July 'a great part of the countrie [was] abandoned to the spoile of the soldiers'. Popish priests were hanged from their church towers. There followed a series of battles, during which 'the fighte was verie fierce and cruell & blooddye'. One encounter took place at Sampford Courtenay itself. With cavalry, artillery and Italian mercenaries with arquebuses, Russell had every reason to be confident, but the rebels put up a good fight. Six hundred of them died in the battle, another seven hundred during the ensuing rout. It did not do Protector Somerset, in London, much good. His mishandling of the rebellion gave his enemies the chance to push him aside; he was executed in 1552. For Sampford Courtenay, the consequences were surely dire, since a large number of its menfolk must have been killed.

Now the handsome church, washed with light from the tall, clear glass windows, would be too big, even if the whole village attended.

*See South Tawton, page 73*

# SANDBANKS
DORSET                                    *The most expensive property in Britain*

Until the promenade at Bournemouth was built in the nineteenth century, the cliffs were vulnerable to the sea. Pounding waves washed off particles of sand, which then drifted along the coast, being deposited on the isthmus that, like the finger of Michelangelo's God, stretches out almost to touch the Adam that is Swanage (the short distance between them is crossed by a chain ferry). This is Sandbanks. The most expensive real estate in Britain is to be found, not in Mayfair or Belgravia, Kensington or Holland Park, but here.

A century ago, Sandbanks was nothing in particular. There were some coast-guards' cottages, but probably nobody expected them to survive on a promontory that was constantly being reformulated by the sea. The spit's possibilities as a holi-day destination were recognised in the 1920s, when some pioneering families made dwellings out of old railway carriages. A pavilion was built in 1928. Thereafter, Sandbanks developed into the British equivalent of Le Touquet, a place where middle-class families could sail and picnic amid the sand dunes. A memory of those days survives in faintly Arts and Crafts houses, looking as though they have been transported from Wimbledon, in their respectably unostentatious uniform of pitched roofs, wrought-iron garden gates, tile-hanging and leaded lights. Paint peels from the garages of those that are still in the original family ownerships. Bicycles can be seen leaning next to wicker shopping baskets and wooden garden seats, while the wisteria blooms mauvely overhead.

Admittedly the Royal Motor Yacht Club (president: The Duke of Edinburgh) sought to keep up standards. Rescuers who attempted to carry a man, who had nearly drowned after falling off the club jetty, into the clubhouse were reput-edly stopped by the Commodore, on the grounds that he was not a member. But not everyone was so pompous (on one occasion, the band leader Billy Cotton succeeded in substituting the Communist hammer and sickle for the red ensign that was run up the masthead). Until the last decade of the twentieth century, Sandbanks was relaxed.

Then fashion descended. During the runaway Brown boom (or, as it might seem with hindsight, bubble) that followed the election of New Labour in 1997, Sandbanks's property values rocketed. The homely, suburban dwellings that had previously lined Panorama Road no longer seemed adequate to the immense fortunes being made in football, entertainment and the City. Advertisements for marine valeting services and art galleries started to appear in the windows of the ferry terminal. A new kind of architecture arrived, as stylistically eclectic as that of the Hamptons on Long Island, New York, and just as keen to show itself off. White modernist boxes with huge windows, Louisiana plantation homes, Odeon-style art deco pastiches, decade-of-love-inspired apartment buildings in funky colours – this has become the new Sandbanks vernacular, as often as not hidden behind security gates. Nobody knows what happened to Sandbanks during the 1824 hurri-cane that did so much damage to Weymouth; there was nothing much there, so little to record. What if another hurricane blew it all away? One can but dream.

# SNAP
## WILTSHIRE

*Vanished . . . in the twentieth century*

By the end of the twentieth century, there was a population drift in Britain from big cities and towns to market towns and villages (the population of London increased, but that was only because of immigration from overseas). Now, it would be difficult to imagine that any settlement could disappear from the bosom of the earth: the inclination has been to load the bosom with more and more houses. But until the 1930s, people were still drifting away from the land, and the village of Snap suffered the consequences. It does not exist any more. The only thing you can see if in wintertime you drive down the byway that leads to the site are some patches of stone and dips in the earth, not readily noticeable beneath the copse that has grown up over them. The last families left after the First World War.

Snap never added up to much more than a hamlet. Lying a couple of miles off a Roman road and not far from the Ridgeway, in a trough of the heaving green waves of the Wiltshire Downs, it does not emerge into written records until the poll tax returns of 1377, paid by nineteen people. By 1812, Snap (or Snape, or Snappe, as it was variously known) had a school for sixteen children; but this must reflect a unique effort of philoprogenitiveness because the community was never big enough to support a pub, church or chapel. This was a rural place, which farmed, among other creatures, rabbits on an epic scale (twenty-four thousand by 1720); those from Aldbourne Warren were famed as 'the best, sweetest and fattest' in England.

The blame for the eventual depopulation must be shouldered by the Ramsbury butcher Henry Wilson. He bought two large farms in the 1890s and – as might have happened at any time since the Dissolution of the Monasteries – turned them over from arable to sheep. Having no work, the villagers abandoned the settlement. The local MP criticised Wilson as oppressive, but was successfully sued by Wilson's sons. There seems, however, little doubt about it. He was.

# SOUTH TAWTON
## DEVON

*The rumbustious tradition of the village ale*

When the fifteenth-century church house at South Tawton was restored recently, the parish revived the tradition of the church ale. During the medieval period, 'ales' of all kinds were an essential part of village life. Brewing ale and then charging people to come to the party was a way of raising money. There were thus bride ales, for marriages, and ales staged by the lord of the manor, at which attendance (and entry fee) were compulsory. But the practice seems to have originated with the church, and was later taken back by it.

*The church house at South Tawton was constructed to accommodate village ales,*
*descendants of Saxon drinking festivals, which raised money to carve the church roof.*

In the Saxon period, villagers would camp out the night before the saint's day of
the church in shelters made from boughs and greenery, clearly a survival of pagan
habits. The fact that a statute of King Edgar's reign in the tenth century was forced to
forbid 'drunkenness and debauchery' on such occasions suggests what some of them
got up to. These wakes survived into the Middle Ages, together with a semi-religious
drinking festival known as scot ale. The church authorities seem to have got the better
of them in the fourteenth century, helped by the mood of austerity encouraged by
mendicant friars and the puritan Lollards, but the principles – or lack of them – took
on a new life when church ales came into the ascendant in the fifteenth century.

Originally they may have been held in the sacred building itself. Until the 1950s,
the first large pew on the right of the church in Chudleigh, Devon was known as
the 'bacon hatch', from the practice of serving food. But ales were so profitable
that church houses were more than self-financing, their numbers growing rapidly
during the fifteenth century, as church naves filled with pews.

That at South Tawton dates from the 1490s. Built of granite beneath a thatched
roof, it is a robust building – in itself evidence of the money that church ales
could raise. A brewery formed part of the kitchen arrangements on the ground
floor, while feasting and (presumably) other parish meetings took place in the
hall above; a central hearth, essential on Dartmoor, sent smoke up into the rafters,
which are still blackened. It is recorded that money from church ales paid for the
carving of the church roof.

Perhaps church ales can be seen as the forerunners of modern fund-raising activities, such as the church fete. Even so, the strait-laced Elizabethan Philip Stubbes took a dim view, accusing participants of becoming 'as drunk as rats, and as blockish as brute beasts'. William Kethe, rector of Child Okeford in Dorset, lamented the merrymaking of the village, typified by the church ale of a neighbouring parish when 'men could not keep their servants from lying out of their own houses .... at night'. At Charlton Horethorne in Somerset, one Robert Smyth was heard to 'whoop and halloe' during the three days and nights that he was drunk. That was in 1607. By then, however, Puritan sentiment was gathering to a head; medieval revelry did not seem compatible with the decorum of the church. Village drunkenness may not have disappeared, but the church ale could not be held responsible. It faded even from its stronghold of the West Country during the early seventeenth century.

# STOKE ABBOTT
DORSET                                          *The knell of passing day*

Every weekday during the summer, David Rawlings enters the lichen-mottled, Ham stone church at Stoke Abbott shortly before 7am and takes a bell rope in his hands. He then tolls the bell a hundred times. This is the curfew. In past centuries bells would also have been rung at fixed times in the evening – indeed, for military reasons, William the Conqueror prescribed a general curfew at eight o'clock in the evening, by which time everyone had to be indoors. (The word curfew is derived from the French *couvre feu*: cover fire, or lights out.)

William I's curfew was repealed in 1100, but a non-enforceable curfew was continuing to toll 'the knell of passing day' when Thomas Gray composed 'Elegy Written in a Country Churchyard' in the mid eighteenth century*. The purpose of the Stoke Abbott bell was simply to call people to work. A century ago, it was rung at 5.30am. At some distant period in the past – its date already lost in the Victorian period – an acre of ground had been given to provide remuneration for the bell-ringer.

Bells used to be an essential feature of the British countryside. They rang out not only for church services, as they still do, but provided a shared reference for time. The earliest mechanical clocks – such as that in Salisbury Cathedral, made in the late fourteenth century – did not have dials and hands, only chimes. They announced time to the ear. This continued with the sounding of the hours and quarters by church clocks and others in public places – valuable to communities that had little other means of telling the time beyond sundials (approximate at the best of times, and useless on cloudy days). In addition, bells would be rung at critical moments of the farming year – the Seeding Bell would be followed, in due season, by the Harvest Bell and the Gleaning Bell. The coming of Lent was preceded by a Pancake Bell, and in an age when most people relied on communal ovens to bake bread, an Oven Bell would declare when they were hot.

Another village that still rings a curfew bell, though only on Tuesday and Thursday evenings, is Cropredy in Oxfordshire. Lost in the fog one evening, the Tudor priest Roger Lupton was able to find his way home only by the sound of the church bell. In 1512, he showed his gratitude by placing £6-13s-4d in the care of the churchwardens to pay someone to wind up the clock, which still had no face. This person was to ring the tenor bell daily both in winter and summer at 4am, the 'grettest or myddell bell by the space of a quarter of an houre and toll daily the Aves bell at six in the morning, at twelve noon and at four in the afternoon, and to toll in winter at seven in the night three tolls and immediately after the tolling to ring the curfew between eight and nine at night'. The 4am bell was rung for fifteen minutes. But even 4am was sluggish by some standards. 'Come, stir, stir, stir! The second cock hath crow'd,' Romeo is urged in *Romeo and Juliet.* 'The curfew bell hath rung, 'tis three o'clock.'

These days, bells in the countryside, which newcomers and tourists expect to be a place of quiet, can cause controversy. Objections have been made to the ringing of church bells on Sundays. At Stoke Abbott, the parochial church council toyed with changing the time of the curfew bell from 7am to 7.45am in 2003, in deference to the sleeping habits of visitors. But they reckoned without the traditionalists in the village, who raised a petition. The bell still rings out at 7am.

*See Stoke Poges, page 198*

# TARRANT GUNVILLE
## DORSET
*Poet into ploughman*

In 1940, John Stewart Collis discovered a longing to work on the land. Born in 1900, he was too old for active service and feared that he would have been given an office job if he went into the army. Farming was a reserved occupation, essential to the war effort because the nation now had to feed itself. But there was still an obstacle. Farmers did not want to have him.

Collis was not deterred. The Irishman, whose wife, Eirene, had left for the safety of the United States, had been seized of an idea and intended to follow it through. He simply presented himself for work, first in Sussex, then Dorset, afterwards publishing the two books that were later brought together as *The Worm Forgives the Plough* in 1946 and 1947. They are an insight into the lives of ordinary country people, in all their peasant limitations, who yet display reserves of endurance, not to mention practical skills, that a Dublin upbringing had not prepared Collis for.

Agriculture still trod much the same furrow as it had in the days of *Tess of the D'Urbervilles.* It had been more or less continuously depressed since the 1870s. There was still a debate about the desirability of machines; hay was piled into ricks, corn threshed rather than combined. What was simply called 'artificial', meaning fertiliser rather than dung, was coming in, but scattered broadcast over the fields; seeds were sowed in the same Biblical way. Thistles might rise higher than the beans.

Like most townspeople, Collis had previously looked on fields as scenes of beauty and peace. That was before he knew the constant, unremitting effort required to make them yield food. Ingenuity was needed to fix broken equipment, but the default position was tedium. A drudge was originally a kind of plough. Of all the jobs on the farm, planting potatoes was the most painful, because of the constant stooping. But almost every job – hoeing, harrowing, pulling up couch grass, forking the cut corn down from a rick – was physically hard and, after a while, mind-numbingly dull. 'I have no objection whatever to standing on a dunghill,' Collis observed, heaving dung-enriched straw from the stables onto carts. 'But for how long?' It was 2pm, an east wind was blowing, there was nobody to talk to, nothing to talk about, and another three and a half hours to go before knocking off.

Camaraderie between the labourers was scant. If someone left the village, he might simply go, without saying goodbye (escaping creditors might have had something to do with it). There was not much conversation, as can be judged from the limited reserves of expression noted in a fellow worker called Arthur. The variations on the theme of a single word beginning with b were almost like song: '"It's a b," "well I'm b'ed", "he's a b", "you can b off" . . . Once, when I heard him preserve silence for a few minutes on account of the proximity of the boss's wife, it seemed unnatural and disquieting, and I felt anxious for him until he started up again.'

However grim and exhausting the work, Collis remained a poet, with a poet's capacity for wonder. Life bursting from tiny seeds gave an intimation of God. Close observation of a flint revealed the form of a sea urchin that died a hundred million years ago. This prompted a soliloquy on dinosaurs, the largest of which, the Brontosaurus, remained the highest being on earth for ninety million years. Unless Man reconnects with some of the truths that Collis learnt through clod-hopping drudgery, his era of supremacy – ten thousand years to date – may be considerably shorter.

# TYNEHAM
## DORSET

*A place of ghosts*

They left, pinning a notice to the church door: 'Please treat this church and houses with care. We have given up our homes, where many of us have lived for generations, to help with the War to keep men free. We shall return one day and thank you for treating the village kindly.' Of course, they did not return. This is Tyneham, the village that the military took over to help tank crews prepare for D-Day and never gave back. Villages were regularly deserted in previous centuries, perhaps because of plague, but more likely because a landowner so willed, or economic conditions changed. But this sort of thing was not supposed to happen in the prosperous south of England in the twentieth century.

The order to go arrived in November 1943. The Second World War had already come to the village, in a way. Ralph Bond of Tyneham House organised the local men – those who had not gone into the armed services – into the Tyneham, Kimmeridge and Steeple platoon of the Home Guard. He had two years' experience of the Officer Training Corps at Eton to call on. They would go off to the gravel pit after church on Sunday and 'pop off a few rounds'. Like so much about Tyneham before the human population decamped, it seemed to belong to a different and distant era.

Helen Taylor's memories of pre-War Tyneham have been recorded. She was the daughter of a gamekeeper and a laundry woman who worked at the big house. They lived in Laundry Cottage. It was a world of hierarchy and deference, which she was not disposed to question, let alone challenge. A favourite treat for the children would be a tea party at Tyneham House. On Sundays, the Miss Bonds would take them, after Sunday School, to pick bluebells and primroses for the church. Helen's special job was to sweep the church steps before the ladies arrived for morning service. In due course she became a seamstress, marvelling at the immaculate lawns and exotic plants growing in tubs along the front terrace of the country house – quite a contrast to their 'little matchbox of a cottage'. Life might not have evolved enormously since the diarist Celia Fiennes ate 'the best lobsters and crabs being boyled in the sea water and scarce cold, very large and sweet', in 1697. The men in stovepipe hats standing around the churchyard in Victorian photographs would have understood about service. Britain moved on after the Second World War; hundreds of country houses were pulled down or became institutions.

Tyneham village stands, its progress arrested. The church, as the villagers hoped, has been looked after. Not so the houses, which look like Pompeii. But something was saved from what is literally wreckage. There has been no unsuitable development. The roads may be potholed, but they haven't been widened; there are no speed-limit signs, no Thank-you-for-driving-safely notices. Half a century as a firing range may have given some wildlife a headache, but it has kept the landscape free of pesticides, fertilisers, over-farming, golf-course developments, caravan parks, shopping malls and petrol stations. Biodiversity is at a maximum. Let us not mourn the sadness of Tyneham, place of ghosts, but rejoice in the accidental richness that it now offers.

# WEDMORE
## SOMERSET
*Island in the Somerset Levels*

The church at Wedmore sits on a mound. When it was built – parts in the thirteenth century, although like so many square-towered Somerset churches, it is
mostly in the fifteenth-century Perpendicular style – the village formed an island
in the watery Somerset Levels: local people still talk of the Isle of Wedmore. The
first efforts to drain the Levels had been made by the monasteries in the twelfth
century; agricultural improvers resumed the task in the late eighteenth century.
But much of the land remained waterlogged until the Second World War focused
minds on the need to produce as much food as possible from home soil.

In the Saxon period, the surrounding fenland – like that of the Isle of Ely, in
the Cambridgeshire Fens – had a defensive role. Marshy at the best of times, it
would flood in the winter to become a lake. No wonder, then, that King Alfred
should have chosen Wedmore as a base when he was fighting the Danes. He is
supposed to have had a palace here, perhaps associated with remains in the hamlet
of Mudgley. After defeating the Danes in 878, Alfred entertained King Guthrum at
Wedmore, bestowing gifts and making peace. The Treaty of Wedmore compelled
Guthrum to adopt Christianity and withdraw from Wessex to the eastern half of
the country – to be known, from its separate legal system, as the Danelaw.

The plan of the Saxon Square at the centre of Wedmore can best be appreciated from the delightful needlework Millennium hanging displayed in the church.
On four streets the houses face outwards, their backs opening onto an area of
gardens and trees. Many of them are built of local limestone, the silvery grey of
the predominant Blue Lias being mottled with dabs of the pinkish Red Lias. It is
doubtful that anything to do with the Saxon Square dates from the Saxon period.
In the High Street, a slender cross commemorates the markets that were held at
Wedmore from 1255. But by the Middle Ages, the great age was over – at least
for anyone not a dairy farmer. All that water produced 'butter pastures': lush
grass, which in turn made rich milk. In recent years there have been rather fewer
cloth caps and old Land Rovers to be seen, as dairy prices have crashed. Even so,
Wedmore has given its name to a cheese.

# WHITCHURCH CANONICORUM
## DORSET
*Shave your head to meet the mysterious St Wite*

Except for Westminster Abbey, the only church in Britain still to contain a shrine
with relics of its patron saint is in Whitchurch Canonicorum. The figure of St Wite
is obscure; there is dispute not merely about her identity, but her sex – some scholars having identified the name with that of St Witta, a Wessex monk who became
a bishop in Germany. Alternatively, she may be the same as St Candida, a Latin

translation of the French St Blanche. However, Wite may not have meant white in Anglo-Saxon, and the most likely explanation is that she was a holy Saxon woman, killed, according to tradition, by the Danes when they landed at Charmouth.

King Alfred himself seems to have built the first church; certainly he bequeathed it in his will to his youngest son. It was of sufficient importance for William I to bestow the living on his personal chaplain, Guntard, who attended him on his deathbed. By now, an abbey was associated with it, and William granted both church and the religious house to the Abbey of St Wandrille in Normandy, where Guntard had become a monk. The Normans rebuilt the church. The suffix Canonicorum – of the Canons – derives from a successful bid made by the sees of Sarum and Wells in 1240 to claim the revenues, which they split between them: chapters of canons ran the cathedrals. Perhaps they were attracted by Whitchurch as a pilgrimage site.

Whoever she had been in life, in death St Wite's relics had begun to work miracles. A stone shrine for them had been constructed in the early thirteenth century. This encases a lead coffin with a Latin inscription, recording that 'Here rest the remains of St Wite'. (When the coffin was opened in 1900 to repair damage to the shrine, it was found to contain what were thought to be the bones of a woman.) In the front of the shrine are lozenge-shaped openings into which worshippers could insert their limbs or clothing, for maximum exposure to the relics' curative properties.

Pilgrimage was a popular activity in the Middle Ages. It provided ordinary people with one of their few opportunities to travel. In Chaucer's *Canterbury Tales*, the Wife of Bath had visited Santiago de Compostela and Jerusalem (three times) and the Knight had fought in Spain and North Africa as a crusader. But the much-married Wife of Bath was rich, and the knight was on campaign. For much of the population, even a journey to the shrine of Thomas à Becket at Canterbury – the destination of Chaucer's pilgrims – would have been too much of an undertaking. There were many lesser sites that were more easily reached, and every county had its relics.

Pilgrims, hoping to secure an easier passage to heaven, or enjoy better health or fertility in this world, gave offerings, which made the churches containing the most fashionable shrines very rich. When Erasmus visited the Shrine of Our Lady at Walsingham in Norfolk, he was dazzled: 'When you look in you would say it is the abode of saints, so brilliantly does it shine on all sides with gems, gold and silver,' he wrote in 1513. By contrast, St Wite's shrine seems to have been a plain affair. But just as pilgrims to Walsingham made the last part of the journey barefoot, having left their shoes at the Slipper Chapel a mile away, so those going to Whitchurch Canonicorum underwent mortification: they had their heads shaved at a place that is still called the Shave Cross Inn.

# WORTH MATRAVERS

DORSET                              *Stone of choice for English cathedrals*

Having taken exercise on the village pond, the ducks at Worth Matravers can retire, up a ramp, to their shed, which is made of wood. It is about the only thing in the village that is. Worth Matravers is in stone country. There are carved stone owls and kingly figures on top of the gate posts, ammonites set into walls. A stone slab in the porch of the church is thought to commemorate an anchorite who lived in a stone cell. The walls of the houses are stone, so are their roofs. The pub is called the Square and Compass – stonemasons' tools – and has been since 1752. Every year it has a stone-carving festival, announced, not by a handwritten notice, but a beautifully lettered stone.

This is the Isle of Purbeck. The Romans quarried stone here: it has been found lining sepulchral cists. During the Middle Ages, Purbeck supplied the pillars of Salisbury Cathedral, and contributed to many other great churches and abbeys. In the ground the stone is creamy yellow; it weathers to the soft grey that is the key-note of Worth Matravers, dusted with silver and mustard-coloured lichens.

There is a museum attached to the pub. As well as a jam jar containing some of the garishly coloured Kinder toys that were part of the MSC *Napoli*'s cargo when it sank off the Devon coast, it displays some of the fossils that have been found locally: fish jaws and crocodile skulls and a complete ichthyosaur. When the stone was formed, this part of Britain – not then in its present latitude, but part of the mother continent nearer the equator – lay under a warm, sheltered sea. The water of the lagoon was so supersaturated with calcium from the shells of tiny sea creatures that nodules formed around grains of sand. Compressed, these eventually formed into limestone. Under a magnifying glass, the nodules, or ooliths, look like fish eggs.

Smooth-grained oolitic limestone is easy to carve when fresh from the ground, but hard once it has been exposed to the elements, which makes it Britain's best building stone. It occurs in a broad sash that slants across the breast of the country, from the coast of Yorkshire to Dorset. Some of the stone in Purbeck was formed in freshwater, from the shells of millions of viviparous snails; this can be waxed and polished to resemble marble, by which name it is popularly known. The waxing and polishing bring out the colours caused by impurities – grey, blue, green and red.

From around 1650, good limestone was not easily available on the surface of Purbeck, but had to be mined in pits known as quarrs. The Ancient Order of Purbeck Marblers and Stone Cutters controlled the stone trade. One of their articles gave them the right to take stone from any land on the Isle, whoever owned it; another restricted the trade to freemen and their sons. The Order still has its headquarters in Corfe Castle; a new charter was awarded in the sixteenth century after the old one was destroyed by fire.

# WRAXALL
*Wonders of guano*

Guano is a word from the Inca language that means 'droppings of seabirds'. It falls in enormous quantities on the rocky, exceptionally dry islands along the Peruvian coast, where, unable to soak into the soil, it is baked by the sun. By the nineteenth century, it had built up to a depth in some places of sixty or seventy feet. The birds that had deposited the guano had fed on fish; the fish, in turn, had ingested mud that had washed off fields into rivers, as well as some of the sewage floating down from cities. As the American *Merchants' Magazine and Commercial Review* commented in 1856: 'The bird is a beautifully-arranged chemical laboratory, fitted up to perform a single operation, viz.: to take the fish as food, burn out the carbon by means of its respiratory functions, and deposit the remainder in the shape of an incomparable fertilizer.' It contained potassium and phosphorus. To Victorian farmers, it was 'a treasure intrinsically more valuable than the gold mines of California'. Tyntesfield House outside Wraxall, overlooking the plain of the Severn estuary, was built on it.

From the 1840s until the 1860s, guano sales boomed in England, as exponents of 'high farming' sought to apply scientific principles to the improvement of land. Before 1841, the only fertiliser bought in quantity was ground-up animal bone. The sole importers of guano, under a monopoly obtained from the Peruvian government, were Antony Gibbs and Sons. Obtaining the guano required little more than a shovel – or, given the quantities in which it was arriving, a large number of shovels. The Gibbs firm organised shipping, distribution and marketing. In return they took around twenty per cent of the wholesale price – and since Peruvian guano was an expensive item (the Gibbses ensured that it remained so, preferring to underpin value rather than maximise sales volume), this did the Gibbs family very well.

After the 1860s, the Gibbses' policy of keeping up prices encouraged the market for cheaper, if inferior, alternatives and the trade declined. By then, however, they had already created Tyntesfield, enlarging an existing mansion into a picturesque composition of gables, chimney stacks and mullion windows – the Gothic style reflecting a strong vein of piety. Nor did they stop there. They constructed stables, farmhouses, saw yards, lodges and cottages, as well as gardens complete with bothies, orangeries, potting sheds and aviary, before having themselves buried in their own tomb in the church at Wraxall, much of which they had built. The estate had its own pumping station to provide water. When electricity came, it acquired an engine room.

This was the self-contained world of a fully functioning Victorian country house, which needed little from the outside world. George Gibbs became ennobled as Lord Wraxall in 1928, and his son, the last of the Gibbs family to live at Tyntesfield, did so as a recluse. When Lord Wraxall died in 2001, the property was bought by the National Trust.

The reek of the Guano Islands may now seem far away, but they should be remembered with nostalgia. The world is becoming ever more conscious of the quantities of fossil fuel needed to produce the modern artificial fertilisers that have replaced bird droppings. Given our fears about climate change, it may seem that guano was preferable.

# ZENNOR
CORNWALL *Rural Cornwall does not take to the Lawrences*

'We have been here nearly a week now,' D. H. Lawrence wrote in March 1916. 'It is a most beautiful place – a tiny granite village nestling under high, shaggy moor-hills, and a big sweep of lovely sea beyond, such a lovely sea, lovelier even than the Mediterranean.' The letter was addressed to his friends John Middleton Murry and Katherine Mansfield, whom he was hoping would join him and his wife, Frieda. 'I know we shall be happy this summer,' he wrote six days later, when they had agreed. When coming to Zennor, the Lawrences had initially stayed at the Tinners Arms, recreated as the Tinners Rest in Lawrence's story 'Samson and Delilah'. They then found a double cottage that they could rent for five pounds a year, the idea being that Murry and Katherine would occupy half and together form a microcommunity.

The Lawrences were never likely to blend into a remote Cornish village, however beautiful. With his red beard – a reason for suspicion in itself – this pallid man had anti-war views. Frieda shared her name with the flying ace Manfred von Richthofen, the Red Baron, to whom she was distantly related. Their Bloomsburyite hatred of convention (and, in Frieda's case, housework) would not have endeared them to neighbours. Fortunately the cottage did not have any. Murry and Katherine arrived in a flurry of distempering, floor staining and buying of second-hand furniture. But they were gone by June. It was a difficult time for Lawrence: the publication of his novel *The Rainbow* had been suppressed for immorality, so there was no money in the household beyond what he could glean from magazine articles, charity and donations from friends and family. He was also ill, with symptoms not unlike the tuberculosis that would eventually kill him. Not that their friends would have found it any more congenial if everything had been going well. Lawrence expected friendship to be intense – a little too much so for the inhibited Murry. Neither the latter nor Katherine could stand the arguments, which, even by bohemian standards, were spectacular.

Once, it took no more than a seemingly innocuous remark about Shelley to set them off. 'Out of my house – you little God almighty you,' Frieda roared. Lawrence, who could be violent, retorted in language that he must have learnt in his youth: 'I'll give you a dab on the cheek to quiet you, you dirty hussy.' This description comes from Katherine, who quit the scene. But a couple of hours later the Lawrences took the argument into her own cottage. After screams and a scuffle outside, 'they dashed into the kitchen and round the table. I shall never forget how L. looked. He was so white – almost green and he just hit – thumped the big soft woman. Then he fell into one chair and she into another.'

Finally, the Lawrences became too much for the village. The rector was, perhaps not surprisingly, suspected of hating them. He may have been the instigator of a police raid. Books and papers were searched, and the pair was sent off to the train, banned from living in Cornwall or anywhere within three miles of the coast. The village had closed ranks.

# SOUTH-EAST ENGLAND

IN PRE-ROMAN times, when it was easier to travel by ship than by land, the English Channel was not the barrier that it later became, and tribes in southern England had strong links with those in France. Proximity to the Continent continued to shape development: Roman engineers built infrastructure, early Christians founded minsters and twentieth-century airmen pegged out the runways used by Spitfire squadrons during the Battle of Britain. Geography has helped the South-East to prosper – too much so for some villages, which have been absorbed into London, although their inhabitants still resolutely defend their 'villageyness'.

Poor transport has been Kent's saviour; the shingle beaches and salt marshes feel like another world after the bustle that goes on inside the M25. Timber and brick (sometimes with Flemish influence) are the materials of the Kentish village, folded, in the mind's eye, among apple orchards and hop gardens. Thoughts of the riots to which its independent-minded inhabitants often contributed have long been superseded by cricket matches and village fetes.

Neighbouring Sussex shares the Weald, an area of forest and scattered settlements, whose ironmasters cast the cannon for Henry VIII's ships. Beyond it came the South Downs, nibbled into its own chalk-based ecosystem by generations of sheep (they begat their own breed, the Southdown, see page 118). The Pre-Raphaelites found much to enchant them at Winchelsea (see page 153), and the conscientious objectors of the Bloomsbury group shocked the parishioners of Berwick by painting murals while their menfolk were at the front (see page 94).

Surrey remains the English miracle: despite all the pressures, still not absorbed into London, landscapes such as the Hog's Back still almost as beautiful as when William Cobbett rode through them – although the locals are considerably more affluent. You would not know that the Victorians and Edwardians had hidden so many big houses among the free-draining pine woods, which they thought to be particularly good for the health. In this crowded county, you can look out over valleys that would seem to be empty of people, were it not for the church spire that hints at a village. Nightingales sing on Bookham Commons (see page 122). Hampshire, where Jane Austen grew up, was a farming county in the Georgian period, red brick and red-faced. The utopianism of the Owenite settlement at Queenwood (see East Tytherley, page 112) never took root, but, later in the nineteenth century, fly-fishing on the trout streams did. The most lyrical of English composers, Gerald Finzi, sought peace at Ashmansworth (see page 92). It is easy to see why.

Across the Solent, the Isle of Wight keeps to itself, a place of refuge from the hectic modern world, with a town hall without a town at Newtown (see page 134), a buccaneering sea captain at Yarmouth (see page 156) and a glory of parish pumps at Whitwell (see page 150). The 1950s somehow kept going here until they became fashionable again.

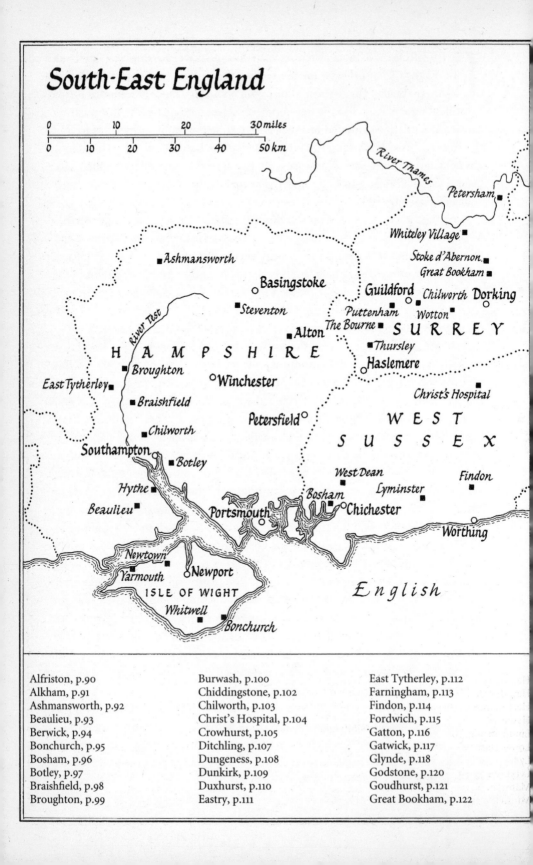

# South-East England

0   10   20   30 miles
0   10   20   30   40   50 km

*River Thames*

Petersham

Whiteley Village

Stoke d'Abernon
Great Bookham

Ashmansworth

Basingstoke

Guildford   Chilworth   Dorking

Steventon

Puttenham   Wotton
The Bourne   S U R R E Y

*River Test*

Alton

Thursley

H A M P S H I R E

Haslemere

Broughton

°Winchester

East Tytherley

Christ's Hospital

Braishfield

Petersfield

W E S T
S U S S E X

Chilworth

Southampton

Botley

West Dean   Findon
Lyminster

Hythe

Bosham

Beaulieu

Portsmouth   Chichester

Worthing

Newtown
Yarmouth   Newport

*English*

ISLE OF WIGHT
Whitwell
Bonchurch

# ALFRISTON

EAST SUSSEX                              *The best village bookshop in Britain?*

It is quiet on Alfriston high street at nine o'clock on Saturday morning, but a light is on in the Much Ado bookshop, and if you look through the glass of the lavender-painted door you will see, behind piles of books, a head of donnishly thinning hair. That head belongs to Nash Robbins, one half of the bibliophilic duo that have set themselves the heroic task of keeping a cultivated, independent bookshop in a country village. He and his wife, Cate Olson, used to run an out-of-print book-shop in New England; four years ago they sold it and bought a cottage in Alfriston. How have they found it? 'I grew up on a farm in Pennsylvania,' Cate says, smiling. 'But there's no American equivalent to the English village.'

The years that they have spent in East Sussex have been an education in the English psyche, magnified through the goldfish bowl of village life. The good and the bad reveal themselves more quickly than in town. 'You understand the power and the glory of gossip,' Cate says. But the couple have been assimilated; being American made them difficult to classify and may have helped the process.

There had been books on sale at 1 Steamer Cottages (the address picked out in elegant lettering above the door) before Cate and Nash arrived, together with a quantity of the sort of ornaments that Cate calls 'dustables'. But Much Ado Books is more a literary experience than a conventional bookshop. In the summer, customers select paperbacks from a cupboard outside the back door and read them in the garden. Reading glasses in different strengths can be borrowed by anyone who has left theirs at home. The whole shop is controlled by what can only be called an aesthetic. You don't have to browse for long before realising that the shop is a subtle indoctrination into the washy-coloured, cross-hatched, nostal-gically English world of Eric Ravilious and Edward Bawden. It's not that there aren't new books aplenty, but they all seem to conform to the general look. This hasn't happened by accident. The appeal of Ravilious and Bawden is regarded here as 'almost visceral'.

Nash offers lavender shortbread, made with herbs from their own garden, and privileged visitors are allowed upstairs into a room full of busts of Shakespeare, library ladders and gorgeously coloured wrapping paper (a teabag is hidden under each bow, so that customers can make a cup of tea to sip while reading new purchases). The timbers of the roof were erected around 1370. You wouldn't guess that from the street, with its chequer-work Georgian facade. But as these boldly venturing booksellers have realised, there are a lot of things about villages that cannot be guessed from the outside.

# ALKHAM
## KENT

*Model of an England that never was*

There are two Alkhams. West of Dover is the full-scale, one-to-one Alkham, its flint walls and tile roofs trying, almost successfully, to hide themselves among yew and chestnut trees. Down in the old Nissen hut of a village hall is the 'oo' version, at least on the day that the Alkham Valley Model Railway Society has come to town. Stalls selling vintage Hornby rolling stock, copies of the National Railway Enthusiasts' Association magazine for September 1982, cups of tea served in the mid-blue crockery that is the indestructible concomitant of traditional village catering, men in their fifties (women do not seem to do it) sitting in rapt concentration in front of miniature switches, the faint, bitter aroma of burnt oil rising happily to their nostrils – the scene is busy with would-be signalmen, guards and engine drivers, talking about the technicalities of life before Dr Beeching's branch-line cuts.

But one figure, spectacled and bearded, sits apart from the hubbub, quietly following the precise instructions that have been printed onto a series of spiral-bound boards ('Arr. Light loco from Dover MPD. Brake van: To exchange siding. To goods loop. To goods shed siding.'). It is Ian Hollis. In front of him is the model Alkham that took him nine years to construct. Ask if it is an accurate picture of the village and he will reply 'Yes' – perhaps a little gruffly if interrupted during a delicate manoeuvre, such as hooking a set of trucks onto the guitar-string coupling of a guard's van. 'Just go outside and look.'

*Forever Alkham: a Kent village as train set.*

In one important particular it is different, however. Alkham never had a railway. Ian was inspired by plans to build a line in the 1870s; they were never realised, but he has imagined what might have happened if they had been. Perhaps a coal mine was sunk nearby, requiring its own spur. But traffic dwindled during the Second World War and by the mid 1950s, when the model is set, the line had become single track. This Alkham of the mind is a well-ordered place, where flowers bloom neatly and mothers in headscarves stop pushing their carriage-built perambulators to pass the time of day with neighbours; no ugliness, barely a whisper of traffic, the trains, of course, running on time.

You might assume this to have been the Alkham of Ian's childhood, but he has never lived there. At the end of the show, he packs his creation into wooden drawers, loads them into a wooden trailer (it is a two-hour job) and sets off to his home on the Isle of Wight. With him goes the Alkham of his dreams, a village where the ladies behind the perambulators wear below-the-knee tweed skirts and the signals are always ready to turn green. Many people think of villages like that. The real Alkham, however, has not done so badly, its amenity protected by a shield of designations (Area of Outstanding Natural Beauty, Site of Special Scientific Interest, Conservation Area). Has it avoided the twenty-first century entirely? No. Would the people living there want it to have done? Probably not.

# ASHMANSWORTH
## HAMPSHIRE                    *An English composer finds solace*

Parry, Elgar, Vaughan Williams, Ivor Gurney . . . English composers have often drawn inspiration from the countryside. So did Gerald Finzi. This intensely sensitive musician, as English as a sky painted by Constable, was not brought up in rural surroundings. His father was a well-to-do shipbroker; both parents were of Jewish descent. He was born in 1901 and spent the first eight years of his life in St John's Wood, London. Then his father died, the house was sold and the family moved to Camberley, which landed the young boy in a school that he hated. Too young to fight in the First World War, Finzi suffered the loss of friends and the death of his three elder brothers. Tragedy turned him inwards; it also strengthened his resolve.

Like others in the 1920s, Finzi found solace in the traditional ways of the countryside, with its echoes of a pre-industrial world. Moving to Painswick in Gloucestershire (see page 344), with its churchyard of floridly carved tombs and green domes of yew, he came into the orbit of the Arts and Crafts architect Detmar Blow and his family at Hilles House. In 1933, he married the beautiful artist and poet Joy Black; a couple of years later they moved to Aldbourne in Wiltshire. Their house was large, with room for a studio for Joy and a badminton court, which could also be used for country dancing, but after children it was not large enough. Finzi needed quiet. He found it in Ashmansworth.

Unimpressed by the houses on the market, the Finzis decided to build Church Farm on sixteen acres near Newbury. Their architect, Peter Harland, already had experience of composers, having designed a progressive house for their friend Arthur Bliss in Somerset. The Finzis wanted space and wide skies (according to his biographer Diana McVeagh, Finzi had developed slight claustrophobia after having been shut in a cupboard as a punishment during childhood), but not white walls and acres of glass. Church Farm's walls are brick, handmade and textured. A long house with a pitched roof, it allowed Finzi's book room and music room to exist at one end, with the children's quarters at the furthest remove. Arts and Crafts furniture filled the rooms; sarsen stones found lying on the surface of the Downs paved the yard. The village was disquieted by the high wall, which appeared to take privacy to an extreme.

The Finzis had little time to enjoy their new home before War broke out. Refugees crowded into it, while Finzi himself toiled in the Ministry of War Transport in London. But he made his contribution to village life by founding the Newbury String Players, an amateur group that took music to unheated churches and halls. After the War, Church Farm became a focus of culture and artistic creativity; young musicians and artists came to enjoy wholesome vegetarian cooking, Finzi's discriminating library and the orchards of rare apple trees. This is the life of beauty evoked by Finzi's music, with its large *oeuvre* of songs setting words by the metaphysical poet Thomas Traherne and Thomas Hardy. In 1938, with Church Farm in progress, Finzi could not afford to buy any of the books at the sale of Hardy's library. But he did acquire his walking stick, now in Dorchester Museum.

# BEAULIEU
## HAMPSHIRE                                              *A watery place*

Beaulieu's natural element is water. The village lies on a creek that, having wound lazily in from the Solent, bellies out into the pond of the mill dam in front of Palace House, made from the remains of the Cistercian abbey established by the otherwise money-grabbing King John. Presumably the Cistercians found not only seclusion but a degree of self-mortifying damp. But they understood about water, piping it from a spring via the Monks' Conduit, still in use when John Murray published a guidebook to Surrey, Hampshire and the Isle of Wight in 1865. In the mid nineteenth century, the Lord Montagu of the day laid on piped water to every house in the village to eradicate a waterborne fever that was threatening to become endemic.

Earlier, the 2nd Duke of Montagu had spotted a watery opportunity at Buckler's Hard, named after the Buckles who had lived there, the Hard being the firm gravel foreshore that breaks out from the otherwise muddy banks of the Beaulieu river. With the abundance of good oaks standing in the New Forest, he established a shipyard. He made an attractive offer of low rent and free timber for house-building to any shipwright who would take him up on it, and in 1743 one arrived. Two rows of houses were constructed either side of a wide space in which timber could be stacked for seasoning. Among the ships that were built in the dockyard was Nelson's favourite, HMS *Agamemnon*. It was floated around to Portsmouth, which had the necessary hoisting equipment for inserting masts.

During the Second World War, the oyster beds became a building site for the vast, reinforced-concrete Mulberry Harbours that were towed to Normandy to act as impromptu landing stages for D-Day. Now the masts of luxury yachts bristle in the marina that Buckler's Hard has become. If you want to see Beaulieu itself, it is best to visit during winter, otherwise you may not be able to glimpse much beyond the heads of the four hundred thousand visitors who pile in during the summer months, lured by the motor museum and other attractions. Tourism has been good to the village shops; there is a photographer, a teddy bear shop and a chocolate maker. You could buy a vintage car from the garage, a bouquet from the flower shop or nail extensions from the hairdresser. What used to be the village bakery is now a tea shop, where wiry cyclists can be heard talking about saddles.

# BERWICK
## EAST SUSSEX
*Bloomsbury on its knees*

There is a noise coming from somewhere near the chancel of St Michael and All Angels at Berwick. You cannot help being aware of it as you study the extraordinary murals that cover the nave walls and chancel arch. They were the idea of Bishop Bell of Chichester and painted by Duncan Grant and other Bloomsburyites from the farmhouse at nearby Charleston. The Bishop can be seen kneeling on one side of the chancel arch, beside the rector Rev. G. Mitchell. It was wartime, and a soldier, sailor and airman are on their knees, opposite the prelate. Above, Christ rises in majesty, his throne supported by angels in colourful Piero della Francesca-ish dresses. But that noise disturbs concentration.

It comes neither from burglar nor rodent, but, as it turns out, the sacristan, a woman in spectacles and quilted jacket who has been rummaging in the vestry and, emerging, now offers to switch on the lights. Mistake her for the vicar and she will firmly dissuade you of the error; this is, and always has been, a High Church sort of church. Sir Kenneth Clark, director of the National Gallery, hoped that the example of the murals would get 'a movement underway'. It didn't, and the church became a unique witness to rural piety during the Second World War. Believable-looking shepherds give reverence to the Virgin, holding a child who looks as though he must be at least three years old (modelled on Quentin Bell). The Sussex Downs open out behind them. The pulpit with its vases of fruits and flowers, and the roundels of the seasons – ploughing, gathering corn into stooks, gathering apples, struggling home over the ice – that decorate the screen, are the most successful elements of the scheme. Bloomsbury struggled with figure painting. The gawkiness of the set pieces might be thought to spoil a good church.

People come from far and wide to see the murals, particularly the Glyndebourne crowd. But the project, carried out by conscientious objectors, affronted young wives whose husbands were at the Front. 'It was very controversial,' the sacristan says. 'My old mama was horrified. She led us out to the church at Alfriston, and it was a tiny congregation even then.' Berwick remains a hamlet, but in the Church of England even hamlets can be divided over ritual. A mile away, the folk of Berwick station do not like to worship in Berwick church; the rector holds a songs of praise service in the village hall.

# BONCHURCH
## ISLE OF WIGHT
*Smashing holiday destination for writers*

There are two churches in Bonchurch dedicated to St Boniface, an Anglo-Saxon missionary from Wessex – hence the name. In one of them, Charles Algernon Swinburne is buried. He spent his childhood here, at a house called East Dene. 'The rambling gardens and lawns of East Dene descend southward to the sea-shore . . . The view from the house south-east is over limitless ocean,' Edmund Gosse wrote. A stick-thin, carrot-headed child, who made odd, involuntary movements with his limbs, Algernon nearly killed himself once, climbing a cliff to prove to Captain (later Admiral) Swinburne that he was brave enough to take part in a cavalry charge (it was the time of Balaclava).

'He loved the sea, in the sense of being by the sea and of swimming in the sea,' his friend Coulson Kernahan remembered. They were constant themes of his poetry. So were death and corruption. His funeral service caused head scratching on the part of the vicar. In order for him to be buried in the churchyard at Bonchurch, as he had wished, some form of Christian rite had to be said, against the express instructions of his will. The grave later inspired Thomas Hardy to write his poem 'A Singer Asleep'.

These days, Bonchurch might seem too richly soporific for poetry, but it inspired others, too. Tennyson came here, cloak and beard blowing in the sea breeze as he stalked over to Farringford, at the other end of the island, where he made his home. Staying in 1859, he went upstairs to get the ledger containing the only copy of what would be *In Memoriam*, on which he had been working for sixteen years, in order to read it to an artist. It was not there. He wrote in a panic to his friend Coventry Patmore in London, who searched his flat. There it was, at the back of a cupboard. For Tennyson it must have been an anxious twenty-four hours.

Ten years earlier, Dickens had also visited. Staying at the seaside always freed up a creative logjam. Restlessly, he had forsaken his usual summer retreat of Broadstairs in Kent and a few weeks on the Isle of Wight set him up wonderfully. As he wrote to his friend John Forster, 'Naples is hot and dry, New York feverish, Washington bilious, Genoa exciting, Paris rainy – but Bonchurch smashing.' Enchanted by a small waterfall, he had a carpenter fit it up into a never-ending shower bath. He took the house from a clergyman friend and, while there, the Dickens children were able to play in the Swinburnes' garden with Algernon. A delightful souvenir survives in the form of a playbill for a conjuring performance by 'the Unparalleled Necromancer RHIA RHAMA RHOOS', who was, of course, Dickens himself.

In July he left to finish *David Copperfield* at Broadstairs. As he prepared to do so, he wrote to Forster, describing himself as 'under the depressing and discomforting influence of paying off the tribe of bills that pour in upon an unfortunate family-young-man on the eve of a residence like this'. He was, as he put it in later letters, oddly like Mr Micawber in his need to be on the move while strapped for cash. How many family men returning from holiday have not felt like him?

# BOSHAM
## WEST SUSSEX                    *Where King Harold had a hall*

Bosham, pronounced Bozzum, is a seaweedy sort of place, positioned like a wisdom tooth in the jagged mouth that is Chichester harbour, with a sailing club, various tea rooms and nautically named dwellings, such as Galleon House. One of them must have been occupied by Grey Wornum, architect of the Royal Institute of British Architects building in London, that elegant piece of 1930s Swedish *moderne*. His last work was to design the gates of Holy Trinity church at Bosham, in memory of his daughter Jennifer, who was drowned, aged 23, in 1950. 'Many waters cannot quench love', reads the inscription on a tablet set into the flint wall.

An image of the church features in the Bayeux Tapestry. The future King Harold, who owned a manor here, is portrayed riding up to it, a hawk on his wrist and a pack of hounds in front of him. He is about to set out across the Channel, on the mysterious but certainly disastrous expedition of 1064, which left him ship-wrecked on the Normandy coast. (While Harold was being entertained by Duke William, the latter tricked him into swearing away the succession over a hidden box of holy bones.) The lower part of the tower and the chancel arch survive from the church Harold knew. While the needlewomen showed the 'Ecclesia' diagram-matically, they used the name Bosham, unusually spelt the same way as today.

Sussex means the land of the South Saxons. In 477, a Saxon warrior called Ella led an army to invade what was then the island of Selsey, near Bosham, and even-tually ruled all the provinces south of the Humber, according to Bede. But the moment of glory did not last. During the struggle between Mercia and Wessex, Sussex seemed to be on a limb. This left the South Saxons to get on with their lives in relative peace. Sticking tenaciously to the culture they had brought

*Early Norman chancel arch of Bosham church,*
*a building stitched into the Bayeux Tapestry.*

with them from Germany, they were slow to adopt the new religion of Christianity. Bede wrote that the Scottish monk, Dicul, set up a small monastery at Bosham in the 660s, but none of the local inhabitants could be persuaded to convert. It took another churchman, the rebarbative bishop Wilfrid of Ripon, exiled from almost everywhere else in England, to do the job in the 680s. Wilfrid established his cathedral at Selsey, but like the rest of the Saxon town there, it has been lost to the waves.

Harold's manor house at Bosham has also disappeared: the Bayeux Tapestry shows him feasting in an upper hall. It is a pleasant scene. After 1066, however, the sleepy, traditionalist South Saxons were in for a rude awakening. Being so close to France, Sussex was the first part of England to be systematically Normanised.

# BOTLEY
## HAMPSHIRE
*Home of England's greatest journalist*

On 9 July 1812, the journalist William Cobbett was released after two years in Newgate Gaol for publicly criticising the flogging of some militiamen at Ely. Making his way home, he was received at Alton in Hampshire with the ringing of church bells. But the bells were silent at Botley, where he had farmed since 1805, because the Rev. Richard Baker – 'that delectable creature, the Botley Parson' – had kept hold of the key to the church. Cobbett had a gift for falling out with people. It was what made him such a spirited writer.

The son of a farm labourer, Cobbett grew up in what seemed, in retrospect, to be a golden age of smock-wearing rural prosperity. There would be a cask of ale in the cellar and a bacon flitch in the pantry. It was a world that he left, however, by joining the army, which took him to Canada. In 1792, he escaped a court martial by fleeing first to France, then America. What a change he found when he came home. In his native Farnham he found his brothers impoverished and dependent upon charity. Two of the three big landed estates round about were now owned, not by aristocrats, but bankers. Farmers were celebrating the high price of grain, while their workers struggled to get sufficient food. Having been a violent Tory, he became an even more vehement radical.

Semaphore towers, education (in general, he didn't approve of it), gentrified farmers, church tithes, 'English country gentlemen', Methodists, Thomas Malthus, mill owners, mechanisation, coastal defences, London (invariably called the Wen), bankers, stock jobbers, yeoman cavalry, potatoes . . . these and many other objects of his scorn were wrapped up with what, in exasperation, he called the THING, meaning the whole putrid system of government, with its sinecure holders, rotten boroughs and terrible public debt.

At Botley, he wanted to recreate something of the countryside of his youth. When evangelical campaigners tried to abolish 'barbarous' country sports, Cobbett responded by organising annual games of single-stick, in which farm labourers, with one hand tied behind their backs and the other grasping a cudgel, attempted to beat each other senseless. A large prize was put up for the winner. So anxious were the competitors to win that one swallowed a tooth that had been knocked out, rather than allow blood to come out of his mouth (the first person to show an inch of blood lost).

'I never saw hospitality more genuine,' Mary Russell Mitford remembered of a visit. With his 'unfailing good humour and good spirits', Cobbett, tall and red like his farmhouse, a red waistcoat stretched over the dome of his stomach, was in his element as the Old English yeoman farmer. It did not last. Having again withdrawn to America, he went bankrupt and lost the farm in 1820. We have *Rural Rides* (on which he set out from his new home in Kensington) as a result.

# BRAISHFIELD
## HAMPSHIRE                                                    *Scrapes in the ground*

They began with a scrape in the earth. The Stone Age family that came to Broom Hill at Braishfield then made a shelter of sticks over it. This is the oldest dwelling ever to have been found in Britain. Nothing exists above ground, but when it was excavated in the 1970s its construction was carbon dated to about 6500BC. Since this hut is grouped with three others, not carbon dated, it can plausibly be called the first village. And it must have been a successful one. According to the Hampshire County Council publication *Hampshire Treasures*, which lists the antiquities of the county, about a hundred thousand 'worked flints' have been discovered, including axes and the tiny stone tools known as microliths. Early men and women must have occupied the site for a long time. The few implements to have been dated span more than a millennium from 6400 to 5260BC.

The huts were not continuously occupied. The people of the late Mesolithic period had little control over their environment. They moved from place to place, according to the season and the supply of food. Braishfield is on the light land of the Hampshire Downs, broad sweeps of chalk where humans could find space to exist among the thin vegetation. It operated as the equivalent of a base camp, to which the hunters and gatherers would return from expeditions or sojourns elsewhere. These days, farmers look with displeasure on the flints that cover the fields, likely to break machinery and obstruct crops. Our ancestors must have eyed them very differently. Unless you could make a blade out of flint, you did not have one. They did not use only those that lay on the surface of riverbeds. They also dug out the stronger nodules of flint that lay within the depths of the chalk, from which precisely shaped, sharp-edged blades could be made.

The Mesolithic site is not the only piece of archaeology at Braishfield. The Romans built a substantial villa here, to which a bath house was added in the third century. The Saxons farmed the land from a series of scattered buildings, including Fairbournes farm, thought to date from the tenth century. By the eleventh century, it had become part of the manor of Michelmersh, which was given by Queen Emma to the clergy of Winchester Cathedral. Later it came to be owned by two Oxford Colleges, which hung onto it until the Second World War.

The area has changed over time; buildings have come and gone, leaving little more than the scrapes in the earth that gave shape to the Mesolithic dwellings. But there is a continuous history of habitation here or hereabouts. We cannot be sure that the structures and boundaries established by residents at any one historical period influenced those of any other, but it seems more than possible that, in some way, they did.

# BROUGHTON
## HAMPSHIRE

*Where Test, the sacred river, ran*

Wet flies and nymphs . . . it would be all too easy to make a joke about the rival methods of catching trout, but Frederic Halford, for one, would not have smiled. He was a self-confessed purist dedicated to the supreme art of dry-fly casting, a sport that he codified in a series of books during the last quarter of the nineteenth century. Born Hyam, he came from a Jewish family that pioneered the mass production of ready-to-wear clothes, and as a young man he went into the business. But commercial life was not incompatible with doing what he liked, even before he retired in his mid fifties. And what he liked was to fish the river Test, one of the gin-clear British chalk streams that have ever since been regarded as the most sublime of trout-fishing beats. He bought The Mill House in Broughton, lying on the Wallop, a tributary of the Test, so that he could do so.

As a boy, Halford was fishing mad. But his quarry were the roach, perch, barbel, chub, pike and carp of the river Thames – coarse fish, whose pursuit came to be regarded as a plebeian activity in comparison to the aristocratic challenge of trout. Coarse fishing requires time, fly-fishing finesse. The latter suited the sporting instincts of an increasingly rule-bound society, the richer element of which could afford to take its leisure seriously. Halford developed his skills on the Wandle, from which Wandsworth takes its name, then a notable trout river. His growing passion coincided with technical developments, such as more powerful split-cane fishing rods and strong, oiled silk lines, which made it possible to cast hooks (suitably disguised) across rivers, even in wind.

Unlike coarse fish, which spend their lives at the muddy bottom of rivers, trout snap up insects on or just above the surface of the water. Fishing's greatest art, Halford thought, lies in imitating Nature. It calls for knowledge: success depends on identifying the insects that will be scudding about when you are fishing. Artistry is required to make counterfeit 'flies' out of feather scraps and thread. Skill and judgement are needed to land the fly just above the point at which a trout is likely to feed. These great truths were embodied in works such as *Floating Flies and How to Dress Them* (1886) and *Dry-Fly Fishing in Theory and Practice* (1889).

Halford's approach was that of a naturalist, who carefully observed the trout as it fed (sucking insects down into the water, while taking them) and even the sound of the 'rise' – 'the heaviest fish being the lowest bass, the smallest the highest treble' – which would be modified by the size of the bug being gulped. But there was another view. It was propounded by the monocle-wearing London lawyer George Edward Mackenzie Skues. Although drifting a 'wet fly' under the surface of the water in order to tempt a fish had come to seem ungentlemanly, Skues championed it. 'Let me impress upon you,' he wrote in the *Fishing Gazette*, May 1911, 'while the dry-fly method is the more spectacular means of taking trout, it is not more scientific nor more sportsmanlike than the wet method.' Debate raged; Halford won. The river Itchen, where Skues loved to fish, was designated as dry-fly only; Skues refused to conform, and at the age of eighty was banned from it. Halford had given trout fishing its code.

# BURWASH
## EAST SUSSEX
*Elizabethan centre for iron*

Richard Lenard, his loose coat tied with a tasselled belt, his legs planted astride, looks a supremely confident man – not one to cross in a hurry, since he grasps a sledgehammer in one hand. Dated 1636, he appears, appropriately enough, on a fireback: he was an ironmaster from Brede, East Sussex. At this date, the Weald was the centre of iron production in Britain. 'Full of iron mines it is in sundry places, where for the making and fining whereof there bee furnaces on every side,' wrote William Camden in his *Britannia* of 1586. The forest rang with the pounding of hammers, powered by watermills. In 1543, the first iron cannon to be made in England was cast at Buxted.

With oak trees to make charcoal, and sandstone whose orange streaks betrayed the presence of ferrous oxide, this was an industrial area. Only in the eighteenth century, when the demand for wood – not just from ironmasters, but from cloth-iers boiling vats and farmers drying hops – had depleted the forest, did iron smelt-ing transfer to the Midlands and North*. As well as possessing raw materials, the Weald had stolen a march on the rest of the country by importing new technology from France.

The old-fashioned method of extracting iron used a type of furnace known as a bloomery: charcoal and ironstone were heaped into a pit, covered with clay, the charcoal was set alight, puffed hard with bellows, and the iron would gather at the bottom in a kind of paste. This produced only wrought iron. The French blast furnaces took the form of towers, through the top of which the iron ore and char-coal would be dropped, while air was blown in at the bottom. Such was the heat that liquid iron flowed out in a stream. It was cast iron, which the ironmaster could turn into wrought iron by another process. A blast furnace is shown on the Lenard fireback, together with other tools (not to mention a shelf bearing large flagons and jugs: iron smelting was a thirsty job). It may be his little dog that jumps up at him, but I rather think it is a pig, the name for a bar of iron – a typical Carolean conceit.

Iron in these parts was the material of choice in the Elizabethan period. Even grave slabs were made from it, the oldest having been erected to a Joan Collins in Burwash churchyard in the fourteenth century. Joan came from the family that owned Burwash Forge, and no doubt the choice of iron for her grave slab was not made from economy. The ironmasters were making money. They were also mixing with the gentry. It was expensive to set up a blast furnace, which meant that they needed partners, who often came from well-off local families; some gentlemen's sons managed furnaces.

Iron money built some beautiful houses, such as Bateman's, outside Burwash, where Kipling later lived. It built the villages of the Weald, too, a wild and fright-ening area, as it had been regarded in medieval times, which – despite the smug-glers at Hawkhurst (see page 124) – became gradually tamed. According to Edward Hasted's eighteenth-century *History of Kent*, Lamberhurst had the glory of supply-ing the railings for St Paul's Cathedral in London: 'They compose the most magnificent balustrade perhaps in the universe, being of the height of five feet six inches, in which there are at intervals seven iron gates of beautiful workmanship'. The ironwork came by water in the autumn of 1714. What a swansong.

*See Taynuilt, page 629. See also Furnace, page 479

# CHIDDINGSTONE
## KENT

*Planning by gavelkind*

Over a parlour fireplace in the row of houses opposite Chiddingstone church are carved the initials G.I.B., with the date 1638. They commemorate, a little late, the marriage of George Beecher and Jane Elye, which had taken place at St Mary's two years earlier. With its neighbours, their house forms one of the most beautiful ensembles in England, as good a demonstration as you could find of the Kentish vernacular – tiled roofs and tile-hanging, stout oak timbers and demurely decorated plasterwork, jetties that oversail the street and gables and dormers that spike the skyline. The Beechers lived in the house with the porch formed by oak columns that supports the projection of the first floor. Lucky them.

The Beecher house was built in the mid sixteenth century; the family had come there by at least 1575. With its gable end to the street, it must have squeezed into a gap, for other dwellings are older. Two of them were owned by men, Roger Attwood and William Hunt, who had stumped off after Jack Cade, the mysterious rebel who led an army on London in 1450. These otherwise solid householders were expressing their dissatisfaction with Henry VI's ministers, the conduct of the Hundred Years War, and what they regarded as unreasonable taxation.

Afterwards, Cade was pursued by the Sheriff of Kent and stabbed to death at Heathfield, East Sussex. Attwood and Hunt were among those who partook of the general pardon and returned home. Hunt's house, now the post office, was the biggest in the row, with a hall and cross wing. It was later bought by Sir Thomas Boleyn, Anne Boleyn's father, who owned nearby Hever Castle. A plaque, half covered by a climbing rose, declares that the street was bought by the National Trust in 1939.

If this were the whole village, there would not be much of it. Originally, there was more. The family that changed its topography lies in the pyramid-shaped mausoleum in St Mary's churchyard. It was built in 1736 for Henry Streatfeild, an ironmaster; he lived in what was then known as High Street House. In the next century, another Henry Streatfeild pumped this seventeenth-century house up into a castle. The result is an unlovable building with crenellations. Naturally, someone with these architectural pretensions was not happy to have an old-fashioned street shambling up to his sham fortification. He therefore walled the park, diverted the road around the outside and pulled down some of the old houses to make a lake.

But that was not, and is not, the end of Chiddingstone. According to the 1851 census, there were then more than twelve hundred people living in the parish, far more than could have crammed into Chiddingstone Castle and the village street. It is a dispersed settlement, with outliers such as Chiddingstone Hoath and Chiddingstone Causeway. Some believe that this reflects the inheritance pattern established by gavelkind, the system of Jutish law that applied in Kent and virtually nowhere else. It does not presume primogeniture to be the default position when a deceased person's estate is assessed; property tended to be divided among several children, creating a large number of small holdings. A more likely explanation is that this part of the Weald was poor. The land was clay and difficult to work; perhaps the difficulty of winning arable land back from the forest tended to make holdings small.

By 1850, the charm of Chiddingstone and villages like it had been noticed by George Devey. He built a rhapsodic cottage development in Penshurst, two miles away, heralding a vernacular revival that would set the theme for thousands of gabled houses with applied half timber on arterial roads and in suburban housing estates built in the early twentieth century. Speculative developers still cannot get it out of their minds.

# CHILWORTH
## SURREY                    *Gunpowder, paper for bank notes – terrible!*

On looking down into the valley of Chilworth, just to the south-east of Guildford, William Cobbett* exploded. 'This valley, which seems to have been created by a bountiful providence, as one of the choicest retreats of man; which seems formed for a scene of innocence and happiness, has been, by ungrateful man, so perverted as to make it instrumental in effecting two of the most damnable of purposes; in carrying into execution two of the most damnable inventions that ever sprang from the minds of men under the influence of the devil!' One purpose was literally explosive, the making of gunpowder; the other was the associated (to Cobbett's mind) activity of printing bank notes. 'Here in this tranquil spot . . . has the devil fixed on as one of the seats of his grand manufactory; and perverse and ungrateful man not only lends him his aid, but lends it cheerfully!' Even for Cobbett, this was going it.

Nowadays, he would not have waxed so vehement: the gunpowder works closed in 1920, and paper making had ceased decades before that. The gunpowder works ran along the valley of the river Tillingbourne, a tributary of the Wey, which in turn flows into the Thames. The first mills were established by the Evelyn family (of which the diarist John Evelyn† was a later member) in the early seventeenth century. By 1626, the East India Company had gone into competition with them, but its involvement was short, and it was another owner who benefited from the high demand caused by the Civil War. By 1677, there were thirteen mills in the area. The eighteenth century was a time of decline, and some of the gunpowder mills were converted to paper making, although the gunpowder business looked up after new owners took over in 1819; sales went up during the Crimean War (1854–56).

In 1885, ownership changed again. 'Brown' or 'cocoa' gunpowder had been developed by German powder makers to propel larger shells, and four German munitions experts were on the board of the newly formed Chilworth Gunpowder Company. It was developed with Germanic efficiency, equipped with the latest machinery and some substantial and ornate buildings – the second biggest gunpowder factory in the country, after the Royal Gunpowder Mills at Waltham Abbey. Several hundred people were employed at the works, generally in safety – although six workers were killed by an explosion in 1901. The site's maximum capacity was reached during the First World War, but demand collapsed with the Armistice and the factory closed. Afterwards, some of the factory buildings were converted to homes, the community – which survived until the 1960s – being known as Tin Town from the corrugated-iron roofs.

Paper making was never so centralised, although it was an important industry on the Wey. It did, however, play its part in the wars against France. In 1793 or 1794, the owner of a corn mill, which had been converted to the manufacture of bank notes, was visited by a stranger, wanting to have a paper with a watermark copied. He returned to repeat the order, with various changes of watermark. After some time, the mill owner discovered that his client had been the Comte d'Artois, afterwards the French King Charles X, wanting to undermine the French currency with forgeries.

*See Botley, page 97. †See Wotton, page 154

# CHRIST'S HOSPITAL
WEST SUSSEX                                                    *School village*

Christ's Hospital is about to break up, or, as they say there, Beat Retreat. It is a grand sight. In long, dark blue cassocks and hairy yellow socks, a band is marching. Oompahing, tootling ranks cross over, double back on themselves and form circles, the drum major twirling a silver-topped cane. It could be the Brigade of Guards. Marching, like music, is an important aspect of school life. Every day the whole school marches into lunch. They are used to it. To outsiders, it is astonishing.

Today, the band is only practising; visitors are not especially welcome on the day itself. It is too emotional. The young people who are about to leave have spent seven years living together, on a campus that covers two hundred acres of the school's estate of twelve hundred acres, perhaps – since this is a charity – to return to homes that are much more cramped.

In outward form, Christ's Hospital is the *chef-d'œuvre* of Sir Aston Webb, architect of the Cromwell Road front of the Victoria and Albert Museum and Admiralty Arch. Confident, red-brick buildings, bacon-streaked with stone, stand around the greensward, leaving plenty of marching room in between. Dotted among these Edwardian structures are memories of a much longer history: a statue of Edward VI; pepper-pot turrets in Tudor style on top of the hall; a 'great picture' of Edward VI and scholars looming over the library; an enormously long painting (by Antonio Verrio) of Charles II and governors in the dining room; a complete Wren facade (Wren was a governor); Frank Brangwyn murals in the chapel. The band is rather a recent innovation, founded in 1866.

Nobody who attends Christ's Hospital could be in much doubt that the school is a Tudor foundation. They are wearing the uniforms to prove it. The institution has been in existence since 1552, when the boy king Edward VI, moved by the preaching of Nicholas Ridley, Bishop of London, endowed a school for the poor, who could no longer be educated by the monasteries. For the first three and a half centuries, Christ's Hospital occupied the site of an old monastery in Newgate Street; when the pupils kicked a ball over the wall, it would land in the yard of Newgate Gaol, which was adjacent.

By 1893, the Hospital was ready to leave the City of London. Since *Tom Brown's School Days* had been published in 1857, the idea that strenuous exercise should form part, if not the basis, of an Englishman's education had taken hold, and many of those schools not already located in the countryside decided to move there. Charterhouse departed Smithfield for Godalming in 1872; King's College, Wimbledon, established beside King's College in the Strand, took up new quarters on the south side of Wimbledon Common in 1899.

Only Christ's Hospital, however, was dignified with its own railway station: a splendid structure when built in 1902, with no fewer than seven platforms in the expectation both of daily traffic to and from the school, and the expansion of Horsham towards it. Admittedly the station's purpose was undermined by the decision that the school would only take boarders, and in the mid 1960s, five of the platforms were closed and the station building demolished. But its survival is a salute to the scale of Christ's Hospital, which is bigger than many villages. Indeed, the site contains its own village, built to house teachers and other staff.

# CROWHURST
SURREY                                        *Immense antiquity of yew trees*

What are the oldest living organisms in Europe? Possibly some of the yew trees gracing British churchyards. The most ancient of all were growing strongly before churches were built beside them; gnarled survivors from a distant past, limbs too heavy to be held up under their own weight, trunks twisted, crowns thin, interiors cavernously hollow. A door was at one point fitted onto the yew at Crowhurst to turn the internal cavity into a room. A cannonball was found inside the tree in 1820, a survivor of the Civil War.

Ancient trees are difficult to date because they are generally hollow (no growth rings to count) and still alive (carbon dating cannot help). The age of old yews is calculated not in decades, nor in centuries, but in millennia. Crowhurst church may have been built on this site because the yew had already made it a sacred spot.

*Crowhurst: the yew trees in country churchyards sometimes predate Christianity.*

Yews, as other trees whose lifespan can be so much longer than that of humans, were an object of reverence to pre-Christian religions – an echo of which may be found in the Tree of Calvary, as the cross of the Crucifixion is sometimes called.

Britain has the greatest number of ancient trees in Northern Europe. In London, Richmond Park alone is said to contain more oaks aged above five hundred years than the whole of France and Germany combined. There may be some very ancient olives around the Mediterranean, records of which are either scant or have been little investigated. Britain, by contrast, has been naming and celebrating its ancient trees since Queen Elizabeth supposedly sheltered in a hollow tree at Cowdray Park in West Sussex (now called, predictably, the Queen Elizabeth Oak).

Our blessing in the matter of ancient trees has little to do with our forestry. We have scant forest cover in comparison to our neighbours, and none of it is in its primeval state. But ancient woods do not necessarily allow individual trees to survive to great age. The competition with other trees causes them to grow tall but thin, so that eventually they fall.

Many of Britain's ancient oaks are a legacy of the royal passion for hunting. From the days of William the Conqueror, kings and aristocrats needed glades of open country to ride over. This parkland included a proportion of free-standing trees. They had to work for their living. They were often pollarded (cut down to a height of six feet or so, above the browsing height of animals) to provide a crop of young shoots that could be harvested as fence poles every few years. Limbs were lopped off to provide timber to build ships – or torn off by gales – causing the trunks to grow outwards rather than up. Gouty and misshapen, invariably hollow, yet with deep roots grappling them to the earth, these oaks have stoically endured all that has been flung at them – 'the King Lears of the natural world', as Thomas Pakenham, author of *Meetings with Remarkable Trees* (1996), called them.

Yew trees can be found growing wild, for example at Box Hill, near Crowhurst. They were domesticated by Tudor gardeners, who appreciated their ability to form dense hedges. Obliging trees, they were capable of being trained and clipped into geometric and animal shapes. When the topiary was abandoned, they grew into billows, their original meaning lost. The Crowhurst Yew is another keeper of mysteries. Torn by gales, its centre empty yet surrounded by a more than ten metre ring of living tissue, furrowed and jowly, it inspires wonder. Like so many other churchyard yews, it represents a root of spirituality that goes deep into British soil.

# DITCHLING
EAST SUSSEX                          *A village that needs its museum*

Ditchling has a museum, and so it should: it is an arty village – the 'place in England that had the greatest vitality and thought in action and craftsmanship', according to the potter Bernard Leach. It was to Ditchling that the sculptor and craftsman Eric Gill moved in 1907, later transferring to Ditchling Common. Fervently religious, he founded the Guild of St Joseph and St Dominic, an Arts and Crafts community living what a guidebook describes as 'a fully integrated artistic life'. Integration was carried to extremes by the highly erotic Gill, for whom sex was an expression of the Creator's love. Wife, lovers, sisters, daughters, the family dog . . . oh dear, the things that go on in the countryside.

Gill was a magnet for other talents, being joined by his disciple Edward Johnston in 1907. In an age when public institutions felt they had a responsibility to elevate the nation's taste, Johnston was commissioned to design the sans-serif typeface used throughout London underground. At Ditchling, his legacy survives in the Edward Johnston Foundation, which is dedicated to raising public awareness of calligraphy both for its own sake and as the basis of typography. They have a growing collection, which so far numbers ten thousand items, housed in a new education and research centre near Ditchling Common. It deserves to acquire a cult following by those who are still old-fashioned enough to use a fountain pen.

Johnston's friend Hilary Pepler, printer and puppeteer, moved his family to a house called Sopers, where he founded St Dominic's Press. To this coterie was added, in 1918, the artist Frank Brangwyn, internationally successful and rich enough to live in state at The Jointure, although he became something of a recluse in the 1930s (among other troubles, he had been devastated by the rejection of his mural scheme for the House of Lords). The poet and painter David Jones took refuge with the Guild of St Joseph and St Dominic after his experience of the trenches.

The museum, reached through a violet-painted door at the end of a lane by the church, was established by the Bourne sisters, Hilary and Joanna, in 1985; Hilary Bourne's woven hangings and altar curtains can be seen in the church. The area remains home to some creative types. Raymond Briggs, whose brush gave us Fungus the Bogeyman, lives two miles away at Hassocks. Pinned up in the window of a cottage is a poem, changed monthly, for passers-by.

Traffic is the besetting evil. Step back to admire the beautifully lettered plaque on the red-and-grey diaper cottage where Gill lived, and you will soon end up with Edward Johnston in the churchyard.

# DUNGENESS
## KENT                                                    *Nowhere else like it*

Dungeness isn't what most people would think of as a village, although the community that lives here calls it one. It is a scattered assortment of black shacks, washed up, like Peggotty's upturned boat, on a shingle beach. This is partly an industrial landscape: pylons stride out from the nuclear power stations, what looks like a black-and-white space rocket turns out to be a modern lighthouse, and there is a general impression of telegraph poles and wire. On Denge Marsh, vast concrete dishes known as acoustic mirrors – a defence experiment of the 1930s, intended to obtain early warning of approaching enemy planes by means of sound – have been abandoned like gigantic pieces of Lego. Yet the shingle, washed up into ridges whose upper layer acts as a mulch to trap moisture between the pebbles underneath, is also a national nature reserve. Colonised by clumps of cabbage-like sea kale and blue-flowering viper's bugloss, it is the only place where the Sussex emerald moth is now found. If you don't see one, enjoy the pretty little smew ducks, with their panda eyes – but watch out for bloodsucking medicinal leeches.

The lighthouse is the fifth on this point. While the coast of Norfolk is constantly being nibbled away by the waves, the shingle bank at Dungeness represents the land's revenge on such behaviour. Slowly it is extending out into the sea. Previous lighthouses (the earliest was built in 1615) became successively landlocked, as the shoreline crept outwards.

Presumably the first shacks were built by fishermen; there are still a number in the community, as can be seen from the boats hauled up on the beach. After the

First World War, however, they were joined by a ragbag of bohemians and people seeking cheap homes. There was a housing shortage, and after the railway disaster at Quintinshill, near Carlisle, in 1915 – Britain's worst: more than 200 people died – during which wooden railway carriages caught fire, railway companies renewed their rolling stock. Redundant railway carriages were given away to railway workers. They could be made into cosy places to live. Looking out from cabin-like rooms, occupants can enjoy the drama of what some regard as the most glorious sunsets on the planet, feeling snug and protected while the wind roars outside.

The film-maker Derek Jarman performed the seemingly impossible by conjuring a garden out of the shingle – supplemented with pebbles, old garden tools and pieces of driftwood – which continues to blow with poppies to this day.

# DUNKIRK
KENT                                              *The Battle of Bossenden Wood*

The last battle fought on English soil was at Dunkirk. The Battle of Bossenden Wood took place in 1838, but in truth, it was not much of a contest. On one side was a rabble of farm labourers who had risen in support of the self-styled Sir William Courtenay, much as their forebears had done four centuries earlier on behalf of Jack Cade*. Courtenay was really a mentally deranged wine merchant from Cornwall called John Thom. He managed to convince some of the simple folk of East Kent that he was Jesus Christ, with the stigmata to prove it. His followers formed a small army. When Lieutenant Henry Bennett of the 45th regiment arrived with a detachment of soldiers to arrest Courtenay, Courtenay's response was to shoot him. The soldiers opened fire, and eleven people were killed. Among the dead were both Courtenay and Bennett.

Dunkirk apparently takes its name from a house once occupied by a Frenchman, who called it after his home town – although it is one of eight Dunkirks in England. Next to the dual carriageway of the A2, it is today more of a straggle than a village, with a couple of plant nurseries, an agricultural supplier and a car showroom under the shadow of a radio mast; the showroom perpetuates a historical memory in its name: Courtenay Cars.

The one remarkable thing about the place is its church. Christchurch was built shortly after the Battle of Bossenden Wood, perhaps as an attempt by the Church of England to rescue villagers from error. It is said that the knapped flints were donated by the Archbishop of Canterbury, who took them from the town walls of Canterbury (an act of vandalism if he did so, given that the walls are Roman and medieval). John Whichcord, Christchurch's architect, had previously been responsible for workhouses at Maidstone and Tonbridge.

To all intents and purposes, this is a church like any other, with a graveyard with flowers and a war memorial. The only outward clue that it is different comes on the door; there is a discreet doorbell in it. Christchurch has recently been turned into a luxurious house.

*See Chiddingstone, page 102

# DUXHURST
SURREY                                              *Colony for Women Inebriates*

Lady Henry Somerset heard the call to commit her life to others beneath an elm tree in the grounds of her house, Reigate Priory, or so it is said. She was intensely religious. A daughter of Lord Somers, an amateur artist, who, as well as Reigate Priory, owned Eastnor Castle in Herefordshire, she had thoughts of becoming a nun, but instead married Lord Henry Somerset in 1872. Marriage would be the cross for her to bear: her husband was homosexual. They separated. After a fight, she obtained custody of their son, and withdrew to undertake charitable work from her family's homes, styling herself Lady Isabella Somerset. According to the *Oxford Dictionary of National Biography*, a close friend committed suicide while drunk and the experience directed her towards the temperance movement. In 1890, she was elected president of the British Women's Temperance Association. She had the means, the connections and the will to drive the cause forward.

After her father's death in 1883, Lady Isabella inherited both Eastnor and Reigate Priory. Between 1892 and 1894, a house at nearby Redhill, possibly belonging to Lady Isabella, was used by Frances Willard, the American president of the Women's Christian Temperance Union, whom she had met in the United States. They toured Britain and America together, addressing temperance meetings. In 1895, Lady Isabella reinforced the Reigate connection by founding the Colony for Women Inebriates at Duxhurst. Its object was to rescue women who had come before the courts as drunkards; what we would now call rehab at the Colony was an alternative to prison. 'There was not a class of society unrepresented,' Lady Isabella's biographer observed, from 'ladies by birth' to jailbirds and even murderesses. Not surprisingly, most of those who were offered the chance took it.

Forty women could be accommodated at a time, on an estate of a hundred and eighty acres. Women lived in elaborately gabled, rustic cottages, half a dozen inebriates to each, which were named after the temperance organisations that had contributed the money (The Isabel having been funded by the British Women's Temperance Association). Lady Isabella devoted much of the rest of her life to the Colony. Two years after her death in 1921, it became Princess Marie Louise Village for Gentlefolk, giving shelter to forty-four poor ladies. After use as a prisoner-of-war camp in the Second World War, the buildings were allowed to decay; they were eventually demolished, leaving only the graveyard of the church and the cottage orné, The Cottage, which Lady Isabella built for herself and made her principal home.

# EASTRY
## KENT

*Iron Age fields – and those wretched Romans*

You are not likely to wander through Eastry by accident – a new bypass sweeps you past it – and you might not find much to detain you if you did. But the pattern of the surrounding fields was formed during the Iron Age. The fields were much smaller then, and there were consequently more of them, but the boundaries that you see today follow the old lines. It was a busy, productive, well-populated landscape: more people lived here during the Iron Age than at any period until the Middle Ages.

Then came Julius Caesar, his legionaries jumping onto the shingles around Deal, a few miles away. The ruthlessness with which the Romans reorganised England can be seen from the road on which Eastry is built. Connecting Canterbury and the coast, the straight line could have been drawn across the earlier field system with a ruler. The so-called Saxon invasion in the fifth century might have been nasty for the ruling elite who may have been killed or sacrificed, but was seemingly of little difference to the peasantry who worked the land. The new arrivals took over the existing structures of the countryside.

Eastry appears to have become very important indeed: as it name suggests, it was the capital of the East Saxons. The seventh-century King Ecgberht is supposed to have had a palace at Eastry, in the hall of which his two young cousins, Princes Ethelbert and Ethelred, were Richard III-ishly murdered. In 2003, someone found a Saxon sword off the High Street at Eastry while digging a soakaway for a conservatory. Naturally some top people were buried at Eastry. They worshipped at nearby Woodnesborough, a pagan shrine whose first syllable derives from Wodan.

Tradition has it that the Saxon palace stood on the site of the present Eastry Court, next to the lovely church. The Channel 4 *Time Team* programme tried to find the whereabouts of the palace, but drew no firm conclusions. It is possible that behind its Georgian facade Eastry Court contains some fabric from the Saxon period. If so, it would surely be unique. While Saxon arches and masonry are found in churches, no domestic architecture of the period is known to survive above ground.

Eastry's importance declined after the Kingdom of Kent was consolidated into a single dominion in the early ninth century, and in 979 the manor was given to the powerful abbey of Christ Church in Canterbury. As such, the buildings continued to receive high-ranking guests: Thomas à Becket is said to have hidden here before escaping in a fishing boat to France.

# EAST TYTHERLEY
## HAMPSHIRE                                   *A memory of utopianism*

You can just about find the remains of Queenwood, if you look. They lie between East Tytherley and Broughton, almost overtaken by the woodland that decorates unproductive pockets of this efficient landscape of corduroy-striped fields and oilseed rape. They are a memory of the longest lived of the cooperative communities founded under the inspiration, although not the leadership, of Robert Owen, the utopian socialist who combined cotton spinning with humane principles at New Lanark in the Scottish Borders.

Like other social reformers since the 1601 Poor Law had established the idea that the poor, where possible, be given work, Owen proposed that self-supporting communities be established. Property and profits would be pooled, a healthy living provided for people who would not otherwise have one, and education dispensed to enable the next generation to get on. The ideal size of these ventures, he calculated, would be between five hundred and fifteen hundred souls; the village, rather than the town, would be the model, although not necessarily in the shape it had evolved over the centuries.

Owen's ideal community would have looked more like a prison, laid out in the form of a quadrangle. Francis Place, a radical tailor of Charing Cross, wrote a critique of the man: 'He told me he possessed the means, and was resolved to produce a great change in the manners and habits of the whole of the people, from the most exalted to the most depressed.' You did not argue with Owen. He was not able to debate, only expound. His self-belief inspired a movement: Socialism. But puffed up into overconfidence, it would also be Queenwood's undoing.

The cooperators arrived at Queenwood in 1839, taking the lease of a 533-acre farm. Owen declined leadership (although he later became President); he said that the project was not sufficiently well-funded to create the kind of community of which he could approve. But it was a beautiful and promising site, and they began building. 'Our days are spent in united industry,' wrote Heaton Aldam, director of agricultural operations, 'our evenings in mutual improvement.' To begin with, all went swimmingly, but the people who joined the community came mostly from the industrial towns and did not have the skills to meet the most urgent requirement of growing food. Heaton resigned; his successor soon died. The agricultural difficulties were overcome. But the community overreached itself in Harmony Hall, an architectural centrepiece conceived on far too lavish a scale. Expenditure had outrun income. Even the £25 charged to boarders at the school – and not all were expected to pay – was less than the nearly £30 a year that they cost to keep.

After six years, the Queenwood community collapsed. But something was saved from the wreckage. 'Will men in a community of mutual and combined interests be as industrious as when employed for their individual gain?' Owen had rhetorically asked in a catechism. Many might have thought the practical answer to be no.

But the cooperators at Queenwood pulled together; they lived frugally; they did not blame one another for failure; they suffered defeat with dignity. More dignity than they might have shown if there had been profits to fight over? Who knows?

# FARNINGHAM
## KENT
*The glory of the village fete*

It is 1.30pm on a Saturday in Kent, near the confluence of the M20 and M25, and a balding singer croons 'Let's take it nice and easy' on Farningham's market meadow. He should tell that to the bus driver in the pretty High Street, all weatherboarding, brick chequer-work and flint. His vehicle can be inched through the traffic only by much sucking of teeth. The village fete has cast its spell.

Here is that Home Counties world that some might imagine had been lost: hats and summer frocks, children playing with shrimping nets under the ancient bridge, bowls of strawberries on a strawberry-patterned tablecloth, everyone from the village joining in. There is bunting. There are flags. The sun shines. Rubber ducks have been indelibly numbered for racing along the river Darent. Small boys in football shirts and baseball caps aspire to the glory of knocking down coconuts – although it would take a nervous coconut to feel threatened by the missiles sailing past into the net. A Squadron Leaderish voice over the public address system thanks the trustees of the village hall for making their lavatories available, which means that people will not have to venture into an adjacent field. Clearly the tea tent has something to answer for.

Farningham puts on a particularly good fete – but is there such a thing as a bad one? The bric-a-brac stall flaunts a naked display of domestic memories: old knives and forks, a pair of blue-and-white porcelain clogs, a souvenir plate of the 1981 royal wedding. A history of the 1st Eynsford and Farningham Scout Group is on offer from the local history society, among other publications. Next door, the kill-a-rat machine is a particularly fine example of its type, the tube being turquoise with yellow curlicues, the lettering Victorian. A jingle of knee bells, a flash of crossed sashes, a grizzle of beards, and the Wadard Morris Men have arrived at the beer tent. 'Has anyone lost a pair of spectacles?' a plummy voice asks over the loudspeakers. 'Unfortunately someone has trodden on them.'

The fete is a ritual of summer. It is a peculiarly British, one might venture to say English, creation. In Italy and France, villages come out to mark saints days with communal feasts and possibly bull running. Germany has carnivals and beer festivals. It is only the English who see the charm of dressing up to enjoy a mixture of tea, old-fashioned games, home-made cakes and the chance of a bargain. Fetes are a representation of the modern village, whose members may not be found in the church pew every Sunday but are happy to turn out in support of the church roof.

Nostalgia has a part in it, but don't think the fete is stuck in the past. It would not retain its popularity if it were. Face-painting barely existed in the days when theatrical make-up was literally greasepaint. Now every parent takes home a Spiderman or a butterfly. The Axstane Players may have performed a series of music-hall numbers at Farningham, but they were followed by a parade of drum majorettes, not to be found in the countryside of one's youth. Fetes announce themselves on the internet, as well as fliers on telegraph poles. Like school sports days, they are about taking part, an act of communion with the village ideal. Modernisation cannot change the fundamentals. 'I open the fete in our Suffolk village every year,' the Countess of Cranbrook says. 'I always give the same speech. It goes down very well.' Hear, hear.

# FINDON
## WEST SUSSEX

*The countryside at war*

In 1944, shortly before D-Day, General Montgomery came to address the troops gathered on Broadwater Green outside Findon. What he said has not been recorded, because the likelihood is that it was not Montgomery at all, but a pseudo Monty in the form of his double, the actor Clifton James, deployed by MI5 as a ruse to confuse the Germans. Sussex, like much of southern England, was intensely engaged in preparations for the Allied invasion. It was a wonderful time to be a child.

At Findon, Canadian troops practised the assault techniques that they would unleash both in the bungled dummy Operation Fabius and the genuine landing on Utah beach. The German position was represented by the Iron Age hill fort of Cissbury Ring. Villagers from Findon put their hands over their ears as the defending machine guns put up their continuous clatter, while the attacking forces inched nearer behind a barrage of high explosives and phosphorus. Bren guns mounted on tank tracks had been converted to flame throwers. At other times, genial Canadian soldiers were happy to give boys a ride on these armoured vehicles. After manoeuvres, local children would assemble alarming caches of shell cases and shrapnel, even guncotton and gelignite. It was all good fun until one lad was badly burned by a thunderflash that exploded unintentionally, and the building of arsenals stopped.

In the early part of the War, the south coast had been overflown during the Battle of Britain, and local people could watch Spitfires and Hurricanes fighting Messerschmitts and Heinkels in the sky. As the prospects of an Allied invasion of France increased, coastal towns were sporadically bombed by the Luftwaffe, which could cross the Channel in minutes. Before D-Day, gliders that would be used to transport troops behind enemy lines were a more common sight; one of them crashed, part of its plywood frame being converted into a hard-wearing gun case by a local shooting enthusiast.

Soldiers would play football with the Sussex youngsters to stave off boredom. Amid the beauty of the South Downs, it must have seemed strangely unmartial, more like a holiday camp than a war. And then they were gone. The countryside emptied; the bangs and flashes ceased. The noise of bombardment was now echoing around beaches on the French side of La Manche. The earthworks of Cissbury Ring had been replaced by the dunes of the Normandy coast.

# FORDWICH
## KENT
*Past grandeur remembered in a town hall*

The Isle of Thanet was once exactly that – an island, separated from the rest of Kent by the Wantsum Channel. Sea penetrated as far as Canterbury, along what would become the course of the river Stour. Fordwich, the highest navigable point on the inlet, became – as well as the ford implied by its name – a port, doing very well from fees extracted from ships unloading at the quay and making use of the town crane. The Caen stone shipped from Normandy to build Canterbury Cathedral passed through Fordwich. Having joined the federation of Cinque Ports (established by Edward the Confessor to defend the coastline) as a 'limb' of Sandwich, it was incorporated as a borough by Henry II.

Fordwich was still supplying Canterbury with coal and timber when Defoe published his *A Tour thro' the Whole Island of Great Britain* in the 1720s. But it was

*The town hall at Fordwich, where juries could condemn malefactors to death by drowning.*

already being eclipsed by Whitstable, and by the nineteenth century the Stour's long battle against silt had been lost. In 1824, the engineer Thomas Telford* wrote of the 'total decay of this Navigation'. Today, Fordwich (population 300) still proudly calls itself the 'smallest town in England', although physically it is no more than a pretty village whose growth was arrested, if it did not go into reverse, centuries ago. The eighteenth-century brick fronts to some of the houses conceal much older, timber-framed structures, some with open halls.

But a witness of past glories survives in the town hall. In the sixteenth century, Fordwich had two communal buildings, the other being the Give-ale House, used for celebrations: a memory of it lingers in the name of Give-ale Cottage, next to the church. A town hall had existed since at least the thirteenth century. The present building probably dates from 1544 – a timber-framed structure with brick nogging, which originally would have been lime-plastered and thatched. The hall itself is on the first floor, jettied out on three sides, the roof being supported by that handsome piece of carpentry known as a crown post.

A length of wood near the entrance forms the bar, at which the accused would stand during trials; the mayor acted as judge, sitting behind a robust, upright table. The jury had its own room off the hall in which to consider its verdicts – a tight enough space for twelve men, provided with a small circular opening in the floor through which they could relieve themselves if their deliberations proved lengthy. The undercroft includes a gaol.

The town crane at the back of the building could become an instrument of justice, when the ducking stool – still in the hall – was attached. And the town had other watery punishments up its sleeve: as a member of the Cinque Ports, it could (according to the Fordwich Custumal, in which the rights of the town were recorded) sentence malefactors to have their hands tied under their knees and be thrown into the thief's well, by tradition identified with a well in Thews Lane. Mary Stretcher, guilty of felony, escaped this fate in 1613. She was merely hanged.

*See Craigellachie, page 547. See also Newtown, page 134

# GATTON
SURREY · *Seven voters, two MPs*

Before the 1832 Reform Act, the right to send MPs to Parliament resided with boroughs. There were different voting qualifications, all of which related to property. The result was a wide difference in the numbers of voters, from around nine thousand in Westminster to fewer than forty in each of the Cinque Port towns. Old Sarum, the abandoned town outside Salisbury that William Cobbett* called 'that accursed hill', had only three voters in 1728, five in 1734. Gatton, twenty miles south of London, near Reigate, was even worse. In this settlement of six houses, the two MPs were elected by a single man. The radical journalist William Hone, writing in *Cobbett's Weekly Register*, imagined the Prince Regent paying Gatton a visit to find out how Parliament was elected. On his arrival, he would be greeted by the proprietor, East India Company surveyor and nabob Sir Mark Wood, who had been recently made a baronet – 'not because he was a borough-proprietor', heaven forbid, but because of some well-hidden merit discovered by a discerning administration. The interview would proceed as follows:

'You are the proprietor of this borough, Sir Mark?' – 'I am, may it please your Royal Highness.' – 'How many members does it send to Parliament?' – 'Two, Sir.' – 'Who are they?' – 'Myself and my son.' – 'You are much beloved, then, in the borough, Sir Mark?' – 'There are not many tell me otherwise, your Royal Highness.' – 'Were there any opposition candidates?' – 'None, Sir.' – 'What is the qualification for an elector?' – 'Being an inhabitant and scot and lot [a property tax].' – 'Only six electors, then? For I see you have only six houses in this place?' – 'Only one elector, please your Royal Highness.' – 'What! One elector, and return two members; how is that? But what becomes of the other five householders?' – 'By buying the borough, I am freeholder of the six houses; I let five by the week, pay the taxes myself, live in the other; and thus, being the only elector, return myself and my son as members at the election.'

Buying Gatton did not come cheap; however, its value rose sharply in the early nineteenth century, making it a good return on the investment.

The right to send MPs to Parliament had been awarded to Gatton by Henry IV, although there is nothing to suggest that it was ever a place of importance. Sir George Colebrooke, Bt, did, however, dignify it with a town hall in the form of a temple, built by Sir Robert Taylor in 1765. It contains an urn of post-1832 date, 'in memory of the deceased borough'.

*See Botley, page 97

# GATWICK
## WEST SUSSEX                                          *Under the flight path*

During the 1980s, a new facility was opened for passengers at Gatwick Airport. It was called Gatwick Village. Still operating, it is of course not a village, but a retail experience made up of shopping outlets and fast-food restaurants – hardly cottage industries. Little sunlight penetrates the aisles; no flowers bloom. Yet the airport authorities recognise that villages possess qualities that modern air travel does not: reassurance, intimacy, friendliness and tradition. It is included here in tribute to the many real villages that are either blighted by airports or have disappeared completely beneath them.

Gatwick has a long history. John de Gatewyk acquired the manor in 1241, and his name (which means goat's farm) stuck. Gatwick Manor, built in 1696, was a fine, William and Mary country house, which survived until 1950. There cannot have been much of a village, but, from 1891, Gatwick had something else – a racecourse, which became a reasonable success.

Nearby was the village of Lowfield Heath. It had grown up around the turnpike road, which ran across the heathland between Crawley and Horley. The Constable family – millers, although not, it would seem, relatives of the painter John Constable* – had a windmill here. It was remembered as 'a small village', with a church, pub, school, post office and store, children's play area and blacksmith's forge. The architect of the church was the irrepressible William Burges, who squeezed the maximum fun and drama out of what must have been a tight budget, incorporating a chancel window of what his biographer J. Mordaunt Crook calls 'staggering power'. St Michael and All Angels survives, almost all of Lowfield Heath that does, among the hangars and towers of the airport; Church of England services are no longer held here, but the eschatological surroundings make it an appropriate locale for the Seventh-Day Adventists, who have taken the church on.

Flying started in 1930. Ronald Waters, a young man who had just learnt to fly at Croydon Airport, bought ninety acres and obtained an airfield licence (cost: one guinea) from the Air Ministry. He started a flying club, operating initially from a wooden hut. A revolutionary circular terminal – the Beehive – was built in the 1930s, and in 1953 Gatwick's future was assured when the government decreed it to be London's second airport. Before that, it had played its part in the Second World War. 'It was still a comparatively small airfield and we could see the main railway line, the end of the old Gatwick racecourse and, later, farm workers haymaking using old-style pitchfork methods,' recalled one of the airmen of 35 Wing, the journalist Robert Hounsome. 'This, one reflected, was what the war was all about.' Would he think the same now?

*See East Bergholt, page 228

# GLYNDE
## EAST SUSSEX                    *For the connoisseurs of good mutton*

The sheep of choice for the aristocratic improvers of Georgian farming was the Southdown. Square and chunky, best for mutton but also producing wool, it was bred by the tenant farmer John Ellman of Place Farm, Glynde.

Sheep and man had lived together for millennia. Originally hill animals, able to survive on whatever scraps of vegetation they could find, sheep accompanied early people on their wanderings. Being light on their feet, they did not poach the ground as they grazed it. The Argonauts of the classical world went in pursuit of the Golden Fleece; Christians were taught to think of Jesus Christ variously as shepherd, Lamb of God and the gate to the sheepfold. Over millennia, the sheep developed as a tough, hardy animal, with different characteristics depending on the terrain to which it had become adapted. Descendants of primitive sheep still found in Britain include the Soay – which somehow found its way to the Scottish islands where, on Orkney, it even learnt to eat seaweed – and the goat-like Jacob.

The Downs of Oxford, Hampshire, Dorset and Sussex were prime sheep-rearing country. In an age before nitrogen fertilisers, their chalky soil was unsuited to cultivation. Sheep, however, thrived: nibbling the grass to its roots, they created a special habitat, rich in wild flowers and herbs. In the eighteenth century, the Hampshire parson and naturalist Gilbert White noticed that, whereas the sheep to the west of Selborne had horns and smooth white faces, the sheep on the Downs were hornless, or polled, their black faces having a 'tuft of white wool on their foreheads'; they also had speckled and spotted legs.

These were long-legged, rangy animals. From 1780, when the twenty-seven-year-old Ellman succeeded to Place Farm on his father's death, he began the process of selective breeding. Within seven years the market price of his animals had risen by a third. By the end of the century, they were being sought after by the greatest agriculturalists of the day. In 1790, the Earl of Oxford purchased a flock of Southdowns and introduced them to Norfolk. Among the many farmers and landowners won over by them was Coke of Norfolk himself. The first Southdown ram to make ten guineas was sold in 1787; in 1802 and 1803, the 5th Duke of Bedford paid three hundred guineas to hire a ram for one season. Folding was the preferred method for raising sheep: they were corralled onto arable land at night (where they manured the soil) and allowed to roam the Downs during the day. Southdowns had legs stocky enough to make the journey.

This was a time when mutton was taken almost as seriously as wine. Alas, when Lord Sligo pressed Bedford to try a fine haunch of Glynde mutton, he had to admit that it tasted rank and was, furthermore, tough. It turned out that the shepherd who had been ordered to kill the 'best' Southdown sheep had actually slaughtered a ram, for which the Marquis had just paid two hundred guineas. In other circumstances, the eating quality of Southdown was regarded as being unrivalled during hot weather.

Downland wool had been much prized in the Middle Ages. But when the Southdown was first introduced, there were grumblings: some experts believed that it was apt to be brittle and lacking the necessary properties to make felt. But as the breed spread across Britain and beyond, the wool quality improved. Feeding on chalky pasture, the original Southdowns might have had to walk long distances to satisfy their appetites (exercise made a finer, but more fragile wool).

Ellman retired in 1829, and sold his famous herd, safe in the knowledge that its reputation had been established. By the Second World War, artificial fertilisers had caused the practice of folding to decline, and the Dig for Victory caused their original Downland home to be ploughed. The Southdown dwindled to the status of being a rare breed, and what used to be the supreme sheep breed of the world is now kept alive by specialist butchers' shops and farmers' markets.

*See also Canon Pyon, page 307*

# GODSTONE
SURREY                                    *Sound of leather on willow*

You would have no idea, sitting under one of the billowing chestnut trees on Godstone village green, that you were only nineteen miles from London. Surrounded by solid red-brick and Edwardian-ish half-timbered houses, it is an idyllic scene – the calm only ruffled by a call, rippling around the chaps in white who are gathered about the little tent-like structure that shelters the scorer, for another umpire. A flag of St George flutters from a flagpole; little wooden cut-outs of rabbits crouch atop the whitened line marking the boundary. This is England at its finest. Yet a good batsman could probably whack a ball onto the M25; it is only half a mile away.

Godstone must be the sportiest village in the country. Cricket was played here in 1749. In that year, the crease was taken by a gentlemanly scallywag called Long Robin (short for Robinson), a friend of prize fighters and hackney coachmen. ('The last time I saw him, he was laid up with two black eyes, and a broken pate, which he got in a midnight skirmish about a mistress in a night-cellar,' *The Ladies' Magazine* sniffed in 1763.) For all his failings, Long Robin was regarded as the best all-round cricketer of his day. The Godstone ground returned to the annals in 1912, when the openers Jack Hobbs and Andrew Sandham, playing for Surrey, put on 347 between them.

A football club was started in the 1890s (still going strong, with only six secretaries in its history, according to the village website). Tennis began in the early twentieth century; it is still played on grass as well as hard courts. The bowls club dates from 1921.

Godstone is also blessed with two charming structures, bearing the nautical names of the Endeavour and the Bounty. The Endeavour is an essay in Surrey vernacular, its old tile roof breaking out into two eyebrows over dormer windows; built in 1937, it houses the Scouts. The Bounty, with various bits of old masonry built into the walls, was added ten years later, to resemble a dovecote. Having proved too small for the Cub Scouts, it is now home to the parish council.

# GOUDHURST

KENT *Sitting on top of the Weald*

The best view of the Weald is from the top of St Mary's, Goudhurst. Beyond the orange-red tiled roofs of the village, the rolling landmass drowses beneath a green eiderdown of fields and oaks. Oaks in belts, oaks in clumps, oaks rising from hedgerows, oaks spreading themselves in the middles of fields, oaks too innumerable to count, all of them billowing with leaf: green in a thousand shades. The conical caps of old oast houses stand out like white beads. Here and there a church tower pokes up, tawny from the ironstone from which it is built (this used to be an iron-making area). On a clear day, you are supposed to be able to see fifty-one churches from this vantage point – assuming that you have a telescope, no doubt.

Weald is the same word as wold, meaning wooded place (as in Cotswolds and the Yorkshire and Lincolnshire Wolds). They are not primeval: by the Roman period, most of the native forest had been felled and the land was farmed. After the collapse of Rome, some of the farmland seems to have reverted to scrub and then back to forest. The Weald was a frightening place to medieval travellers, little populated except by charcoal burners and iron workers, the villages sparsely scattered. 'Nothing more than a waste desart and wilderness, not furnished with habitations', is how Edward Hasted put it in *The History and Topographical Survey of the County of Kent* (1797). There were plenty of pigs, snuffling up the acorns in the woods, but when Queen Victoria came to the throne in 1837 most of the ploughing was still done by ox teams, as it had been since the Middle Ages.

The woody character of the place is enshrined in Goudhurst's name – hurst being derived from the Old English *hyrst*, which means a wooded height. St Mary's occupies the highest ground, with the rest of the village scrambling up the sides of a steep hill to meet it. Wood was such a ubiquitous material that, inside the church, even the painted effigies of the Tudor ironmaster Sir Alexander Culpeper and his lady, Dame Constance, are made of it. Most of the older village houses have a wooden frame, however much they may hide it: the carpentry is concealed behind tile-hanging and weatherboarding to keep out the rain.

The Weald also gave its name to a familiar type of timber dwelling, the Wealden house, although perhaps unfairly, since Wealdens occur throughout Kent, Sussex and elsewhere in the Home Counties. It was a form that emerged around the time of the Black Death, with the upper storeys of the bays to either side of the central hall being jettied out, two curved braces reaching up to the roof plate, and the whole being covered by a deep roof of tile or thatch.

In modern times, Goudhurst has come to exemplify picturesque tranquillity, but it has not always been so. The Weald was still a rough old place in 1747, when a vigilante Goudhurst militia saw off the vicious band of smugglers known as the Hawkhurst Gang in a pitched battle*. Today, they would be lucky to dodge the traffic of the A262.

*See Hawkhurst, page 124*

# GREAT BOOKHAM
SURREY                                   *The common (not so common now)*

Twenty-three miles from Nelson's Column, Great Bookham is more of a commuter sprawl than a village, but it still possesses something that would once have been an essential part of the village economy: a common. You can hear nightingales singing there. Roe deer start as you walk across it, Purple Emperor butterflies sail by. Surrey as a whole has more woodland cover (twenty-three per cent) and a more varied flora than any other county in Britain. Bookham Commons (officially there are three, according to the National Trust, which owns them) are emblematic of this unexpected biodiversity. The scrubby woodland, interspersed with thorn bushes, is particularly valuable, providing a habitat for birds evading predators.

To medieval society, it was the productivity of a common, not its songbirds, that mattered. Although common land was owned by the lord of the manor, villagers enjoyed rights over it, which allowed them to graze their animals and gather brushwood. The lord was not allowed to enclose it without an Act of Parliament, or the commoners' consent. Around London, commons served further purposes: mustering soldiers, recreational walking and shooting practice. An Act of 1593 tried to stop them being enclosed.

Peasants may have found other uses for it, which went beyond their legal entitlement. When William Cobbett* visited the common of Horton Heath in Hampshire in 1804, he found that the surrounding cottages – some thirty of them – had used some of its hundred and fifty acres to create gardens, orchards of apple and black cherry trees, and patches of corn. He saw more than 125 stalls of bees, some sixty pigs, fifteen cows (excluding calves) and not less than five hundred poultry. Beyond these encroachments, the common itself was used to fatten the sheep and cattle of neighbouring farmers. The bees alone provided a good income, and Cobbett calculated that the smallholdings produced 'in food, for themselves, and in things to be sold at market, more than any neighbouring farm of two hundred acres'. This was a momentous lesson to someone who had previously been entranced by the efficiency of enclosing exactly this sort of land. From then on, Cobbett championed peasant agriculture as the system most likely to promote the welfare of the rural poor. His views did not prevail against the Board of Agriculture, wanting to increase the volume of food available for the cities.

For centuries before Cobbett, landowners had been obtaining Acts of Parliament to overturn commoners' rights, divide the commons into fields and farm the land at greater profit to themselves. Enclosure of wasteland continued through the nineteenth century, as the importation of guano (seabird excrement)† from Peru provided the nitrogen to fertilise otherwise impoverished land. The loss of the common was one factor that made the lives of farm labourers, witnessed by Flora Thompson in *Lark Rise to Candleford* (1945)**, unremittingly harsh.

There are now nine thousand commons left in England and Wales, a total of 1.3 million acres. According to the Open Spaces Society, which has been defending them since 1865, nearly ninety per cent of those in England have a national or international designation for wildlife, landscape or archaeology.

*See Botley, page 97. †See Wraxall, page 82. **See Juniper Hill, page 185*

# HAM
## KENT

*Welcome back, strangers*

There is a sign half a mile outside Ham, pointing to Sandwich, three miles away. Ham, Sandwich . . . chortle, chortle. There was at one time a wild rumour that the television presenter turned actress Kelly Brook had booked the Blazing Donkey pub at Ham for her summer wedding to Billy Zane, but the couple then appeared to plump for a Greek island (that did not happen either). It is difficult to imagine Hollywood descending on Ham; it is so scattered that the helicopters might not find it.

Better to spend the evening with a different pair of stars. They have been living on Ham Fen since St Valentine's Day 2004, and are so shy that you would hardly know they were there. Mr and Mrs Beaver are part of an experiment by Kent Wildlife Trust to see if this species can be reintroduced to the wild. Beavers died out in Britain some five hundred years ago. They are large animals – the size of a well-fed Labrador – but you will be lucky to see more than a black nose swimming along. Ungainly on land, they are happiest in water; a rustle of reeds and a ripple on the surface of the stream are the first things to announce their presence. They take a dip as soon as they hear anyone coming. They can hold their breath under water for up to a quarter of an hour.

Reintroductions are controversial. But local farmers have been brought on side by Peter Forest, who runs the seventy-acre Ham Fen reserve, the last fen in the county. He explains that they are European beavers, which do not eat fish. They strip the bark from willow saplings for their food – the shoots are severed as cleanly as though by a saw – but would rarely stray far beyond the riverbank to damage commercial plantations; the bark on older trees is not on their diet. Nor do they seem to dam rivers unless the water is in danger of falling below the eighteen inches they need to survive. And, unlike most rodents, they have small families – just one kit a year – so the population spreads slowly. The Ham Fen couple has yet to breed.

The reserve is not generally open to the public – like other celebrities, the beavers value their privacy – but Mr Forest often takes groups of interested people. Meanwhile, life in Ham – although 'hamlet' would now be a better name – goes on without taking much notice. The nearest proper village, Worth, got going in the seventeenth century, thanks to the activities of Huguenot refugees. Their Dutch-gabled farmhouses can still be seen.

These days, Hawkhurst hardly looks like a centre of organised crime, but in the eighteenth century it was home to a violent band of smugglers, the Hawkhurst Gang. Smuggling was a problem all around the coast of Britain. Sir Robert Walpole's tax on tea was widely resented, generating popular support for the smugglers. There were far too few excise officers, known as riding men, to have any effect.

At sea, smugglers could afford the latest ship-building technology, such as fore-and-aft rigging, giving them an advantage of speed over the excisemen; they also used boats specially suited to their purpose, often equipped with oars, which enabled them to glide into estuaries and generally outmanoeuvre the more cumbersome government ships. In 1783, the Board of Excise informed the Prime Minister, William Pitt, that there were at least two hundred and fifty vessels of more than twenty tons engaged in smuggling around Britain. The Hawkhurst Gang operated along most of the eastern half of the south coast.

Although Hawkhurst is more than fifteen miles from the sea, its position could not have been better. Near the main roads to London from Hastings and Rye, it lay in the Weald of Kent, heavily wooded and still, as a consequence, inclined to the lawlessness belonging to an area into which the eye of officialdom could not easily see. Poverty would have made local people sympathetic to the smugglers' activities; employment had fallen when the local iron industry collapsed (important under Queen Elizabeth, it had transferred to the Midlands by the mid eighteenth century*). Gentry supporting the forces of the establishment were thin on the ground.

The smugglers took up the Jacobite cause as an excuse for anti-government activities, drinking 'Confusion to his Majesty King George' before the 1745 rebellion, according to a riding officer's report. But it was a marriage of convenience. They dropped their political affiliation after Bonnie Prince Charlie's defeat, and went on smuggling from their base at the Oak and Ivy Inn. Occasionally, after some particularly shocking exploit, one might be caught and gibbeted, but often the riding officers were in the pay of the smugglers, if not actually smugglers themselves.

The Hawkhurst Gang had brutal ways of enforcing loyalty. In October 1747, its members raided a government customs house in Poole, stealing the tea, brandy and rum that had been captured from a smuggling ship some weeks earlier. On the way home, the gang rested at Fordingbridge in Hampshire, where one of them, known as Diamond, tossed a small packet of tea to a passing shoemaker whom he recognised, Daniel Chater. Eventually, customs men got wind of the incident, and Chater was compelled to inform.

While he was being taken to identify Diamond by a riding officer, William Galley, they stopped at a pub in Rowland's Castle; unhappily for them it was a smugglers' pub. The smugglers plied them with drink, then brutally seized them, tying them to horses and whipping them as they rode. Chater lost consciousness. Galley's ordeal continued, as he was slung across the saddle, a smuggler called Jackson 'all the time squeezing his private parts'. Finally he was thrown into a sandpit; Chater was kept in a barn for some days before being dumped in a well. The murders were a step too far. The Duke of Richmond, whose seat of Goodwood Park is near Rowland's Castle, went in pursuit of them, and the leader Arthur Gray was eventually executed for another murder. Seven of the other principal actors were sentenced to death, being executed on the Broyle, near Chichester; five had their bodies hung in chains in different parts of Sussex.

The people of the Weald had ceased to see smugglers as Robin Hood figures, their opinion having been made plain in April 1747, when, under the inspiration of a former army corporal, William Stuart, a local militia defeated some of the Hawkhurst Gang in a pitched battle at Goudhurst (see page 121).

*See Bersham, page 460

# HERSTMONCEUX
EAST SUSSEX                                                    *Home of the Sussex trug*

Life is full of little pleasures, and one of them is holding a Sussex trug. This boat-shaped wooden basket, used to carry secateurs, seedlings and freshly pulled carrots around the garden, can become, quite literally, a friend for life. Enthusiasts will take these hardy receptacles, after what may have been forty years of good service, back for repairs. It isn't that their owners can't afford a new one, but, like other pieces of craft made from natural materials, the trug enjoys an intimate relationship with the person using it. They have shared happy garden hours together, at the rising of the sun and its going down, during misty mornings and golden afternoons. You can't throw a trug like that on the bonfire, any more than you would put down an old Labrador before its time.

Trugs came only from Sussex. The epicentre of production was, and remains, the village of Herstmonceux. It was here that this form of basket was invented in the 1820s by Thomas Smith. There had been trugs before. The word derives from the Anglo-Saxon *trog*, meaning a boat-shaped vessel. The old trogs had been circular, like miniature coracles. Then, as now, their dimensions were determined by the amount of grain they held, farmers using them to measure out bushels, gallons and pints. Smith's innovation was to add the handle to carry it by, and little feet on which it could stand without rolling over. It was the dawn of what the encyclopedist and garden theorist John Claudius Loudon* would call the Gardenesque, with its emphasis on individual, exotic plants, cherished not just by working gardeners but by the ladies of the house. The Sussex trug was ideal for carrying cut flowers, plants and vegetables. At the Great Exhibition of 1851, Smith won both a gold medal and an order from Queen Victoria.

*No gardener of sensibility would be without a Sussex*
*trug, made at Herstmonceux since the 1820s.*

Once, trug-makers abounded by the dozen around Herstmonceux, taking their raw materials from the chestnut coppice and cricket-bat willow that grew locally. Now, the only place where they are made in the village is The Truggery, found behind the veranda of an unassuming brick house on the A271. Trugs have been made here since 1899. Some of the old ones, with green trim, are displayed in a glass-fronted cupboard in the shop, with little tickets attached by string explaining their history. The baskets, mostly of the standard half bushel, supplemented by a few long cucumber or sweet-pea trugs, are everywhere – piled on the floor, hung from the ceiling, marching along the keyboard of a piano. Overlooking fields at the back is the sap-smelling workshop, its window blinds permanently down so that sunlight can't distract the craftsman's eye.

Stripped to the waist, Pete Marden – a bald man, orange-bearded – is splitting chestnut. Once split, it is steamed with the bark on for twenty minutes in a converted iron pipe, until it can be bent to form handle and rims. Willow, cut into thin boards and shaved smooth, is used because it is light. Having been soaked in water, the boards become pliable enough to curve into shape. Where does the straight, knot-free willow come from? Offcuts from cricket bats made at Robertsbridge.

*See Great Tew, page 177

# HYTHE

HAMPSHIRE     *The last electric pier railway (privately owned) in Britain*

The sea does cruel things. It overwhelms some settlements, sucking them into the waves, while others it maroons. Hythe was one of the Confederation of the Cinque Ports, formed to provide a makeshift navy from commercial vessels (in return the towns that supplied them received privileges). It was a place of substance. But the port silted up, the sea withdrew and Hythe could do nothing to prevent its place being taken by Southampton, on the other side of the river Test. Three of the four churches disappeared; the civic buildings came to look increasingly like curiosities, given the scale of their surroundings. While huge ocean-going liners docked at Southampton, Hythe now has little more than the ferry that has been bobbing back and forth since the Middle Ages.

But Hythe can still claim one distinction: the last electric pier railway (privately owned) in Britain. It is a plucky little survival, not reliant on a summer trade but fulfilling a workaday transport function throughout the year. The ferry became a steam service in 1836. By 1879, it was necessary to build a new pier, reaching seven hundred yards into deep water. Rails were laid to help take heavy loads down to the boats, but the motive power was provided by hand. A new railway was built in 1922, with a single two-foot gauge track. Then, as now, it was operated by two little locomotives, with four wheels each, left over from the First World War; they had been built for the Avonmouth mustard gas works. Originally they ran from batteries, but before long it was decided to take power directly from a third rail running along the seaward side of the track (pedestrians walk on the other side).

Change has come, even to this last vestige of Hythe's pride. During the twentieth century, Southampton grew away from its historic core around the docks; this has made buses a more practical rival to the ferry. When Iain Frew edited *Britain's Electric Railway Today* in 1983, it seemed that the ferry itself might prove the pier railway's undoing: 'the availability of shallower draught ferries may in fact render the entire structure redundant within the next few years'. The end has not come yet. Admirers of this transport oddity hope it never does.

# LINDFIELD

WEST SUSSEX                              *Village of lime trees*

The crocuses are out in Lindfield. All the way up the hill that forms the village high street, they speckle the neatly kept verges in random purple, yellow and white. Everything is neatly kept in this village. The pavements are laid with brick, the yew hedges trimmed. It is too early in the year to enjoy the lime avenue that rises above the crocuses – no leaves out yet, but the trees will look ravishing in a month or so.

Limes are an essential part of Lindfield's character: the name of the village means open space by the lime trees.

Mid Sussex District Council recently cooked up a plan to fell fifteen of the thirty-four limes, on the grounds that they were too big. Pollarding stopped in the 1980s because it cost too much, and by 2008 the roots were making the pavement uneven. But the Lindfield Preservation Society kept faith with these veterans. The felling scheme was overturned and a new campaign of pollarding begun. Every one of the trees has now been given a tree preservation order. Hurrah! According to Pevsner, it is 'without any doubt the finest village street in East Sussex [sic]'. Vigilance ensures that it still is.

Foliage, though, is the enemy of architecture. You must go before summer if you want to see the grand parade of Sussex vernacular that jostles up the hill – hipped, half-hipped, bonnet-hipped and catslide roofs; walls that display their timbers, or hide them beneath tiles, mathematical tiles or stucco; others built from sandstone or local brick. Houses that cannot rise to Georgian door cases have pretty iron-work porches or verandas. Humphrey's has been a baker's shop since 1796.

There are some really important buildings, notably Old Place, built in 1590 and rescued from use as a poorhouse by the Victorian stained-glass artist Charles Eamer Kempe. It had a significant garden in Edwardian days. Next door, The Thatched House was once a hunting lodge of Henry VII, according to an elegantly lettered notice on the gate. Dr Andrew Boorde, the physician at the court of Henry VIII, who is supposed to have been the original Merry Andrew, lived at a house called Paxhill. (He was merry enough to be put in prison by the Bishop of Winchester for keeping prostitutes, where he died.) The impresario and diarist Philip Henslowe, who built the Rose Theatre on Bankside, was born in Lindfield around 1550.

In the hungry 1820s, Lindfield became the scene of a philanthropic experiment by William Allen, a Quaker chemist who made a fortune in London and bought a house here. He built cottages, allotments and schools that taught useful subjects, such as surveying and botany, hoping to give poor labourers and their children the means of escaping the workhouse. Allen died in 1843. That was two years after the railway came, Haywards Heath being the result. Lindfield could be described as a suburb of this later development – but not by anyone who wanted to leave the village alive.

# LOWER HARDRES
KENT                                                    *Rise of Captain Swing*

In 1786, the Scottish engineer Andrew Meikle perfected his design for a thresh-ing machine. Turning at a rate of three hundred revolutions a minute, a drum supplemented by four scutchers, or mechanical flails, separated the grain of wheat from its husk. Powered, most commonly, by a horse trudging round in a circle, it could thresh between one and two dozen bushels an hour. Threshing by the old-fashioned method using hand flails, little changed since Biblical days, involved several labourers working continuously from harvest until high summer. It was a dusty, monotonous job, as the poet Stephen Duck made clear in 'The Thresher's Labour' (1730)*.

In the course of forty years, the threshing machine became widespread throughout Britain. But the workers so liberated were by no means happy about it. In 1822, riots in protest against the new machines broke out in East Anglia. It was a time of agricultural depression, exacerbated by the return of unemployed soldiers after the Napoleonic Wars. Nothing came of the disturbances, but at the end of the decade, after three successive years of bad harvests, with food prices rising but farmers cutting wages in the knowledge that their workers would receive parish handouts under the Speenhamland System†, some country people felt driven to take action.

Throughout the summer of 1830, ricks belonging to unpopular Kent farmers were set on fire, notably those of magistrates who had sentenced poachers. When fire engines were rushed to the scene, it was found that their pipes had been cut. 'Scarcely a night passes without some farmer having a cornstack or barn set fire to,' the *Maidstone Gazette* reported. The fires were accompanied by letters from the mysterious Captain Swing, a mythical figure whose name may derive from the 'swingel' that is part of a flail, or the popular meaning of 'to swing' – to be hanged.

Swing then directed his anger towards threshing machines. On 28 August 1830, a mob of four hundred labourers descended on Lower Hardres and Lyminge, destroying whichever they could find. The dragoons were called out from Canterbury, but the disturbances continued. To begin with, there was sympathy with the rioters, many of whom were going hungry. The magistrate Sir Edward Knatchbull wanted 'to see as little violence used in suppressing the disorders as possible'. But in October the disorder escalated. Machines were destroyed by daylight. Guns were fired. Bands of rioters roamed the countryside recruiting others, demanding better wages, constant employment and improved parish relief. 'Society is now completely unhinged,' the *Kentish Gazette* stammered in November. Rioting spread across much of southern England, and did not entirely die out until 1833.

The establishment's response was in proportion to the scare it had got. 'I hope that your fate will be a warning to others,' Mr Justice Alderson told three of the rioters, including a shepherd of eighteen and a bricklayer of nineteen, as he passed sentence. They were put in chains and sent twelve thousand miles away to Australia. Four hundred and eighty-one men suffered this fate. Nineteen labourers, still wearing their smock frocks, were hanged. They and the transported were often young men, whose families were left destitute. His Majesty's Poor Law Commissioners produced a report on the riots. A new but no more humane Poor Law was introduced in 1834, squires dispensed charity that engendered subservience, and Parliament made it easier for parishes to create allotments. Otherwise Swing had failed.

*See Charlton, page 24 † See Speenhamland, page 193*

# LYDD
## KENT

*'Colonel' Cody flies a kite*

Perhaps the most remarkable aspect of the Royal Engineers' attempt to develop box kites as a platform for observing the enemy was that nobody got killed in one. Certainly the personnel involved in the experiments outside Lydd in the early twentieth century must have held their breath as a lone spotter made his ascent to heights of more than two thousand feet. Incredibly, the man who oversaw operations – granted officer status for the purpose – was the goatee-bearded Wild West showman Samuel F. Cody, hiding his flowing locks in a bun pinned up under his cowboy hat in deference to military convention. He patented his system of man-lifting kites in 1901, selling it to the Admiralty in 1903 and the army in 1905.

Born Cowdery, Cody first appeared in England performing a Wild West burlesque on roller skates at Olympia in 1890. Claiming, falsely, to be the son of 'Buffalo Bill' Cody, he had considerable success in plays such as *The Klondyke Nugget*. A stunt rider, he was also a crack pistol shot, who would shoot a cigarette from a lady's lips – that lady being, as likely as not, his wife, who not surprisingly retired home to the United States with nervous trouble.

From the theatre, Cody progressed to an equally flamboyant fascination with aeronautics. Where he got his knowledge from, no one knows, but the claim that he was taught to fly kites by the Chinese cook on a cattle ranch in Texas should be approached with caution. If only the British army had had access to kites during the Boer War, it was said, they would not have had to rely on cumbersome gas-filled balloons to peep behind enemy lines. Perhaps providentially, Cody's invention came at the wrong moment to be used in the field. It involved launching a series of four or five kites in tandem, linked by piano wire. These pulled up a steel cable, to which would be attached a man-lifting kite, with Cody or someone else in a basket underneath. As the man-lifter went up, its position above ground could be secured on the cable by means of a ratchet. There were several sudden collapses, which left Cody hanging onto the branches of trees or circling in the sea until rescued.

Cody himself helped make the manned kite obsolete. In October 1908, he was at the controls of the British Army Aeroplane No. 1A, which took off from Farnborough Common in Berkshire and flew for a glorious twenty-seven seconds. (He was later killed when one of his flying machines crashed in 1913.) His was the first aeroplane flight in Britain, but these days, some people in Lydd might be glad if it had not been made. Lydd Airport has got delusions of grandeur, imagining that it is really London Ashford Airport, with the ambition of handling half a million passengers a year; proposals to extend the runway and build a new terminal are currently before Shepway District Council.

Lydd no longer has a barracks, but the military association has bequeathed an exciting landscape on Romney Marsh: concrete blocks, red flags, gravel workings, mobile homes, sheep . . . you never know what is coming next. The air still seems to reverberate with the distant sound of artillery shells on the firing range (the explosive known as lyddite, much used in the Great War, was tested here). Quite a few of the houses survive from the glory days when Lydd was a bustling port, and the triangular stretch of common known as the Rype holds even older memories. It was supposedly given to the Barons of Lydd by the Archbishop of Canterbury, in return for their having repulsed the Danes in 904.

See also Manston, page 132

# LYMINSTER
WEST SUSSEX                                    *Who killed the Knucker?*

English folklore is on the whole rather tame in comparison with that of Russia or the Nordic countries; the horrors of witches and monsters are on a relatively domestic scale, perhaps reflecting the well-tempered landscape out of which they emerged. Sussex is as cosy as anywhere in the Home Counties; nothing to terrify the unwary there, one would have thought.

Except at Lyminster. Here there is a pond. It was supposed to be of fathomless depth: once they tied the ropes of all the six bells of the church together, lowered them down and still could not touch the bottom (it is said). Fed by a spring, the pond has no obvious inlet, although water spills out from it plentifully enough. The water is always cool; it never freezes – indeed, on frosty mornings in winter, when the temperature is warmer than the surrounding air, it steams. There was a monster living in this pond. It is called the Knucker.

Folklorists agree that the Knucker was a terrible creature. It would fly through the air at inconceivable speed, seizing whatever flesh, human or animal, that it could, before taking its prey back to the swamps of Arun to be devoured. The dragon laid waste the country for years, until the King of Sussex, as could only be expected under the circumstances, offered his daughter's hand in marriage to anybody who could slay the foul fiend. At this point, accounts differ. Some say that a gallant knight stepped forward, tracked the dragon to its lair, or Knucker Hole, as the pond is called, and after a ferocious combat killed it. He then married the princess, who was as beautiful as he was brave, and they peopled Sussex with a comely race.

Alternatively, the Knucker was slain by a farmer's lad called Jim Pulk (or Puttock). He baked a huge Sussex pie, hauled it on a cart to the Knucker Hole and hid behind a hedge. The Knucker could not resist the pie; he gobbled it up, cart, horses and all – not knowing that Jim had used it as a piece of gigantic bait, laced with poison. The Knucker keeled over and died. Jim came out from behind the hedge, and cut its head off with a sickle. This put him in need of a pint, which he found in the pub, but when he drew his hand over his mouth as he finished it, some of the Knucker's blood got into his system. Jim fell down dead.

Whoever killed the Knucker, he is supposed to be buried under a medieval tomb at Lyminster church. The stone lid is decorated with a cross, against a background of what could be, at a pinch, dragon's scales. Why Knucker? The word probably derives from an Old English word for water monster used by Beowulf.

Unlike most monsters, the Knucker had chosen an attractive place to inhabit, given that the pond yields only sweet water. He was also spiritually neutral, unlike St George's dragon, which to medieval churchmen was associated with the devil, prevented from polluting the Church (or Virgin) by the epitome of Christian chivalry. But that tale may have had quite a different meaning originally. The dragon symbolised the evil spirits trying to keep back the fertility of springtime; St George's Day is celebrated on 23 April, the beginning of spring.

# MANSTON
## KENT                              *Tailplanes among the cabbages*

The Isle of Thanet is weird. Although the economic geography of Britain has tilted towards the south, the general flood of prosperity stops short of this corner of Kent. Once the site of coalfields, it is so disadvantaged that European development money has been spent to help it catch up.

Manston is pure Thanet. In the centre is the church, a pinched piece of 1870s Gothic, more or less hidden behind an overgrown yew tree: you would miss it were it not for the war memorial in front. The parish noticeboard advertises the Viking quilters, the Manston and District Garden Club, and a new yoga and Pilates group, meeting in the village hall. A Union Jack flies in the front garden of a bungalow. A pub called The Jolly Farmer recalls the era when the few gentry houses were built, and farming wreathed the Garden of England in smiles.

The elephant in the living room of this otherwise colourless settlement is the airfield. It would be more correct to call it Kent International Airport, but this is Thanet. Although the airport emerged from receivership in 2005, it has yet to shrug off the sense that it is an old RAF station in civvies. Shacks are still painted olive green. This was one of the most valiant of Fighter Command's front-line stations during the Battle of Britain, with Luftwaffe airfields in France only ten minutes flying time away. A museum next to the airport shows photographs of debonair young airmen about to sprint to their Spitfires and Hurricanes. Often they did not come back.

Manston's runway was extended to 2,752 metres during the Cold War. Afterwards, the Treasury forced the military to sell up, and now it is not B52 bombers that haul themselves into the air above the village but elderly Boeing 747 cargo planes. At rest, they loom, white and enormous, over the cabbage fields, like hugely inflated seagulls. Perhaps villagers get used to it; to me the sight always comes as a surprise.

# MINSTER

*Queen Eormenburg takes the veil*

The very name of Minster, in Thanet, indicates how the place came into being. It was built around the Saxon minster, a kind of monastery. Before the parish system had been established, minsters were the mainstay of early Christianity outside major centres such as Canterbury. Their canons were similar to monks, except that the latter spent their days in contemplation, the canons devoting more of their time to work outside the monastic enclosure. Kent, where St Augustine converted the Saxon King Ethelbert in 597, possessed several. Often they were endowed by royalty. This was the case with Minster in Thanet, so called to distinguish it from Minster on the Isle of Sheppey, also in Kent; both these minsters were founded in the same year, 670, both for nunneries that would house a princess. Princess Sexburg, who came from East Anglia, lived at the Sheppey Minster; Minster in Thanet was home to Queen Eormenburg.

Villages in Saxon Kent were strung out along the old Roman roads, and sites on these roads were also chosen for minsters. In the case of Minster in Thanet, it was the road from Canterbury to the east coast, via a ferry across the Wantsum Channel, which then separated Thanet from the rest of Kent. At that time Minster was actually on the sea, although it is now some way inland. Its potential for settlement had been already appreciated by the Romans, who built a large villa here in the second and third centuries. Bricks from the villa were later used in the minster building.

Eormenburg (also called Ebba), a Kentish princess, had been married to a prince in Herefordshire. King Ecgberht of Kent gave her the site of Minster in recompense for the murder of her two young brothers*. No fool, she asked for as much land as her tame deer could run over in a day, which amounted to ten thousand acres. She was followed as abbess by her daughter Mildrith, who became the subject of a devotional cult when her remains were translated to St Augustine's Abbey in Canterbury in 1035.

The reason for Mildrith's remains being moved – and their whereabouts were disputed by the canons of St Gregory's Priory in Canterbury, who claimed to have inherited the body from the Minster at Lyminge, near Folkestone – was that the Vikings had come. Minster in Thanet, a rich nunnery, was an easy target. The attacks arrested its growth. The minster was abandoned, the land farmed from a grange. The minster was rebuilt on a grand scale by the Normans, but although impressively housed, this mother church of Kent did not thereafter make much of itself; it is now the parish church.

*See Eastry, page 111

# NEWTOWN

*Town hall – where's the town?*

You would hardly have thought that Newtown would need a town hall, even in 1699 when it was built. The town had long had its day. Blame the French: they burnt the place during a raid in 1377, and it never really recovered. Until then, it had been a prosperous port and the biggest town on the island.

Today, Newtown nestles between the fingers of land and mudflat that have been shaped by the Newtown river. Being sheltered, the creeks made an excellent harbour. There may have been a settlement here before the Conquest, because the burgesses had to pay only rent, being free of other taxes, hence the original name of Francheville; the status may have been a legacy of the Saxon period. The Bishop of Winchester refounded the settlement in 1256, giving it the descriptive, if unoriginal, name of Newtown. Like other planned towns in the Middle Ages, it was laid out on a grid, the streets bearing optimistic names such as Gold Street and Silver Street. Each of the seventy-three plots of land was rented at a shilling a year.

Among the industries that developed were salt works, evaporating seawater in salt pans. The oysters were highly regarded; the oyster men were required to provide enough oysters and a 'good dish of fish' for the mayor's annual feast. 'The oysters are too large to be generally popular,' Edmund Venables observed in 1860. Can oysters ever be too large? He liked their flavour, however, and admitted that 'our neighbours the French esteem them very highly'. Perhaps it was the prospect of supersized oysters that provoked the 1377 raid.

In 1584, Queen Elizabeth granted the borough two members of parliament; presumably this was an attempt to revive it, because Newtown had already fallen behind Newport and a map of 1636 shows only a dozen inhabited buildings. 'The traces of a very large town are met with,' John Albin wrote in 1795, in the second Isle of Wight history to come out that year, 'though it is now dwindled away so as scarcely to deserve the name of a village, not containing more than about ten cottages, and consequently but very few inhabitants.' So why the town hall? Vanity must have had something to do with it. Perhaps the electors were embarrassed still to be sending two quite unjustifiable representatives to Westminster. The town hall gave them an air of civic importance and an elegant room to meet in.

Or perhaps they were conservative enough to feel that the old town hall, which had presumably rotted away, should be replaced, even though there was no longer much reason for it. Whatever the case, the architect A. F. Livesay of Portsmouth produced a creditable building of attractive red brick above a stone base. There are banded stone quoins to the corners and a hipped roof above. Steps lead up to a bold door case; to add to the effect, this side of the building is faced with buff-coloured mathematical tiles in imitation of stone. 'If you build it, they will come,' a modern saying goes. Only in this case no other structures joined the town hall, which could grace a respectable market town. It stands on a plot of grass beside an empty street. Alone.

*See also Fordwich, page 115*

# OFFHAM
KENT                                                              *Running at the Saracen*

'My better parts / Are all thrown down,' Orlando says in *As You Like It*, 'and that which here stands up / Is but a quintain; a mere lifeless block.' The quintain was part of a popular sport, and the only one now left in the country stands on the green at Offham. The sons of villages were unable to take part in the jousts beloved of Henry VIII and other great figures of medieval and Tudor England; they lacked the necessary armour, war horses, esquires and chivalric qualifications. So, instead of a live target in the shape of a galloping knight, they tried their skill at a wooden one (a game also popular with fledgling knights wanting to hone their technique).

*The only surviving quintain in Britain stands on the green at Offham.*

Originally, this might have been no more than a tree trunk or post; a shield was then added, and the post might have been carved into the shape of a barbarous Turk. This was attacked, either on foot or on horse, using a lance. In Italian, the name for this exercise was 'running at the armed man' or 'at the Saracen', and it is described as being practised in Roman times, the Emperor Justinian banning the use of spears with points.

The quintain was a refinement on the wooden dummy. A bar was set on top of a post; at one end of the bar was a shield, at the other a heavy bag of sand. You rode at the shield with your lance, but since the bar swivelled on a pivot, you had to keep up momentum to avoid being hit on the neck by the sandbag and perhaps knocked off your horse. The word quintain is thought to derive from the Welsh *gwyntyn*, meaning vane.

Matthew Paris recorded that, in 1254, a group of young Londoners, riding at the quintain for the prize of a peacock, got into trouble with Henry III for attacking the royal servants who had been jeering at them. Tilting at the quintain was part of the 'solemn country bridal' laid on as part of the stupendous entertainment presented for Queen Elizabeth during her stay at Kenilworth Castle, Warwickshire, in 1575. In *The Natural History of Oxfordshire* (1677), Robert Plot described the sport as still going strong, although 'only in request at marriages, and set up in the way for young men to ride at as they carry home the bride; he that breaks the board being counted the best man'. A variant was the water quintain, which involved a young man in a rowing boat, who would be knocked into the water if his attack went wrong.

The original Offham quintain is thought to have been Elizabethan, although little if any of the sixteenth-century structure can survive in the post and crossbar that remains now. Why does one survive here at all? Quintains were not difficult to make, could be set up quickly and were often erected only for a day. But Kent's Georgian historian Edward Hasted explained that the 'dwelling house of the estate', which stands opposite the Offham quintain, had the duty of keeping it in repair, a responsibility that now rests with the parish council. In former times, married men who were not blessed with children were put onto the quintain and spun round. Sometimes, as P. H. Ditchfield observed in *Old English Sports, Pastimes and Customs* (1891), 'discontented and disobedient wives' shared the same fate. However, the custom has been discontinued.

# OSPRINGE

KENT                                          *Christianity takes over from Rome*

In 601, Pope Gregory the Great directed St Augustine not to destroy pagan buildings during his mission to convert the Saxons to Christianity. Instead, they were to be converted to the new religion. One of the buildings that might have been affected by this ruling is the little ruined chapel at Stone, outside Faversham. It is the only church in Britain, albeit ruined, to incorporate a pagan shrine or mausoleum. The Roman structure, thought to date from the fourth century AD, was constructed from roughly squared tufa stone and rows of tile. Roman tiles can be seen among the flints with which the Saxons extended the little building to form a nave. It may have been used for Christian worship as early as the seventh century. By the thirteenth century, when more work was done, the chapel was dedicated to Our Lady of Elwarton.

Today, the dwellings that the chapel served have gone without trace, leaving the chapel marooned in the middle of a field, next to a copse. The stumps of the walls survive to a height of a metre above ground. They do not look particularly significant, and the spot is a deserted one. It would have been busier in the previous centuries, however: the Roman road of Watling Street ran close by the chapel, and archaeological finds show that the area was well populated. The Roman fort of Durolevum stood somewhere in the area, perhaps on the nearby Judd Hill. The chapel at Stone may have been related to Durolevum, although we do not know how. Certainly it was common for missionaries to build monasteries within the enclosures provided by abandoned Saxon Shore forts, such as Reculver (see page 139), fifteen miles away. Near Stone chapel is a Roman cemetery.

By 1511, the chapel was in disrepair; by the time of the Reformation it had probably been deserted. The settlement had moved east to Ospringe, half a mile away, to take advantage of the trade from pilgrims en route to Canterbury. Ospringe itself is now a hamlet, although the thirteenth-century Maison Dieu, built to accommodate them, testifies to its former importance.

# PETERSHAM
SURREY                                    *Ten miles from Trafalgar Square*

The church of St Peter at Petersham has a new organ, brought over from Switzerland. Installing a new organ is a significant investment, and it is a sign of the dynamism of this congregation that it has been able to achieve it. This may seem all the more surprising, because Petersham is not a self-contained rural parish, but part of the London Borough of Richmond upon Thames, a suburb where one might expect local allegiances to be weaker.

Is Petersham a village? Despite the pressures of its location, nuzzling at the elbow of one of the river Thames's more preposterous loops, less than ten miles from Trafalgar Square, it continues to feel like one. The population numbers two thousand. A third of the parish is a golf course, another third is common land beside the Thames, leaving only a third for housing. This may include former council estates colonised by, among others, a German community attracted by the German school, but it still in general manages to give the impression of Georgian red-brick substance: large houses behind mottled brick walls that suggest vegetables gardens and topiary.

The church began life in the seventh century. Part of a medieval building survives in the chancel. But, this being Petersham, there was already a significant property to the west of this church, which stopped later builders from extending the nave. Instead, the church expanded laterally, into broad transepts with galleries and box pews. (The chancel, unexpectedly, occupies part of what might otherwise be the crossing.) There are a few benches forming 'agricultural pews', for farm labourers who could not afford to pay rents for the grander kind of pew, with doors, in the eighteenth century.

The Victorians came in the person of the great church restorer George Gilbert Scott, who added stained glass (all except a fragment blown out during the Second World War). Otherwise the parish authorities did not feel that St Peter's needed medievalising. It survived, the neat brick exterior consorting comfortably with water meadows too low-lying to be built on, and a graveyard that is valued as a haven of peace.

Grand families worshipped here; some, like Prince Rupert of the Rhine and the late Queen Elizabeth the Queen Mother's parents, the Earl and Countess of Strathmore, chose this church to be married in (some are recorded in the tablets on the walls). Ham House is nearby, and St Peter's was its church. One of the tablets commemorates Captain George Vancouver, who was with Captain Cook when he was killed in the Pacific. After charting the western coast of America, he retired on half-pay to Petersham, where he wrote his *Voyage of Discovery*. He was already suffering ill health and died, aged forty, in 1798. It would not demand much of him as an explorer if he came back to visit his last home. Except for the aircraft on their way to Heathrow, Petersham would, in its bones, seem the same as when he left it. Except for the considerable improvement of the new organ.

# PUTTENHAM
SURREY                                   *Flavouring three million pints of bitter*

September is a busy time on Duke's Farm, on the Hog's Back in Surrey: the hops are harvested. The scene is worthy of a Shell poster from the 1950s. Handsome young men drive tractors, while in the trailers behind, smiling girls pull down the heavy green vines that clamber up strings attached to the system of wires overhead. The air is heavy with a seductively honeyed smell, which to some noses has an undercurrent of marmalade. In a barn, elderly machines rattle the plants so much that the seeds fall away. Then they are carried to the drying shed, fanned with hot air and packed tight into big, sausage-shaped sacks, stamped with the traditional Farnham bell. There used to be dozens of hop gardens around Farnham – three bells marked those within the town boundary. Duke's Farm (one bell) is the last to survive. Its fourteen acres will produce enough hops to flavour three million pints of bitter. Scrabble players will like to know that hops are sold in zentners, or weights of fifty kilograms.

Surrey is a magic land. Standing in the hop garden, you would have no idea that only half a mile away motorists were haring to London on the A3. Like many of the villages around here, Puttenham does not seem to have changed much since Lutyens grew up in these parts (he later built a house here, Lascombe, where you can rent one of the cottages if you like). Its single street of mostly red-brick dwellings has a Georgian air, although the date stones of some houses claim they are earlier.

The Good Intent not only makes a point of welcoming 'muddy boots, dogs and children', but offers a changing round of five real ales. The pub sign shows Oliver Cromwell in his campaign tent dedicating himself to the wellbeing of Britain. Beer was one of the few pleasures he did not ban.

# RECULVER
## KENT
*Goldfinger casts his shadow*

The Ian Fleming villain Auric Goldfinger lived at Reculver, on the coast of East Kent. It was the sort of bleak spot that would have suited him, the gaunt towers of the abandoned church – the Twin Sisters – adding an extra note of desolation to the Roman fort, the caravan park and (out to sea) the phalanx of wind turbines. A few miles away lay Ramsgate, its harbour granted the prefix 'Royal' by George IV, an act of aggrandisement that belies its modest size. 'Quiet little port,' James Bond comments. 'Customs and police who were probably only on the lookout for brandy from France.'

Fleming knew Kent well. In 1952, he bought White Cliffs, a house on St Margaret's Bay, from Noël Coward. He played golf at Royal St George's, outside Sandwich, which became Royal St Mark's when Bond outwitted the cheating Goldfinger by switching balls. It was in the clubhouse at Royal St George's that the author suffered his fatal heart attack in 1964; if he had lived, he would have been captain of the club the following year.

Kent provided inspiration and settings at several points in his career. The young Bond grew up at the perhaps aptly named Pett Bottom, under the guardianship of an aunt; Fleming knew the hamlet from frequenting the Duck Inn, which has now put a plaque on his favourite seat. In *Moonraker*, Hugo Drax's rocket plant lies on the Kent coast between Dover and Deal. In the attempt to stop Drax launching a missile on London, Bond powers his four-and-a-half-litre Bentley along Ebury Street, where Fleming had his London home, at the start of an epic chase, which takes him past Leeds Castle (where Drax forces an Alfa Romeo off the road) before crashing into the rolls of newsprint that the dastardly Krebs has unleashed from a lorry.

Near the Old Palace at Bekesbourne, below Canterbury, which Fleming owned for two years in the early 1960s, is Higham Park, at Bridge. It had been home to

Count Louis Zborowski, a motor-racing driver who died at Monza in 1924, aged twenty-nine; Zborowski had designed cars fitted with aeroplane engines, which he named Chitty Bang Bang. Fleming borrowed the idea for *Chitty Chitty Bang Bang*, written for his son, Caspar, and published in 1964.

Reculver's history, if not so fantastic as the plot of *Goldfinger*, is itself appropriately dramatic, as well as being associated with a wonder of military science. When the Romans built the fort of Regulbium, it stood on the edge of the Wantsum Channel, which separated the Isle of Thanet from the mainland. But eventually the channel silted up, the last of the marshes being drained after the Second World War. The farmland that was created has no settlement on it; the sea off Reculver was chosen as the testing ground for Barnes Wallis's bouncing bomb, used to attack dams in the Ruhr Valley in 1943. One of the (unarmed) prototypes recovered from under the water is now in the Herne Bay Museum.

# ROTTINGDEAN
EAST SUSSEX                                   *Quite a family go to the seaside*

The District Line had arrived; so had speculative builders and streets of semi-detached villas. It was time for the Burne-Joneses to leave Fulham. Besides, the painter needed a break. Something of a Pre-Raphaelite lily, albeit amply bearded, he was easily tired, but the sea always served as a tonic. And so it was that Georgiana Burne-Jones one day walked out from Brighton (her husband did not like Brighton) to Rottingdean, 'straight to the door of a house that stood empty on the village green, and we bought it at once'. Called Prospect Cottage, it was the first they had ever owned: too small by itself, but they solved that problem by acquiring the next-door house, which their friend, the metalworker and architect William Benson covered in black mathematical tiles (very chic). He turned the two residences into one, which they named North End House, partly because it was at the north end of the village and partly in memory of Fulham.

As described by Sir Edward's granddaughter, Angela Thirkell, it was not brilliantly convenient, although with its changes of level and different staircases, it was thrilling for children. Nor did it configure to conventional ideas of comfort. 'As I look back on the furniture of my grandparents' two houses I marvel chiefly at the entire lack of comfort which the Pre-Raphaelite Brotherhood succeeded in creating for itself,' Thirkell remembered. But there was a magic to it. Angela woke up every day to the sight of an angel on the point of drawing her curtains (it had been painted onto the nursery wall by Burne-Jones). North End House became the focus of a family compound that threatened to take over the village.

Because it was quite a family. It included nephew Rudyard Kipling and his cousin, the future Prime Minister Stanley Baldwin (Baldwin had married one of the Ridsdales, who were Old Rottingdean.) The Kiplings stayed at North End

House until their third baby was born, then rented The Elms on the other side of the green. They did not mean it to be permanent, but stayed for five years. They might have stayed longer if it had not been for the sightseers. Thirkell was likely to find a little knot of them around the entrance when she came back from playing with Josephine Kipling. 'All through the summer months charabancs . . . would disgorge loads of trippers at the Royal Oak, and as there was little for them to see in the village besides my grandfather's house and the church, they went a good deal of time round Cousin Ruddy's gate.'

W. E. Henley, author of 'Invictus', came, so crippled he had to be taken around in a Bath chair; James Barrie would go for walks over the Downs; Henry James came over from Rye. The painter William Nicholson, with his 'troupe' of children, bought The Grange, which his friend Edwin Lutyens* remodelled for the lawyer who succeeded him. The artistic moment at Rottingdean could not last; it never does. 'No new houses then straggled out to meet one,' remembered Lady Burne-Jones of her first encounter with the village, 'but the little place lay peacefully within its gray garden walls, the sails of the windmill were turning slowly in the sun, and the miller's black timber cottage was still there.' By the time Kipling wrote his memoirs he would lament: 'To-day, from Rottingdean to Newhaven is almost fully developed suburb, of great horror.'

*See Mells, page 55; Thursley, page 145

# SEASALTER
KENT                                                                   *Salt of life*

'In the providential arrangements of the world, the absolute necessaries of life are either supplied with unsparing abundance, or may be procured with moderate exertion.' So wrote Charles Tomlinson in *The Natural History of Common Salt* (1850). Ah, happy days. In the matter of salt, however, he was right. Layers of salt were deposited, two hundred and fifty million years ago, on what was then the bottom of an inland sea; they are now mined in Cheshire. In the same area, springs bring salt to the surface in the form of brine, which used to be collected in tanks and heated, until the water had evaporated off. At Seasalter in Kent, as at hundreds of other seaside places, seawater could be collected and boiled. It still is. This is how the chef Stephen Harris provides salt to his restaurant, The Sportsman.

Salt has been made at Seasalter since Mesolithic times. The remains of an industry that flourished in the Saxon period can be seen from the sea wall: humps in the marsh reveal the position of huts. They also trapped fish here. Huts, traps and the wood that was burned to heat seawater were made from trees in the great Forest of Blean, which stretched from Whitstable to Canterbury. Surviving fish bones show that the cod caught near shore were huge. Salt was needed to preserve the catch. Meat from the animals grazing the marsh was also salted. Later, some farmers spread salt on their fields as a fertiliser. Clothiers used it for bleaching. Salt was an important commodity.

An Act of Parliament taxing salt (in England and Wales) was introduced in 1694, briefly repealed in the 1730s, then reintroduced (by then across Britain). Although the tax remained in place until 1825, it was clearly ticklish: between 1760 and 1817 no fewer than thirty Salt Acts were passed to get it right. It is no wonder: the hated *gabelle*, or salt tax, was one of the causes of the French Revolution.

In Norman times, salt-making was a cottage industry: the Domesday Book records that at Caister, one of sixty-one places where salt was made in Norfolk, there were forty-five salt pans. The manor of Rameslie in Sussex had as many as a hundred. The landscape around Seasalter has changed since then: the creeks and inlets, marshes and salty pools have been replaced by a uniform shoreline, behind which holiday bungalows and mobile homes shelter.

Chef Harris takes his water directly from the sea, waits for the sediment to settle out of it, then boils it in a cauldron. As it crystallises, flakes bloom on the surface, then what look like miniature stalagmites form at the bottom of the pan. Different consistencies form at different temperatures, but it is the first bloom that Harris favours. Does it taste any different from salt bought in a box? Possibly. It is also part of the narrative of local food: a celebration of an activity that has been practised for millennia on the Kent coast, remembered in this place's very name.

# STEVENTON
## HAMPSHIRE

*Where Jane Austen was born*

The world of Jane Austen revolves around the houses and villages of the countryside. She herself was born in a village – Steventon – and it was where she grew up. Her father, George Austen, after obtaining a scholarship and then fellowship at St John's College, Oxford, had become rector of both Steventon and Deane in 1764. At first, he and his wife, Cassandra, occupied the parsonage at Deane. Like many parsonages in the eighteenth century, Deane's was a pokey house, below the level that would satisfy an educated, if less than prosperous, gentleman and his well-connected bride. They must have been pleased when they were able to move into the freshly renovated rectory at Steventon, although to do so they had to negotiate the lane between the two villages. It was only a mile long, but so deeply rutted that Mrs Austen, in fashionable ill health, could make the journey only on a feather bed laid on other soft furniture. That was in the summer of 1768. Jane, their seventh child, was born in Steventon rectory seven years later.

To Mrs Austen's eye, the landscape around Steventon was unpromising, the chalk hills grazed smooth by sheep, the valleys growing the turnips beloved of Cobbett*. The rectory was a square house at the edge of the village, with sash windows and dormers in the tiled roof. Set a short way behind a simple paling, it would have been regarded as serviceable, rather than elegant, despite new additions at the back. Flowers mingled with vegetables in the garden, in the cottage style. In 1800, Jane heard 'an odd kind of crash which startled me': three of their elms blew down, two of them onto the 'sweep' of lawn that the Austens had created.

Not far away was Steventon manor house, occupied by the Digweed family (they rented it from the Rev. Austen's patron, Thomas Knight). Like the Rev. Austen, the Digweeds farmed, sometimes sharing the purchase of a few dozen sheep. Jane grew up surrounded by turkeys, ducks, chickens and guinea fowl, as well as farm-yard animals and bees. They provided the background, as Jane's sister Cassandra remembered, to a happy childhood.

Somewhat apart from the village stands the church, a sweet thirteenth-century building that contains memorials to some of Jane's family and friends, including her sister-in-law Anne, who died in 1795. The epitaph, recalling 'the Innocency of her Heart, Simplicity of her Manners, And amiable unspotted Tenour of her Life, in every Relation', is a model of its kind; perhaps Jane had a hand in its composition.

Jane lived at Steventon for the first twenty-five years of her life. She wrote *Sense and Sensibility* and *Pride and Prejudice* here, although they were not published until later. In 1801, her father unexpectedly moved to Bath, leaving his eldest son, James, as a curate at Steventon. After George Austen's death four years later, Jane moved, with her mother and sister, to various new homes, before settling at Chawton, also in Hampshire. Chawton Cottage, as it was then called, is now shown to the public by the Jane Austen Memorial Trust. At Steventon, the rectory that Jane knew was swept away in the 1820s by her nephew William Knight, who had taken over the family living and built himself a new rectory. For the sake of the view, he also demolished some old thatched dwellings, rehousing the occupants in new cottages. Jane died in 1817. Readers of *Mansfield Park* can only imagine what she would have felt.

*See Botley, page 97

# STOKE D'ABERNON
SURREY                                    *Celebrity descends with a training ground*

Stoke d'Abernon (*salve, magna parens*) is a hybrid, *stoke* being the Saxon word for 'place' and d'Abernon the name of the Norman lords of the manor. Two of the d'Abernon males can be seen in the church, Sir John the Elder and Sir John the Younger, stretched out at full length as memorial brasses, the older being the most ancient in Britain. There is further hybridity at the railway station, from which the number forty-two train plies its way to Waterloo Station in (if fast from Surbiton) little over half an hour. The name of the station, albeit located in Stoke d'Abernon, is preceded by that of Cobham (Stoke d'Abernon may have lost out altogether if it had not been for the protest of an energetic rector, in the days when the views of rectors were listened to).

Cobham is, or was, a village on the river Mole, with a watermill, a village green called The Tilt (although it never seems to have been a tilting ground) and a sweetly old-fashioned air; within living memory a Swiss-style dairy stood back from the high street behind a spread of lawn. Alas, it outgrew its rural origins, and charm fled like a frightened dryad. Stoke d'Abernon hung onto such signifiers of village identity as field paths, copses and a red-brick manor house, which survive alongside suburban closes within earshot of the M25: a hybrid once again.

Altogether it is a queer animal to be in the limelight, but celebrity has descended, now that Chelsea Football Club operates a training ground off the Stoke Road. The Chelsea Academy was opened in 2004. Since the players are expected to live within easy reach, this has had a radical effect on property prices, catapulting the area into the super league. Once bought for an appropriate price, the football-ers' houses are remade as marble-lined leisure centres, with gyms, indoor pools and bars, hidden (because security is critical) behind electronic gates. A local prep school produces a newsletter, which once advertised second-hand uniforms and the odd used television; the For Sale section recently included an Aston Martin Vantage for £120,000. Bentleys and other luxury cars go past in a blur. A group called the Alliance Against Urban 4x4s staged a protest outside the ground, urging the players to be kind to the planet and buy electric cars.

This has not been Stoke d'Abernon's first brush with fame. In 1993, the violin-ist Yehudi Menuhin became Lord Menuhin of Stoke d'Abernon, taking the name because that is where he had opened his music school thirty years earlier. The Menuhin School is still there, physically half a mile from the Chelsea Academy, yet in a universe which, one suspects, does not intersect.

# THE BOURNE
## SURREY
*Change was never more eloquently observed*

George Sturt did not expect to become a wheelwright, although he was the son of one. Instead, he went away to become a teacher, but, on discovering Ruskin, he became dissatisfied with book learning. When his father died, he returned to the family business. It was 1884, when all the carting and most of the ploughing in the countryside were done by horse. The wheelwright's shop made the farm wagons and dung carts, the barley rollers and ploughs that kept rural life on the move. Wrights had to know the qualities of the wood that wheel hubs, spokes and felloes were made of; they had to understand the needs of the carters, who wanted the back wheels of their wagons to sit in the ruts already made by the front. They had to follow the dictates of tradition, which had introduced elegant curves and dish-ing to the shapes of carts, not to make them look prettier but to reduce the volume and therefore weight of the wood being pulled, or allow a load of dung or turnips to settle comfortably. Starting in his twenties, Sturt was embarrassed to discover that he knew less than unlettered men who had begun at fifteen. He described his experience in *The Wheelwright's Shop* (1923).

To begin with, Sturt lived in the market town of Farnham, but later retreated to The Bourne, then an independent village but now more or less absorbed by its larger neighbour. It was from this village that he took the pseudonym of George Bourne, under which he published *Change in the Village* (1912). This is the finest of the books that chronicle the countryside as it slowly gave up horses and carts and centuries of knowledge about how things grew and worked, replacing them with tractors and machine tools.

These days, The Bourne's paddocks are overshadowed by the garage selling Japanese cars, and the people who live there commute. But a century ago, the village population was largely employed in Farnham's hop gardens, just as its fore-bears had been. Life could be hard, grindingly so, but what Sturt called the Peasant System had the benefit of shared values and culture.

> The 'peasant' tradition in its vigour amounted to nothing less than a form of civilisation – the home-made civilisation of the rural English. To the exigent problems of life it furnished solutions of its own . . . People could find in it not only a method of getting a living, but also an encouragement and a help to live well. Besides employment there was an interest for them in the country customs. There was scope for modest ambition, too. Best of all, these customs provided a rough guide as to conduct – an unwritten code to which, though we forget it, England owes much . . . And it is in the virtual disappearance of this civilisation that the main change in the village consists.

The first inklings of a different order had appeared; up and down the valley signs told of 'the invasion of a new people', unsympathetic to the old ways. Tokens of social disintegration included the lights of villas, impinging on the primordial darkness of the night, the sounds of piano-playing, 'the affected excitement of a tennis-party' and the 'braying' of motor cars. Thank goodness Sturt did not live to see his old village now.

# THURSLEY
## SURREY
*Lutyens country*

Edwin Landseer Lutyens, surely the greatest of all English domestic architects (although we could argue over Sir John Soane), grew up at Thursley. There were fourteen children in the family, of which he was the eleventh. Somehow they all bundled into a house then known as The Cottage – larger, these days, than when the Lutyenses had it, when it must have been a tight fit. Lutyens's father, Charles, who was a kind of Moses in appearance, with rigidly Puritanical views, had been in the army, but made a second career as an artist. Edwin was named after Charles's friend, the successful animal painter Landseer (who wanted to adopt him, but this was not thought quite the thing).

Charles Lutyens himself had enjoyed his day in the sun, but the clouds gathered. Money ran short, and he insisted that the family ate nothing but cabbage cooked in oil, served on newspaper instead of tablecloths. Not surprisingly, Lutyens was a sickly child. He was kept at home, rather than being sent away to school. Later, he thought this may have contributed to an awkwardness with adult company, which he hid behind a barrage of quick-fire jokes – often childish, sometimes rude, always funny. But for the architect that he would become, Thursley and its environs provided an invaluable object of study.

Then, as now, West Surrey abounded in what Lutyens's biographer, Christopher Hussey, called 'all the old English building materials: timber-framing filled with colour-washed wattle-and-daub, mellow brick nogging, sweeping roofs of thatch or tiles, or thick, moss-grown Horsham slabs'. Lutyens would roam around, by foot or bicycle, training his eye to memorise the details of the old cottages and farmhouses that he passed. Instead of sketching them with a pencil, he would hold up a pane of glass in a frame, tracing the lines of the building with a piece of sharpened soap. At home, the glass would be wiped clean for the next outing. By this means, he built up the reservoir of structural and stylistic knowledge that he tapped for his early buildings.

They did not waste time on naming the roads in Thursley: one is called The Street; at right angles to it is The Lane. As you ramble along them, it is difficult not to feel something of a peeping Tom; this is Surrey at its most intimate, with arches over garden gates framing views of tile-hanging and leaded lights. The Cottage is now called Street House, and you can only see one side of it, which is pretty enough, with a Tuscan door case; the garden front hides behind an ironstone wall, its mossy shoulders shawled with ferns. Eventually The Street winds up to the church. In time, Lutyens would design memorials to his mother and his nephew here. Next to the churchyard, at the top of the hill, is a lovely piece of rustic classicism, in mulberry-coloured brick, called Hill Farm, built about 1700. Perhaps Lutyens remembered it when his thoughts later turned to the William and Mary style – or, as he punningly called it, the 'Wrenaissance'. Lutyens paid a tribute to his place of birth by designing the Village Institute, now Prospect Cottage.

Local, yellow-brown Bargate stone is a common building material, generally used in irregularly shaped blocks because it is difficult to cut square. The joints may be 'galletted', with little chips of stone pushed into the lime mortar. Since mortar is soft, galleting* may have been intended to give extra strength; it would also have reduced the quantity of mortar that was required. Lutyens made use of this technique at Munstead Wood and Tigbourne Court.

*See West Dean, page 148. See also Mells, page 55

# UPLEES
## KENT

Sunday the second of April 1916 was a beautiful day. Spring sunshine danced on the Swale marshes outside Faversham in Kent. There was a guncotton factory here, at Uplees. Guncotton had been developed in the nineteenth century, when the chemist Christian Friedrich Schönbein of the University of Basel wiped up a spillage of nitric acid in his kitchen with a cotton apron and hung it over a stove to dry, whereupon, when dry, it exploded. Looking rather like cotton wool, guncotton was the first high explosive, and widely used – but also extremely volatile. The Cotton Powder Company and the Explosives Loading Company shared a site on the marshes. Workers were paid an extra two shillings a week in danger money to work there.

The usual precautions were taken against chance explosions. Only wooden buttons were allowed. The rails of the tramway were likewise wood. Even metal hairpins were forbidden. Horses were shod in brass rather than iron, to minimise sparks. Smoking, not surprisingly, was banned. The factory consisted of a series of wooden huts, guarded by soldiers around the clock. There was a fire brigade, a plentiful supply of water and a large number of fire extinguishers. Arrangements were in hand to install hydrants to the high-pressure water mains, but as yet the contractors had not delivered the pumps. Nor was the boiler house completely safe; it sometimes emitted sparks.

On the night before 2 April, some of these sparks had started a fire between buildings, which had been put out. On 2 April itself, the factory was not so lucky. Some sacks that had been used to store TNT were piled outside hut 833; around noon they caught fire. The fire brigade came out; a human chain was formed to pass buckets of water from the dyke. But they could not prevent the explosions – three of them, in five buildings. They were so powerful that windows were blown out in Southend on the other side of the Thames, so loud that the noise could be heard in Norwich. Every building within a radius of more than two hundred metres was demolished; a huge crater more than four metres deep was left in the ground.

It is thought that 109 people were killed, sixty-nine of whom are buried in a mass grave in the Faversham Cemetery. Nothing now remains of the factory except shattered reinforced concrete from the foundations, twisted metal rods and the remains of the timber loading dock. Snipe and redshank have returned to the marshes.

# WEST DEAN

*Flint through and through*

Everything about West Dean is flint. Just beyond the park wall of the big house (flint, of course) lies the village: flint church, flint school, flint pub, not so fancy as the mansion house, but sparkling as the sun catches the shiny facets of the walls – much like the little stream that hurries beneath its diminutive flint bridge. A flinty-looking gamekeeper came out of a cottage while I was there, on his way to shoot roebuck with a party of Danes. The handsome girl leading the horses looked as if she could strike sparks on occasion, although I would not want to call her a common chert (the type of stone that flint is).

Flint is a genuinely regional building material. It is found only in the chalky parts of the country, the flints having been originally formed from pockets of silica from the shells of sea creatures within the chalk. When the railways came in the nineteenth century, nobody thought to ship flint to other areas, because it was a choice of last resort for anyone who wanted strong walls. Country women and their children went out to pick bushels of knobbly, whitish-grey flints from the fields, just as the crops had started to grow (for some reason, farmers thought that trampling the crops at that stage did them good). Piles of their finds were then left in the furrows for the farmer to cart away after harvest.

When the flints were split, their glassy black hearts cracked into two more-or-less smooth but irregular surfaces. It took a lot of mortar to bind the rest of their Henry Moore shapes together into a wall. The Romans used flints, bonded with courses of tile, for some of their forts; but at Richborough in Kent and Burgh Castle in Norfolk, the walls are several yards thick. Too much mortar in a domestic wall makes it weak.

Various techniques were developed to add strength. Chips of flint were pushed into any spare gaps, reducing the amount of mortar required; since, in builders' parlance, lime mortar 'goes off' slowly, a wall using too much mortar might wobble before it had set. Galleting, as this method is known, had decorative possibilities, not lost on Lutyens* and his contemporaries. In the highest class of work, crafts-men knocked off the knobbly sides of the flint to form 'knapped' surfaces that were more or less square. This was done when the flints had been freshly dug out of the chalk. Exposure to the air hardened them, but to begin with they were more like hard toffee. Even so, like needle sharpening, flint knapping took a toll on the lungs.

It is hard to put this sinister consequence from one's mind when looking at West Dean: the house is such a prodigy of knapping that even the corners are built of flint, rather than the more serviceable brick or stone. West Dean was built for the immensely rich Willie James, a friend of Edward VII (his wife was even more so; their son, the Surrealist collector Edward James, liked to imagine he had royal blood). Given the skill that went into West Dean's flintwork, it is appropriate that the place is now a craft college.

*See Mells, page 55; Thursley, page 145

# WHITELEY VILLAGE
SURREY                                    *The Universal Provider helps the old*

'I believe I am right in stating that a son is speaking to his father?' These words were spoken by Horace Rayner to William Whiteley, the Universal Provider, who had founded the Whiteley's department store in Bayswater. Whiteley's was a Victorian phenomenon, by 1890 employing six thousand staff, who worked, as was customary, from seven in the morning until eleven at night, six days a week. Rayner's mother had been one of the shop girls; after failing to establish himself in a career, and with a wife and young children to support, Rayner, believing himself to be Whiteley's illegitimate son, appealed to the old man for help. When he refused, Rayner produced a revolver, first intending to blow out his own brains but shooting Whiteley instead. He was sentenced to hang, although this was commuted to life imprisonment (he was released in 1919).

In his will Whiteley left a million pounds – a fabulous sum in 1907 – to found, provide and maintain 'homes for aged poor persons'. It was a princely gesture in an age before the State paid old-age pensions (they would come in shortly after his death). There was, however, something of an irony in it. Few Whiteley employees grew old in his service: the hours were too long for them to stay healthy. According to a Select Committee in 1886, the annual death rate of shop assistants between the ages of twenty-five and forty-five was nine per cent.

Whiteley's will specified conditions for the development, which was to 'be in as bright, cheerful and healthy spot as possible'. R. Frank Atkinson won the limited competition held by the Trustees for the plan of the village; with the Chicago architect Daniel H. Burnham he had recently designed a dazzling, mightily classical Oxford Street store for a Whiteley's competitor, Harry Gordon Selfridge. His layout was formal, based around a central green from which avenues radiate, crossing an encompassing circular road and an outer octagonal one. This sets it apart from Letchworth Garden City and Hampstead Garden Suburb, which were Picturesque.

In 1913, the site was ready for the architect Walter Cave to erect a block of model cottages. Although single-storey, they were thought too big, and the subsequent dwellings were smaller. To avoid monotony, half a dozen different architects were chosen to build the rest of the project, in a happy idiom of red brick, tall chimneys, clay tile roofs and lightly worn classical detail. Building started on 21 July 1914, when the Bishop of London laid the foundation stone for a monument to Whiteley in the centre of the village.

Applications were sought from 'persons of good character and of sound mind and not affected by an infectious or contagious disease and not having been convicted of any criminal offence and being male of not less than 65 years and being female of not less than 60 years of age', preference being given to people who had worked in commerce or agriculture (Whiteley's father had been a corn merchant in Yorkshire). They proved difficult criteria to fulfil, but the retired nurse Eliza Palmer met them, becoming the village's first resident: she was awarded a Bible to mark the event. Soon, more than forty old folk had joined her, overseen by a lady warden and two nursing assistants. Numbers swelled to two hundred in the 1920s.

The village remains a haven of calm, tucked away behind private gates on the Seven Hills Road outside Cobham. Its success can be measured in the ages achieved by its inhabitants: a hundred and eight in the case of Mrs Montgomery, who died in February 1996. She had been working in Whiteley's on the day that the Universal Provider was murdered.

# WHITWELL
## ISLE OF WIGHT
*Around the parish pump*

Whitwell, as its name suggests, is a watery place. It means clear water in Saxon, and the wells of Our Lady and St Rhadegund were regarded as holy. Pilgrims came here, landing at Puckaster Cove and walking what is still called St Rhadegund's Path.

*One of the six scarlet-painted cast-iron pumps installed at Whitwell in 1887.*

Water was intensely important to medieval communities (as it is to any community, only now we take it for granted; we may not always). Easy access to it dictated the sites of many settlements. Springs, often found where one geological stratum meets another, were valuable, as were wells dipping into water reserves that were not far below the ground surface. Poorly provided villages, such as some in the East Riding of Yorkshire, had to collect rainwater in butts, filtered through a bit of sacking; when it ran out they had to resort to the pond, where animals drank and unwanted cats were drowned.

In cities, where people lived closely together, it had long been necessary to bring drinking water in from elsewhere. The people needed it, and there were enough of them to form an economically viable market. Not so in villages. Until the Rural Water Supplies and Sewerage Act of 1944 made the provision of mains water a district council responsibility, most houses did not have piped water. The parish pump was, therefore, an indispensable piece of technology. It has come to symbolise village life itself: small in scale, possibly mundane, sometimes emotive. People would meet at the parish pump, because everybody had to go there.

There was no public pump in the Oxfordshire hamlet where the writer Flora Thompson grew up*, because most people had wells in their gardens. In dry summers, these would fail, which meant a walk of half a mile to a pump by some farm buildings. 'Those who had wells in their gardens would not give away a spot, as they feared if they did theirs, too, would run dry, so they fastened down the lids with padlocks.' Cooking water would be saved from one day to the next, George Sturt observed during a dry summer in Surrey†. Nevertheless, a pump, in the right place, was better than a well, which was difficult to dig and required both skill (so that the bucket, when lowered, did not bob off the surface of the water) and strength to raise water.

Whitwell has not one pump but six. Installed in 1887, they are splendid examples of Victorian engineering and design: cast-iron, painted scarlet, their fluted sides declaring them to be classical columns, ornamented with lion's heads and acorns. As was often the case with parish pumps and wells, they were provided with substantial help from local landowners. According to a plaque in the churchyard, W. Spindler of Old Park subscribed half the cost, while the water was supplied by Granville Ward from a spring on land at nearby Bierley. Water still had to be carried into cottages, perhaps with two pails on either side of a yoke, and once dirty it was carried out again to be thrown onto the garden. No wonder people appreciated it.

*See Juniper Hill, page 185. †See The Bourne, page 144

# WIMBLEDON VILLAGE
SURREY                                          *Persistently villagey*

When did Wimbledon cease to be a village? Never, in the minds of its inhabitants, who still resolutely refer to the corner south-east of the Common as Wimbledon Village. Horse droppings on the road are an ever-present reminder of the equestrian establishment, from which crocodiles of horses and riders set off for a plod around the windmill. When John Murray visited for a guidebook to the Thames in 1849, he found it 'neat and respectable' (high praise), with divine services being held in a barn while the church of St Mary was being rebuilt. There was a rusticity about the place, which, perhaps through careful cultivation, it has never quite lost.

As a whole, London has been reluctant to shed its village past. While most Continental cities were, until the nineteenth century, confined by their city walls, London soon burst its corset and spread. The urban tide rolled over one village after another – Mayfair, Clerkenwell, Chelsea, Fulham, Hampstead. What were once winding country lanes became busy roads, along which motor cars, buses and juggernauts now follow the twists and turns once taken by ponies and traps. Village greens are preserved in memory, although not a blade of grass may be seen. This reflects the peculiar English affection for the countryside over the town.

Wimbledon stood out against the imperialist tendencies of the metropolis until 1965. Having no choice in the matter, it then became part of Greater London. But some of its heart remains in Surrey. It still boasts, for example, a Village Club, founded in 1858 to 'afford to the inhabitants, and more especially the working and middle classes of Wimbledon and its vicinity, opportunities of intellectual and moral improvement, and rational and social enjoyment, through the medium of a reading room and library, lectures and classes'.

The Club still occupies the original premises and claims to be the 'oldest social club in England'. But as an attempt to elevate the conditions and moral tone of Wimbledon's poor it did not stand alone. A Cottage Improvement Society was established in 1859 to provide better homes. There was also a Clothing and Fuel Club, Maternal Society, Provident Medical Dispensary, Friendly Society (in conjunction with Fulham), Loan Blanket Charity and Ladies' Working Association. To this list, provided by William Bartlett in a Victorian history of Wimbledon, can be added one from the 1880s: Fire Brigade, Hospitals, Croquet Club, Working Men's Club, Horticultural Society, Musical Society, Parochial Library 'and associations almost beyond number for helping the working-classes and encouraging habits of thrift and temperance'. As the author, Edward Walford, noted, with so many rich local residents to support the charities, the 'local bench of magistrates ought to have an easy time of it'.

So much care lavished on just one village ought to have made it the envy of every other rural settlement in the land. Except that the Victorian benefactors knew that it was no longer a conventional village, or they would not have been living there. By 1865, the sights and sounds of the countryside were being drowned out. 'The bittern and the heron and the beaver have passed away,' Bartlett sighed. Listening just too early to hear the crack of mallet on croquet ball or the twang of tennis ball on racket at the All England Lawn Tennis and Croquet Club, originally located at the bottom of Wimbledon Hill and since 1922 at the top, his ear instead caught 'the ring of the mason's trowel, or the din of the coppersmith's hammer', as a former waste became an 'overcrowded suburb of the greatest city on the earth'.

# WINCHELSEA
EAST SUSSEX                                            *Pre-Raphaelite heaven*

Enthusiasts for the Pre-Raphaelites may have seen Winchelsea without knowing it. The meadows outside the village form the sunlit background to John Everett Millais's *The Blind Girl*, and the wounded child in the same artist's *L'Enfant du Régiment* lies on one of the tombs in the church. Millais went there in 1855, spending so long in the church that (as he would later tell his son, John Guille Millais) the sexton asked him what he was doing. 'Oh,' Millais explained, 'I want to paint the church.' The sexton replied: 'Well then, young man, you need not hang about here any longer, for the church was all done up fresh last year.'

The novelist William Makepeace Thackeray joined the painter, working on the never-finished *Denis Duval*, whose main character is based on Millais. Together they sat in a church pew while an old parson preached, with gestures towards Millais, on the impossibility of emulating God's work in Nature. The friends became almost hysterical in their efforts to suppress giggles.

Winchelsea has not changed much since, being just as peaceful as it appears in Millais's paintings. It was a more bustling place in the Middle Ages. Edward I rebuilt the town after the old one disappeared into the sea. As one of the Cinque Ports – or, strictly speaking, the Two Ancient Towns (the other being Rye) associated with them – it was expected to provide the king with ships to beat off the French. Winchelsea also acquired some formidable gates in case it didn't. In memory of past glories, Winchelsea still elects a Mayor every Easter. The Mayor in turn appoints a body of Jurats, or assistants, jurat being an ancient word for magistrate. A needlework hanging in the church shows them all trotting along to the Court Hall in a late-thirteenth-century house built by Gervase Alard, Winchelsea's first known Mayor and an Admiral of the Fleet of the Cinque Ports.

The story of the church is that of Winchelsea itself: after the Reformation, this once-mighty structure shrank into the space formerly occupied just by the choir. The town itself dwindled to such an extent that the New Gate now stands by itself among fields. Like most town planners since Roman times, Edward I favoured a grid plan, which survives; every street ends in a view of the surrounding marshes.

Dante Gabriel Rossetti, melancholy after the death of his wife, besieged by creditors and overworked, followed in Millais's footsteps on a rare foray made from Cheyne Walk in 1866. He also stayed at the New Inn, in company with the impecunious painter Frederick Sandys. From its windows Rossetti witnessed a procession of 'about seven persons, including the Mayor in splendid robes of scarlet lined with sables, and three officials in blue robes, one of whom was the parish barber and another the carpenter'. The proprietor of the inn went over to Northiam to dig up a remarkable topiary in the form of a box armchair, which Rossetti had bought from a 'poor old woman' who had been tending it for thirty-three years. Transplanted to Chelsea, it soon died.

Rossetti called Winchelsea 'a most delightful old place for quietness and old-world character'. That it remains so is due to George Mallows Freeman, who might have developed the Greyfriars Estate when he bought it in 1908, but didn't. To Queen Elizabeth I, visiting in 1573, Winchelsea was Little London. That wouldn't be such a bad description today. It is too pretty to have escaped the eye of the second-home owner, but money and taste have ensured preservation. One can imagine aesthetic ghosts still setting up their easels.

# WOTTON
SURREY                                        *John Evelyn and his trees*

We owe the word avenue, meaning a double line of trees, to the diarist John Evelyn. Born in 1620, he was the great-grandson of the John Evelyn who brought the invention of gunpowder to England in the sixteenth century*. John's father, Richard, inherited an estate at Wotton, and it was here that Evelyn was born. A sketch in a commonplace book of about 1700 gives an idea of Wotton House: a rambling, originally Tudor building, patched and extended by different generations, its considerable length punctuated by exaggeratedly tall chimneys.

A Royalist but not a fighter, Evelyn lived abroad during the Civil War, returning in 1647, having married in Paris. In 1652, he began the *Elysium Britannicum*, an encyclopedic history of gardens and gardening on which he worked throughout his life. He was interested in many other things besides: he translated scientific books, assembled a library (now in the British Library), attended the Royal Society, published the earliest book on pollution, *Fumifugium* (about the smoke that hung over London as a result of coal fires), wrote about the Dutch wars, and deserves much of the credit for establishing the Royal Naval Hospital at Greenwich, of which he was first Treasurer. He proposed the motto *Decus et Tutamen* (an ornament and a safeguard) that still surrounds the one-pound coin: it was introduced as a device to stop coins being clipped.

Evelyn was especially concerned about trees. He published a book about them in 1664 called *Sylva, or a Discourse of Forest-Trees, and the Propagation of Timber in*

*His Majesties Dominions*. It was a text of national importance. During the previous decade England had conducted one naval war with Holland and would soon be fighting another. It was therefore dependent on its ships. But the timber for building them was in danger of becoming exhausted. *Sylva* stimulated the planting of oak trees, the benefit of which would be reaped a century hence by the builders of Nelson's navy. Some survive today as ancient trees, their trunks hollow, their crowns shrunken, of which Britain has more than any other country in Northern Europe†.

It is said that a line of centuries-old sweet chestnuts at Warley Place in Essex was planted by Evelyn himself. Which shows that Evelyn was not wholly martial in his attitude to trees. With *Sylva* was annexed *Pomona*, a work about fruit trees, as well as *Kalendarium Hortense: or, Gard'ners Almanac*. Evelyn believed, as he wrote to a friend, that 'the air and genius of gardens operate upon human spirits towards virtue and sanctity': principles that were put into practice at his own garden at Sayes Court near Deptford, Kent.

Sayes Court has disappeared. The decline set in when the house was trashed by Peter the Great and his encourage ('right nasty' according to Evelyn's bailiff) in 1698, Peter having taken it supposedly to study shipbuilding. Evelyn is not buried there, but in the church at Wotton, where he received his first schooling, in the little room over the porch. It lies in the most wooded county in England.

*See Chilworth, page 103. †See Crowhurst, page 105

# YALDING
## KENT

'I could wish that every child had had such a place to grow up in,' Edmund Blunden wrote in *English Villages* (1947). The son of a schoolmaster, he was remembering the village in which his childhood was spent before the First World War. Blunden's presence is commemorated by a plaque on Yalding's village green, elegantly engraved with the poem 'Blunden's Beech', written by his friend Siegfried Sassoon: 'no one knew / That this – of local beeches – was the best'.

'Of one thing I am profoundly persuaded,' Blunden announced. 'To the man or woman who is desirous of finding the best in this country I commend the English village.' Let him take us on a tour of his own. 'The chief style of the house on the street is still eighteenth century, an easy, balanced prose style of glowing but not glaring brick, and high roofs with attic windows, and sometimes an ornamental facing of semicircular tiles.'

Physically, little seems to have changed from his day, even if the oast houses are no longer working and the painted advertisement for Coates the grocer's is fading on its wall. Indeed, the greatest difference between Blunden's day and our own lies in Yalding's ability to look after itself. 'The butcher, the grocer, the cobbler, the barber, the saddler, the ironmonger are here, though the brewery has become a haulage concern. There is the chemist's, and the cake shop, and if you want a dressmaker or a tailor we have them . . . you will be agreeably surprised by the supernatural efficiency of our village stores . . . I have been informed on good authority that Mr P.'s line in ladies' silk stockings is inimitably fine, but then so is his bacon and his cutlery; and Mr C. is the man to go to if you are wanting a curious and beautiful tea set or a silk eiderdown quilt.'

You can still get a horse shod or railing fixed by E. P. Stern, farriers and general smiths, but many of the old farmyards and places of industry have been turned into discreet housing developments. Most of the hop gardens and apple and cherry orchards have also gone. But it still looks as though it would be an idyllic place to grow up. A small boy races a miniature quad bike round a meadow. The Scouts and Guides, in their cooler uniforms, are enjoying a renaissance. Open Gardens Day celebrates the English passion for making things grow. As Pop Larkin, himself a Kentish figure, would say, 'Perfick.'

Not that Thomas Gladwish (perhaps not his real name) would have agreed. Writing in the *Baptist Magazine* in December 1838, he denounced the area as 'a sink of wickedness and dissipation from time immemorial'. After eighteen fruitless years of attempting to 'introduce the gospel', he had at last succeeded in renting a cottage as a makeshift chapel, but could not afford the horse to get to it (he lived six miles away and walked on crutches). The Baptist seed, however, took root, to the point that a Baptist Hall could be built. The Scouts and Guides use it in lieu of a Scout hall. They may be saying their own prayers for congregation, which has dwindled in recent years. If it reaches zero, the Charity Commission might require it to be sold.

# YARMOUTH
## ISLE OF WIGHT
*Perilously near France*

In April 1799, George Morland, painter of cottage scenes, fled his creditors in London, not crossing the Channel to Boulogne or Dieppe – popular resorts for the straitened – but over the Solent to the Isle of Wight. He lodged first at Cowes, but rapidly transferred to Yarmouth when his brother Henry overheard some people in a tavern saying that they had discovered his hiding place. Yarmouth was, in its way, just as bad. After a few days, Dorset militia arrested both Morlands on suspicion of spying. George had, after all, been spotted sketching along the shore: what else could they be up to?

They were marched off to Newport, twelve miles away, carrying the supposedly incriminating sketches, where the justices thought badly of the case. At the last moment an acquaintance testified to the artist's bona fides, and the brothers were let off with a caution. They then trudged back to Yarmouth, and although they stayed long enough for George to paint the Needles, it shows that the Isle of Wight was jumpy. Sheltering the Solent, where ships might be becalmed for weeks, it had

*The sea captain and governor of the Isle of Wight, Sir Robert Holmes,*
*captured an uncompleted statue of Louis XIV, to which he had his own*
*head added; it was erected in Yarmouth church after his death.*

a strategic importance, and if the French had invaded the south coast, it could
have been in the front line.

They were right to worry. The French had landed as recently as 1543. On that
occasion, according to a plaque in Seaview, they were 'bloodily defeated and
repulsed by the local militia'. Afterwards, Henry VIII rushed up the last of his
south-coast forts at Yarmouth (preparation for a feared invasion by Spain after
his divorce from Catherine of Aragon), complementing Hurst Castle on the mainland; between them they could close the western mouth of the Solent.

In the seventeenth century, the town assumed greater prominence than it might
otherwise have enjoyed when Sir Robert Holmes, the governor under Charles II,
made it his headquarters. He is remembered by a full-length statue in the church. It is
a sign of his ambition that this apparently began life as a representation of Louis XIV
in classical dress, captured, together with the sculptor, from a French ship. The head
was not completed, so Holmes had his own substituted in place of the French king's.

The Latin inscription gives a succinct, if immodest, account of his career: fighting successfully against the Dutch at sea, seizing the colony of Nova Belgica, better known as New York, from them, and capturing various Dutch West India Company positions along the Guinea coast, which introduced a unit of currency into the language. Samuel Pepys called him a 'rash, proud coxcomb' – Holmes had apparently tried to seduce Mrs Pepys. Charles II stayed with him at Yarmouth in 1671, in the house that Holmes had built, according to the eighteenth-century Isle of Wight historian Richard Warner, 'entirely for his accommodation'. It is now the George Hotel.

Yarmouth's importance declined during the nineteenth century, when the Solent became protected by a ring of Palmerston forts. Granted borough status by Baldwin de Redvers, 3rd Earl of Devon in the late twelfth century, it is now a village, although a memory of its maritime history survives in the great number of masts that crowd its harbour in summertime. Wear deck shoes if you want to blend in.

# THE HOME
# COUNTIES

W HEN THE balloonist Vincenzo Lunardi, waving his hat and eating a chicken leg, floated away from the capital in 1784, the winds took him north, over Hertfordshire, where he touched down at Standon Green End (see page 194). He would have looked out over a green and gentle landscape, a place of stately trees and gentlemen's seats, wooded slopes and cosy villages – a medley of timber and brick, with dormer windows in the tiled roofs. You would not have thought that anyone could starve to death in this fertile land, yet fifteen years earlier, at Datchworth, a family did (see page 171). In the twelfth century, Hertfordshire produced Britain's only Pope, Adrian IV, born at Abbots Langley (see page 164). Nowadays, London may snap at Hertfordshire's heels, but villages such as Aldbury (see page 165), where the energetic Mrs Humphry Ward lived at Stocks, seem sublimely unaware of its existence.

There are two Berkshires: horse-racing and rurality in the west, commuter villages in the east. Among the professional people making the daily journey to the City was Kenneth Grahame, who rhapsodised Cookham Dean (see page 169) in *The Wind in the Willows*.

On the map, Buckinghamshire touches Greater London with its toe. Jordans (see page 184) was sufficiently far away for a Quaker community to find peace; Denham (see page 172) sufficiently close for the film impresario Alexander Korda to create the British version of Hollywood there. The coming of the railway made some of Buckinghamshire's villages pump iron: Gerrards Cross (see page 176) is a village on steroids.

Much of Bedfordshire comprises the broad flood plain of the Great Ouse, rubbed into its present shape by the ice sheets of the Pleistocene period. Flat and watery, the landscape has a placidly Dutch quality. In architecture, brick came to predominate: the chimneys of the brickworks at Stewartby (see page 196) make as dramatic a contrast to the surrounding farmland as do the immense sheds built to contain airships at Cardington (see page 167).

Oxfordshire offers richer fare: 'a fertile country and plentiful', as William Camden wrote. It was a beautiful land full of fine houses, such as the Duke of Suffolk's palace at Ewelme (see page 174) and Lord Harcourt's Nuneham Courtenay (see page 191), but hard enough for the people who worked there: the life of the agricultural workers described by Flora Thompson, remembering her childhood at Juniper Hill (see page 185) at the end of the nineteenth century, allowed almost no time for leisure.

In the twenty-first century, leisure and affluence have descended, and such pubs as survive (dozens across Britain close every week) are likely to have reinvented themselves for a new clientele. Kingham (see page 186) provides an outstanding example. This, however, is the village that has everything – even that rarest of things, a direct train service to London.

# Home Counties

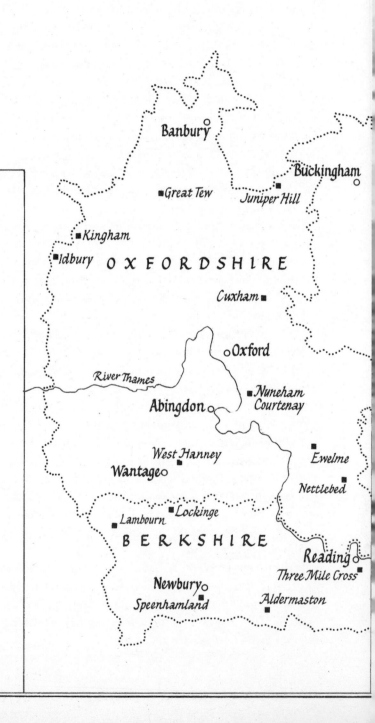

Banbury

Buckingham

Great Tew

Juniper Hill

Kingham

Idbury

OXFORDSHIRE

Cuxham

Oxford

River Thames

Abingdon

Nuneham Courtenay

West Hanney

Ewelme

Wantage

Nettlebed

Lockinge

Lambourn

BERKSHIRE

Reading

Three Mile Cross

Newbury

Speenhamland

Aldermaston

N

Harrold
Turvey
Bedford
Cardington
Stewartby

B E D F O R D S H I R E

Milton
Keynes
Woburn

Stewkley

Dunstable
Luton

Standon
Green End
Bishop's
Stortford
Datchworth

H E R T F O R D S H I R E

Aylesbury
Aldbury

Hertford
Hunsdon

St Albans
Hatfield
Hoddesdon

B U C K I N G H A M -
SHIRE

Abbots Langley
Watford

High Wycombe

Jordans
Gerrards Cross
Denham

M I D D L E S E X

Cookham Dean
Stoke Poges
Brentford
River Thames

Sonning
Windsor

0          10        20 miles
0     10        20        30 km

# ABBOTS LANGLEY

HERTFORDSHIRE                                    *Born unto us, a village Pope*

Abbots Langley was the birthplace of the only British Pope, Nicholas Breakspear, who became Adrian IV. Or so the chronicler Matthew Paris has it. He presumably took his name from Breakspear, three miles away. The origins of Abbots Langley are also enshrined in its name. Langley derives from the Saxon for long meadow or clearing, and in 1045, Ethelwine the Black and his wife, Wynfelda, gave the manor to the Abbey of St Albans, nine miles to the east.

At the time of Domesday, Langley was one of the manors held by the half-brother of William I, Robert, count of Mortain, or his men. The Normans were energetic builders and loved stone, which symbolised what they hoped would be the permanence of their regime. During the course of the twelfth century, Abbots Langley was provided with the church that, with little alteration, survives today. Breakspear was born around 1100. He would probably have known a wooden structure, if there was one. But already St Albans Abbey had been rebuilt. The Norman Abbot Paul of Caen began the work in 1077, using Roman bricks taken from the ruins of Verulamium; it was finished eleven years later.

Guided by the tall tower of the abbey church, Breakspear made his way there as a boy, hoping to become a monk. His father seems to have been a priest; perhaps, as enemies later alleged, a married priest (although if not married, Breakspear would have been illegitimate); he may also have entered the monastery. Nicholas cannot have been a very promising candidate because (if Paris is to be believed) the Abbot rejected him. By some means, Breakspear was able to travel, for we next see him in Arles in southern France, where he studied. Here he succeeded in entering the house of the canons regular at St Ruf, near Avignon; in time he became prior of the monastery and then abbot of the order.

He may have come before Pope Eugenius III as a result of complaints against his rule. That seems unlikely, since, not long after his arrival in Rome, he was made a cardinal and sent on a mission to Scandinavia; his voyage seems to have been made via England. In 1154, he was elected Pope. An effective administrator, stout defender of the papal lands against aggression, a man of foresight and tenacity, he became, in the words of the *Oxford Dictionary of National Biography*, 'something of a role model for later popes'.

By the time of his death in 1159, the journey from Abbots Langley had been a long one. Above all, his story illustrates the internationalism of the Church, and its ability to give startling opportunities to boys from poor backgrounds (Cardinal Wolsey was the son of a butcher). Breakspear did not remember his native village with any endowment once he had risen in life. But in 1846, Abbots Langley became the site of an Elizabethan-style retreat for retired booksellers and their widows, provided by the Booksellers' Provident Institution on land donated by J. Dickinson, a paper manufacturer. It contains, naturally, a fine library.

# ALDBURY

## HERTFORDSHIRE
*The formidable Mrs Humphry Ward*

Aldbury is only thirty-seven miles outside London. But it is still in Miss Marple's England, a village of crowing cocks, reddening apples and apple-cheeked old ladies. Groups of the latter may be found inside the church, investigating a sudden death – that of Sir Robert Whittingham, slain at the Battle of Tewkesbury in 1471 and commemorated, alongside his lady, in a tomb brought from Ashridge in 1575 (unless, as some claim, the tomb is that of his father, also Robert, who died in 1452). Ducks on the green, a backdrop of beech hanger, admirable pubs serving equally admirable beer – what a warm duvet of cosiness to pull around your shoulders as the nights draw in.

Imagine the surprise that villagers must have had when Mrs Humphry Ward, successful late Victorian novelist, niece of Matthew Arnold and friend of Henry James, came to the big house, Stocks, in 1892. Married to an academic, Mrs Humphry Ward – née Mary Augusta Arnold – bought the place out of her own enormous earnings. She used the village as a source of inspiration and testing ground for political ideas. One of the stories dated from the last years of the previous owner, Mrs Bright. While she lay dying, her gamekeeper and his lad disturbed some poachers in a wood. The latter shot the keeper dead and pursued the boy into a clearing, where he was clubbed to death with the butt of a gun. This tale became the subject of *Bessie Costrell*, written in just fifteen days.

In 1910, Mrs Ward gave Aldbury the benefit of her political opinions in a series of Talks with Voters, held to support her son Arnold's campaign to become Liberal Unionist MP for the West Hertfordshire Division. Held in the Aldbury schoolroom, they allowed her to penetrate 'with her usual sympathy and directness into the recesses of the rustic mind', according to her daughter Janet Trevelyan. These colloquies honed her style and enabled her to write *Letters to My Neighbours on the Present Election*, which dealt with the burning questions of that epic election from a strictly conservative point of view (two years before, she had lent her support to the campaign *against* women getting the vote, by heading the Women's Anti-Suffrage Association). Aldbury seems to have taken the electoral excitement in its stride, one of the village women remarking: 'Lumme, sech a fustle and a bustle! And when all's say and do one's out and the other's in!'

Aldbury, according to Mrs Trevelyan, had 'an immense fascination' for Mrs Ward – possibly the feeling was reciprocated. The village may have been 'agape' at the grand folks from London who came to spend their Sundays with her, but no doubt equally struck by the urban poor who came to enjoy moments of rest in the Convalescent Cottage that she had taken. These working people came from the philanthropic project that Mrs Ward started in Bloomsbury, later called the Passmore Edwards Settlement, after a benefactor. The cricket team that they fielded was not well rated by the village children. Near the Convalescent Cottage was Stocks Cottage, lent out to friends, such as George Bernard Shaw.

Mrs Ward rebuilt Stocks in 1907, at great expense. Her later royalties were not equal to it, particularly after a heavy call had been made on them to settle Arnold's gambling debts. Her shade now lingers around the churchyard, where she is buried, but it was probably chased from the house in the 1970s, when Stocks became famous for the wild parties thrown by its then owner, the Playboy executive Victor Lowndes. It is now a hotel. You will find a different kind of stocks, with attached whipping post, on the village green*.

*See Aynho, page 297

# ALDERMASTON
## BERKSHIRE
*The motor car slakes its thirst*

There are some things (décolletage, double entendre, ménage à trois) that sound better in French, and one of them, in the early twentieth century, was thought to be garage. Garage derives from the verb *garer*, meaning to store. From 1902, the *Daily Mail* had used it in preference to the old country-house term of motor stable, meaning somewhere that the car was stored, washed and repaired when not in use. But cars don't need only to be stored; they must also be filled. Before long the term was being applied to those roadside and other pit stops, from the depths of which an overall-wearing mechanic would come, wiping grease from his hands, to operate one of a choice of colourful pumps, pulling a lever on the side until the glass reservoir filled to the necessary level, before inserting the nozzle into the petrol tank. Like chauffeur – a word originally applied to the man who heated up the car before it was driven – a borrowing from French seemed to add tone to the rather grimy proceedings.

The Automobile Association, realising that motorists could not get far without fuel, opened the UK's first garage at Aldermaston in 1920. The village had a difficult twentieth century. As home to the Atomic Weapons Research Establishment that operated from a former airfield, it was the destination of a series of annual marches organised by the Campaign for Nuclear Disarmament after its foundation in 1958. (The marches, which stopped in 1963, the year the test-ban treaty was signed, were revived in 1972 and 2004.) As a consequence, Aldermaston's role in the development of motoring has been overshadowed.

The garage took the form of a weatherboarded hut, next to the AA telephone box. It was not exactly a filling station in the modern sense, not least because it did not sell petrol. The AA wanted to popularise benzole as an alternative to petrol, the cost of which soared to four shillings per gallon after the First World War. Initially benzole was available only in drums, but a pump was installed after the American example (Gulf Oil having opened the first filling station in the world in Pittsburgh in 1913).

Even so, the Aldermaston garage represented a significant innovation. It not only heralded the end of the era when motorists had to carry their own petrol cans to be sure of replenishing their tanks. It formed part of a landscape of motoring that would change the British countryside and its villages forever. Advertising hoardings, 'traffic control robots' (as traffic lights were first called), kerbstones, road widening, white lines, yellow lines, bypasses – all of them would become familiar as part of the furniture of an England seen through the car windscreen. Verges would be mowed, hedges uprooted and trees cut down to improve sightlines.

The tentacles of suburbia reached out along the new trunk roads, lined with semi-detached houses in brick or pebble-dash. As car ownership became general, the old, compact way of building, seen in the traditional village, was replaced by the lower-density development of the suburban estate. Meanwhile, pretty villages became difficult to reach in the 1920s because of traffic jams on the South Downs. Trying to enjoy a day's walking in the countryside, Professor C. E. M. Joad looked with contemptuous wonder on the main road that he encountered. 'The faces of the motorists are strained and angry . . . in the intervals between their spasmodic bursts of activity they glower at one another. From the country they are completely cut off; they cannot see its sights, hear its sounds or enjoy its silence.' Welcome to the Modern age.

# CARDINGTON
## BEDFORDSHIRE                    *The biggest thing since the Graf Zeppelin*

During the last two years of the First World War, two vast hangars were constructed outside Cardington, near Bedford. The structures stand out like a couple of gigantic shoeboxes discarded on the tree-speckled carpet of Bedfordshire's flat agricultural landscape. But if shoeboxes, for what feet! More than two hundred metres long and forty-four metres high, they make the red-roofed houses of the village near them appear Lilliputian. After a two-year gestation, something inside these colossal structures hatched in July 1918. Local people must have looked on in wonder as R31, a whale-like craft of scarcely imaginable size, as unwieldy as it was big, nosed out of a hangar, its crew fearful that this phenomenon of wood and rubberised cotton would be blown sideways and punctured. R31 was an airship. With the infelicity that dogged airship history, the Admirality took it into commission only five days before the Armistice was signed.

In 1916, two German zeppelins, each filled with fifty-six thousand cubic metres of hydrogen, were shot down with relative ease – and to spectacular effect – over the Home Counties. Planes had already shown themselves to be more manoeuvrable than these ponderous craft. It might have been thought that the experience would dampen enthusiasm for the airship as a weapon of the future. Confidence did indeed wobble after the War; for a couple of years in the early 1920s the

Cardington base was closed. But it came to seem that airships would carry cargo and passengers: the German Graf Zeppelin ran a commercial schedule to South America before the first aeroplane had crossed the Atlantic. So in 1924, the Ramsay MacDonald government announced that two experimental airships – one for military use, the other to carry passengers – would be constructed, and Cardington was reopened.

With hindsight, the airships were preposterous structures. The new ones were bigger than ever, their torpedo-shaped frames containing an astonishing 140,000 cubic metres of hydrogen each. Motive power came from engine pods, individually manned, suspended underneath. Yet Lord Thomson, an influential politician as well as Minister for Air, glowed with excitement. 'When complete,' he rhapsodised in *Air Facts and Problems* (1927), 'these ships will provide first-class cabin accommodation for 100 passengers . . . They will have an average speed, under standard conditions, of 63 miles an hour. At this rate, London and Bombay will be brought nearer together, in point of time, than London and Edinburgh were a century ago.'

When Cardington's R101 took to the air, the Air Ministry trumpeted details to the press. A rival team studied the data with what the novelist Nevil Shute, then an engineer, described as 'a faint sense of impending disaster': it was underpowered and did not have enough lift. Whitehall interference in the design process had not helped. Thomson, however, hurried on, anxious that the R101 – the 'socialist' ship, as opposed to the 'capitalist' R100 being built at the same time by private contractors in Howden, Yorkshire – should open a route to India as part of the Imperial Airship Scheme linking Britain with the Empire.

One autumn evening, the village gathered to watch the R101 cast off from the mast and begin its five-thousand-mile flight. 'This old ragbag is never going to make it!' Major Scott, one of the officers, had told his friend Sid Miles, a local hairdresser. R101's structure had been compromised by the fitting of extra gas capacity late in the day, and it leaked. Just after midnight the message came in that the VIP guests, Thomson included, had enjoyed an 'excellent supper . . . smoked a final cigar and having sighted the French coast, have now gone to bed'. As it approached Beauvais, however, the airship lost altitude, pitched forward, nosedived into the ground and exploded in flames. Presumably part of the side had torn off. Of the fifty-four passengers and crew, only half a dozen survived, badly burned. Thomson was among those killed. The hopes that had been built on airships collapsed. During the Second World War, Cardington's expertise in building the leviathans of the air was redeployed towards the making of barrage balloons and inflatable decoy tanks.

# COOKHAM DEAN
## BERKSHIRE
*Kenneth Grahame's 'own little home'*

For more than a century, Kenneth Grahame's *The Wind in the Willows* has been shaping the way that children respond to the countryside. To adult readers it is no less evocative, encapsulating the comfortable drowsiness of the long, sunlit Edwardian afternoon that preceded the First World War. Although published six years before hostilities broke out, it seems already to be impregnated by a sense of loss. At the end of the story, Toad is no longer the self-confident, bumptious figure that he is at the start, and the arcadia of the riverbank, though regained, does not seem quite so innocently immutable as when we are introduced to it. This reflects Grahame's own personality. He was forever haunted by nostalgia, based on his own childhood at Cookham Dean.

Growing up, Grahame spent only two years there. The son of a convivial Edinburgh barrister who was, like other convivial Victorians, given to drink, he could remember the hardness of the upholstery buttons in the railway carriage that took him and his parents to Inveraray when his father – in a last-ditch attempt to mend the family finances – took the job of Sheriff-Substitute of Argyll. He was then a year old. Shortly after his fifth birthday, his mother died. His father collapsed, and the Grahame children were shipped off to Berkshire, where Granny Ingles occupied a rambling house called The Mount.

In one of his first books, *The Golden Age* – which would be better known to contemporaries than *The Wind in the Willows* – Grahame recalled the joy of playing, seemingly unregulated, in the surrounding fields. He acquired a love of 'messing about in boats' from his curate uncle David, a rowing blue. But the idyll was not to last. Mrs Ingles was forced to move from The Mount and Grahame was sent to a barbaric prep school in Oxford, which set him on a respectable middle-class journey towards a job in the Bank of England. But he always longed for the lost innocence of Cookham Dean.

Having risen to the position of Secretary in 1898, Grahame underwent a curious ordeal five years later. A madman, who had come to Threadneedle Street in search of the Governor, produced a gun and shot at him three times. Fortunately he missed. But the experience shook Grahame, who was also suffering poor health. In 1906, he returned, with his wife, Elspeth, and son, Alistair (known as Mouse), to Cookham Dean, first taking a house called The Hillyers, then transferring to a larger property, Mayfield. He put in shorter days at work, striding out towards Paddington Station before four o'clock. Eventually he left the Bank in 1908, the year in which *The Wind in the Willows* (turned down by The Bodley Head and accepted with reluctance by Methuen) was published.

*The Wind in the Willows* reflects a changing world. Toad was much like the Edwardian plutocrats, whose vast and glossy motor cars were said to be overturning the settled structure of the countryside. The stoats and weasels seem to symbolise the forces of disorder (made particularly vivid to Grahame, perhaps, by gun-wielding maniacs) waiting at the gate. And Grahame found that Cookham Dean itself had changed. New houses had been built; they were occupied not by old-fashioned country people but by commuters. When the lease on Mayfield ran out, he moved, with some regret but also thanks, to 'this little old farmhouse' on the Downs at Blewbury, near Didcot. Elspeth became eccentric. As Grahame admitted, 'We live here in a state of primitive simplicity which is almost shocking.'

Mouse, to whom the riverbank stories were first told, was never the brilliant son that his parents were determined he would be; while at Oxford, he committed suicide.

# CUXHAM
## OXFORDSHIRE                                        *A medieval village comes to life*

On the night of the Nativity of St John the Baptist in 1340, John Oldman took a penny's worth of brushwood from the manorial enclosure at Cuxham. It was midsummer, and he almost certainly wanted the fuel for a bonfire to celebrate the event. However, he should not have taken it, and he was duly hauled before the manorial court. We know this because of the exceptional collection of records detailing life on the manor of Cuxham and in its village. The manor was owned by Merton College, Oxford. When Thorold Rogers published the accounts for 1316–17 in *History of Agriculture and Prices in England* (1866), he commented that: 'Out of the many thousand accounts which I have investigated none equal those of Cuxham for intelligence, accuracy, and order.'

In the Middle Ages, a manor was a unit of administration, not necessarily coterminous with the ecclesiastical parish (which might contain more than one manor)*. Generally, there was a manor house, which served as the focus of the estate, where the permanent workforce, known as the 'family', lived. Other folk occupied cottages or smallholdings, often along a stream. At Cuxham, the manor house itself has disappeared, and the grey stone church is the only medieval building to survive. But the village still reflects the medieval layout.

Manor Farm is still a working unit; beyond it lies the Old Rectory. These buildings have the same relationship to each other that they did in the fourteenth century, when the rector paid the farmer 1s 8d to cross a meadow called Nutheys to get to the church, taking a share of the nuts that grew in the meadow as part of the bargain. Next to Nutheys was the vivarium, still marked as Fish Ponds on the Ordnance Survey map. The Ordnance Survey also shows the position of two watermills, together with Mill Farm (there used to be a third mill, but it had gone by 1300).

We know something about the villagers at Cuxham, thanks to the painstaking archival researches made by Paul Harvey in *A Medieval Oxfordshire Village*

(1965). In 1279, there were thirteen lowly cottagers, who possessed little more than a garden; eight villeins, required to work on the lord's land, holding half a virgate (a variable measurement that was generally about thirty acres); and two free-men, who paid rent for a number of acres. Their houses seem to have been built of wood, the main dwelling space being a communal hall, although by the early fourteenth century the villeins and freemen had another room as well. Arranged around their dwellings were barns for their corn and cows, sties for their pigs and stables for their plough horses (only the manor ploughed with oxen). Their land was scattered around three open fields, which were worked in rotation. The idea was that fallow years and animal manure would keep up fertility, but wheat yields steadily declined.

When the Black Death struck in early 1349, the effects were 'immediate and lasting'. Two-thirds of the population, including John Oldman, died. Some of the homesteads along the stream were never reoccupied, and by the sixteenth century all of them were deserted. Today, the village still lines up along the stream, but this is coincidence: it really faces the road that runs next to it.

*See Ewelme, page 174

# DATCHWORTH

HERTFORDSHIRE          *'So shocking to humanity' – a poorhouse scandal*

In January 1769, a family of four starved to death in the Datchworth poorhouse. The poorhouse consisted of a hut with an earth floor and no ceiling, its thatch in tatters and the window frame empty of glass. James Eaves, his wife and two young children were naked (except that Eaves wore a shirt) when they were found horribly emaciated. A third child, a boy of eleven, survived in such a traumatised condition that he could not recall when his parents had died.

This was so evident a scandal – and dereliction of duty on the part of the parish officers charged to look after the poor – that the village tried, literally, to bury it. But word of what had gone on reached Philip Thicknesse, a former soldier, who did what he could to stir up people of influence to take action. In that he failed. Out of frustration he published a pamphlet about it. To Thicknesse, the affair was 'so shocking to humanity, and so alarming in this country, (famed throughout the World for charity and benevolence)' that it 'cannot but make a deep impression on the mind of every reader, who possesses one spark of humanity or feeling for the woes of his fellow creatures.' Even today his account makes strong reading. An engraving shows the horror of the bodies, with only a covering of dirty straw between them and the earth.

Yet the Eaveses' condition had been known. A fortnight before, the overseer of the parish poor had visited, leaving half a crown. This bought a bundle of fire-wood, some brown sugar and a candle. But the wood was never lit, and for the next eleven days nobody thought to enter the house. Neighbours feared that they would catch the fever from which the family may have been suffering. But no apothecary was called, no medical assistance given.

Taking up the case, Thicknesse was told that 'the surviving boy was the only one, for a long time, that was able to crawl out', wearing only a piece of sack. Once or twice he had borrowed an oven lid from a neighbour, who asked him why he did not find employment. 'He replied, because the parish would not cloath him, and no one would take him naked.' The same woman 'did see the poor mother crawl out about ten days ago, with a kettle to get a little water from a kind of pond, at a small distance from the house'. But it had been too much for her to carry back. Having collapsed, she dropped the kettle, 'and crept on her hands and knees into her hovel again'. An older son, who was out at service, had visited at Christmas. Finding his family in such a plight, he went to the overseer's house. The overseer was out, but a woman, in an outburst worthy of Dickens, exploded: 'Send them relief! Send them a halter! – let them die and be d----d!' His employer would not give him time to visit again.

Thicknesse succeeded in getting himself appointed foreman of the coroner's jury. He found, however, that it had been deliberately packed with illiterates, and the coroner himself did nothing to help. Like others in Georgian England, Thicknesse believed that the decencies of life were underwritten by the educated class – gentry, clergymen, substantial farmers. But there were few big houses in Datchworth. In 'extensive but obscure parishes' it was 'usual' for a clique of freeholders to monopolise the parish administration, ensuring that money intended for the poor went only to those who could work for it.

It is clear from Thicknesse's account that his story was shocking even by Georgian standards. But he had heard that a man had starved to death in that very house a few years earlier. Was Datchworth unique? There were many remote villages in eighteenth-century Britain. Inhuman cruelty and shameful neglect cannot always have found a crusader such as Thicknesse to expose them.

*See also Smalley, page 355*

# DENHAM

BUCKINGHAMSHIRE     *Tinsel village, or saving the British film industry*

The Hungarian-born film impresario Alexander Korda did nothing by halves. As the scriptwriter Ian Dalrymple remembered, his advent in a British film industry that had been until that point a pale and stagnating imitation of Hollywood was electric: he 'shot up as if from a trap door in the stage . . . with a flash of red fire, and a chord in the orchestra'. Having established London Film Productions, he personally directed *The Private Life of Henry VIII* (1933) and produced Harold Young's *The Scarlet Pimpernel* (1934): they were hits on the grand scale.

In 1936, after just five years in Britain and brimming with self-confidence, he built Denham Studios in the grounds of a country house outside Denham. They were the largest film studios in the country, with seven sound stages and fifteen star dressing rooms. They were powered by their own electricity-generating station, which was, of course, the biggest of its type, the tunnels that housed the cables doubling as air-raid shelters during the Second World War. They also had their own water supply, zoo, infirmary and swans.

Not everyone liked the studios' linear arrangement, which doomed many of the two thousand employees to trudge unnecessarily long distances through corridors. To make an awkward plan worse, Korda insisted on keeping the 'old house', where his office was furnished with antiques. But aching feet are not apparent in the best of Denham Studios' productions, such as the adaptation of H. G. Wells's *The Shape of Things to Come*, *The Thief of Bagdad*, *The Life and Death of Colonel Blimp* and *Brief Encounter*. People had other things to worry about. As the cinematographer Jack Cardiff recalled, working on Alfred Junge's sets for *A Matter of Life and Death* on Denham's huge stage was 'quite a frightening experience'.

The studios teemed with employees, most of them, notoriously, foreign (causing Korda to announce: 'It's not enough to be Hungarian, you must have talent, too.') Graham Greene was one of those who objected to the proportion of studio work given to foreigners: 'We have saved the English film industry from American competition only to surrender it to a far more alien control,' he fumed in *The Spectator*. The village, by contrast, took the invasion in its stride. One of its residents, at Denham Place, was the diplomat and *littérateur* Sir Robert Vansittart: Korda employed him as a lyricist.

Denham acquired not only a film studio. In 1939 it got Korda himself, newly married to the Anglo-Indian actress Merle Oberon, who was disconcerted to find that the manor house they rented was soon also occupied by Korda's brothers, Vincent and Zoltán, and their families. During the Blitz, Korda scanned the sky towards London for signs of the conflagration that was expected to consume it. The aroma of cigar smoke now mingled with that of the wisteria clambering over the facades of village houses. But rural life held no charm for the impresario, while inactivity caused greater explosions (in Hungarian) than any suffered through bombs ('Oh, where *is* that wretched Goering?' wailed Korda's sister-in-law, the actress Gertrude Musgrove, in desperation at the lack of incident to distract the brothers).

In 1942, Winston Churchill (previously employed by Korda as historical advisor) arranged for Korda to receive a knighthood, possibly in return for housing British secret agents while ostensibly promoting films in America. While the Pinewood Studios were requisitioned for aircraft production, Denham became a centre for morale-boosting war films, such as Noël Coward's *In Which We Serve*. But before the War, it had been obvious that the studios were too grandiose even for Korda. Perhaps to his relief, his backers, the Prudential Assurance Company, took over the studios, allowing him to continue as tenant. In 1952, they closed, and after quietly rotting for a couple of decades, they were demolished and replaced by an industrial estate.

# EWELME
## OXFORDSHIRE
*Playing the get-out-of-purgatory-quick card*

Little survives of the splendid house built by William de la Pole, 1st Duke of Suffolk, and his wife, Alice Chaucer, granddaughter of the poet Geoffrey. They were quite a couple. She had been the widow of the Earl of Salisbury, killed by a cannonball in France. He virtually ruled England in place of the weak-minded Henry VI. (It would not do him much good. Having lost most of the English possessions in France, Suffolk was hauled off the ship on which he was travelling to exile in 1450 and beheaded.) Ewelme Manor has now shrunk to something that looks, from the

*The Duchess of Suffolk, depicted in splendour and as a rotting corpse in Ewelme church.*

outside, like an eighteenth-century farmhouse, with only a buttress, advancing like a medieval foot beneath a Georgian gown, to hint at former greatness. But several of the buildings that had been part of the manorial complex remain.

In the Middle Ages, manors were neither country houses nor villages nor parishes. They were units of administration. Lords of the manor controlled them, farming their own demesnes, holding manorial courts and making a tidy income from fines; the peasants who lived on the manor had various rights, which allowed them to graze their animals on common land, take a specified amount of timber from the lord's woods, fatten their pigs on the acorns, and so on.

Naturally, the hall, where the lord ate with his household, dispensed justice, organised business and where some lowly people slept, was dignified with whatever architecture could be afforded. So were the rooms into which the lord and lady withdrew to escape the smell and noise, which might take the form, as at Boothby Pagnell Manor House in Lincolnshire, of a separate building. But the manor complex did not consist only of these. In the early Middle Ages, manors were something like campsites, the area, perhaps marked out by a moat, being scattered with a number of disparate structures. The kitchen was kept separate from other buildings because of the fire risk. Horses were kept in a stable; grain and wool were stored in barns.

In a great palace such as Ewelme, these buildings would have been magnificent: indeed, they still struck visitors with awe a century after they were built. Naturally they were complemented by a splendid church, rebuilt by the Suffolks. Every medieval community needed a church or chapel in which to seek God's protection from a spirit world that seemed almost as vivid as the material one.

Alice rests inside the church, in the form of her alabaster effigy. It shows her appearance in life, while beneath it lurks an image of what she would become: a rotting corpse. This gives a clue to the Suffolks' motivation for some of their other projects. The Middle Ages knew very well that death was coming, and might be round the corner (for Suffolk, it was). They wanted to get through the tribulations of purgatory as quickly as possible. In this the rich and powerful were at a disadvantage, given the difficulty of getting through the eye of the needle; they believed that a constant round of masses and prayers for their soul would provide a get-out-of-jail card, and so they paid for priests and others to do nothing else.

At Ewelme, the Suffolks established a hospital or almshouse, called God's House, where thirteen almsmen were retained to pray for them. It was a stiff regime: pay was docked if any of the men left the site for more than an hour at a time. They were overseen by two priests, one of whom officiated in the school that the Suffolks founded in 1448.

Church, God's House and school survive – all of them still going strong – as one of the most beautiful compositions to come down from the fifteenth century. Each is subtly placed in the hierarchy by its building material: stone and flint for the church, brick and stone for the almshouse, brick for the school. The village cohered around them. The watercress beds, established in the 1890s, are in good heart, too: they have recently been restored.

# GERRARDS CROSS
## BUCKINGHAMSHIRE
*And then the railway came*

Gerrards Cross in the Chilterns did not exist before 1861. In that year, the Church of England noticed some 560 souls who were inconveniently remote from a church, and created a parish for them. Even so, the village, or settlement, could hardly be said to have come alive before 1906. That was the year the railway arrived. Thereafter, Gerrards Cross – in a quietly affluent way – boomed.

Sam Fay himself lived there, and since Fay was the general manager of the Great Central Railway, the trains were guaranteed to run smoothly. Fay created a publicity department, the first for a railway company, which came up with the simple but effective slogan 'Live in the Country'. This prefigured the Metropolitan Railway's efforts to promote 'Metroland' by a decade. Gerrards Cross became the precursor of scores of developments around the Home Counties that found themselves commutable to London.

The population is now more than seven thousand. This is a village that has pumped iron, taken steroids, grown; the seven-stone weakling has turned into a circus strong man, which has been squaring up to its even bigger neighbour, Chalfont St Peter (population: nearly thirteen thousand), for years. Proposals to merge the two into a single amalgamated rural entity never come off. The yeoman spirit lives on. Rivalry and independence are as much a part of the invented village character as half-timbering.

A century ago, the headmaster of the little school had word that a motor car would go along the Oxford Road one afternoon, and the children were allowed to go across Gerrards Cross Common to watch it. You could hear it coming: there was little other noise to compete. (Before that, the great excitement had been the mail coaches, rattling along the London to Oxford road, sometimes driven, at cracking pace, by Lord Algernon St Maur, son of one of the big houses, Bulstrode Park.)

Change took various forms. The railway, a joint promotion by the Great Central and the Great Western railways, stalked in on a high viaduct, before diving through a deep cutting. The young community required better drainage facilities, and a Steam Motor Exhauster was purchased to flush out the cesspools. Unfortunately, sparks seem to have set fire to the Common, which then burned for three months. Silver birches grew up in place of the heather, for which it had previously been noted. The General Post Office bought a bicycle to speed the delivery of telegrams. The railway made it possible to reach Paddington, nineteen miles away, in twenty-eight minutes; Marylebone in twenty-five.

New roads were built, in what one prospectus called 'that quaint domestic type [of architecture] so characteristic of Buckinghamshire', the best of the houses being in a sub Arts and Crafts style, of brick or rendering and half timber with low-sweeping tiled roofs. Institutions developed. A cricket club played on the Common. There had been proposals to form a joint volunteer fire brigade between Gerrards Cross and Chalfont St Peter; they were scorned, of course, but a bad fire in Station Road focused minds: the Uxbridge fire brigade took nearly an hour to get there. So a local (joint) brigade came into being in 1914. Bulstrode Park became the centre of the Worldwide Evangelisation Crusade started by the cricketer C. T. Studd in 1919.

# GREAT TEW
## OXFORDSHIRE
*Useful and Ornamental: Mr Loudon's ideal*

No one affected the appearance of England in the first half of the nineteenth century more than John Claudius Loudon. An indefatigable encyclopedist of gardening, plants and architecture; a cataloguer of British trees; the designer of England's first public park, the Derby Arboretum; the inventor of the iron glazing bar that made the curves of Victorian hothouses and Crystal Palace possible: he had many careers. Born in 1783, he started work at the age of twelve with an Edinburgh nurseryman; by the age of twenty-one he could write that 'several noblemen and gentlemen' had asked him to lay out their estates, managing woods, draining land and even reclaiming it from the sea.

Despite being self-taught, he had already launched a career as a journalist. Later, he was helped by a fire at Josiah Taylor's Architectural Library, which destroyed the stock of many pattern books that had come out during the past quarter of a century, including John Plaw's popular *Rural Architecture* (1794). This left the stage clear for Loudon's unending stream of utopian but functional advice. Like many journalists, however, he found that writing about a subject was second best to doing it himself. To put his ideas into practice, he took the lease of the estate farm at Great Tew in Oxfordshire from 1809–11. During the course of his tenancy, he rebuilt the farmhouse and farmyard, and probably waved a Tudoresque wand over the village.

The pub in Great Tew is called the Falkland Arms, and this gives some clue as to the estate's earlier history. Lucius Cary, 2nd Viscount Falkland, a dashing but possibly depressive cavalier who was killed by deliberately charging through a hedge lined with Parliamentarian musketeers, presided over a circle of Royalist poets and thinkers: Ben Jonson and Thomas Hobbes came to Great Tew Park. By 1808, Great Tew was owned by General George Frederick Stratton. He had seen a pamphlet on landed property, in which Loudon advocated the 'Scotch' method of agriculture, the nub of which was rationalism and education. Stratton asked

Loudon to value the estate at Great Tew. On the basis that Loudon would double the rental income, he was asked to live there, farming a thousand acres.

Stratton found that the Scottish system involved spending large sums of money (more than thirteen thousand pounds) on improvements. They were never justified. It was, however, typical of Loudon that he did not allow persistent ill health to detract from his labours: confined to his veranda, he communicated to his workmen using a speaking trumpet and French horn. No doubt his efforts were appreciated by the sons of local farmers and gentlemen, for whom he organised an impromptu agricultural college. But his appetite for innovation did not endear him locally. Two Scottish farmers replaced sixteen English ones.

Oxfordshire must have been glad to be rid of him – and it soon was. Scottish farming did not prove to be a financial success, and Loudon feared that his labours at Great Tew would be remembered as a 'ruinous project of wild adventurers'. On that point, however, he was wrong. It would seem (alas, there is no evidence) that a legacy survives on some of the cottages, in the shape of Regency porches and bargeboards that he probably designed. Readers of Loudon's *Encyclopaedia of Cottage, Farm and Villa Architecture* (1833) may conclude that Loudon had no taste of his own – indeed, no eye for beauty. But Great Tew makes one think twice. It is one of the prettiest villages in England. If Loudon cannot alone take the credit, at least he did nothing bad.

# HARROLD
## BEDFORDSHIRE                                    *The astonishing achievement of bridges*

The most intact of the medieval bridges over the river Great Ouse is at Harrold. It must have been a gigantic undertaking for the masons building it, with six principal arches (the great bridge) and a further nine (the long bridge) snaking away over the flood plain. But they and their kind understood about bridges, better even than the engineers of the Roman period (at least those who found their way to Britannia). The only Roman bridges known to have had stone piers were in the far north of England, on the border with Scotland and at Piercebridge, Co. Durham (see page 433); even the Roman London Bridge was built of wood, to judge from what has been excavated of the foundations. But there are around five thousand stone-built medieval bridges still in existence – many of them, as at Harrold, still used by traffic.

The achievement of these bridges appears all the greater by contrast with what must have been the rudimentary state of roads in the Middle Ages. The roads laid by the Romans had gone to pot. Most of the medieval road system grew up from lanes and tracks, the surface of the highway displaying none of the refinements of Roman construction. How did the masons do it? First, they would drive wooden piles into the riverbed to make a kind of open box, which they filled with gravel and rubble. Then scaffolding was made to support the stones of the arches,

*Harrold bridge, snaking across the river Great Ouse: several villages had responsibility for its upkeep.*

great judgement being required to strike it at the right moment: too early and the mortar would not have set, too late and it would have set too hard, allowing no room for the stone to settle. Fortunately, the Great Ouse at Harrold is a sluggish beast, which does not trouble itself to rage much beyond the winter months, so the foundations were not washed away. But the river frequently leaves its bed to sprawl across the meadows of what, at the best of times, is a watery landscape: hence the long bridge, which is really a causeway.

Bridges brought trade and prosperity to the area in which they were built. But they had to be paid for. The King did not often come up trumps and there was no Department of Transport or Ministry of Works, so different methods of finance were devised. At Rochester in Kent, two rich knights paid for a stone bridge in the late fourteenth century, establishing a foundation to maintain it (it survives as the Rochester Bridge Trust). Harrold, by contrast, was a cooperative effort. Since the benefit was to be shared by the area generally, several communities – lords of the manor and their tenants – contributed to putting the bridge up and keeping it in repair. The arrangement can be deduced from the fabric of the bridge itself, the different teams of workers having left arches of slightly varying shape.

For the twenty-first-century vehicles that still cross it, the narrow carriageway may seem something of a tight squeeze (there are traffic lights at either end), but so it was in the Middle Ages: every so often the parapet opens out to provide a space into which a pedestrian could hop to avoid oncoming wagons, although he or she may have preferred to take the wooden walkway (now gone), which was cantilevered out from the sides.

# HODDESDON
## HERTFORDSHIRE

*Country air for the Labour party*

Ramsay MacDonald liked rambling. He believed that it was not 'from the pained life of the crowded towns' that men gained the inspiration to live in 'strenuous endeavour', but 'amidst the green of budding corn, the white of cherry blossoms and fleecy cloud, and the gay blue of the sky.' In this he was typical of the Labour movement. In the years after the mechanised horrors of the First World War, Nature was an essential part of the better world to which the Left strove. Treading the path to it were hikers and ramblers, sunbathers and cyclists, their joy in fresh air being a low-cost antidote to economic gloom.

The Labour League of Youth discovered that rambling and cycling were useful recruitment tools, together with dancing, drama groups, summer camps and education. The socialist newspaper *The Clarion* led the way. In 1895, it had established a cycling club, opening a clubhouse at Broadley Common, near Nazeing in Essex, in 1913. From 1933 it was possible for socialist cyclists to pedal up to the Clarion Socialist Youth Hostel, set in a manor house at Hoddesdon with ten acres of grounds. To London branches of the League, it represented an escape from the blackened, unhealthy streets of the capital.

Walking in the countryside was not the exclusive preserve of the Left. Most of the organisations that had been created during the previous half century to champion the protection of the countryside, such as the National Trust and the Council for the Protection of Rural England, were emphatically non-political. The same was true of the Youth Hostel Association, founded in 1930. But the importance that healthful exercise, preferably taken in rural surroundings, had for socialism represented a new approach to the countryside: at a time when farming was in the doldrums, it was seen as a shared resource, capable both of rebuilding the body and refreshing the spirit.

The idealisation of rural England may seem strange for a movement that had its roots in the industrial towns. Nevertheless, it chimed with Ruskin and William Morris's abhorrence of the ugliness and misery caused by rampant capitalism. Unfettered ribbon development, by which the tentacles of London stretched, via the arterial roads, into previously unspoiled countryside, seemed to personify the selfishness of developers and speculators. Village life was regarded as preserving virtues that the modern town had lost.

Of itself, hiking promoted the sort of shared fellowship that socialists held dear. While walking, much could be talked of; the philosopher and preservationist Cyril

Joad would tramp through the beech woods around Chorleywood while his Fabian companions unveiled 'the new world of Socialism'. In other respects, places such as the Hoddesdon hostel seemed little different from other forms of rural recreation. People swam, boated, played tennis, danced. There was a high-minded element, with talks on 'Socialism and Art' and, a little alarmingly, 'Breeding out the unfit'. But it was not allowed to take the first two syllables out of Socialism. As one hosteller, Grace Oakden, remembered: 'We had a great deal of fun in those days, as well as serious politicking.' Not, of course, the villagers. They do not seem to have been invited.

The second half of the twentieth century was not kind to Hoddesdon. If the Clarion cyclists were to return, they would find little that was bucolic. It would, however, give them an object lesson in the awfulness of failed planning.

# HUNSDON
## HERTFORDSHIRE
*Stop Harlow North*

Autumn sends flakes of gold gusting along the lanes of Hunsdon, as the wind tears the last of the leaves from the beech trees. According to local campaigners, gold is what certain pension funds and property companies see in this patch of Hertfordshire, too. They have been trying to build houses on agricultural land that they bought north of Harlow since 1994.

In 1900, Britain had around seven million homes. A century later, the number was twenty-two million. During the same period, the population rose from less than forty million to about sixty million. Expectations have also risen, together with the rate at which new householders are formed, as children leave home earlier, the middle-aged divorce more frequently and the elderly live longer. House prices in the south of England have soared ahead of what people earn. To economists, the conclusion is inescapable: we need more homes. But the people of Hunsdon would rather keep the existing environment, thank you, and their distaste is shared by communities across southern counties. Villages have become battlegrounds against unwelcome development.

Considering its proximity (thirty-one minutes by train) to London, Hunsdon is unreasonably pretty. The village hall is thought to have been created from a school that was once a house called Harlowes, owned in the fifteenth century by John Harlowe, whose family gave its name, centuries later, to the New Town. This is a green land, and a land of greens. Henry Moore had his studio at nearby Perry Green, and Hunsdon has no fewer than five greens. Brick lodges with diamond-paned windows survive from the days when farming, not pharmaceuticals, was the big industry round here. While Harlow is in Essex, this is horseboxy, flint-churched Hertfordshire: green belt, and defended to the hilt.

Green belts used to be the sacred cows of the British planning system. They were, from their inception in 1955, intended to be permanent. That froze the value of the land, because all parties knew that it could never be built on. Equally, local authorities had an incentive to invest in it, knowing that it would still be there in half a century's time. The degree of permanence, environmentalists fear, is now relative.

Harlow Council backs development, because it hopes that a billion pounds' worth of planning gain will be used to revitalise Harlow. Stop Harlow North, an action group, has a secret weapon. The Rye Meads sewage works on the river Lee, which is next to a protected habitat – an internationally important area of wetland, haunted by bittern, snipe, gadwall and smew – may be full to capacity, and since treated effluent is ultimately discharged into the river Lee, any expansion of this facility would be damned. Dusk sees Hertfordshire's highest concentration of bats take to wing. Bats are highly protected, too.

There are fourteen green belts around towns and cities. For developers, the Hertfordshire part of London's green belt, lying both near the capital and the M11 development corridor, is a double target. Permission has already been given to breach the green belt west of Stevenage with a development of 3,600 houses.

As for Harlow North, the extra houses do not meet a local need. Harlow has one of the highest unemployment rates in Essex. It is unlikely that local employment will suddenly boom. Ostensibly, official policy encourages only sustainable development, which precludes regular commuting, and rightly so. The train services to London are full, the roads are full. Demonstrating its commitment to meeting the modest local housing need, Stop Harlow North has produced a plan to turn the proposed development area into Gilston Great Park – a recreational green lung that would incorporate an ancient deer park, with pockets of housing on the edge of the villages. Surely that would be the sensible way to proceed.

# IDBURY

## OXFORDSHIRE

*Pulling no punches about village life*

One of the great, forgotten books of the twentieth century is J. W. Robertson Scott's *England's Green and Pleasant Land*. It was published in 1925, when Robertson Scott was fifty-nine. Two years later he would found *The Countryman* magazine, a mouthpiece for his leftward-leaning view of rural life. It was a theme he knew well. Life had begun in Cumberland. But his father – commercial salesman and temperance orator – died when Robertson Scott was still in his teens, and he had to support his family. He did it through journalism, writing largely on country subjects. These were bleak decades for farming, undercut by imports from the Empire and elsewhere; and since agriculture was by far the biggest rural employer, times were hard for the wider countryside, too. In *England's Green and Pleasant Land*, Robertson Scott pulled no punches.

After twenty years in Essex, Robertson Scott had just moved to the Cotswolds. Idbury is a hamlet of stone walls and thatch, with a pretty church that started life in the twelfth century. Enchanting stuff for an amateur watercolourist. Robertson Scott saw a different side. Every cottage in the settlement had been reported as substandard. Two of them had come with Robertson Scott's own house, the sixteenth-century Idbury Manor. He could put his hand into the holes in the stone walls, the foundations were slipping and the thatch letting in water. His social conscience would not let him pull them down. The cottages had been made 'trim and snug' by their occupants, their defects and damp concealed by strategically placed furniture. He patched them up. But patching cannot make perfect. At a time when plumbing was being improved in the towns and cities, the villagers of Idbury still had to carry their water from the pump and make use of 'stinking privies', one between two cottages and possibly on the other side of the road.

Rather than strapping country lads, Robertson Scott could see that the village boys were skinny and bandy-legged. The place had lost the means to climb out of its own poverty. 'For years and years most of the men and women of grit had gone away or been driven away. Those who remained had mated with the second-, third- or fourth-rate of their own or some neighbouring hamlet.' There was no kindly peeress to dispense largesse to this community, he noted sourly. As for the Church, he could see seven spires from a local windmill, each with its own parson; seven parsons ought to have been able to do something, but had not. Robertson Scott took on the organising role that they had failed to assume, arranging village meetings in the schoolhouse that might be addressed by George Bernard Shaw.

Robertson Scott was too wise to offer his own panacea, although he noted the coming of the wireless as likely to enlarge village ideas. He was to be astonished at what the next quarter of a century would bring. Writing an afterword to the 1947 reissue of the book, he gasped at the 'three quarters of a million new cottages – besides the thousands re-conditioned' being rushed up. After the Second World War, farming had been revolutionised. 'But the farmers and farm-workers in my parish could hardly have thought of seeing several tractors, a combine harvester, potato lifters and straw-and-hay-balers and having electric light instead of oil lamps . . . and a double-deck motor bus where there was not even a horse bus service.'

What a vision of progress. If only Robertson Scott could have known that, before another quarter of a century had passed, the progressive farming methods that he welcomed would be regarded by a disenchanted public with growing horror. And that a further quarter of a century later it would be difficult to see the cottages – once tumbledown, now expensively fitted out – for the four-by-fours parked outside them. Goodness, he would have written something pithy. I would love to know what.

# JORDANS

## BUCKINGHAMSHIRE

*A village built by Friends*

The simple, red-brick Quaker meeting house at Jordans was built in 1688, during the period of religious tolerance introduced, ironically, by James II (as a Catholic, it was not toleration of Quakers he was after). With its whitewashed walls, unadorned panelling and upright wooden benches, it is still a structure that radiates the Quaker values of equality before God and spirituality – rather than ceremony – as the basis of worship. (Fortunately, the interior survived a fire of 2005, which destroyed the roof, now rebuilt.) William Penn, the founder of Pennsylvania, worshipped here, as did the mystic Isaac Pennington and Milton's friend Thomas Ellwood. By the late eighteenth century, attendance was in decline, and the Meeting House was closed in 1797. But the coming of the railway brought a new community, and in 1910 it reopened.

A group of Friends also bought Old Jordans Farm, which was turned into a hostel. A barn on the farm had, according to an almost certainly spurious but persistent legend, been constructed out of timbers from the *Mayflower*, the ship that took the first Puritans to America. During the First World War it was detailed as a training centre for the Friends' Ambulance Unit, run by the pacifist Quakers as a contribution to the national effort. After the War, with speculative housing on the march, another farm was purchased.

The Jordans Village Estate was begun in 1919 to protect the surroundings of the Meeting House from unwelcome development. The idea was that it should be built in the Quaker spirit, although not occupied exclusively by Quakers. It was to be self-sufficient, growing its own food and offering employment in arts and crafts to the people who lived there. According to Ernest Warner, a Quaker metal broker of antiquarian tastes who had been instrumental in buying Old Jordans Farm and wrote a book, beautifully printed on art paper by the Friends Bookshop, in 1921, 'industries already started or in contemplation' included 'A Dairy Farm. Market-gardening and fruit-growing. Poultry-farming and bee-keeping. Building, wood-work, and metal industries. Brick- and tile-making. Boot-making and hand-loom weaving'. Under the name of Jordan Village Industries, they were to be organised into guilds, while the design of the settlement was entrusted to the Quaker architect Frederick Rowntree.

Rowntree insisted that the aesthetics of the development should come before anything else. The heart of the village was, inevitably, a broad green, overlooked by terraces of cottages, six originally. The style was character-ised by red-orange bricks and handmade tiles, such as those out of which the Meeting House is built, sweeping roofs and tall chimneys giving a feeling of Hampstead Garden Suburb, which had been founded in 1907. It succeeded in its intention of protecting Jordans, as Gerrards Cross (see page 176) worked its way ever closer.

Alas, like so many other Arts and Crafts enterprises, the cottage-industry element of the vision proved short-lived. Jordans Village Industries closed in 1923; the guildhall, opened in 1919, was demolished. But like the Meeting House, the village remains a place of well-ordered calm.

# JUNIPER HILL
## OXFORDSHIRE

*Lovingly chronicled poverty*

'Old men could remember when the Rise, covered with juniper bushes, stood in the midst of a furzy heath – common land, which had come under the plough after the passing of the Inclosure Acts.' So wrote Flora Thompson at the beginning of *Lark Rise to Candleford*, one of the most popular books about village life ever written. The community of the hamlet that she observed was made up of farm labourers. Not so long before they would have had some independence, grazing animals on the common and able to transact some business for themselves. By the 1880s, the era of Thompson's childhood, they were reduced to working for wages; an invariable ten shillings a week. However pretty the surroundings (particularly when transferred to BBC television), work was long and hard – with the prospect of going out to hoe the beans in the garden, whose produce formed an essential part of the cottage diet, when they got home.

Lark Rise was Juniper Hill. It had, by implication, been abandoned by the Victorian hierarchy, because the church, as well as the shop, were in the 'mother village' of Cottisford, a mile and a half away (Fordlow in the book). Taking the place of church, school and improving readings was the taproom of the pub. Thompson had grown up in Juniper Hill, the daughter of a stonemason and a nursemaid, but soon moved away. After Cottisford local school, she became a Post Office clerk at fourteen, and married another. Although she had always written stories, success came late; *Lark Rise*, the first of the trilogy that became *Lark Rise to Candleford*, was not sent to the Oxford University Press until 1938. (Bravely, given that they do not normally publish fiction, they accepted it.) The world she was remembering was that of her childhood half a century earlier.

It was nothing new for girls to leave Juniper Hill. They all did, some as young as thirteen, to take positions in service. Strangers would not therefore have found, at Lark Rise, the 'sweet country girl of tradition, with her sunbonnet, hayrake, and air of rustic coquetry' (Tess of the d'Urbervilles, perhaps). An older girl, if in evidence, 'would be dressed in town clothes, complete with gloves and veil, for she would be home from service for her fortnight's holiday, and her mother would insist upon her wearing her best every time she went out of doors, in order to impress the neighbours'. Conditions for the maids into which they morphed when not at home were dour. The boys stayed behind to follow their fathers into the fields, enjoying a rise in the weekly wage to fifteen shillings in the early 1890s, although this was mostly eaten up by rising prices: 'it took a world war to obtain for them anything like a living wage'.

What is Juniper Hill like now? The hamlet is marooned within the bleakness of huge fields, the four unexpected balls of an RAF station on the horizon, tall-sided lorries passing along the main road on the other side of a hedge. There is a plaque on the one-up-one-down cottage where Thompson lived until the age of fourteen, with her parents and five siblings. But the grinding poverty has gone. So have the pigs, whose killing was one of the highlights of the cottage year; so has the length- ened burr of the dialect, pail being pronounced 'pay-ull'; so has the spirit of soli- darity that caused the women to pet Emily when she declared, quite untruthfully, that the interesting condition in which she found herself had been caused by the son of the big house. Only a sentimentalist would wish it back, and Thompson, in her books if not the television interpretation, was never that.

# KINGHAM
## OXFORDSHIRE

*Village pub, new style*

It is a summer evening. The Cotswold sun is varnishing the landscape with golden rays. The richly green tapestry of centuries-old trees and pastures nestling between woods, of stone walls and stone villages tucked up beneath a blue sheet of sky, needs only one thing to complete its perfection: a village pub. But of course, pubs are closing in droves. The drink-driving laws and smoking ban signed the death warrant. The rise in property values, making premises more valuable as houses than hostelries, delivered the *coup de grâce*. The beer handle will soon be as redun- dant as the village pump.

Where could the weary traveller slake his thirst with a pint or two of local beer, accompanied by some delicately steamed asparagus, gilded by the yolk of a duck egg, and a hog-roast bun, if only of artistically bonsai proportions? Not much to ask, surely – oh, and throw in a view of a village green and some box topiary balls.

You may go thirsty or hungry as you travel the countryside, or you may find that a benign providence directs you to a gastropub such as The Plough at Kingham. The chef-proprietor Emily Watkins trained at the three-Michelin-starred chef- chemist Heston Blumenthal's Fat Duck at Bray, Berkshire. Hang the expense. And you must be prepared to, for it is unquestionably expensive. But it is there. According to figures from the Campaign for Real Ale (CAMRA), thirty-nine pubs across Britain call last orders for the final time each month. But out of this desola- tion has emerged a new type of hostelry.

The experience is not unique to the Cotswolds. There are pubs across the English countryside (less so, perhaps, in Wales and Scotland) that combine the traditional warmth of log fires and jugs of bitter with outstanding, modern food. The best of them, like the Museum Inn at Farnham in Dorset (see page 36), succeed in retaining a local clientele. But they make their money from the new market of affluent incomers, retirees, weekenders and tourists, the income level at Kingham being kept up by a railway station that offers direct trains to London.

Not that pubs have to assume the gastro prefix; some villages are blessed with hostelries that rely on something more, well, traditionally English than the snails-on-toast bar snack offered by the Kingham Plough. David Short stands at the Aga of the Queen's Head in Newton, Cambridgeshire, stirring soup that will be sold according to a colour chart in the bar ('it goes from dark brown through taupe to green, which usually has peas in it'). When he became the publican forty-six years ago, he quickly established a formula that has remained an unvarying constant ever since. Rare roast beef sandwiches and any-coloured soup, washed down with Adnams bitter – what could be done to improve it?

Because the role that the pub plays in a village is as immutable as the menu of the Queen's Head, communities will rally round to stop one from closing. In Nether Wallop in Hampshire, local people have gamely kept the Five Bells swinging until a new publican can be found. The Tiger Inn at Stowting in Kent – named after a tiger that, having escaped from a circus, drinkers are said to have captured in a tablecloth – was saved by a consortium of local people, who bought it. Pubs need communities, and communities need pubs. New style or old, lively pubs have an active village behind them.

*See also Hesket Newmarket, page 390*

# LAMBOURN
BERKSHIRE                                 *When Kettledrum won the Derby*

According to the *Oxford Dictionary of National Biography*, Robert Milman was an 'indefatigable parish priest', which, for a Victorian clergyman, is saying something. Even so, he had his work cut out at Lambourn. It 'had the unenviable reputation of being one of the roughest, wickedest places in England', remembered Margaret Murray, who used to stay at the vicarage, where her uncle John was one of Milman's successors as vicar. For one thing it was isolated, ignored by the railway, little visited and sometimes cut off by snowdrifts. Then there was the influence of the turf. Racing had taken place on the Downs in 1799, and since that time horses, rather than the Church, had been the principal influence on the place. If racing had stopped, training had not. Local men made an extra income as 'zoologers', observing how horses ran and selling the information to bookies – a perilous occupation, since they were given short shrift by the stable lads if caught.

'Burning with religious zeal,' Margaret Murray observed, Milman set about the task of reform, undeterred by stones thrown at him or strings laid across roads to trip him up. When Kettledrum, foaled and trained at Lambourn, won the 1861 Derby, Milman was forced to burst into the bell tower of the church – locked against his arrival – and expel village men who were improperly ringing the bells in celebration. Milman went on to become Bishop of Calcutta; Lambourn followed its destiny by becoming the country's greatest centre for training racehorses, largely National Hunt, after Newmarket. It is one of the few places in Britain where horses are more talked about than cars.

For millennia, people had been passing near Lambourn on the ancient track known as the Ridgeway. There had been a settlement here in Anglo-Saxon times: Lambourn is mentioned in Alfred the Great's will. The key to its success with racehorses is the geology of the Downs. It is solid chalk. The poor grassland was good for nothing but grazing sheep, which have been nibbling away at it – and returning the compliment in manure – since the Middle Ages. The result is a smooth, springy, herb-rich *gazon* of eminently inviting turf, which might have been created for nothing but galloping on. Now the traditional greensward has been supplemented with six all-weather tracks. Fulke Walwyn and Fred Winter trained several notable Cheltenham Gold Cup and Champion Hurdle winners here in the 1960s and 1970s. Their assistants grew up to be the next generation of trainers, of whom there are now thirty in Lambourn. There are 1,500 racehorses stabled in the valley.

Unsurprisingly, Lambourn is not like other villages. Horses attract vets, saddlers, blacksmiths, bookies, equine dentists, bandy-legged stable lads (aged from fourteen to seventy) and sulky-looking girl grooms. It could have been a pretty village if it had tried; instead, too preoccupied by the state of its hooves and fetlocks, it has allowed charm to slip out of the window, functional banality being the rule for most buildings that are not statutorily protected. Yet an aroma of affluence hangs over the place, suggestive of the horse industry's unrivalled ability to recycle owners' surplus wealth. There is even a silk cravat-maker in Lambourn. Nothing more need be said.

# LOCKINGE
BERKSHIRE                    *The Victorian ideal: moral, sanitary, Picturesque*

Lockinge belongs to the second wave of model villages that rolled over rural Britain in the Victorian period. Georgian improvers had wanted to tidy away the broken-down cottages that clung embarrassingly to the skirts of their mansions, in order to improve the view; the new dwellings that they constructed were Picturesque, yet also sanitary. Victorian estate owners put a new value on their own privacy, and were therefore no better disposed to ramshackle habitations close to their seats, but they were also keen to promote moral and physical decency. Their new cottages were sanitary, yet also Picturesque.

The Society for the Improving the Condition of the Labouring Classes was established in 1844, with the Prince Consort as President. Its work was complemented by numerous local societies, which aimed to provide better housing for the poor. The conditions endured by rural labourers were often no better than those of the industrial slums. The Prince himself showed the way, constructing not only model dwellings for the poor in London but also stout and roomy cottages at Osborne and Balmoral. Other landowners took the hint.

At Lockinge, as well as Ardington on the same estate, Lord Wantage found that the existing cottages were – as his wife later remembered – 'fast-decaying hovels', whose wattle-and-daub walls were so ropey that a walking stick could easily be stuck through them. Wantage had recently returned from the Crimean War, where he had distinguished himself on the battlefield, but nearly died of dysentery. Retiring from the army, he made Lockinge – settled on him and Lady Wantage by his father-in-law, the millionaire banker Lord Overstone – the centre of his life.

A man of deep religious conviction, he shared the alarm of contemporaries over the accommodation of working families, where girls and boys might sleep in the same room, perhaps the same room as their parents. Three bedrooms per cottage were now a desideratum. In concert with his wife, Wantage, perhaps inspired by the example of Prince Albert, who had personally selected him as equerry to the Prince of Wales, set about a programme of improvement. The result was modern but not monotonous, or as Lady Wantage put it: 'The picturesque character of the old style of cottage building . . . has been as far as possible retained, with the view of preserving the irregular character and charm of the old Berkshire villages.' She was insistent that the occupants should go to church.

The Wantages built everything they could think of: a reading room or club, a public house that provided tea and soup to those who did not want alcoholic drink, a bakery, a school, a cooperative shop and a stupendous operation – sawmills, carpenters' shops, blacksmiths' shops, painters' shops, wheelwrights' shops, all of the latest kind – dedicated to the maintenance of the estate. Not everybody approved. A reporter from the liberal *Daily News* found the comfortably settled inhabitants in a state of Tory thraldom, unable to so much as keep pigs in their gardens. Pigs near cottage doors, Lord Wantage replied with dignity, might pollute the drinking water in the well, but they could be kept on allotments. He did not see why benevolent paternalism could not be combined with freedom of thought and speech on the part of the neighbours and tenants benefiting from it. The newspaper man, the aristocrat, the village: a potent brew for misunderstanding that still bubbles, long after deference and paternalism are dead.

# NETTLEBED
OXFORDSHIRE                                        *The rise of the village hall*

When the German writer Karl Philipp Moritz visited Nettlebed in 1782, he found that the villagers would assemble in church not just for divine service but to make music and listen to the choir singing psalms on Sunday afternoons. He was charmed. Had he visited a century later, he might have reflected that there were not many other places to meet. It was a matter of concern to Victorian social reformers that the most popular communal spaces were those that served alcohol, namely pubs. The rector might institute a reading room, but, like the pub, that was generally a male preserve, inaccessible to women and children. Schoolrooms were inconvenient because adults could not sit in the chairs.

People of Arts and Crafts persuasion were particularly conscious of the need for meeting places. With the traditions of the countryside weakening, self-conscious efforts had to be made to preserve activities such as folk dancing, and to foster village spirit. What was needed was a shared space, free from the sale of alcohol, where the growing number of social clubs, Boy Scout troops, village bands, choirs and amateur dramatics groups could assemble. It was found, during the years before the First World War, in the village hall.

Nettlebed has an early and splendid example. It was built in 1911, a barn-like structure, with an oversailing roof made from immense timbers, the sort of solid, stylistically unfussy structure that was pure Arts and Crafts. (A telltale sign of the style is the appearance of layers of tile, set in thick mortar, in the piers of the cloister-like forecourt.) The architect was C. E. Mallows, a draughtsman and garden designer as well as an architect, who had grown up in Flatford Mill in Suffolk. Originally it was called the Working Men's Club, although it functioned in most respects as a village hall, with 'quiz shows, musical evenings, plays, dances, gymnastics, rifle shooting, leisure classes, and a cinematograph ("kinema")', according to the local historian Elizabeth Tate. The financier Robert Fleming, founder of the merchant bank Robert Fleming & Co., who bought the Nettlebed Estate in 1903, is supposed to have built it as a peace offering to the village, after having secured an Act of Parliament to move the cricket pitch in order to improve his entrance. It cost £4,500.

The village hall idea gathered pace after the First World War. To some communities, a hall provided a purposeful memorial to the men who never came back, a practical contribution towards the effort to regenerate village life. 'The organisers of the Village Clubs' Association have only been actively at work for a very few months, but in all parts of the country they have visited . . . the demand is the same,' Sir Henry Rew told the National Council of Social Service in 1920. Lawrence Weaver, architectural editor of Country Life, wrote Village Clubs and Halls the same year.

Money was found to build them through a variety of organisations, such as the rural community councils. Village halls could be beautiful, they had to be serviceable, but they were invariably traditional in style. Nostalgia was creeping in, together with the Arts and Crafts beams. But they formed an essential resource, and still do. A new wave of village hall building took place as part of Britain's self-renewal at the Millennium, funded by the first fruits of the Lottery.

# NUNEHAM COURTENAY
## OXFORDSHIRE
*The original deserted village*

'Pretty white cottages, scattered round a small piece of water and shaded with a number of very fine trees'. The old village of Nuneham Courtenay does not sound so bad. Certainly the villagers liked it. But when the 1st Earl Harcourt began land-scaping his newly completed Palladian country house of Nuneham Courtenay, he considered that it was too near his dwelling. To the villagers' dismay, he set about demolishing the old village and relocating them to a new one. We now know, from a comment made by a visiting Bishop, that this was the inspiration for Oliver Goldsmith's poem *The Deserted Village*, scathing in its attack on 'cumbrous pomp', as opposed to the 'bold peasantry' on the green:

> Ill fares the land, to hastening ills a prey,
> Where wealth accumulates, and men decay.

Yet we can also see from Lord Harcourt's correspondence that he was proud of the new cottages, which he appears to have designed himself; they were no doubt more spacious, more solidly built, better equipped with ovens and less hazardous from the point of view of fire than the ones recently pulled down.

Harcourt, 'an empty man', according to Horace Walpole, though a skillful vice-roy to Ireland and for a time tutor (less successfully) to the future George III, began the new village in 1760. There had been planned villages built at the gates of country houses before. One of the first had been Chippenham, near Cambridge (see page 222), built around 1700 after the Earl of Orford, victorious admiral at the Battle of La Hogue in 1692, had allegedly diverted money intended for His Majesty's navy into improvements to his estate. There would be more villagers rehoused against their will: at Milton Abbas in Dorset, Lord Milton, who had inherited a money-lending fortune in Ireland and set himself up as a nobleman, is supposed to have flooded the home of a solicitor who refused to vacate.

Designed by William Chambers, the new Milton Abbas was thatched, but other-wise rather lacking in Picturesque tweaks. Nuneham Courtenay was also a sober production. While the mansion house is of stone, brick (being cheaper) was chosen for the twenty-eight pairs of cottages, dark grey headers alternating with orange stretchers to form a chequer-work pattern. The 'Cornish', as Harcourt called the cornice, is about twelve feet from the ground, with dormer windows in the tiled roof. The layout shows some visual sophistication. At either end are a pair of larger buildings (an inn and smithy in one case, taller houses in the other), so that an approaching visitor does not take in the whole village at a glance. The curate's house is set back behind a small garden, which ought to have been balanced by a similar building on the other side, although this is the one element of the scheme never finished.

In the twentieth century, the cottages were sold to private owners, but the look of the village is stringently controlled. Oliver Goldsmith would be surprised to find that some residents would not live anywhere else.

# SONNING
## BERKSHIRE
*'The most fairy-like little nook on the whole river'*

Henry Taunt's *A New Map of the River Thames* first appeared in 1872 and ran through several editions. It was not just a map, but a photographic record of the life of the river: Cotswold villages seen beyond rushy banks, chaps in boaters edging out canoes into the stream, women in white dresses decoratively fishing, boatyards, bridges, towpaths, weirs, houseboats and locks. Until the coming of the railways, rivers had been principally valued as a source of irrigation and a means of transport. But as the nineteenth century drew to a close, they came to be enjoyed for their affinity with blazers, parasols, picnic hampers and the other paraphernalia of Victorian leisure. It was a world of rowing regattas – the most celebrated of which, Henley, was founded two years after Queen Victoria came to the throne – which appealed both to Varsity men and day trippers from London.

There was a holiday spirit to the Thames. Jerome K. Jerome captured the mood in *Three Men in a Boat* (1889): 'We got out at Sonning, and went for a walk round the village. It is the most fairy-like little nook on the whole river.' Taunt was, characteristically, more sober. He noted the bus times to Reading, the bees kept by the lock-keeper and the architecture of the church. In Saxon days, Sonning had been the site of a minster. It acquired a bishop's palace, and was for a time the centre of its own diocese. Sonning may then have been more important, Taunt observed, 'but could not at any time have been a pleasanter resting-place than at present'.

It was thoroughly in keeping that Edward Hudson, the proprietor of *Country Life*, should in 1899 have chosen Sonning to build the first of three houses that he commissioned from Lutyens\*. *Country Life* had been founded to celebrate both the active world of the country house, with its horse racing and motor cars, and the disappearing one of traditional village England, represented in mistily poetic photographs that resembled watercolours. Nostalgic for old crafts, it was rather longer on aesthetic values than landowners of the old school might have wished; no doubt its readership was as much drawn from London and its environs as from *l'Angleterre profonde*. Indeed Hudson himself was a Londoner. Sonning suited him perfectly.

*Country Life* duly published Deanery Garden in 1903, as a house for a man with a hobby, Hudson's hobby being rose growing and wall gardening. You can get little joy of it from the outside. Hudson, an intensely shy man, had created a *Hortus conclusus*, his house offering nothing to delight the passer-by beyond tall chimneys and low-sweeping roofs. The front door might almost be one of Lutyens's famous jokes, being almost ridiculously modest. One imagines Hudson, to whom Nature had given a lugubrious, bloodhound expression, disappearing through it like Alice after drinking the potion.

Sonning had already acquired aesthetic connotations. While Deanery Garden was rising, the aging, blind Pre-Raphaelite William Holman Hunt had built a cottage here called The Acre. Hunt wrote of Sonning as an 'exceptionally pictur-esque and well-ordered village'. The phrase comes from a defence of the ancient brick bridge, whose widening and ultimate replacement would be as an 'evil' that dimmed the 'attraction of the river not only to Englishmen, but to Colonials and Americans who have across the sea read widely of its beauty'. The letter is quoted by P. H. Ditchfield in a book of 1910, characteristically entitled *Vanishing England*. But Sonning bridge did not vanish; pleasure craft continue to nose through the arches. Boating and art saved the day.

*See Mells, page 55; Thursley, page 145*


# SPEENHAMLAND
BERKSHIRE                              *A formula to keep starvation at bay*


On 6 May 1795, a group of Berkshire magistrates met in the little brick Pelican Inn at Speenhamland, or Speen, now a suburb of Newbury. They were acutely aware of the state of the poor, who had until then been supported from parish funds. For decades, the price of bread had been steadily rising faster than wages. Since the outbreak of war against France in 1793, this had become acute. 1794 saw a bad harvest, and grain could no longer be imported from the Continent. There followed a harsh winter, during which the Thames froze and snow lay on the ground for months.

Economically, the root of the problem was that farmers did not pay their labourers a living wage throughout the year. This was because it had always been assumed that they and their families would be able to supplement their earnings through hand-loom weaving, knitting or some other cottage industry. But since the Industrial Revolution, the top-up from rural crafts was no longer available. Parishes, meanwhile, avoided their duty to support the poor, moving them on when they could. So starvation – and the possibility of rioting – loomed. After the French Revolution, the governing class was acutely sensitive to the threat of riots. The Speenhamland magistrates established a formula that would give poverty-stricken families support as it was needed. The rate of relief was linked to the price of bread: the dearer the bread, the bigger the dole.

The idea owed much to Sir Christopher Willoughby, chairman of the Oxfordshire magistrates since 1778. A progressive farmer, he was a member of the Board of Agriculture, and a friend of its Secretary, Arthur Young. He had bold views about prison reform, not to mention the standardisation of weights and measures, and local government generally. Since the Home Office was staffed by a grand total of thirteen civil servants, he saw that magistrates had to take reform into their own hands. Throughout 1794 he worked, unsuccessfully, to encourage employers to raise wages. The Berkshire magistrates compelled parishes to make up the difference between real wages and those necessary to live. Soon, Willoughby had persuaded the magistrates of Buckinghamshire to adopt the same measures. Eventually the Speenhamland System was adopted throughout most of England.

While charitably intended, the System was widely criticised. Bad farmers, knowing that the parish would supplement wages, had little incentive to reward their labourers properly. The labourers were demoralised through being permanently dependent on support. Thomas Malthus believed that the end result, given that agricultural supply was finite, would be to push up the price of bread, as well as to encourage the poor to engender families that they could not afford. William Cobbett* saw that the system did not prevent suffering. 'What has caused the labourers to rise?' he asked in December 1830. 'Why, want, horrid hunger.' The Speenhamland system was not working. But it had kept the poor in their own homes. The 1834 Poor Law Amendment Act put them somewhere else: in the workhouse†.

*See Botley, page 97. †See Abbey Dore, page 291

# STANDON GREEN END
## HERTFORDSHIRE
*What goes up must come down*

Who was the first aeronaut in Britain? There is not much doubt about it, if you live in Standon Green End. 'Let Posterity Know And Knowing be Astonished,' declares the inscription on a stone in a field there, 'That On the 15th Day of September 1784 Vincent Lunardi of Lucca in Tuscany, The First Aerial Traveller in Britain . . . Traversing the Regions of the Air For Two Hours and Fifteen Minutes In this Spot Revisited the Earth.'

Perhaps the dashing young secretary to the Neapolitan Ambassador was not the absolute first. Some weeks previously, a Mr Tytler, having conquered the problems of a porous linen balloon (he had it varnished), had 'navigated the air' in Edinburgh. But due to a fire (before the varnish was applied, the balloon had been lined with paper), which destroyed the gallery supposed to hold his furnace, he had come down pretty near the spot at which he had left. Lunardi's ascent had been a real flight. Astonishing it must have been to the countrymen and -women who did not know he was coming.

Lunardi, wanting to demonstrate his 'aerostatic machine' to the maximum number of people, had originally chosen the Royal Hospital in Chelsea as his launch pad. But a dastardly Frenchman called Moret had attempted to steal his glory by making an attempt from a nearby location before him. This ruse backfired: Moret, in the stern words of a Victorian historian, 'failed to erect his inflation', and the crowd of sixty thousand, bored and no doubt drunk, stormed the enclosure, stealing whatever they could. Lunardi hurriedly switched his arena to the Honourable Artillery Company's parade ground in the City of London. An even bigger crowd assembled. They were joined by the Prince of Wales.

It seemed at first that Lunardi would meet Moret's fate: a failed inflation. But by shedding a planned colleague and substituting a lighter basket, Lunardi was able to cut the cords. A gun fired; the basket rose; the Prince of Wales waved his hat; everybody waved their hats; Lunardi waved a flag in case nobody could see him, and worked the oars that were supposed to control the balloon so vigorously that one of them fell off. The pigeon that he took with him escaped, leaving only a cat and a dog as company. From the balloon, London looked, as Lunardi put it, like a beehive. He helped himself to a chicken leg and several glasses of wine.

Lunardi must have gone high: it was cold enough to freeze the condensation around the neck of the balloon. The cat became so distressed that he resolved to drop her off in a cornfield. He touched down among a dozen men and women

*Memorial to Vincenzo Lunardi, 'The First Aerial Traveller in Britain', at the point where he touched down at Standon Green End after 'Traversing the Regions of the Air For Two Hours and Fifteen Minutes'.*

who were harvesting oats. With the aid of a speaking trumpet, he warned them from trying to hold onto the ropes of the balloon, which was moving quickly. Contact with the ground was made for just long enough to throw the cat to a countrywoman (she promptly sold it to someone who had been following the flight). Lunardi tossed out the last of the ballast, his chickens and bottles, even his plates, knives and forks. Off he went again.

'At twenty minutes past four I descended in a meadow near Ware,' Lunardi recorded. 'Some labourers were at work in it. I requested their assistance, but they exclaimed they would have nothing to do with one who came on the Devil's Horse.' He finally owed his deliverance to a young woman, who caught hold of a cord that Lunardi threw out and told the men not to be silly.

The stone at Standon Green End records a brave venture as well as a historic one. George III, watching Lunardi as he floated above the capital, told the ministers with whom he had been in conference: 'We may resume our own deliberations at pleasure, but we may never see poor Lunardi again!'

# STEWARTBY
BEDFORDSHIRE                              *Brick village, brick county, brick country*

There is no mistaking where you are at S-T-E-W-A-R-T-B-Y. Its name is emblazoned on one of the towering chimneys of the London Brick Company. It is a brick village, established by a brickworks, for a brickworks, but on the best principles of utopian planning.

By 1900, England had become a brick country. The building material that, handmade, soft and variable, had appealed so much to the fantasy of the Tudors was now being mass-produced and shipped around the nation by the railway-wagon load. Local character suffered. But brickworks boomed, and nowhere more so than in Bedfordshire. The brickfield that Dickens describes in *Bleak House* was transient, the workers living in 'wretched hovels . . . with pigsties close to the broken windows and miserable little gardens before the doors growing nothing but stagnant pools'. Brickmakers would establish themselves next to whichever development was taking place, then move on when it had finished.

When the industry got organised, it set up permanent kilns, not near the places where the bricks were needed but where the raw material could be found. There was no better clay than that covering north Bedfordshire. In the late nineteenth century it had been discovered that, with twenty per cent moisture, it could be pressed into a mould and fired without drying. Because it contains a proportion of carbon it also required less fuel to be burnt during firing. The Bedfordshire brickfields produced most of the brick used in London's pre-Second World War expansion. Manufacturing half a billion bricks a year, Stewartby was the largest brickworks in the world.

The village there was begun by Sir Malcolm Stewart, who succeeded his father as chairman in 1924. Liberal and religious, Stewart introduced welfare and pension schemes, holidays with pay, profit sharing and workers' consultation – novel ideas, whose benefit would be proven in the low incidence of strikes. Over thirty years, Stewartby swept the hamlets of Wootton Pillinge and Wootton Broadmead off the map, replacing them with a model settlement that includes workers' houses, a united church, schools, sports ground, swimming pool, canteens, offices, a research centre and a memorial hall, with overtones of Bournville near Birmingham, the model village founded by the Cadburys in the late nineteenth century. Good architects (Albert Richardson, Oswald P. Milne, Vincent Harris) were appointed. The thin, Scandinavian classicism of the public buildings seems modern but dignified; the vernacular of the houses is reminiscent of the best days of the London County Council's architects' department, which built workers' housing estates around London.

Stewart's experience at Stewartby led him to champion, during the depressed 1930s, the Land Settlement Association, whereby the unemployed from industrial towns would be relocated on smallholdings in the countryside. This won the support of Quaker reformers, then the government. Though not popular with local people, who wanted better housing themselves and were dismayed to see outsiders being given special treatment, the idea was put into practice at Potton in Bedfordshire and Caversham outside Reading, Berkshire.

Brick production at Stewartby ended in 2008, after the chimneys, now listed, failed to meet modern emissions standards; at the time of writing, a tenant is being sought for them. But the village lives on.

*See also Creswell Model Village, page 314; New Earswick, page 429; Saltaire, page 435*

# STEWKLEY
BUCKINGHAMSHIRE                    *The Norman love affair with stone*

There could hardly be a more dramatic example of regime change than the Norman Conquest of England. William I not only swept aside the existing political structure, but imposed a culture on his new territories that in some cases overwhelmed what had been there before. By the time his youngest son, Henry I, was on the throne, its effects were being felt in hundreds of villages across England. The Saxons did not have much skill at stonemasonry, being generally content to worship in wooden churches roofed with thatch. Stone suited the Normans' hard, domineering character, and they loved it. The old Saxon churches were pulled down – some of them were no doubt falling down anyway, from neglect. New, stone-built churches arose. It has been calculated that seven thousand were built during the century after 1066.

Castles express one aspect of Norman rule: ruthless domination of the newly occupied land. But most Normans were also intensely devout, as can be seen from the scale on which they endowed monasteries and churches. The church of St Michael at Stewkley (a warlike dedication, since St Michael is a warrior angel in the fight against Satan) is one of the most complete Norman churches to come down to us. It was built in the third quarter of the twelfth century. The narrow west doorway is almost lost inside a frenzy of zigzag, chevron, rope moulding and beasts (now worn), showing off the Norman decorative repertoire to maximum effect. There was not just one arch, but three.

The embellishment extends to the interior of the church, where a zigzag string course continues round the nave and over the windows. Whereas the Saxons had entered their churches through the base of the tower, the Normans developed building technology to the point at which they could build towers over part of the nave, as at Stewkley. But since there were generally no aisles in Norman churches, it has no transepts to form a crossing.

When George Edmund Street was asked to enlarge the church 'to meet the want of accommodation for the poor' in the Victorian period, he considered lengthening the nave. This would have involved careful rebuilding of the precious west doorway, stone by stone. In the end, however, he was 'extremely glad not to have to alter the fabric at all'. A solution had been found by keeping an earlier west gallery: not without controversy at the time, given the opposition to galleries by the Ecclesiological movement, but something that should earn Street the gratitude of later generations. Street also added a handsome marble and alabaster reredos, as well as a porch: adornments that the Normans had yet to devise.

# STOKE POGES
BUCKINGHAMSHIRE                    *The rude forefathers of the hamlet sleep*

The poet Thomas Gray thought carefully about his funeral, laying down instructions in the will that he wrote a year before his death in 1771. He was not the only eighteenth-century person to do this, but had more reason than most. Having written the most famous poetical reflection on mortality in the English language, 'Elegy Written in a Country Churchyard', he knew that his body was destined to occupy a corner of the very spot where these musings were almost certainly set.

Stoke Poges, a gated driveway or two beyond the last pebble-dashed tentacle of Slough, is not as rural now as it was when Gray would visit his widowed mother and his aunt there. You are not likely to hear the lowing of cattle, far less the 'drowsy tinklings' of their bells. Instead, what sounds like a never-ending waterfall is the rushing of car tyres on Tarmac, and commuters bustle where ploughmen used to plod. But the immediate surroundings of the churchyard were saved in the burst of nostalgia for country England that followed the First World War, by conservationists who gave the adjacent fields to the National Trust. The twenty-first century can elegise, too, if it has the time.

A fellow of Peterhouse, Cambridge, Gray stayed at Stoke Poges every summer. On 12 June 1750, he sent the text of the Elegy to his friend Horace Walpole in London, saying that it was recently completed. The next year, when he got wind of a magazine's intention to publish it without his permission, he begged Walpole to have it brought out privately. His name was not attached, but the secret was soon out. The success of the poem encouraged a whole school of Graveyard Poets in their ruminations on 'skulls and coffins, epitaphs and worms', to quote one of their number, Robert Blair, in 'The Grave'.

The Elegy is a meditation on mortality, reflecting on the lives – with what potential unfulfilled? – of the anonymous villagers who have gone before. To contemporaries, it would have been made more vivid by the state of Georgian churchyards. Gray's 'Where heaves the turf in many a mouldering heap' would have seemed a decorous allusion to the physical condition that resulted from burials having repeatedly taken place in the same small area since the Middle Ages.

In the Saxon period, the dead were not always buried near the church, but consecrated ground came to seem increasingly attractive as a final resting place and by the early Middle Ages church burial had become de rigueur. Increasing village populations were not accompanied by new cemeteries. Knowledge of the location of past burials was left to tribal memory, and bodies whose whereabouts could no longer be remembered would have rotted. It meant that fresh graves cut across old ones, and gravediggers – like the one in *Hamlet* – were often turning up bones. In the eighteenth century, the churchyard at Kirkburton in Yorkshire was recorded as being 'so full thronged with graves that the sexton scarcely knew where to put down his spade'.

No wonder the better-off liked to have their graves marked by stone or slate headstones. A vault was even better. But most parishioners could not make such exclusive after-death arrangements, and churchyards remained not merely gloomy, but grisly places, until Victorian hygiene campaigners brought about reform. In his Elegy, Gray says nothing about the smell.

For his own funerary arrangements, the poet opted for the simplest possible tablet and a coffin of plain wood. Death, however, did not accommodate these plans. After he died in Cambridge at the height of a hot summer, Gray's remains were placed in a coffin whose wooden exterior was lined both with lead and a second layer of wood for the slow journey to Buckinghamshire (the cortège made two overnight stops). By the end of the century, admirers had erected a thumping stone monument by the slapdash classicist James Wyatt – the irony of which should make a poem in itself.

# THREE MILE CROSS
## BERKSHIRE
*A village in five Regency volumes*

'Of all situations for a constant residence, that which appears to me most delightful is a little village far in the country; a small neighbourhood, not of fine mansions finely peopled, but of cottages and cottage-like houses . . . with inhabitants whose faces are as familiar to us as the flowers in our garden.' With these words Mary Russell Mitford opened one of the most popular books of the Regency, *Our Village*. It is a slightly simpering account of what appears to be her life at Three Mile Cross, where every cottage is embowered in jasmine, every inhabitant is a character, and every page seems to have an exclamation mark! She popularised cottage living at a time when gentlefolk were discovering the faux simplicity of the cottage orné.

Miss Mitford may be a recherché taste today, but she gave readers whose sensibilities had been honed by the Picturesque exactly what they wanted: an account of rural life that was as pretty and decorous as a model village by Nash. When Anne Thackeray Ritchie made the journey to Three Mile Cross, three miles south of Reading, to gather material for an introduction to an edition of *Our Village* published in 1893, she couldn't believe what she found. No church, no boys eager to play cricket on the green, no pump, no winding street: instead, only a pub and a scattering of unromantic brick cottages. 'Was that all?' she asked. It is not the image that the book conveys. But Miss Mitford, in all probability, despite her protestations, would not have chosen a village life if there had been any other option. The truth is more interesting than the book. Her father was a rogue.

Born in 1787, Mary Russell Mitford was the daughter of a sometime surgeon, who called himself, on scant authority, Dr Mitford. The Russell reflected her mother's (remote) connection with the Dukes of Bedford. The doctor soon ran through his wife's money, spending it on greyhounds, high living and electioneering. The family home was auctioned, and the Mitfords took lodgings in London. On her tenth birthday, Mary was given a lottery ticket, which won her twenty thousand pounds. There was a brief return to the days of glory, as her father rebuilt a country house in the latest style. Soon that money, too, had gone. Mary, who had begun to make poems, was now reduced to write to support both herself and her parents – her father's affairs having landed him in debtor's prison. The cottage at Three Mile Cross was a sad comedown after what they had known.

No less a figure than Samuel Taylor Coleridge had recommended drama. The sketches published as *Our Village* (originally five volumes, 1824–32) were intended to smooth out the finances between productions. Having nursed her mother until the latter's death in 1830, she was then faced with looking after her father, as well as keeping him amused.

Much of her literary work was done after midnight. And so the light touch, laced with wit, of *Our Village* – 'idyllic realism', one critic has called it – is remarkable. It may be that she encouraged England to sentimentalise the village, a habit from which it is still not altogether free. But the genial twinkle with which, in semi-fiction, she faced the heavy burdens of real life sets a noble example. She grew fat. She soldiered on.

# TURVEY
BEDFORDSHIRE                    *'Wonderfully increased and improved' by lace*

The fine lace that covered the bosoms of Georgian gentlewomen came either from Honiton in Devon or the Midland counties of Buckinghamshire, Northamptonshire and Bedfordshire. Legend had it that lace-making was brought to the latter area by Catherine of Aragon, who spent the years after her divorce from Henry VIII at Ampthill. Certainly lace-makers were still keeping 25 November as 'Cattern's Day' into the Victorian period. At a time when trade was slack, Catherine and her ladies were supposed to have ordered all their old lace to be burnt, so that they could support the industry by buying new. A more prosaic but historically more plausible explanation is that the craft, like that of straw-plaiting for hats, which was practised in the same countryside, was introduced by French immigrants fleeing religious persecution in the second half of the sixteenth century.

Touring Britain in the 1720s, Daniel Defoe found that 'Thro' the whole South Part of this County, as far as the borders of Buckinghamshire and Hertfordshire, the People are taken up with the Manufacture of Bone lace, in which they are wonderfully increased and improved.' For the next century and a half, on summer evenings when cottage doors were left open, every female in a village such as Turvey could be glimpsed at work on her pillow, wooden bobbins deftly twisting clever patterns out of the thread. The activity stood the area in good stead during the hungry 1790s, when other parts of the country suffered the pain of high food prices. Together with straw-plaiting, it provided a supplement to labouring wages that became increasingly necessary in the first half of the next century. It has been estimated that lace-making gave employment to 140,000 women throughout the Midlands alone.

Times were good for English lace-makers during the wars with France, although foreign imports began again after 1815. The Victorian period saw the village improve as the local landowners replaced collapsing thatched cottages with better ones, and a 'handsome' school was built after the 1870s Education Act. Until then, girls had not learnt much beyond their craft, sitting, from the age of seven or eight, in rows in the village's lace schools. But the invention of lace-making machinery, producing coarser but cheaper lace, sent the cottage industry into decline, what little the lace women could make often reduced further by greedy dealers. By the end of the century, straw-plaiting had also collapsed, killed by – who would have thought it? – imports from the Far East.

# WEST HANNEY
OXFORDSHIRE                                              *Oh yes they did*

In the Hanney War Memorial Hall, Mike Page waits patiently in his red and blue spotted dress. Bright red circles are being applied to his cheeks, and the *tout ensemble* will soon be topped off with a baroquely luminous blue wig. Working in payroll and accounts by day, he is Dame Busybody by night. Every one of the week's four performances is sold out. Dancing, stock characters, make-believe, cross-dressing, corny jokes, hissing, magic pumpkins and beans – the pantomime season is upon us, and the Hanney Drama Group's production of *Cinderella Climbs the Beanstalk and Meets Dick Whittington* shows that this ancient and argu-ably great British tradition is alive and well.

Oh no it isn't. Dame Busybody has a gripe. She cannot throw her jelly babies into the audience. Health and Safety thinks that the public must be protected from projectile sweets, particularly those of an unwrapped nature. Which is just about typical, the doomsayers mutter. Pantomime began in the Regency, an unbuttoned, three-bottles-at-dinner age, short on home entertainment. It does not fit into a politically correct modern world, its sense of wonder killed by computer games and wall-mounted televisions. Commercial productions spend too much money on soap stars and not enough on scenery or script. Around this time of year, you are likely to see, hear or read at least one pundit, probably Gyles Brandreth, declaring that the tradition of pantomime is tottering.

But do you know what, boys and girls, they're wrong, aren't they? Because the spirit of panto has only gone into hiding. It may have fled the West End, but it lives on in hundreds of village halls around Britain. In Hethersett, Norfolk, they combined *Jack and the Beanstalk* with robots, *Dr Who* and Norfolk humour. In Somerset's Quantock Hills, Stogumber's Wild West production, *There's Gold in Them Thar Hills*, transported Widow Twankey to the Klondike. The Malborough Amateur Dramatic Group from the village of Malborough, near Salcombe in Devon, goes by the acronym of MAD. But after five shows of *Beauty and the Beast* (to a hall seating 230, on raked seats), who would not be?

# WOBURN
BEDFORDSHIRE                                    *The first agricultural shows*

According to Edmund Burke, the lands belonging to the 5th Duke of Bedford were 'more extensive than the territory of many of the Grecian republics; and they are without comparison more fertile than most of them'. The Duke wanted to make them more fertile still, being one of the foremost agricultural improvers of his age. He was born in 1765. Although some landowners had been enclosing open fields and common lands since the Tudor period, much of England was still farmed as it had been for centuries. Manure from the herds and flocks grazing on wastes was not collected. Farmers followed the three-crop rotation – winter grain followed by spring crops, then fallow – that had been practised since Anglo-Saxon times.

It has been suggested that the poverty of aristocrats returning to England after Charles II's Restoration in 1660 spurred them on to find ways of increasing their revenues. Scientifically minded agriculturalists from Scotland started to migrate south after the union of the crowns in 1707. Books were published, written by men such as the parson Stephen Hales, author of *Vegetable Staticks* (1727), who advocated methods based on observation and research rather than custom. They were of little use to most farmers, who could not read. So it was all the more important for educated gentlemen to spread the word about the new farming methods. By the end of the century, when war with France threatened food shortages, what had seemed like a rewarding interest for progressive landowners became nothing less than a patriotic duty.

With men such as Coke of Norfolk, Bedford helped raise British farming to a position of supremacy that was admired throughout Europe. His platform was Woburn Abbey, where he commissioned Henry Holland to create new farm buildings in the novel (for polite architecture) material of *pisé de terre*, or rammed earth, painted to look like stone. He had five more farms built by other architects. These works provided the necessary background for his agricultural improvements.

Every year, Bedford, like Coke, would invite the countryside to witness what he had done. These Sheep Shearings were the forerunners of agricultural shows, an opportunity for landowners and farmers to see the latest agrarian ideas in action. What was then the market town of Woburn must have heaved with excitement; a Sheep Shearing might be attended by several hundred people. Although it had no fewer than twenty-one pubs, the Duke upgraded the George Inn (now Inn at Woburn).

The *Farmer's Magazine* describes the Sheep Shearing held in the summer of 1800. Royalty, in the portly shape of the Duke of Gloucester, rolled in, and 'the company proceeded, in a grand cavalcade, to the New Farm-Yard, in the park' to inspect the sheep: improved breeding was possible in closed flocks and herds, rather than those that had ranged communally – and promiscuously – on the open fields. There followed showings of fine cattle and prodigious hogs, the demonstration of a threshing machine and 'experiments' with ploughs, the exhibition of the loin of a prize three-year-old wether of 1799, on which 'the fat measured seven inches' and – this being the estate of a Regency grandee – the taking of several bets about different beasts. It was a 'truly rational Agricultural Fete'.

There would be few to come after the Duke's unexpected death following a hernia incurred while playing tennis in 1802, on which his brother, the epicurean 6th Duke inherited, but Woburn showed the way that farms and villages throughout Britain would follow during several decades of prosperity – prosperity, that is, for everyone in the countryside except the old peasant class.

# EASTERN
# ENGLAND

ESSEX IS apt to surprise. People who know only the Essex that abuts London would be amazed at the loneliness of the mudflats and marshes, or to know that it may have the longest coastline of any English county. While the Communist vicar of Thaxted (see page 271) was reinventing folk traditions at the beginning of the twentieth century, a maker of metal-framed windows was building the modernist village of Silver End (see page 266). There have been rebels and utopians in Essex, conservatives and cockneys, their personalities often reflected in the villages that they created or came from. Great Bentley (see page 239) has Britain's largest village green.

Suffolk grew rich on wool during the Middle Ages, but when the trade fell off it had to farm for its living. The landscape that was painted, almost obsessively, by John Constable was an agricultural one. While Constable's father, a miller, did well enough, it was hard to win much from the land, particularly along the coastal strip (until recently, when people started to grow vegetables on it). Poverty bred Dissent, an elegant expression of which is seen at Walpole (see page 276); almshouses, such as those at Long Melford (see page 257), provided relief for some paupers. As late as 1930, when Adrian Bell published *Corduroy*, the rural dialect could seem impenetrable to outsiders. To some of the artists who came to Suffolk, the county's backwardness had charm.

While Suffolk villages, particularly in the eastern part of the county, are often scattered, those of Norfolk tend to be large and nucleated, a reflection of medieval prosperity. Norfolk would become a county of great estates, densely stocked with churches – some of them now standing alone in the fields because their villages have gone. This is a man-made landscape, farmed on a big scale. The reed-fringed waters of the Norfolk Broads result from a different form of human activity: peat-digging in the early Middle Ages. Flint, the only building stone, is seen everywhere, sometimes mixed with the orangey-red brick that became popular under the Tudors. There were good reeds for thatching, unless a roof of pantiles was preferred.

Rich farmland, straight drainage ditches, the peace of a hazy afternoon shattered only by the sudden roar of an RAF plane en route to a bombing range on the coast: that is Lincolnshire. The black earth of the fens did not yield much in the way of building materials, and so mud and stud – a kind of wattle and daub – became the vernacular in some parts; a survival can be seen at Little Steeping (see page 256). There are two Cambridgeshires. Samuel Pepys visited watery Parson Drove, near the Wash, and did not like it (see page 259). But in the booming south of the county, Little Gidding (see page 252) is an oasis of spirituality.

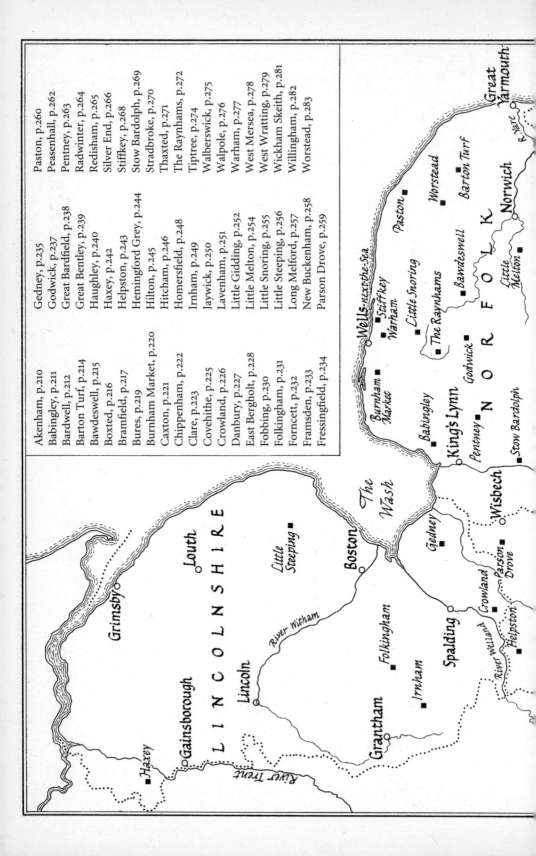

NORFOLK

Great Yarmouth
R. Yare
Worstead
Barton Turf
Norwich
Little Melton
Paston
Bawdeswell
The Raynhams
Little Snoring
Godwick
Wells-next-the-Sea
Stiffkey
Warham
Burnham Market
Babingley
King's Lynn
Pentney
Stow Bardolph
Wisbech

The Wash

LINCOLNSHIRE

Grimsby
Louth
Little Steeping
Boston
Gedney
Parson Drove
Gainsborough
Lincoln
River Witham
Folkingham
Irnham
Spalding
Crowland
Helpston
River Welland
Grantham
Haxey
River Trent

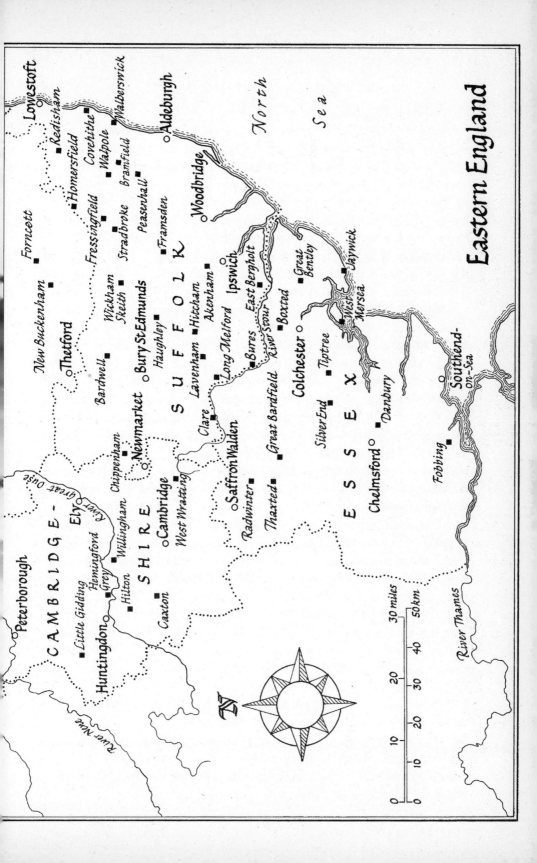

Eastern England

North Sea

Lowestoft
Redisham
Homersfield
Covehithe
Walpole
Walberswick
Bramfield
Aldeburgh
Forncett
Fressingfield
Stradbroke
Peasenhall
Woodbridge
Framsden
New Buckenham
Wickham Skeith
Thetford
S U F F O L K
Bardwell
Haughley
Bury St Edmunds
Ipswich
East Bergholt
Akenham
Great Bentley
Jaywick
Chippenham
Newmarket
Lavenham
Hitcham
Long Melford
Bures
Boxted
River Stour
West Mersea
C A M B R I D G E -
S H I R E
Willingham
Cambridge
Clare
Saffron Walden
Great Bardfield
Colchester
Tiptree
Peterborough
Little Gidding
Hemingford Grey
Hilton
West Wratting
Radwinter
Thaxted
Silver End
Danbury
Huntingdon
Caxton
E S S E X
Chelmsford
Great Ouse
River Nene
Ely
River Cam
Fobbing
Southend-on-Sea
River Thames

N

30 miles
50 km
0  10  20  30  40
0  10  20  30

# AKENHAM

The turning to Akenham is just outside the boundary of Ipswich, but you would not know it: despite the pylons striding across the cornfields in companionable pairs, this is a place of such impenetrable rurality that there is not even a sign. You reach the little church of St Mary down an unmade track. An undercurrent of aggression may haunt the nearby housing estate at Whitton, one of Suffolk's biggest, but Akenham itself seems as withdrawn as it must have been in the nineteenth century. In 1878, however, it leapt to prominence in a highly regrettable way: an argument over the burial of a two-year-old child, Joseph Ramsey. As the son of Baptists, who believe in adult baptism, he had not been baptised; a clergyman of the Church of England, in this case Father George Drury, could not say the burial service in the churchyard.

The Church of England's monopoly over burial rites was unfair. But tensions with Dissenters had been mounting: in 1872, the Bishop of Lincoln refused one of his clergy to allow the title of 'Reverend' to be applied to the headstone of a Methodist minister, thereby precipitating a pamphlet war. Internal tensions within the Church of England were also being felt. Drury signalled his position by espousing the title 'Father'; he was an Anglo-Catholic, whose Rome-leaning style of worship would have seemed papistical to many in the pews. He put candles and a cross for the altar, and preferred the word Mass to Communion. His brother, Father Ignatius, had already scandalised by founding a nunnery at Claydon, next to Akenham, where Father George also officiated. Father George was in trouble with his Bishop; so much so that the Bishop had approved the appointment of a local landowner, Mr Smith of Rise Hall, as church warden, even though he belonged to a Congregational church in Ipswich.

On the day of the burial, Father George found a group of twenty or thirty people standing outside the churchyard, while the Congregationalist minister the Rev. Wickham Tozer conducted the service. What happened next is not certain. Father George's intention, he said, was to escort the coffin into the churchyard. According to the burial party, he attempted to break up the service. Disgusted, Father George stalked back to his rectory, locking the iron gate to the churchyard behind him. The story got about that the child's coffin was left standing at the gate for weeks. In fact, the Rev. Tozer took the burial party onto the consecrated ground through a hedge. Soon afterwards, the *East Anglian Daily Times* published a full account of the proceedings. Obloquy was heaped on Father George.

It was not, however, one-sided. There were strong suspicions that the brouhaha had been anticipated, indeed provoked. It turned out that the Rev. Tozer was not the Ramseys' regular minister; he had probably been brought in because of his known connections with the press. Besides, what were so many people doing at an infant's burial? Such events were commonplace in Victorian England: ten of the Rev. Tozer's own children had died.

Elizabeta nat Calhot    Elizabeta nat Tilney

Ducissa Rorfoltia    ur Thome howard

glass from Holy Trinity church in Long Melford, Suffolk, showing two Elizabeths: chess of Norfolk and the Countess of Suffolk. The former is said to have been the for John Tenniel's Duchess in *Alice's Adventures in Wonderland*. (See page 257.)

BLAISE HAMLET,

To John S. Harford Esq.<sup>r</sup> of Blaise Castle

Picturesque and beautiful Dwellings are Erected.

Gloucestershire in whose Grounds these

this Plate is most respectfully inscribed by

The Publisher.

Pub<sup>d</sup> by George Davey Bookseller Broad S<sup>t</sup> Bristol

John Harford, the Quaker owner of Blaise Castle in Gloucestershire, created a hamlet to house widows and other 'decayed persons' in 1810–11; under the hand of John Nash, presiding genius of Picturesque architecture, each dwelling became a different variation on the cottage theme, with dormers, porches, pigeon lofts and a crescendo of roofing effects in thatch. (See page 302.)

*Opposite above*: The Lizard lifeboat in the 1890s. Lifeboat crews are drawn from families who have been seafarers for generations. (See page 53.)

*Opposite below*: The romance of St Michael's Mount, Cornwall, which can be reached by land only when the tide is out. Beneath the castle grappled to the rock was a village that once had three pubs. (See page 69.)

Once, watercress was sold throughout London as a snack; Broad Chalke in Wiltshire is one of few villages where it is still commercially grown – a testament to the purity of its water. (See page 19.)

Thomas Hardy's 'immutable' Weatherbury in *Far from the Madding Crowd* was based on Puddletown, Dorset. This watercolour by Ernest Haslehust, 1910, shows it with thatched roofs and sheep. (See page 64.)

Not everybody in the congregation of Berwick Church, East Sussex, was pleased to see the Bloomsbury set decorating it while their own men folk were at the front. The baby Jesus was modelled on the three-year-old Quentin Bell; each of the two local shepherds has only one arm. (See page 94.)

The airship R100, brother to the R101, built at Cardington in Bedfordshire, shown next to the tower to which it was tethered. Each of the crafts contained 140,000 cubic metres of hydrogen. With an average speed of 63 miles an hour, they were intended to open routes within the Empire, such as London to Bombay. (See page 167.)

N:1                    London. Publish'd Sep.r 29.t 1809. by H. Humphrey S.t James's Street.

The Life of WILLIAM-COBBETT, _written by himself_
_ " Now you lying Varlets, you shall see how a plain Tale will put you down ! "

1st Plate.

Father kept the sign of the Jolly-Farmer at Farnham. I was his Pot Boy
and thought an Ornament to the profession, _ at Seven Years Old my
natural genius began to expand, and display'd itself in a taste for Plunder
and oppression :_ I robbed Orchards, set Father's Bull Dog at the Cats._
quarelled with all the Poor-Boys, and beat all the little Girls of the
Town,_ to the great admiration of the inhabitants;_who prophecied
that my talents (unless the Devil was in it.) would one day elevate me
to a Post in some publick situation _

Vide : My own Memoirs
in the Political Register of 1809.

The great journalist William Cobbett bought a farm at Botley, in
Hampshire, where he promoted country sports. This cartoon by
Gillray shows him as a boy, outside his parents' pub at Farnham
in Surrey. The sign reads: 'Ye olde jolly farmer' in anticipation of
Cobbett's later character as a champion of British agriculture.
(See page 97.)

The Southdown sheep was bred by the tenant farmer John Ellman of Place Farm in Glynde, East Sussex. Square and chunky, it produced not only good mutton but also wool. (See page 118.)

The Village Church in Rottingdean, East Sussex, painted by Philip, son of Sir Edward Burne-Jones, in 1891. Sir Edward and his wife Georgie settled at Rottingdean after Fulham became too crowded. They were joined by Rudyard Kipling and his cousin, the future prime minister Stanley Baldwin. (See page 140.)

As head of the British Women's Temperance Association, Lady Isabella Somerset built a Colony for Women Inebriates at Duxhurst, outside Reigate in Surrey, in 1895. (See page 110.)

Galley & Chater *falling off their Horse at Woodash, draggs thier Heads on the Ground, while the Horse kicks them as he goes; the Smugglers still continuing thier brutish Usage.*

There were at least 250 smuggling ships operating around Britain in the late eighteenth century. One of the most notorious of the gangs was based at Hawkhurst in Kent; they are shown here perpetrating 'brutish Usage' on an unfortunate customs officer and informant who fell into their clutches. (See page 124.)

This still from the 1964 film *Goldfinger* shows the golf match between James Bond and villain Auric Goldfinger. Ian Fleming modelled the fictional course on Royal St George's, Sandwich, of which he was about to made captain when he died. One of many other places in Kent that he wove into the story is Reculver; it was there that Goldfinger had his home. (See page 139.)

Kenneth Grahame was inspired to write *The Wind in the Willows* by his childhood at Cookham Dean, Berkshire, where he was brought up by his grandmother. This illustration by Arthur Rackham from the 1940 edition evokes the mood of the landscape that Grahame knew. (See page 169.)

In January 1769 James Eaves, his wife and two young children starved to death in the poor house at Datchworth in Hertfordshire. This horrifying woodcut comes from a pamphlet published to shame the authorities. (See page 171.)

The poet Thomas Gray is buried at Stoke Poges, Buckinghamshire, where he was inspired to compose 'Elegy Written in a Country Churchyard' in 1750. By the end of the eighteenth century, admirers had erected a giant stone monument by James Wyatt. (See page 198.)

The bridge at Sonning in Berkshire, 'the glory of this exceptionally picturesque and well-ordered village', according to the Pre-Raphaelite painter William Holman Hunt who lived

Around 1330, Sir Geoffrey Luttrell of Irnham in Lincolnshire commissioned a book of psalms, whose margins teem with scenes of everyday life; here, ploughing (above) and peasants bringing in the harvest (below). The latter accompanies psalm 95, verse 12: 'The fields and all in them rejoice'. (See page 249.)

Lettuces growing on the Fenland soil of Gedney in Lincolnshire. They could not be harvested without migrant labour, these days coming from Russia and Eastern Europe. Over the years, other temporary labour has come from Ireland, the East End of London and, during the miners' strike, the Yorkshire coalfields. (See page 235.)

Edward Bawden (1903–89) lived at Great Bardfield in Suffolk and often took the village as his subject. Here he shows back gardens, with a policeman taking an interest in some sheds. Although Bawden had an eye for decorative effects and Victoriana, he was also a realist, who faithfully recorded a slow-moving, old-fashioned world. (See page 238.)

Little Snoring, Norfolk, was transformed during the Second World War when the airfield was built. Successes against enemy aircraft are recorded on tablets in the church. (See page 255.)

Francis Crittall, whose company made metal-framed windows, established the Modern Movement village of Silver End in Essex with 'an artesian well, modern drainage, electric light, a communal laundry, a cinema, a restaurant, our (I mean your) Co-operative Society, sports, games, playgrounds for adults and for children'. Flat roofs, boxy profiles and corner windows created a machine-age aesthetic. (See page 266.)

Between the wars, Thaxted in Essex was a centre for the revival of folk music and morris dancing – classless, communal traditions that appealed strongly to socialists such as the vicar Conrad Noel, friend of another Thaxted resident, Gustav Holst. (See page 271.)

Father George sued the newspaper for libel and won, but he received no more than two pounds plus costs. The Dissenters carried their point. The Burial Laws Amendment Act was passed in 1880 to guarantee access to consecrated ground with or without the services of any Christian church or denomination. Death had joined the free market.

St Mary's church is now unused, its churchyard forlorn: a notice warns potential thieves against stealing the lead.

# BABINGLEY
## NORFOLK
*Any old iron?*

In 1828, Henry Robinson Palmer invented what would become a favourite rural building material: corrugated iron. Writing *An Encyclopaedia of Cottage, Farmhouse and Villa Architecture and Furniture* in 1839, the progressive John Claudius Loudon* was enthusiastic: 'for barns, sheep-houses, and various other country buildings, and for all manner of sheds, both in town and country, it is particularly suitable,' he opined. It could also be used for cottages: he recommended corrugated iron for roofs, door panels and flues.

Even the ever-practical Loudon, however, did not foresee the application that most fully exploited its capabilities – complete buildings in the form of mass-produced corrugated-iron kits. The Phoenix Iron Works came up with this development in 1844. Across the Empire, new frontiers were being conquered, creating a demand for buildings that could be erected cheaply and quickly, without skilled labour. Anything from a pigsty to a cathedral could be made from corrugated iron; in 1854, thirty thousand kit buildings were shipped to Australia alone.

They did not suit the climate perfectly. Once the trade had been interrupted by the Crimean War, Australians had time to reflect that timber construction might be cooler. Still, the trade to other parts of the Empire continued, as a glance at the brightly painted rum shops of the Caribbean confirms. Corrugated iron was the dominant building material of the California Gold Rush of 1849, and returned to prominence after the San Francisco earthquake and fire of 1906.

Meanwhile, in Britain, the demand for coal and iron that boomed during the Victorian period created a need for instant buildings in out-of-the-way places, such as the Welsh valleys and Durham coalfields. The cheapness and durability of corrugated-iron sheeting also appealed to farmers during the agricultural depression that began in the 1870s. The sight of rusting barn roofs would, for aesthetes and conservationists, blight country walks for a century to come.

But the church of St Mary and St Felix at Babingley shows that corrugated iron can also have charm. It stands on the Sandringham estate. There had been a church at Babingley since the Middle Ages, as befitted the spot where, by tradition, St Felix the Burgundian made landfall on his mission to convert the East Angles to Christianity in the seventh century. But by the time the future Edward VII, as Prince of Wales, acquired the estate in 1862, it had fallen into ruin. Besides, like many Norfolk churches, it stood by itself among fields, the village having migrated to the main road.

'Up to the last year of his life he was continually improving his domain, repairing churches, spending money on the place in one way or another,' a friend remembered of Edward VII after his death in 1910. Babingley's chance came in 1880. But instead of rebuilding the old church, the Prince constructed a new one, in what was then a more convenient location, and he built it out of a kit. Boulton and Paul of Norwich were probably the manufacturers. They supplied a cruciform structure, of the kind known as a tin tabernacle. By a stroke of genius, the agent at Sandringham had it thatched.

In recent years, the Church of England found it surplus to requirements in this county of many churches. However, it has found a new congregation in the British Orthodox church, an association of the Eastern orthodox churches, whose numbers were swelled by dissident Anglicans after the established Church's decision to ordain women as priests.

*See Great Tew, page 177

# BARDWELL
## SUFFOLK

*Blowing in the wind*

Bardwell has a windmill. There were ten thousand across Britain in their eighteenth-century heyday. Now those that still have sails and machinery number just a few hundred. Twentieth-century millers, such as the one in Adrian Bell's *Corduroy**, could not wait to be shot of the temperamental technology of the wind machine, preferring a diesel engine. Yet in more susceptible hearts, windmills arouse strong feelings of fascination and romance. Villages take pride in having one.

While more than five thousand watermills are mentioned in the Domesday Book, the windmill had yet to appear. It is thought to have reached these shores in the twelfth century, perhaps via the Middle East, where the wind had been harnessed for centuries. Conditions in Britain meant that the sails had to be large, in order to catch enough wind on still days, yet the whole structure had to be strong enough to withstand storms and gales. As a result, windmills stood out prominently in the landscape.

The earliest were built around massive central posts. These post mills acquired wooden cabins, known as bucks, which provided a sheltered space for the miller to work. The whole superstructure could be turned to face the wind, above a base of brick or stone. In the seventeenth century, the smock mill, taking its name from the bell-shaped miller's smock, was introduced from Holland. In this, the sails were attached only to the topmost 'cap' of the mill, which was the single part that

*The glory to which the windmill at Bardwell is being restored.*

turned; it was guided, from the mid eighteenth century, by a fantail, a small set of blades at the back of the cap. Smock mills are generally of wooden construction. Tower mills, built of brick, could be taller, a particular requirement in the nineteenth century, when milling was done on a bigger scale, with competition from steam.

As the windmill's commercial importance declined, its appeal as an aesthetic landmark grew. 'One of the loveliest sights I know is that of a windmill at work, the sails turning steadily against a blue sky'. So opens Rex Wailes's *The English Windmill* (1954). The Society for the Protection of Ancient Buildings formed a Mills Section in 1931. Increasingly, traditional milling attracts a public disenchanted with factory-produced flour and bread. But the road to restoration is not necessarily a smooth one.

At Bardwell, the conical black tower mill, prettily topped with a white headdress of cap and fantail, has been undergoing its second restoration. The first had only just begun when the 1987 hurricane tore off the wooden cap and sails. Enid

Wheeler and her late husband, Geoffrey, had to start again. Readers who took the *Eagle* during the 1960s will be familiar with Geoffrey's work as a draftsman: he drew the cutaway pictures of steam trains for that serious-minded comic. A windmill suited his passion for machinery.

The Bardwell mill was built in 1823, the shutters of the sails being adjusted by a central mechanism that worked even as the sails turned. At the time of writing, two sails, made of wooden shutters, have been completed, while a third is laid out beneath the lean-to roof of a workshop; it is hoped that this will soon be in place. Then milling will resume, accompanied by its satisfying soundtrack of wooden creaks and knocks.

Bardwell is a perfectly modern village. But one foot seems to have become wedged in the past. A field at the entrance appears to have been planted with dilapidated lorries and other motor vehicles, among which pigs run. There is a double-decker bus parked hard up against Bardwell Hall on the other side of the road, not to the improvement of its looks. But then, Bardwell would have its peculiarities – it was used as a location for *Dad's Army*.

*See Redisham, page 265

# BARTON TURF
## NORFOLK
*The origin of the Broads*

The second part of Barton Turf's name seems likely to derive from what was the Norfolk Broads' principal industry: turf-cutting, or digging peat. It was this activity that formed the watery landscape in the first place. The Broads themselves – lakes – appear not to have existed at all in the early Middle Ages, since they are not mentioned as place names. Instead, there was a wide river estuary, whose flooding in the remote past had caused the conditions in which collapsed freshwater vegetation could form peat.

Norfolk was a well-populated county with a high demand for fuel. This was supplied by peat, dug out of the turbaries (turf-cutting areas) using long-handled spades. Some parishes were producing two hundred thousand turves a year in the 1260s, yet Norwich Cathedral alone was consuming twice this volume in its kitchens. Peat-digging was a right of common. The people of Barton Turf must have done well on it, to judge from the size of the church.

In time, when the best peat was used up, they went lower, digging up mud and sand together with semi-decomposed vegetation; they shaped this material into bricks and dried it – it would still burn. Then, perhaps as the result of terrible storms, the peat workings flooded. This is when fishing starts to be mentioned in the documents. The landscape had formed into the pattern of lakes, connected by rivers, that we know as the Norfolk Broads.

To anyone in a sailing boat, the Broads may seem idyllically natural, but a number of features proclaim them as man-made. The sides of the lakes do not shelve gently as they would if they were the remains of an open estuary that had silted up; instead, they are strikingly steep. Little islands sometimes cross the lakes, and when one is joined to another, they form a straight line. These are the remains of baulks of turf that were left between the peat workings. They correspond to boundaries: the part-submerged ridge in Barton Broad appears to mark the boundary between two parishes, each with a right to dig peat. It has been calculated that, to form the Broads, nine billion cubic feet of peat must have been removed, an astonishing volume but not impossible, given that the industry persisted for three hundred years.

After the early fourteenth century, the area lost its most valuable resource, and Barton Turf shrivelled into a hamlet. It took half a millennium for the next big thing to arrive: tourism.

# BAWDESWELL
## NORFOLK                                          *The legacy of war*

Shortly before nine on the night of 6 November 1944, Bawdeswell was riddling its fires and thinking of bed. There were clouds overhead, and the middle of Norfolk must have seemed as safe as it was possible to be, now that the Allies were fighting their way into Germany. It was then, however, that an RAF Mosquito bomber, limping home to Downham Market after a raid on Gelsenkirchen, crashed into the centre of the village.

Aerial warfare destroyed more of London, Coventry and other cities on which the ferocity of the Blitz was concentrated, than rural areas, but villages were not immune. The first building on mainland Britain to be damaged in the Second World War was the Argyll Hotel in Bellochantuy (by a British test pilot trying out the machine guns on his plane, rather than enemy action). German planes soon appeared over Devon, dropping bombs and strafing ferries*. Kent suffered collateral damage while the Battle of Britain raged overhead – villages such as Smarden and Bearsted were hit by V1 'buzz' bombs and V2 rockets, falling short of their intended target of London. The toll on the countryside increased as the War drew to an end and the Luftwaffe found it increasingly difficult to penetrate British defences. Bombers scattered their payloads over the countryside before turning back. Most fell in fields, but some unlucky people were killed. At Bawdeswell, only the aircrew lost their lives. But the crash destroyed the parish church.

Bawdeswell is an ancient village. Chaucer made it the home of the Reeve in *The Canterbury Tales*. On the road between Norwich and Fakenham, it acquired four coaching inns as well as a toll house for the turnpike trust. The church had been medieval. It might have been replaced by a modern structure. But East Anglia, in the twentieth century, was a bastion of architectural conservatism. In Constable's Stour valley, Dedham became home to the architect Raymond Erith, whose vigilance and design skills, later reinforced by those of his partner Quinlan Terry, ensured that the little town remained one of the most harmonious in the country.

At Bawdeswell, the architect chosen to rebuild the church was James Fletcher-Watson, better known as a watercolourist who followed in the Norwich School tradition of John Sell Cotman. He had grown up in Norfolk. During the War, he used his architectural training to build runways in Burma for General Slim. An uncle, Cecil Upcher, was also an architect, with a practice in Norwich, and he joined it. The design he made for Bawdeswell is a pleasing essay in restrained classicism, its simplicity recalling the churches of New England, though with flint walls that anchor it securely to Norfolk. These were, on the whole, dark days for British architecture, and Bawdeswell must have considered itself pretty lucky to have obtained such an elegant result.

Fortunately, the countryside did not lose many buildings during the Second World War. The great legacy lay in the fields. Britain had been given a scare, when, having allowed farming to fall into the doldrums during the 1930s, it found a U-boat fleet threatening to cut off imports of food. There followed the most concerted drive to maximise agricultural production that Britain has ever known. It continued into the 1970s. Ponds were drained, downland ploughed up, hedgerows ripped out, nitrate fertilisers and pesticides sprayed on. Insect life was eliminated, and with nothing to feed on, farmland birds were pushed to the edge of extinction. In recent years, the landscape has recovered something of its former vitality, but there remains a long way to go.

*See Churston Ferrers, page 27

# BOXTED

ESSEX                                            *Onward, Christian settlers*

George Herring, born in 1832, was an unlikely friend of the Salvation Army. Having perhaps begun life as a carver of boiled beef in the City of London, he built up a huge fortune as a bookmaker. Towards the end of his life, however, he became a philanthropist. Like General Booth, the Salvation Army's founder, he believed (in the words of the novelist H. Rider Haggard, a Salvation Army Commissioner) 'that many of the great and patent evils of our civilisation result from the desertion of the land by its inhabitants, and that crowding into cities which is one of the most marked phenomena of our time'. To find an alternative, he offered Booth a hundred thousand pounds. With it Booth bought a four-hundred-acre farm at Boxted, three miles from Colchester; it was divided into sixty-seven smallholdings varying from four and a half to seven acres each. Herring was able to inspect the site shortly before his death in 1906.

From religious crusading, Booth had turned increasingly to social work of a Christian hue. Having witnessed the numbers of rough sleepers on the bridges of

London, he wrote *In Darkest England and the Way Out* (1890). He estimated that three hundred thousand people were starving in London, and half a million in dire want. The Salvation Army had already opened a shelter where women could sleep, wash, eat, sew, knit and attend the Army's 'rollicking' version of evening service. Shelters were now opened for homeless men, where a condition of breakfast was going to church. Such measures could only be palliatives. One of the problems, as Booth saw it, was London itself. There were too many people. Those who did not have work fell into abject destitution.

There had been attempts to found smallholding communities before, notably by the Chartist leader Feargus O'Connor in the 1840s*. With the possible exception of Whiteway, the Tolstoyan community in the Cotswolds (see page 363), none of them had been a conspicuous success. Where Boxted would be different was in the selection procedure. Only good workers, of good moral character, were approved. Most of them were married; sensibly, it was expected that they should have country backgrounds, and have kept in touch with vegetable growing through working allotments. Total abstention from alcohol was de rigueur. The families moved into well-built, three-bedroom cottages, grouped in pairs, with a tool house, pigsty and a chicken house that could be moved around on wheels.

Rider Haggard interviewed the settlers, chosen at random, and found them 'happy and hopeful'. 'I should like to point out,' he wrote, 'that this venture is one of great and almost of national importance, because if it fails then it will be practically proved that it is impossible to establish smallholders on the land by artificial means, at any rate in England, and at the present prices of agricultural produce.' Alas, it did fail. There were 'ugly scenes', according to the *Victoria County History* of Essex, when some smallholders were evicted for non-payment of rent in 1912. In 1916, the estate was sold to Essex County Council, which intended to use it to resettle servicemen after the First World War. Elsewhere in Essex, Booth's vision lives on. The Farm Colony that he established around Hadleigh Castle in 1891 still continues, despite the unpromising character of the land; it is being revitalised as an organic community farm, supplying Marks and Spencer with beef from its Hereford herd. It will be the site of the Mountain Bike races during the 2012 Olympic Games.

*See Dodford, page 317

# BRAMFIELD
SUFFOLK                                          *Lapidary lives*

Bridgett Applewhaite died in 1737, after an unhappy life and miserable end. She is the sort of anonymous gentlewoman about whom we would know nothing of interest, were it not for the information recorded on her memorial inside Bramfield church. Memorials and tombstones, particularly if their epitaphs are written with unselfconscious sincerity, form an archive of the otherwise forgotten.

In the Middle Ages, only the rich were able to afford inscriptions carved onto stone. The middle rank of medieval society – priests, gentry and wool merchants – made do with incised brasses, laid into the wall or floor of the church; today we have more of them than any other country in Europe. The poor had no memorial at all, their bodies being buried one on top of the other until the surface of the tussocky graveyard rose several feet above the surrounding level*.

Tombstones became more frequent in the seventeenth century, and the application of epitaphs to them had become sufficiently common by 1631 for John Weever, in *Ancient Funerall Monuments Within the United Monarchie of Great Britaine and Ireland*, to suggest rules: the composition should list 'the name, the age, the deserts, the dignities, the state, the praises both of body and mind, the good or bad fortunes in the life, and the manner and time of the death, of the person therein interred'. During the next two hundred and fifty years, the bare facts of existence were often used to draw morals, quite possibly in verse. But occasionally the vivid light of lived experience broke through. 'These four youths were suddenly called into eternity on Tuesday the 6th day of April 1819', records a tombstone in Little Dean, in the Forest of Dean, a coal-mining area, 'the link of a chain employed to lower them into Bilston Pit breaking they were precipitated to the Bottom of the Pit'.

Bridgett Applewhaite's epitaph begins with an account of the 'Fatigues of a Married Life/Borne by her with Incredible Patience/for Four Years and three Quarters, bating three Weeks'. The death of her husband bestowed 'the Enjoiment of the Glorious Freedom/Of an Easy and Unblemisht' Widowhood', but after four years she was tempted to 'run the Risk of a Second Marriage-Bed'. Then disaster struck:

> Death forbad the Banns –
> And having with an Apoplectick Dart
> (The same Instrument with which he had Formerly
> Dispatch't her Mother)
> Touch't the most Vital part of her Brain;
> She must have fallen Directly to the Ground,
> (as one Thunder-strook)
> If she had not been Catch't and Supported
> by her Intended Husband.
> Of which Invisible Bruise,
> After a Struggle for above Sixty Hours,
> With that Grand Enemy to Life,
> (But the certain, and Merciful Friend to Helpless Old Age,)
> In Terrible Convulsions Plaintive Groans, or Stupefying Sleep,
> Without Recovery of her Speech, or Senses,
> She Dyed . . .

It is a grim story, told in a little more detail than the twenty-first century may feel entirely comfortable with, although it is the very candour of the account that stirs us to feel a common humanity with poor Bridgett. There is no pious reflection about her religious faith or hopes for salvation. Those things came later in the eighteenth century, once the natural phlegm of the Church of England had been stirred up by Methodism and the Sunday School movement†.

*See Stoke Poges, page 198. † See Painswick, page 344*

# BURES
SUFFOLK                                                      *Village fit for a king*

Outside Bures is St Stephen's Chapel. It was looted at the time of the Reformation and left derelict: the cult of St Edmund, ninth-century king of the East Angles, had attracted such enormous wealth to the Abbey of Bury St Edmunds, where his relics lay, that the greedy Henry VIII was particularly anxious to suppress it.

Almost nothing is known of Edmund's reign, beyond the fact that it lasted several years and ended in 869, when he was killed by the Vikings. More than a century after his death, a monk visiting Ramsey Abbey wrote an account of the king, apparently based on memories relayed by Edmund's armour bearer. According to this, Edmund was a saintly figure, who volunteered to be martyred as a means of avoiding other bloodshed. *The Anglo-Saxon Chronicle* suggests a different picture: a king who died either in or after a battle. No matter: the story of Edmund as a Christ-like figure, who became, like St Sebastian, a kind of human pincushion from the number of arrows shot at him, before his head was cut off, gained the upper hand.

He was duly canonised. Bury St Edmunds had been a royal vill; so had Bures. The twelfth-century chronicler Galfridus de Fontibus wrote that King Edmund was crowned at Bures, or Burum.

At some point, the ruins of St Stephen's Chapel were turned into cottages. In the 1930s, the family that owned them turned the building back into a chapel. One end is bargeboarded, the other has stone walls pierced by lancet windows; the transept is half-timber over brick. With its thatched roof, the chapel is a charming structure, the interior containing monuments to the de Vere Earls of Oxford, which once stood in another casualty of the Dissolution, Colne Priory. But visitors must persevere if they are to find it. There are no signs, the track to it crosses a farmyard, and the door will most probably be locked.

The king is remembered in St Edmund's Hill, St Edmund's Lane and St Edmund's Way. Otherwise modern Bures has other things on its mind. With one foot in Essex and the other in Suffolk, it has become quite a large settlement – or agglomeration of settlements, Bures Hamlet merging with Bures St Mary and Bures Green (Little Bures, or Mount Bures, is nearby). The slatternly river Stour, apt to lounge out of its bed to spill over water meadows and somebody's patio table, forms the county boundary, with a Second World War pillbox rustily standing guard over the bridge in case Hitler had chosen to invade by way of Dorking Tye. The Suffolk side has the best of the bargain, not only possessing the grand terminus for H. C. Chambers and Sons' fleet of motorbuses, resplendent in their livery of terracotta with cream lettering, but the church of St Mary.

A letter of 1721 describes an extraordinary haul of fish that was taken from the Stour by a drag net: 'full forty bushels of fish, eight gallons to a bushel, most part of them Roach, the other Pikes and Perch'. There is, however, no suggestion that this miraculous draught could be ascribed to St Edmund.

# BURNHAM MARKET
## NORFOLK
*Chelsea on sea*

It is just before Easter and the builders are out in Burnham Market on the North Norfolk coast. Surely there has never been so much carrying of toolboxes, parking of white vans, sawing of planks and touching up of sash windows in the history of villages. Even the church has scaffolding climbing up the tower. The interior of the nave is covered in plastic sheeting and ladders. Burnham Market is sprucing itself up for the summer, and does not want to have a hair out of place.

This is the epicentre of North Norfolk fashionability, where a two-course meal for one washed down by half a bottle of Chablis will set you back sixty pounds. The last time Burnham Market had it this good was in the thirteenth century. Then the area was doing so well as to support half a dozen Burnhams, one of them being Horatio Nelson's birthplace, Burnham Thorpe. But they lost the battle against silt, their harbours became unusable, and only a trained eye would detect the medieval dwellings that lie behind the neat Georgian facades. By the time William White had published his *History, Gazetteer and Directory of Norfolk* in 1836, it had become 'a small humble village'.

It reached a low ebb in the long agricultural depression that set in during the late 1870s, days when selling wild rabbit skins provided a useful source of income to impoverished families. For the first eighty years of the twentieth century, the North Norfolk coast was so difficult to reach by car that the summer population was mostly composed of Cambridge academics and families that had acquired holiday homes during the *Poppyland* era, around 1900. Then came the M11, which reached Cambridge in 1980, and other transport improvements. By the end of the 1980s, long-timers were heard to make comments such as: 'Sweet house, but I'll always remember it as the post office.'

There is nothing humble about Burnham Market now, except the delicatessen, which is called Humble Pie. As Pevsner commented, there isn't a false note – as long as one averts one's eyes from the Roman Catholic Church of St Henry Walpole, S. J., the only building with a pointed gable facing the street. This is Farrow and Ball country; even the estate agents' signs are elegantly proportioned.

Burnham Market still clings to the remnants of its old ramshackle charm. The wonky RAC sign on the green has been left to rust happily. Gurneys fish shop advertises its catch in gaily coloured lettering on a blackboard. Aubretia spills spontaneously over a flint wall. But otherwise the tidiness is overwhelming – it might be an idea to wash the car before coming. Nearly 70 per cent of the houses here are second homes, whose owners support an economy of grass mowers, house cleaners and decorators, though few tradesmen could afford to live here. The London crowd spends money in several dozen local businesses: butcher, baker, hardware shop, chemist, clothes shops, Gurneys and a bookshop – but surely no village needs so many art galleries.

# CAXTON
## CAMBRIDGESHIRE                          *Going with the money*

Villages can move. When you see a church on its own among fields, the explanation could be that the village it once served petered out. But it could also be that the village relocated to a more favourable position. This happened, probably in the second half of the thirteenth century, at Caxton.

The earliest map showing routes across Britain, the Gough Map in the Bodleian Library in Oxford, was made around 1360. The travellers who saw it were lucky. Few people made journeys in the Middle Ages. Peasants were tied to their villages, and that was where they found their friends and marriage partners. Only the rich had horses to take them further afield. Those who did travel – lawyers, soldiers, royal messengers, members of the great international network of the Church – were unlikely ever to see a map, much less use one. They relied on itineraries: lists of places, strung together like beads on a necklace. It was not such a crazy way of doing things: today, routes printed from the AA website or created by satellite navigation use the same principle. Still, medieval men and women had little idea of how one part of their country related to another.

Rivers are shown on the Gough Map fat as eels, reflecting the fact that it was generally best to travel by water. Roads are nothing more than red threads, whose skimpiness suggests the loneliness of travelling on them. Clusters of roofs and church towers depict settlements of varying importance: London, Winchester, Lincoln, York, Cambridge, Ely . . . and Caxton, in what is now Cambridgeshire. Why Caxton? Probably because it had gone to some pains to make itself a conspicuous and hospitable feature on one of the more important of those red threads, the road from London to the North.

The Romans built Ermine Street, connecting London with York and, eventually, Scotland. But their road system – little improved until the advent of turnpike trusts in the eighteenth century – fell into decay after the legions left. The Saxons who founded Caxton did not think of building their houses on the abandoned road; instead the settlement grew up around the parish church of St Andrew. But after the Conquest, Ermine Street came back into use. The village found itself bypassed, and missing out on trade. So it said goodbye to the church, left its old houses to rot, and built new ones beside the road. The move was probably inspired by Henry III's grant of a charter to hold markets in 1247. Gradually the village expanded over the fields away from the road, and what had been tracks became lanes of houses.

Presumably Caxton had become a noted stopping place by the time of the Gough Map. If so, during the succeeding centuries the road brought more prosperity, as can be seen from the number of sixteenth- and seventeenth-century buildings that survive, including three (former) inns. In 1663, the first Turnpike Act was passed to improve Ermine Street, but the toll gate erected at Caxton was not a success: it could easily be circumvented. Turnpikes were to be Caxton's downfall. After an Act of 1773 they led to such an improvement in the Great North Road from London to Edinburgh that the Caxton route came to be known as the Old North Road. The village never recovered its confidence. One reminder of the coaching days does survive, however: Caxton Gibbet, a mile and a half north of the village, a modern reconstruction of a gallows where highwaymen were hanged.

# CHIPPENHAM
## CAMBRIDGESHIRE

*Improving an estate? First move the village*

Edward Russell was a grumpy, difficult, red-faced man, strongly motivated by vanity and prone to sulk. He was, however, prepared to stick his neck out. Not only was he one of the eight aristocrats who invited William of Orange to England in 1688, but four years later he led the English fleet to victory against the French in the five-day Battle of La Hogue. Appointment as first Lord of the Admiralty put him in a prime position to profit from Navy funds, and it is probably this, added to a fortune made from illegal trading when he had been posted to Tangier, that enabled him to purchase the estate of Chippenham in 1696. He had great ideas for the house, the landscape and the village, being one of the first landowners to roll all three into an aesthetic whole. By 1712, his work was done, and he celebrated it by commissioning a splendid map from a surveyor called Heber Lands, now in the Cambridgeshire Record Office.

Chippenham derives its name from a Saxon called Cippa. The map shows the higgledy-piggledy character of the old settlement, whose few dozen buildings lurch in bucolic disorder along the roads. Some of the existing village was allowed to remain, but dwellings that Lord Orford (Russell had now been raised to the peerage) deemed to be too near the mansion house were erased. They were replaced by fourteen neatly pretty new cottages, each a single storey with dormers and hipped roofs, set behind what are now generous lawns (cottage gardens originally), and rubbing shoulders with an elegant red-brick schoolroom (arched windows, pilasters) of 1714.

Orford's works make a striking contrast with the old village. Even so, the historically important thing was not so much the look of the new cottages as their position outside the park that Orford created from land bought from yeoman farmers. Look carefully on the 1712 map and you can see the traces of old habitations. Two intact cottages seem to have been marooned among the deer, far away from any other building. Orford's tenants would not have had any say in whether, where or how they were rehoused – or even if they were to have houses at all.

To the Orfords of the countryside, 'emparking' was a form of enclosure and made economic sense (better to have cattle, sheep or deer grazing your greensward than peasants scratching an existence from strip farming). It also provided the canvas on which Capability Brown and improvers of the Picturesque movement would paint their pictures, made from the living landscape by planting woods, digging lakes and, in extreme cases, moving hills. The map shows that Orford's own landscape ideas were more Baroque (trees planted in avenues) than naturalistic. But he started something. The first act of any Picturesque improver was to move the village away from the mansion house.

What did this mean for villages? For some it could be devastating, but the transformation of Chippenham may have been less traumatic. Research has shown that the village population reached its zenith long before Orford's arrival. In the twelfth century, the manor was owned by the Knights Hospitallers*; they had 150 tenants and probably as many families. After the Black Death, that number was cut by half. The village never recovered its previous numbers. A survey undertaken for the new owner after the Dissolution of the Monasteries showed that there were still only sixty householders in 1544. Picturesque improvers were often accused of arrogance in depopulating villages. Orford was certainly arrogant, but by rebuilding Chippenham, or part of it, he probably did the village a favour.

*See Ysbyty Ifan, page 513. See also Nuneham Courtenay, page 191

# CLARE
## SUFFOLK

*Long continuity of habitation*

Suffolk's golden century dawned around 1450. The next hundred years saw spectacular profits from the wool trade, part of which went to build the great churches – square-towered, airy, angel-roofed – which now seem so bafflingly huge, given the size of the villages that support them. By 1700, the boom was over, and the county had to get by as best it could. Its settlements ceased to grow; some – such as Hitcham (see page 246), which used to have its own guildhall, but is now a hamlet – shrank.

The Luftwaffe and post-War planners may have wrecked Ipswich, and Bury St Edmunds has ballooned in recent years, but lack of money meant that Suffolk's villages and small towns slept through most of the twentieth century – woken only by the roar of Wellingtons and Lancasters leaving airbases such as Mildenhall during the Second World War. They have arrived in the twenty-first century with much of their architectural character intact, a witness, in the case of Clare, to long continuity, stretching back to the Roman period and before.

Clare began life as a prehistoric camp (cottages were later built into its banks); it acquired a castle, a friary, became a borough, its lords being enormously powerful in the Norman period and Middle Ages. Richard de Bienfaite had been William the Conqueror's friend and supporter, being rewarded with ninety-five estates in Suffolk alone. Had the family's allegiance not been divided with Tonbridge in Kent, the castle would have become more magnificent; as it was, Clare became the administrative centre of a huge aggregation of estates throughout East Anglia, known as the Honor of Clare.

The presence of these powerful lords in Clare was a mixed blessing for the town. It was overawed. The borough never sent representatives to Parliament. It preferred to pursue a quiet life, doing well from weaving the coarse cloth known as bays and says until the industry declined in the seventeenth century. These days, you could hardly call it a town: it is run by a parish council.

There are two Suffolks. Towards the coast is flint country, and villages have a dispersed character, loosely grouped around greens. Austere rectories and gentleman's houses were built from the Regency onwards; there are few large buildings of earlier date. Clare, whose name may derive from the clear water flowing in the river Stour, lies in the interior, on the border with Essex – a land of winding roads, undulating fields, deep ditches and scattered woods. The villages in this part, such as Lavenham (see page 251) and Long Melford (see page 257), are more coherently planned, their burghers showing off in timber-framed halls that are jettied and flamboyantly carved.

As the timbers of old Clare settled and sagged, the streets became, to Georgian eyes, embarrassingly higgledy-piggledy, so the wand of propriety was waved: some of the old timber structures disappeared behind new fronts of tawny-pink or East Anglian 'white' (really yellow ochre) brick, or mathematical tile; the tipsy-looking, unreformed Tudor houses seem to lean on them for support. Clues to the much older buildings that lie behind them are sometimes visible from the outside. This is the case with Richmond House, which presents to the world a front of flat plaster, colourwashed in the prevailing pink, complete with classical door case, sash windows, parapet and a rippling tiled roof. Look at the chimneys, though: they are Tudor. The main part of the house may be earlier still.

# COVEHITHE
*Neptune gets his own back*

Covehithe had ideas above its station. In the fifteenth century, the rich benefactor William Yarmouth funded the construction of one of Suffolk's many spectacular churches, lit by the immense windows of the Perpendicular style. It can only have had a small congregation even then. Presumably Yarmouth imagined that the community would grow.

It did succeed in producing an outstanding individual in John Bale, a churchman, who became Bishop of Ossory and wrote the oldest known play to be written in English verse. As for so many poor boys, the escalator that took him to the heights of success was the monastic system, his formal education having been provided by the Carmelite convent at Norwich, which he entered at the age of twelve (although he later became a vehement polemicist for the Protestant cause).

But the population of Covehithe never exceeded three hundred. The churchwardens stoutly defended their church against the depredations of the Cromwellian iconoclast William Dowsing, by denying him ladders to reach the windows, but by 1672 the community was forced to recognise that it could no longer maintain such a big building; another church was built, crouching amid William Yarmouth's walls.

It was a foretaste of further shrinkage. Covehithe was to suffer the same fate as its neighbour Dunwich, a major town at the time of the Domesday Book, served by six churches, which lost its battle against the sea in 1328. Violent waves shifted the shingle spit offshore, blocking the harbour; ships were diverted to Walberswick (see page 275). No longer being worth the cost of erecting sea defences, Dunwich was allowed to crumble away, and is now little more than a single street. In the 1880s, Covehithe was losing, on average, eighteen feet of land to the sea every year. In 1887, sixty feet disappeared. Half eaten away, the village street now ends above the toffee-coloured cliffs, with a notice strongly advising visitors not to risk going further. There are but half a dozen houses left in the village. Their fate is uncertain as the sea continues to chew at the cliffs, biting off more each year.

Further along the coast is Happisburgh in Norfolk, where Sir Arthur Conan Doyle was inspired to write the Sherlock Holmes story 'The Adventures of The Dancing Men' by seeing a coded signature, written by the landlord's son, when staying on a motoring holiday at the Hill House Hotel. Since his visit in 1903, the shoreline has been stolen – houses, trees, sections of cliff have all gone. The culprit is not difficult to name. What to do about it, as sea levels rise, is proving an unfathomable riddle to people who live by this coast.

*See also Hallsands, page 40*

# CROWLAND
## LINCOLNSHIRE

*The greatest curiosity in Britain*

Crowland, like Ely, used to be an island. Cut off from the rest of the world by the black waters of the Fens, overhung by fog and infested with demons, it had been a good place for St Guthlac and two companions to build a cell when brought here by a local fisherman around 700. From this beginning grew Crowland Abbey. Though watery, the countryside was not unproductive. In the summer, land that dried out could be used to graze cattle, even if they had to be taken there by boat. There was fishing, caught in traps and weirs, and a huge abundance of eels (Ely takes its name from them). Wildfowl could also be trapped.

Crowland was still known for being 'in a Morasse and Fenny ground, so that an horse can hardly come to it', when Thomas Fuller published *The History of the Worthies of England* in 1662. But evidently Fuller had not been there recently, because he could not say whether it had not already acquired 'more firmnesse than formerly' from the drainage of the Fens.

Striking testimony to Crowland's condition both before and after drainage survives in the middle of the village. Trinity Bridge is an exceptional construction. The eighteenth-century historian of Crowland Abbey, Richard Gough, called it 'the greatest curiosity in Britain, if not in Europe'. The triangular bridge appears to have been built over a point where the river Welland divided into two streams. Three arches meet in the centre, the three-in-one symbolising the Trinity. A bridge of this form, probably of wood, may have existed as early as the tenth century; this one, however, was constructed in the late fourteenth century, and is a geometrical tour de force.

*Bravura engineering at Trinity Bridge, Crowland, where*
*the three-in-one arch symbolises the Trinity.*

As a bridge, it can never have been highly functional. The rise is unusually steep, impracticable for a horse and impossible for a cart, since it has been laid as steps. On the other hand, the arches were so tall that it was possible for a carriage, as well as a cart, to pass underneath, which, in its later stages of use, they often could, the water having been reduced to a bog. Presumably the bridge had a ceremonial purpose as much as a practical one, perhaps marking an abbey boundary, or making a grand first impression on visitors arriving by water. (Or a point of departure: both Henry VI and Edward IV are recorded as having set sail from the bridge.) It may have supported a tall cross. At some point a seated figure was attached to the south-west wall, at various times described as a Saxon king holding a loaf or even Oliver Cromwell (hardly likely, since Cromwell's forces attacked the abbey). It is probably a figure of Christ with an orb, taken from the west front of the abbey.

But the bridge is now high and dry. In the eighteenth century the Welland was diverted away from the (then) town, and the land dried out – so much so that, in 2002, innovative means had to be found to compensate for the shrinkage of the underlying soil, which was causing the bridge to crack. The engineer responsible was Richard Waters, whose professional eye saw the bridge, not as an extravagant oddity, but a 'very unusual and economical solution to the crossing of two watercourses at their confluence, reducing the need for three separate bridges to a single structure with three abutments'. A curiosity? Yes, but an intellectually elegant one.

# DANBURY
## ESSEX
*The twelve days of turkey*

There is quite a scene at Springate Farm, Danbury, on Christmas Eve. So many people are collecting their turkeys that a couple of police officers have been laid on to direct traffic from the lane. Springate Farm is home to the famous Kelly Bronze, described by the very Secretary of the Department for Environment, Food, and Rural Affairs himself, Hilary Benn, as 'much sought after' – although not, presumably, for the Benn household's Christmas feast, since he is a vegetarian. Paul Kelly inherited the farm from his father, who started the flock in 1971, when Paul was eight. He personally hands the turkey to each customer, while, one imagines, Dickens's Spirit of Christmas Present beams down from above. The box in which it comes is printed with a quotation from, of all unlikely authors, John Ruskin: 'There is hardly anything in the world that some man cannot make a little worse and sell a little cheaper, and the people who consider price only, are this man's lawful prey.' Splendid.

Danbury is an interesting village, well stocked with timber-framed, plaster-walled, tile-roofed houses, one of them being the sixteenth-century Griffin Inn. The church sits within an Iron Age hill fort, not very easy to spot, overlooking the green. In 1779, workmen were digging a grave in the north aisle when they discovered a stone slab. Beneath lay a coffin containing the perfectly preserved body of a man, apparently pickled in a mixture tasting (imagine someone tasting it) like mushroom ketchup.

There was a time, a quarter of a century ago, when the turkey farm offered a useful source of income to village people in the run-up to Christmas. Mr Kelly has forty thousand turkeys to pluck, truss and pack and these days, folk from Danbury would rather not do it. Since turkey farming is an almost wholly seasonal business, Mr Kelly worried if the enterprise could survive without what had previously been a happy supply of casual labour. Enter the Poles. 'I could kiss and cuddle them every time they turn up,' he says. They seem a cheerful crew, twenty-five men with moustaches flaring beneath their compulsory throw-away hats, smiling broadly despite the necessarily low temperatures in which they work. One of their tasks is to take the sinews out of the drumsticks when the turkey's feet are removed, an attention to detail that has become rare.

The secret of the Kelly Bronze's success is age. It is a slow-growing bird, sold when mature, unlike the majority of the ten million Christmas turkeys consumed in Britain, which are fast-growing Whites, eaten flavourlessly young. Not only are all the Springate Farm birds free range, but some enjoy an even wilder life than the rest, having been released into a wood at a very young age and left to get on with it. A turkey's feathers quickly adapt to sleeping under the stars, while an electric fence ensures that their rest is undisturbed by the night-prowling Mr Fox.

# EAST BERGHOLT
## SUFFOLK
*John Constable goes to school*

The painter John Constable struggled. He struggled against his father, Golding Constable, a prosperous miller, barge owner and coal merchant, who did not want him to become an artist. He struggled with his art, which he found difficult to master (he used to draw directly onto a pane of glass to improve his perspective). He struggled with the Royal Academy, slow to elect him to membership and prone to hang his paintings in unfavourable positions. He struggled to produce the great six-foot canvases, in which this difficult, sometimes waspish man remained true to a personal and not especially popular vision. He struggled to convince the rector of East Bergholt, the village where he grew up, that he should marry his grand-daughter Maria. The young couple had to wait seven years before he relented. He then struggled to live up to his wife's ambition for him. All those biscuit tins have done him a disservice.

Like Cézanne, Constable's vision was closely associated with a single geographical area, the Stour valley. He painted other subjects – Salisbury Cathedral, the Lake District, Hampstead Heath, Waterloo Bridge – but only because he had

*The bell cage at East Bergholt, erected as a temporary measure, when work on the church tower ceased after Cardinal Wolsey's downfall in 1530, and never replaced.*

encountered them personally. Most of the six-footers, like so much of his *oeuvre*, show scenes that he knew as a boy. Visiting those scenes today is like walking the battlefield at Waterloo. The area is much smaller than one might expect. The compass hardly extends beyond the walk from the family home in East Bergholt to school in Dedham, and around his father's mills at Dedham, East Bergholt heath and Flatford. A dozen viewpoints for paintings lie within a few hundred yards of one another.

Constable was an obsessive, constantly exploring the landscape of his childhood and returning to it, with almost photographic accuracy, long after he had left to further his career in London. It was not subject matter calculated to win worldly success. Constable eschewed Turner's homages to the Sublime; there is no overlay, however slight, of historical, classical or Biblical reference. One reason that his works were poorly hung at the Royal Academy was that the committee saw them as mere topography. The scenes must have possessed a strong emotional meaning for him. And yet we can only guess at it. No symbolism, no pathetic fallacy is there to guide us towards an interpretation of the view.

Golding Constable's four-square brick mansion has gone from East Bergholt. So have the elms and black poplars (a useful tree in the age of carts, from its habit of denting without splintering*). But in other respects, after nearly two centuries, the village is much what it was: 'large and well-built . . . with several handsome mansions and well-stocked shops', as William White described it in 1833. The church has still not acquired its steeple, so that the bells lie in a wooden cage in the churchyard, to be rung by hand (a perilous activity that has not yet, thank goodness, been banned by Europe).

It was a prosperous countryside in Golding Constable's day. There are always people working in Constable's paintings: building boats, shovelling muck, driving horses, fishing. But the buildings in this working environment were left to look after themselves. A thatched boathouse near Flatford Mill, shown in *The White Horse*, eventually tumbled down and disappeared. Those structures that still exist are kept up to the nines; there is little sign of the rotting posts and mossy roofs that Constable loved.

Every inch of Constable's Suffolk had a commercial value. Cattle grazed up to the edge of the river. Willows were not allowed to grow beside the path as they do now; they would have got in the way of the horses that towed the barges. Constable naturally understood every incident of this working landscape – the barges being poled into position, horses being ferried across the river when the towpath changed sides. *The Haywain* shows a Suffolk hay cart, not crossing the ford, as you might think, but cooling its wooden wheels in the water of the Stour after a long morning's work. The cart is now empty. Visit the spot and you will know why it is not fording the river: the canal banks are too steep for it to get out on the Essex side. Besides, there is a bridge only a few yards upstream.

*See Aston on Clun, page 295

# FOBBING
## ESSEX
*Thomas Baker makes a stand against taxes*

To reach Fobbing, you must first (if you are going from London) traverse the landscape of the damned that is the Thames estuary. It is easy to imagine that the Peasants' Revolt started here, although the topography was somewhat different in 1381. There were no pylons, no flyovers, no power plants. You would have looked east from the ridge occupied by the village across marshes (bleak enough on a winter's day, but full of wildfowl) to Vange Creek, cranking into the river Thames, its sprawling course marked by the sails of the ships making their way to and from London.

To Thomas Baker, the problem was taxes. We know little about this Baker, beyond the name of his land holding – 'Pokattescroft alias Bakerscroft' in Fobbing. But when John Bampton arrived to collect a second instalment of the poll tax – a measure that fell on both rich and poor, to finance the war in France – Baker led the village in repulsing him. They refused to give anything, and drove him away. Robert Bealknap, Chief Justice of the Common Pleas, was sent out to punish the malefactors, but he and his party did not get beyond Brentwood. The country began to rise. Used to sailing backwards and forwards across the estuary, the people of Essex quickly stirred up their friends in Kent. Wat Tyler emerged as the leader in Maidstone, spiritually supported by the itinerant priest John Ball. Like so many other rural uprisings over the centuries, it was largely futile and brutally suppressed. Wat Tyler was struck down with a dagger in front of the young Richard II at Smithfield; Ball was hanged, drawn and quartered at St Albans. Baker met the same end at Chelmsford. With him were seven others from the village.

Interestingly, at least one of these Fobbing rebels, William Gildeborne, was well off. He owned goods, including seventy-two sheep, and around a hundred acres of land. Baker, if his name signified his trade, would also have been a figure of substance in the village. Here was something new. The revolt was not a riot of the dispossessed, who had nothing to lose. Indeed, this suggests the extent to which the Peasants' Revolt blew up against a background of change in the village. For village life had evolved rapidly since 1348, when a third of England was killed by the Black Death. Before, the manor had kept a tight grip on the supply of land, and it had been difficult for a peasant to increase his holding. But with so many people dead, there were vacant plots to be had. Ownership became unequal. The sense of solidarity among the leading families – against landless vagrants below them, against the demands of the lord of the manor above them – decayed. The lack of common purpose that they might have felt with their peers in the thirteenth century left them exposed to fight alone, should any point of friction arise with the lord. The old certainties had gone. Individualism was a heady draught.

One can imagine the misplaced self-confidence that Thomas Baker felt in his dealings with unwelcome poll tax collectors. Although his stand seems to have been issueless, it was part of the slow evolution that turned medieval villages into Tudor ones.

# FOLKINGHAM
## LINCOLNSHIRE
*An 'extremely neat' House of Correction*

To John Britton, writing *The Beauties of England and Wales* in 1807, Folkingham was 'a small town, pleasantly situated on the summit of a hill, abounding with springs'. Since then, it has not succeeded in maintaining its character as a town, and is now a large village, but a particularly harmonious one, having been almost entirely rebuilt in the decades around 1800. In 1825, the topographer James Creasey's admiration knew no bounds. 'The change in the appearance of this place, from what it was forty or fifty years ago, is such, that, to a person acquainted with it then, it would scarcely be thought the same.' Previously, it had 'consisted of little else than a mass of irregularly built and dirty-looking thatched cottages; even the Inn itself was but a miserable hovel, compared with the present elegant structure'.

The town had come into the ownership of Sir Gilbert Heathcote, and had been comprehensively improved: new inn, tidied-up marketplace, 'the more humble dwellings of the poor' hidden from view. One of the buildings to have disgraced the old market square was the House of Correction, built in 1611. This was replaced with a new building inside the walls of the castle in 1808.

The Folkingham House of Correction was part of the wave of gaol building that followed John Howard's campaign for prison reform in the eighteenth century. Some architects took their cue from George Dance's Newgate Gaol, from the 1770s, whose massive rustication expressed the oppressive character of incarceration in stone; Newgate was followed by Roger Mulholland's even more forbidding Belfast House of Correction. A different approach was taken at Folkingham, whose gatehouse took the form of a splendid, if severe triumphal arch (now all that survives), while inside the chapel was, according to Creasey, 'extremely neat', with each prisoner able to see the minister but not other prisoners.

One of the 'latest improvements' was a treadwheel. 'This piece of machinery is admirably calculated to effect its intended purpose, viz. that of affording both labour and punishment to the prisoners at the same time; the former being obtained by the vexatious and fatiguing exercise on the wheel, and the latter by a knowledge that all their vexatious labour is entirely in vain . . .'. The labour was not quite in vain, the treadmill sometimes being attached to a pump. Nowadays, what remains of the House of Correction fulfils an altogether more benign function as a holiday cottage let by the Landmark Trust.

# FORNCETT
## NORFOLK

*A hopeless rebellion*

Around 1492, Robert Kett was born in the Norfolk village of Forncett (a bipolar settlement that divides into Forncett St Mary and Forncett St Peter). He became a tanner in the local market town of Wymondham. Leather being essential in Tudor life, tanners tended to be well respected and prosperous; Kett's wife, Alice, came from a family of minor gentry. Also in the town was his brother William, a butcher, with whom Kett no doubt worked closely, given their professional interests in cattle. Norfolk, being well supplied with gentlemen, did not require tanners to serve in government; a state of affairs that may have piqued Kett, but made it unlikely that he should ever cause much of a stir. And yet he did. A settled man, approaching sixty, he decided to throw in his lot with a disorderly mob, which he led in a spectacular, if unfocused, rebellion.

Why? It is a question one might ask in relation to Watt Tyler, Jack Cade or any of the leaders of medieval and Tudor revolts, who must surely have known that they would not be treated kindly when caught. Kett may have been cross with Protector Somerset's government for introducing new regulations for tanners. He is known to have defended Wymondham parish church, then part of the Abbey, from depredations after the Dissolution. In doing so, he fell out with a lawyer called John Flowerdew, who had torn part of it down. It was not only Kett who disliked Flowerdew; in the summer of 1549, the lawyer became the subject of vigilante action by local people, who opposed his efforts to enclose common land. Finding his hedges and ditches about to be levelled, he paid the rioters to attack Kett's enclosures instead. Kett seems to have sympathised with the mob. Rather than defending his own works, he joined them, and was soon their leader.

Organised by Kett and possibly others, the rebels formed an effective band. By the time they marched on Norwich, the second most important city in the country, they were twenty thousand strong. Kett is supposed to have kept them in order by dispensing justice from beneath a tree called the Oak of Reformation. The rebels took the city, then attacked Great Yarmouth.

Only a small army could be spared to the Marquess of Northampton, who was sent to cut their supply lines. The government was appalled when it was forced back to London, defeated. Then France declared war on England. The sideshow in Norwich had to be ended, and it was. The Earl of Warwick set off with another army, whose cavalry eventually cut down the insurgents and captured Kett, but not until after Kett's forces had captured the artillery and bombarded Norwich. Militarily, Kett had done well to keep the field for seven weeks.

Politically the list of twenty-nine grievances published by Kett and the rebels is something of a bran tub. The first demand concerned enclosure, but only in so far as it related to 'saffron grounds' (the fields on which crocuses were grown for saffron, a valuable spice). The other articles are similarly specific, with the exception of a call to free 'bond men' on the premise that all mankind had been made free by the Crucifixion. They were modest demands. To the end, Kett saw himself as an ally of the King against the greed of landowners. He was, of course, somewhat naive.

Robert and William Kett were both hanged, the former from the walls of Norwich, the latter from the steeple of Wymondham church. Kett's lands at Forncett were seized by the Crown, on the advice, among others, of Flowerdew.

# FRAMSDEN
## SUFFOLK

*Suffolk fights back*

There are people living in Framsden, as in many villages, who can still remember it as a self-sufficient community. After the Second World War, it could boast two blacksmiths, two butchers and an abattoir, two windmills, a carpenter, a wheelwright, a hurdle maker, a brickmaker, cobbler, tailor, grocer's shop, and a horse-drawn carrier plying backwards and forwards to Ipswich. The village is lucky that it still has a pub, the Doberman Inn. But the post office and village shop – the last vestige of commercial Framsden – closed in the early 1990s.

There is little remarkable in this; Framsden's tale is typical of that of hundreds of other villages, which have come to depend increasingly on the motor car to reach shops and other services. The closure of sub-post offices has been to the late twentieth and early twenty-first centuries what the Beeching cuts to the national railway network were to the 1960s. Some post office functions have been superseded by the internet; on the other hand, you have only to think of Amazon and eBay to recognise that parts of the internet are dependent on being able to post and receive parcels.

As a county, Suffolk is fighting back. In 1997, the Countess of Cranbrook took on Tesco, after the supermarket chain applied to open a store on the edge of Saxmundham, fifteen miles from Framsden. Deploying a lined exercise book, in which she noted down the comments that she collected from eighty-one local shops – small outlets, which sourced their food from nearly three hundred local and regional suppliers – Lady Cranbrook won. If the arrival of a supermarket had forced the shops to close, towns and villages would have lost their heart; folk without a car would not have been able to buy the necessities of life; the local food economy would have collapsed, and young food businesses would have been unable to get off the ground.

While the Alde valley is hardly famous for its culinary tradition, it now boasts what Lady Cranbrook calls 'one of the country's most vibrant, innovative and employment-rich local food economies', celebrated each autumn at the Aldeburgh Food and Drink Festival held at the Snape Maltings. Jam makers, cheese makers, bakers, piemen, farmers making burgers from Red Poll cattle, others growing organic chickens or making boneless joints from Suffolk game – these are among the thirty new businesses that have come into being since 1997. The Festival's opening dinner takes place in a sheep barn. Sitting on straw bales, guests barbecue their own hazel-stick Alde Valley Lamb kebabs in a barn that, every winter, is used to lamb sheep.

There are many villages over which this new dawn has yet to break, Framsden, with its population of only three hundred, being one of them. But a farm shop has opened at adjacent Helmingham, in the kitchen garden of Helmingham Hall. The blood of commerce is, albeit sluggishly, circulating; there is hope.

# FRESSINGFIELD
SUFFOLK                                             *'So lewd a place' for an Archbishop*

Born in Fressingfield in 1617, William Sancroft rose to become Dean of St Paul's at the time of the Great Fire of London. In 1677, he was raised over the heads of all the other Church of England Bishops to become Archbishop of Canterbury. It was not that Sancroft had sought the position; he was of a retiring temperament, more at home at Emmanuel College, Cambridge, where he had been a fellow and Master, than at the forefront of politics. Charles II, however, had identified his unwavering belief in the divine right of kings. As Charles grew old and his brother James did not increase in popularity as his successor, this was a considerable recommendation.

As Archbishop, Sancroft crowned James II as king in 1685. Within three years, James had cast Sancroft, together with six other bishops, into the Tower of London. In an attempt to bolster his position as a Catholic, James had promulgated a declaration of indulgence, allowing freedom of worship. To the Church of England, it seemed that this would not only unleash the horrors of popery but combine them with encouragement for Dissent. Irreligion itself would be allowed a foothold in the establishment, if all religious tests were removed.

The King required that the declaration should be read out in church. Sancroft and his fellow protestors refused, on the grounds that it was not for the King to exercise 'such a dispensing power as may at pleasure set aside all laws ecclesiastical and civil'. In June 1688, they were tried for seditious libel and acquitted, amid general rejoicing. Six months later, the King fled the country, as the Prince of Orange advanced on London, supposedly to protect the inheritance of his wife, Princess Mary. Sancroft, scrupulously maintaining James's right to be king, refused to crown the new monarchs. His archbishopric was removed from him. In August 1691, he returned to Fressingfield.

It had been intensely important to him throughout his life. He had been deeply attached to his parents and often returned to his birthplace, Ufford Hall: a house on the scale of a large farmhouse, which he had shared, when growing up, with an elder brother and six sisters. Despite well-intentioned efforts to pair him off, he maintained his 'steddy resolution . . . never to marry'. He was not deeply attached to the rustic life: during the years he had spent at Fressingfield during the Civil War and Commonwealth, he referred disparagingly to a place turned to mud by heavy rains as 'Sloughland' and 'the land of dirt'. He laughed at the idea of the countryside being called High Suffolk; it was altogether 'so lewd a place'.

But he had many good friends there and loved his extended family. With Ufford Hall full to the rafters, he built a new house at the bottom of the garden. There he served as his own chaplain, refusing to participate in the rites of a Church of England that William and Mary's accession had, he believed, made schismatic. A nonjuring clergyman buried him at Fressingfield in 1693.

# GEDNEY
## LINCOLNSHIRE    *Migrant labour at the edge of the known world*

Do you want to know a way of amusing yourself in the Fens? Sit on the sea bank as darkness falls and watch the RAF Chinooks shoot up the bombing range at Sutton Bridge. This is the great tablecloth of agricultural land that England spreads before the Wash in colours of chocolate brown and vivid green. The brown comes from the peaty earth that clings to the celery in Cambridge market (or used to, before Spanish imports), the green from the vegetables and salad crops that grow in stripes.

To the urban visitor, this farming landscape may seem to belong to a different country – open, empty, endless, the silence broken only by the boom of a fighter plane overhead or the roar of a motorcycle being put through its paces on the long straight roads. Otherwise the blades of the wind turbine may be all that moves in this landscape of low horizons and wide drainage channels. But do not call it provincial. Anyone who wants to buy some Polish sausage or sour cream, or even to tune into a Polish-speaking radio station, will not have to look for long.

The magnificent church of St Mary Magdalene at Gedney is called the Cathedral of the Fens. It has a congregation that only just squeezes into double figures. By contrast, the Roman Catholic church at Holbeach, a few miles down the road, is an architectural misery, whose low-pitched roof could be mistaken for a suburban villa. But it is said to be 'bursting at the seams', thanks to the influx of migrant workers from the former Communist countries of Eastern Europe. They pick the lettuces and staff the canning factories, pack the flowers and sort the potatoes. More have come to this area than anywhere else in Britain. It has been calculated that twenty thousand migrant workers are employed in the sixteen-mile stretch between Boston and Spalding.

When England crashed out of the European football championship in 2004, Boston suffered a small riot – two police cars set ablaze, an off-licence in flames – thought to have been directed against Portuguese workers (it was Portugal that defeated the English team). The Portuguese began to arrive in the 1990s, forming a community of six thousand in Thetford. They are said to be none too happy about Eastern Europeans undercutting them and working below the minimum wage. Tensions can run high, although – with an unusually low level of indigenous unemployment – ill feeling is more likely to take the form of grumbling than fights. Wearisome, back-breaking, cold, unremitting – the tasks undertaken by migrant workers are often shunned by the local young, who feel they can put their schooling and possibly degrees to better use.

To David Piccaver, growing eleven thousand acres of leafy salads, foreign workers are essential; he would not be in business without them. Lettuces are harvested from April until early November; about a hundred pickers are needed at the peak of the season. In recent years the labour has been provided by students, mostly from Poland, Bulgaria and Romania, with some Russians, housed in a camp on the farm. To avoid friction, the students rarely come into contact with the local population. Gedney's pubs are off limits.

The arrival of so many Eastern Europeans, in so short a time, has had its difficulties. Children have appeared at the local school, unannounced and unable to speak English. The infrastructure has not always coped. And yet, as most people are prepared to recognise, the Fens have always relied on seasonal help coming from outside. After the Second World War, it was the Irish, harvesting potatoes; when the coal mines were closed in the 1980s, ex-miners arrived from Sheffield – and are remembered as working 'jolly hard'. The countryside grumbles, but it is capable of absorbing change.

# GODWICK
## NORFOLK

*One of England's vanished villages*

Godwick is a village of ghosts. It began life in the Saxon period, to judge from the name (wick meaning dairy farm; the first syllable derived from its owner, Goda). But the cottages disappeared centuries ago, leaving only hummocks and hollows to show where they once housed a community. It has been calculated that around two thousand villages have vanished from the British landscape. Plague is often assumed to have been the cause, but often abandonment followed the Dissolution of the Monasteries; new owners wanted to maximise the return from their land, and old villages, established to support traditional open-field farming, could be in the wrong place. Little kindness was shown to the cottage folk who were dispossessed.

In Godwick's case, it seems simply to have been that the poor soil yielded too little to support many people. There were only eight or nine dwellings left by the time Sir Edward Coke bought the manor in 1580. Coke, a Norfolk man who later rose to be Queen Elizabeth's attorney-general, was then in his late twenties. The year before, he had (successfully) argued his first case before the court of the king's bench. In 1585 he built a mansion, large if conventional, and his household accounts show that he was enjoying capons, pullets, ducklings, eggs, a pig and other food there in July 1597; he also bought 'a bushel of oatmeal to make the poor folks porage'. When, having become Lord Chief Justice in the reign of James I,

*The church at Godwick, already a ruin when the lawyer*
*Sir Edward Coke bought the estate in 1580.*

Coke employed his talents in attacking royal abuses, he found himself in the Tower of London, where he occupied himself by writing Latin verses in which he wished himself at Godwick.

True to type, Coke also enclosed some of the village lands and built a barn across what had been the village street. The barn, still in use, is all that survives of Coke's time. The mansion lasted long enough to be photographed by a Victorian gentleman, but succumbed to the mania for demolishing country houses that possessed the post-Second World War decades (1962 was Godwick's fatal year). In truth, Coke himself preferred his house at Stoke Poges in Berkshire (see page 198), being nearer to London; this was where he died. He never built up the church at Godwick, which was already a ruin when he came. Even so, Godwick has fared better than most of the other two hundred or so lost villages in Norfolk, evidence of which has been erased by ploughing. Godwick may be occupied only by ghosts, but they do at least have something to haunt.

# GREAT BARDFIELD
## ESSEX                                              *Artist in residence*

In 1949 the artist Edward Bawden published *Life in an English Village*, a King Penguin, though rather a small one, the plates being sixteen lithographs. They show a bald vicar contemplating his sermon in the vicarage study, cleaners in the parish church and the Methodist chapel, children leaning over their desks in the schoolroom, and mothers with infants at the Child Welfare Clinic in the village hall. A stoutly built farm labourer's wife peels potatoes beneath the sleeves of her husband's shirts, which are drying overhead in the cottage kitchen, and a gloomy Sunday evening is spent in a more prosperous home, with deer's heads and a grandfather clock. Then come the trades: repairing agricultural machinery, cabinetmaking, keeping the pub and the village shop, baking, butchering, tailoring, boot mending and tending chrysanthemums in a glasshouse, presumably belonging to the big house.

The setting was Great Bardfield, where Bawden came to Brick House in the High Street in 1925. At that time he shared it for weekend visits and holidays with his friend and fellow artist the dashing Eric Ravilious, killed while serving as a war artist in the Second World War. Bawden's father gave Brick House to Edward and his wife, Charlotte, as a wedding present when they married in 1932, and from 1935 it was their home. Unlike Ravilious, Bawden was shy and sometimes difficult to get on with, but, being a man of strong decorative instinct, he turned his home into a statement of his artistic tastes, painting the dining-room walls when Charlotte was out.

In the text of *Life in an English Village*, Noel Carrington, brother of the Bloomsburyite Dora, describes how the countryside had been opened up, first by bicyclists, then the motor car. Most of the artists who ventured into it with their watercolour boxes belonged to the 'wobbly line' school, which 'managed to make all the old buildings look a bit more wobbly than they were'. The country-side seemed doomed to quaintness, and the standard of living of the countryman along with it. But Carrington's tale is not exclusively one of demoralisation and decay. He also looks hard for signs of a village renaissance and finds them: in the availability of allotments, the development of village schools, the village bus, the housewife's full shopping basket. The town dweller was returning to the country-side, and commuting from it. 'The tempo of village life will be altered,' Carrington considered. 'There will not be . . . the same touching of caps, but there will not be so much boredom, nor so much rheumatism from damp floors.' Physically the village would have to change because the agricultural engineer could not be expected to occupy the premises that might recently have been vacated by the village blacksmith.

Wars have generally brought prosperity to farmers. The decades after the Second World War would see agriculture riding high. Not everything turned out so happily as Carrington had hoped: much of the slow-moving world that Bawden recorded vanished completely – not least the unconscious visual charm. Perhaps it was ever thus. Even Bawden had a backward-looking susceptibility to Staffordshire dogs, old-fashioned teapots and Victorian wirework *jardinières*. But as for the village renaissance, one was definitely apparent at Great Bardfield, where the arrival of Michael Rothenstein and Duffy Ayres, Bernard Cheese and Sheila Robinson to join the Bawdens created a colourful artists' colony in the grey post-War years.

# GREAT BENTLEY
## ESSEX
*The largest village green in Britain*

Great Bentley has the largest green in the country. One might think that the village would therefore compose into a typically English scene, but the reverse is the case. At forty-five acres, the green is so big that you can barely see the houses that line one side from the other. Where is the church? Oh, now I've got it, a dumpy tower folded away to the side. A quite large, lemon-coloured Georgian house has settled itself down in the middle of the green, without anybody much minding. It does not seem to be the sort of green where villagers could stop and gossip, because they might not pass within hailing distance of one another when walking across it. However, it reminds us of the origins of most village greens, which lie in commons.

Originally, commons were areas of land, owned by the lord of the manor, that were not used to grow crops. Village families had rights over these wastes, allowing them to graze livestock, collect firewood or dig peat. In the early Middle Ages, the common was likely to lie outside the village; in some places it might have been a clearing in a wood. It suited some people to be nearer the common, at least for a few months of the year, and so they built huts – just a few to begin with, but gradually others joined them. It was convenient for the new habitations to be grouped around a shared open space, where animals and ducks could be kept.

Before long, the green had become the natural meeting place of the village, a place of fetes and cricket matches, where older folk passed the time of day while younger ones played leap-frog or courted the opposite sex. It was an arena for hawkers to show off their wares, travelling shows to set up their booths and the local pig killers to erect a bench for slaughtering if there was no room elsewhere – in fact a secular focus to complement the church that may or may not have been built next to it. There are exceptions: planned villages in the North-East were laid out around greens after the Conquest, and it has been suggested that Eltisley in Cambridgeshire was planned in the Saxon period, complete with green. But even these planned greens were still likely to be governed by rights of common – and as commons, were vulnerable to landowners wanting to enclose them.

George Eliot describes a classic green near the beginning of *Adam Bede*: on one side a line of thatched cottages leads to the church while an uninterrupted view of the 'gently swelling' countryside opens out on the other. Any Englishman can picture the scene: it is part of his cultural DNA. There are fewer greens in Wales or Scotland, and the idea seems not to have travelled beyond these shores. Irish villages tend to sprawl, French ones are laid out like miniature towns. England turned the village green into a national icon. Approximately one in three English villages has one: 3,650 are registered, according to the Open Spaces Society (contrasting with only 220 in Wales). They are so recognisable, so desirable, that even in the heart of London, a memory of what were once greens, belonging to independent villages before they were swallowed up by a greedy conurbation, has been kept alive, for example in Chelsea and Pimlico, where not a turf of grass is to be seen.

Why did Great Bentley choose to stretch itself around the perimeter of its common, rather than separating off a more conveniently sized morsel to form a classic green? We do not know. But its development was fixed around the time of the Napoleonic Wars, when the landowner gave the green to the village.

# HAUGHLEY
## SUFFOLK
*The organic movement begins*

Square-jawed, with a beret on her head, Lady Eve Balfour was not someone to let the grass grow under her feet. She had been born into a political family, her father having been Gerald Balfour, 2nd Earl of Balfour, brother of the Prime Minister Arthur Balfour and himself an MP; her mother was the daughter of the 1st Earl of Lytton, Viceroy of India. Unconventionally for a woman, she was attracted by farming and, in 1915, went to Reading University to study it. Claiming to be older than she was, she persuaded the Women's War Agricultural Committee to let her run a farm in Monmouthshire. After the First World War, she bought her own farm at Haughley. There she campaigned against tithes, played saxophone in a dance band, gained a pilot's licence and wrote successful detection fiction.

In 1938, she encountered a book written by the future Lord Portsmouth called *Famine in England*. It predicted that Britain would be unable to feed itself, not because of the coming war (Portsmouth's sympathies were pro-Nazi) but because the expanding urban population would overwhelm the countryside's productive capacity. He was a ruralist, who sought to promote a more sustainable attitude towards soil. Lady Eve seized on the message. She at once organised trials on her farm at Haughley. 'This pioneering experiment,' she told an audience of the Soil Association in 1977, 'was the first ecologically designed agricultural research project, on a full farm scale.'

By 1943, the trials were sufficiently advanced for Lady Eve to publish *The Living Soil*. This developed ideas formed by the agronomist Sir Albert Howard, who, as imperial economic botanist to the government of India, came to respect the way in which Asian agriculture maintained soil fertility and kept plants healthy; another influence was Robert McCarrison, who, having noticed the fine physique of the Hunza tribesmen on the north-west frontier, found that this could be explained by their diet: whole grains, vegetables, fruit and milk, with little meat or alcohol. It was a revolutionary insight at the time.

Lady Eve concluded that the vitality of the soil was an essential ingredient in good health, not just for the plant or the animal that ate it, but for mankind as the ultimate consumer. The consequences of neglecting the soil had recently been demonstrated by the disastrous dust bowls created by drought and over-farming in the United States. 'As Europe is in revolt against the tyrant, so is nature in revolt against the exploitation of man,' Lady Eve observed. After the War ended, she was instrumental in founding the Soil Association, still the keeper of the flame of the UK's organic movement. Four per cent of UK land is now managed organically.

Organic was never a word that appealed to Lady Eve; she preferred the term 'biological farming' because of its emphasis on life. Although the first grants for organic agriculture were made, by chance, soon after her death, she was conscious of the argument that, in the short term, her system would not produce the same volume of food as conventional farming. Her answer was that 'organically grown food goes further. When the inevitable change in life-style takes place I predict that we shall find it easier to feed the world population than we think, perhaps easier than now because Western Nations will presumably have become less gluttonous. I predict also that we shall all be healthier!' Words that have not come to pass since she spoke them in 1977, but which may yet prove to be prophetic.

# HAXEY
## LINCOLNSHIRE

The Haxey Hood is not what it was. In former times, the Fool, who is an essential part of this highly ritualised Twelfth Night sport, was swung from a tree, while being 'smoked'. Beneath him was a fire of wet straw, and when he was showing the first signs of suffocation, he would be cut down, so that he dropped into the fire, and left to scramble out as best he could. Smoking the Fool is now a comparatively health-and-safety-conscious affair, with the wet straw lit behind him as he coughs his way through his speech. The speech contains a summary of the succeeding game: 'Hoose agen hoose, toon agen toon, if a man meets a man knock 'im doon, but don't 'ot 'im.' Although the smoking part of the ceremony may have been sanitised, the rough and tumble is still as vigorous as ever, as dangerous as Harry Potter's Quidditch and almost as complicated.

The focus of the game is a leather 'hood', in the shape of a cylinder (or rather a series of hoods, because in a kind of warm-up some extra ones are thrown to the crowd, which has to carry them off the field, pursued by the Boggins or marshals . . . only a flavour of the action can be given here). A kind of four-way rugby scrum known as a sway forms around the hood, its different factions trying to push the mass of humanity – or, rather, the hood that it surrounds – in the direction of one of the local pubs. It is often a slow process getting it there. There is no fixed time on the game, which, starting in mid afternoon, might take a couple of hours, but could go on through the night. There may be two hundred people forming the sway, which – despite the best efforts of the Boggins – is a slowly moving vortex of destruction, taking down hedges, walls and anything else in its path.

The game supposedly originated in an act of rustic chivalry, when Lady de Mowbray, the fourteenth-century wife of a local landowner, lost her riding hood in the wind; a gang of farm workers ran after it, and returned it. As a reward, she gave thirteen acres to the village on condition that the pursuit of the hood would be re-enacted every year. Maybe. But the general scrimmage may not have been very different from other communal games of the Middle Ages*, nearly all of which have now died out.

Why did the Haxey Hood survive? Haxey's location may have had something to do with it: the village is part of the Isle of Axholme, a remote area of North Lincolnshire that was sometimes cut off until the drainage of the Fens. But Victorian ideas of propriety penetrated even here, and various moralists noted that the 'coarse amusement' had all but lost its following during the nineteenth century. The village seems to have made a conscious effort to revive Throwing the Hood as part of its commemorative activities after the Great War. The world yearned to recover contact with the immemorial past, through the folk traditions of the countryside. To judge from the numbers who participate in Haxey Hood today, it still does.

*See Hallaton, page 328

# HELPSTON
CAMBRIDGESHIRE                    *The poet John Clare is not at home*

If you had been visiting Helpston, north-west of Peterborough, in the 1820s, it is possible you would have called on John Clare. He might not have thanked you for it. The son of a thresher and wrestler, he had been brought up to a village existence among people who were mostly, like his mother, illiterate. He called them 'clowns'. His own education had been limited to a Dame school in Helpston – then in Northamptonshire – and a vestry school at nearby Glinton, but as well as being able to read and write he had an intense ability to observe.

He tried various jobs, working as a plough boy, as a pot boy at the Blue Bell Inn, as a gardener at Burghley House, as a lawyer's clerk, before joining the Northamptonshire militia (he was not much of a soldier and was soon back home). But all the while he was writing his own poetry, scribbling it down on scraps of paper he kept inside his hat. Through a Stamford bookseller he came into contact with Keats's publisher John Taylor. His first book, *Poems Descriptive of Rural Life and Scenery*, was published in 1820, soon followed by *The Village Minstrel*. He was acclaimed by literary society. Some of it beat a path, literally, to his cottage door.

It was the cottage where, in 1793, he had been born. Limestone built, but whitewashed, with a thatched roof, it was one half of a pair of cottages – and not even that. In Clare's father's time, the half had been subdivided so that the Clares had only the ground floor, with a russet apple tree in the garden whose fruit provided much of the rent. Clare described it in 'My Early Home':

> The old house stooped just like a cave
> Thatched o'er with mosses green
> Winter around the walls would rave
> But all was calm within
> The trees they were as green agen
> Where bees the flowers would kiss
> But flowers and trees seemed sweeter then
> My early home was this –

Unlike George Crabbe*, a country doctor who, in revealing the misery behind the picturesque exterior of rural life in *The Village*, wrote with the moral superiority of a magistrate, Clare described the world as he found it. He was a sharp-eyed naturalist and an equally keen student of women. To begin with, he composed with the Augustan phrases of James Thomson's *The Seasons* ringing in his ears, and more than a nod to Oliver Goldsmith's *The Deserted Village†*. These early poems, derivative and self-consciously literary, were to prove his most successful. As he developed, his mode of expression became increasingly direct. He employed the vocabulary of Northamptonshire people, which might have seemed barbarous to his polished audience in London.

But Helpston did not celebrate Clare's literary triumphs; if anything, it turned against him. He found it increasingly frustrating to be immured within the confines of the village. In 1832 his friends helped him to move from Helpston to Northborough, a few miles away; though geographically close, he found it a terrible dislocation. Perhaps he drank; he may have suffered from venereal disease. He descended into insanity, becoming a voluntary inmate of an asylum in Epping Forest. From there he escaped and walked the eighty miles back to Northborough, feeding off grass.

The last twenty-three years of his life were spent in the Northampton General Lunatic Asylum. 'Restless revels of rhyme' had sapped his memory, he wrote in his unpublished autobiography. 'I knew nothing of the poets experience then or I should have remaind a labourer on and not livd to envy the ignorance of my old companions and fellow clowns. I wish I had never known any other.'

&ast; See Muston, page 340. †See Willingham, page 282

# HEMINGFORD GREY
## CAMBRIDGESHIRE
*The romance of old stones*

During the reign of Edward I, the people of Huntingdon were cross with Roger de Grey. Holding the manor of Hemingford, to which his surname became added to distinguish it from the Abbot of Ramsey's Hemingford Abbots, he diverted the course of the Great Ouse through his mills. As a result, boats going to and from Huntingdon found themselves beached. More recently, the problem has been not too little water but too much. 'Everywhere there was water,' Lucy Boston wrote, describing the place at flood time in the 1950s, 'not sea or rivers or lakes, but just senseless flood water with the rain splashing into it.'

The village faces away from the river but cannot forget about it, and the Environment Agency has been hard at work trying to improve defences. Nevertheless, it remains a tranquil, undisturbed spot – the sort of place that would, around March, inspire underground animals and town dwellers to say 'bother spring cleaning' and set off for the riverbank. You cannot miss the gardens. The path by the river goes right through one of them, planted with hyacinths. The owners of River House have thoughtfully made an opening in the wall so you can look through and enjoy their lawn and old trees. The garden of the Manor House is open to the public. You put a pound in a jam jar freighted with stones.

The Manor House at Hemingford Grey is one of the oldest houses in the country. Norman windows give into a hall that dates from the late twelfth century. You can visit by appointment unless the owner is still clearing up after the fall of a ceiling, but even then, as she says, the house has been standing for nine hundred years and will still be there when you come back. This is a proper English house, with old yew trees and a friendly jumble of old bicycles and buckets beneath the pantile roof of the wood store. The garden has a graceful parade of topiary chess pieces. Beehives can be glimpsed among daffodils on the other side of the river-bank. But that riverbank: Ratty would have skulled off somewhere quieter when the Environment Agency was there. The bleeps from reversing dumper diggers drove the gardener mad.

Still, the noise is over now, and we are left with the house. What gives it such charm? In the late 1930s, Lucy Boston came here, when the Manor House was an architectural muddle; she devoted the next thirty years of her life to it. Hemingford Grey became Green Knowe, the setting for a series of children's stories that evoke the romance of the place. *The Children of Green Knowe*, published in 1954, was the first; that same year saw her first adult novel, *Yew Hall*, in which the manor, thinly veiled, also takes centre stage. It was the beginning of her literary career, and she was already sixty-four.

Hemingford Grey wove its spell around her – and she wove her spell around it. When she first saw the house, while punting in 1915, it was 'wrapped' in 'primeval quietness'; later, she was nearly deterred from buying it because so many people came to the river that punts had to be reserved in advance. During the Second World War, she filled the house with music and art, sharing it as fully as she could with the young men of the bomber squadron stationed nearby. Meanwhile – from the fact she had once lived in Austria and wore a dirndl skirt – the rest of the village thought she was a spy. You feel her presence still.

*See also Hammoon, page 41*

# HILTON
## CAMBRIDGESHIRE
*Quaint mazes in the wanton green*

The verb 'to amaze' derives from maze, suggesting that its labyrinthine paths not only bamboozle but astonish. Their origins seem to be just as perplexing as their intricate shape. There was a great labyrinth in Egypt near Crocodilopolis, visited by the Ancient Greek historian Herodotus, who found it 'greater than words can tell'. Nobody knows what its purpose was. Similar mystery surrounds later mazes, for example those sometimes found on the floors or walls of medieval churches. It has been suggested that they symbolised the perplexities that beset the Christian life, or the entangling nature of sin. They may have played some function in penances imposed on the faithful as a result of confession (did the penitent have to complete the maze on his knees?), a possibility supported by the name by which they are sometimes known, *Chemin de Jérusalem* (Road of Jerusalem).

At Hilton there is a turf maze – a form special to England. Unlike hedge or topi-ary mazes, where the path is followed between walls of greenery, turf mazes are horizontal; as at Hilton, they are often set into the sward of a village green, and the path is formed by a ribbon of raised turf. Turf mazes are vulnerable to being ploughed over, neglected or, in the case of the Shepherd's Ring (mazes were often given names) at Boughton Green, Northamptonshire, dug up by soldiers making trenches during the First World War. As Titania observes in *A Midsummer Night's Dream*:

> . . . the quaint mazes in the wanton green,
> For lack of tread are undistinguishable.

Fortunately the Hilton example is particularly well preserved because the design was originally laid down as a bed of pebbles.

As the quotation above shows, turf mazes existed during Shakespeare's day, and their origins may be much older. They often look like ecclesiastical mazes, suggesting that they could originally have served a similar function (whatever that may have been). By the seventeenth century, they were used for rustic games. Describing Julian's Bower at Alkborough in Lincolnshire and Troy's Walls at Appleby, the Yorkshire antiquarian Abraham de la Pryme refers to 'a hill cast up round them for the spectators to sit round about on to behold the sport'. Writing in 1686, John Aubrey describes the maze at Pimperne in Dorset as being 'much used by the young people on Holydaies and by ye School-boies'. Hilton is unusual because we know when it was made: 1660. This is recorded on a stone sundial in the middle of the maze, together with the name of the man responsible, William Sparrow, Gent., who was born in 1641 and lived until he was eighty-eight. Since he was nineteen at the time, and it was the year in which the repressive Commonwealth, with its disapproval of country sports, ended and Charles II was restored, it may well be that the purpose of this maze, at least, was fun.

# HITCHAM
## SUFFOLK                                                   *Botanist turns rector*

John Stevens Henslow, Charles Darwin's mentor at Cambridge, became rector of Hitcham in 1837. He was not someone to take a fat income while leaving religious duties to a curate. With a wife and young family, he went to live in the comfortable vicarage, which had been remodelled by the previous incumbent, in 1839. He had reformed the teaching of botanical studies at Cambridge; now he set about reforming the parish.

On being made professor of botany he had, as he later admitted, known 'very little indeed about botany', although he 'probably knew as much of the subject as any other resident in Cambridge'. Henslow revived the botanical gardens, gave lectures, ran field classes and entertained undergraduates to soirées at his house overlooking Parker's Piece. His open personality captivated his students, who, although awed by the extent of his knowledge, felt, in the words of one of them, 'completely at ease with him'. Darwin, not a particularly brilliant student, fell under his spell, regarding the encounter with Henslow as the most formative event of his career.

At Hitcham, Henslow found 'a woefully neglected parish, where the inhabitants, with regard to food and clothing and the means of observing the decencies of life, were far below the average scale of the peasant class in England'. His brother-in-law Leonard Jenyns, who wrote a memoir of Henslow, filled out the picture of 'a people sunk almost to the lowest depths of moral and physical debasement'. It had been a flourishing place once, with a sixteenth-century guildhall. Now it had sunk to being little more than a hamlet.

Only a handful of people went to church. Henslow set about recalling 'his flock from sin and idleness to habits of soberness, honesty, and industry', not by preaching at them, but by giving them something constructive to do. He organised a cricket club. He got up a subscription for Hitcham Parish School, to replace the old Dame school, which was run by a woman who had 'no knowledge of the art of teaching'. The parishioners lived in wretched hovels, with leaky thatch and sometimes no drainage, in which they ate a diet composed principally of bread and potatoes. Henslow promoted self-help clubs, by which they could save for winter fuel and medicine.

As a magistrate, the rector was, in the manner of the day, severe on those who took self-improvement too far into their own hands: fifteen years' transportation was the sentence for rustling a sheep. Farmers did not escape censure, however; at a time when rick burning was common, they were reminded that worse could follow if they did not do more for their labourers. For this Henslow got little thanks. Without a squire in the big house to support him, he ploughed a lonely furrow. Like Cobbett*, the Suffolk farmers thought education impractical. They particularly objected to Henslow's attempts to establish allotments. The effort that labourers put into them would, they believed, reduce the labour that they could give their employers. Eventually Henslow found enough land for more than fifty allotment holders to have a quarter of an acre each. Conditions improved; discontent subsided. When Henslow died ten years later, his funeral was as simple as possible, but a large number of the village labourers asked to attend.

*See Botley, page 97

# HOMERSFIELD

SUFFOLK                                    *Britain's first concrete bridge*

Concrete and the countryside: they do not always seem to go comfortably together. To many people, concrete is an alien material, incapable of harmonising with the scene amid which it sits because the materials from which it is made generally come from elsewhere. Nor is it apt to mellow attractively with age; on the contrary, it streaks and spalls and looks dreary when not maintained. Architects love it, because of the obliging way in which it can be poured to form any three-dimensional shape that they might invent; in the decades after the Second World War, it became synonymous with not just new buildings, but a new, brighter future in the towns and cities. Village people did not on the whole welcome it; they did not think it fitted in.

Yet concrete – a mixture of sand and gravel or broken brick, stuck together by a binding agent (cement) – is an ancient material. The Romans knew about it; their binding agent was a ground-up volcanic rock called pozzolana. In Rome, the dome of the Pantheon – forty-three metres across – is made of concrete, and still stands after nearly nineteen hundred years. When the Roman Empire ended, the technique was lost.

It was James Smeaton, requiring a mortar that would set underwater to build the Eddystone Lighthouse, who rediscovered pozzolana, which had been described by the Roman architect Vitruvius. Galvanised by this work, he conducted a series of experiments on other cements, which he published in 1791. Lime* was the most commonly used cement in Britain; it was thought necessary that the resulting concrete had to be dropped into place from a height (three metres, in the case of the Houses of Parliament's foundations) to be effective.

Not only does concrete have a history, some early manifestations of the material can be found in and around villages. Lord Ashburton was experimenting with concrete cottages as early as 1868 at All Cannings in Wiltshire: he began with what may have been a challenge to one of his tenant farmers, who built a pair of cottages in brick while – on the adjacent plot – Ashburton built an identical one in concrete. Presumably Ashburton was pleased with the new material, since he went on to build several other village houses out of it.

What is called mass concrete can withstand compression, but, unlike steel, cannot withstand much lateral stress. When, however, steel reinforcements are put inside the concrete, the virtues of both materials are combined. Reinforced concrete (and the variant of pre-stressed concrete, where the steel wires are put under tension before the concrete is poured) became the twentieth century's favourite material for road bridges. A precursor of such bridges had been built at Homersfield in 1870. An iron cage was constructed, then filled with concrete. It spans the river Waveney in a fifty-foot arch, surmounted by a stout cast-iron railing.

This was the first concrete bridge built in Britain. Quite how much the people responsible knew about structural engineering is uncertain, but they built soundly:

the bridge has served for a hundred and forty years, and is now resplendent after a restoration. The earliest examples of truly reinforced concrete bridges are credited to Louis Gustave Mouchel, a Frenchman who acted as UK agent for the Hennebique system. Mouchel's first bridge in Britain was built in 1901 at another country location: Chewton Glen in the New Forest.

*See Barrow upon Soar, page 299; Limekilns, page 599

# IRNHAM
## LINCOLNSHIRE
*Pictures of medieval life*

Meet Sir Geoffrey Luttrell, lord of Irnham. With his wife, Agnes Sutton, and his daughter-in-law, Beatrice Scrope, he is shown – a fully caparisoned knight, stepping out on his warhorse – in a miniature in the book of psalms, or psalter, that he commissioned around 1330. Sir Geoffrey liked to make a mark: unusually, the scribe has written the words 'Dominus Galfridus Louterell me fieri fecit' above the miniature, leaving no doubt as to the patron.

Perhaps he also had strong views about the decoration, because the Luttrell Psalter, now one of the treasures of the British Library, stands apart from other devotional works in its vivid record of medieval rural life: the sights that would have greeted Sir Geoffrey daily when he rode around his estate. The margins of the book teem with activity. In between images of the Crucifixion and the Virgin Mary, we see food being cooked, dinner served, a lady at her toilet, sports and games (such as archery practice), a windmill, a watermill, eel traps in the river, a goose and goslings being attacked by a hawk, a grindstone, a boy in a tree stealing cherries (to the displeasure of the tree's owner below).

What relevance have the illustrations to the text? Sometimes they provide a visual equivalent of the words. The psalmist's observation (in the Vulgate, or Latin, translation by St Jerome) that 'the foolish man shall not know; nor will the stupid man understand these things' is accompanied by a picture of a fool. The reference to 'a pelican in the wilderness . . . and as a sparrow all alone on the housetop' inspires a small bird and a large pelican on branches. A leper, being wheeled in a kind of barrow, his begging bowl by his side, evokes famine. Other images seem to be puns on words or parts of words, or fantasies suggested by words reassembled in a different order. Fabulous creatures and strange hybrids – a fiddler with animal legs, a man whose head is located on his backside – co-exist with the plodding round of oxen at the plough, harvest being gathered in, and peasants taking corn to their lord's mills.

Seven centuries on, the arrangement of Irnham is much as it would have been in medieval times. St Andrew's church stands on the rise of a small, wooded hill, the big house lies just beyond it, and there at the bottom of the hill sit the fishponds that would have provided Sir Geoffrey's household with its Friday dinner.

Where Sir Geoffrey Luttrell's countryside would have been busy with cowled folk bent over their tasks on the land, today's fields are empty: most of the people who live in modern Irnham do not work here. But the village has not stood still. About ten years ago, the Benton Jones family, owners of Irnham Hall – a rambling Tudor affair, which seems to have absorbed fragments of Sir Geoffrey's hall – decided to expand the village, doing so with remarkable tact. The dozen or so houses that they built using traditional materials are already beginning to look mellow with age. At the church, fund-raisers have been so successful in raising money for repairs that they could treat themselves to a new bell, as well as a door designed by Ptolomy Dean.

# JAYWICK
## ESSEX                                   *Chaos or individual expression?*

There is a moral in Jaywick: it shows what could happen in a Britain without planning laws. In 1928, the developer Frank Stedman bought twenty-four acres of fields and salt marsh near Clacton-on-Sea. Since the building of the pier in 1871, Clacton had ballooned into a popular seaside resort for Londoners, and Stedman thought that he could attract a similar clientele to buy chalets. He parcelled up the land into small plots, and sold them around the East End.

It was in some ways a democratic undertaking, on the model of Peacehaven in Sussex, which, since 1914, had spilled itself along a previously idyllic five miles of the south coast. Social campaigners, such as the utopian William Morris, had been inveighing against the evils of the smoke-choked city since the mid nineteenth century. The Salvation Army* had established a colony at Hadleigh in Essex, where 'the residue of unemployed and unemployable labour' – as Beatrice Webb observed when she visited in 1908 – could be introduced to healthful self-sufficiency in the countryside. Not that Stedman could be accused of idealism. He seems to have been motivated entirely by money. To the cockneys who were his market, however, a place by the seaside, on its own little piece of land, seemed a heavenly alternative to the crowded, blackened terraces of the East End.

There was talk of a lake, sports facilities, landscaping. None of it materialised. One of the problems was the attitude of the local authority. Wanting to scotch the development, the planning office refused to allow the first houses to be connected to mains drainage. Stedman redefined the settlement as one of beach huts, equipped with portable lavatories that were emptied daily. The settlers, building their own bungalows or modifying those that could be bought off-the-peg, ignored the council's efforts to restrict Jaywick occupancy to the summer months. Their supposed beach huts had bedrooms – as many as six in some cases. They developed their own vernacular style, applying decorative woodwork to asbestos panels and pushing out porches and bay windows. The result was anarchy, not because of the architecture so much as the absence of infrastructure. Its spirit reflected that of the early years of mass motoring – many of the roads are named after brands of car (Austin, Hillman, Vauxhall, Bentley, Daimler). Ironically, one of the failures of Jaywick was the chronic state of the roads.

Although beside the sea, Jaywickers could not actually see it from their bungalow windows: the development is below sea level, protected from the waters by a stout concrete wall. On 31 January 1953, when it was blowing a gale on a night of high tides, the greatest storm surge ever experienced in the North Sea breached the sea defences along the East coast of England. At Jaywick, the sea level rose by a metre in quarter of an hour; thirty-five people drowned. The community rebuilt itself, although by the early twenty-first century it would be recognised as one of the most socially deprived in Britain. Architecturally, an effort was made to address this in 1999–2000 with a development of weatherboarded, environmentally excellent houses, built so that, once their occupants were rehoused, some of the original chalets could be demolished. Demolition, however, was fiercely resisted. Despite its flimsy, frontier-town character, Jaywick has succeeded where many more architecturally prestigious schemes have failed: it has personality, and woe betide anyone wanting to threaten it.

*See Boxted, page 216

# LAVENHAM
SUFFOLK                                                    *The riches brought by wool*

The carved wooden figure of St Blaise peers out of a parclose in Lavenham church. He was combed to death. This martyrdom does not make him the patron saint of hairdressers, but of the wool trade; the weavers of Lavenham would have been familiar with the iron, long-tined combs on which St Blaise met his fate. Like the Cotswolds, Suffolk was a centre for wool, and prosperity showed itself in the proudly jettied houses, ornately carved guildhalls and dramatically oversized churches of Lavenham and many other small towns along the Stour valley.

The parclose provided a chapel where masses could be said for the soul of the clothier Thomas Spring III. The rise of the Spring family can be seen on the flint tower of Lavenham church. At the base, begun in the 1480s, their merchant badges mingle with the coat-of-arms of the de Vere Earls of Oxford who, as lords of the manor, were other donors. By the time the parapet was reached in the early 1520s, the Springs had been granted their own arms, which are emblazoned around it. Thomas Spring III, who left two hundred pounds on his death in 1523 'to the finishing of the steeple', was so immensely rich that he could look the aristocracy in the eye. He left sixteen Suffolk manors, seven Norfolk manors and property in nearly a hundred villages.

Lavenham made woollen broadcloth. The industry boomed under the early Tudors, with exports being sent as far as the Middle East. By the end of Elizabeth I's reign it was in retreat. Initially politics caused the decline. Nearly all Suffolk's coloured cloths were sold to countries such as Spain and Portugal, but the Armada dealt a blow to that trade. The Thirty Years War in the early seventeenth century put other markets beyond reach; Suffolk's last cargo of coloured cloth took ship to Smyrna in 1657. Fashion also played a part. The Flemish, who came to England as refugees in their hundreds, introduced new kinds of cloth (called bays and says), and broadcloth went out of style. Its half century in the sun seemed to have drained Suffolk of commercial energy, and it went back to farming.

Only the architecture was left to suggest what Lavenham had been before 1530. There are private houses, but many of the most elaborate have gone: they were surplus to requirements after money ebbed away from the town. Instead what survives, apart from the church, are the guildhalls. There were originally at least five. They were not to protect a craft – Lavenham was too small for guilds of that type – but were a cross between religious societies and self-help groups. Motivation came from the gnawingly awful prospect of purgatory; it was believed that the time someone's soul would spend there could be reduced by prayers and masses after death*. While the Thomas Springs of the world could afford to hire priests to say masses for their souls in their own chantries, guilds allowed members to have their names read in masses held for several people at once.

They also provided a kind of insurance, in case members found themselves on hard times. Membership conferred prestige on those who belonged; guilds took a prominent role in the ceremonies of the parish. They built appropriate structures in which to meet and show off their status. At Lavenham, the richest of the guild-halls, dedicated to Corpus Christi, is owned by the National Trust. Among the objects on display there is a mummified cat, found in the roof of a nearby house. It would have been placed there – presumably not mummified at that stage – to ward off evil spirits. In matters spiritual, Lavenham did not take chances.

*See Ewelme, page 174

# LITTLE GIDDING
## CAMBRIDGESHIRE                          *A powerfully spiritual place*

In 1624, the Virginia Company, which had founded the American colony of Virginia in 1607, was wound up when the King withdrew its charter. It had been appallingly managed since its foundation. During the final years, its deputy, John Ferrar, tried to make what sense he could of its affairs, but he found himself embroiled in the catastrophe; he was on the point of being ruined. A solution was found, which involved the purchase of the manor of Little Gidding by John's widowed mother, Mary, from a bankrupt former partner. John, Mary and John's brilliant younger brother, Nicholas, decided to go and live there. They wanted to pursue a spiritual life. An outbreak of plague meant that they left London sooner than they intended. They arrived at Little Gidding in 1626.

*Little Gidding: a centre of refined Royalist spirituality, later celebrated by T. S. Eliot.*

The manor had been all but abandoned. An Elizabethan owner had enclosed it, possibly evicting some of the inhabitants, whose numbers had been already reduced by plague. None of the houses was occupied, the church had not been used for sixty years, and only a shepherd was still living there, in a hut. Before anything else, Mary Ferrar cleaned the church and said prayers. The manor house was then put right, and the land let. Under Nicholas's leadership, the family followed a regime dedicated to a timetable of prayer. They lived austerely. John looked like a priest, and Nicholas went some way to becoming one, being ordained as a deacon by Charles I's Archbishop of Canterbury, William Laud. Although they worshipped according to the *Book of Common Prayer*, word got around that they were Papists.

When John, Nicholas and Mary Ferrar were joined by John and Nicholas's sister Susanna, with her husband, John Collet, and their family of many children, the household grew to forty people. They printed books, played and wrote music, and Nicholas, in the hours between the almost constant round of services and prayer, translated Latin texts. Medicines were dispensed to local people, and children taught. The little ones followed a dry curriculum, consisting principally of Bible study, but it was not unkindly done. To make their learning more enjoyable, they were set the task of composing concordances, or harmonies: lines of the printed texts of the four Gospels were cut out and pasted into one book in the correct order; the pages were decorated with appropriate prints.

In the spring of 1642, King Charles visited. By this time Nicholas was dead. Charles would soon raise his Standard at Nottingham, opening the Civil War. For now, he could delight in the community (he already owned two of their harmonies), the young princes being fed with apple pies and cheesecakes in the buttery. 'Little Gidding is a happy place,' he said. 'I am glad to have seen it.' He would see it again, as his star fell to earth in 1646: he had escaped from Oxford, and was making his fugitive way north, in the hope of finding sympathy from the Scots. Little Gidding was too hot for him to stay there; John Ferrar took him somewhere safer, to Coppingford Lodge.

After the Ferrar family was dead, Little Gidding remained a powerfully spiritual place. One evening in 1848, William Hopkinson, a solicitor from Stamford, happened to see that the estate was for sale, and bought it sight unseen. 'The possession of this spot was through an extraordinary impulse and I feel a solemn duty is to be performed towards it,' he wrote to a friend. T. S. Eliot visited on a spring afternoon in 1938; afterwards he wrote the last of his great reflections on time and interconnectedness, *Four Quartets*.

# LITTLE MELTON
## NORFOLK
*Painted ladies in church*

Medieval churches have been called sermons in stone, because they incorporated so many carved and stained-glass images to reinforce the teaching of the Church to an illiterate congregation. They were also sermons in paint. Most of the painted decoration has disappeared, or been destroyed during the waves of Puritan iconoclasm that followed the Reformation. But the number of fragments, and occasionally whole schemes, that survive suggests that painting was commonplace. It also began early, certainly with the Normans, perhaps before.

Like the sermon from the pulpit, murals tended to emphasise correct behaviour. Scenes from the Gospels seem to occur rarely. The Seven Deadly Sins, however, were a popular subject; so were the Seven Works of Mercy. In the charming flint church of Little Melton, two elegant women can be seen conversing on a bench. They lean gracefully towards each other, comparing what might be costly rosaries, just as though they were two Ladies Who Lunch (or do not lunch very much, because, like their modern-day equivalents, they are slim). Their clothes, falling in long Gothic pleats, are the height of 1370s fashion for Norfolk, one of the women fastening her bodice with large round buttons.

Attractive – and believable – though the scene looks, it is intended as a warning. There is (difficult to see now) a devil sitting beside them; there may originally have been one behind. The women are Idle Gossips. Rather on the wartime basis that dangerous talk costs lives, medieval society believed that excessive chatter endangered the soul. The devil Tutivillus had the job of collecting together all the syllables that had fallen unheard during church services. Perhaps he balanced them with the surplus syllables that were produced without need. At Slapton in Northamptonshire, two gossips are overshadowed by a very large devil; gossip was a sin to be taken seriously.

There cannot have been many individuals like these women on the medieval manor; was their inclusion a jibe at the lord's household? Gossip, to judge from the frescoes, was regarded as a feminine vice. Perhaps it was also seen, even then, as one to which the more affluent were especially vulnerable; uneducated peasants, whose lives were spent within the same parish, cannot have had time to join the chattering classes, or much to chatter about.

# LITTLE SNORING
NORFOLK                                      *The wind sock still flutters*

'Give Way to Aircraft'. The sign, anchored to an old car tyre, proclaims this is an active airfield. You would not know it; the sign itself is so weathered that you can hardly read it. Only an orange windsock stands out stiffly in the blustering wind. Beneath it, the brick control tower is derelict, the man in the car next to it here only to inspect his owl boxes. Two of the runways are overgrown. Little Snoring Airfield, Class A, built by Taylor Woodrow in 1942–3, is not what it was when Bomber Command's Number 115 squadron arrived, with a thunderous roar of Lancasters, during the Second World War.

But those days are not forgotten. In St Andrew's church, with its round flint-built Norfolk tower and Norman doorway, three wooden panels list in golden italics the 'Victories' for the fighter planes that came to replace the bombers. A fourth panel records Awards and Decorations. In November 1944, Squadron Leader Marlin, who had already been awarded the Distinguished Service Order and the Distinguished Flying Cross (with bar, meaning he won it twice), gained the second bar to his DFC.

The boards form a remarkable set of documents from an age when the Church of England was not shy about commemorating feats of arms. It is right that Little Snoring's war should have a record. The airfield revolutionalised life in what had previously been a sleepy Norfolk community. At its height, it was served by more than two thousand RAF personnel, who lived and ate on eleven different sites around the village. Like dozens of other unpretending little places around East Anglia, Lincolnshire and the south coast, Little Snoring (population: 272 in the 2001 census) was shaken into life. After the War, it subsided into its previous torpor. Almost.

Back at the airfield, at the other end of the one maintained runway, a hangar, labelled McAully Flying Group in enormous letters, shows that the initial impression of abandonment is mistaken. The flying club is named after its founder, Elwyn McAully, who was killed while practising for an aeronautical display in 1960. Membership is growing. From half a dozen members, it has reached thirty and waiting. Flying has grown in popularity in the countryside. Little Snoring is waking up.

# LITTLE STEEPING
## LINCOLNSHIRE
*A local vernacular*

Mud and stud is a form of construction found only in Lincolnshire. It was always rather flimsy. In most areas of the country, timber-framed houses were built of robust oak members – although the quality, as well as quantity, of the wood used declined in proportion to the improvements in carpentry and the appearance of better cladding materials, such as weatherboarding, tile-hanging and plaster, in the seventeenth and eighteenth centuries.

Mud and stud is similar to wattle and daub. The frame, although generally oak in early examples, was skimpy, consisting only of upright studs joined at top and bottom by a cross rail. (When oak became scarce during the eighteenth century and later, it was replaced by pine imported through King's Lynn and Boston from the Baltic.) Thin staves made of ash were attached to the outside of the studs, the whole thing banged together with nails and daubed – with the aid of a two-pronged daubing fork – with a stiff mixture of mud, straw, animal hair and dung. Usually the laths were braced with a rail, to which they were nailed.

When the daub, which covered both the inside and outside of the dwelling, had dried, it was limewashed. Mixed with animal fat or oil to render it weatherproof, the limewash would have to be reapplied every year or possibly every six months, because it was washed off by rain. Originally roofs were usually thatched, later being laid with the pantiles that are much seen in Lincolnshire.

Documentary evidence of mud-and-stud building is scant. There is what appears to be a reference in the Saleby parish overseer's account in 1696, but the earliest parts of Heggy's Cottage, a rare example of an unaltered mud-and-stud cottage at Haconby, date from around 1500, when the cottage would have been open to the roof. It was later floored. Little Steeping has an example of a mud-and-stud cottage from the mid eighteenth century, Mill Hill cottage. It is in the care of the Lincolnshire Heritage Trust, which restored it as a holiday cottage in 2000 (it is sometimes open to the public, or can be rented through the Vivat Trust). Once, there would have been thousands of mud-and-stud buildings across the county, but they were small (in the case of cottages, a ground floor plus attic) and, if allowed to decay, insanitary; many have been swept away. Only about three hundred and fifty are now known to exist, most of them, like Little Steeping, in the district of East Lindsey.

# LONG MELFORD
SUFFOLK                                   *Private beneficence of the almshouse*

If ever there was a local boy who did well it was Sir William Cordell. He was born near Long Melford, where his father was major-domo to Sir William Clopton of Kentwell Hall. Clopton's antecedents can be seen in Long Melford church, not only in effigies but a glorious sequence of stained-glass windows, one of the ladies being taken by John Tenniel as his inspiration for the Duchess in *Alice's Adventures in Wonderland*. Cordell was blessed with wits rather than ancestry, and used them to become Master of the Rolls and Speaker of the House of Commons. He married Mary Clopton, granddaughter of his father's employer, and having acquired the manor of Long Melford from the Crown, proceeded to build an even more splendid house than Kentwell: Melford Hall. You do not get much impression of the man's dynamism from the alabaster sculpture on his tomb. But it shows his red hair. True to type, he was energetic and self-willed.

Cordell's hall is visible to all, opposite the church; being on the other side of the river, however, what residents still generally call the village (although to judge from the number of shops down the long street, it must surely verge on being a town) is kept at a respectful remove. Cordell remembered the villagers by building them an almshouse called Trinity Hospital. It was founded to accommodate twelve poor men and two poor women in 1580, the year before Cordell's death. As an MP, Cordell would have been well aware of the crisis of poverty that had developed in sixteenth-century England. An effect of the Dissolution of the Monasteries had been to close the infirmaries operated by the monks. There had been eight hundred of them across England in the mid 1530s. Hardly any were left thirty years later.

During Edward VI's reign, the Duke of Somerset and Duke of Northumberland, who acted as regents, stripped the chantries, which gave homes to the poor in return for prayers for the dead, and guilds, self-help groups that might provide social provision*, to augment the royal purse and their own. With few institutions to help them, the poor, particularly wounded soldiers and sailors, were forced to beg. Cordell had been part of the Parliament that passed the 1572 Poor Law, which required parishes to collect a poor rate for the relief of the aged, the sick and the poor. An Act of 1576 allowed for the creation of poorhouses. But public provision remained rudimentary and inadequate to the problem, which continued to get worse as the century drew to a close; it was no match for private munificence.

Munificent the Trinity Hospital certainly was. It followed in the tradition of Thomas Sutton's Charterhouse in London and Lord Leycester's Hospital at Warwick, but whereas they incorporated old monastic buildings, Cordell started from scratch. The site that he chose was at the top of the green, opposite Melford Hall. It was built of red brick; a row of tall double chimney stacks suggests the warmth of the rooms, those of the male pensioners being disposed around three sides of a sheltering courtyard, with the fourth side occupied by the women and two wardens. The result is a splendid exhibition of philanthropy, cannily made when Cordell's own need for the money was over (it was mostly built after his death). Purgatory – the hope of reducing time there having been the motive for bestowing chantries a century before – was no longer a doctrine of the Church of England, but a route to heaven could still be provided by good works.

*See Lavenham, page 251; Ewelme, page 174

# NEW BUCKENHAM
## NORFOLK
*A Norman plantation*

The twelfth-century canon who wrote the Waltham Chronicle had a low opinion of William d'Aubigny, 1st Earl of Arundel. Having married Henry I's widow in 1138, d'Aubigny 'became arrogant and inordinately conceited . . . and anything that our world possessed that was special, apart from the king, was worthless in his eyes'. Nevertheless, like other Normans, he was a great builder of castles, religious foundations and what he hoped would be towns. One of his castles was Castle Rising, a palatial structure built to provide an appropriate setting for the Queen, who was now his wife.

New Buckenham, with its settlement, is just as interesting. D'Aubigny's father had been lord of Buckenham, now to be called Old Buckenham, a mile and a half away, and it already had a castle. D'Aubigny went to some expense in acquiring the new site, since he had to buy it from the Bishop of Norwich. Having done so, he threw himself into building, not waiting for the new castle to be built before demolishing the old. Perhaps because building with flint makes it difficult to form corners, as can supposedly be seen from Norfolk's characteristically circular church towers, he pioneered the circular plan years before it was taken up for military reasons (corners came to be seen as vulnerable to undermining). Old Buckenham became the site of a monastery – one up on the leper house that d'Aubigny established at Castle Rising.

He also pulled down the old village and laid out another outside the gates of the new castle. Although Old Buckenham Priory, with its prior and eight canons, was so close, his ambition for New Buckenham can be seen from his decision to include space for a church. This would not have been popular with the Church hierarchy, whose rectors were in receipt of lucrative privileges from the existing parish structure. Only a powerful lord could have done it.

Over the centuries, the settlement fared better than the castle, which has been reduced to a ring of flints on a motte, surrounded by a water-filled ditch and banks. Even so, it may not have fulfilled all of d'Aubigny's hopes. Other Norman planned settlements became notable towns, for example, Selby, where the abbot transformed the village next to the abbey founded in 1069 by building a market-place and staithes (abbots, like lords, wanted to profit from the revenues that property development could generate).

New Buckenham never grew much beyond the boundaries that d'Aubigny set. Like Pleshey, so completely surrounded by its castle walls that it looks like a green side plate left out on the chequered tablecloth of Essex fields, it is now nothing more than a village. But its failure to grow has left its Norman shape easier to read. It follows a grid pattern, symmetrical around the central axis of Chapel Street. To the east lies the common, grazed for eight hundred years. The church was not built in d'Aubigny's time, but came to occupy the space he had left for it almost exactly a century after New Buckenham was begun.

# PARSON DROVE
## CAMBRIDGESHIRE                                *Samuel Pepys in the Fens*

On 17 September 1663, Samuel Pepys stayed at Parson Drove in the Cambridgeshire Fens. He had made the journey from Brampton, where his uncle Robert Pepys lived, with 'much ado', his horse sometimes sinking up to its belly in water. After a hard ride, he found Parson Drove 'a heathen place', his uncle and aunt Perkins, with their daughters, living as 'poor wretches, in a sad poor thatched cottage, like a poor barne or stable'. They were poorly dressed and engaged in peeling hemp, which would later be made into rope. The Swan Inn was 'miserable', his cousin Frank sang a 'country bawdy song', and Pepys felt ashamed to have his relations to supper. To cap it all, one of their horses was stolen out of the stable, Pepys being 'inwardly glad' that it was not his. Bed at midnight led him to 'a sad, cold, nasty chamber', his only consolation being that he was able to kiss the 'indifferent hand-some' maid. Well, at least the horse was later found. By morning Pepys discovered that he had been bitten cruelly by the dreaded fenland gnats.

Poor Pepys, one might have thought he would have had better luck. Ten years earlier the Commissioners of Sewers had announced that the drainage of Parson Drove Fen was complete, and the Earl of Bedford and thirteen other 'gentlemen adventurers' took possession of it – all 95,000 acres – as payment for their work in draining the Bedford Level. Part of it is still known as Adventurers' Land. They had been at the work since 1630. Pepys might have seen the Old South Eau and Lady Nunn's Old Eau, and certainly the ancient drain known as the Cats' Water, which the adventurers had cleared of weeds. These took a winding course, unlike the fer-ociously straight canals, such as the North Level Main Drain, made in the nineteenth century. Bedford's object was to make the Fens into summer grazing, which might flood during winter. The name of Parson Drove suggests that local people, when not fishing for eels, made a living from cattle – drove meaning somewhere that cattle were driven. The name of a village pub, the Butcher's Arms, suggests another connection with animals. This Drove was called 'Parson' because it had a chapel.

Despite Bedford, Parson Drove remained fever-wracked and isolated well into the nineteenth century. That, however, did not stop Frederic John Gardiner, writing his *History of Wisbech and Neighbourhood During the Last Fifty Years* in 1898, being nettled by Pepys's comments. 'Although this may have been a faithful picture of the village, 233 years ago, the improvements that have since been made would now justify a very different description.' The Swan Inn had undergone 'considerable alterations'. As for being 'heathen', Parson Drove was now its own parish, the vicar to whom the living was given having previously been the chaplain of the chapel. To date, he had ministered to his flock for fifty-four years, for forty-three of which he never missed a single Sunday. Could there be a more salubrious village?

# PASTON
## NORFOLK

*A medieval family on the rise*

In the Middle Ages, many people took their names from their place of origin. The Paston family came from Paston. We first hear of them in the late fourteenth century, and by the middle of the next century they had propelled themselves into the ranks of the gentry – and were aiming higher.

It was the law that had done it. William Paston, given a grammar school education and sent to the Inns of Court by an uncle, became a Justice of the Common Pleas in

*Monument to Dame Katherine Paston in the church at
Paston: her family is known through its letters.*

1429. Then came two advantageous marriages, his own and that of his son, John I, which together brought them a dozen manors in Norfolk. John I was also a lawyer, perhaps none too scrupulous: the will that he made for the aged Norfolk grandee Sir John Fastolf, considerably more substantial (financially) than the Falstaff whom Shakespeare supposedly modelled on him*, made Paston the sole legatee. This led to a dispute with other claimants, more powerful locally and at court than the Pastons.

The civil war that broke out did not help their cause; John I hitched his hopes to stars that were falling to ground. The family survived, and returned to prosperity when a twist in national politics brought them a new protector in Norfolk. A century and a half later, a second civil war sank their fortunes completely, through the fines suffered for supporting King Charles. They were rewarded with a peerage by Charles II, but before long the family had died out. Their finances were also extinguished.

We know about the Pastons through their letters. They are some of the earliest written in English. As lawyers, the Paston men were often in London (occasionally in the Fleet prison), and the letters were sent largely to keep track of their interests at home. The correspondence starts around 1430; perhaps the lawyer's interest in documentation kept the collection together until they were published by antiquarians in the eighteenth century. Between talk of writs and inheritances, barley and wool, the Pastons dropped comments about their daily lives, which form a rare observation of life in the fifteenth-century countryside.

It was an intensely religious world, in which a letter seldom ends without an invocation to the blessed Trinity or Almighty God to keep the recipient safe. It was also almost casually violent. Men wore daggers and would go after enemies with them. Women, who ran the estates in their husbands' absence, might have to barricade themselves in to keep out attackers and, to protect their possessions, organise armed defence.

'Right worshipful husband, I recommend me to you, and pray you to get some crossbows, and windases to bend them with,' Margaret Paston wrote to her husband, John I, in 1448. In 1465, she had to report that the manor of Hellesdon had been ransacked by the Duke of Norfolk's men, who made off with the 'lead, brass, pewter, iron, doors, gates and other stuff of the house'; they also broke into the church. This was nothing, though, to John's attempt to keep Fastolf's newly built Caister Castle: it was surrendered only after a siege. A family on the make, such as the Pastons, hung onto whatever it could get; but the rich and powerful were equally greedy.

This was a handmade age, where personal possessions were few. Coarse, durable cloth was the normal wear, day in, day out. The purchase of a gown was an event, its colour ('a goodly blue or else a bright sanguine') left to chance. To us, it might seem a harsh, uncertain and cheerless existence, lacking charm. Which may be why John Paston II, a jolly and personable character, did notably better than his grasping father, John I.

*See Almeley, page 293

# PEASENHALL
## SUFFOLK                    *A tale of everyday life – and murder*

The case of the Peasenhall Murder captivated Edwardian society because the killer, whoever he or she was, got away, even though somebody was tried for it twice. The course of the trial, however, illuminated the life of a Suffolk village, revealing some of the pressures that existed in a small community where most people spent the whole of their lives.

Peasenhall, famous today for Emmett's, supplier of hams to the late Queen Elizabeth the Queen Mother, was, during the nineteenth century, dominated by an agricultural business: the factory where Smyth and Sons made seed drills. The seed drill had been invented by Jethro Tull in the eighteenth century. Previously sowers had walked through the fields, scattering seed broadcast, as they had done since Biblical times. Tull's machine made it possible to plant seed in rows, minimising the chance that it should fall on stony ground and allowing enough room for people to hoe.

In 1800, twenty-three-year-old James Smyth perfected an improvement, which would come to be called the Suffolk Seed Drill. It was one of a number of innovations by Suffolk manufacturers – notably Ransomes of Ipswich, which introduced the metal plough – that made it possible to exploit Suffolk's agricultural potential (the metal plough, in particular, made it possible to turn the heavy land in the west of the county). The Suffolk Seed Drill was sold throughout England and to the rest of the world. Hands came from villages all around Peasenhall to work at Smyths', their hours regulated by the factory hooter, which blew at 8am, 1pm and 6pm.

One night in May 1902, the foreman of the carpentry department of Smyth and Sons, William Gardiner, stood at his doorway; a thunderstorm was brewing, as he remarked to a neighbour who passed. An illegitimate child of a feckless mother, Gardiner had been born in a Suffolk workhouse, but in the subsequent forty-odd years had climbed the alp of Victorian respectability, becoming a pillar of the Primitive Methodist congregation, going to the chapel at Sibton with his wife and six children. The first stirrings of scandal had lapped around his boots when some lads from the works had spotted him going towards the Doctor's Chapel, a thatched hut owned by the Congregationalists. Shortly before, a young housemaid called Rose Harsent had set off to clean it. Well, there may have been nothing in it; but when William Harsent, Rose's father, called on her place of work with some clothes that her mother had ironed, he found her in the kitchen with her throat cut. She had been pregnant.

Initially the rural police thought, incredibly, that it was suicide. Later, they arrested Gardiner. Twice the jury could not come to a unanimous verdict. In November 1902, his wife wrote to *The Times*, appealing for funds: 'I am the wife of William Gardiner, accused of the Peasenhall murder . . . I am penniless and heart-broken. I know that my husband is innocent, and I cannot allow him to go undefended, if it can be avoided, at his next trial. Would you help me, and ask the public also to help me?'

At the end of the second trial, the prosecution entered a *nolle prosequi*, indicating that charges would be abandoned, although not clearing Gardiner's name. Afterwards, he went to London to lead a new life as a grocer's assistant. His wife and family also left Peasenhall; it is not known whether their new life was pursued with Mr Gardiner.

# PENTNEY
## NORFOLK                                   *A Saxon treasure is discovered*

At some point between 925 and 950, somebody in the village of Pentney, in the wide-open farming country between Swaffham and King's Lynn, hid his valuables. Perhaps he had to leave in a hurry; it could have been because of some commotion such as a Viking rage. He dug down at some place he could recognise, deposited his bundle, expecting to come back. But he never did.

More than a millennium later, in 1977, William King, a sexton, was digging a grave. He had reached a depth of four feet when he decided to take a break. After a cup of tea, he noticed a metal disc protruding from the edge of his hole. He pulled it out, and five others came with it. Having cycled home with them in his pocket, he consulted the rector; the latter said he would find out more about them, and put them in a box. They stayed in the box until he retired three years later. That is where they were found by the new rector, the Rev. John Wilson, who took them to the Castle Museum at Norwich. The curators arranged for them to be seen by the British Museum.

The discs were not horse brasses, as had been thought, but silver brooches; they are now on display in the British Museum, highly intricate pieces of work, with crosses in the centre and interlacing foliage around the outside. Only one of the six shows much sign of wear. Perhaps the man who hid them was a silversmith, or trader; they seem not to have been made by the same person.

These silver objets de luxe are like stars in an otherwise impenetrable night sky, as regards Pentney's Anglo-Saxon history. There was a Roman settlement here. It lies on the river Nar, not far from a Roman road. In 1075, the Norman who held the manor invited some Augustinian canons to found a monastery, which they did very successfully. Unusually well run, it maintained its regime of prayer, preaching, education and tending the poor for half a millennium; the flint-and-stone gatehouse still stands, though nothing else of the abbey buildings.

But no building from the Saxon period has come down to us. We can only imagine a world peopled by folk who, like others in many cultures throughout history, appreciated fine craftsmanship and ornaments denoting high status; who enjoyed adorning their cloaks with brooches that might be applied, it would seem, in pairs; but whose peaceable life could be sometimes dramatically overturned.

As the finder of the Pentney hoard, King was awarded £137,000. He gave £25,000 to the church.

# RADWINTER
## ESSEX
*William Harrison remembers his youth*

Before writing his *Historical Description of the Island of Britain,* published in 1577, William Harrison, the rector of Radwinter, asked the old people in the parish how the material circumstances of this corner of England had changed during their lifetimes. The reminiscences he collected were full of senescent wonder at the luxury of modern times. The quantity of furniture, tapestry, linen and expensive plate to be found in prosperous households had marvellously increased. Material comforts had even spread to the village.

The consensus was that there had been three great changes. First, chimneys were now commonplace. Earlier in the sixteenth century, only great houses had possessed them, the rest of the population managing with an open fire in the centre of the hall. ('Full sooty was her bower and eke her hall,' wrote Chaucer of the poor widow in 'The Nun's Priest's Tale'.) Needless to say, there were some who thought the new-fangled chimneys to be morally degenerate and bad for the health.

Secondly, many villagers were sleeping more soundly than before. 'Our fathers (yea and we ourselves also) have lain full oft on straw pallets, on rough mats covered only with a sheet, under coverlets made of dagswain or hopharlots (I use their own terms), and a good round log under their heads instead of a bolster or pillow.' A mattress stuffed with prickly straw and leaves, with only sacking to cover the sleeper, does not sound very welcoming, although Harrison's mention of a 'good round log' suggests that there could be nostalgia even for rigours such as these. But on the eve of the Armada, sleeping arrangements had become warmer and softer – likely to sap, in the opinion of the Radwinter old folk, the moral fibre of the nation.

'The third thing they tell of is the exchange of vessell,' Harrison continued. Whereas wood had been used for almost everything in the Middle Ages, wooden platters and spoons were being replaced by tin or even silver ones. Radwinter was rolling in it. With moist eyes, the elderly seemed to behold the rise of a Loadsamoney generation, not unlike that which would appear four hundred years later, in the 1980s.

Harrison's account gives a rare glimpse into the world of ordinary people in an Essex village. He himself was far from ordinary. A fiery Protestant preacher, he held several livings, both in London and at Wimbish, next to Radwinter, agonising about the propriety of such 'pluralism'. His interest in time did not stop at the memories of local ancients. He was obsessed with abstruse chronological calculations, which enabled him to date the origin of the world to the zodiacal phase of Leo in the year 3966BC. Radwinter today does not look much like the village that he knew. Despite – or because of – those chimneys, most of the village was destroyed by fire in 1874, to be rebuilt in Queen Anne Revival style by the jovial architect William Eden Nesfield, a friend of Harrison's successor as rector, the Rev. John Bullock.

# REDISHAM
SUFFOLK                                                          *A farming classic*

When Adrian Bell's book *Corduroy* was published in 1930, it was an immediate success. Why? It was about the author's initiation into farming. As the son of a news editor, he had been educated at Uppingham (chosen by his mother on the advice of the Army and Navy stores), and might have been expected to occupy a place in the Chelsea bohemia, which, after a few months spent behind a harrow and on the hunting field, he came to reject.

Farming was not doing well in 1930; on the other hand, it had yet to be changed by machinery and chemicals. Bell learnt to plough using Suffolk Punch horses, and would continue to do so at various locations, including Redisham, where he bought a derelict smallholding, Brick Kiln Farm, out of the profits of *Apple Acre* in 1942, after most of his neighbours had acquired tractors. The farming that he saw being practised, and would practise himself, stretched back to the John Bull era of the eighteenth century – indeed, some of the round-faced farmers he met seemed to be reincarnations of that English type. The popularity of *Corduroy* reflects the yearning of a nation scarred by the First World War to rediscover a different, if vanishing tradition; to some readers, it would come to represent what they were fighting for in the next War. Through it they could sniff the English countryside, and think of home.

Bell wrote at a time when virtually the whole of Suffolk derived its living from agriculture. Needless to say, the language was sometimes impenetrable to a townie ('there are some traps set by the wellums,' he might be told, a wellum being a waterway beneath an arch in an earth bridge over a ditch). But life seemed in other ways to be beguilingly straightforward. Looking down on the local village, he saw a windmill and church forming the two principal monuments. 'This is my bread,' the village seemed to say, 'and this is my belief.' Being an atheist, he did not find out much about the belief, but he mounted the tower of the windmill. 'The miller was a small, rosy man with a powder of meal on his face, which gave him the complexion of a débutante. He was as unemotional as a dumpling, despite his stirring trade.'

While his father had enjoyed the *Sturm und Drang* thrill of being up in the mill during high winds, when the sails revolved madly, the present miller saw it as nothing but inefficiency, and longed for the day that he could replace it with a nice diesel-powered equivalent*. The blacksmith (who, like the rest of the village, knew all about Bell within hours of his having arrived) accepted that his trade was being killed by the motor car, and with it the forge 'as a meeting place second only to the inn'.

This is not a sentimental book. Turkeys gang up on hens, systematically pecking them to death; they in turn, if allowed to roost in a tree, are mesmerised by the fox, and simply fall off into his jaws. But it speaks of a simpler time, when it was possible for a man of sixty to say that he had eaten nothing but pork, four times a day, all his life, and still lift a bucket filled with water using his teeth. Diet is only one of the areas in which the modern, metropolitan world would not see eye to eye with the country ways that Bell described. With *Silver Ley* and *The Cherry Tree*, the books with which it forms a rural trilogy, *Corduroy* is a minor masterpiece.

*See Bardwell, page 212

# SILVER END
ESSEX                                                    *Brave new world*

'Silver End – what a delightful name for our new venture!' wrote Francis Crittall to his workforce in 1926. Crittall was doing well. He had established a company to make metal-framed windows at Braintree in 1889. After the First World War, the shortage of timber coincided with a new aesthetic, in which the geometry of the machine was preferred to the wavy lines of traditional hand-craftsmanship. Houses had to be built, and standardisation would get them built quickly.

Crittall understood about mass production, having used it to halve the cost of the eighteen-pound bombs that his factory had been consigned to make during the War. In 1918, he set about demonstrating its virtues in an estate of sixty-five houses on the edge of Braintree: flat roofs, metal-framed windows, concrete block construction. They are possibly the first examples of what came to be known as the International Style, although they have never received the recognition that they deserve, because the architect responsible, C. H. B. Quennell, was an Arts and Crafts man.

Across Europe, the demand for Crittall windows boomed. So did the Crittall factory, and the number of workers (often *mutilés de guerre*) that it employed. This in turn generated a local housing need. Crittall did not want to meet it by building at Braintree: like many of his generation, he had a horror of town dwelling because of the slums. On the other hand, villages lacked the amenities of towns. Crittall set out to solve the conundrum, as he told his Readers, Friends and Fellow Workers in the company magazine, by acquiring 'a farm of 200 acres, beautifully situated, on which we propose to erect a village . . . with all the advantages of the town . . . at Silver End there will be water from an artesian well, modern drainage, electric light, a communal laundry, a cinema, a restaurant, our (I mean your) Co-operative Society, sports, games, playgrounds for adults, and for children, where they can make their own mud pies, all as it were inside a ring fence.'

There had already been garden cities (Letchworth and Welwyn in Hertfordshire) and garden suburbs (Hampstead in Middlesex); Silver End was a garden village. The plan was drawn by C. Murray Hennell, who had worked with the architects Parker and Unwin at Welwyn. Quennell built Crittall's own house, The Manors, 29 Francis Way: symmetrical around a modest pediment, beneath a low-pitched roof.

Altogether 476 houses were built. To avoid monotony, Crittall employed several architects to design them. Most are in the neo-Georgian garden city style, although, not surprisingly, metal-framed windows were de rigueur. Sixty-five, however, are different. These were the contribution of the Glasgow firm of Sir John Burnet and Partners, the chief designer being Thomas Tait, assisted by Frederick MacManus. Tait designed Le Chateau as the home of W. F. 'Pink' Crittall, Francis's son and an enthusiast for the new architecture. It was rectangular, with a flat roof and corner windows. Wide windows let in the sunshine and fresh air and gave a sense of horizontality to the design; the rendered surfaces were colour-washed, as though a little bit of the Mediterranean had breezed into the Essex countryside. This set the tone for the streets of workers' houses designed by Frederick MacManus, some with projecting balconies, some with tall triangular fins on the front elevation, the windows of which light the staircase. Traditionalists gasped.

Later, purists criticised the Silver End houses for not going far enough. But they were a signal that something new was afoot, and it concerned more than architecture. Like Sir Ernest Debenham at Briantspuddle in Dorset (see page 18), Francis Crittall wanted to create a self-sufficient community, supplied with healthy food from its own farm. To this end he acquired seven hundred acres next to Silver End, building not just poultry houses and piggeries (one of them so splendid that it was mistaken for the church) but a sausage factory and bakery. Instead of a village shop, Silver End had the Department Stores (twenty-six departments) to sell the produce. The Central Building included a four-hundred-seat cinema, club rooms, portrait gallery and infant welfare clinic. A church was created out of an old barn, but with an invitingly modern interior, which was meant to rival that of the cinema.

During its first decade, Silver End was cited as the healthiest village in England, with the lowest death rate and highest birth rate. That cannot entirely be explained by the architecture: its population was young. Even so, it seemed to fulfil the modernist ambition of creating a setting for youth, sunshine and, quite possibly, sex.

# STIFFKEY

## NORFOLK

*A parson's fall from grace*

The Rev. Harold Davidson lies buried in the graveyard of his church at Stiffkey. So lie hundreds of country parsons, near the paths along which they walked countless times to take holy service. Few, however, have ended their lives so dramatically as Davidson: he was mauled to death by a lion, while working as a menagerie entertainer in Skegness. But little about Davidson's life conformed to type.

Stiffkey, pronounced Stewkey, at least in Davidson's day, is a fishing village on the Norfolk coast, famous for its cockles. They are called Stiffkey blues, from the colour they take on from the mud. Davidson arrived there as rector in 1906. As a young man, he would have preferred acting to the church, but his clergyman father thought differently; he went to Oxford and, with some difficulty, succeeded in taking a degree and, thereafter, holy orders. His wife, Molly, a strong-willed Irishwoman, had been an actress.

Stiffkey offered little opportunity either for Davidson's theatrical bent or his conception of ministry. The seedy nightlife of London provided a bigger canvas and greater challenge. He sought out fallen women, or those who might be about to fall – young country girls, who found themselves at sea in the capital. Sometimes he would spend the whole week in London, returning to Norfolk only at weekends. With him might come some of those he had rescued.

It might be that Davidson was naive; a mission to rescue prostitutes was open to misinterpretation, as W. E. Gladstone had discovered. He might have been something of a nuisance, pursuing women while not wearing the dog collar that would have declared his position. His life was not free from other troubles; the fourth child that was born while he was serving as a naval chaplain during the First World War was, as he realised, not his. In 1925, having become ensnared by a swindler while trying to stretch his modest income, he was declared bankrupt and forced to commit much of his future earnings to pay creditors.

Despite his absences and eccentricities, Davidson remained popular in his parish. But a dramatic debacle came when the Bishop of Norwich decided, for reasons that are not clear, to prosecute him for indecency, and hired a firm of private detectives to gather evidence. The resulting trial gripped the nation. During it, Davidson's own evidence was curious (he claimed not to know the meaning of the word 'buttock'), but the prosecution was able to make little of its case stick. That is, until it produced – perhaps appropriately, given Davidson's thespian leanings – a *coup de théâtre*: a photograph of Davidson with a fifteen-year-old girl. She was naked. It may, as Davidson claimed, have been a stitch-up, but he was found guilty on all counts.

In adversity, Davidson resorted to showmanship; he exhibited himself in a barrel on Blackpool's golden mile. His death came in 1937. He had enjoyed, or endured, an obsessive, probably misunderstood life: a victim, perhaps, of the freedom that the Church of England gave to its clergy in country parishes to interpret their ministry according to their own lights. Without the occasional oddball, there would not have been the poets or naturalists, either.

# STOW BARDOLPH
## NORFOLK

*An uncanny Georgian likeness*

Meet Sarah Hare. She died in 1744, and has been living in a mahogany cabinet in Stow Bardolph church ever since. Or rather her effigy has, but because of the provisions of her will it is weirdly, if not ghoulishly, realistic. She asked to be perpetuated as a waxwork, dressed in her own clothes. And there she is, plump of feature, double-chinned, her bosom swelling above the bodice of her dress, a curl of hair on her forehead, and an unblinking stare. You feel that you have met her before, behind a market stall or at a Rotary club dinner. Over her head and around her shoulders is draped a sumptuous crimson silk cloak. She must have been quite a woman. Usually the case is kept closed.

*At Stow Bardolph, Sarah Hare asked to be commemorated as a waxwork in her own clothes, not as a sculpture in stone.*

Effigies had been made of royalty since the Middle Ages. Originally, the custom was to display the corpse of the deceased monarch so that there could be no doubt about his being dead, and people could see for themselves any signs of foul play. The earliest record of an effigy refers to the one made of Edward II for his funeral in Gloucester Cathedral. In his case, there had indeed been foul play (although the assassins apparently chose a murder weapon that would leave no visible trace), and furthermore the delay of two or three months between murder and funeral made it impossible to show the body.

Several royal effigies survive at Westminster Abbey, the earliest being that of Edward III. Made of wood or wax, they were dressed, like Sarah Hale, in the clothes of the deceased. The Abbey also has a waxwork of Nelson, made to provide a rival attraction to St Paul's Cathedral, where he is buried. Sarah Hare's effigy is the only one of a commoner to survive. It has overtones of the auto-icon made of Jeremy Bentham, kept in a case at University College, London; the seer, who died in 1832, is similarly displayed in a case, wearing his own clothes and with a wax head, but his own body parts are incorporated (the head is kept in a safe to stop it being stolen by students).

Sarah Hare's effigy is made all the stranger by contrast. Stow Bardolph has exceptionally fine monuments. Sir Thomas Hare reclines in Roman dress. Sarah's sister Susannah was immortalised by no less a sculptor than Peter Scheemakers, his only work in Norfolk. You can lift a glass to the family at the Hare Arms: despite its name, no body parts there.

# STRADBROKE
SUFFOLK                     *Life's journey of a twelfth-century village lad*

People from humble backgrounds can be mocked for their lack of polish, and so it was with Robert Grosseteste, thought to have been born at Stradbroke around 1170. Stradbroke is not a bustling place today, nor was it in the twelfth century; the parish church was rebuilt in its present form long after Grosseteste's time, during Suffolk's wool boom*. It would be difficult to think of anyone who rose so thoroughly above the limitations of his early life as Grosseteste. As Bishop of Lincoln, the largest diocese in the country, he was one of the most important men in England, deeply involved in the turbulent politics of King John's reign, and probably the first Chancellor of Oxford University.

Aristocrats were charmed by his courteous and graceful manner, and impressed by his management of money. A lover of music, he kept a private harpist. The metre that he used for a long poem that he wrote in French, *Le Château d'Amour* – despite the title, a perfectly proper work for the Bishop, being an exposition of Christian theology – was later used by Sir Walter Scott for the *Lay of the Last*

*Minstrel.* When his tomb was opened in 1782, it was found that he was exceptionally tall for his era, more than six feet: his physical size must have reinforced his naturally commanding presence.

Some of this may make him seem a figure of the remote past, wrapped in theological speculation and courtliness. But in one respect he helped lay the foundations for the modern world. Bishop Grosseteste was a scientist. Born into a tradition that took the ancient authors, as well as the Bible, on trust, he sought to understand the world by testing it. It helped that his early career was spent in the diocese of Hereford, which was then the centre for scientific study in England. There he wrote treatises on time, astronomy and sound, as well as the first commentary on Aristotle's *Posterior Analytics*, in which the Greek philosopher examines what can be known about matter.

His most original work, however, was done at Oxford. Two things are striking about it. First is the primacy he gave to light, a theological rather than scientific premise based on Genesis, light being God's first act of creation. It enabled him to imagine the universe expanding from a single concentrated point of light – an idea not unlike that of the Big Bang. Secondly, Grosseteste tested his hypotheses through experiment. His theories about rainbows, for example, were supported by a study of light passing through a glass flask filled with water. Furthermore, he combined natural observation with mathematics, believing that geometry in particular held the key to many natural phenomena. For these reasons Grosseteste has been regarded as the founder of the scientific method (a distinction also claimed by Roger Bacon, who was his pupil).

Grosseteste was a figure of his time, vitriolic against the Jews, because of their money-lending activities (the only trade open to them). But his life's journey was extraordinary for a village lad.

*See Lavenham, page 251

# THAXTED
ESSEX                                                    *Folk song and Fabianism*

'It was a feast – an orgy,' the composer Gustav Holst wrote to his friend William Whittaker at Whitsun, 1916. Well, an orgy of early singing was what he meant, punctuated with morris dancing. Holst had come to Thaxted in 1914, having tramped there in knickerbocker tweeds on a week's walking tour. He was entranced by the authentically Tudor feeling of what had once been a prosperous town, since declined into a village, but still with a handsome timber guildhall and stone immensity of a church. Early photographs show Thaxted – its name derived from the thatch that covers some buildings – deserted except for the odd pony trap and occasional small child in the middle of the road. After the rigours of teaching in London, the very air was refreshing. Holst fell into conversation with the vicar, Conrad Noel. A cottage in Monk Street (thatched) came up for rent and he took it for weekends and school holidays.

Holst's daughter, Imogen, was six at the time. 'It was so quiet that we could hear the bees in the dark red clover beyond the garden hedge,' she remembered. There were congenial spirits, too. Conrad Noel was not only a theologian (he founded the Thaxted Movement, questioning orthodox ideas of the Trinity) but a socialist, who was prepared to excite the parish by running up a red flag on the church tower on May Day. He styled himself a Christian Communist (a position not incompatible with high Anglicanism, with a liturgy that included not only Latin but Greek). Soon the leftward-leaning Holst was coaching the church choir. For the 1916 Festival, local talent was supplemented by the choirs of St Paul's Girls' School and Morley College in London, where Holst taught. They sang in the church, which was decorated with earthenware jugs of wild flowers for the occasion. They also sang in fields, in people's houses, on the train home. They sang for fourteen or more hours a day. Perhaps it did deserve to be called an orgy.

Music-making and socialism went hand in hand – folk music, that is. Folk songs were being collected by Cecil Sharp, himself a socialist at the time (though not later). Fabianism had inherited a belief in the countryside and its traditions from William Morris. Folk song and country crafts were examples of truly popular culture, because nobody knew who had first composed or designed them. Country dancing seemed to epitomise the classless, communal joy that was the socialist goal. George Bernard Shaw danced at Fabian summer schools. The Labour politician Barbara Castle grew up in a household that erected a maypole each spring. Thaxted became, and remains, a focus of morris dancing.

It took some time for the Holsts – or von Holsts as they were then – to settle down. Initially the village was suspicious of a German-sounding man, who bicycled much and asked questions. They eventually took to 'Our Mr Von', while he took himself to them, moving to a house in the centre of the village, beside the guildhall. It was on the grand piano that he squeezed first into the cottage and then into The Steps, Town Street that he composed *The Planets*. The tune of 'I Vow to Thee, My Country' (adapted from 'Jupiter') is called 'Thaxted'.

# THE RAYNHAMS
NORFOLK                                     *Progressive agriculture, and proud of it*

Charles Dickens was not a great friend to the aristocracy, but he admired Charles, 2nd Viscount Townshend. 'Surely here was a benefactor to the human race,' his magazine *Household Words* observed in 1853, 'whose monument history has raised, by calling him "Turnip Townshend".' Together with Jethro Tull, who invented a seed drill, and Robert Bakewell, who bred the new Leicester sheep and long-horn cattle, Townshend has always been regarded as one of the pioneers of the

Agricultural Revolution, which transformed British farming in the eighteenth century. It may be that historians have in the past overstated his influence, given that his innovations were not always taken up quickly or widely across the country. There is, however, no doubt that he revolutionised his own corner of Norfolk and showed that farming could bestow a fortune on those who caught onto it.

Born in 1674, Townshend's first career was in politics. 'Nobody heard him with patience,' his friend Lord Chesterfield commented; yet despite his difficulty with spoken English he became ambassador at The Hague and served as secretary of state to the King. His beautiful second wife, Dolly, was the sister of Robert Walpole, a Norfolk squire's son and Prime Minister. Walpole – new, profligate and venal – fell out with his strait-laced brother-in-law after Dolly's death, and Townshend retired from government in 1730.

Thereafter Townshend found a new fulfilment in agriculture. It suited him. Coarse-looking, blunt in manner and without a courtier's command of language, he retained the character of a countryman, and – unlike some other aristocrats – loved home. He came from a family of agriculturalists. Before his time, part of the family estates had been enclosed so that a flock of twenty-four thousand sheep could be run on it. As early as 1661, marl – a kind of calcium-rich mud – was being dug out of pits to be spread on the sandy soil, improving it for crops. Townshend made further enclosures, and continued the marling. He also made an immediate improvement in profitability by introducing what became known as the four-crop Norfolk rotation.

Previously, farmers had practised a three-crop system, in which every third year the land was allowed to take a rest, lying fallow; this fallow year, however, produced nothing more than rough grazing. Townshend's system allowed the land to be cropped continuously, with the inclusion of clover and sainfoin – leguminous plants, which, as we now know, return nitrogen to the soil. These were grazed by animals, whose dung further enriched the land. The famous turnips allowed animals to be kept over winter. When sown, they were not scattered broadcast, but drilled in rows, using one of Tull's seed drills, and hoed. A century later, making his *Rural Rides*, William Cobbett* would regard the condition of a farm's turnips as an index of good management.

The rewards of the new system were considerable. Land that had previously been heath, good only for furze bushes and rabbit warrening, was brought into production. Over thirty years, the rent of one farm went up from £180 to £800 a year. In West Raynham, Townshend built what is now the post office. Although anything else he may have done was lost beneath a Victorian rebuilding in Norfolk flint and brick, it remains a bustling, smart village. Townshend amalgamated the living of West Raynham church, now a ruin, with that of East Raynham, next to Raynham Hall. St Mary, East Raynham, was carefully rebuilt in the 1860s by Clark and Holland from Newmarket, a statement of what medieval inspiration combined with the income from an efficient agricultural estate could do. How well it looks in summer, beyond fields of golden wheat.

*See Botley, page 97

# TIPTREE

## ESSEX

*High farming and jam*

You may say that Tiptree is too big to be a village, but having none of the appurtenances of a town, it can surely be nothing else. It grew out of two agricultural enterprises. The trouble is that it grew and grew.

Before 1841, Tiptree Heath was an area of poor clay soil, which had all but forgotten it was once part of the Great Essex Forest. That year, John Joseph Mechi, a successful London cutler and alderman, purchased a farm there, with the intention of improving it and showing the rest of the country how to farm. Most farmers, he believed, did not invest enough in their fields. Mechi could have been said to plough money into his. The Mechi system required covered yards, drainage, horse-drawn reaping and mowing machines, and attention to the feed given to animals – not least the farm horses, since farmers had to consign a fifth of their land to feeding them. Steam was the way forward: steam for ploughing, so that deeper furrows could be turned; steam for threshing; steam for cutting up straw into chaff. It can't have been particularly pretty; the first thing he did on coming to Tiptree Hall Farm was to tear down all the fences and trees.

Not everyone subscribed to Mechi's views on the sewage question. It was lamentable, he thought, that human excreta from London should be discharged, via Bazalgette's sewers, into the sea: 'The agricultural mind can scarcely realise such a gigantic and suicidal throwing away of valuable property.' However, another kind of fertiliser was essential to Mechi's progressive style: guano, the nitrogen-rich excrement of fish-eating birds, which was being imported in industrial quantities. Unprofitable wastes could be made to yield corn.

This highly capitalised agriculture was known as 'high farming'. There were other high farmers – Lord Bateman at Uphampton in Herefordshire; Lord Lonsdale at Lowther Hall in Cumbria; the Prince Consort at Windsor – but Mechi, indefatigably publishing his balance sheets and waving them at sceptical farmers' meetings, was the movement's apostle. At Blennerhasset in Cumbria, William Lawson recognised this by calling his high farming enterprise Mechi Farm. (Lawson's farm didn't pay; and for all his protestations to the contrary, it is difficult to think that Mechi's could have done either – but he had deeper pockets.)

Inevitably, in a paternalistic age, Mechi's desire for improvement did not stop at the farm gate. As he could claim two years before his death in 1880, 'Wretched hovels are being superseded by decent cottages, and, in fact, all round here we are on the "improved track". Church, chapel, and school accommodation has marched with the rest, and we are a changed, and, I believe, improved people.' The Ecclesiastical Commissioners were approached to make Tiptree Heath into an Ecclesiastical District and then a parish, which it became in 1858. In the census three years later it was found to have a population of 877.

Meanwhile, the Wilkin family continued to farm at Tiptree Heath, much as they had done for more than a century. Their revolutionary moment came in 1885, when Arthur Charles Wilkin formed the Britannia Fruit Preserving Company. Tiptree's future would not, as it turned out, be high farming, but jam. The population has been well nourished on it, having reached about 9,500.

# WALBERSWICK

SUFFOLK                                        *Art nouveau beside the mudflats*

In 1914, the Glasgow architect Charles Rennie Mackintosh was in crisis. His depression fed by alcohol, he had been forced to resign from his old practice and set up on his own, but the work did not come. In need of a holiday, he and his wife, Margaret, went to Walberswick, a fishing village. Three weeks later, war broke out, and they decided to stay on.

On the face of it, Walberswick may seem an unlikely choice for one of the most advanced art architects of his day, even if the local flora provided a subject for Mackintosh's delicate watercolours. It is a place of pantile roofs and crabbing boats, and winds coming off the North Sea. Beach hut territory – but, unlike Southwold, its bustling neighbour across the mudflats of the river Blyth, where the huts break out into rainbow hues, Walberswick paints hers black. Suffolk has always nurtured a tradition of Puritanism and Dissent; it has also harboured artists*.

As a town, Walberswick's zenith came in the fifteenth century. In 1426, the parish elders instructed their chosen stonemasons on the building of Walberswick church: flint walls and stone panels after the pattern of Tunstall, near Orford, with a west window as good as the one at Halesworth. By the middle of the century, the parish was busy building a guildhall. The church, when finished in 1493, was, like so many Suffolk churches, a beacon of faith, a wonder of Perpendicular tracery – and, soon, far too big.

William White, writing in 1833, put Walberswick's decline down to Henry VIII. By changing the country's religion, he quashed the nation's appetite for fish – previously de rigueur on Fridays and during fasts. In the late seventeenth century, the parish admitted defeat, and started dismantling the greater part of the church nave, keeping only the south-west corner for services. What had been a town adapted itself to reduced aspirations as a village, until in the nineteenth century it found itself to be a haunt of artists. According to the *Art Journal* in 1880, 'a yearly increase' in them could be noticed.

It was the railways that did it. Before their advent, landscape painters had to make tours, lasting two or three months, in search of subject matter. Better communications allowed artists to live in their favourite locations, which they often did – favourite locations being otherwise devoid of arty small talk – in groups. Fishing villages, in particular, spoke to the soul. Men of almost Biblical austerity faced the dangers of the sea, while their womenfolk stoically awaited the return of the boats: theirs were harsh, simple lives, laced with storytelling possibilities. On the Continent, art colonies were formed in Brittany and at Scheveningen in Holland. Stanhope Forbes and the Newlyn School discovered Cornwall. In Devon, artists put Clovelly (see page 28) on the map in the 1850s, and by the end of the century it was thronged with visitors. Walberswick was one of several East Anglian destinations, including Blythburgh, Blakeney and Aldeburgh. The Mackintoshes followed a well-beaten path.

At other destinations, tourists and second-homers may have displaced the artists, who have moved on to rawer haunts. Walberswick, through its reserve, has retained the loyalty of creative types, albeit well-heeled rather than bohemian.

*See Walpole, below. See also Broadway, page 305

# WALPOLE
### SUFFOLK                                        *A tradition of Dissent*

In the year of Charles I's execution, 1649, 'ye saints in and about Coukley' asked local Puritans for 'ye right hand of fellowship in this their great undertaking'. The undertaking was to establish a congregation of Independents, extreme Dissenters who did not acknowledge the authority of any established church. They were led by Samuel Manning, who would be their minister for half a century; among their number was John Tillinghast, nephew of Robert Tichborne, one of the regicides who had signed the King's death warrant. They believed that worship should consist principally of reading and preaching the word of God; Manning did not wear a surplice or make the sign of the cross, and there was certainly no incense. To begin with they met in one another's houses. Then, at some point in the late seventeenth century, they acquired a farmhouse at Walpole, which they converted into a chapel.

Walpole Old Chapel is a symbol of the Dissenting tradition. Except for the eleven years of Cromwell's interregnum, Dissent had to keep a low profile until freedom of worship was granted under William and Mary's Act of Toleration of 1689 (although Nonconformists were not able to enter university or Parliament for another century and a half). Appropriately, therefore, the chapel looks like a pair of cottages: casement windows cut into the bumpy skin of plaster that hides the timber frame, the whole covered by a tile roof. The interior, however, was gutted. It became a single space, held together by arched braces that run up the walls and meet at the apex of the roof. Pride of place – although pride was a sin – was given to the pulpit, placed, to throw maximum light onto preacher and lectern, between two tall, arched windows. The preacher was visible to everybody, and everybody was visible to him. There is a gallery to hold extra members of the congregation. Downstairs, they sat, from the eighteenth century onwards, in upright box pews, made out of humble pine.

Throughout the years of persecution the Independents were supported by sympathising gentry, including the MP Colonel Humphrey Brewster, who had commanded a troop of cavalry in the Parliamentarian army, and Lady Brooke, a zealous royalist, who nevertheless believed that Dissenters should be brought within the Anglican Church. In 1689, the Independents bought a lease of their building from the Corporation of Southwold; perhaps this was the time of its remodelling. Later, the population declined as people drifted away, and so did the congregation; the opening of a Primitive Methodist chapel in the 1860s divided the loyalties of those who remained. In 1993, it was taken into the care of the Historic Chapels Trust.

# WARHAM
NORFOLK                                   *A saviour for Norfolk's many churches*

Services at St Mary Magdalene's church in Warham can be held only during the summer, since it has neither heating nor electric light. Whereas most villages, with congregations that may rarely exceed single figures, struggle to keep one medieval church in good order, Warham on the North Norfolk coast is blessed with two. No wonder St Mary Magdalene has never been modernised.

Technically, though large enough in its own right, it is a chapel of ease to All Saints, less than a mile down the road. Yet what a treasure it is, the pure Perpendicular Gothic of the exterior contrasting with a complete fitting-out of Georgian carpentry inside: box pews, three-decker pulpit, communion rails, the lot. The church was restored in 1801. Presumably this was when the fragments of what Sir John Betjeman called 'fine sixteenth-century Rhenish glass' were arranged as pairs of heads in the windows, to charming effect.

In the Middle Ages, Norfolk was prosperous and crowded with villages; it now has the greatest concentration of medieval churches of any area in the world: 659 of them. Thirty-one survive within the city walls of Norwich alone (there were sixty-one in the Middle Ages; three were lost to enemy bombs in 1942). The numbers are not exceptional for a successful city; London's spiritual needs were just as well supplied, the Square Mile containing a hundred churches. Nor is it remarkable that Norfolk's villages should have had places of worship; most villages did. Norfolk's churches are simply evidence of the way that the county's economy boomed during the Middle Ages. Later, wealth flooded out again. The villages often shrank into hamlets, and then the hamlets dwindled away, leaving a church, alone in the fields, as the only memorial.

A peculiarity of Norfolk churches is their round towers, once thought to have been a form forced on masons who built from flint, without good stone to form quoins. It is now thought that this was a stylistic choice, because round towers were favoured even where stone was available. The shape introduced geometrical puzzles: how to join the tower to the west end of the church, for example. At Warham, sensibly, St Mary Magdalene has a square tower, while All Saints has no tower at all.

Recognising the challenge posed by Norfolk's oversupply of churches, Lady Harrod formed the Norfolk Churches Trust. Born in 1911 into a gentry family in Norfolk (a direct ancestor was the prison reformer Elizabeth Fry), Wilhelmine – invariably known as Billa – Harrod was the model for Fanny in Nancy Mitford's *Love in a Cold Climate*. She became briefly engaged to Betjeman, at the same time, confusingly, as his future wife; she did not marry him, but they remained friends, Norfolk churches being a shared love. After some years in London, she lived in Oxford; she married the economist and Christ Church don Sir Roy Harrod in 1938. But they holidayed in Norfolk and, in 1962, bought a house at Holt.

These were the dark ages during which the Diocese of Norwich was advised to demolish the churches it could not use. Billa Harrod saw churches not merely as architectural monuments, but flag bearers for the Christian faith: 'If people see the symbols being allowed to crumble away they think the whole thing is over,' she would say. St Mary Magdalene is one of many churches that, through the efforts of the Norfolk Churches Trust, continue to serve the purpose for which they were built. Lady Harrod's own funeral took place there in May 2005.

# WEST MERSEA
ESSEX                                           *The oyster is my world*

West Mersea is a day out. It is separated from normality by the Strood, a causeway that may first have been built by the Romans, now incorporated into the B1025, which disappears beneath water during twice-daily high tides to play a joke on visitors. The Strood gives an ever-changing view of the mudflats: opalescent when caught by the rays of a low sun, creased and leathery as elephant skin if the sky is dull, a paradise for wading birds. This same mud, below water level, is also the reposeful home of the 'natives' of this place, the imprecisely named Colchester oysters – the town is nine miles away – that connoisseurs regard as a prince among bivalves.

The outworks of the village have run to bungalows and executive homes, but persevere and you come to the yacht club and boatyard. This is the picturesque end of West Mersea, with houses leaning into the wind as though they had shipped a tot too much rum in the great age of sail. Opposite the Dabchicks Sailing Club is a cottage called the Old Victory, with a veranda and a Union Jack on the flagpole. In short, this is a properly salty place, with a sailmakers, a vendor of anti-foul paint and men in blue overalls for whom mustard-coloured gumboots are the footwear of choice.

Life does not offer much better around one o'clock than half a dozen native oysters and a glass of crisp white at the authentically tarry and pine-tabled West

Mersea Oyster Bar – except a dozen natives, of course. These small, round-shelled delicacies have been appreciated since the Strood first came into existence; probably longer. The borough of Colchester sent them by the horse-load to Queen Elizabeth and her courtiers, to curry favour. In Philip Massinger's play *A New Way to Pay Old Debts*, published in 1633, Judge Greedy declares that he had not eaten much before breakfast beyond 'a barrel of Colchester oysters'.

To gourmets brought up to think that oysters should be eaten only when there is an R in the month, it may come as a surprise to find that the opening of the oyster season at Billingsgate was, in the nineteenth century, 4 August. There was such excitement surrounding the date that the gates would be flung open at midnight on 3 August, 'when, in the rush to obtain the first supply of oysters, it being dark, a life or two was lost annually', according to an account of 1851. The size of the oysters being dredged was regulated by law, the minimum being depicted by a model of an oyster cast in brass and kept by the magistrates or water bailiff.

These days, oysters come purified to EU specifications, but there are fewer than in the days when Dr Johnson fed them to his cat. Henry Mayhew calculated that half a billion oysters were sold at Billingsgate in 1850. But the boom, like many booms, was followed by a collapse. A Royal Commission of 1863 missed the causes – overfishing and pollution. By the twentieth century, oysters made but a rare appearance in most British homes, attempts to open them being apt to endanger thumbs.

West Mersea may still be salty in parts – too salty, at times, to judge from the pile of sandbags on the front. Oyster dredging continues, bravely, but the streets that cluster round the florist, physiotherapist, dry cleaners and bank show that domestic development has got the upper hand. The tone of the new West Mersea was set as long ago as 1923, when Baillie Scott, the decoratively minded Arts and Crafts architect, built Casa Pantis. Googling for a translation of pantis throws up some most untoward websites. Spare your blushes; it was intended to mean 'of the pantiles'.

# WEST WRATTING
## CAMBRIDGESHIRE          *'I'll take that one': the arrival of evacuees*

Operation Pied Piper began on 1 September 1939. War had been declared, and the government wanted to move hundreds of thousands of British children aged between five and fourteen from the cities to the countryside. Railway carriages, fleets of buses and even ferry boats were pressed into service, and the immense Ford Motor Company works at Dagenham came to a halt as it was turned into a marshalling yard for East End children about to begin a new life. Newspapers printed photographs of excited youngsters waving enthusiastically from train windows as their journeys began. Such was the propaganda view. For some children the reality was cruelly different, not least because of the bureaucratic muddle in which the whole exercise was conducted. In Berkshire, 46,722 children arrived to occupy 23,915 billets. With too many children, the authorities encouraged hosts to select whoever they wanted. 'I'll take that one,' became, for the evacuees, ominous shorthand for a process that could be part lottery and part slave market. In a more trusting age, there had been few checks on the suitability of welcoming households. Some of them turned out not to be so very welcoming. Children might be savagely beaten, or worse.

But the experience was not universally dismal. For many children, the most lasting impressions were made by country ways on minds that had been brought up in quite different surroundings. No doubt the families who took evacuees at West Wratting included both good and bad. It was a typical destination as regards the bewilderment that urban children may have felt in being deposited amid turnip fields and milking parlours. One of them was Anne Cole from Edmonton, who wrote down her experiences. Her memoir is published on www.1900s.org.uk.

The coach bringing the evacuees was full of East Enders. 'Very few, if any, had ever seen the countryside.' They were to find a world that, after half a century of agricultural depression, had not kept pace with the town. There was mutual misunderstanding, made worse by the language barrier. The cockneys spoke in a way that was virtually incomprehensible to Cambridgeshire children, and vice versa. Years later, Anne's evacuee friends told her how 'awful' it had been. 'Many were exploited or neglected. The children were billeted on any home which had room and were not really welcome.' For reasons of space, the village school had to run on segregated lines, with village children being taught in the mornings and evacuees in the afternoons. They picked wild flowers in the spring (in autumn, it would be rose hips for the government programme of making rose-hip syrup for vitamin C).

Anne was luckier than many because she stayed with her grandparents. Even so, it was very different from home. Her memories are focused on the practicalities so important to children. Towns and cities already had mains drainage and piped water, but throughout the countryside water was still being carried in buckets from a standpipe or collected from rainwater butts. 'Every drop of water was precious.' So after clothes had been washed in the immense copper in the garden wash house, the soapy water was used to wash floors and the rinsing water heated for baths. Behind the wash house stood the lavatory: 'a wooden bench with a hole and bucket; newspaper for toilet paper; hurricane lamp for the dark nights'. Milk was fetched from the farm in a jug. Food was entirely seasonal and home-made, down to the cough mixture concocted in autumn from blackcurrants, honey and vinegar.

One summer night the evacuees watched an aerial dogfight between a British and a German plane; then, one day, a German plane came down in a field. Eventually the War was over. Anne's father, whom she had not seen for five years, returned from Palestine. Only the memories of the countryside persisted – for some people deeper than they would have wished.

# WICKHAM SKEITH

SUFFOLK                                    *Last witch dunking in Britain*

King James VI of Scotland helped to popularise dunking. This was the practice of 'swimming' supposed witches to see whether or not they would float. It was a classic catch-22: if they sank (and risked drowning), they were innocent; if they floated, they were guilty (and subject to mob justice). The King wrote about the practice, until then confined to the Continent, in his *Daemonologie*, first published in 1597 and reissued when he ascended the English throne. He had a special interest in witches: that is why Shakespeare inserted a gaggle of them into *Macbeth*.

Trial by freezing water, like trial by hot irons, had been an ancient test for felony, though not for women, even before it was outlawed by the Pope in 1215. Since then, ducking stools, which immersed the victim in the duck pond, had been used as a punishment for, among other things, scolding – regarded as a uniquely female offence. There was therefore an association with women. It seems to have taken a few years for the idea of swimming witches to catch on, the first verifiable case being that of Mary Sutton, thrown into a Bedfordshire mill pool in 1612. The episode was described in the pamphlet 'Witches Apprehended', published the next year.

By the middle of the seventeenth century, the practice had become so widely known that the accused themselves asked for it, as a means of clearing their names. At this time, 'Conjuration, Witchcraft, Enchantment or Sorcery' were subject to the Witchcraft Acts (typically, they had been strengthened when James I became King), which regarded them as a felony, and as such punishable by death. John Wesley was one of their most passionate opponents, and, in 1735, a new Witchcraft Act was passed; now witches were treated simply as vagrants or frauds.

But dunkings continued. The last dunking did not take place until 1825. An old pedlar called Isaac Stebbings had been accused of using sorcery to send a thatcher's wife and a farmer out of their minds. Stebbings was duly carried by four men into the village pond, known, poetically for this purpose, as the Grimmer; the parish constable himself was on the scene, simply to ensure, as he said later, that matters did not get out of hand. Stebbings floated, not once but three times, but demanded a retrial. This time, however, the clergyman and his churchwardens took action, and the swimming party was disbanded. It was not quite the end of the matter, however. A local cunning man was paid three pounds to ensure that Stebbings suffered a lingering death.

# WILLINGHAM

*A bishop and his allotments*

In 1806, the Rev. George Henry Law gave the Fenland village of Willingham, where
he was rector, its allotments. The weekend presence of men with garden forks on
their shoulders, carrying freshly pulled leeks in plastic bags, confirms that allotments (perhaps not on the same site) are still there. These days, the allotment has
become part of the British identity, an expression of the national *furor hortensis*
that grips the working man in his potting shed as much as the great lady with
her trug*. The opportunity for cultivation that it offers is becoming increasingly
popular as people worry more about their food.

The notion that labourers should be allowed a parcel of land to dig for them-
selves has deep roots. In 1589, Queen Elizabeth had decreed that every cottage in
England should have four acres to go with it; this was never enforced, but showed
that independence had been identified as a means of supporting the rural poor.
In practice, many peasants did have smallholdings, a state recollected by Oliver
Goldsmith in *The Deserted Village* (1770):

> A time there was, ere England's griefs began,
> When every rood of ground maintain'd its man;

But the ability of England's 'bold peasantry' was being whittled away, as their
commons and open fields were taken away from them by enclosure, and the
Industrial Revolution killed the market for cottage-made goods.

With the outbreak of war against France in 1793, the plight of the farm labourer
and his family became acute. Having followed the unfolding horrors of the
Revolution on the other side of the Channel, landowners were anxious to support
social order. Yet they had no desire to increase the cost of poor relief, given that
they were the ones paying for it. One solution that was eagerly canvassed in some
quarters was the allotment.

The agriculturalist Arthur Young, secretary to the newly formed Board of
Agriculture, was an unexpected supporter, since he was also an apologist for
enclosure. He believed that the government should turn the wastes or commons –
scrub and open land on which villagers had previously grazed animals – into smallholdings. As a temporary measure, farmers allowed their workers to grow potatoes
on fallow land, which relieved some of the worst distress. In 1796, a group of evangelicals, William Wilberforce among them, founded the Society for Bettering the
Condition and Increasing the Comforts of the Poor. Allotments would help keep
the labourer out of the beer house. They appealed to the belief that the 'Poor's way
to Bettering their Condition' lay through greater industriousness.

Willingham was not the first village allotment; others had been instituted
during the 1790s, notably in Wiltshire. They were all private initiatives, since the

attempts of campaigners and parliamentarians to persuade the government to act had signally failed. Law's effort is significant because of his later career. In 1824, he became Bishop of Bath and Wells, and was able to spread the allotment idea through the West Country. He established allotments at Banwell and Wells, the latter on a hundred-acre site. He personally rode down to inspect them every morning. A visitor in 1838 wrote of Law's 'terrestrial paradise . . . they say that hundreds of men, women and children would be almost in a state of starvation without the land.'

Law's example must have encouraged other clergy to do likewise. At Willingham, the skills learnt on the allotment may have stimulated what one writer called the 'rapid leaps and bounds out of a purely agricultural parish into a living centre of horticulture', which, by the end of the nineteenth century, was making the village good money from hothouse grapes, flowers and asparagus.

*See Herstmonceux, page 125

# WORSTEAD
NORFOLK                                        *Cut according to the cloth*

Worstead is one of those freaks of topography, a place that is now so small as to be barely noticeable, which yet gave its name to an item known throughout the world – in this case, the woollen cloth used for men's suits. Needless to say, it was once somewhere of importance, served by two churches. One of the churches has gone, but the survivor is appropriately splendid. There is also a lingering sense of the town about Worstead, which has a square where markets used to be held. It is, however, modest in population, being home to well under a thousand souls.

Cloth weaving was probably brought to Norfolk by Flemings. We can guess this because of a linguistic quirk. They wove a wool known, in Flemish, as *hierland*, but the first letter was often dropped; in Norfolk, this came to be known as cloth of Ireland, or Irish cloth. The industry was underway in the eleventh century. The Flemish community was reinforced during the reign of Henry I, when more came as a result of floods in their own country.

The cloth to which Worstead gave its name (it was also made in Aylsham) was distinguished not by its wool but its yarn. It was made from the greasy tops of sheep's fleeces, whose oil gave it greater strength. Among the presents sent to the King's justices and ministers by the City Chamberlain of Norwich in 1301 were 'cloths of Worstead and cloths of Aylsham', showing that worsted had already achieved a reputation. Its importance is reflected in an Act of Parliament of 1497, Taking of Apprentices for Worsteads in the County of Norfolk – the oldest kept in the record office of the House of Lords. By this date, worsted accounted for most of the cloth woven in Norfolk, although its production was now centred in Norwich. Worstead's last weaver was John Cubitt. He died in 1882, aged ninety-one.

# THE
# MIDLANDS

'WHATEVER I forget, I shall never forget the Haggs,' the novelist D. H. Lawrence wrote to his boyhood friend David Chambers. 'The water-pippin by the door – those maiden-blush roses that Flower would lean over and eat and Trip floundering round. – And stewd figs for tea in winter, and in August green stewed apples.' Lawrence grew up in a Nottinghamshire mining community but he could walk out to Haggs farmhouse, where the life and landscape were rural. That experience typifies the English Midlands. Its great plains, seeming to stretch away in an infinity of trees and hedgerows and church spires when seen, for example, from the limestone ridge at Long Clawson, Leicestershire (see page 336), look as though they were made to be farmed; and farmed they have been for centuries, as you could have seen, after the Second World War, from the quantity of corduroy-striped ridge and furrow that survived.

Rather less of that exists now, after years of ploughing, but it can still be found in Northamptonshire, Leicestershire and other Midlands counties. At Laxton in Nottinghamshire (see page 333), a version of the medieval open field system is still practised. That village still contains fourteen farms. But in the century since Lawrence was a young man, urbanisation has increased across the Midlands. The Worcestershire-born Stanley Baldwin, twice prime minister in the 1920s, liked to present himself as a tweedy countryman, delighting in the now-vanished sound of the corncrake, but his fortune came from the typical Midlands industry of metal bashing (see Wilden, page 365).

Dramatic scenery excited early industrialists, as well as Picturesque tourists; the fast-flowing streams of Derbyshire's Peak District powered waterwheels in the eighteenth century. Now, the industry that distinguishes Castleton (see page 308) is altogether more decorative – the mining of the fluorspar known as Blue John. Although the banks of the Severn river in Shropshire were once aglow with iron foundries, places such as Clun (see page 311) had fallen into a rural torpor by the time E. M. Forster tramped through them. Trees are still sacred here.

Industry never found its way into the Herefordshire hills – Old Red Sandstone country, where the colour of the soil is complemented by the reddish-brown coats of the white-faced Hereford cattle. Herefordshire's black-and-white architecture, some of it erected by the carpenter – or 'architector' – John Abel, buried at Sarnesfield (see page 351), perfectly suits the scale of rural life. We know what that life could be in the English Midlands around 1700, thanks to the history that has come down from the appropriately named village of Myddle in Shropshire (see page 341). It was not all a bucolic idyll by any means.

Gloucestershire might not like to think of itself as a Midland county: the Cotswolds has become too fashionable to remember the wool from which it once made its living. By the end of the nineteenth century, industry had fled, leaving the sleepy, limestone towns and villages to be kissed awake by William Morris and the Arts and Crafts movement. They have been lovingly cared for ever since.

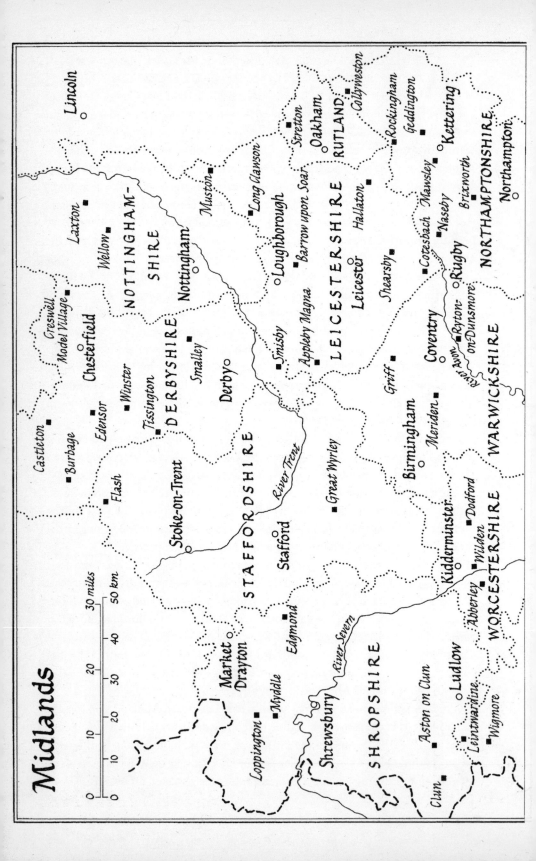

# Midlands

Lincoln

NOTTINGHAM-
SHIRE

Laxton
Wellow
Greswell
Model Village
Chesterfield
Castleton
Burbage
Edensor
Winster
Tissington
Flash
Smalley
DERBYSHIRE
Derby
Nottingham
Muston
Long Clawson
Stretton
Oakham
RUTLAND
Collyweston
Rockingham
Geddington
Kettering
Mawsley
Naseby
Cotesbach
Brixworth
NORTHAMPTONSHIRE
Northampton
Loughborough
Barrow upon Soar
Hallaton
Leicester
LEICESTERSHIRE
Shearsby
Rugby
Ryton-
on-Dunsmore
Coventry
Meriden
WARWICKSHIRE
Griff
Smisby
Appleby Magna
River Trent
Stoke-on-Trent
STAFFORDSHIRE
Stafford
Great Wyrley
Birmingham
River Avon
Kidderminster
Dodford
Wilden
WORCESTERSHIRE
Abberley
Market
Drayton
Edmond
Myddle
Loppington
River Severn
Shrewsbury
SHROPSHIRE
Ludlow
Aston on Clun
Leintwardine
Wigmore
Clun

30 miles
50 km
0  10  20  30  40
0  10  20  30  40  50

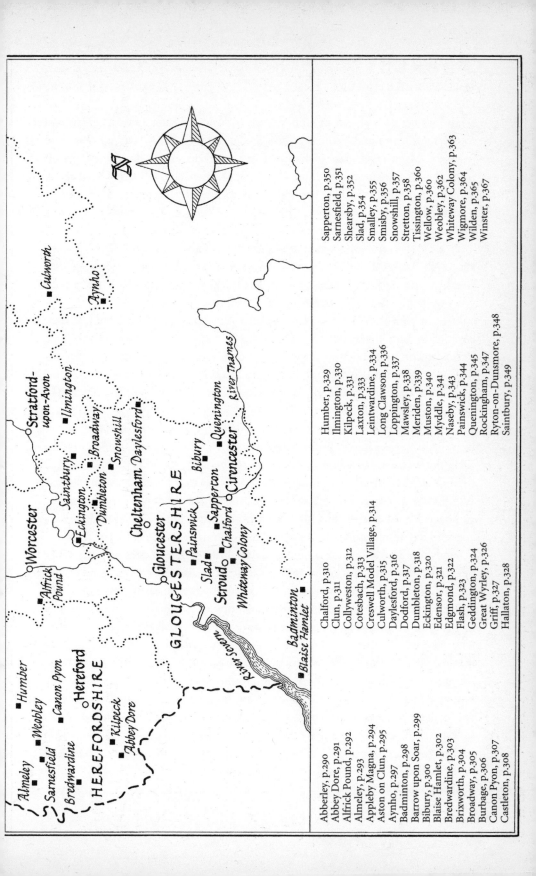

# ABBERLEY
*The story of the stones*

Some people look at old buildings from a distance. Peter Oliver, director of the Herefordshire and Worcestershire Earth Heritage Trust, gets up close and personal. Magnifying glass in hand (it is kept permanently dangling from his neck), he approaches the Norman church of St Michael in Abberley, a village of some five hundred souls near the Malvern Hills, and under magnification another landscape springs into view. The lens turns the surface of the sandstone into a previously unsuspected microcosm of ridges, valleys and crags.

To Dr Oliver, Abberley is a kind of geological theme park. The village demonstrates all the local building stones, predominantly a buff-coloured sandstone, streaked with dark grey traces of iron. His imagination ranges back 310 million years to the time when Worcestershire – then, like the rest of Britain, occupying a different part of the globe – was covered with tropical rainforest and immense river deltas. Sand that had been washed down by the rivers could no longer be held in suspension by the deltas' sluggish meanders, lakes and lagoons. The deposits that built up eventually became fused into sandstone, found near seams of coal made from the compaction of plant material shed, over millions of years, by the rainforest.

The Normans used the local stone to build St Michael's. Some of the blocks are from beds that became streaked with iron oxide, as groundwater penetrated the rock; the iron can be seen in brown lines in the stone, or sometimes an overall reddish colour. Mixed in with the sandstone are occasional blocks of mulberry-coloured and pale green mudstone – a product, as its name suggests, of the compacted mud of river and lake bottoms. A Saxon tomb displays gritstone, a coarser kind of sandstone, this one probably coming from the Forest of Dean.

Sandstone makes a poor building material: the surface flakes away as water penetrates the tiny gaps in the stone. St Michael's also suffered by a disastrous miscalculation made in the fourteenth century, when the roof was raised; the flying buttresses that were built proved insufficient to contain the thrust formed by the extra weight, and although the roof was then lowered, the structure eventually collapsed. All that survives now is the chancel, turned into a chapel, and the footings of a few walls. The Victorians again used the local sandstone to build the grand new church of St Mary in 1852, to the chagrin of their successors, who have had to replace some of the blocks. This, however, was the railway age: prosperous local families commemorated themselves with headstones and tombs of indestructible granite brought from Cornwall* and elsewhere, formed from molten rock deep within the earth's crust. Under the geologist's lens, the fabric of the British village becomes a history of the world.

*See Mousehole, page 60

# ABBEY DORE

## HEREFORDSHIRE

*It is Christmas Day in the workhouse*

'For the poor always ye have with you,' St John's Gospel says. In the Middle Ages, the destitute around Herefordshire's Golden Valley would have looked to the Cistercian Dore Abbey for support, although even before the Dissolution of the Monasteries, attempts were being made to provide for paupers in other ways. As the smallest unit of administration, it fell to the parish to assume the responsibility – an honour of which the parish was, until the onus was removed in the twentieth century, often shy. When the monastic system was broken up by Henry VIII, parishes assumed greater responsibility for the poor, sometimes with the help of donations from private individuals. In 1601, the Act for the Relief of the Poor made such care a legal duty for parishes in England and Wales. The able-bodied poor had to be given work, the aged and infirm shelter.

From the seventeenth century, some parishes provided special accommodation for the people they were required to support. They were known as workhouses, to emphasise what was otherwise quite obvious: life on the parish was no free ride. Taxpayers tended to resent the burden of the poor rate, and did what they could to humiliate those who received relief. An act of 1697 required them to wear badges, comprising two letters: P for pauper, and the initial letter of their parish.

Workhouses were thought to be cheaper than dispensing money to allow the impoverished to stay at home. Often they were made out of existing residential buildings, although one or two were specially built: possibly forbidding, but on a small scale, which allowed the poor to stay near the place where they had grown up. Various efforts were made to improve matters: Gilbert's Act of 1782 required able-bodied workers to be kept at home; the Speenhamland System topped up wages to meet the rising cost of bread*. But for the first quarter of the nineteenth century, village England was living one step ahead of starvation. Desperation led to riots, and eventually the authorities took notice.

The new system was introduced by the Poor Law Amendment Act of 1834. Workhouses were back. Only now they were constructed not by single parishes, but by unions of several parishes. They were bigger and more systematically organised. The first was constructed at Abingdon in Oxfordshire in 1835, on the panopticon principle used in prisons: three wings radiated from a central point, surrounded by a hexagonal perimeter wall. Thirty-eight parishes were served by it. Local opinion can be gauged from an attempt to murder the governor shortly after it was opened. Nothing daunted, workhouses were built across the country. Abbey Dore got its one in 1839.

The Dore Workhouse was lucky. For much of the nineteenth century, its Board of Guardians was chaired by the Rev. Archer Clive, a benign country clergyman. Shortages of blankets were remedied, medical care appears to have been admirable, the children (although separated from their parents, just as husbands and wives had to live apart) went to school. Not all were so humane. According to Charles Dickens, writing the postscript to *Our Mutual Friend* in 1865, 'I believe there has been in England, since the days of the Stuarts, no law so often infamously administered, no law so often openly violated, no law habitually so ill-supervised.' That law stayed in force until the Local Government Act of 1929 passed responsibility for maintaining the poor to local councils. The Dore Workhouse now offers accommodation of a rather different kind, having been converted into a development of cottage dwellings known as Riverdale.

*See Speenhamland, page 193

# ALFRICK POUND
WORCESTERSHIRE                                    *Locking up the strays*

A familiar feature of every medieval manor would have been the pound or pinfold. This was the animal equivalent of the lock-up. The entitlement of each farmer to horses, cattle, hogs, sheep or geese was strictly limited, as were the places where they could be grazed. Under the open field system, straying animals must have been commonplace, but they were vigorously resented by those whose crops they had eaten. Strays were therefore rounded up on a regular basis, and locked into a communal green space, with a water supply. There they waited until the owner appeared, with evidence that he had paid the necessary fine for their release. This evidence took the form of a notched stick, which had been split down the middle. If the half presented by the owner matched the half retained by the 'pindar', who kept the pound, the animals would be released.

Most pounds must have been made of wood and have disappeared, but some had stone or brick walls, survivals being commonest in the Midlands, where the open field system continued in operation longer than elsewhere*.

Pound and pinfold are interchangeable. Pinfold tended to be used more in the North. As Hensleigh Wedgwood explained in *A Dictionary of English Etymology* (1862), the word sounds as though it means a fold where sheep are penned, as in sheepfold. But this would be tautologous, because a fold is, by definition, somewhere that animals are penned. Instead pinfold comes from an old word meaning a pawn or pledge. The word was well known to Renaissance dramatists, Shakespeare using it in *The Two Gentlemen of Verona* and *King Lear*. 'Is it your master's pleasure, or your own, To keep me in this pinfold?' Isabella asks in Thomas Middleton's *The Changeling*. To which Lollio replies punningly: ''Tis for my master's pleasure, lest, being taken in another man's corn, you might be pounded in another place.' The attendant spirit in Milton's *Comus* complains of being 'pester'd in this pinfold here'.

Presumably it was the pound that gave Alfrick Pound its name; certainly the remains of a pound are still there to be seen, announced by a wooden sign. Other examples exist at Higham and Tockholes in Lancashire. Norwell in Nottinghamshire and Hutton-le-Hole in North Yorkshire both have circular pounds, the one built of brick, the other of stone. Some pounds were combined with lock-ups (Sandiacre in Derbyshire; Clophill in Bedfordshire). 'The most unusual one to survive,' in the opinion of R. J. Brown in *English Village Architecture* (2004) 'is at Raskelf, North Yorkshire, which is an open crenellated polygon with arched and barred door and window openings.'

*See Laxton, page 333

# ALMELEY
## HEREFORDSHIRE

*Falstaff was here*

What is in a name, or a reputation? Shakespeare's Sir John Falstaff, the gutsy, lustful, elemental buffoon of *Henry IV, Parts One and Two*, evolved out of a figure who, in real life, was extraordinarily different: Sir John Oldcastle, a conviction-driven Lollard, one of a sect of early Protestants who believed that the Bible should be read in English (they were called Lollards from the mutterings they made while they read).

The Oldcastles came from Almeley, in the Welsh Marches. They were knights, but by no means rich, possessing only one manor. Presumably the name derived from their dwelling place; there is indeed a castle in Almeley, which is marked on the Ordnance Survey map as Oldcastle, although it cannot have been very old when the first of the Oldcastles emerged in the early fourteenth century, not being recorded in the Domesday Book or early lists of border strongholds. The name might have been applied to the ruins of the Roman camp on whose site the castle was later built. It then transferred itself not only to the Oldcastle family but to the hamlet around them.

Our Sir John Oldcastle seems to have been born in the mid 1370s. He grew up amid some of the most beautiful scenery in Britain, a land of fast-running streams and wooded hills. It was, however, remote from the centres of power, ambiguous as to its identity, Welsh or English, and a shelter for heretics, including Lollards. Sir John Clanvow, who owned estates near Almeley, wrote a pious tract called *The Two Ways*, declaring his sympathy with the heretic Lollards. The rectors of Almeley and nearby Whitney-on-Wye were thought by their bishop to be capable of sheltering William Swinderby, a Lollard evangelist.

Perhaps Oldcastle heard him as a teenager. Whatever he believed might not have mattered much, had he stayed put. He was trusted as a military commander, active against Owain Glyn Dŵr's rebellion and attending Parliament as one of the knights of the shires. His ways would have lain in respectable obscurity if his wife (or wives – there may have been two) had not died. We know little about this lady or ladies, but his next marriage, to Joan Cobham, propelled him into a different sphere.

The thrice-married granddaughter of Lord Cobham, Joan needed a fourth husband to help manage her estates. His more prominent position attracted attention to his views. He was tried for heresy but not executed, merely sent to the Tower to recant. But he escaped, and organised a futile, although widespread, revolt. After its failure, he went on the run, finding shelter round and about the Marches, eventually being captured at Broniarth. The old soldier put up quite a fight. When taken, he was sent to London, where he was promptly hanged and burnt.

The process by which Oldcastle became transformed into Shakespeare's rollicking anti-hero at the end of the sixteenth century is puzzling. But he acquired the reputation of having been an evil friend of Henry V's youth, and Shakespeare originally used his name, before the tenth Baron Cobham ensured that it was changed to that of another knight, Sir John Fastolf (a distinguished Knight of the Garter with no living relatives). The mask slips once, when Hal calls him 'my old lad of the castle'; but to the Protestants, Oldcastle had become a martyr, and Shakespeare had to remove all doubt by denying any connection with Oldcastle in the epilogue of *Henry IV, Part Two*. Doth he protest too much?

# APPLEBY MAGNA
LEICESTERSHIRE                              *This Noble Foundation*

The grandest village school in the country is at Appleby Magna. To call such a splendid establishment a village school is faintly ridiculous: the design was supplied by Sir Christopher Wren, the scale is that of a country house, and there were originally dormitories for boarders. But it was erected to serve local needs, having been built at Appleby because, as its founder Sir John Moore wrote in 1695, 'there I drew my first breath'.

*The handsomest village school in England: Appleby Magna.*

Sir John, a younger son who went into trade, became a successful City merchant, concerned particularly with the export of lead. Shrewd investments in the East India Company and New River Company multiplied his fortune. In James II's reign he became one of the City of London MPs. During the same difficult time he served as Lord Mayor, treating the King and Queen to a 'very splendid and magnificent' entertainment when they visited the Mansion House. Having no children, he spent his latter years disbursing his money on charitable causes, notably the Christ's Hospital schools, then in the City, and what became the Sir John Moore Foundation at Appleby.

The progress of the building works can be followed through Sir John's letters. By then in his seventies, he watched them from London, through the eyes of his nephews Thomas and George Moore. The original idea had been for Wren's master carpenter at St Paul's, Thomas Woodstock, to execute the design, but he died in 1694. This left the way clear for the forceful local builder Sir William Wilson to take control, as far as he could. Of a bullying temperament, he seems to have bulldozed Thomas Moore, leaving George to lament over alterations and overspends to his uncle. Round windows appeared, as did lengths of cornice, and Wren's hipped roof was replaced by a flat one (although this, to be fair, was to accommodate the boarders, whose presence had not been foreseen at the beginning). 'I am very glad to hear the Schoole is all covered with lead and well done,' Sir John wrote in December 1695. 'I thank you for your care in keeping all materiall from embelzment [sic].'

There was a prolonged wrangle over payments, which lasted until the eve of Sir John's death in 1702. Wilson's final act of self-promotion was to carve the (not very good) statue of Moore in the school hall. The inscription beneath it, approved by Moore, makes plain his intention of endowing a school 'for ye Education of ye Male Childern [sic]' in adjacent parishes and towns. The most famous old boy is William Huskisson, who, having entered the school in 1782, used his copperplate writing to great effect, becoming a civil servant, an MP and president of the Board of Trade; he died after falling in front of Stephenson's Rocket at the opening of the Liverpool to Manchester Railway.

# ASTON ON CLUN
## SHROPSHIRE                                    *Sacred importance of trees*

The black poplar does not have the folkloric resonance of the oak or the ash. It is now rare, the reason for growing it having been lost. It produced a light wood, which tended to dent rather than splinter; it was therefore especially useful for the bottoms of carts. It was also slow to catch fire, and so farmers in the Home Counties chose it for the floors of oast houses, where hops were dried. Another characteristic, which might have attracted the notice of tree-worshipping ancestors, is that male and female trees are quite different, rather than unisex, and since in Britain there is a sexual imbalance (too many males), seedlings are rare. Still, they did not attract a cult.

Except at Aston on Clun. Every year the villagers dress a black poplar with flags. This happens at the end of May, on what is called Arbor Day. The original Arbor Tree, or last mature one, collapsed in 1995. It was then a typically ancient tree, hollow, misshapen, its trunk gnarled and encrusted with warts. Flags on long poles would protrude from it, giving the appearance of a St Sebastian suffering martyrdom, or the practice of acupuncture on a grand scale.

The meaning of Arbor is open to speculation; perhaps it has something to do with the wooden buildings that were known as harbours or arbours in seventeenth-century Shrewsbury, in which case it would have denoted shelter. Indeed, the meaning and antiquity of the ritual are equally uncertain. There is no published reference to it before the early twentieth century. Legend associates it with a marriage that took place in the late eighteenth century between John Marston, a local landowner, and Mary Carter. After the ceremony, the wedding carriage was pulled home by local people, who stopped at the tree in the centre of Aston on Clun. The bride was so enchanted by the decorations put in it that she gave money to ensure that they were repeated each anniversary.

It seems likely there was a connection with Oak Apple Day, the celebration instituted by Charles II to remember the return of the Stuart dynasty; with a telling eye for a story, he associated it with his own escape after the Battle of Worcester in 1651, when he hid in an oak tree at Boscobel House. Parliament required people across the country to participate in 'hearty public praises and thanksgivings unto Almighty God' for the Restoration. The day chosen was 29 May, Charles II's birthday. It is also Arbor Day. The custom may have older roots even than that. A Celtic fertility goddess called Brigit (after the coming of Christianity, she seems to have morphed into the Irish St Brigit, who was, strangely, a nun) was worshipped by the decoration of trees.

Is it significant that the Arbor Tree has associations with a marriage? We do not know. We have to accept it as a mystery. If the ritual is a very old one, it cannot have been performed even with the previous ancient tree, which, since black poplars do not have the longevity of oaks or yews, could not have been more than three centuries old. Today, the ceremony takes place around a relatively young tree, grafted from its predecessor, with the flags (temporarily) attached to a scaffold.

# AYNHO

*A place for drunkards to reflect*

In 1837, a labourer called Richard Howes was put in the stocks at Aynho for being 'drunk and riotous' on Coronation Day. Well, what did they expect? It was the dawn of the Victorian age. The stocks can still be seen, two wooden boards that clap together with holes for the feet; like most stocks, they are a double seater, allowing two offenders to suffer the indignity simultaneously. We do not know if the unfortunate Howes was the last person to sit in them, but elsewhere the stocks continued in use as a punishment for some years.

At Stanningley in West Yorkshire, John Gambles was, perhaps appropriately, convicted of Sunday gambling in 1860 and sentenced to sit in the stocks for six hours. In 1872, the old stocks at Newbury in Berkshire were disinterred from the town hall cellars, where they had rested for fourteen years, so that Mark Tuck could be consigned to them. Some things had improved, however. Since it was raining, they were set up in the Shambles, which was covered, rather than the Market Place, and a policeman stood by during the four hours that Tuck was in them, to make sure he was not unreasonably pelted. Early ages showed no such squeamishness. The stocks, indeed, were often associated with a pillory, as well as a whipping post for corporal punishment.

The Saxons seem to have known about the stocks; there is an illustration of them in the ninth-century Utrecht Psalter, thought to have been made near Reims. From 1351, a statute required every township in England to maintain a set, as an attempt to control workplace relationships after the Black Death. Every manor was ordered to have stocks in 1405. The misdemeanours that could land people in them were various. In Henry VIII's reign, children who did not work on the farm could be whipped, and anyone who did not make them work could be put in the stocks.

The most common categories of people to find themselves in the stocks were drunkards and vagabonds. A law of 1605 confirmed that the stocks should be the punishment for drunkenness, and in some places they must have been much in demand. An old photograph from Marden in Kent shows a couple of rough-looking characters in the stocks – one smoking a short clay pipe, the other looking resigned beneath his broad-brimmed hat, both with hobnailed boots projecting towards camera – with the slogan 'Drunk Again' chalked onto the board. Vagabonds were beggars or rogues who roamed from parish to parish – an alarming prospect to the Elizabethans, because they might form into marauding bands or, worse, become a burden to the parish (poor relief was designed to support only the needy who were born in the parish). Their length of time in the stocks was therefore particularly severe: three days on bread and water, at the end of which they would be moved on.

Many villages let their stocks fall into disrepair, for which they were upbraided by the court. People may have had mixed feelings about them; they certainly did about the pillory. Exposing miscreants to sundry projectiles thrown by the mob effectively turned them over to rough justice. Daniel Defoe got away with it in 1703: having satirised the Church, he was forced, among other things, to stand in the pillory three times, but the crowd garlanded him with flowers. A public informer got a different reception at Seven Dials in London: he was stoned to death.

# BADMINTON
## GLOUCESTERSHIRE
*Country of the Houyhnhnm*

Look at the countryside around Badminton: here is the English country idyll. Piles of logs, trailers parked in driveways, cattle grids, places with picturesque names, such as Old Sodbury – these deceptive signs of ramshackle rurality rub up against avenues and lodges and urns, suggesting that a great country house is round the corner. There are cottages in the village, to be sure, but the quality of the topiary suggests that they are occupied by doctors, lawyers and, on occasion, architectural historians, rather than peasants. What may once have been created as an agricultural centre has been purified and distilled into a place of unapproachable Cotswold stone beauty. Unapproachable, that is, to those who cannot see a pretty cottage without wanting to buy it. As the universal cold custard of the paintwork proclaims, nothing in Badminton is likely to come onto the market. This is an estate village, and the Duke of Beaufort ain't selling.

What, beyond exceptional care over the architecture, gives Badminton its special character? We are in the kingdom of the horse. Autumn, in these parts, comes as colourful as a coral reef, and with it a new season for the Beaufort Hunt. Hounds have been kept at Badminton since the seventeenth century, when Henry Somerset, the Royalist who would become the 1st Duke of Beaufort, was constrained to spend some years living quietly after the Civil War. Originally it was a harrier pack, chasing hares; then a pack of staghounds was added. As yet the fox was regarded merely as vermin, not a quarry fit to be hunted. But from the mid eighteenth century its status changed, as gentlemen came to realise the thrill of galloping across a landscape that was often newly drained.

The 5th Duke is supposed to have given his hounds over entirely to fox-hunting in 1762, after a dull day in pursuit of the stag: a fox, accidentally started, provided an exciting run. At that time, there were relatively few foxes in the countryside. The new passion for hunting them coincided nicely with the aesthetics of landscape improvement. Capability Brown's swathes of grassland dotted with clumps of trees created an environment in which foxes could live and breed happily – until such moment as they were compelled to streak away with a pack at their tails. Since the Hunting Act of 2004 the tradition has (temporarily, its supporters hope) been modified: hounds follow pre-laid trails, rather than live foxes.

Hunting is not, however, the only equestrian activity for which Badminton is famed. Each May, 165,000 people flock to the Horse Trials, a crowd that divides into fresh-faced, pony-mad girls and hard-bitten, horsey Old Sodburies. Great Badminton occupies a no-less-iconic position in property circles. Estate agents, unable to get their hands on much in the village itself, have invented a kind of Greater Badminton, in whose aura all the surrounding villages are deemed to bask. Even houses at Wotton-under-Edge are advertised as being 'near Badminton', when, according to the AA route-planning website, it is half an hour away. By the same token, Tormarton becomes 'Tormarton, Badminton'; a less romantic description would be 'off junction eighteen of the M4'.

See also Caldbeck, page 379; Exford, page 34

# BARROW UPON SOAR
## LEICESTERSHIRE
*Salute the Plesiosaur*

Barrow upon Soar salutes the past. It is a remote past, sometimes. The village symbol is a plesiosaur, after the unusually complete specimen that was discovered in a lime pit in 1851. A label in the Oxford Museum of Natural History describes the plesiosaur as having the head of a lizard, the teeth of a crocodile, a giraffe neck of forty-one vertebrae, the body of a serpent, the tail of an ordinary quadruped, the ribs of a chameleon and the 'Padelles' (meaning flippers) of a whale. It was an odd-looking dinosaur, which, using its Padelles, rowed itself around the warm seas that covered Leicestershire about two hundred million years ago, when Leicestershire was somewhere on the shores of the supercontinent Pangea, lapped by tropical waves. Locals call it the Barrow upon Soar kipper.

There are fossils all around the village. A huddle of ammonites can be found on the wall of the Trap pub. A huge drop of Jurassic amber is suspended above the old Catholic church. Lizard-like kuehneosauruses run across a wall on Beveridge Street. Trilobites, those prehistoric crabs that look somewhat like woodlice, are out in force. Your eye is constantly being caught by shells, skeletons, organic forms – part of a sculpture project. (Alas, one trilobite was destroyed when a joyrider crashed into it, and the kuehneosauruses were stolen; both works have been replaced.) It might seem that Barrow upon Soar has lodged its sense of identity firmly in the Jurassic period. And rightly. Without its Jurassic heritage, the village would not have made its living in a more recent era.

The warm Jurassic seas were so full of creatures – tiny ones, as well as the huge plesiosaurs – that the calcium of their shells saturated the water. As the organisms died, their carcasses floated to the seabed, where, during countless thousands of years, the shells piled up into beds that could be dozens of feet thick. Limestone would be the result: a fine thing to build with, but also a more workaday material. Ground up, limestone can be burned to make lime, which was even more important to builders than stone: it was an essential ingredient in mortar, plaster and the protective limewash with which many buildings were sealed. No wonder C. Gray, writing in W. H. Pyne's *Microcosm* of 1808, should have written that it was 'an article of great consideration, not only from its utility for various purposes, but from the employment which the manufacturing of it affords to thousands . . . It forms an important item in national expenditure'. By the time when the Barrow Plesiosaur was discovered, lime was also being used in agriculture to balance the acidity of soil and add calcium.

Lime burning was a hazardous activity; regulations would not allow it to be undertaken these days without masks and protective suiting. It began at Barrow in the Middle Ages. The scale of production during the nineteenth century was formidable. There were eleven quarries, known as delphs, in operation in 1845. Hundreds of kilns have been found around the village. The lime trade was Barrow upon Soar's most important industry until the beginning of the twentieth century. By then Portland cement had replaced lime, to make a stronger and quicker-setting mortar. Increasingly the virtues of lime mortar, which is softer, but more able to move and breathe than Portland cement, are being appreciated; its admirers should salute the Plesiosaur.

*See also Limekilns, page 599*

# BIBURY
## GLOUCESTERSHIRE

*William Morris: 'surely the most beautiful village in England'*

People did not make much of Bibury until the nineteenth century. Alexander Pope, writing to Jonathan Swift in 1726, remarked on its 'pleasing prospect', nothing more. The diarist John Byng, the future Lord Torrington, who visited in 1794, enjoyed 'two basins of snail tea' (good for the lungs) and the 'pastoral trout stream full of fish (for this is a famous spot for fly-fishing . . .)'. You can still see the fish from the garden of the Swan Hotel, formerly a coaching inn, by looking cautiously over the low wall where they lie with their noses upstream, waiting for something appetising to float down (if they circle, they are 'on the rise').

Byng 'procured the key of the church (a key the size of Dover Castle), and admired it as lightsome, and well-glazed'. Had he lingered, he might have noticed the hourglass beside the pulpit. An earlier vicar used to turn it frequently in the course of his two-hour sermons, during which the squire would slip outside to smoke a pipe, returning for the blessing. There was no suggestion, however, that Bibury was anything out of the ordinary.

It took William Morris to call it 'surely the most beautiful village in England'. In 1871, he bought the lease of Kelmscott Manor, a house that was so thoroughly one with its setting that it seemed to 'grow out of the soil'. From Kelmscott, he would

*Essence of Cotswolds: cottages at Bibury.*

take friends to see the countryside, including villages such as Bibury, twelve miles away. Fashion had not yet descended on the Cotswolds. It was still seen with the eye of a farmer, as an unpromising area of exposed hills, good for sheep but not prosperous. Indeed, Morris's early biographer J. W. Mackail wrote that the country around Kelmscott was 'among the sleepiest and loneliest of southern England'. Under Morris's influence, however, attitudes were soon to change. Bibury became specially admired, and in the course of the next century the cottages that form Arlington Row became one of the most photographed scenes in the country.

Morris and his friends looked at Bibury as artists, not social reformers. They saw an exceptional harmony in its streets, where both walls and roofs were made of limestone – often said to be golden, but more often, after weathering and growth of lichen, silvery grey. In an age that extolled the virtues and creativity of anonymous craftsmen, they seemed to be the equivalent of folk art, created by skilled but unlettered men. The walls of the houses appeared to be solid, and so they were, being up to a couple of feet thick. This did not ensure, however, that they were free from damp, which could penetrate through the rubble filling.

Arlington Row dates from the seventeenth century, when Arlington Mill, powered by a waterwheel, was in operation. Weavers occupied the cottages, and their first-floor gables and dormers, which poke into the great stone expanse of the roof, lit the workshops where the looms stood. At the mill, the woollen cloth was soaked and beaten until it became felt.

# BLAISE HAMLET
## GLOUCESTERSHIRE
*Taking Picturesque to extremes*

Blaise Hamlet is the apotheosis of the Picturesque village. These days, it stands at daggers drawn with the suburbs of Bristol, at which it can look with countrified disdain, being owned by the National Trust. But originally it stood at the entrance to Blaise Castle, property of John Scandrett Harford. Harford came from an old line of Bristol merchants, iron founders and bankers. Like the Frys and some other successful families in the city, Harford was a Quaker. But this was long after the Quakers had been distinguished by their plain dress and austere ways, and Harford had entered the landed gentry (his son consolidating the process by converting to the Church of England). His Quaker conscience told him to house the poor; his status as a gentleman encouraged him to do it in the most decorative way possible.

Fortunately, Harford had come into contact with John Nash, a very un-Quakerish architect, who was the presiding genius of Picturesque architecture. His career had begun with country houses, designed in the manner of Tuscan villas. He crossed Harford's bows in 1804, creating an elaborately thatched dairy for Blaise Castle. The Blaise Hamlet commission came in 1810, the year before Nash embarked on the grand juggling act that led to the creation of Regent's Park and the Picturesque parade formed by Portland Place, Regent Street, Piccadilly Circus, Lower Regent Street and Waterloo Place.

In association with George Stanley Repton, a son of the landscape architect Humphry Repton, Nash lavished attention on each of nine cottages. The ruling principle was to make each one a musical variation on the cottage theme, the more inventive the better. Exorbitantly tall chimneys with Tudor brickwork; a plethora of dormers; fantastic roofing effects that seem to rise in a crescendo of ornament, sometimes in thatch; pillars made from rustic logs – these are some of the ingredients. The result is a suite of buildings that might be designed for a mantelpiece as much as their bucolic village green, such is their extreme and beguiling quaintness.

Historians have noticed that the accommodation concealed by this meringue of ornament was not spacious. Tenants were allowed a room on the ground floor and a couple of bedrooms above. The cottages were, however, to quote *The Architectural Magazine*, 'chiefly occupied by widows and decayed persons'. No doubt a labourer's family could have crammed into one, but the social purpose was housing for the elderly, the hamlet lacking the services that would have given it an independent existence. A decayed person might well have thought a Blaise Hamlet cottage to be better than the parish house to which he or she might otherwise have been consigned – even with the disadvantage of being on view to tourists who had Blaise Hamlet on their itinerary more or less from the day it was built.

# BREDWARDINE
## HEREFORDSHIRE
*An intimate picture of parish life*

On Quinquagesima Sunday, 3 March 1878, the Rev. Francis Kilvert walked in the churchyard at Bredwardine. 'The sunny air was full of the singing of the birds and the brightness and gladness of the Spring,' he wrote in his diary. Looking at the tombstones, crowding together, of different sizes but all facing the same way, 'it seemed as if the morning of the Resurrection had come and the sleepers had arisen from their graves and were standing upon their feet silent and solemn, all looking toward the East to meet the Rising of the Sun.'

Kilvert was then thirty-seven. He had become vicar of Bredwardine the year before, but would not have long to enjoy his vicarage, with its pie-crust parapet. In August 1879 he married; the next month, shortly before his thirty-ninth birthday, his tombstone was added to those in the churchyard, when he died of peritonitis. The diary that he left behind – the little of it that survived burning by the niece who inherited the notebooks – is an intimate picture of parish life.

Kilvert came to Bredwardine from Clyro in Radnorshire. Once, it had been a place of some consequence, with a castle. By Kilvert's day, it had sunk into being a rural backwater. A fine brick bridge had been built over the Wye in 1769, although the river was still capable of carrying away a coach and horses during flood. Such was the steepness of the ground that Kilvert's vegetable garden lay on the other side of the river from his house, where they could find flatter land. In November 1878, they had to escape as best they could, wading knee-deep through water with the children on their backs, when the Wye broke its banks. Later that winter it got so cold that the Wye froze. On Christmas Eve – a day of 'very hard frost: Brilliant sunshine on sparkling snow' – he visited the Davies family at the farmhouse known as the Old Weston, where David Davies was a shepherd. 'Little Davie' Davies had died, after seeing a vision of 'some pretty children dancing in a beautiful garden' with sweet music. 'I never saw death look so beautiful.'

Events in the wider world seem rarely to have penetrated the Welsh Marches. The exception was the news of Rorke's Drift (or more accurately, the Battle of Isandlwana that preceded it, when Lord Chelmsford's base camp had been destroyed). News of the disaster arrived when Kilvert was having dinner at Hay Castle. The 727 regulars who had been killed belonged to the 24th Regiment of Foot, later known as the South Wales Borderers, based at Brecon. 'Col. Thomas much affected by the news and obliged to leave the concert room. He knew the officers intimately.' Death came to Victorian England in many ways.

# BRIXWORTH

NORTHAMPTONSHIRE  *Northern Europe's greatest seventh-century building*

All Saints in Brixworth has been described as 'perhaps the most imposing architectural memorial of the seventh century yet surviving north of the Alps'. Set on a rise that puts it a little apart from its Northamptonshire village, the gaunt, tawny walls of this commanding edifice run for more than a hundred and twenty feet. Originally, Brixworth was a minster, whose priests, living in a monastery, would have preached Christianity around the countryside; the scale of the building shows that the new religion, brought to Kent in the sixth century, had become firmly established in Mercia*. The original monks had come from Peterborough around 675.

When built, All Saints (not its original dedication, which is unknown) took the form of a basilica: an aisled building composed of nave, presbytery and apse, with a crypt beneath the altar and a narthex (a kind of porch) at the west end. The single-storey aisles were not open, but divided up into chapels. There had been basilicas in Kent, known, for example, through the outline presented by foundations at Reculver (see page 139); ultimately they derive from the Roman building type.

Since the apse at Brixworth was polygonal, rather than semi-circular, it has been suggested that the architect knew about the Middle Eastern basilicas, such as Qalb Lozeh in Syria; if so, Anglo-Saxon Mercia was more outward-looking than one might have thought. Maybe an influence was Wilfrid, the stormy, unstoppable Bishop of Hexham, who often travelled in France and Italy and probably brought back craftsmen to build the many churches that he founded. The round-headed arches, however, are a survival from Roman practice; the builders also quarried tiles from a Roman villa to make the heads of the arches, and there is a carved eagle (the emblem of a legion?) beside the door.

The difficulty of constructing a church of this size can be seen from the hotch-potch of materials. Every stone had to be quarried, hauled into position, shaped and placed by hand, supplemented only by the brawn of oxen and horses. Mustard-brown ironstone predominates. Iron workers had been digging this stone out of the Forest of Rockingham (see page 347) since Roman times; in the twentieth century, great gullets of it would be gouged out of the Northamptonshire landscape to feed the Corby steelworks, a few miles away. Dozens of people must have been employed in the construction of Brixworth church, which would have lasted decades.

Then came the tenth century. Although Brixworth is about as far from the sea as anywhere in England, it was nevertheless found out by Danish raiders. They pillaged the monastery. Later, only the church was restored, for use by the parish. Presumably the chapels had tumbled down, because the aisles were removed and the arcade filled in. The scar bears witness to what must have been a terrible episode for the village. The rebuilding did, however, give them a tower.

When the Anglo-Saxon enthusiast Percy Withers brought A. E. Housman – classical scholar, poet and all round dry stick – to Brixworth, he was astonished by the transformation that came over him: Housman's cynicism slipped away, his face glowed with wonder, and if he did not actually 'burst into exclamation' – a unique occurrence, reserved for the next Saxon church that they visited, St Peter's in Northampton – he came very near to it.

*See Minster, page 133*

# BROADWAY
## WORCESTERSHIRE
The Cotswold ideal

Broadway is an institution. So much is it everyone's ideal of a Cotswold village that it is hardly possible to walk down the street for visitors during the summer. Many of them are American, attracted by the chip off a metropolitan grand hotel hiding behind a facade of Cotswold stone, the Barceló Lygon Arms. Antique shops abound. Both Americans and antique shops have been associated with this village for more than a century, and were essential to its revival, or reinvention, as an immutable example of visual harmony. There was a period before that, however, when Broadway was on its uppers. As with so many villages, its resurrection was due to art; where art goes, money follows.

Broadway owed its original prosperity to the wide street that curves through it, and from which it takes its name. It was busy with coaches, carriages and carts on the main road between Oxford and Worcester. But the railway did away with all that; during the Victorian period Broadway did not even have a station. Its decline could be read in the architecture, as yeomen's houses were divided into cottages, and knocked about in the process. Cotswold towns and villages were not sufficiently dramatic or highly coloured for the Victorian taste. Broadway languished, its Cotswold stone roofs letting in water, its best house, Abbey Grange, used variously as a workhouse and lock-up.

But to those with an eye for it, neglect did not impair its charm. The first person to sing its praises was William Morris*. He came in 1876, and subsequently described one of its old farmhouses in a lecture as 'beautiful, a work of art and a piece of nature, no less'. After that, it was discovered by a band of painters and illustrators in the 1880s. They worked for *Harper's Magazine* of New York. They included the dapper Edwin Abbey, an American, specialising in historical scenes from the Renaissance and eighteenth century, and the Englishman Alfred Parsons, an illustrator and garden designer. They set up studios in Abbey Grange. John Singer Sargent came, giving Japanese lanterns to two little girls in white dresses, whom he painted in the dusk of the garden as *Carnation, Lily, Lily, Rose*.

There was much boisterousness between the artists, who painted within shouting distance of one another – fun condoned but not embraced by Henry James, another summer resident, who was not known to unbend beyond an indulgent smile. Urbane and comfort-loving, he was horrified by the American actress Mary Anderson's decision to turn the dilapidated Court Farm into a home for herself and her husband, the sportsman and barrister Antonio de Navarro. 'You, if I may say so, have made yourselves martyrs to the antique, the picturesque,' he wailed. 'You will freeze, you will suffer damp. I pity you, my poor dears.' He need not have worried. Court Farm became as comfortable as only an American house (before the Second World War) could be: the note was that of 'an aristocratic inn of the eighteenth century', one visitor commented.

The railway did arrive eventually, in 1903, just as Sydney Bolton Russell was eyeing up the Lygon Arms. He bought it, and whereas Anderson turned her manor house into an inn, he decorated the inn as a country house, with antique furniture restored by his son Gordon. Gordon Russell, originally a craftsman in the Arts and Crafts mould, although later frowned upon by Arts and Crafts purists for his willingness to increase output by using machines, opened a workshop here. These influences have helped turn Broadway into the place of artful loveliness that it is today. Best to go out of season.

*See Bibury, page 300. See also Walberswick, page 275

# BURBAGE
## DERBYSHIRE
*Everyman's music: the brass band*

It was the piston valve that allowed the brass band movement to flourish in the nineteenth century. This development made it possible for instruments that could play every semitone in the scale to be manufactured sufficiently cheaply for working people to buy them. The piston valve was invented in the 1820s, and brass instruments with the system became widely available in the 1840s. The Burbage Brass Band was founded in 1861. A golden age had begun.

Before 1800, few amateurs had tackled brass instruments. There were not many in currency: only trombones, trumpets and horns. The trombone, whose blaring tone made it popular in the Tudor period, had fallen from favour, its place, from the reign of Charles II, taken by the trumpet. But trumpets and horns, with their restricted range, were not highly adaptable, and therefore held little appeal for lone musicians. They found a home, however, in the bands that often accompanied militia regiments, where they might be joined by clarinets, flutes, fifes, bassoons and serpents, as well as the indispensable percussion.

Such bands were financed by the commanding officers of the regiments concerned, and drew musicians from the bands that accompanied travelling shows, such as Wombwell's Menagerie. The possibilities of virtuosic brass playing were at the same time being demonstrated by the conductor Louis Jullien, whose touring light orchestra relied on its ability to dazzle provincial audiences: it was not unknown for the combined, welkin-ringing blare of twenty cornets, twenty trumpets, twenty trombones, twenty ophicleides and twenty serpents to be deployed for a rendition of Bellini's 'Suona la Tromba' (sound the trumpet) from *I Puritani*.

Bands of only brass instruments began to emerge in the 1830s. By 1850, Dickens's *Household Words* magazine was commenting on the 'brawny workmen' trained into a band by the Messrs Strutt of Derby, while 'another set of harmonious blacksmiths' could be found in the brass band established at the Cyfarthfa works in Merthyr Tydfil. The Burbage Brass Band was founded by Robert Broome, the owner of the local limestone quarry, and fellow industrialists. Victorian employers tended to believe that music-making was a force for good among working people, because it provided a constructive leisure activity that encouraged self-discipline and comradeship.

At Burbage, the patron was the Duke of Devonshire. To some ears, the sound of a brass band will always evoke northern collieries and industrial towns, but the strains of the Burbage Brass Band have also been – and are still – a joyous accompaniment to the many prize-givings and gala occasions celebrated on the lawns of Chatsworth House throughout the summer. As the band's historian, David Apthorpe, comments, Burbage 'proudly maintains its original aims and objectives . . . to teach music without charge, provide a healthy and constructive pastime, develop community spirit and entertain'.

*See also Sedgwick, page 395

# CANON PYON
## HEREFORDSHIRE                         *O, the Roast Beef of Old England*

Roast beef is a dish synonymous with England, and the chances are that, in the great age of beef-eating, the Victorian paterfamilias who wielded his knife at the head of the table would have been carving a Hereford. This attractive breed of cattle, with its white face and reddish-brown coat, became one of the most successful of all time, conquering not just Britain but the main cattle-raising countries of the world.

While Robert Bakewell of Leicestershire is famous for breeding the longhorn during the Agricultural Revolution, it was not an achievement that outlasted him; after his death in 1795, the animals soon lost favour to other breeds. Benjamin Tomkins and his son, also Benjamin, christened beneath the leaning arcades of Canon Pyon church in 1745, were Bakewell's contemporaries. Until 1800 no effort was made to sell Hereford cattle beyond the county boundaries of Herefordshire, so the Tomkinses are not as celebrated as Bakewell. Nevertheless, the breed that they and their neighbours created in the second half of the eighteenth century would go from strength to strength.

In the Domesday Book, only the counties bordering Wales are listed as having bovarii – ox men. There is some debate as to what bovarius means, but it suggests that the area was particularly associated with oxen, which were used throughout England for ploughing, the last teams surviving on heavy ground until the dawn of the twentieth century. In Herefordshire, the animals were descended from the Red Cattle that once roamed the Welsh Marches. They were valued for their brute strength, and farming remained primitive in this damp, if beautiful, county, where agriculture had never much thrived.

The Tomkinses' achievement was to take native brawn and turn it into the beef that would become a symbol of national pride for those who could afford to eat it. Like Bakewell, they stopped the old practice of keeping both sexes in the field together, and bred only from selected partners, in order to develop specific traits. It would be wrong to give the Tomkinses sole credit. In 1694, one William Town is recorded as having sold 'nine Hereford oxen for 52l' – a hint that local animals were sufficiently distinctive to be identified as a type. Even so, eighteenth-century breeders accepted that none of them, not even the Tomkinses, had a monopoly on the best sort of Hereford. Different strains were characterised by shades of face: mottled, grey or white. As a result, no herd book – recording and restricting the breeding of pedigree herds to ensure the greatest conformity to breed type – was established until 1845.

But that was typical of the Hereford. It is a rugged, practical animal, whose ability to look after itself explains why there are more Herefords in New Zealand than any other breed. Growing slowly, its beef is praised by connoisseurs. Modern demand, however, is for animals that mature quickly and reach bigger sizes. In Britain the Hereford has been eclipsed by Continental breeds. But the numbers are increasing again, and the result is as attractive in the landscape as it is on the plate: the reddish coat of the Hereford forms a perfect harmony with the reddish soil of its native county. And the lowing of cattle still punctuates the sermons in Canon Pyon church.

# CASTLETON
## DERBYSHIRE
*The gem of the Peak*

Blue John is derived from the French *bleu et jaune*. A kind of fluorspar, with radiating concentric rings of purple or blue and white or yellow, it was probably discovered by Roman miners, looking for lead. The Romans made urns and vases out of the stone. It is difficult to carve, because of its loose texture. But around 1800, its sumptuous striations of colour proved so irresistible to Regency taste that the skill was mastered. Kedleston Hall in Derbyshire, the palatial house that Robert Adam built for Lord Scarsdale, has a fine suite of vases carved by the celebrated Richard Brown, as well as the ultimate luxury of Blue John inlay in the music-room fireplace. Chatsworth House in the same county also has fine Blue John ornaments – and so it should. For this is not only a ducally opulent material, but local. There is only one place in the world where Blue John can be mined: above Castleton.

*Cups and urn made from Blue John, mined at Castleton.*

J. M. Hedinger, describing the steep and winding descent into the village in 1823, made the most of its Sublime qualities. 'Here nature presents herself in her rudest forms: down the road the prospect is bounded by the rugged rocks projecting in the most romantic manner, bare and sterile.' After this savage introduction, the landscape opens out into a scene of fine trout streams and productive agriculture. 'Here, traveller, stop and collect thyself! View this fertile valley as one of the greatest gifts of Providence, who has bestowed on the inhabitants of this place all the climate can produce.' To have, as well as this bounty, the rich possibilities of a Blue John mine made it a very heaven.

The village takes its name from the Norman castle that overlooks it, perched above a steep bluff. In this wild stretch of country, out of which heaves the limestone ridge of Mam Tor, Castleton must once have had the feeling of a frontier town, inaccessible and populated with miners. But since the Victorian period it has been 'resorted to by thousands in this country in their excursions or pleasure', as William Adam put it in *The Gem of the Peak* (1843), 'and the foreigner seldom fails to take it in his way during his tour through England. The fame of Castleton and the "Wonders of the Peak" associated with it, have been trumpeted far and wide'. One of these wonders was, of course, Blue John.

It has become more difficult to find the ball-shaped lumps in which Blue John occurs, but it is still worked. The trick is to impregnate it with resin before it is carved, which helps to bind the crystals together.

# CHALFORD
## GLOUCESTERSHIRE
*Pickling, but not as generally understood*

The smells around Chalford in Gloucestershire may be art. Damien Hirst, born in Bristol, has a studio here. It is on quite a scale, occupying a former car components factory whose roof is now covered with what *The Gloucester Citizen* has claimed to be the second biggest photovoltaic system in the country. It includes an abattoir rail and fish preparation area, part of the equipment needed to turn sharks, sheep and other species into sculpture, preserved in formaldehyde. There was an unfortunate episode outside the old studio in the summer of 2004, when the delivery van expected to collect waste failed to arrive and a plastic crate of animal parts was left to attract maggots and neighbours' complaints. Nevertheless, Hirst, who also owns a house in the village, is always at the head of names expected to contribute to local causes, from works against flooding to a new village hall.

Chalford is not classic Cotswolds. Outside the working town of Stroud, it lies in the Golden Valley – a name of ambiguous derivation, which may originate from the colour of the trees in autumn or the fortunes of the mill owners who turned sheep fleeces into money. Flocks had thrived on the hills since monastic times, and Stroud broadcloth was famous. Having been woven, it was beaten with hammers in one of the fulling mills on the river Frome; teasels were then used to raise a nap, which in turn was cut short with enormous shears to leave a soft pile. The broadcloth came in three colours: scarlet for soldiers' uniforms, white for the clergy, green for the baize of billiard tables. It is still used as a covering for tennis balls. Chalford clung to the steep sides of the valley. Until the 1930s, donkeys with panniers were used to make deliveries to village houses; the Chalford Donkey Project, started in 2008, has been trying to reintroduce the service.

Now one of the biggest local employers is Pangolin Editions, the largest bronze foundry in Europe. Husband and wife Rungwe Kingdon and Claude Koenig, who met at Gloucester College of Art, started by casting a conservatory in 1985. Proximity to the sculptor Lynn Chadwick at Lypiatt Park helped establish the business, which now employs eighty-five people. In October 2008, the *Daily Telegraph* reported: 'The place is an incredible hive of activity, with men and women spraying, scraping, hammering, welding, picking, rubbing, polishing and painting objects that range from a surreal 30ft bronze elephant riding a tricycle to a variety of bronze figures, heads, limbs, animals and other objects that defy explanation.' Whatever the noise of metal bashing, bronze has this advantage over other artistic media in the vicinity: it does not rot.

# CLUN

In 1907, E. M. Forster went on a solitary walking tour of Shropshire, arriving at Clun. It was not Clun's first brush with literature: Sir Humphry Davy praised its river in his *Salmonia: or, Days of Fly Fishing* (1828). Forster came because of the intense affinity that he felt with A. E. Housman's *A Shropshire Lad*, 'kidding himself', as he later put it, 'into thinking the scenery beautiful and not yet looking out for its lads.' Housman had celebrated Clun in lines that are probably derived from a traditional jingle:

> Clunton and Clunbury,
> Clungunford and Clun,
> Are the quietest places
> Under the sun.

The town had some importance until the decay of its castle in the late thirteenth century, but, despite the possession of two silver maces that are now in the safe-keeping of the charming little museum, thereafter declined to the size of a village, its name famous to farmers only through the Clun Forest sheep.

Forster paid tribute in *Howards End*, where Clun became Oniton, 'dreaming between the ruddy hills . . . a market town – as tiny a one as England possesses'. Evie had the whim of getting married from it, and it briefly stood back to let the motor cars pass. 'Right away from everywhere,' is how Mr Wilcox describes it to Margaret, 'up towards Wales.' But the family lost interest, and Oniton, like Clun, went back to sleep.

On a darkling autumn evening, Clun is best found with its toes turned up in front of the fire in the White Horse, one of three pubs here, hung with horse halters and brass plates. With a convenience store hidden away discreetly inside what looks like an old bank, a library (in the garage), doctor's surgery, primary school and two – *two!* – butchers, not to mention the headquarters of leather designer Matt Fothergill, whose bags sell in the Conran Shop, Clun has as much as is needed, nay more, to support life. But the luminous green landscape of an Area of Outstanding Natural Beauty starts as soon as the last farmyard is passed. Tree-fringed streams, sheep (whether or not of Clun Forests) dotting the fields like large puffballs, buff-coloured cattle, square-towered grey churches, the occasional white-walled farm-house and hills, hills, hills – this is as quiet as Housman described it. The zephyr of change hardly rustles the leaves.

Which you might have thought would make it an unlikely resting place for an Angry Young Man. Yet in 1994, the playwright John Osborne was buried in the churchyard. The Angry Young Man was essentially an urban figure, but by 1988 Osborne was ready to move, with his fifth wife, Helen Dawson, to The Hurst, a

Regency house sitting in thirty acres of Shropshire, overlooking the Clun valley at Clunton. He liked to say that he had 'the best view in England', and quite possibly he was right. 'Together they enjoyed for twenty years the accoutrements of his success: handsome houses, acres of land, horses and dogs,' ran Helen's 2004 obituary in the *Daily Telegraph*. 'Together they would dispense liberal quantities of Champagne to visitors, and chain-smoke their defiant cigarettes.' The Hurst is now a centre for writers and literary students.

# COLLYWESTON
## NORTHAMPTONSHIRE                      *Synonymous with stone roofs*

In 1375, nine thousand, five hundred stone slates were bought for the roof of Rockingham Castle (see page 347). There was a repeat order for four thousand, five hundred slates fifteen years later. In 1383, Oakham Castle in Rutland acquired five thousand 'sklat'. They came from Collyweston, the most famous medieval quarry for stone roofing slates, worked since Roman times. The stone roofs seen on grander village and country houses are part of the essential character of this part of the East Midlands, the more humble structures being thatched.

The stone is a particular form of limestone, from the band known as inferior oolite. (This does not mean that it is any worse than oolite proper, merely that it occurs underneath it.) Similar beds appear at Hinton, near Bath, Stonesfield in Oxfordshire and in Yorkshire's Cleveland Hills. The Collyweston stone is what geologists call 'fissile'; it splits easily. A bluish colour when first exposed to the air, it is called 'pendle' at the quarry. Beds are between six inches and a few feet thick, separated from one another by a kind of sand, or 'race'. Large blocks, or 'logs', of pendle generally fall down under their own weight when the supporting race has been removed.

When a hard frost is likely, the logs are drenched in water, which turns to ice; as the ice expands, it forces the bedding planes apart. This process is repeated, although the stones may still need to be 'clived' or split. Traditionally, the resulting slates were kept in place by an oak peg. The weight of a Collyweston slate roof is enormous, and requires impressive carpentry to support it. In time, the slates weather to the greyish buff that provides one of the visual keynotes of the area.

Collyweston's reputation was such that it roofed the Guildhall in London and several Cambridge colleges. The accounts of Lady Margaret Beaufort, Henry VII's mother, contain, not surprisingly, references to it: she was lord of the manor. One of her duties, unrelated to the profitable quarry, was to preside over the court before which John Stokesley, principal of Magdalen Hall, Oxford, and later Bishop of London, was brought in 1506. He was accused of sacrilegiously baptising his cat, as part of a ritual designed, it was said, to discover buried treasure. He was let off.

# COTESBACH
## LEICESTERSHIRE

*'Tumultuous assemblies of lewd persons'*

In 1607, the Midlands were in a bad mood. For decades, landowners had realised that there was money in sheep, and that they could increase their revenues by putting the old open fields, worked by peasant families, down to grass. They were brutal in doing so. Peasants were dispossessed. Those who were not needed to look after the sheep were left without any means of sustaining themselves. Murmurings of resentment had been made during the Pilgrimage of Grace, after Henry VIII's break with Rome, but the gentlemen leading that revolt ensured that it was quickly refocused on religion. During Edward VI's reign, Protector Somerset had been forced to issue a proclamation against the 'tumultuous assemblies of lewd persons' who were rioting throughout southern England, but again the anti-enclosure grievance was lost beneath the stir made by what Somerset called 'sondery priests for these martyrs of religion'.

Throughout the second half of the sixteenth century, resentment against the enclosures continued to build. Sir Edward Montagu, a Northamptonshire MP and landowner, who did not himself agree with the cause, felt compelled to report the complaints about the loss of open fields and consequent depopulation to Parliament in 1604. Three years later, by what seems to have been a process of spontaneous combustion, uprisings broke out across the Midlands, motivated by peasants' anger and despair at what one petition called the 'incroaching Tirants', who forced the poor to live destitute among 'fatt hogges and sheep' only for 'theyr owne private gaine'.

One of the tyrants was John Quarles, a London draper. He had got hold of the manor of Cotesbach in 1596, and was squeezing it for all it was worth. Having recently gone bankrupt, he needed the money. In June 1607, five thousand insurgents gathered at Cotesbach. They tore down (or levelled) Quarles's hedges, filled in his ditches and ignored the gallows set up as a warning. They were not terribly effective. Eventually Quarles was hauled up before the Star Chamber for depopulating the village, but by then half the residents had left. At least no one was hurt.

That was not to be the case a week later at Newton in Northamptonshire, where a thousand levellers assembled under the leadership of a mysterious Captain Pouch, whose leather pouch was reputed to have magic powers. The Crown had recently sold part of the ancient hunting forest of Rockingham (see page 347) to a member of the spreading Tresham family, who promptly evicted the squatters who had been living on the land, sometimes for generations. Montagu, the very man who had represented the strength of anti-enclosure feeling to Parliament, led a cavalry charge of gentry and their servants against the rustics, who were armed with pikes, staffs and stones. Forty or fifty levellers were killed (the wonder-working pouch was found to contain only a piece of green cheese). Oliver Goldsmith was still lamenting the 'tyrant's power' of the enclosing landowner in his poem *The Deserted Village*, published in 1770.

# CRESWELL MODEL VILLAGE

DERBYSHIRE                                    *In the shadow of the pithead*

About 3.45am on 26 September 1950, an underground conveyor belt in the Creswell colliery overheated. A rip in the fabric had been noted the day before but not repaired. Now friction with the roller that drove the belt caused it to catch fire. The High Hazel Seam where this happened was two and a half miles below the surface. More than 230 men were underground at the time. A pump failure meant there was little water to fight the fire. Eighty men died in the disaster, some of the bodies not being recovered for nearly a year. Creswell Model Village went into mourning. Death had come to every street in the two-thousand-strong community. One family lost three sons. A woman who had been married only three weeks lost her husband. It was the worst pit disaster Derbyshire has ever suffered.

The Model, as it was known, was built by the Bolsover Colliery Company in 1896. Mining had been taking place since the 1860s, but construction of the village was well-timed: a big seam was discovered the next year. The BCC employed a little-known architect called Percy Houfton to plan the settlement; he was probably influenced by Lord Leverhulme's Port Sunlight on Merseyside in providing a geometrical layout combined with open space. The village takes the unusual form of a double octagon – an inner and outer ring – surrounding a large green with a bandstand. The two hundred and fifty houses, in mottled red brick with white-painted casement windows and sometimes Dutch gables, have the faintly Arts and Crafts feel of some of the new London County Council estates.

Residents felt that they were part of a community. Everybody worked for the pit; tenants were vetted by the estate's owners (latterly the National Coal Board); there was no unemployment. In 1903–04 the Creswell Drill Hall was built for the Boys' Brigade (run by the colliery manager, whose wife took charge of the Girls' Bugle Brigade). Emerson Bainbridge, the prominent anti-union boss who founded the Model, hoped for three things: 'the absence of drunkenness, the absence of gambling and the absence of bad language'.

It did not suit everybody. Some people called it a 'white collar village', where you could not go outside without being properly dressed. 'You were absolutely under t'control of Bolsover Company,' one resident remembered. The houses did not have vegetable gardens attached to them, for fear of spoiling the architecture, but there were allotments elsewhere in the village. However, when the Model was sold 'to a private consortium down south', shortly before mining ceased in 1991, many villagers were dismayed. Pride went out of the estate. Fortunately, the residents' association was able to pull it back from the brink, applying for a Heritage Lottery grant to restore the green, bandstand and an initial eighty houses. It was such a success that the whole scheme has been restored.

*See also New Earswick, page 429; Saltaire, page 435; Stewartby, page 196*

# CULWORTH

*The gang that terrified Northamptonshire*

To geographers, Culworth is a remarkable example of village development. Originally there were two distinct hamlets, Culworth and Brime; in the twelfth century, the lord of the manor created a marketplace between them, in conjunction with his new castle. This explains the shape of the settlement, which opens out like two butterfly wings on either side of the central green. Considerations of this kind were not, however, uppermost in the minds of Northamptonshire gentry when Culworth was discussed in the late eighteenth century. They were more likely to associate it with the word 'gang', perhaps qualified by an adjective such as 'notorious'.

The gang – a shifting entity of up to fifteen people – was in operation for more than a decade. Most of the principal members were farm labourers, such as John Smith and his sons John and William. But they were joined by artisans, such as the carpenter Richard Law and the shoemaker William Abbott. Shoemakers seem often to have been more literate than their village neighbours, and Abbott was also the parish clerk at Sulgrave, supposedly carrying pistols when he performed his duties in church. When the end came, Sulgrave church was found to have been the hiding place for Abbott's share of stolen goods.

Having begun as poachers, the gang graduated to housebreaking and highway robbery. 'It is sufficient to show that they were wholesale plunderers, not merely your petty larceny men,' James Beesley observed after cataloguing some of their crimes in the magazine of the Banbury Mechanics' Institute in 1837. The fact that they could terrorise Northamptonshire for so long reflects the inefficiency of the law officers, who were appointed parish by parish (the constables in Thomas Hardy's *The Mayor of Casterbridge*, 'shrivelled men' who became 'yet more shrivelled than usual', hid their official truncheons up a drainpipe at the first outbreak of public disorder).

Culworth is not a large place; the gang's activities must have been known to other people in the village, but presumably they were too frightened to take action. Eventually two gang members, Richard Law and William Pettifer, travelled to Towcester in 1787, putting up at an inn. They told the landlord that their bags contained fighting cocks, but he was suspicious; he knew they came from Culworth. Once they had gone upstairs, he managed to open the bags and found that they contained smock frocks and masks, the same disguises worn by the perpetrators of various recent burglaries. The constable was called; they decided to watch and wait; when another housebreaking was committed in a nearby village, Law and Pettifer were arrested.

They soon implicated other gang members, and the whole confederacy was broken up. Six of them were hanged, Abbott transported. After sentencing, they confessed to forty-seven robberies, which most authorities assume to have been only part of their activity. John Smith the elder wrote out a sermon to his sons, urging them, rather late in the day, not to go the same way as him. He asked his wife to 'take care of these lines and cause them to be read to my children every Sabbath day, and I hope that God will give them grace to take warning'. About two years later, John Smith the younger was executed at Warwick for highway robbery, his body being brought back to Culworth for burial, after nightfall, on a donkey. William Smith went straight.

# DAYLESFORD
GLOUCESTERSHIRE                               *The ultimate in organic chic*

Lady Bamford has an exceptional kitchen garden. It forms a heart-shaped enclosure of two acres, surrounded by brick walls eighteen foot high, raised in the year of the French Revolution, 1789: part of the legacy of the nabob Warren Hastings, who built Daylesford House. Some years ago the Chelsea gold-winning gardener Rupert Golby brought it back to life. But not even a country house like Daylesford can consume everything that it produces. Lady Bamford therefore conceived the idea of sharing the harvest of gorgeously misshapen organic tomatoes and weird gourds with the wider world, and the Daylesford Farm Shop was the result. It is a phenomenon.

Visit Daylesford village, 'entirely built by the late Mr. Grisewood', as the relevant volume of the *Victoria County History* (1913) observes, and you could miss it. The shop occupies a group of barns on the main road. Externally, apart from the parking area, they look rural, and the timber framework has been kept on the inside, too. But the feeling is . . . well, not quite the happy rustic confusion of other farm shops. It is cool and pale and modern. Most of the women shopping here match the decor: blonde and expensive and tanned. At one point a chef was flown in from Thailand to cook Thai dishes. There are twenty different types of bread, all made on the premises. To the original shop has been added a dairy, where you can watch the Friesian herd being milked from a viewing platform, and the milk being turned into cheese.

Daylesford is part of the reinvention of the countryside that took place after 2000. A catalyst for many enterprises was the outbreak of foot-and-mouth disease in 2001, the official response to which was to burn several million animals. Afterwards, farmers trying to rebuild their lives and businesses were encouraged to look to the towns; the great money fountain of the South-East was throwing up a new market of well-off, food-aware, health-conscious shoppers who wanted to be entertained. A different kind of elite was emerging – distinct from the new money of the 1980s boom, which aped the lifestyle of the traditional upper class. They were making money younger, and the source of their fortunes was just as likely to be software or biotechnology as finance. The country seemed a healthy place for their children to grow up; buying a house there did not mean giving up on design.

By the early twenty-first century, it had become so easy to flit between the Cotswolds, Norfolk or even Cornwall and London that the two worlds enmeshed as never before. Celebrities who were normally seen at gala premieres and exclusive restaurants acquired country homes. For a while, Madonna reinvented herself as the chatelaine of a country estate. The Daylesford Farm Shop, which spawned the brand Daylesford Organic, purveyed food of impeccable provenance at Harvey Nichols prices, in a setting where supermodels (Kate Moss) and actresses (Liz Hurley) could feel comfortable. As Alex James, formerly of rock band Blur and now resident at nearby Kingham, commented, it was 'so fabulous it has gentrified the entire surrounding area'. Daylesford is more than a destination or shopping experience. It shows that the countryside has become chic.

# DODFORD

WORCESTERSHIRE        *A system to develop 'all the virtues of our nature'*

Feargus O'Connor, the Chartist leader, stood on a platform, waving a giant cabbage. It was 1847. The enormous Chartist petitions, delivered to Parliament in 1839 and 1842, had failed to win working people the vote, but, nothing daunted, O'Connor had immediately taken a new line. If property qualifications were necessary to obtaining the franchise, working folk – thousands of them – would become landowners. To this end, he established what would become known as the National Land Company, to create allotments on which miners, weavers, printers, cobblers, lime burners, printers, smiths, tailors, stonecutters, grocers, nail makers, postmen, thatchers, carpenters, slaters, grinders, warehousemen, hatters and a schoolmistress could pursue a healthier life than that offered to them in the cities.

Within a few years, seventy thousand members had bought shares at 1s 6d. Having rejected Devon as a 'land of Parsons, sour cider, and low wages', O'Connor established the first settlement at Heronsgate in Hertfordshire, which he called O'Connorville. It was at the official opening in 1847 that he brandished the cabbage. Further settlements were created at Minster Lovell in Oxfordshire, Snigs End and Lowbands in Gloucestershire, and Great Dodford (it has since lost the 'Great') in Worcestershire.

As early as 1843, O'Connor, editor of the *Northern Star* newspaper, published *A Practical Work on the Management of Small Farms*, as a self-help manual for his new agriculturalists. On a four-acre plot, a labourer could grow enough to feed his family and make a profit, after taxes and rent, of a hundred pounds a year. Although Chartism had begun as a movement of the towns, it was lurching, unexpectedly, towards a new idealism located in the countryside. Snigs End made the wagon on which, drawn by four horses and decorated with streamers of red, green and white, the last Chartist petition set off to Parliament in 1848.

Alas, on examination, the 1848 petition was found to have far fewer than the nearly six million signatures O'Connor claimed – less than two million, and those included Queen Victoria and the Duke of Wellington. Ridiculed, O'Connor lost his grip, drank, became unstable and was locked up. Without his leadership the land settlements foundered. Schools had been built but there was no money to run them. O'Connorville reverted to its old name of Heronsgate, and became a place of suburban villas. For Snigs End, Lowbands and Minister Lovell, the problem was the size of the plots; O'Connor had been wildly optimistic in his predictions of what they would yield. Great Dodford, by contrast, kept going until the First World War. Its secret had been to grow strawberries and plums instead of cabbages and potatoes; near Birmingham and the Black Country, the smallholders had ready markets to which they could drive their carts.

You can still see a handful of the original thirty-nine cottages, one of them restored by the National Trust. Built of brick beneath slate roofs, they are, *avant la lettre*, bungalows. The projecting central bay contained the combined living, dining and kitchen area; there was a bedroom to either side, services at the back. The houses also had an attached dairy, back hall (containing a well and a pump) and storehouses, while the piggery faced the coal house and privy across the yard. The family in Rosedene, as the National Trust cottage is called, must have done well, because later in the nineteenth century they built a stable for a horse.

Social campaigners held up Great Dodford as a success. Between the Wars, the residents were tempted away to Austin motor works at Longbridge, nine miles distant. The dream of independence was dead.

# DUMBLETON
## GLOUCESTERSHIRE                              *Land Girls get down to it*

Joan Betteridge, married for fifty-two years, met her husband at a dance in the Dumbleton village hall. It was 1943, and she was staying with nineteen other girls in Dumbleton Hall, converted to a hostel for the Women's Land Army. The WLA had been set up to help meet the shortage of farm labour, at a time when many able-bodied men had been conscripted. Before 1939, with agriculture in the doldrums, seventy per cent of food had been imported. Now imports were threatened by a fleet of predatory U-boats, so it was imperative that food production should be increased if Britain was not to go hungry.

Socially, like so much that happened during the Second World War, the WLA overturned the established order; at its height, eighty-seven thousand young women, generally from towns and cities, were translocated to farms and hostels in rural villages. Land Girls encountered at first hand the tough, sometimes primitive monotony of the countryside, and were generally healthier for the time that they spent in the open air. It was better than the alternative of a munitions factory. Dumbleton was one of nearly seven hundred WLA hostels across Britain.

Betty Olsen, clutching a Gladstone bag in each hand, left Leeds on 31 August 1942, destined for Norfolk. She did better than one girl, whose suitcase came undone while changing trains at Peterborough station, leaving all her clothes on the line. At every station, some of the Land Girls would alight. Betty's turn came at Fakenham; like Joan Betteridge, her billet would be a grandly old-fashioned house called Shooting Box Hostel, on the Holkham estate. She had a uniform of brown corduroy breeches, green jersey and a velour slouch hat – the recruiting posters made ploughing look chic and refined. But legs and bodies had to be wrapped in sacking tied with string when they were harvesting the sprouts and cabbages: 'we looked like Bill and Ben the flowerpot men', she remembered.

They hoed fields of a hundred acres. Betty must have been a good worker. Not all Land Girls were; besides, even the best knew next to nothing about farming when they started. 'Wash this one down after I've finished,' said one cowman to a new recruit, as he milked. Looking up from the next cow, he was astonished to see her cleaning the whole animal, rather than just the udders as he had intended. Some farmers were resistant to taking them. The National Farmers' Union hated the scheme. Successful Land Girls had to work twice as hard to overcome initial prejudice.

Needless to say, it was organised on a county basis, by a redoubtable county lady: Gertrude, or Trudie, Lady Denman, who had been given the three-thousand-acre Balcombe Place in Sussex as a twenty-first birthday present by her father, the construction magnate Lord Cowdray. Born in 1884, she had been at the forefront of establishing Women's Institutes during the First World War, and had since used her energy and wealth in philanthropic causes, such as family planning. Balcombe Place became the WLA's administrative headquarters. Leadership involved standing up for the organisation; in frustration she resigned in February 1945, when the government refused to grant the Land Army the benefits it had given to women in the civil defence and armed services.

For Britain, the Land Army had, like evacuation, decanted part of the town into the countryside, and perhaps added to the high repute in which farming was held during the decades after the Second World War. For the individuals involved, it provided a healthful existence, with comradeship and, in many cases, romance. It could be an indelible experience. 'I'm a 79-year-old lady now,' Joan Betteridge recalled in 2001, 'but I'm still a twenty-year-old Land Girl at heart.'

# ECKINGTON

*The wrong sort of water*

The Iron Age left two hill forts to scowl over the Vale of Evesham, a summer dream of asparagus and plums. In the shadow of one of them lies Eckington, its twelve-hundred-strong population busy about car boot sales, open houses, cycle rides, Mums-and-Minnows groups, bowls tournaments and the other events advertised on the village website. There is not much wrong with it, according to Arthur Ore, chairman of the parish council. Not only does Eckington have a school, a shop, two 'fantastic' hairdressers and a 'fabulous' village hall, it also has the spectacular Bredon Hill, one of the most important wildlife sites in England. On most days, sinewy-thighed, sun-hatted ramblers can be seen stalking their way up this imposing, isolated outlier of the Cotswolds, treading carefully to avoid the rare violet click beetle.

But then one Friday in July 2007, Arthur visited Evesham, about twelve miles away. Rain deluged down with tropical abandon. Trapped by the floods at a friend's house, he was unable to return for two days. At 7.30am, Jackie Phillpotts went into the fields at Eckington Manor Farm to look after the Highland cattle, and everything was well. By midday, the lane separating the fields from the farmhouse was four feet deep in water. 'I moved forty cattle on my own,' she remembered. 'They were having to jump ditches and wade through water. I had to struggle across the ditches, up to my knees. It was frightening the speed at which water was coming up.'

Water is becoming one of the great issues for the countryside. Some areas are running short of it, particularly on the east side of the country: use by agriculture and domestic appliances (in all the new houses that have been built) has increased, just as rainfall patterns have become more unreliable. As a result, the aquifers are running dry. Elsewhere, water comes all too abundantly, and in a rush. Eckington was luckier than Elford in Staffordshire when the rivers Tame and Trent burst their banks in the summer of 2007: some families found themselves waist-deep in water and hundreds of farm animals were killed.

At the height of the floods, Eckington's red sandstone bridge – a round-arched eighteenth-century structure, standing on earlier foundations – disappeared completely beneath the torrent. A month later, holidaymakers had returned to the picnic tables, and were once again enjoying the tranquillity of the riverside; the Avon had slunk back into its bed again. Only some festoons of rotting vegetation, which the flood waters had hung on the hedges, survived as evidence of the catastrophe. While the Birmingham Anglers' Association lost the fish that it stocks in the lake, one lady in the village was luckier. Although sofas and floorboards were ruined, she was principally concerned by the fate of two goldfish, which disappeared from the pond in her garden. She found one in a puddle and replaced it. Then, when the car on the drive was moved, there was the other one, in a damp patch underneath.

The fish survived, and so did Eckington. The countryside has taken stock and moved on. It always does. But the fear remains that flash floods such as that suffered by Eckington could become a commonplace unless – difficult to think how – the countryside is re-engineered.

# EDENSOR
## DERBYSHIRE

*Proud to serve the great house*

The Dukes of Devonshire got on with their servants. Evidence of this can be found in the churchyard at Edensor, the village in the park at Chatsworth where many of them are buried. John Phillips died in 1735, having been housekeeper for sixty years. His epitaph looks forward to the Resurrection:

> Then do I hope with all ye Just
> To shake off my polluted dust,
> And in new Robes of Glory Drest
> To have access among ye Bless'd.

It sounds like the completion of a great spring-clean, such as he must often have organised on earth. James Brousard, d.1762, is remembered in less accomplished but nevertheless touching verse:

> Ful forty years as Gardener to ye D. of Devonshire,
> to propagate ye earth with plants it was his ful desire

William Mather's tombstone of 1818 hints at a sudden end, perhaps brought on by carelessness or drink:

> When he that day with th'Waggon went,
> He little thought his Glass was spent;
> But had he kept his Plough in Hand,
> He might have longer till'd the Land.

These vignettes hint at the life of the village: feudal, slow-changing, rustic. But in 1838–42, the 6th Duke considerably improved its amenity by relocating and rebuilding it. His passions were art, building, buying libraries, collecting coins and medals (sold, in a moment of crisis, at a thumping loss), and the new Edensor was created with the bravura that would be expected of the man who commissioned Joseph Paxton to build the glasshouse that inspired the Crystal Palace. Paxton had a hand in Edensor, but he was enormously busy, so the architectural details were left to his assistant, John Robertson.

Robertson had worked as a draughtsman for J. C. Loudon* and came thoroughly versed in Loudonesque principles of Picturesque cottage architecture. Edensor was to be decorative, but also serious. For the sake of variety, every cottage followed a different design. For the sake of solidity, each was constructed out of stone. For the sake of Victorian earnestness, the stylistic detail was faithful to the original inspiration, be it Tudor or Swiss. The result, as *Gardeners' Chronicle* put it in 1842, was 'a perfect compendium of all the prettiest styles of cottage architecture from the sturdy Norman to the sprightly Italian'; a dish of many influences, flavoured with pointed gables, Tuscan towers and snug porches. All the woodwork is painted in the estate colour of peacock blue.

A walk along the street was a geographical and stylistic education. A school was provided, as well as a soaring church by Sir George Gilbert Scott. No less striking were the arrangements that the Duke had made for the village livestock. It was allowed to roam the park, on easy terms, according to James Caird, who described the arrangements in *English Agriculture in 1850–51* (1852). 'We are persuaded that this is a plan which might be advantageously adopted on many large estates,' being useful to the tenants and ultimately more beneficial to the landowner than keeping his own animals on the land. Everything about the village added to the glory that is Chatsworth.

*See Great Tew, page 177

# EDGMOND
## SHROPSHIRE
*Coldest place in England*

In the seventeenth century, the river Thames would freeze so hard that enterprising tradesmen held frost fairs on the ice, which was strong enough for them to erect printing presses and light fires over which animals could be roasted. In the nineteenth century, skating was a popular wintertime activity – even though Mr Pickwick fell through the ice. But the coldest temperature ever measured in England was not recorded in those periods of regularly cold winters. Nor was the reading taken on a mountain top. The village of Edgmond claims the honour, a temperature of minus twenty-six-point-one degrees Celsius having been recorded on 10 January 1982 at the Harper Adams agricultural college: an area of open countryside.

It was indeed an exceptionally cold winter. Troops were called out to clear snowdrifts as deep as ten feet. In Ludlow, a farmer was dug out of the snow after he collapsed and died, despite having set out wearing two pairs of trousers and two overcoats. Bill Burrell, who made the reading at Harper Adams, remembered: 'It had snowed the night before but had cleared up and it was a lovely day – just bitterly, bitterly cold. It was painful to breathe.'

The conditions for low temperatures were, indeed, perfect. A covering of snow sucks heat out of the ground, while its insulating properties prevent that heat warming the air above. So the ground became extremely cold. Since it was a still day, the lowest layer of atmosphere did not mix with the levels above. As a result, the air nearest the ground cooled dramatically. Freezing air had also been accumulating in the valley bottoms, making them colder and colder. This happened to be one of the first winters for which satellite images were available. The Met Office used the accurate data they provided to track the progress of the cold snap. They showed that the most intense cold was felt in wide, snow-covered valleys such as those of the upper Severn and Thames.

# FLASH
## STAFFORDSHIRE                                    *Highest village in England*

On the edge of a Continent, the British Isles are not stupendous for mountains. Instead, the remarkable aspect of their geology is that it has been so scrunched up as a result of the movements of the earth's crust, leaving an unusually varied and intimate mosaic that includes all the different geological periods in history.

Mankind's interaction with this landscape can cause surprises. If, for example, the uninformed observer were to begin a search for the highest village in Britain, he or she might start in the Highlands of Scotland; but this would be a mistake. The government's brutal suppression of Highland life after the 1745 rebellion and lairds' preference for sheep over crofting, mean that Tomintoul in Moray (see page 632), built in 1775 to bring a degree of order to a previously lawless area, is the highest Scottish village to survive in the Highlands. But at 345 metres, it is not the highest village in Scotland; that position is claimed by Wanlockhead (467 metres) in the upland border country of Dumfries and Galloway (see page 635).

The highest village in England is not far behind it: Flash, on the windswept Staffordshire moors, is situated at 463 metres. Bleak and remote, it sustained a way of life that was as tough as its surroundings, and not always within the law. It is part of a parish called Quarnford, meaning mill by the ford. Flash may derive from a word for sudden stream. While cattle were kept here during the Middle Ages, and cheese made in the 'vaccary', the chapel was not built until 1744 (it was remodelled in 1901). The breezy situation promoted longevity; a headstone in the graveyard records a mother and son who died in the late eighteenth century, aged 104 and ninety-one:

> Our glass is run, our time is past,
> For age will bring you down at last.

When William White published his *History, Gazetteer and Directory of Staffordshire* in 1834, an attempt to civilise the inhabitants had been made by establishing a free school for thirty children, at the expense of Sir George Crewe and Joseph Tunnicliffe of Macclesfield. But the village, however educated, continued to shelter characters who preferred to live beyond the eye of the authorities. It was a notorious centre of bare-knuckle fighting and the printing of 'flash' or counterfeit money. As well as being difficult to get to, Flash had the advantage of being near Three Shires Heads, the point where Staffordshire meets Cheshire and Derbyshire. In the early days of policing, the officers from county constabularies were compelled to stop a pursuit at the county boundaries.

With snow blowing from the moors and tops of stone walls and making a royal icing of the roads during winter, the well-named Travellers Rest is a welcome sight. Yet only five miles away are the amenities and domesticated landscape of Buxton. What a land of contrasts it is.

# GEDDINGTON
## NORTHAMPTONSHIRE    *Things that make villages worth living in*

The Geddington Volunteer Fire Brigade is a remarkable organisation. It has never put out a fire; it would not be allowed to, by the health and safety bureaucracy that puts concerns about insurance above those about properties burning down; it might not want to, never having been trained. But it has a fire engine, a big red one, with a silver bell on the outside. Built in 1953, it was going cheap when it was decommissioned several decades later, and people who know about machinery restored it to glory. The force of the water jetting out of the nozzle (big pump, narrow-gauge hose) is something terrific. The fire brigade used to meet in a room over the old working men's club. Then, in 2000, it went one better, by building its own station.

It has, of course, a fireman's pole. The walls are covered with fire-brigade memorabilia, such as historic boots, vintage helmets and badges. The theme has become a long-running joke, together with the masonically convoluted rituals and hierarchy that go with it, the point of which nobody can quite remember. Essentially, the fire brigade is a body of men (only men are members; it is a contentious point), which does good work in the village. Every village should have one.

There was a perceived need for fire persons once. The brigade has its origin in the firemen's strike of 1977. A local farmer thought it would be a good thing for the village, much of which is thatched, to form its own service. Farming was a reserved occupation during the Second World War, and he had served in the Home Guard; perhaps he rather enjoyed it. Once formed, the volunteers never disbanded. During the strike, they were called upon to remove a fallen tree from a road, and then the official firefighters went back to work before further incident. In the days before a berm, or dry ditch, was built to relieve the build-up of water at an angle in the brook, the fire engine was pressed into service, pumping out houses that had flooded.

*The Queen Eleanor, pride of the Geddington Volunteer Fire Brigade.*

Otherwise, the brigade's activities are non-fire combative. It ensures that the village is kept in good order. Every autumn it lays on a dinner for elderly residents. Money is raised by a variety of stunts, which have in the past involved the fire engine – she is called the Queen Eleanor, after Edward I's Queen Eleanor of Castile, whose image appears on a thirteenth-century cross in the village – being driven through Spain under police escort (they did not have to stop at a red light once). And every Boxing Day, there is the Squirt, a contest between the volunteers and the local fire brigade, to see who can hose a barrel, hanging from a wire, across the brook first. The regulars have the advantage of nozzle control; the volunteers have the more powerful jet.

This is the thing about village life. The size of the community is right. It is big enough to contain a sufficient number of people with the energy and commitment to get an enterprise going. It is small enough for residents to know one another. This dynamic can make villages creative places – where pre-existing traditions to satisfy the deep human need for belonging do not exist, they can be, and often are, evolved. The Geddington Volunteer Fire Brigade may not put out fires, but it provides some of the glue that makes the village a place worth living in.

# GREAT WYRLEY

## STAFFORDSHIRE                    *An uncomfortable story of race relations*

In 1876, Shapurji Edalji was appointed vicar of Great Wyrley in Staffordshire. This Church of England clergyman had been born a Parsee in India in the early 1840s. Although by all accounts amiable and conscientious, he ministered to a parish of agricultural and colliery workers, who had little experience of their own county, let alone the world beyond British shores. In the late 1880s, a dismissed servant girl scrawled threatening messages on walls around the church. This initiated a campaign of abuse, which progressed to rubbish being tipped onto the vicar's lawn, and a series of cruel practical jokes. The local chief constable, who had a self-confessed hatred of blacks, came to the surprising conclusion that the most likely culprit was Edalji's own teenage son, George, then a pupil at Malvern School. Edalji did not believe this for a moment, but the matter was allowed to rest there. George became a solicitor practising in Birmingham.

In the first half of 1903, more alarming goings-on visited Great Wyrley. In an echo of Jack the Ripper's crimes, sixteen sheep, cattle and horses had their stomachs ripped open in an inexplicable series of mutilations. Letters to the police accused George Edalji of being the Great Wyrley Beast Killer. The miscarriage of justice that followed would be barely believable, were it not for the intense suspicion of outsiders felt by rural communities.

George was arrested, and circumstantial evidence in the form of bloodstains and hair was found on his clothes. From prison, he offered a reward of twenty-five pounds – all his savings – for information about the true perpetrator. No evidence was forthcoming, except for the febrile confession of Harry Green, a farmer's son, who was quickly put on a boat to South Africa to recover his mental balance. The mutilations continued after Edalji had been locked up. Yet at the trial he was found guilty, his sentence being seven years in prison. It was said that the animals had been sacrificed as part of a black magic ritual.

There was considerable disquiet in the legal profession at the verdict. Perhaps this explains why Edalji was released after three years for good behaviour. After his release, Edalji's story reached Sir Arthur Conan Doyle, inventor of the detective story. For once, he turned detective himself, demonstrating that the police 'evidence' was entirely bogus. Horsehair had got onto Edalji's clothing because the van in which he had been taken into custody contained a horse's mane. The blood on his cuff had come from a Sunday roast. What was supposed to be blood on his razor was actually rust. Being badly short-sighted, Edalji could not have set off on animal-mutilating expeditions after dark; besides, his father had given sworn testimony that they slept in the same room, behind a door that was locked.

For technical reasons Conan Doyle was unable to secure a retrial, but the Home Secretary granted Edalji a pardon and the Law Society had him readmitted to the roll of solicitors. The campaign helped establish the creation of the Court of

Criminal Appeal in 1907, providing a forum in which victims of bad justice could get redress.

Perhaps the unhappy story could have taken place anywhere, but from the standpoint of the twenty-first century, its rural setting is uncomfortable. You do not see many people of black or Asian descent living in villages. It is possible that they do not feel welcome.

# GRIFF
## WARWICKSHIRE                           *George Eliot's England*

George Eliot grew up in Warwickshire. 'In these midland districts,' she wrote in the introduction to *Felix Holt, the Radical* (1866), 'the traveller passed rapidly from one phase of English life to another: after looking down on a village dingy with coaldust, noisy with the shaking of looms, he might skirt a parish all of fields, high hedges, and deep-rutted lanes; after the coach had rattled over the pavement of a manufacturing town, the scene of riots and trades-union meetings, it would take him in another ten minutes into a rural region'. The ambiguity present in the surroundings in which she grew up is, in a different way, still with us.

Griff, where Eliot grew up, was part of the Arbury Estate, where her father was the land agent. This was farming country and, born in 1819, Eliot grew up at a time of uneasy agricultural triumphalism, before the price protectionism of the Corn Laws was repealed in 1846. The workers in this landscape did not benefit much from the profits enjoyed by the landowners; they were hungry and restless. She would have known handloom weavers no doubt; but they were already a threatened species, their artisan ways being undercut by factory production in the mills. It may seem that rural England had little in common with the towering factories and rows of mean workers' housing that characterised the industrial cities. And yet coal was dug on the Arbury Estate, too. Out of the guts of the countryside came the energy that powered furnaces and steam engines, brickworks and bottle kilns.

George Eliot, a forensic analyst of the Victorian hierarchy and its emotions, is not generally known as a countryside writer. Yet her upbringing at Arbury glazed her descriptions of the disappearing midlands countryside with a powerful nostalgia. Thus the opening to chapter twelve of *Middlemarch*:

The ride to Stone Court, which Fred and Rosamond took the next morning, lay through a pretty bit of midland landscape, almost all meadows and pastures, with hedgerows still allowed to grow in bushy beauty and to spread out coral fruit for the birds. Little details gave each field a particular physiognomy, dear to the eyes that have looked on them since childhood: the pool in the corner where the grasses were dank and trees leaned whisperingly; the great oak shadowing a bare place in mid-pasture; the high bank where the ash-trees grew; the sudden slope of the old marl-pit making a red background for the burdock . . . These are the things that make the gamut of joy in landscape to midland-bred souls – the things they toddled among, or perhaps learned by heart standing between their father's knees while he drove leisurely.

These were indeed the scenes that Mary Anne Evans (to give George Eliot her original name) toddled among, if she can ever be imagined as a toddler. To a more hurried age, the fine detail becomes a generalised blur. Since her childhood home is now the Griff House Beefeater Grill and Premier Inn, overlooking a giant industrial/retail estate, that might in some respects be just as well.

# HALLATON
## LEICESTERSHIRE
*Go, before the EU bans it*

The Hallaton bottle-kicking takes place on Easter Monday. For every other day of the year, the village is a haven of tranquillity, remarkable for its butter cross – which, in a fit of classical geometry and Enlightenment rejection of religious symbolism, takes the form of a cone with a ball on top. Hallaton Hall stands almost in the middle of the village, and must have kept an eye on things from behind its high wall.

Not that this feels like an estate village, because it rambles so, and the architecture is various. Hallaton is on the junction of the stone and brick countries. You see dark yellow stone, orange in places, from the iron content, and orangey-red brick, sometimes laid in a chequer-work pattern with alternating black headers. Quite a few buildings are thatched. Through arched openings you glimpse the wide Leicestershire landscape, opening out into fields at the end of village gardens. It seems not to have been a particularly prosperous village, to judge from the number of households that were excused hearth tax in 1670 (ninety-two out of 165). But there are some elegant monuments inside and outside the church, most splendid of all an elaborate tomb to the Rev. George Fenwicke, rector for thirty years. All very attractive, all very correct – a world removed from the mayhem that descends over Easter.

Bottle-kicking is a throwback to football's early roots. There is no ball, no rule book. Always played against the neighbouring village of Medbourne, the game is a cross between a rugby scrum and civil war; as people often reflect, it is amazing that the forces of health and public order allow it to continue. Nobody has been killed playing it (at least within memory), but there may be broken limbs. Possession of the 'bottle' (in fact a small barrel of beer) has little to do with skill and more with players being pulled to the ground, in what is emphatically a contact sport. According to one of the landlords, serious players start to get into condition on Saturday night, downing pints of ale.

Play is preceded by the blessing of a hare pie on the steps of the church. True to form, the pie is in fact made of beef, although hares were originally used. Half of it is consumed by churchgoers, the rest cut up and thrown to the crowd. In former times, the cut pie used to be scattered on Hare Pie Hill, presumably in memory of an ancient fertility rite; hares have always been regarded as magic animals. One of the Rev. Fenwicke's successors tried to ban the ceremony on the grounds of its pagan associations, but was forced to back down after the slogan 'No Pie, No Parson' was daubed on the rectory wall.

The barrel is thrown into play by the eldest resident. The object is to roll, carry or otherwise propel it to one of two boundary streams. There are refinements in the scoring system; in essence, it is the best of three. The victorious team celebrates around the cross, using the contents of the final bottle. Afterwards, the village picks itself up, dresses its wounds and prepares to sleep through another Leicestershire year, until Easter comes round again to provide a rude awakening.

*See also Haxey, page 242*

# HUMBER
## HEREFORDSHIRE

*Ley lines start here*

'I have read of a lad who, idly probing a hill-side rabbit hole, saw a gleam of gold, then more, and in short had found a royal treasury.' So wrote Alfred Watkins, describing how he discovered the theory of ley lines. According to Watkins, ley lines are previously noticed prehistoric trackways, which link monuments such as barrows, earthworks, standing stones and tumps. 'The sighting line was called the ley or lay,' he announced in *Early British Trackways* (1922). He believed that the word survived in place names such as Weobley (see page 362) and Tumpey Ley.

The idea came to him on 30 June 1921, when he visited the parish of Humber – specifically the part of it called Blackwardine, site of a Roman camp – in his native county of Herefordshire. As he studied the map, he noticed 'a straight line starting from Croft Ambury, lying on parts of Croft Lane past the Broad, over hill points, through Blackwardine, over Rising Camp, and through the high ground at Stretton Grandison, where I surmise a Roman station'. As this passage, with its intimate knowledge of the landscape, demonstrates, Watkins was nothing if not a Herefordshire man.

Watkins had been born in the Imperial Hotel, Hereford, in 1855. His father owned it. It became the basis of a series of Hereford businesses, including a brewery and flour mill, all brought under the Imperial banner (Watkins's sisters were known as Their Imperial Highnesses). Once the brewery had been sold in 1898, Watkins had enough money to devote himself to his enthusiasms. He energetically embraced the innovations transforming late Victorian society, such as photography and motoring. He made his first camera from a cigar box. Realising that the key to photography was the equation between the speed of the film and length of time the shutter allowed light to reach it, he developed an early exposure meter that sold around the world.

But dressed in a tweed suit, albeit one with fourteen pockets, and a neatly trimmed beard à la Edward VII, he was also a country-minded, Elgarian figure, captain of the Hereford Rowing Club and a member of the Hereford Bee-Keepers' Association. Ley lines satisfied several of Watkins's interests at once. For example, he spent much time recording the monuments of Herefordshire (including 120 market crosses, which he photographed and measured, the results being published in *The Standing Crosses of Herefordshire* in 1929). Many of these monuments were staging posts along the onward march of a ley line.

Since Watkins's death in 1935, archaeologists have been intrigued rather than convinced by his theories. Believers in the supernatural, looking for confirmation that the everyday world hides codes to explain its meaning, if only those codes could be found, have been more receptive. Ley lines have taken their place in the new spirituality, together with crystals and homeopathy. Watkins himself might have been happier with a legacy closer to that described by the *Daily Express*: 'A good citizen died yesterday,' it wrote on 9 April 1935, 'the kind which keeps the public life of the countryside on the highest plane of any in the world. His name was Alfred Watkins.'

# ILMINGTON
## WARWICKSHIRE                                    *No elms, but plenty of fruit trees*

A damson tree reaches over the churchyard at Ilmington. When it is a good year for fruit, damsons lie in a thick purple pall on the grave, appropriately enough, of the man who owned the adjacent orchard. It is a glorious orchard, its trees – apples, plums, pears – so old that they have sometimes been brought to their knees, and struggle to defy gravity as they push fruit-laden branches into the air. Ilmington, originally Elmington, was the place of elm trees. Since the advent of Dutch Elm Disease in the 1980s, the elms have all gone, but the village continues an arboreal tradition. Now it is the place of orchards.

Old maps show that the village used to be unusually rich in them, their blossom decorating the bosom of this Cotswold landscape like lace. In the late twentieth century, the artist and gardener June Hobson started a project to celebrate this heritage by embroidering an Apple Map for the church. Making the map was a parish activity, with children and old folk, the skilled and the less so, all plying their needles. It depicts the golden stone of the village houses nestled among apple blossom and pillowed on the great shoulder of Ilmington Down, the highest point in Warwickshire, the object being to show where the orchards used to be, and often still are.

The village still contains as many as thirty-eight different varieties of apple. Villagers set out on an Apple Walk every autumn to pay their respects. It is a stiff course, with some steep gradients on the Down, but rewarded with views over the great, gently rising plain of fields and hedgerows that stretches north across the whole of the county towards Warwick and Stratford. There is nowhere better to sit on a stile, crunch an apple and contemplate the visual delight of the countryside.

Apple consciousness in Britain has risen since the dark days of the 1980s, when the Common Agricultural Policy paid farmers to grub up their orchards to make way for imports of the inappropriately named Golden Delicious from France. Apples bulk up more quickly in other countries, but Britain has the perfect climate to grow apples that are crisp and flavoursome and smell like, well, apples. Recently, British apple growers have been fighting back, but the trees that they have been planting in Kent and Sussex do not resemble those that Samuel Palmer painted, their blossom heaped up like meringue. These days, trees that produce fruit for the table are mostly of dwarf varieties, their limbs trained to wires or tied down to the ground for easy pruning and picking.

You have to go to Herefordshire and Somerset to remind yourself what the old days were like. There, cider orchards – old ones, too – have survived, on odd parcels of land that are too steep to plough up. Nobody minds about the blemishes in apples that are going to be pressed. They shake the trees to bring down the crop.

*See also Crosthwaite, page 383*

# KILPECK
HEREFORDSHIRE                                  *All the wonders of Creation*

If you want to know what it felt like to live in the Welsh Marches during the Norman period, visit Kilpeck church. The building is covered with carvings by a group of masons so individualistic as to be called the Herefordshire School. They also worked at Leominster, Eardisley and elsewhere in the county, including the now-vanished church at Shobdon.

The most elaborate scheme to survive is at Kilpeck. Looked at with an un-tutored eye, it seems terrifying. The human form, when it appears, suggests only anxiety and gloom, while goggle-eyed, jawless masks, extraordinary animals and ambiguous symbols evoke a world haunted by spirits and monsters – a comfort-less place, where the life to come is no more welcoming than what precedes it. This is a subjective interpretation, but since scholars do not agree on the meaning of the carvings, perhaps it is as good as any other. Herefordshire in the early twelfth century, when these carvings were made, was not a joyful place.

Kilpeck was part of an ancient Welsh mini-kingdom. William the Conqueror's kinsman William fitz Norman claimed it by erecting a (wooden) castle. The Normans who held this borderland were pioneers. The picture given by the

*Elaborately carved doorway at Kilpeck, entry to a freakish*
*Norman vision of goggle-eyed masks and weird animals.*

Domesday Book in 1086 is of a wild area, its settlements apt to be devastated and whole districts given over to hunting. Life here must have seemed particularly precarious, even in such an uncertain age. Although brutal and, in some cases, almost psychopathically aggressive, the Normans were also pious. They endowed monasteries and rebuilt nearly all England's churches in stone. William fitz Norman's son, Hugh, styled de Kilpeck, built the church around 1140.

The carvings at Kilpeck are characterised by long, waving leaves, fat serpents curling around plants, stylised birds, male heads with vines flowing out of their mouths, interlacing bands and forest creatures. There are men, their clothes folded into what look like ribs, plants snaking around their calves; they wear caps (somewhat in the Phrygian style of the French Revolution), baggy trousers and what may be soft shoes. They seem to be figures from the everyday world, Herefordshire types, translated into the language used by the carvers, as stylised as the visions of El Greco.

Presumably the purpose of the carvings was to interpret the teaching of the Church to people who could not read. If so, we have now lost the code; with the exception of St Peter, holding his key, we can only guess at the identity of most of the participants, human or animal. But it is obvious that Kilpeck's spirit world does not derive wholly from the Bible; it was an age of superstition and credulity as well as faith. It would be easy to imagine that some of the weird forms were spooks from the lonely woods and wastelands.

Not that even the strangest creatures, supposedly real or self-confessedly supernatural, would have been incompatible with the accepted religion. 'Who knoweth not in all these that the hand of the LORD hath wrought this?' Job asked, referring to the beasts of the earth, the fowl of the air and the fish of the sea. God's ways were often unfathomable, and so were the wonders – and peculiarities – of His creation.

# LAXTON
## NOTTINGHAMSHIRE                                      *Last of the open field system*

In 1635, a surveyor called Mark Pierce was employed to map the farmland around Laxton by the estate's new owner, Sir William Courtenay, an Anglo-Dutch merchant. He did so in nine sheets, now in the Bodleian Library, Oxford. The map shows the village surrounded by four enormous open fields, between them divided into 2,280 strips of land. Open field farming, with land sliced up into small parcels between villagers, who then, since there were no field boundaries, were forced to farm in cooperation, was still practised much as it had been in the Middle Ages. Extraordinarily, the system survives, in modified form, to this day. Laxton is the only place where it does so.

Laxton is mentioned in the Domesday Book as having six plough teams. Since each team of eight oxen was able to plough about 120 acres (a 'hide'), the village must have possessed about 720 acres of cultivated land. The division into four fields, rather than two or even one, came later. But the details would have been much as Pierce showed them. One might have expected the strips to be laid out in long, unvarying lines. But, in fact, the fields look more like a patchwork quilt of differently striped blocks. This is because the strips, separated by ridges that had been built up over the years by ploughing, needed to follow the contours of the rolling land, in order to allow water to drain off most effectively. Families would work more than one strip so that the better land was shared out equally with the worst.

Running through the pattern of strips are areas of uncultivated land, often the banks of streams, their sides too steep to plough. These are the sykes, left as useful pasture. Pierce showed animals grazing on them, as well as a shepherd guarding a flock in a meadow at the end of one of the fields. The sykes also provided lanes by which the strips could be reached. Woods played an important part in the village economy: the medieval world relied on trees to provide logs for the hearth, timber to build with, wood to make carts and ploughs. The Laxton woods are shown as neat blocks, as no doubt they would have looked, being intensively managed to supply a valuable resource.

The open field system allowed villagers to feed themselves and their families; they also had to work the lord's land, or demesne. Not much was left over to sell. It was the way of farming that dominated the middle and south of England for centuries. Enclosures, which hedged the open fields into sheep runs, changed all that. They provided the landlord with an internationally tradable commodity, wool, that could be raised with a minimum of manpower. Agrarian capitalism of this kind was more efficient than the old way, but it left dispossessed families destitute.

At Laxton, the Pierrepont family, who became Dukes of Kingston and Earls Manvers, never got round to enclosing it. It became an oddity, then a rarity, before being recognised as a precious and unique survival; as such it was bought in 1952 by the Ministry of Agriculture. It was sold by Mrs Thatcher's administration to the Crown Estate in 1981; the relatively low price of one million pounds reflected the need to subsidise this method of farming. Order over the fields is maintained by an annual court, a streamlined version of the medieval Court Baron and Court Leet, which respectively would have decided questions of ownership and matters affecting the common farming effort.

Whereas farmers elsewhere have moved out of the villages they might once have occupied, their old stackyards being converted to homes and holiday lets, Laxton contains fourteen working farms, occupying premises that were often built in the eighteenth century. Therefore it is full of farmers, too. In the twenty-first century, that makes it a wonder.

# LEINTWARDINE
## HEREFORDSHIRE
*The besetting evil of bureaucracy*

There is jubilation in Leintwardine, an ancient settlement in the Welsh Marches. The BIG Lottery Fund and Advantage West Midlands (funded with European money) have given a total of £586,000 towards restoring the village hall and the community centre. But the committee that runs both these halls does not look to the future with unalloyed joy. After twelve years of fund-raising and making do, it is worn out. These days, fewer people are willing to serve on village committees. Bridget Sudworth, chairman of the Leintwardine Village Hall and Community Centre Committee, might stand down if there was anyone to take over.

It used to be that villages could rely on farmers to shoulder such burdens. There are fewer farmers these days, and those that are left work harder, perhaps on their own, to stay afloat. The wives and partners who might once have had some free time now often have jobs, and are too exhausted to volunteer. Retired newcomers are as likely to form the backbone of the parish council as traditional village types.

Step forward Richard Sudworth, Bridget's husband. Since leaving Bristol in 1997 and retiring in 2006, this former dentist has thrown himself into local life; he is, among other things, chairman of the Leintwardine Group Parish Council.

The couple had known the area before moving here. For eighteen years, they rented a weekend cottage at nearby Downton, one of the three villages making up the Leintwardine Group. Leintwardine is a working village. It is not overwhelmingly pretty. But with a population of only seven hundred, it has (at the time of writing) a bank, a filling station-cum-shop, post office, butcher, two pubs, a fish and chip shop, a September Goose Fair, a summer Coracle Regatta (held at Mortimer's Cross) and those two village halls (the community centre was formed out of the Victorian village school when the present school was built in the 1960s).

This is not a retirement community; Leintwardine has a primary school, and there are plenty of young local people. But the village feels itself under siege. Rising house prices are a serious matter for those involved with Herefordshire's traditional industry, agriculture, while developers want to pounce on sites that could provide glorious views of the Welsh Marches for well-heeled outsiders. Vetting plans is an important function of the parish council.

Like many people who run village institutions and events, the Sudworths are daunted by the amount of red tape that the voluntary sector now faces. Health and safety certification creates a disproportionate amount of work and expense. In an increasingly litigious society, many people do not want the anxiety. Insurance for fund-raising activities that would normally have taken place in private gardens has become so alarming that such events may not happen.

But Leintwardine and villages like it must not despair. When Flossie Lane, publican of Leintwardine's The Sun Inn, a parlour bar run from the house where she was born in 1914, became frail towards the end of her long life (she died in 2009, aged ninety-four), regulars rallied round. They formed a kind of guild, known as the Aldermen of the Red-Brick Bar, appointing an annual mayor, clad in a squirrel-skin cape made by the butcher. The Aldermen supervised the honesty system by which The Sun continued once Flossie was too immobile to run it, money chinking into a row of jam jars, one for each denomination of note and coin.

Local spirit can still come to the fore when needed. But the mounting pressure of bureaucratic rules has pushed it underground during the past ten or twenty years. Filling in forms out of a sense of public duty, or getting on with some gardening in one of the most beautiful spots in England? Not everyone would choose the former.

# LONG CLAWSON

LEICESTERSHIRE                                    *And it is long, too*

There are moments, when travelling around England, that deserve to be called epiphanic. One of them comes on the approach to Long Clawson from the west. Crest the limestone ridge, and the Vale of Belvoir stretches limitlessly before you, hedges and trees and black-and-white cows spread like a heavenly tablecloth. Long Clawson, unfolding itself along the lower slope of the ridge, lives up to its name. It is long. A mile and a quarter long, in fact. The journey from the beginning of the West End to the end of the East End winds through no fewer than fourteen sharp bends. When you think the village has finished, it goes on to unpack some more of itself. It is like an improvisation that never stops. What can explain it?

Villages take different forms. Some have a focal point – the village green with the church off it, or a market cross. These nucleated villages tend to exist in lowland areas, and may reflect the rise in population that took place from the late Saxon period until the Black Death in the fourteenth century; concentrating the village workforce in one place made better use of resources. Quite a number of these villages show a degree of conscious planning, perhaps because they were laid out by a lord or an abbot. In some areas, squatters settled on waste land, often in old forests; their encroachments, being unofficial, indeed illegal, were disorderly, and if they later coalesced into villages, they are likely to be loose and haphazard.

Linear villages, such as Long Clawson, are the commonest form. They grew up along roads, with the church at the higher end and cottages and farmhouses strung out along the main street. From here, gardens and orchards went back in long strips, perhaps to a back lane that marked the limit of the settlement. There is a Back Lane at Long Clawson, although it skirts Castle Field next to the church, presumably the site of the manor house, since medieval earthworks can still be made out there.

Long Melford in Suffolk (see page 257), Combe Martin in Devon and Piddletrenthide in Dorset are all linear villages of more than a mile in length. Their main streets, however, are reasonably straight. The exceptionally cranky line taken by the street through Long Clawson shows that it was never an important thorough-fare. This is suggested by the frequency with which its name changes, turning from Barnard's Place to West End and Church Lane until it leaves the village as East End, or Hose Lane. The church guidebook suggests that ownership by two manors, one Saxon and one Danish, may have had something to do with it. Each manor may have had its own settlement, which fused together laterally. Equally, since the village seems to have oriented itself in accordance with a line of springs, perhaps a desire to take advantage of them led the villagers to spread themselves out.

The next village to the east is Hose, also an old-fashioned term for stockings. It gave rise to the Leicestershire saying, 'There are more whores in Hose than honest women in Long Clawson.'

# LOPPINGTON

SHROPSHIRE                    *A less than charming memory of rural life*

This decent enough village of red brick and black-and-white houses contains an unusual survival. Set into the ground is an iron ring. This may be the only remaining physical evidence of what had been, until 1835, the popular pastime of bull baiting. That this should be found in a village is not wholly expected. Bull baiting often took place in market squares, before the unfortunate bulls were slaughtered; the Bull Ring in Birmingham preserves a linguistic memory of its following in towns. While the equally brutal sport of cockfighting* appealed not only to plough boys but at court – there was a cockpit at Whitehall – bull baiting did not cross the class boundary. It remained the preserve of tradesmen, farmers, factory hands, miners and rustics, with butchers, for obvious reasons, playing a prominent role. In the Middle Ages it was laid down that bulls should be baited before they were slaughtered, in order to release bad blood and improve the meat.

The sport involved tethering a bull to a stake or ring, and setting dogs on it, the bulldog having been bred for the purpose. The dogs attacked singly, their object being to fasten onto the bull's muzzle. The bull sought to throw them into the air with its horns. If the bull was successful, the dog's owner and friends would try to soften its fall by getting their backs or a pole underneath it. The dog would then go back to the fray.

'Sometimes a second Frisk into the Air disables him for ever from playing his old Tricks,' the seventeenth-century French writer Henri Misson recorded. 'But sometimes too he fastens upon his Enemy, and when once he has seiz'd him with the Eyeteeth, he sticks to him like a Leech, and would sooner die than leave his Hold. Then the Bull bellows, and bounds, and kicks about to shake off the Dog . . . In the End, either the Dog tears out the Piece he has laid Hold on, and falls, or else remains fix'd to him, with an Obstinacy that would never end, if they did not pull him off.'

Bull baiting took its place in a round of diversions that included cock throwing (tying a cock to the ground and attempting to knock it down by throwing pieces of wood), wrestling, cudgelling, single-stick†, quoits, skittles, football, cricket and bell-ringing. In fairness to our ancestors, it should be said that by the time bull baiting was outlawed by Parliament in 1835, it had been subjected to various local prohibitions. Opposition reflected a change in the nature of Britain, whose middle class was developing what would soon be regarded as a characteristically British sentimentality towards animals (expressed in the paintings of Edwin Landseer). It has been argued that cockfighting was not banned because of the cruelty, but because gentlemen were wagering too much money on it. This was not the case with bull baiting. People had come to find it disgusting.

*See Dalston, page 386. †See Botley, page 97

# MAWSLEY

NORTHAMPTONSHIRE            *Have we forgotten how to build villages?*

Mawsley is a new village. Until the eve of the Millennium, the site had been unremarkable Northamptonshire fields, bounded by copses and shaggy, overgrown hedges – over or through which the Pytchley Hunt would sometimes jump. The neighbouring village of Faxton, mentioned, as a manor, in the Domesday Book, gave up the ghost in the 1950s; people preferred comfortable factory jobs in Northampton to getting soaked, frozen or broiled on the land.

Half a century later, thanks to the motor car, the population drift has reversed. So many people want to live in the countryside, while working elsewhere, that existing villages cannot accommodate them. While many have been expanded, this can only be taken so far without sacrificing the character of the original settlement. New villages can provide a large number of dwellings in one hit. To some planners, they seem an obvious solution. Few, however, have been built.

Mawsley perhaps explains why. By 2000, the planning system had digested the example of Poundbury, the Duchy of Cornwall's development beside Dorchester. Previously, the architecture of new developments had been subservient to the rule of the highways engineer. Priority had been given to the passage of cars through the streets, which was made as safe as possible by avoiding sharp turns and removing anything that impeded the driver's vision. The result was the characteristic form of late-twentieth-century development – not *rus in urbe*, nor (to borrow the motto of Solihull) *urbs in rure*, but suburbs in every direction: visually bleak developments that were threatening to pedestrians and dangerous to playing children.

The planners had failed to appreciate that the easier they made streets to drive along, the faster drivers were likely to go. Poundbury championed the 'walkable community'. Everything needed to sustain life was available within walking distance. It was made deliberately difficult for cars to negotiate, so they had to slow down. They were made to park out of sight. Architectural pundits raged over Poundbury's vernacular and modestly classical idiom, both for and (mostly) against, but its achievement was to put humans ahead of machines.

Although Poundbury is sometimes described as a village, it is not one; it is an urban extension, docked to the mother ship of Dorset's county town. Like scores of other developments across Britain, Mawsley adopts Poundburyish principles – the planning system expects nothing less. With some six hundred and fifty homes, it makes a reasonable fist of its vernacular design: the red brick, gables and bay windows can be seen on farmhouses round about. It combines five-bedroom 'executive homes' with terraces of small houses – a standard component of old towns and villages, reintroduced at Poundbury. There is a primary school, a doctor's surgery, even an NHS dentist. Residents can socialise or attend church in a building known as the Centre. The community has established a WI, a football club, an allotment association, a baby and toddler group and a walking group. A lake adds to the attractions.

Yet Mawsley misses the point of Poundbury. It is the car again. Real villages grew up because they had a purpose; they provided work for the people who lived there, and in order to live there, residents surrounded themselves with shops, pubs and places of worship. Mawsley is a place with no reason to exist except that people need homes. You cannot live in one of these homes without a car. You sleep here, then you drive off somewhere else. Mawsley is not ugly. But it is only a stage set, a skin-deep representation of a village, without the option of a change of scenery in the next Act.

# MERIDEN
## WARWICKSHIRE

*It says it is the heart of England*

Meriden thinks that it is at the centre of England. It has a cross and a metal plaque to prove it. The old market cross was rebuilt when the green was done up as part of the 1951 Festival of Britain, and the plaque makes bold the claim that this village represents England's geographical bull's eye. There are those who disagree, among them the Ordnance Survey, which in 2002 found, by use of the gravitational method of mapping, an alternative centre, on a farm near Fenny Drayton in Leicestershire, grid reference SP 36373.66 96143.05. According to the BBC, this was a considerable surprise to the farm's owners, who were then in their late eighties.

The Midland Oak, between Lillington and Leamington Spa in Warwickshire, is another contender: the ancient oak that stood here for centuries was replaced in 1988 with a new tree, and a plaque to trumpet its claim. But long-established ideas are hard to shake, and Meriden has been under the impression of being the centre (as it still maintains it is) for half a millennium. Here, according to its own lights, is Middle England at home.

'A pleasant and cheerful village,' was how Francis Smith described it in *Warwickshire Delineated* (1820). Originally it was called Alspath, but acquired its present name from the road that was much travelled in the fifteenth century: 'myre' signifying dirt and 'den' a bottom. 'I can well vouch for the propriety of the appellation, before the institution of turnpikes,' Thomas Pennant commented in *The Journey from Chester to London* (1782).

Once, the Forest of Arden covered Warwickshire and parts of adjacent counties, and Meriden, whatever its other pretensions to centrality, was at its heart. The Woodmen of Arden held their meetings in the village, their present hall by Joseph Bonomi dating from 1788. A great archery contest was still being held at Meriden every August into the 1930s. 'There are picturesque costumes, and quaint ceremonial, and the whole affair is a most interesting survival,' George Long observed in *The Folklore Calendar* (1930).

When the aristocrat John Byng, later Lord Torrington, visited in 1789, he noted the views of a cottager about the enclosures that had taken place. 'We had our garden, our bees, our share of a flock of sheep, the feeding of our geese; and could cut turf for our fuel – now all that is gone!' By contrast, Byng noted, the archery green that had lately been turfed by Lord Aylesford was in splendid condition, being 'in the style of an extended bowling-green'.

During the Second World War, Meriden acquired a new industry, when a factory for Triumph motorcycles was built. By the 1970s, these heavy British machines, with their throaty roar and air of untamed masculinity, had lost ground to cheaper, more sophisticated imports from Japan. The workers responded to threats of closure by organising a sit-in; production ceased, and only resumed when Tony Benn, as Industry Secretary, funded a workers' cooperative. Alas, this brave adventure went into liquidation eight years later, although the Triumph marque was saved. Motorbikes bearing the famous logo, the tail of the R swooping down and along to become the crossbar of the H, are now made at Hinckley in Leicestershire. But a tall obelisk on the green commemorates the cyclists who were killed during the First and Second World Wars.

# MUSTON
## LEICESTERSHIRE
*When plenty smiles alas! she smiles for few . . .*

George Crabbe's career as a parish clergyman was not glorious; holding several livings, he lost the congregations he could not personally attend to the preaching of Nonconformists. But then he had not thought of taking holy orders until the Tory politician Edmund Burke suggested it as a means of obtaining a livelihood. The Church – or those who controlled its patronage – proved generous. Crabbe was able to devote that considerable part of his energies not consumed by parish duties to writing poetry, such as *The Village*. In this and other works he reflected on the bleak monotony that was the sum total of many country existences. While sophisticated people might have longed for the 'simple life' (surely Crabbe was the first to use the expression), the poet's experience was quite different:

> Rapine and Wrong and Fear usurp'd her place,
> And a bold, artful, surly, savage race.

Crabbe's own life as a young man had been hard. Born in 1754, he grew up in Aldeburgh, a Suffolk town that had been half eaten away by the sea. It would later provide the material for *The Borough*, which contained the story of the sadist Peter Grimes that inspired Benjamin Britten's opera. Attempts to establish himself as an apothecary and surgeon failed, and he left for London. He was set on becoming a poet, but the patronage necessary to keep him alive proved elusive. 'My Existence is a Pain to me,' he wrote in desperation to Burke; he had 'only to hope a speedy End to a Life so unpromisingly begun'.

Fortunately Burke heard the note of desperation and took Crabbe under his wing. Crabbe first became a curate at Aldeburgh. Then Burke's recommendation secured him the congenial position of chaplain to the Duke of Rutland at Belvoir Castle. The second half of *The Village* contains an otherwise baffling eulogy, which destroys the form, to the Duke's brother, Robert Manners, who had died as a naval captain from wounds suffered in the Battle of Dominica. Important friends secured a number of Church of England livings for him, including Muston, to which he moved in 1789. When the 4th Duke died, Crabbe placed curates in his Belvoir parishes and transferred to a house that his wife had inherited, in Suffolk.

It was, perhaps, ironic that Crabbe was living in Belvoir Castle when he wrote *The Village*. His account of the farmhand's unremitting toil and destitution makes an implicit social comment: 'When plenty smiles alas! she smiles for few . . .'. His castigation of absentee clergy seems equally ripe.

Crabbe's work would have been understood in the eighteenth century as a literary exercise, concerned as much with unseating the worn-out pastoral tradition, with its swains and shepherds, than with righting social wrongs. Nevertheless, descriptions such as that of the parish poorhouse were immediate and shocking – perhaps more so because of the heroic couplets in which they are contained:

> Behold yon House that holds the parish poor,
> Whose walls of mud scarce bear the broken door . . .

Crabbe's interest in Leicestershire was not only poetic; he contributed to John Nichols's eight-volume *The History and Antiquities of Leicestershire*, with accounts of natural history and Belvoir Castle. He returned to Muston in 1805, to a hostile reception from inhabitants who had heard the strange rumour that he was a Jacobin and against the war with France. During his absence, many of the congregation had attached themselves to Dissenting chapels, including two of his own servants. He consoled himself by finishing 'The Parish Register', a long poem, narrated by a clergyman, made up of character sketches inspired by entries in the record of baptisms, marriages and burials.

*See also Helpston, page 243*

# MYDDLE
SHROPSHIRE                    *Peace and tranquillity? You must be joking*

In November 1704, Richard Evans was going to London. He rode into Myddle, carrying some money, accompanied by an unreliable character called Price. Price was hailed by a comrade, who, like him, had been in prison for debt, and they all went to the alehouse. Before leaving Myddle, Evans went to say goodbye to a friend; the latter, however, had got drunk and had gone to bed. Instead, Evans found Matthew Hinton, a weaver, and Laurence Bassnett, a shoemaker, in the house – they had probably also been drinking. Words were exchanged, Evans whipped out his sword, on which Bassnett prudently shut the door and continued the conversation, evidently a heated one, through the window. Evans walked back to his horse but never got there, Bassnett having hit him over the head with a poker and Hinton with a long-handled shovel. Price hurried off for the constable, but Evans was dying by the time they returned. Bassnett was caught, tried and found guilty, but was able to claim benefit of clergy; soon afterwards he was impressed as a soldier. Hinton got away.

We know about this randomly brutal episode because of Richard Gough's extraordinary account of *The History of Myddle*, begun in 1700. Gough was a yeoman farmer. His plan for organising the account was based on the pews in the parish church, each of which was assigned to a family: as he mentally went round them, he wrote down all that he could remember about their occupants. Near the Welsh border, Myddle had a population of six hundred, small by today's standards, yet Gough's *History* is shot through with acts of stupid but extreme violence, often associated with drink.

Someone called Clarke was approached by a bailiff and a servant of Sir Edward Kinaston to collect a debt. He and his sons were cutting peat on Haremeare Mosse. As the servant approached, his sword drawn, 'one of Clarke's sons, with a turf spade, which they call a peat iron (a very keen thing) struck Sir Edward's man on the head, and cloave out his brains'. Clarke's son escaped, but was later killed by a neighbour called Hopkin during an argument over some hay. Before long, Hopkin had also been murdered as he walked home, 'having been knocked on the head with the foot of a washing stock'.

On another occasion, a gang led by Hugh Elks burst into a house while the family was at church one Sunday. A dairymaid had stayed to make cheese. The men were wearing masks but the unfortunate girl saw Elks's features. 'Good Uncle Elks, do me no harm,' she cried, upon which he cut her throat. Fleeing, the would-be robbers left Elks's dog shut in the dairy. It was found on the churchgoers' return 'almost bursting with eating the cheese'. The dog waddled back to Elks's house; Elks was found guilty and hanged.

The twenty-first century may value the countryside for its sense of peace and security. But in an age when men routinely carried arms, some people drank to excess, an organised police force did not exist and the virtues of self-restraint, as preached by the Methodists, were as yet little to be seen, hot-headed villagers could all too easily destroy other people, not to mention themselves.

# NASEBY

*Ghosts of the Civil War*

Naseby is a watershed, and full of springs. Three big rivers are supposed to rise here. Over one of the garden walls you can see an ancient metal cone declaring, in Regency script, that what appears to be a garden pond actually constitutes the origin of the Avon. That river flows west all the way to Bristol. The Nene and the Welland also have their beginnings nearby; they run the other way and empty into the Wash.

Naseby has grown and grown since the Second World War. The old village shop closed, the shopkeepers having become demoralised when the Post Office did not compensate them fully after a burglary; but a new and improved version has opened on another site. The village school makes a satisfactory volume of noise at break time, and the congregation of the church is sufficient to have at one point perpetuated bad feeling with the riding establishment across the road, by parking its cars during services so that the horse lorry could not get out. (Relations have improved since the lowest ebb, when an electrical fault meant that every time the church central heating was switched on, the metal parts of the stable yard became electrified.)

The older domestic architecture includes some Victorian cottages, and a few bigger houses and farms, some of them Georgian. Most of the more modern homes appear to have arrived in Naseby only by chance. They could have been built anywhere. Recently, the planners have been trying harder, and the newest development is a clump of cottages, with white walls and thatched roofs. Only they are not cottages in size. They are like cottage-shaped hot-air balloons, which have been blown up until they are jostling for space and might lift into the sky and float away. If only they would. Naseby deserves to be treated with greater care. It is one of the most stirring words in the English language.

It was on a great plain outside the village that the army commanded by Charles I lost the decisive battle of the Civil War, to what the Royalists had underestimated as the New Noddle Army – the New Model Army created by Oliver Cromwell. The King's nephew, Prince Rupert, led a famous charge, swept away the opposition's left wing, but did not – or perhaps, on overexcited horses, could not – stop. They found the Parliamentarian baggage train, laagered outside Naseby, and pillaged it. By the time they returned to the battlefield, the Royalist 'hedgehogs', squares of men bristling with long pikes, had been overwhelmed by superior numbers. It was too late.

Well into the twentieth century, the place from which King Charles was supposed to have directed the battle was marked by the King's Oak. As Thomas Guy Paget wrote in *The History of the Althorp and Pytchley Hunt* (1937), it 'sheltered innumerable litters of foxes beneath its roots'. There are also two monuments to the battle, one an obelisk, the other a column with a ball on top. Before the battle, Cromwell is believed to have stayed in a thatched cottage at Naseby, now called Cromwell Cottage. A party of his troops surprised the Royalist rearguard, a number of whom were about to eat supper. Having killed some and driven the others away, they sat down to eat the food that had been prepared – or so W. H. Holloway has it in *The Story of Naseby* (1923). 'Cromwell's table', a robust nine-foot-long piece of oak furniture of seventeenth-century date, can be seen in the church.

# PAINSWICK
GLOUCESTERSHIRE        *The transformative influence of Sunday School*

These days, Painswick is famous for its Rococo garden, a private exuberance on the part of Benjamin Hyett, the eighteenth-century owner of Painswick House. But the village at its gates did not participate in the froth and frolic. It was a low-church sort of place, with a nonconformist tradition that goes back to the sixteenth century. A Quaker congregation appeared as early as 1655, and by the end of the century there was a Quaker school. Admittedly, the village would seem to have let itself down at its annual festival: 'Drunkenness and every species of clamour, riot, and disorder . . . filled the town upon this occasion' according to Robert Raikes. It was fertile ground for Raikes to plant one of his new Sunday Schools in 1784.

Raikes was a journalist and printer. His father, also Robert, had founded the *Gloucester Journal*, which Raikes continued. Flamboyant and self-advertising, he was known locally as Bobby Wildgoose. 'Mr Raikes is not a man that, without a previous disposition towards approbation, I should greatly have admired,' sniffed Fanny Burney, visiting when Keeper of the Robes to Queen Charlotte while the Royal family were at Cheltenham. 'He is somewhat too flourishing, somewhat too forward, somewhat too voluble' – a typical journalist, in short – 'but he is worthy, benevolent, good-natured, and good-hearted, and therefore the overflowing of successful spirits and delighted vanity must meet with some allowance.'

The first object of his philanthropy had been prisons, where prisoners awaiting trial were not even fed. Opposite Gloucester Prison one Sunday, he saw the children of chimneysweeps running wild in Sooty Alley, Sunday being the only day on which they did not work. In 1780 he opened a Sunday School to teach them the Bible, with the literacy to read it, and Christian decorum. Other schools had been opened on Sundays, but Raikes could use the *Gloucester Journal* to champion the cause. A movement was born.

Painswick, with its Protestant tradition, may have been particularly receptive to the idea that the day of rest might be spent in 'quietness and good order'. Certainly an account of the Painswick festival, written by Raikes in a letter two years after the Sunday School was founded, suggests a remarkable transformation. Instead of going to the alehouse the crowd headed for church, 'which was filled in such a manner as I never remember to have seen in any church in the country. The galleries and aisles were thronged like a playhouse.' Three hundred and thirty-one children presented themselves. 'Young people lately more neglected than the cattle in the field; ignorant, profane, filthy, clamorous, impatient of every restraint, were here seen cleanly, quiet, observant of order, submissive, courteous in behaviour, and, in conversation, free from that vileness which marks our wretched vulgar.'

The advantages both of Bible study and the basic literacy that made it possible were quickly appreciated by the objects of Raikes's philanthropy. In the nineteenth century, Sunday Schools became a popular institution run by and for the 'respectable' working class, transmitting the values of thrift, self-discipline, self-improvement and hard work that parents hoped would not only enable their children to know God above, but to get on in the world below.

# QUENINGTON
## GLOUCESTERSHIRE
*Sculpture does furnish a garden*

'Roses grow in every garden, clematis relieves with its rich purple shade the walls of many a cosy little dwelling-house, and the old white mills, with their latticed windows, and pointed gables, are a feature of every tiny hamlet through which the river flows.' J. Arthur Gibbs wrote that of the villages of the Coln valley in Gloucestershire in 1898, and Quenington is still the same, only more so. It is a place in which the aesthetic possibilities of the English summer have been raised to a high plane. As the river cranks its leisurely way round the village, it passes through an arcadia of gardening and summer hats and teas on lawns and people asleep in hammocks after lunch. There is poetry to this village, so carefully looked after, the tympanum of its Norman church restored; it is of the kind that lulls you to sleep.

But for a fortnight every other summer that changes. Buses arrive; there is bustle; the street is full of amiable people whom the village does not know. It is the time that the Quenington Sculpture Trust puts on its biennial show. The shows were started in 1992 by Lucy and David Abel Smith, who live in the Old Rectory; they established the Trust five years later. The idea is to promote sculpture that can be enjoyed outdoors. It takes all forms. Although the show introduces sculpture to a wider public, some of whom might buy the pieces that they see, a certain amount, inevitably, remains at the Old Rectory: the Abel Smiths can't resist adding to their collection. And so a walk round this part of the Coln valley is a bit like a children's treasure hunt, where exciting things are hidden in shrubberies and crooks of trees.

Out of a stone trough, shaded by vegetation, a crop of thin, brown, asparagus-like objects wriggle – on closer inspection they turn out to be distinctly phallic.

*Sculpture emerging from the lawn at Quenington, scene of a biennial sculpture show.*

A monolith of blue glass, one half of which is bubbly, the other smooth, literally colours the view that unfolds beyond it: river, meadow and trees. Beside the wooden bridge – too ingenious to negotiate with ease – is a stone hut, its pyramid roof half lost beneath the scrambling rose. Outside hangs a different kind of flower, an enormous one, with petals made of sharp steel. The trunk of a tree is wrapped with the words 'The Soul of Man resembles the Water, the Fate of Man resembles the Wind'. It is a memorial to the Abel Smiths' gardener, Esme Bradburne, who died in 2000.

On the lawn, a swimmer emerges from the turf: head, shoulders and hands all that are visible, eyes darting a somewhat suspicious look at people who live above ground. A library has been made in the form of a circular dovecote; the big double doors open out so that it becomes a stage. Plays are acted here, beside the river. They are almost certainly mounted to raise money for some local cause, which is right and proper, but as everyone knows, something of an excuse. The real purpose is to celebrate the pleasures of the countryside, in this age of peace and plenty. Of all the sculptures in this remarkable place, there is no altar to flute-playing, goat-footed Pan. Perhaps there should be.

# ROCKINGHAM
## NORTHAMPTONSHIRE

*At the heart of a royal forest*

The village of Rockingham exists because of the Castle, and the Castle exists because of Rockingham Forest. William the Conqueror decreed the Forest, and it ran from Northampton in the south to Stamford in the north, with the river Nene forming its eastern border and the river Welland that on the west: an area thirty-three miles by eight. It was not all woodland; long before the Saxons had come, making settlements in the valleys, the uplands had been occupied by prehistoric people, who began burning and felling the primeval forest that once covered all of Britain.

Charles Kingsley gave an evocative description in *Hereward the Wake* (1866): 'Deep, tangled forest filled the lower clay lands, swarming with pheasants, roe, badger, and more wolves than were needed. Broken park-like glades covered the upper freestone where the red deer came out from harbour for their evening graze, and the partridge and plover whirred up, and the hares loped way innumerable . . .'. Kingsley knew the Forest well, having grown up nearby, at Barnack.

The defining feature of a Norman forest was the system of laws. Forest laws existed to protect the king's venison, or deer, which he hunted, and the vert, or habitat, that it lived in. Poachers could expect to be blinded if they were caught. The peasants who found themselves living in a royal forest may have felt disadvantaged; their dogs were brutally lamed to stop them running after game. On the other hand, they had plenty of pasture on which to graze their animals: being preserved for the benefit of the deer, it was not whittled away by greedy lords of the manor wanting more land for themselves.

The Forest also supported trades. Iron was smelted in movable furnaces, using charcoal made from the trees. (Smith seems to have been a common surname, from the fact that three people called Smith kept their pigs in the Forest, eating acorns, in 1295.) Charcoal was also used in potting and lime burning. There was a primitive glass industry in some forests. Bees were kept, nuts gathered, birds trapped; wood was taken to make carts, wheels and boards. It was not always taken legally but, by 1300, the draconian punishments could be 'amerced' or replaced by fines; indeed, law-breaking was accepted, if not encouraged, because of the income it generated. Similarly, far more deer were killed for the table or given as presents than actually hunted by the King.

There was no monarch more greatly besotted by hunting than James I. Yet such were the holes in the Stuart finances that he was forced to sell off parts of the royal forest. Sales to rich grandees continued until the end of the eighteenth century, creating a landscape of great agricultural estates. Interspersed with pockets of industry, or former industry, it pertains to this day.

William the Conqueror often came to Rockingham. So did King John, who loved hunting. Among its attractions was a vineyard, established during the reign of Henry I. In the twentieth century, Rockingham land was sold to develop the steel town of Corby, whose furnaces were the descendants of those in the medieval Forest. Once you pass the castle gate and look out over a great plain of fields and hedges, with the thatched village of Rockingham at your feet, you are in a different England: one that may have changed enormously since the Norman period, but still makes hunting folk smile.

# RYTON-ON-DUNSMORE
## WARWICKSHIRE                                    *The importance of droving*

As the sun rises on a November morning, a group of people, wearing heavy coats, will be seen gathered around a stone in a field off the A45 in Warwickshire. They are witnessing what may be the oldest ceremony in Britain, held almost continuously (there was a short break during Queen Victoria's reign) since at least 1170. It may be much older than that. This is the collection of the Wroth Silver, a tribute paid by eight parishes to the Duke of Buccleuch, in the person of his steward, the Duke being lord of the manor.

The stone is all that survives of a wayside cross that originally stood here. The payment, placed into a hollow in the top of the stone, consists of the following: a penny from each of eight parishes, two and a half pence from seven parishes, four pence from five parishes, a shilling from one parish, two shillings and tuppence from another, with representatives saying 'Wroth Silver' as they toss the money onto its place. The fine for not paying can be computed in money (twenty shillings for every penny not produced) but is otherwise a white bull with red nose and red ears.

Nobody quite knows what it all means, but cattle have something to do with it. 'Wroth' could be derived from an Anglo-Saxon word meaning roadway, although there have been other suggestions. The best guess is that Wroth Silver was originally a payment for a right granted by the lord of the manor, perhaps to drive cattle through his land.

Droving is an ancient activity. According to Kenneth Bonser in *The Drovers* (1970), 'the early inhabitants of Britain moved large herds of cattle and sheep, raiding or in search of fresh pastures'. Traditionally, Welsh cattle were driven across the Midlands to the lush pastures of Northamptonshire, where they were fattened before being sold to the London market. Perhaps one of the routes passed Knightlow Hill. The lord of the manor would certainly have wanted payment to allow the drovers onto his land; the cattle created wide paths, or a parallel series of paths, unless the lie of the land prevented them from spreading out, in which case they turned the surface of the track to mud, making it sink. The drovers themselves would not have been seen as great ornaments to the locality. The Welsh had a particularly bad reputation; an eighteenth-century cleric thought they would go to Hell for their bad practices.

After the ceremony, participants and spectators conclude in traditional form, although this part of the ritual is not quite so ancient as the rest. They repair to the Queen's Head at Bretford for breakfast, accompanied by rum and hot milk, a churchwarden pipe (no longer smoked indoors) and a recitation of verses. There was an attempt to ban the ceremony in 1685, but the then lord of the manor would not hear of it; he wanted the money. Now, the cash value of Wroth Silver has, like that of the Royal Maundy, declined in real terms. But the Maundy services date only from the fifteenth century. The Wroth Silver ceremony is of much greater antiquity, and the Duke of Buccleuch is prepared for it to continue, as long as there are local people willing to take part.

# SAINTBURY
GLOUCESTERSHIRE                                    *The Jacobean Olympics*

In 1608–9 Robert Dover from Norfolk married a daughter of the Dean of Lincoln, Sibella Sanford, and moved to Saintbury, where he practised law. His name lives on in Dover's Hill, between the village and Chipping Campden, where, in 1612, he sought to revive the Olympic Games.

Dover's Olympic ideal was hardly that of the Baron de Coubertin, who founded the modern Olympic movement in 1894. Jovial and large-minded, he probably grafted his interpretation of the Greek athletic festival onto a traditional Whitsun event featuring rustic sports. The Puritans looked with disfavour on such rumbustious festivities, associated with drinking and all that ensued from it. Dover was of a different persuasion; he wanted to legitimise them and keep them going.

We have some idea of what went on from a book called *Annalia Dubrensia: upon the yeerly celebration of Mr. R. Dover's Olimpick games upon Cotswold Hills*, published in 1636. This included no fewer than thirty-three poems by notable poets, including Michael Drayton and Ben Jonson, some of whom appear to have attended the games. (It is unlikely, as has been argued, that Shakespeare ever went, although he may well have known Dover.) The frontispiece shows the games taking place. Dover presides: an impressive figure wearing a suit of James I's old clothes, provided for him by the courtier Endymion Porter, who employed Dover and lived nearby. Around him can be seen men in Jacobean doublets and ballooning breeches throwing spears, fighting with staves, wrestling, tossing hammers, coursing and horse racing. One competitor is standing on his head. For the ladies there was dancing, and the event was rounded off with an open-air feast in front of the tents, at which one of the diners is shown conspicuously raising his glass.

The games continued under Dover's supervision until 1644. Suppressed by the Commonwealth, they were revived at the Restoration and continued until 1852, when they once again incurred the displeasure of religious prudes, who found them unseemly. In 1951, the Festival of Britain, reaching out from its base on

London's South Bank in an attempt to embrace the whole country, staged them anew, but without the more dangerous of the bucolic exercises, such as shin-kicking. And so they continue, with climbing the greasy pole and the sporting activity that goes, in every sense, from strength to strength: tug of war. There is no evidence that tug of war was part of Dover's games; it seems to have enjoyed a new lease of popularity following its introduction as a pastime on ships such as the *Cutty Sark* in the late nineteenth century. It did, however, form part of five of the Olympiads in Ancient Greece.

# SAPPERTON
GLOUCESTERSHIRE *Could the Cotswolds redeem urban man?*

In 1893, two London-trained architect-craftsmen, Ernest Gimson and Sidney Barnsley, followed what was becoming a well-beaten path to the Cotswolds. Since William Morris had settled at Kelmscott Manor* in 1871, the Cotswolds had become Arts and Crafts country. This was an area that had changed little since its last burst of prosperity in the eighteenth century. Farm workers wearing smocks and corduroys threw hay onto wooden carts carved in the wheelwright's shop.

It was a land blessed in architecture, its lovely stone – so easy to carve into urns and door hoods when freshly quarried – forming delightful harmonies out of marketplaces and village streets, old-fashioned manor houses and unimproved cottages. After the soot-blackened, slum-ridden, noisy, hectic and overcrowded capital, the round-shouldered hills, which had seemed somewhat bleak to the eye of Georgian agriculturalists, appeared to offer a new beginning.

Gimson and Barnsley, soon joined by Barnsley's brother Ernest, took a lease on Pinbury Park from Lord Bathurst. Typically, this seventeenth-century gentry house, where the avenue was said to be haunted by the ghost of a nun-housekeeper rolling a Double Gloucester cheese, had fallen down the social scale, becoming an out-of-repair farmhouse. Its new tenants were enthusiastic members of Anti Scrape, as they called the Society for the Protection of Ancient Buildings. Before starting on careers dedicated to furniture and the building crafts, they set about repairing it, so that after six years it was once again 'a fine old country house in a setting of great beauty', to quote a younger craftsman, Norman Jewson.

So successful were they that Lord Bathurst, who had recently married, decided to take it back to live in himself, giving Gimson and the Barnsleys generous terms for the lease and the choice of sites on his estate to build houses, which he funded himself. They did not go far; the hamlet of Sapperton was a mile away, and that is where each of them created a home: Ernest Barnsley from a pair of derelict cottages; Gimson a quarter of a mile up the valley; Sidney Barnsley midway between.

Ernest Barnsley worked as an architect. Sidney followed a pure Arts and Crafts path, making furniture, to his own design, exclusively with his own hands (it was often inspired by local farm implements, such as hay rakes). Gimson practised the craft of decorative plasterwork himself, sometimes helped by his wife, but he was frustrated by the limits of his own ability as a maker; he therefore designed metalwork and high-quality furniture that was made by other craftsmen, whom he supervised.

It was an austere community. Relaxation came from listening to folk music of the kind recorded by Cecil Sharp, or early instruments revived by Arnold Dolmetsch; both Sharp and Dolmetsch were friends. It must have been an intense life in the little hamlet. Predictably, the farm labourers in the other cottages did not feel entirely comfortable with the arty newcomers, and some disagreement caused the Ernest Barnsley and Gimson households to fall out. Communication was never restored.

Even so, there were achievements. Gimson and the Barnsleys 'preached to a world that had ceased to use its eyes the beauty of the Medieval or Early Tudor [or more often seventeenth-century] style of farm-house building', remembered the Bloomsburyite Gerald Brenan, who grew up nearby. 'By so doing they reformed the art of restoring early buildings, thus helping to put an end to the vandalism of the Victorian era.' There was another consequence, however. 'Farm-houses that in 1914 were worth £500 were sold in 1934 for £5,000.' That is a trend with which one can readily identify today.

*See Bibury, page 300

# SARNESFIELD
## HEREFORDSHIRE *Naming an architect in black and white*

John Abel lies buried beneath a table tomb, decorated with angels, near the porch of Sarnesfield church. He was a carpenter. In this land of black-and-white villages, where schools, town halls and even churches are built of wood, that meant more than it would today. 'This craggy stone a covering is for an architector's bed,' his epitaph reads. 'That lofty building raised high, yet now lies low his head.' He was born around the year Francis Drake set out to circumnavigate the world; he died ninety-seven years later. His almost century of existence had been a dramatic period for England, even in rural Herefordshire. Although buried in an established churchyard, Abel was a devout Roman Catholic; at times it must have been dangerous.

Generally we know little about individual carpenter-architects, despite their high status in society. The fact that Abel can be identified by name has encouraged some writers to ascribe almost any timber-framed building in the Welsh Marches to him. Rather little even of Abel's output can be documented. Allowing for this, and without wishing to overstate his productivity, we must imagine that he contributed significantly to local market towns and villages, as well as building

spectaculars such as the old Town Hall in Hereford (now demolished). His fondness for Latin tags sometimes helps identify his work. Perhaps that reflected his
adherence to the old Religion; he was hauled before a church court in 1618 on
the grounds that his marriage was conducted in secret. The case was eventually
dismissed, but his name can be found on a list of Catholic recusants in 1627.

Abel's first known commission was to rebuild the roof of the church at
Vowchurch, which was threatening to push out the walls. He went on to design
the old town hall at Brecon, the market hall at Leominster and, in 1633, to convert
the ruins of Dore Abbey* into a parish church. With a High Church patron in
Lord Scudamore, who was a friend of Archbishop Laud, Abel was able to create
a complete Laudian interior, with a superb chancel screen. The contract for Dore
Abbey survives, showing that he used 204 tons of timber in the church.

During the Civil War, Abel sided, not surprisingly, with the King, and his
skill was of some use to the cause. When a Parliamentarian force was besieging
Hereford in 1645, he found himself, for some reason, inside the city, able to design
and build hand mills to replace the gunpowder mill that the Roundheads had
burnt down. This siege was lifted (although Hereford fell at the end of the year to
Colonel John Birch†). For Abel's services Charles I awarded him the title of King's
Carpenter. He later designed a kind of wooden tank, called 'the Sow', with the
hope of capturing Canon Frome castle, but while it was being dragged into position by oxen it was surprised by Parliamentarian raiders whose 'shout of triumph
made the valleys ring'.

After the Civil War, Abel resumed his career. Perhaps he went on constructing
richly fantastic timber structures until he died.

> His line and rule, so death concludes, are locked up in store;
> Build those who list or those who wist, for he can build no more.

*See Abbey Dore, page 291. †See Weobley, page 362

# SHEARSBY
## LEICESTERSHIRE                                    *A country spa*

Shearsby gives the impression of a village that tried to pull itself up in the Georgian
period. The church, St George's flag bravely flying beside it, was rebuilt in 1789;
its tower has urns on the corners and a stumpy octagon on top. From its hillock, it
surveys a settlement that seems to be loosely scattered around the green (with one
farmhouse dated 1669 just off it), but whose pretensions to Georgian town planning can be seen from The Square. It does not have any obvious characteristics of
a square, but that is what it is called. The effort to improve itself reached its apogee
when, in 1807, Shearsby opened a spa half a mile out of the village.

Typically, the site had previously been regarded as a holy well – one of the many ponds that formed naturally and replenished themselves on Leicestershire's limestone shelf. For example, the parish of Sapcote possesses not only the Golden Well, on Bath Street, its name probably related to the water's high sulphur content, but also the less appetising Soap (or Sope) Well – according to Sapcote's Victorian historian, the Rev. Henry Whitley, the 'remarkable soft water' was supposed to 'wash without soap, hence the name of the well'. The curative properties of some waters had been respected since the Middle Ages. Leicester Abbey once maintained a lazars' house at St Mary's Well at Papillon Hall. With its high iron content, the chalybeate water was supposed to be beneficial. In the early eighteenth century, the hall was occupied by the sinister David Papillon, who was believed to have hypnotic powers, and claimed magical properties for his Everlasting Well.

Throughout the eighteenth century, as Bath and other watering holes became increasingly fashionable, entrepreneurs saw such springs as business opportunities. Once their health benefits, real or supposed, had been established, doctors and apothecaries could make money from treating patients and putting them up. Proprietors were anxious to emphasise that the curative properties of their water were purely local; it would, as Dr James Taverner observed of the water from Witham Spa in Essex, 'make its escape upon carriage, tho' the bottles are ever so carefully cork'd and cemented'. Dr Taverner was one of dozens of medical practitioners prepared to vouch for the qualities of their local spa, with which they were often commercially associated.

Shearsby's virtues lay not in drinking the water: it contains various sulphates and iron oxide, in an unpalatable cocktail. The complaints that it was supposed to be capable of ameliorating were many, however. They included skin diseases, indigestion, rheumatism, bilious problems and nervous disorders. A county history of 1831 describes Shearsby as having 'accommodations on the spot enabling invalids to take the benefit of bathing and drinking the water with convenience and comfort'. By which was presumably meant the Bath Inn, which still exists.

In 1807, the prospects seemed bright. 'This spring, if properly taken care of, and secured by a building over it, and the recommendation of a few MDs might be as beneficial as several in the kingdom, which owe their celebrity more to the fashion, than the convalescence, of their visitants.' So wrote the county historian J. Nichols. The landowner, Mr Reeve, duly built, but the result was only modestly successful. There was no doctor to puff it. Besides, fashion had moved on. Since the 1780s, the Prince Regent had been going to the seaside at Brighton, not taking the waters at Bath. Sea bathing, not holy springs, had become the route to health.

# SLAD

Laurie Lee created the nostalgia industry. By the time of his death in 1997, *Cider with Rosie*, published in 1959, had sold six million copies. The book describes, in a poetically heightened and, contemporaries would claim, not wholly accurate way, his boyhood in Slad, a village outside Stroud in the Cotswolds. His mother moved there during the last year of the First World War, when Laurie was three. His first memory was of the grass, as tall as he was, from which he was scooped by one of his many sisters.

The father was absent in London, and did not return to live with them. It was an emotionally intense but physically hard life, with cabbage for dinner and bone-marrow-freezing winters during which the old of the parish would be carried off. There was a murder, a suicide, incest, sex; the schooling was primitive. But the intimacy of this unsophisticated existence was a quality that had been long lost by the time of the book's publication, and readers for whom the post-Second World War years were proving a slog yearned for its almost Mediterranean warmth (in fact Lee had written much of it in Ibiza).

Lee chronicled a time of change. 'The last days of my childhood were also the last days of the village,' he wrote in the last chapter of *Cider with Rosie*. 'I belonged to that generation which saw, by chance, the end of a thousand years' life.' He had been born into a 'world of silence', where farm workers bent their backs over the soil and the white roads between villages were rutted with hoof prints and cartwheels; where the horse was king and his people supplied him with fodder and smithies, stables and paddocks in tribute. Then came the 'brass-lamped motor-car . . . coughing up the road'. Journeys could be made by bus, rather than cart. 'But the car-shying horses with their rolling eyes gave signs of the hysteria to come. Soon the village would break, dissolve and scatter, become no more than a place for pensioners.' Gloucester, once almost a foreign city, came within range for shopping trips. The squire died, and the big house became a nursing home. The vicar caught Lee reading *Sons and Lovers*, and destroyed it, but couples were getting married in registry offices. The church would lose its grip.

Lee's childhood home had been carved out of a small manor house, which had later served as a pub; 'it had decayed even further by the time we got to it, and was now three poor cottages in one'. He ran away from it to bohemian London and the Spanish Civil War. Publication of *Cider with Rosie* enabled him and his wife, Kathy, to buy another place, Rose Cottage, from which they moved next door to Littlecourt. They kept their flat in London, where Lee enjoyed the convivial literary world, but he also became a fixture at the Woolpack Inn. Like other writers, he found that he had started a tourist route, with himself as one of the monuments. The Slad of his childhood had become a place of memory and imagination. Asked if certain incidents in *Cider with Rosie* were true, he would reply, 'It's in the book, isn't it?'

# SMALLEY

## DERBYSHIRE

*The inhumanity of a Parish Overseer*

Births and deaths – the most important events in village, or any other, life – find their record in the parish register, kept for centuries in a chest in the parish church. They are usually dry, factual documents, kept because the parish was, since Elizabethan times, the unit of English administration. But vicars and their clerks might also use the register to record momentous events, as at Smalley. In 1656, the register records, three members of the Holland family were struck by lightning. In 1779, smallpox was visited upon the parish; of the forty-three people who caught it, a dozen died – a considerably higher rate than at nearby Morley, which might be attributed, the rector thought, to the greater cleanliness there.

On the whole, the entries do not reveal much about the response of those who wrote them. But an exception comes after the common was enclosed, for the benefit of progressive agriculture, in 1785. That year, Samuel Liggett, a pauper, died – 'starved to death', as the Rev. Robert Wilmot set down bitterly, 'by the humanity of the Parish Officer'. This dreadful event – by no means the only one of its kind to have occurred in Georgian Britain – exposed an obvious flaw in the parish system.

Led by the two churchwardens, a body known as the vestry was responsible for administering the parish; it was supposed to keep the peace, maintain the roads and support the destitute. Answering jointly to the Bishop and local magistrate, it was chaired by the vicar or – as at Smalley, which had only a chapel – his curate. The churchwardens had responsibility for church affairs, from providing the candles to securing a vicar. An Overseer was appointed to determine the contribution each householder had to make towards the poor rates. The churchwardens ratified the Overseer's accounts, and it is surely impossible to think that bribery ever tempted them to amend the lists.

Serving on the vestry was an honour that many people could have done without, but the law did not allow them to decline it. Not everyone, therefore, was activated by higher feelings, and the connection between the money raised through the poor rates and that spent on relieving want was all too immediate. It was an incentive to treat hardship meanly. Paupers who appeared from elsewhere were driven on, in the hope of transferring the expense to another community. The native poor could be kept on short rations.

At Smalley, a Standing Overseer – the Parish Officer castigated by the Rev. Wilmot – had been appointed by householders anxious to keep down the poor rates. 'A meeting of parishioners was held to appoint a man to this office distinguished for extreme parsimony and hardness of heart,' the rector wrote. 'The result of the appointment was cruelty and oppression to the poor and Samuel Liggett was absolutely starved to death. I was from home when he was buried and did not known of his death till many months afterwards when, although I obtained sufficient information to convince me of the fact, I could not obtain evidence to convict the Overseer upon it, and therefore he escaped the punishment he deserved.'

The vestry system tottered on until the Great Reform Act of 1832, after which paupers were consigned to large workhouses (a dubious improvement)*. But the parish constable was still expected to apprehend criminals until the formation of county constabularies in 1839. And the parish waywarden kept the burden of maintaining local roads until county councils removed it in 1888. He also kept charge of the parish bull.

*See Abbey Dore, page 291. See also Datchworth, page 171

# SMISBY
## DERBYSHIRE
*A room of one's own*

To nineteenth-century visitors, Smisby was steeped in romance. Everyone had read *Ivanhoe*, written by Sir Walter Scott in 1819 after he stayed with Sir George Beaumont at Coleorton. Much of it is set around Ashby-de-la-Zouch, and one of the most memorable scenes takes place on the Tournament Field at Smisby. Scott imagined the Norman aristocracy and Saxon gentry watching Sir Wilfred of Ivanhoe slog it out with all comers. Villagers used to take advantage of their literary fame by displaying swords that were supposed to have been found on the field.

With their heads full of this stirring tale, the Victorians would not have been interested in anything as humble, even unseemly, as the village lock-up, yet it seems a remarkable structure to the twenty-first century. Lock-ups are a fairly common survival of the years before permanent police forces, when individual parishes had to keep order for themselves, and employed their own constables to do so. Drunks would be put in the lock-up overnight; worse offenders had to languish there until taken to court.

The architectural form of the lock-up was, of course, unregulated, leaving room for a certain amount of caprice. Some lock-ups are unadorned cells (an unusually robust example, built out of roughly shaped stone, exists at Nunney in Somerset, completed in 1824); others wooden boxes (Barley in Hertfordshire's is formed of open slats). Deeping St James in Lincolnshire has one made out of the base of a market cross. Shenley in Hertfordshire boasts a dome of rum-baba form; a rather more sophisticated dome, capped by a cupola, can be found at Alton in Staffordshire. The Smisby lock-up is one of a number graced by a tall pyramidal roof, utility being combined with ornament. Built of brick on an octagonal plan, it has a string course of stone, and a stone ball sits on the top. A heavy door shut the malefactor into a cool, lightless chamber – not a good place for an arachnophobe. Lock-up spotters will want to compare the similar examples at Ticknall in Derbyshire and Breedon on the Hill in Leicestershire.

The variety of forms taken by village lock-ups reflects the idiosyncrasies of the system; policing, as organised by parishes, was a hit-and-miss affair, adequate for rounding stray livestock up into the village pound, coming down hard on poachers, discouraging misbehaviour and swearing, but hopeless as an answer to all but the most incompetently committed crimes. Malefactors who fled to other parts of the country generally got away. After the County Police Act of 1839, county police forces under chief constables started to replace the parish constable system. The Derbyshire Constabulary was formed in 1857, although, with changing attitudes towards punishment, the Smisby lock-up had probably closed its door, prisonerless, before then.

# SNOWSHILL
## GLOUCESTERSHIRE
*The fantastic Mr Wade*

Charles Wade's first contact with Snowshill Manor came in a field canteen during the First World War, when he saw it advertised in *Country Life*. Returning home, he found that it was still for sale and bought it. Externally, the stone-built, Queen Anne house with its deep roof, the facade being a slightly lopsided composition of old-fashioned mullion and Georgian sash windows, became, like the village of which it is part, an example of loving conservation. But the interior would be filled not only with Wade's many collections, but with his spirit. Enter Snowshill, and you enter a world of contrast and surprise. There are little objects in tight spaces, such as the sides of a doorway; large cabinets in eighteenth-century panelled rooms; bicycles in the attic; the side of a coach on a corridor, and Japanese warriors on guard in what should be a bedroom. It sounds peculiar. It is – and so was Charles Wade.

He must have made an extraordinary impression on the village. 'A face like a death mask of Henry Irving topped with a thick fuzz of grey-black hair, cut like a sponge,' was how Lutyens\*, quite accurately, described Wade to his wife. His costume of moleskin waistcoat, brown knee breeches and buckled shoes never varied. Visitors would be startled as he materialised eerily from behind secret doors or burst out suddenly, his locks streaming, from a concealed corner of the fireplace. Some people called him the Necromancer of Snowshill.

But he was also an architect and an artist, who had worked, chiefly as an illustrator, for Parker and Unwin, then designing Hampstead Garden Suburb. With an income from a sugar plantation on St Kitts, Wade did not have to market his skills; instead he used them to create a private universe, a refuge from an uncongenial reality. (He was not the only member of his generation to react against the times. In 1933, John Betjeman wrote to him: 'I haven't an income big enough to let me live in the past, I loathe the present and the future fills me with fear. I hope you reply before I have committed suicide.')

One of the few things Wade had enjoyed during schooldays in Eastbourne was the chance to learn carpentry, which became all-absorbing. It gave him an Arts and Crafts perspective, which made the Cotswolds, where William Morris had lived at Kelmscott†, an obvious destination. Like many manor houses, Snowshill had sunk to being a farmhouse when Wade acquired it. He supervised a team of twenty-eight workmen from all over Gloucestershire to repair it. So good was their work that Lutyens pronounced the house to be 'untouched': the highest praise.

No one captured the experience of entering Snowshill better than Wade's friend R. A. Kayll. 'The house was dark and scented. The pungent smell of wood smoke and the sharp tang of turpentine and oil lamps impinged on the nose.' This was not a house with carpets, much less the expected carpet beaters of the period. Photographs, fountain pens, coal – all were too new-fangled to be entertained. Instead, visitors encountered the weird, the old-fashioned and the finely wrought, in wonderful juxtaposition: 'A painted wooden cat, a leather porter's chair, a trundle chair on wheels like a trolley with drawer beneath, spits, bundles of old umbrellas racked overhead, glass apothecaries' jars reflecting sharp points of light from polished steel and brass in this room of Rembrandt half tone and shadow different from anything I had experienced.'

Wade loved English pieces but he also loved colour. It led him first to explore the reds, golds and blues of Spanish and Italian furniture; from these he turned to Persia and eventually to the Far East, particularly Japan. Religious statues also attracted him because of the gilding. The result may seem promiscuous or magpie, but the *tout ensemble* remains as English as the village in which the Manor is set. Since the days of the Grand Tour, eclecticism in collecting and decoration has been second nature. Admittedly, Wade took it to an extreme (which seems all the more remarkable given the Arts and Crafts desire to reconnect with local traditions). But then he was a type to whom the word eccentric can be justly applied. Nowhere better does eccentricity flourish than in a village.

*See Mells, page 55; Thursley, page 145. †See Bibury, page 300

# STRETTON
RUTLAND                                    *Location, location, location*

The pub in Stretton is called the Jackson Stops Inn, after the estate agent. The thatched building used to be a farmhouse; in 1955 it was put on the market, and stuck there so long that it seemed the Jackson-Stops & Staff signboard would never come down. When the new owner turned the house into a pub, he translated the board into an inn sign. It is thought to be the only pub in the country named after an estate agent. And in a way that is strange, because estate agents have done more to change the character of villages than anyone.

For most of the history of villages, life was static; before the drift to the towns that accompanied industrialisation, the same names recur in parish registers generation after generation. The girls moved away when they took husbands, but perhaps no further than the next village. When property changed hands it was generally because of death or marriage, and it probably made little difference to most of the villagers, because they did not own their homes.

They may not have been watertight structures at the best of times. Victorian reformers were scandalised by the state of the cottages occupied by the rural poor, which were just as bad, in their way, as the slums of the towns. Providing houses for the village was a matter of philanthropy as much as business; it made a poor return on capital. For much of the twentieth century, landowners with villages were advised to sell them, because the cost of upkeep exceeded the rents. The 1977 Rent Act, which gave tenants the right to stay almost indefinitely, was regarded with horror.

Then something happened. People stopped wanting to rent and turned to mortgages instead. Mortgages had been around before the Second World War, particularly to help the purchase of the speculative semi-detached houses that were marching down the Acacia Avenues of the suburbs. But it was only after 1945 that Britain's building societies and life assurance companies were able to offer products that suited all homeowners. The austerity years were a time of saving, not least because there was little enough to spend money on. This swelled building society funds. In 1969, the Labour government allowed mortgage interest to be set against income tax. When inflation took off, bricks and mortar (or stone and thatch) seemed the only investment by which ordinary people could build up capital. Besides, much of the protection tenants had come to enjoy was removed in the 1980s.

Most established firms of estate agents began as land agents, managing farmland, or auctioneers. Jackson-Stops & Staff had its origins in the livestock auctions held by Herbert Jackson-Stops at Towcester from 1908. By the end of the century, such had been the transformation of the property market that it had thirty-nine offices all over the country. Village populations, which had once been settled, became increasingly transitory. Pretty houses in charming locations were a more-or-less finite (some would say diminishing) resource; prices spiralled, and young people on local incomes lost out when cottages were sold to well-heeled commuters and weekenders who could afford to pay more*.

On the upside, domestic property has never been in better condition than it is now. Owners have an incentive to keep it in good repair. Estate agents have become regarded as one of the least trustworthy professions. But they are also one of the most vulnerable: Jackson-Stops & Staff became a 'democratic consortium' after a management buyout during the early 1990s. Still, the property carousel goes round and round. At the time of writing, the Jackson Stops Inn has just been sold.

*See Helford, page 43; Pooley Bridge, page 394

# TISSINGTON

DERBYSHIRE *The decorously pagan tradition of well-dressing*

There are six wells in Tissington: Hall Well (near Tissington Hall), Hands Well (named after an inhabitant called Hand), Yew Tree Well, Children's Well, Town Well and (from its shape, nothing else) Coffin Well. On Ascension Day, each April, they are decorated or 'dressed' with large flower pictures. Well-dressing is practised by other villages in Derbyshire and some in Staffordshire, in fact the custom seems to be increasing. In Tissington, it has been related to the Black Death, which the village escaped. In 1350, the wells were dressed as a thanks offering for the purity of the water, whose virtue was thought to have preserved the villagers (although we may now think that the dreadful state of the roads, combined with Tissington's inaccessible location, had more to do with it).

In the twentieth century, dressing involved the construction of a large frame, filled with clay mixed with salt water (so that it will not dry out easily). Into this are pressed bluebells, young larch buds, grains of rice, mosses and lichens, the different colours composing to form a brightly coloured scene, surrounded by a decorative border and topped by a religious text.

It is likely that the origins of well-dressing pre-date 1350. There are springs and wells throughout Europe that have been venerated since pagan times. They may heal diseases (the British Isles has nearly four hundred that are supposed to cure eye problems, in some cases, perhaps, because the water contains vitamin A), or have magic properties – most obviously to grant wishes, if an offering is made to the resident nymph or divinity in the form of a coin or (in former days) pin. Quasi-pagan celebrations did not, on the whole, appeal to the Victorians, but well-dressing was decorous and polite. The event involved hymn singing and a Christian service at each well. In 1827, William Hone observed that the Tissington ritual was 'a festivity which not only claims a high antiquity, but is one of the few country fetes which are kept up with any thing like the ancient spirit'.

# WELLOW
NOTTINGHAMSHIRE *Tallest maypole in Britain*

North Nottinghamshire is not, on the whole, a land of pretty villages. So rich was it in great country houses, however, that it became known as the Dukeries. There are not many Dukes around now. Having grown rich on the coal that lay on their estates in the nineteenth century, the noble families took wing in the twentieth; Charles Barry's palatial Clumber Park was demolished in 1938, causing Pevsner to observe that the twentieth century 'has few wealthy men with the inclination or means to go on with them'. Slag heaps and pinched mining villages were left interspersed with beautiful but houseless parks and remnants of old forest. Now the slag heaps have been flattened, and you would not know that this stretch of the country had been anything but farmland. With its russet brick walls and pantile roofs, Wellow fits comfortably into the new landscape. It has always been a country village, boasting the tallest maypole in Britain.

Wellow was founded by Cistercian monks. They came to Rufford Abbey in the twelfth century and, wanting seclusion, displaced the village that was already there*. (Rufford became the seat of the Savile family; half of it was pulled down in 1959.) Perhaps the monks gave the village a hand in building the church of St Swithin, the earliest parts of which belong to that time. As well as the church, the villagers built a defensive ditch and bank around their settlement – George Dyke – which can still be walked. Sherwood Forest would become famous for the outlaws who robbed the rich and gave to the poor; Wellow, however, was taking no chances.

It was in the second half of the fourteenth century that maypoles became established in Britain. Their origin is unclear. There is nothing to suggest that they were phallic, or associated with fertility rites. Were they memories of the world ash tree celebrated (as Wagner remembered) in Nordic mythology? It is an attractive idea, but unsubstantiated by evidence. As part of popular folk ceremonies, they were associated with misrule – some communities being none too particular about whose tree they took to make the pole. On the other hand, the dancing that took place around them appears to have been decorous, with couples joining hands together to form a ring. The interleaving of ribbons is a late development, not known before the eighteenth century.

Puritans frowned on maypoles. Which popular festivities did they not disapprove of? By the late nineteenth century, however, Victorian romantics had come to see them as an emblem of the old-fashioned countryside, idealised as a place of self-sufficiency and fulfilling craft work. They had not been entirely abandoned. In Gloucestershire, a Victorian clergyman found himself unable to establish a cricket club because 'the young men preferred to dance together on the village green'. But many villages had been letting their maypoles rot away since the eighteenth century. They were therefore a prime target for John Ruskin, in his campaign to revive pre-industrial traditions. Under his influence, one was raised at Whitelands College in Chelsea, a women's teacher-training college, as the centrepiece of the May pageants that were held from 1881 onwards. With help from the English Folk Dance and Song Society, the revival gathered steam.

Maypoles combine well with village greens. At Wellow, the triangular green is shared with a chapel built by the Primitive Methodists in 1847, in a harmoniously Georgian style. They cannot have been easy companions, since the Methodists inherited the Puritan suspicion of popular festivals, particularly those where strong drink and dancing were involved. But the chapel was converted to a private home in the 1980s. The maypole is still going strong.

*See Old Byland, page 431

# WEOBLEY
## HEREFORDSHIRE

*Passions of the Civil War shake a timber village*

The Throne that stands on Hereford Road in Weobley is not a chair, but a house. Charles I stayed here on 5 September 1645 – hence the name. Weobley was then a prosperous borough, entitled to send two members to Parliament since 1295. There is nothing to suggest that Weobley was highly exercised by the passions that raged during the Civil War, although it probably inclined towards Parliament, the lord of the manor – Robert Devereux, 3rd Earl of Essex – being a Parliamentarian general. Charles came as his sun was setting after the Battle of Naseby (see page 343). It was a last-ditch attempt to raise fresh support. He was in Weobley again on 19 September, but this time only passing hurriedly through to avoid being cut off.

The Throne was then the Unicorn Inn. It would not have seemed so quaint as it does now. Weobley is a wooden village, but then so was most of Charles's kingdom. Now The Throne leans at various out-of-the-perpendicular angles, bulging here and reclining there; it probably did then. The carpenters who assembled the frames of timber buildings used green oak, so that the joints locked together as the wood dried and shrank. The Throne had been standing for half a century before Charles's visit: enough time for it to have taken on the organic character that makes Weobley houses seem as though they are whispering into one another's ears.

Weobley's streets have made themselves into an essay in timber construction. The earliest were built using crucks, or naturally curved timbers, perhaps taken

*Weobley is an essay in timber architecture, some houses being supported by curved pairs of crucks, others having upper floors jettied out over the street.*

from the point at which a bough leaves the trunk or from a tree that had grown in a gorge and was naturally bent. Pairs of timbers were matched, or one tree was split to make two identical crucks; these were then joined with a cross beam to make an A shape, then hauled or walked up into position. One pair of crucks was joined to another to make a bay, and as many bays could be added as the owner required. A cottage would be only one bay.

Walls were made out of a timber grid, filled with woven laths covered by a daub of mud, horsehair and manure, limewashed to keep out the rain. It was a green way of building, if not very thermally efficient. A pair of crucks can be seen at the end of the Red Lion Hotel. By the seventeenth century, the cruck system had long been abandoned. Houses were now built like boxes, but with exuberant overhangs to the first floor. Carved and pierced bargeboards decorated the gable ends. Just outside the village, timber was used to even greater decorative effect in a beautiful farmhouse called The Ley.

But the church is a great cliff of red sandstone. Inside, a bombastic monument depicts Colonel John Birch, the Parliamentarian soldier who took the besieged city of Hereford after a brilliant ruse and, after the Restoration, bought Garnstone Castle (now demolished). He is supposed to have tried to persuade the vicar to marry him to his mistress while his first wife was still alive; on the vicar understandably refusing, he said the ceremony himself. As one of the Weobley MPs, he was 'the roughest and boldest speaker in the House', according to Bishop Burnet, but deplored factional vindictiveness. It was therefore unfortunate that the inscription on his monument, which appeared to cast aspersions on 'King Charles I of ever blessed memory' and justified 'the late iniquitous rebellion' (to quote the case made before an ecclesiastical court), should have caused such offence that Bishop Ironside of Hereford had the offending words effaced. They were restored after the Bishop's death in 1701.

# WHITEWAY COLONY
GLOUCESTERSHIRE                              *Tolstoyans keep the faith*

In 1898, Daniel Thatcher, a journalist, and Joseph Burtt, who had worked in a bank, purchased Whiteway House and forty acres of land in Gloucestershire for £450. They were Tolstoyans. Tolstoy, the author of *War and Peace*, had been a Russian aristocrat who had freed his serfs and adopted the life of a peasant. He did not form a perfect example in every respect (he had an unquenchable sexual appetite), but his principles of anarchism and self-reliance were an inspiration to men and women of the *fin de siècle*, who were in search of a new beginning.

Thatcher and Burtt were joined by seven other men, four women and two children, some of them refugees from the bigger Purleigh Colony in Essex, where disagreements had developed over who should be permitted to join. It was the beginning of a community, the Whiteway Colony, which, unlike most utopias, would survive to the present day. The first thing to do was to burn the deeds to the property, symbolising an end to individual ownership and authority. Initially, the communards lived in the existing house, but as they attracted more recruits other structures – self-built huts, with corrugated-iron roofs – appeared. Tools were made in their own forge, cloth for garments woven on their own loom. As a boy growing up in nearby Miserden, Gerald Brenan* was fascinated by glimpses of 'some wild-eyed man, all tangled hair and beard, who called up in my mind John the Baptist'.

Vegetarianism was obligatory, nudism optional. When the rector called, the door was opened by a naked woman, who invited him to step inside. 'Not till you have finished your toilet,' he replied with composure, before racing off on his tricycle. By the time Brenan was old enough to take a more informed interest, the Colony had changed. 'Although sandals lingered on, both nudism and white smocks had vanished . . . A bearded Russian known as Peter wove linen, an unbearded Oxford MA called Prothero had a bakery which sent out bread all over the country.' Prosperity, he concluded, had sapped some of the primitive rigour from the venture. However, the sexual permissiveness that had been one of the founding tenets remained. 'Those of us who were attempting to go the full length of the Tolstoyan teaching welcomed the idea of free unions as a great improvement on legal marriage,' remembered Nellie Shaw, an early Whiteway historian.

It was not easy keeping the faith. In the 1920s the Colony was infiltrated by the Home Office, anxious about revolutionary tendencies. The *Daily Express* also got in: 'no idea can be given of the indolence and sheer animalism of the Whiteway Arcadia', it blustered. Yet Whiteway endured. Now about 150 colonists live in sixty-seven different properties. Once a month, a meeting is held in the hall, purchased in 1924 from a tuberculosis sanatorium, to decide who can be accepted into the community in the event of a property being sold (houses are individually owned but not the land on which they stand). As Joy Thacker, who has written a book about the Colony puts it, 'There were no rules at the beginning, and there are no rules today.'

*See Sapperton, page 350

# WIGMORE
## HEREFORDSHIRE

*Saxon borough becomes stronghold of the once-mighty Mortimers*

Before the Norman invasion, Wigmore was the only borough in Herefordshire. Afterwards, it was quickly snaffled by Ralph de Mortimer, and his family prospered there. Power over the Welsh Marches was effectively franchised to a number of Marcher lords, such as the Mortimers, who could do more or less anything they liked in return for subduing the Welsh. Several kings were entertained at Wigmore Castle. In Edward II's day, Roger Mortimer went one further, taking up with Queen Isabella, the She-Wolf of France, organising her husband's murder in Berkeley Castle and being created Earl of March.

Mortimer got his comeuppance from Edward III; but from its commanding position Wigmore Castle exudes a sense of the power that the family wielded. Eventually a Mortimer ended up on the throne as Edward IV. On his way to it, he won 'an obstinate, bloody, and decisive battle' nearby at Mortimer's Cross, commemorated by an eighteenth-century stone monument. But the male line of the Mortimers died out, and once the Tudors had amalgamated Wales with England, border castles lost their *raison d'être*.

From its bluff, the castle looks proudly out over a broad plain, once a glacial lake and, in the Mortimers' day, a swamp. You get an impression of the structure from the eighteenth-century engraving by Samuel Buck. But even then the walls had decayed. Now it is so spectacularly overgrown that you hardly know it is there until you march into a thicket of trees. English Heritage has decided to keep it that way, as a romantic ruin – something of a departure for its conservationists. It reasons that the silt stone from which the castle was built, although beautifully cut, has become so badly decayed that nothing short of major rebuilding would restore its character. The site is being stabilised as far as possible, but otherwise left undisturbed.

Often, villages cluster around castle walls. In this case, the former borough is quite a way off, at the bottom of the hill. You descend past dappled grey horses, glimpsing a farmyard and ancient tractors below you. Halfway down, almost hidden among yews, is St James's church, built of the same greenish stone as the castle, with the wooden porch that is a feature of Herefordshire. Founded by the Mortimers, its walls still contain substantial sections of Norman masonry, pierced by round-headed windows. It became a college around 1100, but lost out when Wigmore Abbey was founded seventy years later; it was at the latter that the Mortimers chose to be buried. The Abbey survived looting by the Welsh in 1221, but not the depredations of Henry VIII. The few remains stand in a peaceful valley about a mile from the village.

# WILDEN
## WORCESTERSHIRE                                    *Industry and Englishness*

Sensitive people are apt to wince when they see industrial estates outside small villages, and Wilden is all but overpowered by the Wilden Works. But do not think that it has been put there by some slip of the planner's elbow, which upset an ink bottle over what should have been virgin countryside. Industry has been on the site for centuries. A fuller called William Baylly built a watermill here in 1511, its wheel being turned by the fast-running river Stour. It was the first of seventeen different types of mill at Wilden. An ironmaster's forge was built in the mid seventeenth century.

The Foleys, who owned the forge, became rich and ennobled. By 1812, however, the 3rd Baron Foley had got through the money and it had to be sold. It became a wire works, then the Wilden Iron and Tin Plate Company, whose owner introduced steam-powered machinery and went bust. In 1840, an ironmaster from Stourport, George Baldwin, took over the firm, running it, together with other concerns, with the help of his many children and brothers. George Baldwin's son Alfred developed the business, changed the name to Baldwins Ltd and became the MP for the pretty town of Bewdley. It was at Bewdley that his son, Stanley, was born in 1867. Stanley followed his father's example, working as an industrialist until entering politics: he succeeded his father as Bewdley's MP on the latter's death in 1908. He became Prime Minister in 1923.

Outwardly, Baldwin comfortably occupied the tweedy image of a countryman, effortlessly fusing his own history with the deep, slow-moving rhythms of the land. 'There could have been no more typical English surroundings in which to cherish the earliest memories,' he told a Bewdley audience in 1925. 'I remember as a child looking up the river from the bridge into that mysterious and romantic land of Shropshire, so close to us, from which my people came only three generations before, and watching the smoke of the train running along the little railway through places bearing names like Wyre Forest, Cleobury Mortimer, Neen Sollars and Tenbury – names steeped in romance and redolent of the springtime of an England long ago passed, but whose heritage is our own.'

Addressing the annual dinner of the Royal Society of St George in 1924, Baldwin concluded: 'England is the country, and the country is England.' Although he had grown up in a town and the family money came from metal bashing, the town was small and the tinplate works sat amid fields. The images, sounds and smells that most evoked England were therefore rural ones.

The sounds of England, the tinkle of the hammer on the anvil in the country smithy, the corncrake on a dewy morning, the sound of the scythe against the whetstone, and the sight of a plough team coming over the brow of a hill, the sight that has been seen in England since England was a land, and may be seen in England long after the Empire has perished and every works in England has ceased to function, for centuries the one eternal sight of England.

Wild anemones, bringing home hay, wood smoke . . . these were things that, in Baldwin's words, 'strike down into the very depths of our nature'. Only six years had passed since the Armistice, and romantics such as Baldwin yearned to re-establish their connection with the peaceful country traditions that represented the natural order of things, as opposed to the aberration of the First World War. The feeling gave rise to the Council for the Protection of Rural England, founded in 1926. England was changing, but a memory of springtime remained.

# WINSTER
## DERBYSHIRE
The amenity of a market house

The main building in Winster is the market hall. Even in 1824, Winster was 'but a small town', according to Ebenezer Rhodes in *Peak Scenery*, since then it has declined into a village. The market hall, however, holds a memory of greater days, having been built in two bouts out of stone and brick – perhaps to replace an earlier wooden structure – from the fifteenth to the seventeenth century. The early stage is represented by the ground floor, with pointed arches opening onto the trading space; above this is a later chamber, made of brick with mullion windows.

The prosperity of the settlement was founded on lead mining. The miners lived in the 'gennels', or narrow alleyways between the East and West Banks of the town. So many mines were sunk in the area that, according to Rhodes, the springs were drained, leaving as the only source of water a well that was a mile out of town. Although Derbyshire can be wild and craggy, its inhabitants, even in the remotest places, loved music. The people of Winster were therefore forced to think hard when a local gentleman offered (in Rhodes's account) to finance either a water supply, brought by pipe from the well, or an organ for the church. They chose the organ. They did, however, allow themselves one other comfort: their markets could be held under cover.

The right to hold markets and fairs was highly prized during the Middle Ages. Between 1198 and 1483 some two thousand grants were made to towns and lords of the manor; the latter liked them because they could charge the stallholders tolls, as well as selling their own produce. Days were appointed so as not to clash with neighbouring markets. Often they were held around crosses. Preaching crosses stood in churchyards and served as a natural focus for commercial as well as religious activity.

In time, marketplaces acquired their own crosses, the more elaborate of which could be decorated with sculpture. They often took the form of pillars, with little cross-like about them at all, but the symbolism was important – markets were highly regulated, with fines imposed for trading out of hours, and the cross signalled the solemnity of the compacts being made. Crosses might be raised up and surrounded by steps, which were useful places to sit. The one at Cheddar in Somerset is enclosed by an arcade that provided shelter to market traders gathered beneath it. Elsewhere, the combination of cross and roof, perhaps held up on wooden pillars, as at Harrold in Bedfordshire (see page 178) and Abbots Bromley in Staffordshire (both hexagonal), was known as a butter cross: the shade would have been valuable to dairymen and -women selling butter and cheese on hot days.

Winster went one better. The market was held at street level, with people coming and going through the broad openings. Above it was a good-sized room, which could be used for guild meetings, collecting tolls or as a town hall. Here, the market cross or market house became the fulcrum of the community. Elsewhere it became a place of punishment as well as trade: malefactors were flogged or even hanged by the market cross at Wymondham in Norfolk.

# NORTH-WEST ENGLAND

THE MOUNTAINS of the Lake District were heaved out of the earth around five hundred million years ago. They are far older than the Alps. It is not, however, their age that has made them such an iconic landscape, but the interaction that they have had with man. This also began a long time ago: it is thought that Neolithic people were chipping tuffs, pieces of extremely hard volcanic rock, and polishing them to make axes from 4000BC. One use to which the axes were put was the chopping down of trees. Once the fells were cleared, fields were created: some of the drystone walls forming their boundaries may be prehistoric.

In *The Prelude*, William Wordsworth could attribute his moral education to 'the winds and sounding cataracts' that he experienced amid the lakes and mountains, but, growing up at Cockermouth in the late eighteenth century, he did not encounter Nature as a wilderness. Cumberland and Westmorland supported a breed of independent farmers known as statesmen; their old-fashioned, dove-grey houses, built of stone often split from the rock, were in perfect harmony with their surroundings. Their presence can still be felt at Troutbeck (see page 399). While the Lake District is the most iconic landscape of the North-West, it is not the only one. Downham, lovingly preserved by the estate that owns it, lies in the lush pastures of the Ribble Valley in Lancashire (see page 387). A feeder of the Ribble, the river Loud, powered the busy mills of Chipping (see page 380). Villagers could use the local limestone to build their houses. The red sandstone of the Triassic period can be seen in Hale church, next to Liverpool's John Lennon Airport, where a giant is buried (see page 389), as well as in Cumbria's beautiful Eden Valley.

Jutting like a pugnacious chin over the Cheshire plain, Alderley Edge (see page 375) glitters with an iridescence of many colours – blues and greens, pinks and yellows; minerals have been mined here for centuries. Zigzag up into the Pennines to the east side of Cumbria and you will find a different kind of mining landscape: the lonely moorland amid which Nenthead (see page 393) was built to exploit the lead seams.

In Border country, villages such as Milburn in Cumbria were built for defence (see page 392). Edward I died at Burgh by Sands (see page 377), still shaking his fist at the Scots. It was not the last that the folk living south of the Solway would know of them: they built churches that doubled as strongholds in which they could shelter from the Scottish raids. At Burgh by Sands, the stone came from a fort on Hadrian's Wall.

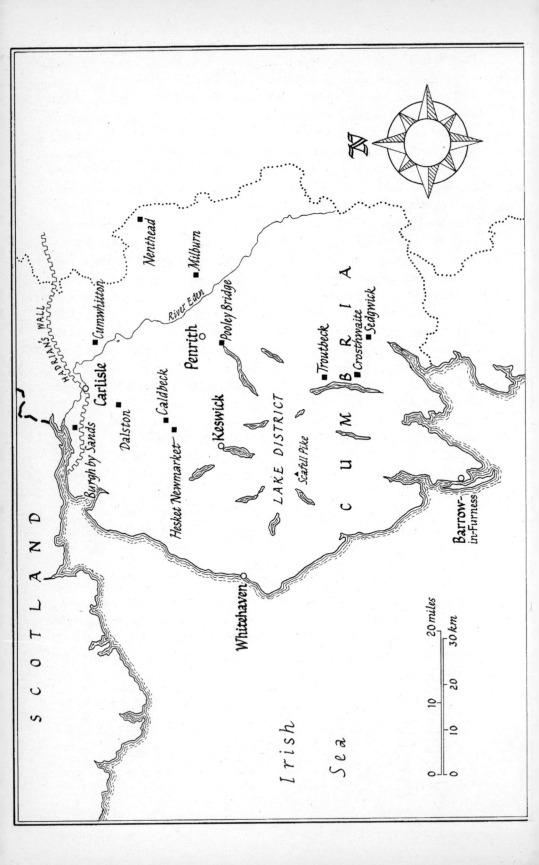

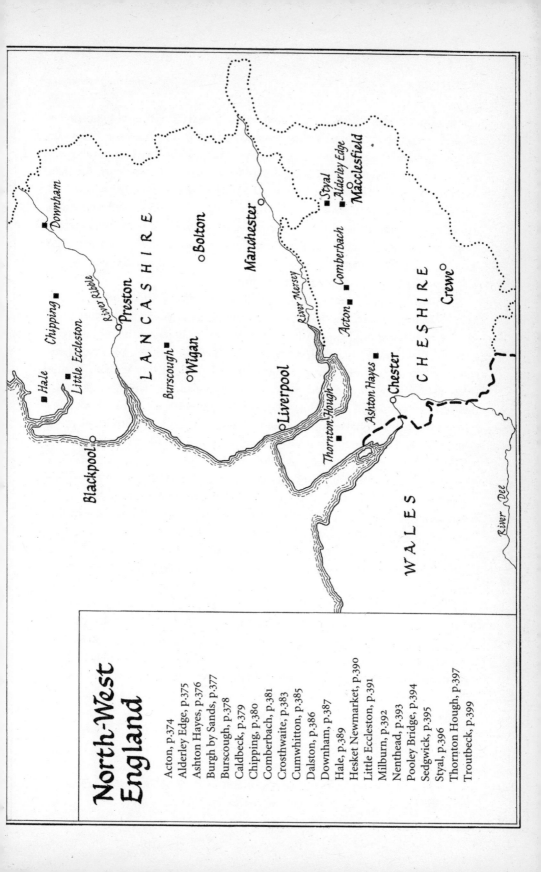

# North-West England

Blackpool

Downham

Hale

Chipping

Little Eccleston

River Ribble

Preston

L A N C A S H I R E

Burscough

Wigan

Bolton

Manchester

River Mersey

Liverpool

Thornton Hough

Ashton Hayes

Chester

Acton

Comberbach

C H E S H I R E

Styal

Alderley Edge

Macclesfield

Crewe

W A L E S

River Dee

Charles Darwin was interested in gooseberries. 'The fruit of the wild gooseberry is said to weigh about a quarter of an ounce or 5 dwts, that is, 120 grains,' he wrote in *The Variation of Animals and Plants under Domestication* (1868); 'about the year 1786 gooseberries were exhibited weighing 10 dwts, so the weight was more than doubled'. More was to come. In 1852, the 'London' variety of gooseberry achieved the 'astonishing' weight of more than 37 dwts, or 896 grains. Improved cultivation played a part in the achievement, but so did selective breeding by growers such as J. Banks of Acton, Cheshire, who raised the 'London' and introduced it in 1831. The 'London' maintained its position as champion berry for thirty-six seasons and won a total of 333 prizes. Why did anyone bother?

The first gooseberries arrived in Britain during the Middle Ages, when they were among the trees and bushes that Edward I planted in the Tower of London. They were red gooseberries; the pale variety arrived from Flanders at the beginning of Henry VIII's reign. Writing in *The Names of Herbes* (1548), when a gooseberry was still a novelty for most people, the Tudor physician and divine William Turner wrote that it 'groweth onely that I have sene in England, in gardines', although the Germans cultivated it in fields. However, the piquant fruit had become sufficiently common by Shakespeare's time for Falstaff to declare that virtues other than valour and quickness of wit 'are not worth a gooseberry'.

The *Oxford English Dictionary* sees nothing to indicate that the plant did not have some association with geese, although it cannot explain why. One possibility is that it was used in a sauce for goose; an alternative theory suggests that it is a corruption of gorse-berry (the plant being supposed to look like a gorse bush). Like other plants, it has gone by different names in different parts of the country. If J. Banks had been an old-fashioned man, he might have called it by the Cheshire word of feaberry (abbreviated to feabe, pronounced 'fape'). In Scotland gooseberries are grozers or grozets, from *groseilles*.

In *The Practical Fruit Gardener* (1724), Stephen Switzer praised the gooseberry – apparently a 'Fruit below the Regard of the Curious' – as the first fruit that you can pick: 'It leads us to the Feast' that summer will produce. As the century wore on, it became something of a cult. Gooseberry clubs were established, the first in 1740. They grew varieties mostly identified by colour ('Hairy Red', 'Great Amber', 'Great Oval Yellow', 'Large White Crystals' and 'Champagne'), with a couple of googlies such as 'Hairy Globe', 'Great Moghul' and the alarmingly named 'Large Ironmonger'. Competition between growers – and showers – was fierce. From 1786, the Gooseberry Growers' Register, published in Manchester, listed prize winners, varieties and the individual weights of champion berries. By the mid nineteenth century they were being produced as big as hen's eggs, by drastically pruning the bushes and reducing the number of fruit grown on each to two or three.

In the twentieth century, gooseberries went out of fashion. Consumption fell, and not just of the fruit: in a sadly diminished market for jams of all kinds, gooseberry jam has passed out of general knowledge. In an episode of *Dad's Army*, made in the 1970s, Captain Mainwaring, hospitalised with an ingrowing toenail, eats one of the grapes he has been brought by Corporal Jones. They are not really grapes, Jones announces as Mainwaring pops one into his mouth, but gooseberries that have been shaved. The fruit had come to seem so sour that it was funny. Tastes had adapted to the citrus and other Mediterranean fruits being flown in by plane. The gooseberry's place became once again 'gardines'. But competitive gooseberry growing continues, and Banks's jumbo 'London' has been exceeded. No other variety of gooseberry, however, ever had such a good run.

# ALDERLEY EDGE
CHESHIRE                    *Geological phenomenon, beloved of footballers and WAGs*

Geology shaped Alderley Edge. Between 190 and 230 million years ago, the area was a great sandy plain, dry for most of the time, occasionally inundated. It was hot; this was before the continents had separated and what is now Britain sat nearer the equator. Sand, pebbles and mud lay on top of one another, like stripes in a Neapolitan ice-cream. Over time, they were crushed together to make rock, through which water percolated – water that was saturated with minerals. The continents moved apart, and the beds of rock heaved themselves upwards, until the top of them formed an abrupt ridge from which the land falls away with dizzying suddenness, overlooking the Cheshire plain. Where the rock was exposed, it glinted with a peacock's tail of iridescent colours, the surface expression of the minerals inside. Among the liveries of everyday metals, such as copper, iron and lead, there is the esoteric sparkle of cobalt, malachite and azurite.

Stone Age people seem to have settled here, to judge from the tools left behind. Lead may have been worked on the Edge from the Neolithic period, copper from the Bronze Age. The Romans, who knew how to exploit the earth, are unlikely to have missed the promise of the coloured rocks: Roman coins have been found in the Engine Vein Mine. In recorded history, copper and lead-silver mines first emerge towards the end of the seventeenth century. The first ventures were not highly successful, but their legacy is the sixty or so trial boreholes that pit the surface. By the 1860s, however, lead, cobalt, copper and iron were all being extracted. At its peak, the Alderley Edge Mining Company was mining up to fifteen thousand tons of copper a year. The company folded in 1878; mining continued fitfully for the next forty years, but ceased altogether in 1919.

By then, another consequence of the Edge's geology was being recognised. With the coming of the railway in the 1830s, the ridge seemed a choice place to build houses. Manchester businessmen were encouraged with the offer of free travel. The village of Alderley Edge was established, accompanied by villas. 'The higher up the Hill, the richer the people', a local saying went, 'and the slower they are to pay their bills.' The Edge's popularity with the Manchester well-to-do was such that Lord Stanley threw his grounds open for them to enjoy. Rumour had it that the Stanley ladies were less happy with the railway's proposal that special excursions should be run to different parts of Alderley Park. But change was afoot. In 1938 the Stanleys sold their 4,600 acres, and while the Misses Dorothy and Margaret Pilkington were able to purchase a block of woodland, which they gave to the National Trust, the rest went as building plots. Thus the ground was prepared for Alderley Edge to become a prime residential enclave of the Manchester elite, business people, Coronation Street actors and footballers. Perhaps the dreams of some of them are visited by the Wizard of the Edge. His legend, first recorded in 1805, reveals that a cavern within the Edge contains a sleeping army: when England is in danger, its warriors will awake. In time for the next World Cup, perhaps?

# ASHTON HAYES
## CHESHIRE                      *The first carbon-neutral village in Britain?*

Ashton Hayes is a typical Cheshire village: mulberry brick cottages; tall-steepled Victorian Gothic church with village hall en suite. In January 2006, its thousand-odd inhabitants decided to make it a beacon of environmentally responsible living. They have set themselves the task of becoming the first carbon-neutral village in Britain. According to their website, www.goingcarbonneutral.co.uk, 'We want our children and future generations to know that we tried to do our bit to stem global warming and encourage other communities to follow suit.' Their efforts bore fruit even more rapidly than they expected: in the first year, they succeeded in reducing their carbon use by twenty per cent.

A few enthusiasts started the project, calling a meeting in the village school about climate change. To their delight, three-quarters of the adult population came along. Together, the villagers set themselves an objective – zero carbon emissions – which the parish council duly endorsed. This has made them intensely interesting to environmental campaigners keen to demonstrate what communities can do for and by themselves. Stories about Ashton Hayes have run in the national press, and the village effort has been cited at international conferences.

Its success, however, is its lack of pretension. The school has been equipped with a solar panel to heat the water used to wash classroom floors; this has been supplemented by a wind turbine fitted to the roof. At home, people have changed to low-energy light bulbs and taken other small measures. Alison Ambrose, a midwife with three sons, told *The Observer*: 'I have switched to a power supplier that takes some from green renewables, got myself a compost bin, stopped using the tumble drier and scream at the children to turn the lights off . . . I'm not an angel about it, I do it when I remember.'

Added together, these small measures can amount to something big. Village conversations now crackle with words such as recycling and carbon footprint. Cheshire County Council has built a new footpath so that residents can walk to the station. In 2007 the Department for Environment, Food, and Rural Affairs gave Ashton Hayes a £26,500 grant to publicise its ambition. Roy Alexander, RSK Professor of Environmental Sustainability at the University of Chester, is establishing a green energy micro grid, whereby energy from bio-fuels or woodchips can be exchanged locally, with the surplus being sold to the National Grid.

It has had other benefits. More people have become involved with village life. As resident Kate Harrison described to *The Guardian*: 'I have conversations with people I used to know only by sight. Groups in the village interact a bit better: the WI, the gardening club, the church, the school. Although English village life can be thought of as competitive, I've never heard anyone bragging or being smug about what they've done. Maybe you're more likely to be a bit apologetic for things such as booking flights. We're all more aware. I hate recycling, but I can't not do it now.'

# BURGH BY SANDS
## CUMBRIA
*Edward I dies within sight of Scotland*

The church of St Michael at Burgh by Sands, in the lonely plain that borders the Solway Firth, does not have a west door; the square tower is impenetrable from the outside. Inside, the entrance to it is guarded by an iron grille, which was probably originally encased by wooden planks. It is enormously strong. Whereas blacksmiths had been elaborating the hinges of oak doors to give the wood added strength, the ironwork of the Burgh by Sands door is more like a portcullis, with huge bolts and loops for greater reinforcement.

There is a tradition of formidable church doors in this border region. Great Salkeld has a spectacular example, the oak planking being encased within a cage, each side of which is bolted to the other. With so much ironwork and carefully considered hinges, such doors would withstand burning. Church towers, built of stone several feet thick, were expected to double as fortresses in which the village could shelter from Scottish raids. The arrangement at Burgh by Sands would have pleased Edward I, Hammer of the Scots. It was in this church that his body lay after he died on Burgh Marsh in 1307.

The year before, Robert the Bruce had crowned himself King of Scotland. At sixty-eight, Edward was so ill that he could travel only by litter. Indomitably, he ordered an army to muster at Carlisle. On reaching that city, a last surge of energy enabled him to forsake the litter, which he offered up in the cathedral; he got to Kirkandrews-on-Eden on 2 July, but the final two miles to Burgh Marsh took three days. He died on the Marsh, in view of Scotland on the other side of the river Eden. A monument in the form of an obelisk was raised by the Duke of Norfolk in 1685, to be replaced by a tower, erected by Lord Lonsdale in 1803.

It is said that Edward wanted his body to be boiled in a cauldron so that his skeleton could lead his troops into Scotland after his death. If so, his wish was not granted; his body was taken back to London to be buried in the Valhalla of the English that is Westminster Abbey. His son Edward II hated soldiering; it was a further seven years before he led an army over the border and it was then defeated disastrously at Bannockburn. For Burgh by Sands and other border villages, the outcome probably made little immediate difference. The church of St Michael, whose tower would soon be fortified so impressively, stands within an older military position – the most westerly of the Roman forts on Hadrian's Wall. Whichever dynasty was on the throne of Scotland, and whatever the occupant of the English throne thought about it, this would remain frontier country until raiding ceased to be a way of life in the Borders. That did not happen until the seventeenth century.

# BURSCOUGH
## LANCASHIRE                                           *Canal life*

You can still find recordings by Emma Vickers, her bright, confident voice a little breathless at times, since she must have been an old woman when they were made. She sang and played the melodeon, sometimes to the tunes of hornpipes that accompanied clog dancing. Emma came from Burscough, or, to be exact, Burscough Bridge. Burscough itself had been an agricultural settlement, which prospered after the draining of the marshes around the freshwater lake of Martin Mere – mosses, as these old expanses of coastal dune were called. Peat cutting for fuel remained a sideline for farmers well into the twentieth century.

Burscough Bridge, now almost attached to Burscough but originally a different entity, has a different history. It owes its existence to the Leeds and Liverpool Canal, dug in the late eighteenth century. The bridge itself, on New Lane, was originally a wooden swing bridge, turned by a long wooden arm; it was replaced in the twentieth century by a less picturesque concrete structure. Emma Vickers's father worked on the canals. Bargemen had plenty of time to practice clog dancing. They were better off, in this respect, than the weavers traditionally associated with it, who perfected their steps while standing at the loom.

The canal took coal to Liverpool and brought grain to businesses such as Ainscough's Flour Mill beside the canal. From Liverpool came horse manure from the city's stables and human waste from its middens to spread on the land: a useful source of nitrogen before the importation of guano in the mid nineteenth century*. The produce that grew with its aid was then sold back to Liverpool or some of the cotton-spinning towns that were hungry to be fed. Passengers, too, came to Burscough Bridge, where they could transfer to coaches on the turnpike to Preston.

So many boatmen and their families lived in the area that almost every aspect of life was coloured by the canal: religion, dialect and clog dancing. A memory of its prosperity survives in the British Waterways Board maintenance yard, in the shape of warehouses, the wharf-master's house and a swing crane. The pub now called the Lord Nelson was originally the Packet House Hotel. One of its windows is still emblazoned with the words Cyclists Room; presumably Edwardian cyclists used the canal when touring.

The railway came in 1849, but did not leave Burscough high and dry. Burscough Junction was a stopping place on the line between Liverpool and Scotland, the only one other than Preston before Carlisle. Wagons loaded with produce from the fields would queue for a mile to get into the depot. Meanwhile, the canal held its own, still transporting nearly two and a half million tons of cargo in 1906. Emma Vickers's father must have been at work then; barge work would provide boatmen with employment for several decades to come.

Now, an infill of modern housing has almost soldered Burscough to Burscough Bridge, creating a single Burscough to allay old rivalries. Both were united in their opposition to being swallowed by nearby Ormskirk in the 1930s.

*See Wraxall, page 82

# CALDBECK
## CUMBRIA  *For the sound o' the horn caw'd me fra my bed*

One evening about 1829, John Woodcock Graves was sitting in the parlour of his home in Caldbeck, amid the hills of the Lake District, with his friend John Peel. They would be out early the next morning, in the mist, hunting. Large flakes of snow floated down. As they relived the adventures of the chase by the fireside, one of Graves's daughters came up, asking for the words to the song with which Granny was putting her brother to sleep. It was an old tune called 'Bonnie Annie'. As Graves later remembered when he was an old man, by then living in Tasmania: 'The pen and ink for hunting appointments lay on the table. The idea of writing a song to this old air forced itself upon me, and thus produced impromptu "D'ye ken John Peel, with his coat so gray". Immediately after, I sung it to poor Peel, who smiled through a stream of tears which fell down his manly cheeks, and I well remember saying to him, in a joking style, "By Jove, Peel, you'll be sung when we're both run to earth."'

Without the song nobody would remember John Peel. He led an unspectacular life. The son of a farmer and horse dealer, he was born in Caldbeck in 1776 and stayed there, farming and horse dealing, until his death in 1854. Like his father, he ran away with a local girl to Gretna Green, nine miles away. While his father had baulked at the cost of the marriage licence, Peel and his sweetheart, Mary, came home married. It was apparently a happy union, bringing them thirteen children. History does not relate what Mary thought of his hunting. We know what Peel thought of it; he thought of little else. With a small income from money that his wife had been given after the marriage, he neglected business. Neighbours reproved him for hunting on the day that his son died. He replied that the boy would have been with him if he had lived, and put the brush of the fox that was killed in his coffin.

The popular image of Peel is of a jolly man, but he does not seem to have been one. Wiry and hollow-cheeked, he always wore a long blanket of a coat, made from undyed Herdwick wool, extremely tough and still bearing traces of the salve (rancid butter, tar, sometimes a little milk) that farmers put on the skins of their sheep as extra weatherproofing. The country he hunted lay in a triangle between Carlisle, Cockermouth and Penrith. Some of it Peel got over on a shaggy, light-coloured pony called Dunny, his long legs drawn up on exceptionally short stir-rups. But the fells could be navigated only on foot. He was after the foxes that would doze daylight hours away among the bracken of the crags; he also hunted hares, but he regarded them as second best.

When he got back from hunting, Peel would drink with his Caldbeck cronies. Canon H. D. Rawnsley, one of the founders of the National Trust, remembered a local man telling him: 'As for drinking, by goy, he wad drink, wad John Peel, till he couldn't stand; and then they would just clap him on't pony and away he wad gang as reet as a fiddle.'

Caldbeck was more populous in those days. With a wool market, a weaving shed, bobbin mill, brewery, paper mill, flour mills and saw mills, it was a little town of two thousand people. After Peel's death, friends put up a singularly ugly grave-stone in Caldbeck churchyard, remarkable for being carved with hunting horns, vine leaves and hound as well as the conventional urn.

*See also Badminton, page 298; Exford, page 34*

# CHIPPING
LANCASHIRE                                                        *Mills on the river Loud*

Chipping means market or trading place – somewhere, during the Saxon period, where news and ideas, as well as goods, would have been exchanged. It reflects the development that had slowly begun to penetrate the fell country south of the Lake District, on what is now the border between Lancashire and Yorkshire, before the Norman Conquest. Subsequently, its remote location was a boon. The Scots raided in 1322, laying the place waste, but otherwise it was too far out of the way to have been anything but peaceful.

Chipping was not a place that bred great ambitions; in the mid nineteenth century its inhabitants were described by Canon Richard Parkinson as 'plain, homespun, dialectal, retiring, home-loving dwellers, having little and needing less'. But Chipping had by then had its moment of dynamism. Rushing down from Parlick Fell, filled with water from the rain that falls copiously on the hills, the river Loud was an ideal power source during the early Industrial Revolution. The village of Chipping had, at different times, no fewer than eight mills, used for spindle making, corn milling, brass founding, furniture making, nail making and cotton spinning.

The highest was Wolfen Mill, a corn mill, which gave its name to the Wolfen Mill Dairy Company; Henry Procter, a miller who came from a family recorded as making cheese since the sixteenth century, took a lease on the mill in 1718, and his descendants used it as a creamery until 1968. (The Procters still make and mature cheese on the outskirts of the village; the Ribble Valley, into which the waters of the Loud ultimately flow, is the Lancashire cheese capital of the world.)

Cotton spinning began at the Saunderrake Factory in 1824. Wharf Mill was in existence by 1844, and continued in operation until the 1960s; its breast-shot waterwheel (meaning that the water powering it is delivered at mid point, rather than above, as in an overshot wheel, or below, as in an undershot one) is still in place, next to the sandstone mill buildings. Kirk Mills was originally a cotton mill, but it was acquired by Henry James Berry, whose father, John Berry, had established a furniture-making business forty years earlier. Alas, H. J. Berry and Sons Ltd went into administration as this book was written. But a memory of Chipping's commercial, if not manufacturing, past survives in what claims, rather boldly, to be Britain's oldest continuously operational shop, created by John Brabin, a London cloth merchant, in 1668. Having been, at different times, a baker's, a grocer's, an undertaker's, a post office and a butcher's shop, it is now a gift shop and tea garden. On his death in 1683, Brabin left the money to establish a school. The building is a school no longer, but Brabin's name is still emblazoned above the door.

# COMBERBACH
## CHESHIRE
*The all-but-lost mystery of mumming*

'In striving to become a great and prosperous nation,' mused the Rev. P. H. Ditchfield from the study of his Berkshire rectory in 1891, we may 'have ceased to be a genial, contented, and happy one.' Ditchfield chronicled changing village life at the end of the nineteenth century in books such as *Old English Sports, Pastimes and Customs* and *Vanishing England*. In the ancient of days, each year would open with an extension of the Christmas holidays that lasted until Twelfth Night on 6 January. One of the traditions of this season was the arrival of the mummers, a group of male performers (it would be too much to call them actors) who travelled from one site to another, wearing ribbon-bedecked costumes that were, for some reason, put on over their ordinary clothes. Comberbach is one of the few villages in which this ancient and ritualistic form of entertainment is still practised.

Mummers plays are of various types. There may be a combat between characters; there may be a sword dance, in which one of the characters dies through having swords interlocked around his neck; there may be a love interest, where a woman (played by a man) is wooed by a clown. They all, however, share certain features. A character dies; he is brought back to life, probably by a boastful and highly implausible doctor. Scholars believe that the plays – or, perhaps better, ceremonials – have their origins in pagan fertility rites, in which the Sun or the Year dies and is resurrected with the return of Spring.

Curiously, although mumming is assumed to be of great age, the earliest written description purportedly dates from 1685 (we know it only from a manuscript copy of 1800). The performance, which took place in Dublin, included St George, St Dennis, St Patrick, some Turks, Oliver Cromwell (always a vivid figure in Ireland), a doctor, an old woman and Beelzebub, 'with a frying pan upon his shoulder and a great flail in his hand threshing about him on friends and foes'. Clearly it was something of a gallimaufry.

In *The English Mummers and their Plays* (1969), Alan Brody speculates that pre-Christian memories have become jumbled over the centuries, and overlaid with extraneous material. Mummers plays do not take place in theatres, but in agreed places that may be indoors or out. The plays therefore start with an invocation to clear a circle, in which the play can proceed. Thereafter the action continues – or should do, if authentic – with an absence of dramatic zest.

Why? Thomas Hardy, who introduced the Egdon mummers into *The Return of the Native*, put his finger on it. 'A traditional pastime is to be distinguished from a mere revival in no more striking feature than in this, that while in the revival all is excitement and fervour, the survival is carried on with a stolidity and absence of stir which sets one wondering why a thing that is done so perfunctorily should be kept up at all.'

The Comberbach Swilltub Mummers, whose motto is Never Knowingly Over-Rehearsed, do their best to conform to Hardy's definition (the name Swilltub comes from an old epithet attached to villagers, probably because of the number of pigs that used to be kept).

After the Second World War, the mumming tradition died out, even in Comberbach. But there was a resurrection; the group was re-formed in 1985 by a band that included some of the sons of the last mummers, as well as one man who had appeared with them.

They perform the village's Soulcake Play, a popular form of the genre in traditional Cheshire, which faded out in the twentieth century. The action centres on a battle between King George and the Black Prince, the latter being killed and brought back to life by a Quack Doctor. (Fortunately the text was collected by Arnold Boyd and published in his book *A Country Parish* in 1951.) It is not, however, performed at New Year, but around All Souls' Day (2 November), perhaps originally as a means of raising money for farmhands, to see them through the winter. In former times the soulcakers would be rewarded for their performance with soul cakes, a kind of biscuit 'once tasted, never forgotten', as one of the mummers describes it. But now they give them out to the audience instead.

# CROSTHWAITE
## CUMBRIA
*Heart of damson country*

The damsons of the Lyth Valley in Westmorland were so famous that Lord Haw-Haw, the Nazi propagandist, mentioned them in one of his Germany Calling broadcasts during the Second World War. That was the era when chara-bancs of visitors and crocodiles of hikers would come during mid April to see the blossom, which turned the fellsides white. Lorries would come from jam makers around the country to carry away hundreds of tons of fruit at the end of summer. But as the twentieth century wore on, the damson – a small, inkily dark-skinned plum, with (unsweetened) a sour but intense flavour – fell out of fashion. It cost too much to pick the fruit, and they were left to rot on the trees. Orchards were left unpruned.

*Damson blossom once attracted charabancs to Crosthwaite in the Lyth Valley.*

In 1996, a rearguard action was mounted by Peter Cartmell, scion of a local landowning family, who remembered the sea of blossom that he had seen as a boy. He wrote to *The Westmorland Gazette*, asking whether anyone would join him in a campaign to revive the orchards. The Crosthwaite village hall was booked in the expectation that a few people would turn up; in the event, it was packed, one grower even reciting a poem that he had written. The Westmorland Damson Association was born.

Damsons are not, strictly speaking, native to Britain. Their exotic origin is reflected in their name: they came from the countryside around Damascus. They may have been popularised by the crusades, but were known in Britain before that. From the number that grow around Roman camps, it has been suggested that the Romans introduced them. Damson stones have been excavated from the Viking settlement at York. The Victorians ate damsons in many forms – damson fool, compote, vol-au-vent and soufflé; venison with damsons, grouse with damson gin gravy, and damson cheese, a fruit paste similar to the *membrillo* that the Spanish make out of quince. These delicacies are all described in Victoria Barratt's *A Taste of Damsons* (1997), published by the Westmorland Damson Association. She herself sells damson gin from Cowmire Hall, a seventeenth-century house incorporating a pele tower* at Crosthwaite.

Valerie and John Harrison used to run Crosthwaite's village shop and post office, until they retired in 2005. In 1999, Valerie published a little book of walks called *Damson Country* – it is now out of print, but the community website www. crosthwaiteandlyth.co.uk has put the whole of it online. Change has not been wholly arrested: walks can no longer start from the village shop, because it has become the Old Post Office. But this is an area that has clung to many of the old ways. Walk eleven leaves from the church of St Anthony, Cartmel Fell, a simple embodiment of plain faith that seems hardly to have been touched since it was built in 1504. The whole of the interior lurches downhill towards the altar, between walls that have long given up the effort to stand straight. Behind the three-decker pulpit, dated 1698, are ancient family box pews, and the Ten Commandments have been inscribed beneath paintings of bare-breasted female torsos with wings, either angels or griffins. Damsons must have seemed one of God's blessings.

The poet Robert Southey is buried in Crosthwaite – but not this one. The other village lies outside Keswick, where Southey lived for forty years at Greta Hall, dying in 1843. His monument in St Kentigern's church – 'none perhaps in any part of the kingdom . . . forms a finer object from the surrounding country,' he wrote – has an epitaph by Wordsworth.

*See Burgh by Sands, page 377. See also Ilmington, page 330

# CUMWHITTON
## CUMBRIA
*At home with the Vikings*

In 2004, Peter Adams was metal detecting along a piece of footpath outside the village of Cumwhitton near Carlisle. As he was about to go home, he discovered a brooch; he thought it was Victorian, but the Kendal Metal Detecting Club looked at a book. It was Viking. Told that such brooches often come in pairs, he went back and found another one. Oxford Archaeology North excavated the site and found a Viking burial ground. At the end of the 1990s, the only known Viking cremation cemetery – fifty-nine mounds containing evidence of funeral pyres – was excavated at Heath Wood at Ingleby, Derbyshire: it has tentatively been identified as a burial place for soldiers from one of the Viking Great Armies of the 870s. The Cumwhitton find, dated to the early tenth century, is the only known example of a Viking cemetery where bodies were interred.

The Viking invasions of the eighth, ninth and tenth centuries had a lasting impact on British culture, as can be seen from the hundreds of place names of Viking origin – notably ending in 'thorpe' or 'by' – along the eastern half of England, from East Anglia to Northumberland. The first longship appeared on the Isle of Portland around 789, its passengers murdering the King of Wessex's representative, who had bustled down to the beach to meet them.

During the next century, Viking pirates would appear with terrifying suddenness to raid unprotected monasteries and churches, navigating the rivers, where necessary, to penetrate far inland. They used blackmail to extract protection money. From the end of the ninth century – the time of the Great Armies – the attackers not only camped over winter but some took land and stayed. These ferocious raiders, who were ruthless in stripping sacred sites of everything valuable, could also be peaceable craftsmen and traders. The eastern half of England became subject to Viking rule and law.

What relations did the Viking settlers have with the native population? The fact that so few Viking burial sites have been discovered suggests that few existed. This does not seem to equate with the extent of their cultural influence. Maybe they were happy to be buried with the local Saxons; they almost certainly took Saxon wives. Were they happy to adopt Saxon practices? In Scotland, some of the Picts – particularly those living in Orkney, Shetland and the islands of the Hebrides – found themselves swamped by Viking influence, to the extent that even their language changed.

The position in England is more ambiguous. The victories of the Great Armies could have been followed by mass settlement by Danish peasants, whom one would expect to have brought their own ways, not least as regards burial. Or the remnants of the Great Armies might have seized political control – and imposed their own place names – despite being few in number. It may be that the Great Armies numbered as many as forty thousand warriors; at the other extreme, they might have comprised just a few hundred. Initial settlement by ex-soldiers could have provided a screen behind which a second, much bigger wave of immigrants arrived from Denmark. Or perhaps the armies were big enough to furnish enough settlers from their own ranks, and these powerful individuals quickly assimilated local ways. Paradoxically, by eliminating warring local rulers they paved the way for the unification of England. One possibility is that the settlement of the Danelaw was less violent than may be imagined. It was sparsely populated, and there was little competition for land. While the Danish newcomers may not have made welcome neighbours, they took over unpromising land that had previously not been much farmed. Their influence on the English village was that they developed the countryside, creating a need for more settlements.

# DALSTON
## CUMBRIA                                        *Alas, a centre of cockfighting*

Oliver Cromwell was not all bad: he banned cockfighting. It was an unpopular activity with puritans such as Philip Stubbes: 'They flock thicke and threefold to the Cock-fightes,' he wrote in *The Anatomie of Abuses* (1583), '. . . where nothing is used but swearing, forswearing, deceipt, fraud, collusion, cozenage, skoldyng, railing, convitious talking, fighting, brawling, quarrelling, drinking, and which is worst of all robbing of one another of their goods, and that not by direct, but indirect means and attempts.'

The message, however, did not get through to Dalston near Carlisle. When cockfighting returned, together with more forgivable forms of misbehaviour, at the Restoration of Charles II (if, in that distant part of the country, it had ever gone away), it was followed by all classes of society, one venue being Rose Castle, seat of the Bishop of Carlisle. Dalston became the sport's Cumbrian epicentre, to the delight of the Herculean eighteenth-century Bishop Nicholson. Dalston Black Reds were supposed to be one of the best fighting breeds. They remain the village emblem.

Cockpits are now rare; the Arundel Arms on Dartmoor is one of few pubs where one survives. But quite a number of pubs go by names such as The Fighting Cocks. The sport united both the aristocracy – crowding into the cockpit at Whitehall established by Henry VIII and favoured by the Stuarts – and country people, who lived with animals and were, in some measure, inured to their suffering. Cock throwing, in which participants attempted to smash a pot in which a cock was immured, and 'threshing the fat hen', in which a hen was killed with a flail, were brutally popular Shrovetide amusements. Eggs were forbidden during Lent; you might as well kill off the chickens and – in a society that had enough of its own suffering to worry about without getting exercised over animals' – garner such amusement as you could while doing so. The crowd that went racing often enjoyed the spectacle of sporting cocks slashing one another to pieces with sharpened spurs; race meetings were often preceded by cockfights.

Cocks are naturally aggressive when they meet each other. This fierce natural trait has been exploited since primitive times. The Romans held cockfights, and may have brought the entertainment to Britain. It was already fashionable in the Middle Ages, first mentioned during the reign of Henry II. Whatever Cromwell thought, cockfighting was probably the most popular sport in Georgian England. However much we may now be aghast, the terminology has entered the language: the pit in a theatre derives from cockpit; pilots sit in the cockpit of a plane; someone's hackles rise like the feathers on the neck of a bird that wants to fight.

'On Monday there's a cock-match at Winchester—do you love cock-fighting, Harry?' says Viscount Castlewood to Henry Esmond in the novel by William Thackeray, '—between the gentlemen of Sussex and the gentlemen of Hampshire, at ten pound the battle, and fifty pound the odd battle to show one-and-twenty cocks.' As this passage shows, the excitement lay not so much in the contest as in the betting that went with it. It is a world away from that of Victorian decorum, but there is a hint of things to come. Cockfighting was organised on county lines. Once it had been banned in 1849 (largely because it encouraged young men to lose fortunes through gambling), the need of one geographical district to battle against another found an altogether different and more beatific expression: cricket.

*See also Loppington, page 337*

# DOWNHAM
## LANCASHIRE
*Nothing less than a work of art*

Downham is like The Knight Whose Armour Didn't Squeak, who so annoyed Sir Thomas Tom in the verse by A. A. Milne:

> The trotting horse, the trumpet's blast,
> The whistling sword, the armour's squeak,
> These, and especially the last,
> Had clattered by him all the week.
> Was it the same, or was it not?
> Something was different. But what?

Something is different in Downham. But what? The absence of a vexatious irritant; the feeling that, in an improved world, all villages would be like Downham. They could be. It is a simple proposition: this exceptionally picturesque village at the foot of Pendle Hill has no street signs or road markings.

Street signs have been with us since the Romans built their arrow-straight roads across the countryside, marking the distances to forts with milestones. The General Turnpike Act of 1773 encouraged another phase of road building. Fingerposts were erected to show the way, together with milestones marked with distances, allowing travellers to calculate the tolls. The advent of the bicycle, capable of zipping around the countryside at perilous speeds, created the demand for a different type of sign, warning of hazards, such as steep hills and sharp bends. It has been calculated that there were four thousand signs on British roads by the end of the nineteenth century.

The modern era for signage began in 1903. This was the year of the Motor Car Act, which allowed local authorities to put up their own signs. It introduced the standard of the red circle (prohibition) and the red triangle (hazard), with a white ring for speed limits. Since then it has been deemed that motorists need to be shepherded around the countryside with an ever-increasing quantity of signs: brown ones, piloted in Kent in 1986, to indicate tourist attractions; signs to indicate speed cameras*; signs to welcome you; signs to say goodbye.

Tarmac offered another canvas for the sign maker. White lines came in at the end of the First World War. Cats' eyes arrived during the 1930s. Yellow lines, to indicate parking restrictions, appeared in the 1950s. Daubed onto the road at surprising expense, single and double yellow lines proliferate in many villages, in places where, on the whole, decisions about parking could be left, without harm befalling, to individual judgement.

Downham has none of them. Other villages may have been bossily fitted out with eight, ten, a dozen speed-limit signs, such is the efficiency of local authority traffic officers, anxious to let no thoroughfare, be it only a farm track, escape. Not Downham.

How has this been achieved? Downham is an estate village; it lives under the benign despotism of the Assheton family, in the shape of Lord and Lady Clitheroe. So the skies are as clear as the landscape. The view in other villages may be obscured by telephone wires hanging in festoons; in Downham, they have been buried underground. The woodsmoke that wreaths out of chimneypots has no bristling television aerial to play with. No whey-faced satellite dishes turn towards the moon. Visit the church and you will find a clue to this phenomenon. The stained glass of the east window was designed, burnt and put together by two Assheton brothers in 1869. The family has artistic genes. It cares about beauty. Could not some of the Downham effect be enjoyed in other places?

Traffic in many villages does not move fast, and studies show that motorists are inclined to take more care on roads that do not have markings, precisely because they have to think for themselves. Country people have to use cars, given the inadequacies of public transport. But the internal combustion engine need not rule the roost.

*See Chideock, page 26. See also Littlebredy, page 51

# HALE
## LANCASHIRE

'Here lyeth the bodie of John Middleton the Childe of Hale. Nine feet three.' So reads the dark stone slab in the churchyard of Hale, a little village beside the Mersey, a couple of miles south of Liverpool's outer rim. Lancashire abounds in giants, mythological and real. In a romantic legend, the two giants Alder and Alphin were rivals for the love of a nymph who lived in the Chew Brook. Alphin of Pots and Pans Hill was victorious in love, but defeated in a contest with Alder, marked by the hurling of boulders; Alphin was killed, the nymph threw herself from a mountain top, and Alder and Alphin are now commemorated in the names of two peaks above Saddleworth Moor.

In Norman England, Eliseus de Workesley, or Worsley, who was an associate of the Conqueror, joined the First Crusade. According to the seventeenth-century antiquary John Hopkinson, he was 'a reputed giant, and in old scrips [writings] is often called "Elias Gigas"'. The Regency boxer Robert Gregson went by the name of the Lancashire Giant when he fought in London. But no mortal – not even the famously tall Jack o'Legs from the Hertfordshire village of Weston, whose supposed grave is very long – could beat Middleton's nine three. Assuming it to be true.

*John Middleton, the giant known affectionately as the Childe*
*of Hale, remembered in the village inn sign.*

That the Childe existed is beyond doubt. Born in 1578, according to his tomb-stone, he was employed as the Jacobean equivalent of a bouncer, protecting the landowner Sir Gilbert Ireland of Hales Hall. Ireland took him to court, kitted out in a suit of purple, red and gold. There he fought the King's champion and won, receiving twenty pounds from James I, which he is supposed to have lost on the way back to Lancashire. En route, he stopped at Oxford, where he so astonished the academic community that a full-length portrait was painted; now in Brasenose College, it shows him bearded with long curly hair, wearing a lace ruff and balloon-ing Jacobean breeches. The artist makes much of his hands, as well he might – they were enormous, measuring seventeen inches. In 1668 Samuel Pepys paid the butler of Brasenose two shillings to take him into the cellar to see a cast of one that was kept there. The Childe's tombstone gives his death as 1623.

In 1768, the parish clerk and schoolmaster Mr Bushell investigated Middleton's dimensions, disinterring and measuring his bones. He concluded that his thighbone was as long as the leg of 'an average sized man'. We tread in the footsteps of giants.

# HESKET NEWMARKET
## CUMBRIA
*Britain's first cooperative pub*

With his long beard, Jim Fearnley looks like Moses on Mount Sinai as he stands, in the photograph, on top of one of his favourite fells. The tablets, if he received any, must have had something to do with beer. Jim founded the Hesket Newmarket brewery in 1988, naming one of his most popular bitters after his mother-in-law, Doris, for her ninetieth birthday. The strength of the brewery's following was demonstrated in 1999. When Jim retired and closure threatened, local people got together and bought it as a cooperative. Four years later, another cooperative was formed to buy the Old Crown pub, out of which the brewery had been born. 'It's the future,' announces the man with the ponytail and green felt hat to anyone he might collar in the bar. 'If you value what you've got, you've got to take ownership.'

Jim's influence still reigns. 'Walkers are welcome,' a notice on the door reads. His photograph and that of his wife, Liz, hang beneath the alpenstocks and other climbing gear that are suspended from the bar ceiling. The village, however, has changed in recent years. It has smartened itself up. The door cases on the village street, each painted a jaunty and different colour, give it the air of Kilkenny, the Irish festival town. The gaiety speaks of second-homers and retirees, the sort of people who may have come to the village because it has a good pub but in some cases will not use it more than four times a year, according to the man in the green hat. So the hundred-plus members of the cooperative are not all village people, but admirers of a good beer and a warm pub, who may come from ten or fifty miles away. Perhaps that says something about the modern village and its appur-tenances: it is as much about idea as location.

Green hat loves the brewery, where he works part-time. The ceilings are so low that the stainless-steel vats are doubled up because there is no room to install bigger ones. A carpenter is at work creating more storage space over the stairs. Where an office might put filing cabinets, this establishment has lines of boxes containing squashed green hops. The scummy fermenting vat teases the nostrils with misleading associations of warm bread. An eighteen-pint container awaits collection by someone who likes to drink his Doris at home. 'Beer,' reads the poster over the pool table. 'Helping Ugly People Have Sex since 1862.' Only since 1862? After another pint of Doris, who cares?

*See also Kingham, page 186*

# LITTLE ECCLESTON
**LANCASHIRE** *Survival of turnpike England*

There are fewer than twenty toll bridges in the UK, the Cartford Bridge at Little Eccleston being one of them. They are oddities in a land where people have come to expect public services to be free at the point of delivery. It was not always so: the eighteenth-century turnpike roads, which put much of the country, for the first time, within visiting distance for tourists with a carriage, were financed by tolls, or the expectation of them (and built by paupers). In operation, some tolls were easily avoided. The system collapsed altogether after the railways made road transport, for a time, obsolete. Britain did not in general fund twentieth-century road improvements through tolls.

Each toll bridge is a curiosity. The wooden Whitney-on-Wye bridge outside Hay-on-Wye is not highly practical, in most people's opinion, but too charming to remove. The original entrepreneurs who built these bridges were granted Acts of Parliament to levy tolls. It would take other Acts of Parliament to rescind the right and, frankly, they are too much trouble.

Roads in the North-West had to be improved as the eighteenth century progressed, to take the traffic generated by textile mills. Canals could carry bulky cargo, but barges were too slow for energetic capitalists. The first turnpike trusts in the region having been formed in the 1720s, the scene was set for expansion: from 1750 until 1775, twenty-seven trusts were created in Lancashire alone. There were sixty-five in existence by the 1820s.

Where ferries had previously plied the rivers Mersey, Ribble and Wyre, bridges were now built, among them Shard Bridge and Cartford Bridge. While Shard Bridge crosses the mouth of the Wyre, Cartford Bridge, which dates from 1831, is geographically disadvantaged, being further upstream (besides, it appeared just as steam trains were beginning to get up puff). One cannot, however, fault the motives of the main projector, the Squire of Out Rawcliffe. A servant girl and her friend were crossing in a ferry, which had to be pulled along a rope; they lost their grip and were washed downstream. They both survived, but the Squire felt it was time for a bridge. The toll now is forty pence for a car. There is a Victorian toll house. Does everyone stop and pay? 'Ninety-nine point nine per cent of them,' the toll keeper says. But do not talk to her about cyclists.

# MILBURN
## CUMBRIA
*A village planned for defence*

The Normans were energetic builders. Milburn is an example of one of their villages, planned with the efficiency that characterised their military campaigns. Militarism and village formation were not unconnected; after William the Conqueror's Harrying of the North in 1069–70*, which squashed insurrection by devastating the towns and villages that lay between the rivers Humber and Tees, burning stocks of grain to ensure that the inhabitants starved over winter and scattering salt on the land to make it infertile, new settlements had to be founded. Further north, where the land would remain subject to raids from Scotland until the Tudor period, settlement was a necessary part of securing the territory. Milburn is the classic example of a village planned for defence, where the inhabitants could hope to beat off the marauding Scots if they were lucky and, above all, protect their cattle and sheep from rustlers.

The village was probably laid out at the time that the church of St Cuthbert was built, around 1100 (St Cuthbert was a seventh-century Anglo-Saxon monk whom the Normans honoured by rebuilding Durham Cathedral). The church is a simple structure, built, like the rest of Milburn, of pinkish local sandstone. In the centre of the village is a four-and-a-half-acre green, where animals could be corralled. Around it, on a rectangular plan, the houses are grouped, standing shoulder to shoulder with only the corners left open. They could be easily closed in time of attack; beasts could be penned here, in safety. Over the centuries the Norman dwellings were replaced, but the plan has been preserved.

Beneath the lowering Cross Fell, life in Milburn was never easy. The place is famed for the strong east wind known locally as the Helm. Warm air, having risen from the lower slopes of the Pennines, cools and then rushes down the western slopes of the Fell: another reason for Milburn to turn its back to the outside world. Wordsworth's enthusiasm for mountain scenery was almost certainly not shared by generations of Milburn villagers, their efforts in wresting a hard living from the land made more difficult by the constant fear of attack.

*See Appleton-le-Moors, page 407

# NENTHEAD

CUMBRIA                                    *The first industrial village in England*

There was only one occupation around Alston Moor in the nineteenth century: lead mining. Activity of this kind had taken place since Roman times, but development gathered pace in the seventeenth century. Some of the most prominent entrepreneurs were Quakers. Quakerism had deep roots in fell country: a crag on Firbank Fell is still known as Fox's Pulpit in memory of George Fox, who preached to a great crowd there in 1652. One of the Quaker tenets was that Friends should reject worldly oaths. As a result, fifteen thousand were imprisoned under Charles II for refusing to swear oaths of obedience, and many died in gaol. But three years after the Toleration Act of 1689, a group of them founded the London Lead Company.

According to legend, their involvement was inspired by two Quaker women, who visited Alston Moor and were distressed by the conditions of the miners. The subsequent history of the company showed that even Quakers are human: when the banker John Freame became governor in 1728, he was forced to prosecute some of his fellow assistants (directors) for malpractice during the South Sea Bubble. Nevertheless, the Company cared sufficiently for its workforce, labouring in a rugged landscape four hundred metres above sea level, to build an industrial village – the first in England – at Nenthead.

They began in 1692 with a few, toughly built houses for senior employees, such as smelters and mine officials. Schools and a Sunday School* were opened. Eventually thirty-five cottages were constructed around a market hall with clock tower, school, chapel and eventually an iron-canopied pump. Efforts were made to improve the local farms, and to provide miners with smallholdings. The Company started its own nursery for trees, and by 1840 grew all its own timber. In 1823 it built Masterman Place, or New Middleton, at Middleton-in-Teesdale, from the 'chaste' designs of the neoclassical architect Ignatius Bonomi. According to a contemporary account, the new homes were awarded to 'their most deserving workmen, thus combining general utility with the reward of personal merit'. Libraries followed, together with post offices, a water supply, baths and a public wash house. A system of ready-money shops was established to keep money lenders out of the temple.

While the Quakers here, as at Bournville in Birmingham, were no doubt exemplary employers, they were not alone in providing workers' accommodation: no organised workforce could have existed without it. Greenwich Hospital, the charitable foundation that was given the Earl of Derwentwater's estates after he was beheaded for joining the Old Pretender's rebellion, took great care over the design of the cottages it built around its smelt mill at Langley, Northumberland in the 1760s.

*See Painswick, page 344

# POOLEY BRIDGE
CUMBRIA                                        *Keeping life in the village*

The Women's Institute has been out in force in Pooley Bridge village hall. The whole of one side is occupied by trestle tables laden cheerfully with Scotch eggs, brightly filled sandwiches, rolls of smoked salmon, Cumberland sausages and Herdwick lamb kebabs. Chairs are arranged in arcs; the lectern is dusted and waiting. The very rafters seem to shake with excitement; the curtains, their subdued floral pattern bespeaking an indefinable, immemorial Englishness, tremble. The Prince of Wales is coming. He has been sighted. He is in the village shop. He is in The Sun pub, bravely downing a half pint of Cocker Hoop beer, although it is still only 11am. The hall's knees give out; it sits down. The Prince arrives. It stands up again. With a creak of polished brogues, he squares up to the lectern, launching an initiative called 'Creating a Sense of Place: a Design Guide', which is a plan for low-cost rural housing. Pooley Bridge has been chosen because Heughscar Close, if not wholly exemplifying royal ideas, certainly meets with the Prince's approval.

Like others, the Prince of Wales is concerned that the sons and daughters of village families cannot find places to live in the areas where they grew up. The problem is not entirely new; in previous centuries, answers to homelessness were proposed by almshouses, church houses and, ultimately, the hated workhouses of the Victorian period. By the end of the twentieth century the State had assumed responsibility for housing the population, although renting a council house came to be regarded, by some tenants, as second best – Margaret Thatcher's right-to-buy scheme, which enabled council tenants to buy their homes, was one of her most popular policies.

The disappearance of council housing into the private sector caused a particular problem for many villages. Country cottages had become popular; competition meant that prices rose. People working locally, for the modest pay that is standard for rural jobs, found that there was nothing they could afford, either to buy or rent. As a result, young men and women drifted away from villages, either to the verges of local towns or further afield.

Six years before the Prince's visit, youth was haemorrhaging from Pooley Bridge. But then Debbie Lowis, a newly qualified primary-school teacher, joined forces with the Eden Housing Association and set about building Heughscar Close. First, planning permission had to be obtained, in the face of opposition from holiday-home owners, who feared the scheme would strike the wrong note. It took five years to complete the scheme. When Prince Charles inspected Heughscar Close, its six houses and two flats had become home to thirteen people: builders, bar managers, occupational therapists, signalmen and marketing executives, as well as three children. They all worked in the Eden Valley, and most had family there.

Children are once again waiting for the school bus. Local pubs no longer have to rely on summer tourists; the takings on Friday and Saturday nights are up tenfold.

Without Heughscar Close, many of its residents would be living, not at Pooley Bridge, but around Carlisle. Ultimately this would have had a cost to social services, not to mention the wellbeing of the people concerned: when different generations of a family live near each other, they can give daily support. And at Heughscar Close as elsewhere, one thing leads to another. With home life secure, Debbie and her boyfriend, Gary Binks – 'a local lad from Penruddock' – got engaged. Wedding bells rang soon after HRH's visit.

# SEDGWICK
CUMBRIA                                  *The hills are alive with the sound of . . .*

One day in August 1885, three quartets of voices gathered on the tennis court of the Wakefield family home in Sedgwick, each of them singing R. J. S. Stevens's glee after Shakespeare, 'Ye Spotted Snakes'. Mary Wakefield had instigated this modest competition. Having trained as a singer, she needed an outlet for her energies, being unable to pursue a performing career due to her father's Quaker objections. She was a natural organiser, who would later become a committed suffragette.

Out of the glee party would grow the Sedgwick Festival, later held at Kendal and renamed the Westmorland Festival in 1900 (then the Mary Wakefield Choral Competition after her death in 1910). By then its growth had been 'phenomenal', according to *The Musical Times.* 'What was at first a small local competition, that concerned merely a few score of villagers, has expanded to an undertaking interesting the whole country side [sic] and drawing into its attractive fold scores of choirs of all kinds, village orchestras, and other musical organisations, most of which were brought into being by the festival scheme.' Already sixteen similar festivals had been founded on the same model. By 1914, there would be seventy-five, including the Leith Hill Festival in Surrey, coached and conducted each year by Ralph Vaughan Williams.

Singing in choirs was nothing new for the English; there had been a strong tradition of doing it since Handel wrote the *Messiah.* Miss Wakefield's competition, however, was targeted at the countryside. It used professional talent to inspire and organise, but did not seek to professionalise the participants. Instead the object was philanthropic: to stimulate music-making among a largely agricultural population, whose lives often lacked spiritual enrichment. It is no coincidence that she was a friend of John Ruskin, who wanted workers to increase the satisfaction that they derived from labour by practising crafts. From the 1870s, Ruskin was a Lake District neighbour at Coniston.

The idea that country people could enjoy more music coincided with the decline of popular musical culture of the kind recorded by Thomas Hardy (for the Mellstock Choir in *Under the Greenwood Tree* he drew on the memories of his father, grandfather and uncle; the choir that they had sung in at Stinsford ceased in 1841). The memory of folk song was being lost. The festival movement seemed another way of regenerating the native musical tradition at a time when folk songs were being written down by collectors such as Cecil Sharp. 'Miss Wakefield,' according to her obituary in the *Journal of the Folk-Song Society*, 'though not an important collector of folk songs, took an active part in making them known.'

As the movement took off, rules were introduced to keep the competitive element within bounds; only local choirs could enter. The composer and music historian Sir Hubert Parry fully understood its multifarious benefits. 'I do indeed think these Competition Festivals are splendid things – quite among the most hopeful signs of the times in this country,' he wrote in 1904. 'Showing people how really enjoyable good music is when you come to know it . . . and giving people something to work for and exercise their faculties upon.' The Mary Wakefield Westmorland Festival continues in the same spirit today.

# STYAL
## CHESHIRE
*'Happy days' . . . but the mill hands still go on strike*

In 1826, the great American bird painter and naturalist Audubon visited Styal as a guest of the Greg family. The Gregs were mill owners. Samuel Greg had established the dynasty in 1784 when, in his mid twenties, he built the towering, red-brick Quarry Bank Mill in the sylvan Bollin valley. Unlike other industrialists, he came from a prosperous background, having been educated at Harrow school and more or less adopted by his childless Manchester uncle, Robert Hyde. But he seems to have conformed to type in being a Dissenter (although his own views are uncertain, he married a Unitarian).

With its cupola and pediment, the mill also conformed to type. Belts running from the great waterwheel (rebuilt in 1817) powered 130 looms on several floors. Initially, a provision for labour was made with the building of an Apprentices' House, where children slept in dormitories; they were used to do work for which adults were insufficiently nimble, including crawling under the looms while they were still running to carry out repairs. Samuel built Quarry Bank House as a residence for himself. By 1832, the year of Samuel's retirement after being attacked by a stag, Quarry Bank was the largest coarse spinning and weaving concern in the country.

Unlike his fourth surviving son, Samuel, Greg was not a philanthropist. But he saw the need to build a village to supply workers. Samuel II introduced such improving institutions as a debating club, which Audubon visited with him and his brother, William. The visitor's recollections are quoted by Mary B. Rose in *The Gregs of Quarry Bank Mill* (1986): 'on the way we passed a chapel and a low row of cottages for the workpeople and finally reached the schoolroom, where about thirty men had assembled. The question present was "which was the more advantageous, the discovery of the compass or that of the art of printing". I listened with interest and later talked with the men on some of the wonders of my own country in which they seemed much interested.'

There was a mechanics' institute to help workers better themselves. Samuel II himself taught the drawing, geography and natural history class, which met on Saturday evenings. He established an Order of the Silver Cross to be given to girls of high moral character, 'which has been a most powerful weapon in my hand to forward my great object in refining the minds and manners of our cottage maidens'. As one mill worker remembered, 'Eh! Those were happy days.' But that did not, however, stop them going on strike in 1846, when they thought new machinery would threaten their jobs. Samuel, convinced that his efforts had been worthless, suffered a nervous breakdown and withdrew from the mill.

Wages at Quarry Bank were low, but so were the rents charged for cottages. Workers could also grow their own food. Despite the fears of the 1840s, the Gregs did provide support during downturns, such as that caused by the American Civil War, when southern cotton-exporting ports were blockaded. When the blockades caused the mill to shut down, the hands were given work on the Gregs' estate, while those under twenty-one were sent to school for free and women were organised into a sewing group. 'The Greg family did nobly in furnishing employment for all their factory employees,' recalled Thomas Tonge, a Greg worker. 'In fact, anything to tide them over hard times without humiliating their pride.'

Another bout of philanthropy came at the end of the nineteenth century, with the opening of a Village Club in opposition to the Ship Inn. Henry Philips Greg did not ban the sale of alcohol; he merely limited its consumption to two pints per person. Sales financed the club, where villagers could read, debate, attend lectures, play games and put on concerts. By now, however, it was not entertainment that the village needed, but people. Mechanisation had reduced the number of workers required at Quarry Bank; people drifted away to other jobs; the village waned. In 1939 the mill buildings and village were given to the National Trust, more for the sake of the surrounding woodland that any merit perceived in the architecture. Earlier Gregs would no doubt have been astonished to find that the mill is now a museum of the cotton industry.

# THORNTON HOUGH
CHESHIRE                                        *He couldn't stop building*

According to his obituary in *The Times*, William Lever, 1st Viscount Leverhulme, managed his employees throughout the world with 'benevolent despotism'. The words could also have been applied to relations with the village that expanded its lungs healthfully around the green outside the gates to his country house, Thornton Manor. He virtually rebuilt it. Soap manufacture was his business, philanthropy his passion, building his recreation. The profits of industry could, he believed, build a better world.

*Entrance to Lord Leverhulme's home, seen from the
village that he rebuilt at Thornton Hough.*

With his bottomless energy, reforming conscience, profound civic sense and commitment to fresh air and exercise, Leverhulme, born in 1851, was a great Victorian. His guiding lights were the Congregational church and Samuel Smiles's manual for pulling yourself up by your bootstraps, *Self-Help* (1859). He was also a marketing genius: having identified a new way of making soap, from vegetable oil rather than tallow, he called it Sunlight, wrapped it in eye-catching packaging and advertised hard.

These are modern business principles. Lever also had advanced ideas on profit-sharing, the six-hour day and decent housing, the most famous manifestation of which is the model community he built for his soap workers, Port Sunlight on Merseyside. It became famous throughout the world, an arm of the Lever Brothers company of which Leverhulme was chairman or 'chief'. By contrast, Thornton Hough was his personal domain: with the accompanying estate of six thousand acres it was financed by his own money and symbolically closed off from the curiosity of others by a gatehouse. Hair standing vertically up from his forehead, wing collar invariably set off by a black-and-white bow tie, Leverhulme could here enjoy the traditional, if not old-fashioned, trappings of wealth.

Lever and his wife, Elizabeth, bought the estate in 1891. An unstoppable collector, he needed a country house in part to store the ever-burgeoning quantity of paintings, furniture and porcelain that were being amassed. This pressure slacked only after the Lady Lever Art Gallery at Port Sunlight, begun in 1914, was opened in 1922. Yet it was typical of the man that the house had its allotted part in his larger business concern. Dinners with senior staff took place at least once a fortnight.

Staff parties were held in relays at New Year, while the summer months were filled with Sunday School picnics and garden parties. The latter helped determine the size of the garden, which in turn dictated the scale of the house, which – reflecting Leverhulme's dynamic and restless personality – grew and grew.

Within a few years of arriving, Lever had acquired most of the village of Thornton Hough. His son, William, the 2nd Viscount, remembered it as having been picturesque. But thatched roofs and whitewashed walls hid damp, dark and unhealthy interiors. 'In fact, the more picturesque the exterior of the cottage, the more impossible did the internal arrangements appear to be, and Lever saw that complete demolition was the only remedy,' William wrote in 1927. Not all the villagers were happy – even unwholesome houses can contain memories – but he persuaded them (did they have an option?) that rebuilding was necessary.

Cottages arose, each with three to five bedrooms. Then came blocks of houses, in a solid, tough, serviceable style, mixing red brick and curly gables and black-and-white walls and sandstone – not quite pretty, but, as you might say, full of Vim (another Lever Brothers brand). The land in front of the parish church was left as a green for football, cricket, tennis, bowling and quoits. Lever's old friend Jonathan Simpson designed a school, his son J. L. Simpson a new Congregational church. The old smithy that was demolished to make way for the church was replaced with one next to – as any smithy should be – a spreading chestnut tree. A Liberal Club, reflecting Lever's own politics, was provided for social events. After the First World War, 'with the altered spirit of the times', its name was changed to the Village Club: the benevolent despot felt he had to back off.

# TROUTBECK
CUMBRIA                                  *The wholesome life of the statesman*

People around Troutbeck lived to a great age, according to the village historian S. H. Scott. They were independent farmers, or statesmen – a word that may derive from 'estate', or alternatively 'stead' (as in homestead), and equates with yeomen in the South – 'men of respectable education', as Wordsworth called them, 'who daily labour on their own little properties'.

Their houses, strung out along the valley, are particularly beautiful, the sombre local stone being dove grey in its native state, or bright with whitewash. The stones were split from the rock, rather than shaped or squared, then laid almost without mortar. Tapering circular chimneys rise above roofs of green slate from Applethwaite Fell. They were often entered by a double-height porch, which gave into a 'hallan' or passage, where sacks of corn would be stored before market day and pigs hung after they had been killed. 'Between the joists, a collection of sickles was generally to be found. A shell over the door served as a receptacle for the hammers, nails, and other carpentry tools of the farmer,' Scott wrote.

They had their own terms for the features of their houses, and just as well, because some of them were peculiar to Westmorland. But the general arrangement was medieval. The family would eat and spend most of its indoor time in a room called the house place or house, a survival of the halls of the Middle Ages. But they were not indoor people, and most of their hours were spent outside, which for men meant the fell.

The fell was home to the Herdwick sheep that provided their main source of income. Until the hills were divided up with stone walls around 1840, a great meeting would take place once a year, during which the ownership of different sheep was sorted out. It was a huge social event, accompanied by athletic contests (wrestling was a popular sport) and several days of hunting. 'Cocking', or cockfighting, was practised with enthusiasm before, and probably after, it was banned*.

The almost complete absence of garden vegetables from the statesman's diet should not have been a route to longevity. Onions were the only ones regularly eaten, although nettles and other wild flowers were consumed as a relish. Not much bread was made, due to the difficulty of growing corn or oats. Rich households could afford to salt beef for winter eating. The poorer statesmen, however, ate meagrely; this, coupled with the dampness of low-lying cottages in this wet climate, made them vulnerable to 'agues'.

The cures were many and various, albeit of doubtful efficacy. 'When Jesus did see the Crosse whereon his body should be crucified, his body did shake,' began one that a statesman called Christopher Burkett wrote in his commonplace book. 'The Jew did aske him if he had an Ague. He answered and said whosoever keepeth this in mind or in writing shall never be troubled with an Ague nor a feavour soe Lord help they servants, they that put their trust in thee.' Perhaps it worked. At the beginning of the twentieth century, Westmorland had the lowest death rate in the kingdom.

*See Dalston, page 386

# NORTH-EAST ENGLAND

IT HAS been said that Yorkshire is not so much a county as a state of mind. That may reflect the fact that the mini kingdom of God's Own Country is made up of strikingly different landscapes. The Sykes family did so well out of the farmland of the East Riding that they built Sledmere (see page 437), house, village, estate and churches (sixteen of them built or restored by one generation alone during the Victorian period). Without much building stone, except for that transported by water for some of the churches, this is a land of brick, its use encouraged, during the Middle Ages, by the port of Hull's trade with the Low Countries. Perhaps it is not surprising that very large stones had special significance to prehistoric people here: the tallest monolith in the country is outside the church at Rudston (see page 434).

The Dales, by contrast, take their architectural character from the limestone, revealed on the surface of the ground in 'pavements' scoured by the action of glaciers ten thousand years ago, cracked by the icy winter rains. It was used to build bridges and stone walls, as well as cottages. Here, too, is millstone grit, a coarse, hard sandstone once used for millstones in Pennine villages and generally found near coal. Like limestone, it turns dark grey when exposed to the air, so West Yorkshire villages, however attractively presented to the world, are apt to wear a stern mask. And that is appropriate enough, for these were places that worked hard. Some grew into the factory towns amid whose thundering road system the Moravian settlement of Fulneck (see page 422) survives as a haven of calm. The orange hues of iron oxide run through the stone around Sheffield and the North York Moors; it was mined to make steel.

The Romans camped at Piercebridge in Co. Durham, and built the first bridge there (see page 433). Later, the Vikings came to the North-East, leaving a memory of their presence in place names such as Wetwang in the East Riding of Yorkshire (see page 444). Northumberland – another limestone county – is still wild and sparsely populated, the ceremony of Bale fire at Whalton perhaps being a pagan survival (see page 445). Austere orders of monks sought out remote locations, such as Blanchland (see page 412), bringing order to the landscape, at least economically; in a later century, John Wesley preached to lead miners there. Kirkharle (see page 427) produced a figure who would order landscapes around Britain according to different principles: Capability Brown.

In the nineteenth century, Bowes in Co. Durham (see page 413) was sufficiently remote for an atrocious kind of boarding school to have flourished, taking children whom their parents would prefer to forget. Thank goodness for Charles Dickens: one of them inspired Dotheboys Hall.

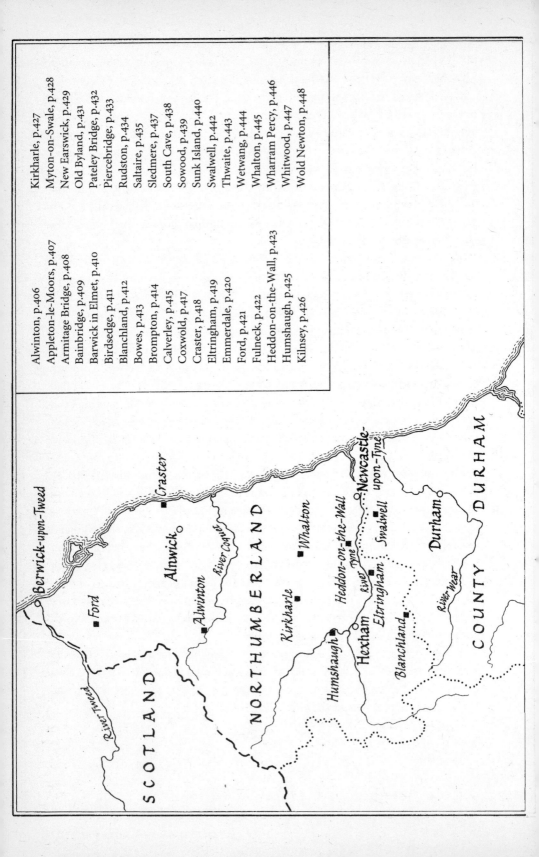

SCOTLAND

NORTHUMBERLAND

COUNTY DURHAM

River Tweed

Berwick-upon-Tweed

Ford

Craster

Alnwick

Alwinton

River Coquet

Kirkharle

Whalton

Humshaugh

Hexham

Heddon-on-the-Wall

Newcastle-upon-Tyne

Eltringham

River Tyne

Swalwell

Blanchland

Durham

River Wear

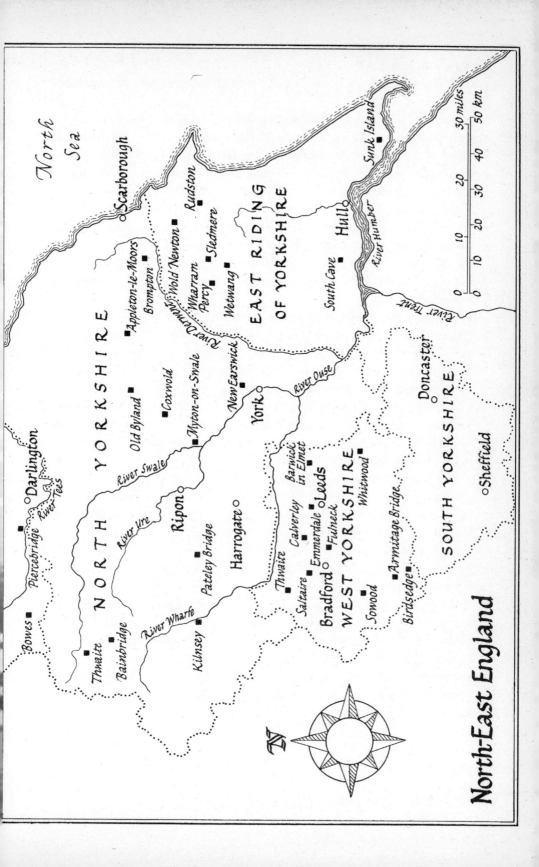

# North-East England

North Sea

Scarborough

NORTH YORKSHIRE

Darlington
River Tees
Piercebridge

Bowes

Thwaite
Bainbridge

Kilnsey
River Wharfe

Pateley Bridge

River Ure

Ripon

River Swale

Harrogate

Thwaite

Saltaire
Calverley
Bradford
Emmerdale
Fulneck
Leeds
Barwick in Elmet

Sowood
Whitwood
Armitage Bridge
Birdsedge

WEST YORKSHIRE

Sheffield

SOUTH YORKSHIRE

Doncaster

Old Byland
Coxwold
Myton-on-Swale

New Earswick

York

River Ouse

Appleton-le-Moors
Brompton
River Derwent
Wold Newton
Wharram Percy
Rudston
Sledmere
Wetwang

EAST RIDING OF YORKSHIRE

South Cave
Hull

River Humber

Sunk Island

River Trent

30 miles
50 km
0   10   20   30   40
0   10   20   30

# ALWINTON
## NORTHUMBERLAND

*Long live the Border Shepherds Show*

In 1761, George Wilson got married at Alwinton. He was, according to John Sykes's *Local Records: or Historical Register of Remarkable Events* (1833), 'upwards of 100 years' – a testament to the healthy outdoor life of the Coquetdale fells. His bride (his fourth) was about half a century younger, being fifty-one. Wilson died two years later, aged 104, 'and possessed great vigour till within ten days of his death'.

Now, as then, this is a farming area, the parish of Alwinton covering more than forty-six thousand acres. Just as George Wilson had been press-ganged into being a soldier in 1688, so the military are still present. Landowners were not sorry when the Ministry of Defence leased their land to extend the Otterburn firing range after the Second World War: it had long been a struggle to make farming in this remote hill country pay.

Yet it continues, and is celebrated every October at the Alwinton Border Shepherds Show. Alwinton is the last of the Border shows, and one might have thought that only the boldest of shepherds would brave the Northumbrian weather in that month. But mud is an inescapable dimension of Coquetdale life. You hardly notice it, if you wear the right boots. Only a visitor from the soft south would think of mentioning it. Better to get on with the tug of war, to the sound of Northumbrian pipes, or watch the traditional wrestling, mostly the preserve now of children, who begin by linking fingers behind their opponents' backs: it is said to have been introduced by the Vikings.

This is a land of terrier racing for dogs and fell racing for humans. Today's sports are mild in relation to those of the past. Football matches used to be played 'in the real old border fashion', which 'frequently finished up with a friendly fight', according to a history of Upper Coquetdate, published in 1903. Terrier men would meet at Alwinton to try their dogs against badgers or, failing that, wild cats or hedgehogs. 'The trails generally ended in a general dog-fight, which led to a battle royal amongst the tribes represented,' a correspondent to *The Field* wrote.

Village life is not so cruel as it was. But it is just as difficult to sustain. Although Alwinton was such a healthy place in the nineteenth century, its population nevertheless fell. The population is falling now. Returns from hill farming have been low; during the twentieth century, farmland was not only lost to the firing range but put under forestry, reducing the number of jobs. Long live the Alwinton Border Shepherds Show. It is the heart of this community: the pulse may have weakened, but it still beats.

# APPLETON-LE-MOORS

NORTH YORKSHIRE                    *William the Conqueror's clean slate*

The northern counties are unusually well off for planned Norman villages: there are three hundred in Yorkshire alone. It seems that they came into existence because, in the late twelfth century, little else existed. The countryside had been systematically and mercilessly scorched bare by William the Conqueror in 1069–70, during the so-called Harrying of the North. Two years after 1066, the northern earls Edwin and Morcar had rebelled against the new regime; William marched north and garrisoned York. But that garrison was massacred the next year, and another insurrection, supported by a Danish army, took place. William concluded that the only way to prevent the North from rebelling each time his back was turned was to devastate it so thoroughly that the reduced and weakened population would not have the strength or numbers to rise up. His men set about their task of genocide with horrible efficiency.

The most thorough account of this episode is given by Orderic Vitalis, who was born, to a Norman father and English mother, in 1075. At the age of ten he was sent away to a monastery in France, and later became a historian in the tradition of Bede. 'In his anger he commanded that all crops and herds, chattels and food of every kind should be brought together and burned to ashes with consuming fire, so that the whole region north of the Humber might be stripped of all means of sustenance.' Orderic stated that a hundred thousand people died of famine – a figure that may in detail be open to dispute, but signifies a very large number. Some of the refugees who fled northwards were enslaved by the Scots, who erupted over the border in 1070.

Villages that had been profitable in Saxon times – Calverley (see page 415), the clearing with calves, for example – were described in the Domesday Book as 'waste'. (This is not as straightforward as it might seem: waste could indicate common land, which was used for grazing. Nevertheless the picture is of low population and unprofitable use.) The destruction of so many settlements gave the lords and monasteries that held the land the opportunity to lay out new villages, sometimes based on a surviving Saxon church. The usual form was to create a symmetrical structure, with dwellings neatly aligned along a main street and garths, each a hundred yards long, running back from them; there would be a church and a green.

Appleton-le-Moors near Pickering is such a case. Once equipped with these elements (except for the green), it seems to have been content to stay at its original size. This makes the layout unusually easy to read, but as a planned village, it is not unusual in the area. Of the twenty-nine villages in the Vale of Pickering, about two-thirds show evidence of planning.

What the Normans destroyed as brutal conquistadores they also – in their alter ego of generous benefactors to the Church – built up again. Around 1070, St Mary's Abbey had been founded; it was probably the efficient estate managers of that institution who, wanting to improve revenues, laid out the village, amalgamating it with its neighbour Baschebi, which ceased to exist.

# ARMITAGE BRIDGE

WEST YORKSHIRE                    *England's oldest family business*

Yorkshire is a conservative place. The business that is now John Brooke and Sons has been around Armitage Bridge since the sixteenth century, perhaps before; it claims to be the oldest family business in the country.

Armitage Bridge is a Norman name, one of few in an area that was laid waste as part of William the Conqueror's Harrying of the North\*, during which houses, barns, livestock and winter fuel supplies were destroyed so that the populace starved during winter – salt was scattered on the ground to render it infertile before spring. It was originally Hermitage Bridge, presumably because a hermit lived there. Roger Brooke inherited some land in the upper reaches of the river Holme during Henry VIII's reign; it had been used by the nuns of Nostell Priory to graze sheep. His son John Brooke leased a couple of fulling mills, where woollen cloth was beaten with hammers to turn it into felt. In the seventeenth century, William Brooke acquired what is now New Mill at Greenhill Bank.

A picture of the West Riding's cloth workers around 1724 is evoked by Daniel Defoe in *A Tour thro' the Whole Island of Great Britain*. Abundant springs provided water; coal pits the means of fire. With these necessities 'at every Dwelling . . . they dwell thus dispers'd upon the highest Hills, the Convenience of the Manufactures requiring it'. Scattered about were 'an infinite Number of Cottages or small Dwellings, in which dwell the Workmen which are employed, the Women and Children of whom, are always busy Carding, Spinning, &c. so that no Hands being unemploy'd, all can gain their Bread, even from the youngest to the antient; hardly any thing above four Years old, but its Hands are sufficient to its self'. Consequently, few people were seen out of doors, but they were busy enough indoors, one of the factories revealing 'a House full of lusty Fellows, some at the Dye-fat, some dressing the Cloths, some in the Loom, some one thing, some another, all hard at work'. This was the era when Yorkshire was toppling East Anglia and the West Country from their previous pre-eminence in the wool industry†.

John Brooke and Sons was founded in the mid 1780s. It was expanded with the aid of a dowry, which (his son) William brought to the family on marriage to Hannah, niece of Sir Thomas Clapham, MP for Leeds. The present site at Armitage Bridge was bought as a result. Unlike many mill owners, the Brookes enjoyed good relations with their workforce, particularly after they supported the restoration of homes that had been burnt to defeat a cholera epidemic in 1854. Like most of the British textile industry, Armitage Bridge suffered catastrophically during the twentieth century, as imports came in from the Far East. The mills are now a Heritage Office Park, home to a range of new, growing businesses. Will any of them last for five hundred years?

\**See Appleton-le-Moors, page 407.* †*See Lavenham, page 251*

# BAINBRIDGE
## NORTH YORKSHIRE

*Village for foresters*

Every evening between Holy Rood (27 September) and Shrovetide, a horn sounds at Bainbridge. It is blown at 10pm, long after it has become dark. Nobody quite knows the origins of the custom, but it may date from the days when the surrounding area was the Forest of Wensleydale: foresters guided themselves home by its sound. (The horn is now kept at the Rose and Crown Hotel.) Bainbridge owed its origin to the Forest. Whereas we can only speculate about the early history of many villages, piecing it together from evidence on the ground, the reason for Bainbridge is known. In 1227, a certain Ranulph, son of Robert, claimed that his ancestors had established it to house a dozen foresters, each with a house and nine acres of land.

Medieval forests were not densely planted with trees: woods were interspersed with open glades, scrub and peasants' fields. There were settlements, too. Life in the forest was subject to forest law, which protected the deer and their habitat for the lord. The Bainbridge foresters would have been part of the enforcement brigade. But peasants also had rights, allowing them, for example, to graze their pigs on the acorns at certain times. (Large piggeries were kept by the manorial lords, commemorated in names such as Swincliff in Nidderdale.) Sometimes they encouraged their sheep and cattle to nibble away at young growth, and surreptitiously felled a tree or two, and before long had succeeded in 'assarting' a field – claiming it from the forest. The manorial courts pretended to take a dim view by imposing fines, really more akin to a tax.

Holly was planted as a form of winter feed for animals (holly woods are remembered in the name Hollins). In order to ensure that the lord and his retinue had plenty of deer to eat and hunt when the party arrived, deer parks were created from the thirteenth century. Barden Tower in Wharfedale survives as an example of a hunting lodge, although the 'Shepherd Lord' Henry Clifford made it his main base in preference to Skipton Castle when he inherited in 1485; it was remodelled as a result.

*A horn is blown at Bainbridge to guide foresters home after dark.*

Before the foresters came, Bainbridge had already been home to Roman legionaries, sheltering in a fort called Virosidium, which now survives as a low rectangular platform in what must have been a well-ventilated position above the present village. It was first constructed out of earth ramparts and wooden palisades in the first century, then rebuilt in stone at different times until the fourth century. As Richard Muir observed with masterly understatement in *The Yorkshire Countryside* (1997), 'no one can imagine Virosidium being regarded as an idyllic posting'.

And these days? On a summer's morning, fortified with the knowledge that stone cottages are now generally weatherproof, a visitor might well think, as he or she contemplates the broad greens, the occasionally handsome house or chapel, and the river Ure tumbling through the Yorkshire Dales National Park, that idyllic is the *mot juste*.

*See also Rockingham, page 347*

# BARWICK IN ELMET
## WEST YORKSHIRE

*Tum tee-tum tee-tum tee-tum,*
*tum tee-tum tee-tum tum*

Every weekday evening and for an hour on Sundays, a good proportion of Britain's listening public makes contact with Barwick in Elmet, quite possibly without knowing it. 'Barwick Green' is the official title of an orchestral work better known as *The Archers'* theme tune, announcing an everyday radio soap about country folk. It depicts a maypole dance. The composer Arthur Wood was famous for his light orchestral pieces, often evoking his native Yorkshire in the folkloric style popular after the First World War. 'Barwick Green' forms part of the suite *My Native Heath*, published in 1925, of which the other movements are 'Knaresborough Status', 'Ilkley Tarn' and 'Bolton Abbey'. Other works include *Three Dale Dances*, *Yorkshire Rhapsody* and *Barnsley Fair*. Wood was born in Heckmondwike in 1875.

What of Barwick's Green? It does not exist. Like Sherburn in Elmet, the name Barwick in Elmet remembers the Celtic kingdom of Elmet, but human activity had taken place here long before that: the village contains the site of an Iron Age hill fort. Nineteenth-century books say that the village was 'the ancient seat of Northumbrian kings; and its extent and magnificence have been attested by the discovery of many interesting remains in the Saxon style'. Later, the Normans built a motte and bailey castle; a Norman window survives in the church.

So many things, but not a green. A maypole is, however, raised every three years on a paved area by the war memorial, around which dancing takes place. Did Wood make a mistake about the setting? As so often happens with nostalgia, the reality became heightened in memory. But what a jolly tune.

# BIRDSEDGE
## WEST YORKSHIRE
*The hills are alive with . . .*

My big mistake was wearing shorts. The marquee at Birdsedge, in the Yorkshire Pennines, was getting a little cool by 9pm. My thoughts kept straying from folk music to the warming hot dog I had ordered for the interval. This was the opening night of the Birdsedge Village Festival.

There had been a village fete in Birdsedge since the 1940s; then, twenty years ago, Jacey and Brian Bedford, two-thirds of the folk group Artisan, came to live in the village and staged concerts to raise money for the village hall. For the past decade or so, the musicians and the fete committee have been combining forces to mount a festival, attracting performers from – it is only a slight exaggeration to say – around the world.

Festivals have become a feature of the countryside. The biggest is the literary festival at Hay-on-Wye, tented like the Field of the Cloth of Gold. Smaller, even miniature versions of this book fair are held in cities, yes, but also in villages, wherever a community building, country house or converted church exists to house them. The Dorset hamlet of Plush – not much more than a small Victorian church, the Brace of Pheasants pub and a village noticeboard – is home to the Music at Plush festival. The pianist Alfred Brendel lives there, and the musical director is his son, Adrian, an internationally successful cellist. For Thomas Hardy, Plush, despite its comfortable name, was the model for Flintcombe-Ash, the 'starve-acre place' where Tess of the D'Urbervilles scrapes a living picking turnips. High culture was very far from the scene.

At the headwaters of the river Dearne, Birdsedge is of a different stamp. It was, and partly remains, a mill village: a finishing mill still operates. Behind the old Sovereign inn, a quarry has been revived to supply fresh quantities of the millstone grit from which the village is built. Millstone grit turns black when it is exposed to the air, giving a tough character to the terraces that line the A629. Despite its size, the village still has a school (neat rows of lettuces in the vegetable patch, kites painted with simple words flying in the windows). Musicians ran workshops there during the festival.

On the ridge above Birdsedge you can look into the Peak District in one direction and, so it is said, see as far as the towers of the Humber Bridge in the other. There are about 150 houses, if you include the hamlet of High Flatts, a Quaker settlement, nearby. Not much to support a festival, but the Birdsedge event is – for now, at least – a home-made, local affair. All festivals begin like this; some grow into international brands, although habitués may shed a tear for the intimacy they have lost.

My Birdsedge concert opened with the Australian folk duo Cloudstreet singing, quite beautifully, a song about syphilis. Hilary Spencer, the third member of Artisan, gave a hair-raising rendition of a traditional ballad about a young man escaping from fairies. Brian Bedford performed some of the ingenious songs that he writes himself. 'Does it clean the carpet?' someone from the audience shouted, when one of the musicians put a bagpipe under his arm.

On the Saturday, as many as a thousand people walked through the gates. Tombola, white elephant stall, children's fancy dress parade and dog agility demonstration continued the fete tradition, while a continuous programme of folk music went on in the marquee and the village hall. Out of a village of three hundred people, seventy-five came forward to help.

*See also Sedgwick, page 395*

# BLANCHLAND
NORTHUMBERLAND                    *Built in the Abbey ruins*

Blanchland is a village created out of a monastery. An order of canons, the Premonstratensians, came here in 1165; they took their name from Prémontré near Laon, where they had been founded forty-five years before. They wore white habits – hence Blanche-land. Like the Cistercians, the order was austere, and at Blanchland they found as remote a location as the Pennines could offer. The valley of the Derwent is deep and narrow here, and they could easily have been overlooked by Scottish raiders; unlike some of the many other abbeys in Northumberland, Blanchland was not fortified. There are records of Scots robbing granges or farms that belonged to the abbey, but not the abbey itself. Folklore has it that at one time of danger, after fervent prayers by the canons, the abbey was enshrouded in a providential mist (all too likely in this part of the world), which prevented the Scots from seeing it. Unfortunately the canons then rang the bells in celebration, which gave away their existence.

Although remote, Blanchland was not without industry: there were lead mines in the area. Lead and silver smelting was carried out within the abbey precincts, although not necessarily during the period of the monks. Even so, when the abbey was dissolved in 1539, nothing much was done to replace the community with another settlement; the abbot's own residence was converted into a manor house for the Forster family, but for a century and a half the other buildings lay in ruins. In 1701, Fernando Forster was murdered; fourteen years later, the co-heir Thomas Forster was caught up in the 1715 Rebellion. Through the other co-heir, Dorothy Forster, half the estates had passed to the 3rd Baron Crewe, who was Bishop of Durham; he now acquired Thomas Forster's portion. At Crewe's death in 1721, Blanchland was left, with other property, to be administered as a charitable trust.

When John Wesley preached at Blanchland in 1747, it had not been rebuilt. 'I rode to Blanchland,' he recorded in his Journal. 'The rough mountains round about were still white with snow. In the midst of them is a small winding valley, through which the Derwent runs. On the edge of this the little town stands, which is little more than a heap of ruins.' As so often, he preached out of doors, to a congregation of lead miners, standing on a large tombstone. 'The whole congregation drank in every word with such earnestness in their looks, I could not but hope that God will make this wilderness sing for joy.' Whether it sang or not, Blanchland did not remain a wilderness for long. The village was rebuilt, on the template already provided by the Abbey ruins.

Part of the wall of the monastic nave survives as the garden wall of the Lord Crewe Arms. The pub itself was made out of the main range of monastic buildings, with some Gothick additions. This stands on the village square, based on the abbey's outer court, which would have been lined with barns and workshops. The gatehouse, four square and battlemented, survives more or less intact (it now houses a gallery), and there is another building with battlements that may have been the abbot's lodge. Fragments of medieval carved stone are built into walls all around the square. As the great walker Alfred Wainwright (not generally one to make much of the works of man) wrote in *A Pennine Journey* (1986), 'When you set foot in Blanchland, you step into the Middle Ages . . . Your imagination is indeed impoverished if you can enter this picturesque village for the first time and not thrill at the spectacle it affords.'

# BOWES

CO. DURHAM *'Education – At Mr. Wackford Squeers's Academy'*

'Youth,' the Victorian business card reads, 'are carefully instructed in the English, Latin and Greek languages . . . Common and Decimal Arithmetic, Book-keeping, Mensuration, Surveying, Geometry, Geography and Navigation . . . No extra charges whatever, Doctor's bills excepted. No vacations, except by the Parents' desire.' This was the promise made by William Shaw's academy in the village of Bowes, then in Yorkshire. There were many similar schools in the area. They specialised in children whom their parents or guardians did not particularly want to see again, hence the ominous 'no vacations'. On this point Shaw was as good as his word, but a look at surviving exercise books suggests that little was taught except writing, with the copious copying out of passages from textbooks.

In January 1838, Charles Dickens, a few days short of his twenty-sixth birthday and worn out by writing, made a northern tour, partly to freshen his spirits and partly to gather material for his next novel, *Nicholas Nickleby*. In that book he immortalised the Yorkshire schoolmaster Wackford Squeers and his establishment, Dotheboys Hall, Dickens's imagination being reinforced by the work of his principal illustrator, Hablot Knight Browne, otherwise Phiz, whom he took with him to the North.

Dickens may have heard about Shaw from a disgruntled teacher, since he made a note in his diary to look out for newspaper accounts of a case in which Shaw had been prosecuted for gross neglect of some children in his care who had gone blind. The reports would have certainly fuelled his imagination. Days began with pupils extracting the fleas from their beds with quills; they were beaten if they failed to remove all of them. When some of the boys started to lose their sight, they were banished to the wash house, from which they emerged completely blind. Shaw had to pay £600 in damages, but returned to Bowes and his school.

Dickens, although travelling under an assumed name and supposedly on a mission to help place a child in a school, seems not to have received a cordial reception; perhaps his identity had been guessed. In the churchyard he found the thirty-four tombstones of children who had died in local schools during twenty-four years, among them George Ashton Taylor, who had died suddenly, aged nineteen, at the Shaw academy. His stone, in the shade of a yew tree, bears a grim epitaph: 'Young reader, thou must die, but after this the judgement.' Thick snow was lying. Dickens felt that Taylor's ghost put the character of pitiful Smike, broken by Dotheboys and unable to escape its clutches, into his head 'upon the spot'. Then Dickens and Phiz were off again, back to London. Their trip had lasted a week.

Dickens did his best to cover his tracks, observing, in the preface to *Nicholas Nickleby*, that 'Mr Squeers is the representative of a class, and not of an individual'. But secretly there was no doubt as to the origin of the character. As he wrote to Mrs S. C. Hall, the Irish writer whose husband would soon have the misfortune of inspiring the odious Pecksniff in *Martin Chuzzlewit*, 'His name is Shaw.' Bowes has since done what it can to put Dotheboys behind it, by opening an otter sanctuary, displaying the remains of a Roman fort and making much of its Norman castle. William Shaw lies securely buried beneath his own tombstone: a large one.

# BROMPTON
NORTH YORKSHIRE     *A Yorkshire gentleman pioneers manned flight*

On the village street at Brompton, near Scarborough, is a squat stone building of semi-octagonal form, with a large sash window to light the interior. It was Sir George Cayley's workshop, and out of it, in 1853, came the first heavier-than-air flying machine to carry a man in flight. The man in question was Sir George's coachman. It launched from a bank on Brompton Dale, flew unsteadily across the dale for a few hundred yards before, in the words of Cayley's granddaughter, coming 'down with a smash'. The spectators rushed to the crash site, upon which the coachman 'struggled up and said, "Please, Sir George, I wish to give notice. I was hired to drive and not to fly."' In the words of Orville Wright, one of the brothers who successfully made the first powered flight fifty years later, Sir George was 'a very remarkable man'.

Sir George can be forgiven for not manning the glider himself: he was nearly eighty at the time. The experiment came at the end of a lifetime's interest in aeronautics. In 1804, he had summed up the challenge of flight in the words: 'The whole problem is confined within these limits, viz., to make a surface support a given weight by the application of power to the air.' He had already, in 1799, designed a machine in what is recognisably identifiable as the form of a modern aeroplane, with fixed wing, fuselage, cruciform tail unit with moving surfaces, cockpit for the pilot, and a means of propulsion. It was the last element that defeated Cayley. Revolving flappers, although embodying the idea of a propeller, were inadequate, and most of the other options available in the steam age were too heavy; in addition, Cayley's idea of an engine powered by gunpowder, not unlike the internal combustion engine, was unreliable.

Nevertheless, the baronet had cracked the basic principles upon which manned flight would depend. Previous ideas had assumed that the secret would be learnt from birds, whose wings provide both forward movement and lift. Cayley realised that only forward movement was necessary, if the wings were shaped correctly. Inside the workshop at Brompton, he constructed a machine with a whirling arm to test the aerodynamics of models. In 1804, he built the world's first heavier-than-air flying machine, a glider, which undertook a successful test. 'It was beautiful to see this noble white bird sail majestically from the top of a hill to any given point of the plain below it with perfect steadiness and safety,' Cayley wrote.

The problem of heavier-than-air flight preoccupied Cayley, on and off, throughout his life, together with other subjects, such as ballooning, the safety of railways, the design of artillery shells and 'Sir George Cayley's Universal Railway', for which he took out a patent in 1846 – a forerunner of the caterpillar tractor. Although he served as an MP, he was happiest at home in Yorkshire, where his energy as an inventor never dimmed. 'Just lately I have been making a breech-loading gun,' he told a friend in 1855, when he was eighty-one, and 'the eternal air engine is still on the stocks', in 'a temporary wooden shed at the north end of the Broad Walk'.

*See also Standon Green End, page 194*

# CALVERLEY
## WEST YORKSHIRE
*Stresses of Jacobean life*

In seventeenth-century England, many gentry and aristocratic marriages took place between young people who hardly knew each other. If they were lucky, affection, respect and even love could develop and sustain a union devised for family advantage. If not, misery could ensue. One reason proposed to explain why Walter Calverley killed his two little children on St George's Day, 1605, was that he did not believe them to be his. In an age before psychiatry it must have seemed the only plausible motive for such an enormity. The true story is probably rather different, and more believable.

Walter Calverley's marriage to Philippa Brooke was mismatched. The Calverleys were a gentry family who, like others in the North, remained true to the old faith at the Reformation. They were locally important, but being recusants (people refusing to attend Church of England services), they did not flourish: their house, Calverley Old Hall, although a fine place, built of blackened Yorkshire stone, was old-fashioned. By contrast, the Brookes had aristocratic and court connections. Philippa's grandfather, Lord Cobham, had been one of the peers who tried Anne Boleyn. But at the age of nineteen, Walter Calverley had already inherited the family estate from his father, and stood to receive more from his mother. He and Philippa apparently liked one another. Marriage seemed like a good piece of business. It gave Walter a lot to live up to.

In the language of the time, Walter was an 'unstayed' young man, lacking self-restraint. Before marrying Philippa, he had jilted a girl from Nostell Priory, one of the great houses of Yorkshire. Afterwards, he moved with his new bride to London and immediately fell victim to its temptations, gambling and soon ending up in the Fleet Prison for debt, nearly dying of fever. He recovered, Philippa gave birth to a son and Walter brought his family back to his home village. Albeit tormented by fears of witchcraft – four local people were convicted of it in 1605 – Calverley was doing well from weaving cloth, which the weavers carried on their heads to sell in Leeds: prosperity was expressed in the new altar and font cover in the parish church.

By contrast, Walter's own position was collapsing: 'down goes the house of us, down, down it sinks,' his character says in *A Yorkshire Tragedy* (1608). Thrown into a pit of clinical depression, he believed his family would be reduced to beggary. It seemed better to kill them, and, presumably, himself. In the event he succeeded only in stabbing to death two of his boys. Philippa was saved by the whalebone in her corset. Galloping to kill his third son, who was at wet nurse twelve miles away, he was thrown from his horse, and was captured before he could get there.

At Wakefield Assizes, Walter was condemned to have the breath crushed out of him, by lying under a board loaded with weights – *peine forte et dure* – after which he was buried at St Mary's, Castlegate, in York. Village tradition has it that his body was dug up again and reburied with his ancestors in Calverley church. Children had a game for raising his ghost, dancing in a circle as they chanted:

> Old Calverley, old Calverley, I have thee by th'ears,
> I'll cut thee in collops unless thou appears.

# COXWOLD

## NORTH YORKSHIRE

*The Life and Opinions of
Rev. Laurence Sterne*

'I am as happy as a prince, at Coxwould,' wrote Laurence Sterne in 1767, seven years after he had arrived there as perpetual curate, 'and I wish you could see in how princely a manner I live – 'tis a land of plenty. I sit down . . . to venison, fish and wild fowl, or a couple of fowls or ducks, with curds, and strawberries, and cream . . . with a clean cloth on my table – and a bottle of wine on my right hand to drink your health. I have a hundred hens and chickens about my yard – and not a parishioner catches a hare, or a rabbet [sic], or a trout, but he brings it as an offering to me.'

For what he was about to receive, the Lord had made him truly grateful. But to some senior clerics, the writing of *The Life and Opinions of Tristram Shandy, Gentleman* was an odd way to repay it. The tale is shapeless, quixotic, bawdy, scatological and hilarious – not the sort of work that divines expected to see from the pen of a clergyman. The opening chapter speculates about the effect on Shandy's future personality when, at the moment of conception, his father is interrupted by a question from his mother: 'have you not forgotten to wind up the clock?' It goes on from there.

But then Sterne had plenty of material to draw on from his own life, not least the descent of his first wife into madness, when she thought that she was the Queen of Bohemia. Rackety friends made at Oxford did not help, and the fact that Sterne hung onto them afterwards has been used against him by those who cannot reconcile his role as man of the cloth with the subject matter that he chose as novelist. Perhaps a life spent as a rural clergyman (he was vicar of Sutton-on-the-Forest near York before coming to Coxwold) contributed something to his outlook.

Coxwold is an orderly village, but was never big. His neighbours were country people, living in crowded homes, in close proximity to their animals; the natural processes of the farmyard were on constant view, and personal privacy would have been scant. Sterne's own dwelling, which friends christened Shandy Hall, had some of the characteristics of his novel: a fifteenth-century timber house, whose hall was divided horizontally in the seventeenth century; the brick veneer of an eighteenth-century facade, possibly built by Sterne, at one end was at odds with the enormous medieval chimney at the other. Typically Sterne would refer to it as 'my Thatched Cottage', even though it was roofed with slate and pantiles.

As might be expected, Sterne was not an original theologian, but, on the other hand, he did not ignore his calling. As well as box pews, he put a three-decker pulpit in Coxwold church, and no doubt preached, as he did at Sutton, when invariably 'half the congregation were in tears'. (The church's great note of eccentricity, a communion rail that projects from the altar in the form of a long horseshoe, so that members of the congregation kneel facing one another, probably arrived after his time, when the chancel was rebuilt in 1774.) In 1765, Sterne was forced to leave Coxwold, touring France and Italy for the sake of his health. It did not cure his tuberculosis (he died in 1768), but *A Sentimental Journey* was the result.

# CRASTER

NORTHUMBERLAND     *The 'perfit golden blandishment' of the kipper*

'Why cannot a kipper be a meal or refreshment?' The person asking this pertinent question was Lord Goddard, in the Queen's Bench Division of the High Court. The year was 1956, and a shopkeeper had been caught selling a kipper on a Sunday, allegedly in violation of the Shops Act. Meals or refreshments could, however, be sold under the Act. So the question exercising some of the greatest legal minds of the day was: could a kipper be eaten without cooking? Hotel guests, for example, might be surprised if they were to be served a raw kipper, but, as Lord Donovan opined, some people did eat their kippers raw.

No doubt the case was followed closely in Craster, which has always been famous for kippers. The idea that they are a specifically northern delicacy is probably wrong. Smoking is an ancient method of preserving food. There are also some very old references to kippers, although the etymology is confusing: a kip is a bony extension of the lip that male salmon grow before mating, in order to do battle with rivals; as a result, male salmon used to be called kippers.

However, we know that herring were smoked in Elizabethan England, because Thomas Nashe described the process, and celebrated the joyous result, in *Lenten Stuffe* (1599). By a transformation comparable to alchemy, the tin-coloured

*Craster, a village whose reputation rests on its kippers.*

herring came to exhibit 'a perfit golden blandishment', such as noblemen might adopt for their armour. The kipper – or, as Nashe called it, the red herring – was an outstanding piece of 'English merchandise', a national achievement whose virtues were specially to be appreciated during Lent. In the nineteenth century, the removal of the salt tax in 1825, coupled with railway transport, ensured something of a Victorian kipper boom.

At Craster, L. Robson and Sons have been smoking kippers for four generations. Beside the harbour, the blackened stone smokehouses, with louvres in the roof, add a distinctive tang to the ozone. The poor herring girls who used to split the fish are now spared the task by a machine. After soaking in brine, the herring are hung on tenterhooks and slid into the smokehouses, where whitewood shavings and oak sawdust smoulder away for as much as sixteen hours. The plumper the herring, the better the kipper: after decades during which the connoisseur's enjoyment has been marred by small fish and a surfeit of bones, we must hope that the shoals will recover and that once more we can have kippers that flop off the side of the breakfast plate.

*See also Findon, page 571*

# ELTRINGHAM
## NORTHUMBERLAND

*The engraver Thomas Bewick's much-loved childhood home*

Eltringham, some miles to the west of Newcastle-upon-Tyne, nearly became 'Little Birmingham' in the eighteenth century. An ironmaster called Laidler wanted to establish a works there, making it a centre of industry. Workmen came to get the thing done as quickly as possible. The mill race that they dug was three-quarters of a mile long. The fall, however, was not steep enough, and the volume of water that came out of it insufficient to power the wheel. The cut was filled up the next time the Tyne flooded. Local people who had thought they would do well from opening pubs lost the money they had put out. As quickly as the works had begun, they ended. Laidler sold up and left. The turmoil that had so excited the village subsided, and it went back to the sleepy life it had known before Laidler's arrival, just about resisting the embrace of the next door coal and brick town of Prudhoe, which began to expand in the late nineteenth century.

While Laidler was at Eltringham, he stayed at Cherryburn House, then a modest, thatched farmhouse attached to a barn belonging to the tenant farmer and collier John Bewick. His son Thomas became a wood engraver, famous for vignettes of rural scenes and animals and the illustrations for the *General History of Quadrupeds* and *History of British Birds* published in conjunction with his partner, Ralph Beilby. Bewick left a *Memoir*, which, while frustrating art historians with its light treatment of engraving techniques, gave a loving account of his childhood at Cherryburn, a house that he left with difficulty to pursue his trade at Newcastle and to which, when established, he returned to live until the expiry of the lease in 1812.

The house lay a little way out of the village, not far from the Tyne. Cherry and plum trees grew in the dean – hence the name of the house – and Bewick affectionately described the trees that grew on the property, including an oak 'supposed to be one of the tallest and straightest in the kingdom'. When he was growing up, the countryside was 'beautified with a great deal of wood', but needy gentry sold the timber, leaving it, in the 1820s, 'comparatively, as bare as a mole-hill'.

He also remembered the common: 'mostly fine, green sward or pasturage, broken or divided, indeed, with clumps of "blossom'd whins", foxglove, fern, and some junipers, and with heather in profusion, sufficient to scent the whole air'. Cottagers kept their few sheep, cows and geese on the common, together with their beehives. Some of them had built hovels with their own hands, being careful to scoop up the horse dung left on public roads to manure their gardens. Bewick was indignant when the common was enclosed and divided up between large farmers in 1812: 'The wisdom which dictated this change is questionable, but the selfish greediness of it is quite apparent.'

Wordsworth wrote in 'The Two Thieves' that he wished he had Bewick's skill; the compliment seems not to have been returned, since Bewick left no recorded opinion of Wordsworth. He appears to have been happy with his lot, so long as Cherryburn and its surroundings did not change. Change did come, however: the cottage in which Bewick had been born must have looked hopelessly old-fashioned by the time of his death in 1828, and a new farmhouse was soon built next to it. But that was all. Since then time has been arrested by the National Trust.

# EMMERDALE
## WEST YORKSHIRE
*Film set for a country soap*

In 1972, a man in a tan leather coat arrived at Beckindale. It was the day of his father's funeral. The cortège, consisting solely of the hearse and an old Humber car, wound its way between stone walls, over old bridges and across moorland. You would have known it was Yorkshire without the cloth caps and ''appen nots' of the vernacular – but they were thrown in as well. This was the first episode of the television soap opera *Emmerdale Farm*, something of a minority taste until, as might happen to any village, a plane crashed onto it, killing four residents. Eighteen million people watched the episode of 1993 when that took place. Thereafter, Beckindale became Emmerdale, and the series dropped the Farm from its title.

*Emmerdale* is not filmed in a studio. Since 1998, it has had a corporeal, out-of-doors presence on the Harewood Estate in West Yorkshire. Timber-framed houses faced with stone were built with supposedly temporary planning permission for a ten-year period, after which they might have been torn down if the planning permission had not been extended; there is also a school, a cricket pavilion and The Woolpack pub. You can see the backs of them if you peer over a high wall; visitors are not encouraged. Of course, you can see why: Emmerdale, even without plane crashes, is a dangerous place. Viv Windsor and Shirley Turner were held hostage by an armed man in 1994; Shirley did not get out alive. Ashley Thomas nearly lost his leg in a terrible storm in 2003. The Kings' house exploded in 2006; that was the year that the millionaire Tom King was kidnapped, but survived – only to be pushed out of a window to his death on Christmas Day. All of which makes Emmerdale an unusual village, but for those who fictionally inhabit it, the occasional adrenalin rush of terror must make up for the otherwise slow pace of country life, to which few of them would seem to be suited.

# FORD
## NORTHUMBERLAND
*The improving properties of art*

The village hall in Ford is also an art gallery. On its walls is a mural cycle on Biblical themes by Lady Waterford, wife of the 3rd Marquess of Waterford, who died after a hunting accident in 1859. While her husband was alive, the Waterfords had lived mostly on his Irish estates; upon his death they were inherited by his brother, and at the age of forty-one, Lady Waterford, who had no children, moved to Ford, with what was then the handsome income of £10,000 a year. She was an artist. She was also an evangelical Christian. She put her time, her money and her art at the service of the people of Ford, whom she hoped to bring into a closer relationship with God. (Principally, that is to say, during the winter months; in time she inherited Highcliffe Castle in Hampshire, her childhood home, and spent summers there.)

Ford Castle is a hundred yards from the church. She set about rebuilding both. It cannot have been comfortable for this highly focused woman to find that the rector, already in place for forty years at the time of her arrival, was of a different liturgical persuasion. The Rev. Thomas Knight followed what she called 'the very highest of High Church doctrines' (he had, furthermore, pursued a bitter, costly and successful lawsuit against her husband over tithes). He never retired, the living becoming vacant on his death in 1872.

In architecture, however, Lady Waterford had a free hand. The village street was rebuilt, a trifle grimly, with a smithy incorporating a horseshoe-shaped doorway at one end and a granite column, supporting an angel, commemorating the late Marquess, at the other. The *chef-d'œuvre* was the school. Lady Waterford decorated it with murals in watercolour, applied to canvas that was then stretched onto frames. Begun in 1861, they took twenty-one years to complete and covered all of the walls of the schoolroom. Ruskin was no warmer to the work of this female artist, albeit a Marchioness, than to that of other women: 'Well, I expected you would have done something better than that,' he announced upon entering. (Ruskin, she had already concluded, was 'the reverse of the man I like, and yet his intellectual part is quite my ideal'.) How could she spend her time decorating a schoolroom, rather than copying threatened frescoes in Tuscany? He had, however, missed the point. Aesthetic considerations took second place to Lady Waterford's mission.

As we know from Victorian novels, many rich women visited the poor and the sick – but few, perhaps, had Lady Waterford's zeal. In an age before women priests, she took as much of a part in services as she could (particularly after the installation of the new rector, Hastings Neville), reading from the Bible and leading hymn singing. The murals, with their emphasis on childhood innocence, operate in the same emotional territory as Mrs Alexander's hymns (*Once in Royal David's City* is one of hers). They were a means of reaching out to possible new churchgoers, the model for baby Jesus being the son of a miner from the community at Ford Moss, for whom she had enlarged the church.

Lady Waterford died in 1891. She is buried at Ford. The school is now Lady Waterford Hall, doubling as a village hall and museum.

# FULNECK
## WEST YORKSHIRE
*Let the doors be shut softly*

Pudsey is a sprawling, multi-cultural suburb of Leeds. But when you turn through the gates of Fulneck to the south, overlooking a scrap of farmland not devoured by the surrounding motorways and conurbation, you enter a different world. It is quiet, handsomely proportioned, spiritual, a single street that was laid down in the eighteenth century, built up in the nineteenth, and frozen in the twentieth as the sect responsible for it declined.

The Moravian Church originated in Bohemia. Protestant before Luther, it was founded by followers of John Hus, who was martyred for his beliefs in 1415. In the seventeenth century, the Moravians were forced underground, only emerging back into the light when Count Nicholas von Zinzendorf became the leader of the movement in 1727. He introduced a highly original form of liturgy based on Christ's teaching. The whole of a Moravian's life became an act of worship. They lived, where possible, communally, in conditions that combined monasticism with aristocratic refinement.

Unlike other Protestant churches, the Moravians sent missionaries to other parts of the world. Zinzendorf came to Halifax in 1743; he looked northwards, across a green valley to what was then the little town of Pudsey, having 'such a sweet feeling and deep impression of the place' that he determined to establish a settlement there, to be called Lambshill. Land was bought, the settlement arose, but the locals could not get used to Lambshill; they called it Fallneck ('Fall' from the steep side of the valley) or Fulneck, as they always had.

Order and calm were presiding Moravian qualities. They were expressed in the architecture, which resembled that of the squares and terraces being built in Georgian towns. Through these buildings people passed with as little noise as possible. As an order of 1752 has it: 'Let the doors be shut softly and . . . all things be done in stillness and Order.' Separate dwelling houses were made for men and women, with meeting rooms, work rooms (for the women) and dormitories. Once or even twice a day both sexes would worship together, though separated, in the central Congregation House, or Grace Hall, where services might end with the congregation prostrating themselves on the floor.

Although this regime may sound extreme, there was room also for beauty. With its tall windows and galleries, the Congregation House was an elegant space, which might be completely decorated with cloths of different colours for special occasions. At a time when many Church of England graveyards were in an appalling condition*, the Moravian graveyard was a garden. Its beauty provided a considerable attraction to converts, as did the emphasis on music. The choir was the unit of organisation: people were buried with their choirs; they were also educated with them.

Moravian education, perhaps influenced by the more than usual number of aristocrats who were attracted to the congregation, was exemplary. Children, like the adults, lived communally, grouped by age and sex and separated from their families. After basic instruction from the age of three until twelve, students had the opportunity to specialise by moving to schools in other Moravian communities. One of those who went through the system was Benjamin Latrobe, architect of the Capitol in Washington, whose father, the Rev. Benjamin La Trobe, was the head of the Moravian congregation in England. After Fulneck, Latrobe continued his studies at Niesky in Saxony. Ironically, for him as for others, Moravian experience led to discontent. The presence of so many aristocrats made him idealise wealth and country houses. He broke with Moravians at the age of nineteen, writing emphatically in later life that, after school, 'I have never had any connection with that society.'

*See Stoke Poges, page 198

# HEDDON-ON-THE-WALL
NORTHUMBERLAND        *Lamentable origin of Foot and Mouth, 2001*

In 2001, Heddon-on-the-Wall earned the unenviable reputation of originating the outbreak of foot-and-mouth disease that devastated the country's livestock and tourism industries. FMD, as the media soon learnt to call it, was first spotted on 19 February, at an abattoir in Essex. After a few days it had been traced back to Burnside Farm, where Bobby Waugh fattened pigs at Heddon-on-the-Wall. In due course, Waugh would be convicted on nine counts under animal welfare legislation, but by then it was too late.

The Labour government, out of touch with (if not antipathetic to) the farming community, was slow to ban animal movements after FMD was discovered. Officials were further hampered by the need to coordinate their action with the European Union. With frightening rapidity the disease took hold across Britain, and the policy of slaughtering infected and suspect herds, then burning their carcasses, led to appalling autos-da-fé across the livestock-rearing counties. The smoke hanging over Cumbria made it look as though it had been laid waste by a vengeful general in some primitive war.

The inability of government officials and scientists to get on top of the disease until the summer revealed some previously hidden practices in the sheep industry. It emerged that sheep were routinely shuttled around the country to be traded, sometimes serially, in livestock markets, so that farmers could take advantage of subsidies that were then paid per head of livestock. (There was an obvious incentive to increase the numbers of sheep on the farm shortly before the inspector called.)

At Heddon-on-the-Wall, Waugh was found to have fed his pigs untreated swill from the leftovers of human meals, bought cheaply from schools and army-catering establishments. It is thought that this is how the infection entered his herd, presumably from meat that had been illegally imported from a country with FMD. In the squalor of Burnside Farm, Waugh failed to notify the authorities that the disease was present, allegedly because he had not observed it. Pigs act almost as factories for the production of the FMD virus, snorting it into the air in far greater quantities than sheep or cattle.

That summer, the countryside closed down. Animal movements were banned, pedigree herds destroyed, county shows cancelled, tourism in areas such as the Lake District and Devon brought to a halt. The army came to the aid of overtaxed slaughtermen. Heaps of dead animals would be left beside farmhouses, sometimes for a week, before teams could burn them. Perhaps more than ten million animals were 'culled'. The strain for many farmers was too much, and in this sometimes lonely profession, with firearms to hand, several killed themselves. Afterwards it was acknowledged that vaccination offers a more humane alternative to mass slaughter, even though it may hurt farmers who rely on exporting their stock.

The crisis is estimated to have cost Britain eight billion pounds. Bobby Waugh was electronically tagged, subject to a three-month curfew and banned from keeping livestock for fifteen years.

# HUMSHAUGH
NORTHUMBERLAND                                    *Young Knights of the Empire*

In the summer of 1908, Robert Baden-Powell, the hero of Mafeking, visited a
tower house in Northumberland, which had a depiction of the seven Christian
virtues carved over the 'noble fireplace' of the hall. Scouts needed one more, he
concluded in *Young Knights of the Empire* (1916): Cheerfulness. 'The important
point is that when you know what is the right thing to do, you should jump to it
and do it cheerily with a smile.' Baden-Powell had seen the fireplace during the
first Scout camp that he had attended, at Humshaugh. Camping for a troop of
boys (drawn from Boys' Brigades and cadet corps) had been first tried at Brownsea
Island in Poole Harbour, but that had been in 1907, before Baden-Powell had
published *Scouting for Boys* in 1908. The camp at Humshaugh in August that year
was another pioneering, self-reliant stride towards the establishment of Scouting
in the national consciousness, the boys who attended coming from Scout troops
across Britain. By the end of the year, fifty thousand Scouts had joined up.

Humshaugh already had military associations. It was near Hadrian's Wall, and
in the eighteenth century a local mill had produced paper on which fake French
money was printed with the object of destabilising the French economy during
the Revolutionary Wars. There were also associations with Arthurian legend,
which Baden-Powell liked. He knew the area, having crossed it in a car, converted
into a motor caravan, while commander of the Northumbrian Territorial Force
(he did not want the bother of staying with friends or putting up in hotels). 'What
a country for fighting and romance we are in,' he wrote from the camp. Henry
Holt, who acted as Camp Quartermaster, summed up the spirit of the adventure in *The Scout* magazine: 'The scenery is really lovely, and wherever the eye
wanders it falls upon something beautiful, and what with the undulating landscape, the verdant woods and a thousand and one attractions in this picturesque
spot, if a boy cannot be happy amid such surroundings he must be a very strange
boy indeed.'

Thirty-six boys arrived at the now-disappeared Fourstones railway station on
22 August, to be marched a mile north to the campsite. Most of them had won a
competition in *The Scout*. They were split into patrols called Kangaroos, Curlews,
Ravens, Bull and Owls; a sixth patrol, called Wolves, contained boys, such as
Baden-Powell's nephew Donald and the Etonian Edward 'Teddy' Wynne, who
had been specially asked.

The boys were issued with diaries. They recorded physical exercises, setting up a
loom in the woods, building a hut, making bivouacs and straw mattresses, sewing
ration bags, making bread without yeast or chemicals, games such as Bang the
Bear and, more conventionally, football – and rain, rain, rain. At night they sang
songs around the campfire, accompanied by Scoutmaster J. L. C. Booth's banjo.
It must all have been of considerable interest in the village. The town of Hexham

was thronged with people wanting to see Baden-Powell, the Edwardian equivalent of a superstar, and his Scouts when they came through.

In 1929, a rough stone was erected as a cairn by which to remember the camp. Alas, several of the Scouts who had camped with Baden-Powell at Brownsea and Humshaugh were no longer alive. The First World War had intervened. Among the casualties was Teddy Wynne, who joined the Grenadier Guards after Oxford and died of wounds in 1916. Scoutmaster Booth fell at Gallipoli. The Young Knights of the Empire rested with King Arthur.

# KILNSEY
## NORTH YORKSHIRE                                    *Home on the grange*

The Cistercians were a reforming order. They wanted to return to a literal observance of the rule of St Benedict, unlike the Benedictines, who had gone distinctly soft. When they arrived from France in the eleventh century, they sought out sites that were remote, wild and uncomfortable. To twenty-first-century eyes, these qualities (the first two, anyway) make them beautiful: Tintern, Abbey Dore (see page 291), Fountains and Rievaulx are among the Cistercian foundations. The rugged landscape amid which such abbeys were set had another advantage in the Middle Ages. The fells and mountains, moors and dales that surrounded them proved to be ideal conditions for farming sheep. Often the abbeys controlled immense tracts of land, which had previously been next to worthless; with sheep they could be made to pay.

The village of Kilnsey grew out of a Cistercian grange. Granges were farming outposts, run by lay brothers working under the control of the monks of the abbey, who acted something like a board of directors. Kilnsey belonged to Fountains Abbey. In theory, granges ought not to have been more than a day's travel distant from the mother house, and Kilnsey is only twenty-three miles away. But you would have had to be extremely fit to make that journey on foot in a day, given the difficult terrain; it would have been impossible in winter. The brothers managed an area covering ninety square miles. Sheep were their main business. Other granges specialised in iron and lead (Brimham), arable crops (Stainburn) and horse rearing (Horton). Once a year the Abbey's huge flocks of sheep were driven into Kilnsey to be sheared.

Remote granges such as Kilnsey had a profound effect on the countryside, effectively colonising areas that had previously been empty wastes. It is easy to picture the desolation that a scene such as the spectacular limestone outcrop of Kilnsey Crag, rising bald and sheer over the river Skirfare, would have presented: 'the whole of this astonishing mass of limestone stretches nearly half a mile along the valley', Thomas Langdale observed in 1822.

The grange itself was approached through a gatehouse, presumably giving access to a service court around which stood the brew house, the bake house and the two barns; a second gatehouse gave access to a hall, a chapel, the court house and a hostel for receiving guests. It was, of necessity, a self-sufficient establishment; other buildings included two mills, drying kilns and lime-slaking kilns. Fish could be netted from the stew ponds to eat on the many feast days. Among the visitors staying in the hostel would have been Italian wool merchants. Cistercian granges accounted for half the wool produced in England, at a time when wool was one of the few items that had to be traded across the otherwise self-sustaining world of the Middle Ages.

The West gatehouse is all that survives today. Most of the buildings, since this was essentially an agricultural enterprise, would have been flimsier than those at Fountains Abbey. Happily, the fishponds are still in use by the Kilnsey Angling Club. They are used to breed trout to restock the river Wharfe, which boasts some of the best fly-fishing in the country.

# KIRKHARLE
## NORTHUMBERLAND *Fertile surroundings for a gardener*

It is no great surprise that a hamlet such as Kirkharle should have produced a gardener; everybody would have had a cottage garden when Lancelot Brown was born there in 1716. It was a farming community, surrounded by great sweeps of open countryside, glorious but empty. Landowners needed gardeners, and Brown duly became one at the age of sixteen. The surprise is that it should have produced someone who had such a new idea of landscape, and successfully imposed it on scores of gentlemen and their country estates. It may be too much to say that Brown transformed the English countryside (even he could not be everywhere), but he certainly changed the way people saw it, and his legacy is still enjoyed today. A landscape such as that which unfolds around Milton Abbey in Dorset – which the original client, Lord Milton, can have seen only as mud planted with saplings – is now in its magnificent prime.

Brown was the son of a farmer. Educated at Cambo, he began work for Sir William Loraine of Kirkharle, leaving in 1739. Two years later he had sufficiently impressed Lord Cobham to be appointed as under gardener at Stowe in Buckinghamshire, which was then developing into Britain's greatest garden of allegory and ideas. There he worked with William Kent, the mercurial one-time theatre designer who had transformed himself into a connoisseur, an authority on gardens and a Palladian architect, under the patronage of Lord Burlington. Kent had travelled in Italy; he also knew Alexander Pope, who had written that 'All gardening is landscape painting'. No doubt Brown imbibed these ideas, together with some of Kent's confidence. In 1749, he set up on his own and, after a couple of years, was almost continuously in demand. He worked on nearly 150 estates, mercilessly destroying the avenues and Baroque parterres that had previously adorned them in favour of developing their naturalistic 'capabilities' – hence his soubriquet of Capability Brown.

The park at Alnwick, in his native Northumberland, was one of his biggest projects. Before his arrival, the surrounding country had been 'naked and bleak', according to George Tate's *The History of the Borough, Castle, and Barony of Alnwick* (1866–69). The forests and woods had been destroyed by border warfare in earlier centuries. Brown planted clumps of trees on the tops of hills and scattered other copses and long belts of plantation over the slopes; large forests were planted in the valleys, while the old park was extended and enclosed by a high wall. This was 'landscape painting' on a huge scale, the carriage driving or 'ridings' extending for miles. As the *Oxford Dictionary of National Biography* comments: 'The images that he created are as deeply embedded in the English character as the paintings of Turner and the poetry of Wordsworth.'

In the single paragraph that he is ever known to have written about his designs, Brown described the qualities required in gardening as 'a perfect knowledge of the country and the objects in it, whether natural or artificial, and infinite delicacy in the planting etc.'. Sensibility, innate or acquired, was not enough: to it had to be married a knowledge of the natural world, such as Brown had absorbed during his Northumbrian childhood. He was called Brown; his colour was green, in every shade of luxuriance and variety.

Little of Brown's time at Kirkharle now remains, beyond a stone erected by his first employer (replacing an earlier one that had decayed) remembering his ancestor Robert Loraine, 'barbarously' murdered by Scots raiders in 1483 'as he was returning home from the Church'. Legend has it that, to strike terror into the hearts of Loraine's allies, his body was cut up into tiny pieces and sent back in the saddlebags of his horse.

# MYTON-ON-SWALE
## NORTH YORKSHIRE
*A bloody battle, but life goes on*

Villages were at the mercy of events. This was particularly so around the Borders of Scotland, where marauding armies might arrive without notice, adding to the lawlessness of the reivers, as freelance raiders were known*. The people of Myton-on-Swale in North Yorkshire might have felt far removed from the Scottish wars, but in September 1319, five years after Bannockburn, they found an elite, battle-hardened Scottish army encamped near the junction of the rivers Swale and Ure, protected on three sides. Led by the Earl of Moray, they wanted to lift the siege of Berwick-upon-Tweed, then in Scottish hands, by capturing Edward II's queen Isabella, who was in York. Their presence, however, had been discovered by the Archbishop of York, who led a militia to attack them.

The Archbishop had raised a lot of men – twenty thousand by some accounts, including his personal household and some three hundred monks dressed in white habits. But they were neither well armed nor experienced. Their best hope of victory was to catch their enemy unawares. The first part of the Archbishop's strategy went to plan: he managed to cross the Swale unopposed. But his attempt to sneak up on the Scots across the fields was less successful. Whether because they were not trained, or unable to regroup between crossing the wooden bridge and meeting the enemy, or even because they were attempting not to draw attention to themselves, the English were spotted, advancing raggedly. The Scots response was to set fire to some haystacks, creating a smokescreen, behind which – trumpets sounding – they formed up into a tight, heavily armed wedge. As this battle group advanced, the English fled, without having exchanged a blow.

The Scots mounted infantry galloped down to the bridge, cutting off the English retreat. The fleeing troops were forced to stand and fight, or else escape, if they could, through the waters of the Swale. It is thought that as many as four thousand of them may have been slaughtered or drowned. Well-mounted, the Archbishop managed to get away; his monks were not so lucky. Their dead bodies gave a derisive name to the fight: the White Battle, otherwise the Chapter of Myton. Fortunately it had taken place in the afternoon, and the coming of darkness put an end to the killing; otherwise it could have been even worse.

Since many of the English besiegers at Berwick were local troops, now anxious about the vulnerability of their homes, Edward II had no option but to lift the siege. Moray withdrew to Scotland. We do not know the sufferings inflicted on Myton-on-Swale, as the defeated English sought desperately to hide and the pursuing Scots, their blood up, bore down on them, happy to wreck the place after stealing what they could, and treating the local people in the traditional manner of a medieval army on the rampage. But it recovered.

Historians now argue over where exactly the battle took place. The medieval bridge has vanished, replaced with a cast-iron one on a different site. Tradition, supported by such topographical references as occur in contemporary descriptions, says that the battle ended on Myton pasture (although since these water meadows are on a flood plain, why would the hayricks – too precious to risk being lost to flooding – have been there?). There is an information board about the battle, but no monument; most people know nothing about it.

*See Carlenrig, page 540

# NEW EARSWICK
## NORTH YORKSHIRE                    *Chocolate is not always bad for you*

Joseph Rowntree, born in 1836, was generally a step behind his fellow Quakers, the Cadburys. They came up with the more innovative products, such as high-quality cocoa essence and the milk chocolate bar; Rowntree, a mild and courteous man, was more cautious. He followed their example, too, in creating a model village in the spirit of the garden city movement. The Cadburys began Bournville on the

*The folk hall at New Earswick, the Quaker Joseph Rowntree's early-
twentieth-century contribution to the housing debate.*

outskirts of Birmingham in 1893; Rowntree started to build New Earswick on the
edge of York ten years later. Both are in an umbrageous Arts and Crafts idiom,
although there may be a touch more merry England about Bournville, and a more
progressive feel to New Earswick, with the expressive roof of the folk hall descending almost to the ground.

Rowntree came late to the game because of the time it had taken him to establish his
confectionery business. His career began in his father's grocery shop. It had been his
younger brother Henry Isaac who acquired the cocoa and chocolate company belonging
to another Quaker family, the Tukes. Henry Isaac, however, had no head for business,
and after some years, Joseph felt bound to help him out. In 1881, the firm introduced a
line of pastilles, previously imported from France; in 1893, they launched into gums.

By now, Henry Isaac having died, the concern was getting onto its feet. Sales
quadrupled in the 1890s; they quadrupled again in the 1900s. By 1906, Rowntree
was employing four thousand people. Victorian employers had been paternalist,
because they could treat each employee as part of a great family. Rowntree felt
that such an approach did not suit a large business, where it was impossible for
the founder to know everyone. He therefore set about organising a welfare structure that did not depend on personalities. The post of female welfare officer was
created in 1891; this was followed by sick and provident funds, schools, a doctor's
surgery, a savings scheme and a pension scheme.

In 1904, Rowntree put half his fortune into three trusts. One was the Joseph
Rowntree Village Trust, whose child was New Earswick. Three years before,
Joseph's son Seebohm Rowntree had published a study of the living conditions of
working-class York, which revealed the squalor among which many poor families
were compelled to live. New Earswick was intended to prove that better housing
could be achieved for people without much money to spend.

Presciently, Rowntree entrusted the design of New Earswick to Barry Parker and Raymond Unwin. It was their first commission, and they used it to try out some of the ideas that would be brought to fruition in Letchworth Garden City. The settlement was separated from the chocolate factory and the rest of York by a green belt of playing fields and rough land. Cottages are grouped in terraces around communal greens or walks, with the cul-de-sac making an appearance towards the end of the process. Village green and folk hall are at the centre of the scheme. The feeling that the architects sought to achieve was, in their own word, 'reposefulness'. There were to be no more than eight dwellings per acre.

It was not an immediate hit. To begin with, it looked, inevitably, raw. The roads were rough; there were no street lights or buses. Attitudes changed as the village matured. A primary school was built in 1912, one wall of which, in a revolutionary gesture, was all glass; a senior school opened in 1939. More than a century after it was built New Earswick seems a model of an architecturally well-tempered community. In only one respect did it fail. The Trust did not find that it was commercially viable to provide decent housing for people on the lowest wages without subsidy; council houses were needed to do that.

*See also Creswell Model Village, page 314; Saltaire, page 435; Stewartby, page 196*

# OLD BYLAND
## NORTH YORKSHIRE                    *The monks want solitude*

The monks who founded Byland Abbey had a hard time of it. A group of twelve had left Furness Abbey in 1134, only to have their new foundation destroyed by King David of Scotland four years later. In 1143 they came to what is now Old Byland; but here they were within earshot of the bells of Rievaulx Abbey, which caused confusion, and they moved again. Only in 1177 were they able to found Byland on its present site. The monastic buildings at Old Byland have disappeared; nevertheless, the monks' presence can still be felt here, because it was they who laid out the village.

Solitude was a requirement of the monastic life, yet gifts of land to abbeys might include villages, and they might disturb the peace of the monks, particularly if they occupied a site earmarked for building. The monks generally had a straightforward way of resolving the conflict: they demolished the village. This happened at Begesland, a settlement that preceded Old Byland. But the villagers were fortunate. Rather than being expelled as though from the Garden of Eden, they had a new village built for them a mile away, on a plateau above the river Rye, which was suitable for the village fields. The form of the village can still be seen.

Central to it was the green. In one corner is the church, which the monks provided. The roads bypass the green, coming in and leaving with a right-angled bend. The reason all this is so clearly visible is that the village never developed; it is more solidly built and has better plumbing than in the monks' time, but it is not much bigger.

Byland Abbey belonged to the Savigniac order, which merged with the Cistercians in 1147. The Cistercians were ruthless in suppressing villages that disturbed their tranquillity. The Pope himself (Eugenius III) was called upon to judge whether the Abbot of Kirkstall was right to destroy a parish church that he thought might compromise the Abbey's seclusion. Villages and hamlets that occupied sites required for sheep walks were regularly swept away, or 'reduced' to become granges*. We cannot say what, if any, discomfort was suffered by the villagers, but the practice was inveighed against by the chronicler monk Gerald of Wales. Old Byland may have had reason to be grateful to the monks; certainly their action places it in a select band of villages whose origins are known and dated.

*See Kilnsey, page 426

# PATELEY BRIDGE
## NORTH YORKSHIRE
*The problem of yoof*

Danny, an eighteen-year-old who lives in Pateley Bridge in the Yorkshire Dales, is only too happy to show off a few stunts on his BMX. Trail riding is his passion. And, to be honest, it is nine o'clock at night and he and two female friends have been sitting on a bench next to the car park, watching the traffic go by, for the past hour or so. There is not a lot of traffic in Pateley Bridge. Nor is there much else to do.

An hour and a half earlier, a meeting of the town council opened in the council chambers opposite the police station. The first item on the agenda was parishioners' representations. All of the half dozen parishioners present were vocal about what might be called, in shorthand, the Danny problem: young people hanging around the car park and behaving like, well, young people. Which may be alright when they are Danny and his friends at 9pm on a weekday; a different crowd takes over at 1.30am on Saturday night.

Youths use the car park as a race track, music booming at such a volume that nearby residents cannot hear their televisions unless they are turned up full. The air vibrates with the throb of modified exhausts, as cars roar off down country lanes, screeching as they are put through handbrake turns. Girls roam the streets, 'screaming their heads off', according to one resident. When another tried to video-tape the proceedings, she had bricks thrown at her windows. The telephone box allegedly serves as a drug exchange.

When inconsiderate, foul-mouthed youngsters terrorise neighbourhoods from Brixton to the Bronx, why should Pateley Bridge be any different? To answer that, you have to go there. In size, Pateley Bridge (population: two thousand) is no more than a village, set amid one of the most beautiful landscapes known to man.

Beautiful scenery does not, of course, guarantee beautiful behaviour – although the place makes its living from tourists in search of rural quiet. But whereas an inner-city trouble spot will be closely watched by the constabulary, Pateley Bridge does not merit much police attention.

There is a strong presumption, in some quarters, that the countryside should be an idyll. It can be – but only, as often as not, if you close your eyes to manifestations of the twenty-first century that you would rather not see. Outside Pateley Bridge is RAF Menwith Hill, a listening station used by the United States Department of Defense. Anyone entering the five-mile security zone around it may find him- or herself being searched at machine-gunpoint. The American military personnel and their children do not always harmonise with the indigenous people of the Dales, but then neither did the folk who founded Pateley Bridge: it began life as a settlement for lead miners, as tough as they come.

Offcomedon is the word they use here for newcomer. There are plenty of offcomedons in Pateley Bridge, perhaps as much as a third of the population having settled from elsewhere, often to retire. None of the angry parishioners at the town council grew up in the village. One person who did is the bike-mad youngster, Danny. Once he and his friends have told me how boring they find it in Pateley Bridge, I ask him where he would live when he is older. 'Here,' he tells me emphatically. 'It's brilliant.'

# PIERCEBRIDGE
## CO. DURHAM

*The image of a Roman ploughman*

In the Department of Prehistoric and Romano-British Antiquities at the British Museum, there is a tiny bronze sculpture that was found at Piercebridge. Made in the second or third century, it shows a ploughman working his plough, behind a pair of oxen. The man is wearing the sort of clothes that would still be peasant garb a thousand years later: hood, cloak and leggings. One of his legs is braced against the plough, the other straightened to give it a push.

It is a plough of the kind that was then common throughout Northern Europe, shaped like an anchor. The oxen, strangely, are not well matched, being a bull and a cow; this is not an arrangement that would have existed in real life, because it would have unbalanced the team. A suggestion has been made that the carefully made object had some kind of religious significance, perhaps related to the founding of a town. Classical authors describe how male and female oxen were used when making the furrow that would describe the boundaries of a new settlement. If so, could that settlement have been Piercebridge?

Piercebridge was founded about 270. There may have been a village here before that date, but it was swept away by the new construction: a fort that the Romans may have called Morbium. It guarded the crossing of the Tees. After

York, reached from Londinium by Ermine Street, the road that came to be known, in the Middle Ages, as Dere Street continued northwards. Its line can be clearly seen in the present B6275, which leaves the A1 as it veers to the east towards the coast, and continues as straight as an arrow towards another Roman fort at Bishop Auckland. The importance of the crossing can be seen from the bridge, built of wood but with stone foundations – and not even London Bridge had those (stone foundations are, in fact, found only at Piercebridge and the bridges on Hadrian's Wall). Great slabs of stone were laid to prevent the mud around them being washed away.

As regards military engineering, Morbium was an old-fashioned conception: a fort of what is known as the playing-card type (rectangular, with rounded corners), whereas the upcoming forts of the Saxon Shore, such as Burgh Castle in Norfolk, had massively thick ramparts that broke out into projecting bastions. Unlike Burgh Castle's mighty walls, the more modest fortifications at Piercebridge have been excavated. The fort's construction would have been related to troop redeployments, perhaps associated with the reinforcement of the east and south coasts.

As elsewhere, the Romano-British population would have felt keenly exposed when the province of Britannia was abandoned. When the legions left in the fifth century, the architecture of the fort was taken over by native people, no doubt pleased of the protection afforded by the walls that the army had left. The present village grew up on its footprint. Prosperous citizens, used to farming and trading under the protection of a professional army, would have found themselves at the mercy of the warlords who emerged when Roman authority collapsed. But for the peasant, pushing his plough, it probably made little difference. Life under one master might have been much like that under another.

# RUDSTON
## EAST RIDING OF YORKSHIRE                    *Tallest of sacred stones*

The tallest monolith in Britain stands in Rudston. By any standards it is an extraordinary monument: nearly eight metres high and nearly two broad, it is at the same time surprisingly thin, like a giant iPod Nano. After digging down at the base, the eighteenth-century landowner Sir William Strickland concluded that as much was buried below ground as showed above. Its pinkish grey contrasts with the creamy yellow stone of the church it stands close to. It is gritstone, which must have been hauled from Cayton Bay, ten miles away, before being erected. Clearly it was of enormous significance to the Neolithic community that went to these lengths to install it. It may have been worshipped as an idol.

Yorkshire is remarkably short on stone circles and the circular earthworks of the type known as a cursus (early antiquarians mistakenly thought that they had been

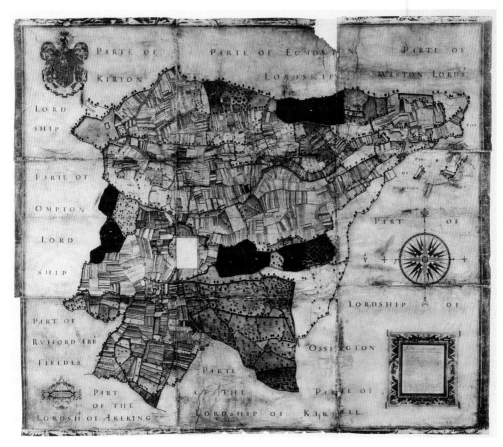

Mark Pierce's map of the 'whole mannor & Lordship of Laxton with Laxton Moorehouse in ye county of Nottingham', 1635. It shows the strips of the open fields, interspersed with woodland and winding bands of permanent rough pasture known as 'sykes'. (See page 333.)

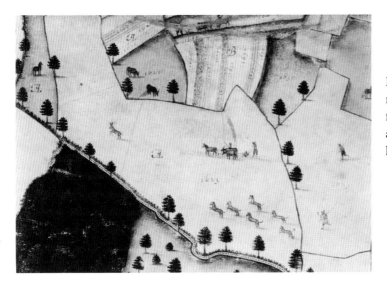

Detail of Mark Pierce's map, showing a farmer ploughing and a huntsman urging hounds after a hare.

*Above*: The outlook from the churchyard in West Wratting, Cambridgeshire. Rural ways were found to be primitive in comparison with cities by the evacuees billetted on local families during the Second World War. (See page 279.)

*Below*: A study of elder made by Charles Rennie Mackintosh at Walberswick, Suffolk. After its fifteenth-century zenith, Walberswick declined – until it became one of many art colonies established in villages around the British coast. In the wakes of the artists came holidaymakers and second-homers. (See page 275.)

The spire of St Mary's, Painswick, emerges from the mist of a Cotswold valley. One of the first Sunday Schools in the countryside was founded here in 1784. Robert Raikes found that its influence filled the church: 'the galleries and aisles were thronged like a playhouse'.
(See page 344.)

Well-dressing at Tissington, Derbyshire. Pictures are made from petals pushed into a frame filled with damp clay. Whatever the origins of well-dressing (possibly pagan), the tradition was sufficiently decorous not to be censured by the Victorians. (See page 360.)

At Hallaton in Leicestershire, the Easter bottle-kicking is a kind of mob football, without the ball. Played by Hallaton against the neighbouring village of Medbourne, the object of this emphatically contact sport is to roll, carry or otherwise propel a 'bottle' – a small barrel of beer – to one of two boundary streams. (See page 328.)

The maypole at Wellow in the Nottinghamshire 'Dukeries' is one of the tallest in the country. Maypoles became established in England in the second half of the fourteenth century. As part of folk ceremonies, they were associated with misrule; the interlacing of ribbons seems to have developed in the eighteenth century. (See page 360.)

The Tolstoyan community of Whiteway in Gloucestershire was established in 1898, to further the social ideas of the Russian novelist and sage. It is still going. (See page 363.)

Milburn in Cumbria was laid out, probably around 1100, to protect the central green. Animals could be corralled there over night, safe from marauding Scots and rustlers. (See page 392.)

The monument to Sir Tatton Sykes, 4th Baronet, at Sledmere, in the East Riding of Yorkshire, erected by friends and neighbours in 1865. Psychologists might wonder about the effect of Sir Tatton's personality, as expressed by this monument, on his son, also Sir Tatton, 5th Baronet, who had some eccentric ideas. The latter was also remarkable for building or restoring sixteen churches on the estate. (See page 437.)

After her husband's death from a hunting accident in 1859, the Marchioness of Waterford moved to Ford in Northumberland. An evangelical Christian and an artist, she decorated the school with a cycle of Biblical murals. The model for baby Jesus was the son of a miner from the community at Ford Moss. (See page 421.)

A village in its landscape: Bainbridge, North Yorkshire, was founded to house foresters who worked in the forest that once covered Upper Wensleydale. (See page 409.)

In the 1890s, six reservoirs were built in the Elan Valley, Radnorshire, to supply Birmingham with drinking water. A wooden camp sprang up to house the huge numbers of navvies working on the project, approached by a narrow bridge at one end of which workers were searched for liquor. The engineers were housed in fine stone houses which still exist. (See page 475.)

Cenarth in Carmarthenshire was a centre of coracle making. Coracles were often used in pairs to net fish in the river, but could also be used for herding sheep. (See page 469.)

Penry Williams' view of Furnace, in Ceredigion, in the nineteenth century. As the name suggests, the village grew up around an ironworks, seen here at its most sublime. (See page 479.)

Penrhys in Mid Glamorgan was a pilgrimage centre in the Middle Ages, having a wonder-working statue and holy well. The statue was burnt at the dissolution of the monasteries; the modern Statue of the Virgin Mary looks out over the roofs of pit villages lower down the valley. (See page 501.)

John Prichard Jones (1845–1917), one half of the London department store Dickens & Jones, built the Prichard Jones Institute in his home village of Newborough on Anglesey. In the Edwardian age, many of London's most famous shopkeepers were Welsh. (See page 499.)

In the nineteenth century, 3,000 people lived in the Highland village of Applecross. It was a remote community, reached only by the last of the parliamentary roads (built after Bonnie Prince Charlie's rebellion) in 1822. Although a coast road was constructed in the 1970s, the population is now just 200. (See page 527.)

When the tenants of Glen Calvie in the Highlands were cleared from their land in 1845, they gathered in Croik Church, some of them scratching their names on the glass. In Calvinistic fashion, they put their misfortunes down to their own wickedness. (See page 550.)

Sir Walter Scott's novel *Old Mortality*, 1816, took its name from the stonemason Robert Paterson, who devoted his life to the preservation of Covenanting monuments. Scott met him in Dunnottar churchyard in Aberdeenshire. This illustration from Scott's book shows Paterson dying by the roadside, next to his faithful pony, with the tools of his trade by his hand. (See page 559.)

In 1662 a coven was sent to trial and convicted of witchcraft at Crook of Devon in Perth and Kinross. Eleven people were either strangled or burnt. (See page 552.)

The village of Tobermory on Mull was one of the most successful of the settlements associated with the British Fisheries Society in the late eighteenth century. The BFS built a pier, replacing the previous landing stage formed out of the stern of an Armada galleon. Some Victorians compared the bay to that of Naples. (See page 631.)

William MacGregor's painting of Crail, 1883. The painters known as the Glasgow Boys took many of their subjects from fishing villages such as Crail in Fife. They didn't have to dodge the traffic. (See page 549.)

Glenfinnan viaduct: twenty-one arches were built to allow the catch landed at the little fishing port of Mallaig to be rushed to London and other markets. Glenfinnan station contains a museum to celebrate 'Concrete Bob' McAlpine who built it. More recently it has formed part of Harry Potter's route to Hogwarts in the Warner Brothers films. (See page 584.)

built as Roman games tracks and named them after the word for 'course'). There may, however, have been a henge at Rudston. According to Rodney Castleden in *Neolithic Britain* (1992), 'when the findspots of Duggleby axes, Seamer adzes, maceheads, chisels with polished edges, and polished knives are plotted on a map, it becomes apparent that there is a very marked and systematic increase in density as Rudston is approached; it was clearly a focus for high-status goods.' Most Yorkshire finds of 'grooved ware', an apparently luxurious kind of decorated pottery, have taken place around Rudston. Presumably people were coming to the monolith carrying precious objects.

Later, a Roman villa was built nearby, its location convenient for the Roman road that ran between York and the coast. What did its occupants make of the enormous, slim stone, which stands on a knoll in a crook of the Gypsey Race, that prehistory had bequeathed them? They brought different deities, among them a jiving Venus with streaming hair (the mosaic, together with a charioteer and busts depicting the seasons, is in the Hull and East Riding Museum).

Early Christians seem to have been determined to take over, or neutralise, its powers. They built a church right next to it. At Stanton Drew in Somerset, the church that was built in a stone circle was placed to block the view of the sun. The power of the Rudston monolith may have been diverted by another means: since the name Rudston means stone cross, it is likely that they put a cross on top of it. Whether as a result of this, or lightning, or some other cause, the top got damaged, and has for the past two centuries been sheltered by a lead cap: an apparently unique decoration for a standing stone. As so often, Christianity found that it could live with, if not benefit from, sites that had been held sacred by other cults. This suited the instinct of the English village, which has always been to recycle what it can.

The stone continues to inspire veneration. On the ground before the monolith and hidden in pits and fissures of its worn surface are coins that people have left as offerings.

*See also Avebury, page 8*

# SALTAIRE
## WEST YORKSHIRE                    *Mill owner does right by his hands*

Saltaire is the magnificent creation of one man's paternalistic vision for the betterment of his employees. Sir Titus Salt was born in 1803. His father, a wool stapler, had moved to Bradford in the 1820s, when that town was becoming the world centre for worsted production. The young Titus joined his father selling wool, particularly from Eastern Europe. His technical breakthrough was to find a means of spinning long-fibred alpaca so that it could be woven with wool. This made his fortune. By 1850, he was the owner of five mills.

In the early phase of the Industrial Revolution, factories were often scattered through the countryside, to be near the rushing streams that drove the waterwheels. As steam power took over, they could be located in towns. Their scale increased as weaving and combing were mechanised. In the first half of the nineteenth century, Bradford's population increased from thirteen thousand to more than a hundred thousand. But lying on 'a little pitch-black, stinking river', the town's rapid expansion had been an urban disaster. According to Friedrich Engels in *The Condition of the Working Class in England in 1844*: 'Heaps of dirt and refuse disfigure the lanes, alleys and courts. The houses are dilapidated and dirty and are not fit for human habitation.' Overcrowding in the mill towns forced brothers, sisters and lodgers of both sexes to sleep in the same room as parents – 'and consequences occur which humanity shudders to contemplate'. Salt had intended to retire at fifty. Instead, he set himself a new project: building Saltaire.

The name is a hybrid of Salt's own and that of the river Aire. There was nothing on the site except a watermill when Salt acquired it, although it was crossed both by railway and canal. First he built what was regarded as a stupendous six-and-a-half-acre factory. Borrowing an innovation from the Crystal Palace, he made the wall of the engine room a sheet of glass, proudly displaying the beating heart of the enterprise to anybody who cared to see it from the train window. Then houses of different grades were built for the employees. The rents of those dwellings gave a return of four per cent on the capital, but the cost of most of the public buildings was shouldered by Salt alone.

In 1859 came the Congregational church, with a Wesleyan chapel (built by public subscription on a donated site) nine years later. New buildings for the elementary school, previously in temporary accommodation, went up in 1868. Drainage was provided; there was an infirmary and dispensary, baths and wash houses. Almshouses were built and endowed, and the occupants provided with pensions. The factory had a canteen, selling meat for tuppence and soup for a penny. Like other Nonconformists, Salt disapproved of alcohol, so there was no public house. Instead, people could relax in the club and institute (1871), which had a library, art school, lecture room and laboratory, concert hall, committee room, bagatelle room, billiard room, gymnasium, drill room and armoury. Salt was nothing if not thorough.

By later standards, the density of the development – eight hundred and twenty dwellings on nearly twenty-six acres – was high; but the streets, designed by Bradford architects Lockwood and Mawson in a faintly Tuscan manner, are pleasant and, built from stone, certainly solid. Salt also provided a fourteen-acre park. Altogether it was an outstanding achievement, recognised by the bestowal of a baronetcy in 1869. It was a beacon of the best civic values at a time when examples of good practice were badly needed. Only a rich philanthropist could have done it; that made it difficult to copy.

*See also Creswell Model Village, page 314; New Earswick, page 429; Stewartby, page 196*

# SLEDMERE

The memorial to Sir Tatton Sykes, 4th Baronet, at Sledmere rises to a hundred and thirty metres, a gesture of titanic Gothic emphasis, if perplexing content, paid for by public subscription. Any son raised in the shadow of such an erection could be forgiven for being a little odd, and Sir Tatton, 5th Baronet, who inherited the estate on his father's death in 1863, was exactly that. Believing that it was important to keep the body at a constant temperature, he would wear several layers of clothing (six overcoats, two pairs of trousers), peeling off the surplus garments as required. Milk puddings had to be served wherever he might be in the world to satisfy his dietary notions.

His father, vicious and tyrannical at home, had been a racing man and popular with his tenants; Sir Tatton II, having raised rents during the prosperous 1870s, came to be hated during the long agricultural depression that set in during the next decade. Home life was no warmer; he became estranged from his beautiful wife, Jessica, thirty years his junior, and she converted to Roman Catholicism. Whether or not she intended to spite him, that must have been the effect, for Sir Tatton's passion was Anglican churches, particularly building and restoring them.

Sir Tatton built six churches on his estate and restored a further ten, supplying them with parsonages and schools as necessary. For an architect he had begun with John Loughborough Pearson, but after three years of marriage, Pearson's wife died and for a time work in his office stopped. Sir Tatton brooked no delay; he went straight to George Edmund Street. In the Master of Sledmere, Street found, according to his son Arthur's memoir, a client anxious 'not only to give every village a building where the people could meet for public worship, but such a building as should be an incentive to worship, and should, by the purity and beauty of its architecture and the completeness of its arrangements, insensibly affect for good those who were gathered together within its walls'.

Sir Tatton spent open-handedly, urging Street to ever greater displays of richness. The interior of St Andrew, Kirby Grindalythe, for example, is dominated by the remarkable mosaic of the Ascension of Christ, installed in 1893 by the Venice and Murano Glass and Mosaic Company: metallic tesserae set into the robes of the adoring saints glow opulently through the gloom. Every inch of St Michael, Garton-on-the-Wolds, is covered with murals by the firm of Clayton and Bell, better known for their stained glass, recreating the decorative effective of a church in the Middle Ages.

Street, worn out by designing the Royal Courts of Justice, died in 1881. For Sir Tatton's home church of St Mary, a little way from Sledmere House, he commissioned Temple Moore. In 1893, Moore had designed a new aisle for the church at Helperthorpe; then, three years later, an Eleanor cross in Sledmere village, which was converted to one of Sledmere's two war memorials in 1920. As an

Anglo-Catholic, Moore's taste for the beauty of holiness was naturally attuned to Sir Tatton's, and the result was, to the architect H. S. Goodhart-Rendel, 'one of the loveliest churches of England'. The reddish Whitby stone of the exterior is no preparation for the rhapsody of craftsmanship inside, with clustered columns, carved reredos, carved chancel screen and ravishing stained glass. On a window-sill at the back of the church is a small white marble bust of Sir Tatton: sensitive, determined, anxious, wearing an overcoat. A copy was placed in each of the churches he built or restored.

# SOUTH CAVE

## EAST RIDING OF YORKSHIRE     *From a schoolmaster's point of view*

In 1804, Robert Sharp took up his appointment as schoolmaster at South Cave, on the edge of the Yorkshire Wolds. He might not, to us, seem an obvious choice – until then, he had been a shoemaker – but he could read and write; indeed, he was generally employed in the other village posts where reading and writing were required, such as tax collector and census taker.

From 1826, he began keeping a diary, a record of family and village affairs, which he sent in sections to his son, William, who was working for a publisher (Longman's) in London. There are plenty of nineteenth-century parsons' diaries, written by university men who were a cut above most of their flock. Sharp's diary is much more unusual, being written by someone who felt on a par with the village tradesmen, such as his friend Old Willy Atkinson, the cobbler, and farmers: well to do, but not gentlemen. It is a portrait of village life from the inside.

Being responsible for the census, Sharp knew exactly how the village was made up. In 1831, there were 173 inhabited houses, occupied by 833 people. Nearly two-thirds of the 181 families in South Cave were 'engaged in Agriculture'. It was therefore a sign of Sharp's independence that he strongly supported William Cobbett's* opposition to the Corn Laws, which were keeping up the price of bread. He also stood up, like Cobbett, for the Catholics, who were to benefit from one of the first acts of civil reform in 1829.

He had a similarly robust attitude towards the Church of England, albeit that his brother Thomas was in orders. Sharp's job demanded that he went to church, but he came out fuming. 'The ignorance or selfishness of many Clergymen is truly wonderful, they must certainly fancy that the Church of England came down from Heaven, with a Bishop to bear it company and a prayer Book in his hand,' he fulminated in 1827. He was also implacably opposed to the National School system, his own school being financed by subscription. It was a war he waged until his death, still teaching, in 1843.

Sharp was not an adventurous man. His weekly round was centred on the school-house and the market, where he hobnobbed with the farmers while receiving their taxes. On Wednesday evenings, he would smoke a pipe with Richard Marshall, the miller; on Saturdays he would take himself to the blacksmith's shop, traditionally the place to catch up on gossip. Sundays began with 'a peep at the Paper when I have one', followed by two church services, arriving 'when the Bells cease ringing and the Organ Grinder blows up his bellows to greet the Parson as he stretches down the Aisle'.

Perhaps it was a limited existence, but the village seems always to have been full of people, whose old-fashioned remarks Sharp enjoyed (a sermon preached by Thomas had 'no botheration or belch about it', said Billy Kirby, 'it was as easy to understand as A.B.C.' – which, since Kirby could not read, made Sharp smile). And there were occasional excitements, such as the hot-air balloon that went up from Beverley, the early mastectomy that was performed on the doctor's wife, the defaulting lodger who was thrown into the beck. Sharp seems not to have wanted more.

*See Botley, page 97

# SOWOOD
## WEST YORKSHIRE                                          *Mapping the land*

One of the crucial attributes of the modern world is that we know where we are. We have a more or less exact picture of the land around us. It has been mapped. In Britain, this was not the case before Queen Elizabeth's reign. The medieval world was more interested in theological relationships than spatial ones. After the Gough Map, now in the Bodleian Library, had been made in the 1360s, showing tiny veins of roads and fat rivers dividing up a land mass that is recognisably that of Great Britain, cartography went quiet. Even sailors had no reliable outline of the coast to help them navigate.

For an increasingly centralised state, the absence of reliable maps raised problems for administration. 'See, how this river comes me cranking in, / And cuts me from the best of all my land,' Hotspur explodes in *Henry IV, Part One*, studying how England and Wales will be divided after he and Glendower have defeated the King. Shakespeare was being anachronistic. No map that the conspirators could have found in 1403, the date of the Battle of Shrewsbury, would have been worth quarrelling over.

Now, by contrast, we can pinpoint a village such as Sowood precisely. It lies a little to the north-west of Huddersfield. Without going there we can see that it is a modest place, overlooking a steep-sided valley through which runs Black Brook. It has a pub, a public telephone, a patch of forest, but no church. Various disused quarries lie scattered around the surrounding moor, while on the other side of the M62 is the site of a Roman fort. The place has been mapped. For that we must thank a native of this place, Christopher Saxton, the first person to make an atlas of England.

Saxton was born at Sowood in the early 1540s. He went to Cambridge, and then apprenticed himself to John Rudd, the vicar of Dewsbury, who was also a cartographer. Saxton helped him complete a map of England 'both fairer and more perfect and truer than it hath been hitherto'. This may have been the map published by Gerardus Mercator in 1564.

Saxton's own survey of England and Wales took place in the 1570s. In 1577, Queen Elizabeth granted him the sole right to publish his own maps for ten years, guarding him against plagiarism. The atlas appeared two years later. It takes the form of thirty-four county maps, sometimes combining more than one county. The endeavour was of keen interest to the Queen's ministers, with Lord Burghley anxious to obtain early proofs. The project's importance can be seen by the scale of Saxton's rewards: the grant of Grigston manor in Suffolk and permission (contrary to a previously declared royal prohibition) to build houses on an area of waste ground in the City of London.

The one thing about Saxton that is poorly mapped is his own life. He would seem to have returned to the West Riding to die. Was that in 1610 or 1611? Nobody knows.

# SUNK ISLAND

### EAST RIDING OF YORKSHIRE  *What the sea takes, it may also give back*

In 1399, Henry Bolingbroke landed at Ravenspur, on the Humber estuary, during his campaign to become Henry IV. He was followed in 1471 by Edward IV, come to grab the throne back from Henry VI. They could not have done it now. Ravenspur, once a flourishing port, has disappeared, together with Ravenser Odd and other features of the coastline*. The sea has compensated, however, by producing Sunk Island.

*Sunk Island: the strangely empty landscape of an area that
emerged from the sea in the seventeenth century.*

It first came to notice during the reign of Charles I. This sandbank was formed either out of the silt washed down by the Ouse and Trent or clay eroded by the sea from the Holderness coast – probably a combination of both. Grass was noticed growing on it, but it could hardly be exploited agriculturally until the ground level was higher than that of the spring tides. Since it had emerged from the riverbed, Sonke Sand, as it was known, was Crown property. Charles II granted a lease of it to Colonel Anthony Gilby, Deputy Governor of Hull, and he was confident enough to build a house, Old Hall, in 1668. Engineers helped Nature in the process of land formation by 'warping': embankments were erected to trap every other tide, the water being released only when it had shed its burden of sediment.

By 1787, according to John Saint-John's *Observations on the Land-Revenue of the Crown*, 'This derelict waste [had] been so successfully improved, that there are now upward of sixteen hundred acres of the land imbanked and in tillage, producing a rent of 900 pounds a year, with a chapel and several farm-houses erected on it.' In 1831, it was colonised further, when Sunk Island was formed into a parish, the chapel (rebuilt in 1802) being turned into the parish church. There was a school in the churchyard. In 1736, five people returning to the island by boat were drowned. The channel separating it from the mainland was then two miles wide; by the mid nineteenth century it had been nearly 'warped up'.

Eventually Sunk Island ceased to be an island at all. Grown to around eight thousand acres, it is a cowpat-flat expanse of rich farmland, with immense skies and moody creeks, where one of the few sounds on a hot August afternoon is the crackle of the wheat waiting for harvest. From the seventeenth century, various farmhouses and cottages had been put up to keep pace with the island's growing land mass and agricultural potential. The Victorians decided to regularise matters, employing Samuel Sanders Teulon, the least digestible of Gothic revival architects, to rebuild the estate. Ewan Christian pulled out all his slightly limited range of stops to build the church (now a heritage centre) and (former) vicarage.

At the end of the First World War, someone had the bright idea of making the east end of the island a place to resettle soldiers on smallholdings. Not surprisingly, in view of the remote and featureless location, the Crown Colony, as it was called, was not a success. Presumably the colonists did not include many birdwatchers; they would have loved it.

* See Covehithe, page 225

P. G. Wodehouse's short story 'The Custody of the Pumpkin' turns on the fate of a giant vegetable grown by the Earl of Emsworth, or, more precisely, his head gardener. Lord Emsworth wants to win the Shrewsbury Show, and has justifiable hopes of doing so. (In the end he does. Sorry if that has spoilt the story.) Alas, Lord Emsworth was a fictional creation. Outside the enchanted world of Wodehouse, Shropshire grandees did not care much about pumpkins, however massive, the cultivation of aberrantly huge vegetables being associated with the working-class towns and villages of the North.

You would not look for a Herculean cabbage, more than four feet tall, in a country house. You would begin by scouring the countryside around, say, Newcastle-upon-Tyne, paying special attention to vegetable patches and allotments. And if your search had been undertaken in 1865, you might have found such a cabbage in Swalwell. It weighed 123 pounds.

Immense vegetables were once the stuff of folklore. Jack's beanstalk leads up to the sky and has an ogre living at the top. Cinderella's coach is the metamorphosis of a pumpkin (though of uncertain size). Now they are routinely exhibited at the Giant Vegetable Championships held each year at the Bath and West Showground in Shepton Mallet. Parsnips at this event are routinely fifteen feet long. Pumpkins can be moved only with the aid of lifting equipment. The world record for a carrot stands at more than nineteen feet. These vegetable Gargantuas spend their lives under glass or polytunnel. The Swalwell Cabbage would take its place alongside such modern phenomena. But the remarkable thing about it was its authenticity. Despite the northerly clime, it was grown outside.

It was an amateur grower called William Collingwood who wrought this horticultural marvel. Collingwood is a famous name around Newcastle: Admiral Cuthbert, 1st Baron Collingwood, was Nelson's second in command at Trafalgar, an indomitable man who spent all the years of his life post 1805 at sea. William the gardener was employed by Ridley's steelworks, but friends called him 'Tar', from Jack Tar, a tribute to his nautical namesake. He lived next to the Buck (now Poacher) Inn at Swalwell, and – once the stalk had been sawn through and the garden gateposts removed to get it out – it was in that pub that the cabbage was triumphantly displayed. It was mentioned in the obituary published in the local paper after Collingwood's death in 1895, and was an inspiration to other allotment holders labouring on land covered with cinders and slag. Their feats of leek and rhubarb husbandry were the talk of local shows.

But P. G. Wodehouse was not entirely wrong: Lord Emsworth had one thing in common with the vegetable-growing steelworkers and miners of the industrial North and Midlands. They were men, old men at that. There are some places that women and boys do not go.

# THWAITE

*On the road to David Attenborough*

Richard and Cherry Kearton grew up in Thwaite, with wildlife all around them. The brothers dedicated their lives to capturing it on the relatively new medium of film, both of the still and moving varieties. They were certainly pioneers, they might easily be called natural scientists, and, like many early photographers, they were sensitive to the artistic possibilities of their discipline.

Discipline, however, it was. With wooden frames and brass fittings, cameras were not easily portable objects; the large-format glass plates that were exposed in them were also heavy. Long lenses were unknown. Part of the Keartons' self-imposed challenge was to find a means of getting close to their subjects without arousing suspicion. The lengths they might go to were demonstrated by the Stuffed Ox – a hide in the form of an artificial cow, into which one or other of the brothers would insert himself to capture images of ring doves and turtle doves. Other habitats required other disguises: the stuffed sheep on moorland for sandpiper and wheatear; artificial rock for ouzel and dipper; a sod house on the peat land of the golden plover; a stone house for the oystercatcher's rocky shoreline. High-nesting woodland birds were pursued using a long-legged tripod, operated by a photographer balancing on another man's shoulders.

Eyes accustomed to the dazzling photography of the *National Geographic* magazine might find that the Keartons' work sometimes lacks glamour. A song thrush sitting on a flint in a pool of water is (or was, until the species' decline) a fairly humdrum sight. Glamour was not, however, the quality aimed at. Even pictures of commonplace birds had the wonder of total fidelity to the subject. In 1903, Richard Kearton compared the way that robins had been portrayed in the eighteenth and nineteenth centuries with the images possible from photography. The exercise proved 'how rapidly the world has advanced during the last two hundred years towards truth and accuracy'.

Where, then, is art? It is in the way that the brothers opened the minds of their contemporaries – as they can still open ours – to the extraordinary world that lies, unobserved, at our feet. Quite literally at our feet in the case of *Daisies Asleep and Daisies Awake*, showing a field of daisies alternatively with their petals closed and petals open. Consider the way in which they marked New Year's Day, 1900. 'The closing days of the nineteenth century were so mild that primroses were in bloom in many woods through the south of England,' Richard Kearton remembered. 'Wishing to celebrate the commencement of the new century by some photographic exploit, we got a root of these flowers under focus during the last evening of the old one, put a plate into the camera, charged our magnesium flash-lamp with powder, and waited for the last stroke of midnight to boom from a neighbouring church steeple. Directly that happened, we fired, and secured a record during the first moment of the twentieth century.'

That century was to open new horizons; while Richard continued his research into wildlife, Cherry became one of the first makers of wildlife documentary films, beginning with his record of former president Theodore Roosevelt's safari to the East Africa Protectorate, *With Roosevelt in Africa*, released in 1909.

# WETWANG
## EAST RIDING OF YORKSHIRE

*The Vikings' linguistic legacy*

Wetwang, Crackpot, Ugglebarnby, Thwing, Booze . . . Yorkshire abounds in what can seem, to an ear trained on Saxon and Norman derivations, outlandish place names. Often they have Viking roots. Wetwang has nothing to do with damp; it is thought to derive from the Old Norse for a field of trial. The pot in Crackpot meant cave, or, in this case, crack in the limestone (it is a composite name: the first syllable comes from the evocative Old English *kraka*, meaning crow). Ugglebarnby was the farm belonging to a Viking called Owl-beard (it would be easy to picture him riding a Harley-Davidson; less so the man after whom Brocklesby in Lincolnshire was named – it means, for reasons one can only guess, 'without breeches'). Thwing means strip of land. Booze? Perhaps it was just something that the Vikings knew plenty about.

These names occur in the area of England that was controlled by Danish rulers and subject to Danish laws – the Danelaw, mostly on the eastern side of England, north of the Wash\*. There is a particular concentration in Yorkshire, where Jorvik, or York, was an important Viking centre. Just as Norse has given the English language words such as berserk, walrus and axle, as well as egg, steak, thrust and want, so the Vikings left their presence embedded in the gazetteer of the English countryside.

Not surprisingly, the Vikings were vilified as murdering barbarians by chroniclers such as Æthelweard, who was Anglo-Saxon; in Scandinavia they are remembered differently, an altogether nobler image of loyalty and daring having come down through the sagas that recorded their raids. Not all of them wanted to stay in the lands they attacked; from the rune stones in the Scandinavian countryside, put up to commemorate the achievements of a usually deceased family member, some were quite glad to take the Danegeld, or blackmail money, with which they were paid off, and put it into the farm at home.

The Danelaw must have seemed like the Wild West; the chronicle of Ramsey Abbey in the late twelfth century records that Æthelric of Dorchester bought some land from two Danes, who had left England because they were afraid of being murdered by their workers. Place names are often the only clue we have to who settled, because little written evidence survives. Sometimes, the Vikings seem to have imposed their identity on pre-existing settlements, such as Kirkby and Derby – the one having a church, the other a deer park. But they do not seem to have created the chaos that Normandy suffered in the eleventh century, when changes in place names were so common that abbeys, perhaps far away, could not keep track of their lands (possibly a deliberate ploy).

The most common Viking names are those ending in by (village, equivalent of the Saxon ton) and thorp (farmstead). Other suffixes are dale (valley), ness (headland), vik (bay), ey (island) and thwaite (clearing in a wood). Gradually local people came to think it politic to adopt Scandinavian family names, but this trend was quashed completely by the Norman invasion in 1066: from then on, the smart thing was to sound French. The flag of St George flies over modern Wetwang, a farming village of plum-coloured brick. No need to worry about longships.

*See Wedmore, page 79

# WHALTON
NORTHUMBERLAND                          *Celebrating the sun god with fire*

Britain changed from the Julian to the Gregorian calendar in 1752. This was achieved by dropping eleven days from that September, so that Wednesday the second was immediately succeeded by Thursday the fourteenth. Thereafter an extra day every leap year was introduced to synchronise the calendar and the solar years. The change brought us into step with the Continent, but like other attempts at 'harmonisation', it was deeply resented. One of Hogarth's Election series shows protesters, who believed that the reform had taken the missing time out of their lives, demanding 'Give us our eleven days'.

Presumably the midsummer festival at Whalton, known as the Bale fire, had been in existence long before then, because the date was never changed. It still takes place on midsummer's eve, Julian style – 4 July. The Bale may be an ancient survival. Bale derives from the Saxon word for fire, associated with the sun god Bel or Baal. There are other Baal fires in Northumberland; they take place in winter. Originally, there would have been many more, celebrating the different stages of the sun as it moves through the year. In recent decades, New Age people have taken to marking the summer solstice at Stonehenge, a ceremony that may have taken place in prehistoric times but died out thereafter. It is possible, by contrast, that the Bale at Whalton is a genuine survival from pagan days. There is a carnival atmosphere, with morris men and sword dancing, fiddlers and bagpipers.

Then the smoke clears and Whalton goes back to its existence as an unusually handsome and outwardly demure village, largely stone-built and eighteenth-century, with one gem: Whalton Manor. It was formed by Sir Edwin Lutyens* out of two existing houses, by linking them over an archway; Gertrude Jekyll designed the garden, which is delicious.

*See Mells, page 55; Thursley, page 145

# WHARRAM PERCY

NORTH YORKSHIRE                    *Digging deep into the Middle Ages*

Villages form, grow, shrink, change shape, grow again. Many towns began their existence as villages, many villages would once have been regarded as towns. Not infrequently, villages have ceased to fulfil the economic function that would ensure their continuance; inhabitants have drifted away or been expelled, leaving their buildings to sink into the ground, visible only as hummocks and declivities in the grass. There are three thousand deserted villages in Britain. The one that has been most fully investigated by archaeologists is Wharram Percy.

It is difficult to imagine that the hollow in the Yorkshire fields would once have been a noisy village street, ringing with the shouts of children, the barks of dogs and the cries of people; hens would have pecked among the rubbish, geese have gone down to the pond; there would have been the smell of life – and a pretty strong smell, too. Now it is silent. The last generation of villagers was evicted in the fifteenth century.

Until then, it had been like thousands of other villages. There were, for example, two manor houses – or manorial complexes – in the thirteenth century. The South Manor was the home of the Chamberlain family, the major landowners until the Percy family gained control in 1254. It did not take the form of a single structure. Instead, buildings were scattered around a compound, in the manner of a campsite. Archaeologists have found pieces of stone that have allowed them to reconstruct the shape of the chamber block, to which the Chamberlains would have withdrawn after dinner, glad to escape the rough noises, rank smells and rodent-friendly straw of the hall (of which no evidence has survived). At some point after the ascendancy of the Percys, the South Manor was pulled down, its materials no doubt reused in the peasants' houses that replaced it. The North Manor also comprised several structures: hall, chamber blocks, kitchens, brew house, dovecote, barn.

Other villages hug the brook that was so important to their existence. Wharram Percy stands back from it, to make room for the mills along its course – two in Wharram Percy itself and no fewer than sixteen along the whole length of Wharram stream. The village street starts down in the valley; this is where the church stands, a modest, ruined place whose form, over the centuries, reflected the waxing and waning of Wharram Percy's population. It began as a nave and chancel, acquired a tower, expanded into aisles, then shrank back into the present ruin, the marks on its walls telling the story of its previous metamorphoses. As the street crept up the sides of the valley to the level ground at the top, it passed between some three dozen peasants' houses – long houses, built around pairs of mighty curving timbers called crucks. They would have been well-anchored dwellings, the animals in one end, the family in the other, all under a single thatched roof. Each stood in its yard or toft; behind them stretched large gardens, or crofts, in which they grew vegetables and fruit.

The end came when the Hilton family, who acquired the village in 1403, found that it was more profitable to farm sheep than charge rents. They turfed out the villagers, and we do not know their names or what happened to them. Through the archaeologists at English Heritage, however, we do know a surprising amount about how they and their predecessors lived and died.

# WHITWOOD
## WEST YORKSHIRE

*Radically Arts and Crafts*

Charles Francis Annesley Voysey made only one attempt to build a village, or other workers' housing. It is at Whitwood, and the unusual commission came to him through a wholly orthodox source: the owner of the colliery whose workers were to be housed. A. Currer Briggs had already asked him to design a substantial holiday home in the Lake District: Broadleys, overlooking Windermere. In theory, Voysey should have been more at home with model villages than with what William Morris called 'the swinish luxury of the rich'. He was of a Puritanical disposition and Quakerish tastes.

The son of a clergyman, he had been brought up, initially, in Yorkshire; but his father, a man of strong and inflexible opinions, lost his living and, at the age of fourteen, Voysey found himself growing up in Dulwich, a prosperous suburb of London. Perhaps the sudden change reinforced a sense that the Voysey men followed their own line. He was a radical, and there was not a lot his clients could do to soften his attitude – or, indeed, the surfaces they were required to sit on.

The Voysey look was one of deep overhanging eaves, banks of windows, green shutters, hand-wrought latches, interiors of plain oak, one of the few pieces of decoration being a heart motif cut out of radiator covers and the backs of chairs. Compared to the overstuffed clutter of mid-Victorian houses, the Spartan aesthetic was revolutionary. But Voysey was insistent that personal convenience took second place to purity of design. Or, as he put it: 'Cold vegetables are less harmful than ugly dish covers. One affects the body and the other affects the soul.'

One might have thought that workers' housing, where simplicity was a requirement of the budget, would have been especially congenial to Voysey. Certainly there was a need for it. From 1850, Titus Salt had tried to answer it at Saltaire (see page 435). But more than seventy per cent of the housing stock in Leeds remained back-to-backs. They were, surprisingly, popular with occupants, who valued the low rent (they were cheap to build) and thermal efficiency (not so much heat escaped through the back wall), but deplored by social and medical campaigners, who saw sunlight and fresh air as essential to good health.

Like other go-ahead industrialists, the better colliery owners not only wanted to see their workforce decently housed, but saw a commercial advantage to it; in 1886, the board of Henry Briggs, Son and Company Ltd, proposed that 'the secretary and Managers be recommended to make early arrangements for building by contract or otherwise, at least one hundred cottages; in order to obtain more hands, and increase the business of the Company'. It was nearly twenty years, however, before the Briggs Company put its good intentions into action at Whitwood. In the end, only part of the scheme drawn up by Voysey was completed. It comprises an institute building – square and embryonically castellated, with a clock on one face and weathervane on top – and a single terrace with rough-cast walls, red tiles and tall chimneys. After that, Currer Briggs ran out of money.

If only Voysey had been given more opportunities of the kind. But why did he not find them? Perhaps his biographer Duncan Simpson has the answer. He was 'a quite fearful, though quite unmalicious, snob'.

# WOLD NEWTON
EAST RIDING OF YORKSHIRE      *Most definitely an object from space*

On an overcast afternoon in December 1795, three farmhands, who worked for Captain Topham of Wold Cottage at Wold Newton, were in a field when they heard what seemed to be two loud cannon shots. Then came a rumbling noise. A young ploughman, John Shipley, glanced up just in time to see a large stone hurtling into the ground, close enough to where he was standing to spatter him in mud. It weighed fifty-six pounds, and had been travelling so fast that it penetrated a foot of soil and six inches of the limestone beneath.

The men must have been terrified. They rushed over to find the stone, which was black, warm and smoking; it smelt strongly of sulphur. Immediately after its appearance, a heavy rain started to fall. When the stone was inspected more closely, it was found to contain shiny particles, and to ring like limestone when struck. It is now obvious that it was a meteor. What had sounded like cannon shots would have been sonic booms as it broke the sound barrier. None of this was known at the time. Most people simply regarded it as a 'phenomenon'.

Meteorites – or aerolites, as they were originally called – had been known since the days of the Ancient Greeks. Various explanations were given for them. Some thought they were made when exhalations of the earth condensed so far as to make them solid. This was a view taken by the seventeenth-century scientist Johannes Kepler, who excluded meteorites from the science of astronomy. Aristotle held that they had either been sucked up into the ether by hurricanes, or flung into it by volcanoes, whereupon they caught fire. Diogenes of Apollonia had a remarkably sound idea of their origin, when he argued that they were invisible stars that fell to earth. He was derided by Pliny. By the end of the seventeenth century the idea that they were chips fallen from the moon had taken hold.

*The fall of a meteorite at Wold Newton must have scared local farm workers,*
*but the publicity it received helped convince the scientific community*
*that objects could arrive from beyond the earth's atmosphere.*

The Wold Newton fall took place just as scientists were working out the correct answer. The year before, Ernst Chladni had published a book boldly stating that meteorites, coming from outside the earth's atmosphere, existed – a proposition with which the people of Wold Newton would have readily agreed, although it took decades to achieve universal acceptance because it challenged the Newtonian universe (in which space was empty) and proposed a baffling theory in its place. Chladni believed that they were the same as shooting stars, basing his deductions on observations of the meteorites that were in museums.

Wold Newton played its part in establishing the validity of such ideas. When Captain Topham, who had been living in London, heard of the extraordinary event on his land, he hurried back to Yorkshire and interviewed the three witnesses under oath. An editor, pamphleteer and something of a showman, he then ensured that the occurrence achieved the maximum exposure by carrying the stone back to London and exhibiting it for a shilling a time in Piccadilly. In 1804, he sold the stone to the natural historian James Sowerby, who wrote that it had fallen to earth like 'Phaeton from Heaven'. His heirs sold it to the British Museum.

Although Wold Newton lost the stone, its memory has been kept alive by a brick obelisk erected by Captain Topham. Its tablet records that 'Here on this spot, December 13th, 1795, fell from the atmosphere An extraordinary stone! . . . the weight of which was fifty-six pounds!' Surely he may be allowed the exclamation marks.

# WALES

GEOGRAPHICALLY, THE principal characteristic of central Wales is its mountains. The Romans never conquered them. New ideas were slow to penetrate, myths and superstitions slow to die. It is a land of waterfalls and saints. The men who brought intelligence from beyond the Marches to west Wales were the drovers, walking great cattle herds towards the fat pastures of England, assembling at Tregaron (see page 509). They became bankers, too. Later, a dam was built in the Elan valley, together with some equally solid houses for the senior engineers, and the valley was flooded (see page 475). Birmingham needed water more than sheep.

Men such as John Prichard Jones left the Principality to become shopkeepers in London (Jones, however, did not forget his home village of Newborough on Anglesey, see page 499). You might not have expected the first British branch of the Women's Institute (founded in rural Canada) to have been in Wales, but the rural crisis was acute there; the Lisburnes of Trawsgoed gave a cottage (see Llanafan, page 483). The population dwindled until better roads were built and the tranquillity came to be appreciated by artists, writers and the Good Life generation of the 1970s. In the footsteps of the bards came poets, such as the mystic Henry Vaughan, the clergyman R. S. Thomas and the bohemian Dylan Thomas. Although he wrote in English, the cadences of the Welsh language permeate Thomas's verse, and perhaps that of the others, too. Until the mid twentieth century, many people were happier speaking Welsh than English, and after a period of decline, the language is now being actively revived. John Wesley, an English speaker, could not make headway here; that was left to the great Welsh preachers, such as Daniel Rowland, speaking the language of their congregations and making them quake. For many Welsh people, dressed in their Sunday clothes, chapel became the centre of life.

Lady Llanover attempted to establish an alternative Welsh identity, to do with harpists and a bogus national dress derived, it might seem, from Mother Goose (see page 493). This was the Wales sold to tourists. Sublime landscape was the offer at Devil's Bridge (see page 472), where a hotel was built during the Regency; Portmeirion (see page 502), overlooking the sands of the Dwyryd estuary, brought the colour and charm of the Mediterranean to an Austerity Britain unlikely to experience the real thing.

The holidaymakers did not spend much time in the Valleys. Coal mining created staunch communities and a way of life. Industry could be a tyrant; the ironmasters at Nantyglo (see page 498) built themselves castle keeps to show who was boss. But villages as rural as Efailwen (see page 474) could echo to the sound of splintering wood when the Rebecca rioters tore down the toll gates of the turnpike trusts. Cosy is not a word that can be applied to Wales. It can be a hard land, but it is a land of dreams.

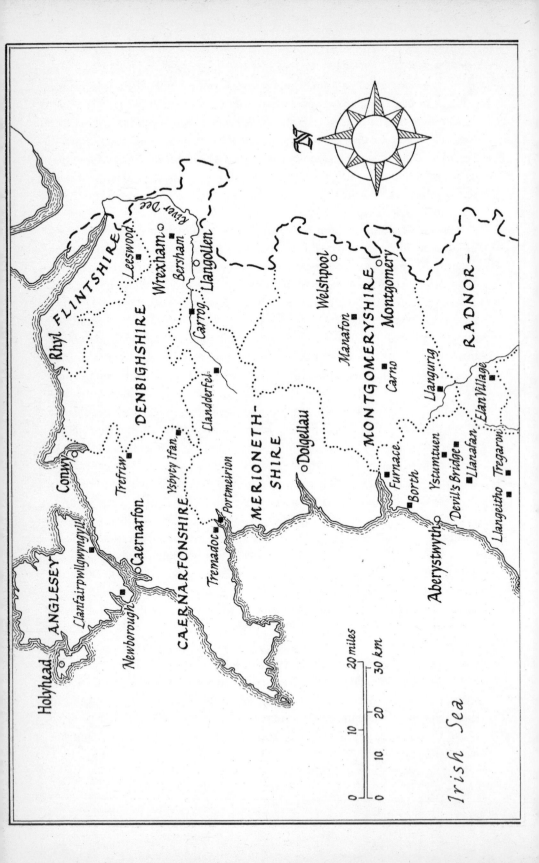

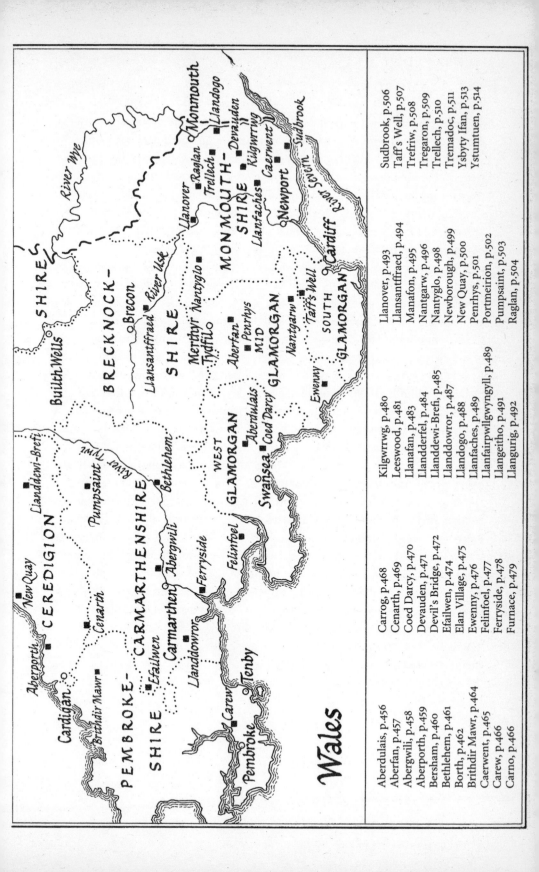

# Wales

# ABERDULAIS
## WEST GLAMORGAN

Waterfalls are as much a feature of the Welsh countryside as the wisps of wool caught on barbed wire. The wide, rushing torrent at Aberdulais was painted by Turner and became a favourite subject for Victorian lady watercolourists. Its waters were at that time used to drive bucolic corn mills (although the peace was shattered during the 1820s, when stone from the gorge was blasted to build the Tennant Canal to Swansea, changing the shape of the falls). But long before Aberdulais was appreciated for its scenic beauty, it had caught the eyes of industrialists. The force of the water was harnessed; the village of Aberdulais grew up as a result.

We first hear about Aberdulais when the German engineer Ulrich Frosse established a copper-smelting works here in 1584. The ore, which, as Frosse reported to one of the principals, was 'very strong to melte', came from Cornwall; the area around Neath supplied coal, used in conjunction with charcoal, while the torrent powered a waterwheel. It was an innovative venture: the furnace was of the German reverberatory type, perhaps the first time it was used in Britain. By July 1585, Frosse could report to Cornwall that 'we have founde out a waye to melte 24C [hundredweight] of owre everye daye w'th one furnas, the Lorde be thanked, and if we maye have owre anoughe from yo'r side we maye with God's helpe melte w'th two furnases in 40 weekes 560 tonnes of owre'. But like many of the early industries here, the venture was short-lived: it had folded by 1600. Sporadic attempts to work iron and full cloth did not last long. Aberdulais was either too far from the raw materials needed, or too far from the end markets.

But the cascade of water never ceased. After Turner packed up his watercolours, another period of industry was initiated by the Aberdulais Tinplate Company. From 1831 to 1877, the tinplaters produced so much spoil that the floor of the gorge is now two metres higher than it was. The works are now ruined, but the National Trust installed a new waterwheel on the site of the old ones in 1991; more than eight metres across, it is the largest such wheel in Europe, and generates eighteen kilowatts of electricity. At the same time, a mighty underground turbine was put in, capable of generating two hundred kilowatts. What may have seemed curiosities in 1991 have come to appear ever more prescient, given the need for alternative energy generation: the new wooden visitor centre, built in 2006, is connected to the turbine and runs off renewable energy, while surplus electricity is sold to the National Grid.

# ABERFAN
## MID GLAMORGAN

Pantglas means green hollow in Welsh, and the setting of Pantglas junior and senior schools in Aberfan was certainly green. Perhaps it was no longer the 'truly lonely little place' that George Borrow had found in 1854, but the hills still 'exhibited pleasant enclosures and were beautifully dotted with white farmhouses'. But that was not all the hills exhibited in the mid twentieth century. Above the village were seven tips started at different times since the First World War. They contained waste from the Merthyr Vale colliery, whose presence had brought the village to exist about a century earlier.

John Nixon came to south Wales from Durham in 1840. Having obtained a contract to supply the French navy with Welsh coal, which had been found to burn better than that from his native area, he began to buy and open pits in the valley beside Merthyr mountain. Excavation at the Merthyr Vale pit began in 1869. Miners came not just from Wales but Ireland and Scotland, living in terraces put up for their benefit; one of them opposite the colliery bears the name of Nixonville.

On 21 October 1966, Pantglas junior school opened at nine o'clock in the morning. A quarter of an hour later, the headmistress was in her study, the clerical assistant was collecting dinner money and the teachers were in their classrooms, when a rumble like a low-flying aircraft was heard. Earlier that morning, the men who were piling coal waste onto Tip Seven noticed that the point of it had collapsed by nine or ten feet. They could not telephone the office, because the telephone wire had been stolen. They had been on the point of moving their crane further back when they decided to have a cup of tea first. It was then that the tip's depressed crown rose up again, and hundreds of thousands of tons of pit waste rolled in a great wave down through the morning mist, engulfing a couple of cottages on the mountainside and crossing a disused canal and railway embankment, before thundering over the junior school and part of the senior school (which, mercifully, did not open until nine-thirty) and destroying some of the village houses. It left 144 people dead, of whom 116 were children. Aberfan entered the language alongside the scenes of pit disasters such as Senghenydd (1913, 439 killed) and Gresford (1934, 266 killed).

The subsequent inquiry found that a number of the tips, including Tip Seven, had been built over watercourses and springs. Tip Seven was, furthermore, built partly of 'tailings': the fine particles left over after the last tiny pieces of coal had been extracted by a chemical process. It was known that the tailings turned to quicksand when it rained, because sheep had been lost in them, and sometimes small children had to be pulled out. There had been complaints that flooding washed greasy black water into the village of Aberfan for decades. Tip Seven had already partly slipped in 1963.

The dead at Aberfan are buried in two long communal graves. At the burial service, the congregation sang 'Jesu, Lover of my Soul' to the tune of 'Aberystwyth', composed by Joseph Parry, a native of Merthyr Tydfil. The site of the junior school is now a memorial garden. A greater memorial is the transformation of Britain's mining land-scapes, as slag heaps were levelled or re-contoured, erasing the visual memory of mankind's often bitter relationship with the blackness at the heart of the earth.

# ABERGWILI
## CARMARTHENSHIRE
*Pure, godly, diligent and Welsh*

ESGOB oedd ef o ddysg bur – a Duwiol,
Diwyd oedd mewn llafu;
Gwelir byth tra'r YSGRYTHUR,
Ol gwiw o'i ofal a'i gur.

Readers who do not speak Welsh may need a translation of these lines by the bard Tegid, which are inscribed on the wall monument to Richard Davies, Bishop of St David's, in the chancel of Abergwili church: 'He was a Bishop of pure and godly learning, was diligent in labour; the traces of his care and pains will be ever seen while the Scriptures last.'

The little village outside Carmarthen has a long association with bishops. A college of priests was founded here in 1287, and their buildings caught the eye of Bishop Barlow after the Reformation. St David's is an immense and geographi-cally challenging diocese; Abergwili being more centrally located than St David's itself, Barlow converted the college into a bishop's palace in 1542, and would have moved the Cathedral here, if he had not been translated to the bishopric of Bath and Wells in 1548. He also made Abergwili the centre of diocesan administration, although the accusation that he cemented this move by stripping the beautiful bishop's palace at St David's of its roof is now said to be unjust.

Only part of the old church survives. During the Civil War, it was pillaged by the Puritans and partly pulled down. It was repaired after the Restoration, but by the Victorian period was again in a sorry state. Much of it was rebuilt, not very sensi-tively, in 1843, the wide nave apparently reflecting Bishop Thirlwall's reluctance to return to his episcopal seat for ordinations. Clumsy workmen managed to smash the stone that originally covered Bishop Davies's tomb, but his coffin was found, the body quickly turning to dust once the lid was lifted.

Davies was born in 1505, the son of a priest who should not, before the Reformation, have taken a 'wife', although this was a common practice in Wales. At Oxford, he became a reformer, which recommended him to the ultra-Protestant Edward VI. He lost his livings under Queen Mary, but returned to favour under Elizabeth I, becoming Bishop of St David's in 1561. It was a difficult see to administer, being mountainous and sparsely populated, with poor livings for the clergy, who were thin on the ground. Furthermore, most people in it spoke Welsh, and there was as yet no translation of the Bible or prayer book.

It was at Abergwili that Davies set about remedying this deficiency, inviting the scholar William Salesbury to stay with him at the bishop's palace. They produced a translation of the New Testament, with Davies himself being responsible for several books. The antiquary George Owen praised Davies not only for 'excellency in learning', but the 'public hospitality and liberality' that he maintained, not least, presumably, at Abergwili. Davies's palace burnt down in 1903. Its successor now houses a county museum.

# ABERPORTH
## CEREDIGION
*Thunderbirds are go!*

'A little fishing town, pleasantly situated in a small cove at the entrance of the river which flows by Blaen porth.' That is how Aberporth seemed to John Britton, writing *The Beauties of England and Wales* in 1815, and so it remains. Unless you are looking at it with the eye of an aeronautics expert, specialising in Unmanned

*Aberporth, where the RAF tested early surface-to-air missiles, such as the Bloodhound.*

Aircraft Systems (UASs). Then the outstanding feature of the place will be ParcAberporth, a technology centre that includes a hangar and runway, a convenient buzz away from the Ministry of Defence's Aberporth missile-testing range. Once, folk in Ceredigion would have thought that a drone was a kind of bumble bee; now it is likely to be a UAS, of the kind regularly used by British and American forces against the Taliban in Afghanistan and elsewhere, as well as (soon) patrols by British police forces and the coastguard.

In the nineteenth century, Aberporth made its money by fishing, lime burning and carrying coal – 'a brisk trade . . . with Milford, Swansea, and Liverpool' employing 'numerous sloops and seamen', with the herring fishery also giving occupation to a 'great number of hands' according to Samuel Lewis in 1845. A holiday trade had started by 1900, not to the improvement of the local streetscape, which – like a man in a deckchair after a good lunch – started to sprawl.

The village was woken by the firing of a Thunderbird missile in 1951. Before the Second World War, Britain had been almost wholly ignorant of the principles of rocket propulsion being developed in Germany, which came to fruition in the V2 'vengeance weapon' first launched in 1944. The Thunderbird – a.k.a. Red Shoes – was a guided anti-aircraft rocket, 6.4 metres long. Bloodhound followed. Sea Slug and Blue Sky were also trialled.

RAF Aberporth, from which the tests took place, closed in 1984. It was, however, but a small step from guided missiles to unmanned aircraft, or aerial vehicles, as they should more properly be known. Next to ParcAberporth is the West Wales Airport, developed from the old RAF facilities; now that the runway has been extended, it can take planes of up to eighty seats.

# BERSHAM
## DENBIGHSHIRE
*Iron mad*

Bersham was one of the most important sites of the Industrial Revolution. You might not think so now. The buildings that survive from the great iron foundry here look little different from corn mills – indeed, that is what one of them became. But this is where John 'Iron Mad' Wilkinson developed the most sophisticated works for making cannons and cylinders of its day. Out of it came guns that did not 'burst', or blow up when being fired, to the destruction of the gun crew and anyone else nearby; it was to Wilkinson that James Watt went to make the cylinders for his steam engine, patented in 1769. They did 'not err to the thickness of an old shilling in no part', Watt's partner Matthew Boulton reported in 1776.

There had been a foundry here in the seventeenth century, owned by two brothers, John and Robert Davies; from their forge came the sumptuous gates of nearby Chirk Castle and St Giles's Church in Wrexham, as well as those to Sandringham House in Norfolk. While Tudor ironmasters had used charcoal to smelt their ore, the depletion of forests and the need to preserve timber for shipbuilding turned their successors to coal. There was a supply of coal near Bersham: tunnels from the Bersham colliery (actually sited at Rhostyllen) eventually undermined Erddig House, nearly destroying it when they collapsed in the twentieth century. Limestone, required to remove sulphur and other impurities, was also found locally. Waterpower came from the river Clywedog.

Bersham's possibilities were recognised by John Wilkinson's father, Isaac, who took over the works in 1753, making iron pots, pipes and cannon. However, it did not prosper. John, who had acquired some capital from his first wife who died a year after the marriage, was able to take control when he married the concern's largest shareholder in 1763.

It might have been a difficult year for a business that made guns: the Seven Years War ended. But orders were placed by the East India Company and others, and the foundry also produced iron for workaday purposes, there being little that Wilkinson did not see as being better in iron. He promoted the Iron Bridge at Coalbrookdale in Shropshire, launched an iron barge, presented an iron pulpit and window frames to a Methodist chapel and was himself, in 1808, buried in an iron coffin.

One of Wilkinson's technical innovations was a new method of boring cannon, which made them stronger. During a period of peace with France, Wilkinson was approached on behalf of the French government, which was keen to adopt his manufacturing techniques. As a result, Wilkinson's brother, William, spent eight years in France. It was an arrangement that would bring about the end of iron making at Bersham: William tried to get his hands on it; there was a legal case; Bersham never recovered, partially closing in 1795 and fully in 1812. (In any case, John had opened a new furnace at Brymbo, a few miles away.)

Its demise was perhaps inevitable, and for causes that John Wilkinson had done much to further. His precise castings contributed to the development of the steam engine. Once steam had replaced water as the driving force of the Industrial Revolution, it was no longer necessary for foundries to be located beside fast-flowing streams.

# BETHLEHEM
## CARMARTHENSHIRE                              *You can get there from Nazareth*

In 1588, Bishop William Morgan, then a parish priest, brought out his Welsh translation of the Bible. It was a mighty work, and would not only make the scriptures comprehensible to ordinary people, but as a literary vehicle would help to keep the Welsh language alive after the decline of the bards. The Welsh read the Bible avidly, so much so that they became famous for being well steeped in it. The evidence is embedded in the place names of the land.

At Christmas time, the folk of Caernarfonshire can make their own journey from Nazareth (or Nasareth) to Bethlehem in Carmarthenshire, 120 miles away. There are three Bethesdas in Wales, three Bethels, five Carmels. Nowhere else in Britain echoes the Holy Land in this way, attaching names from the hot, dusty Middle East to a land of ferns and waterfalls.

Wales's Biblical place names are part of the Nonconformist legacy. In the course of the Victorian century, chapel became the centre and foundation of many Welsh lives, confining Celtic exuberance and imagination within the bounds set by teetotalism and self-restraint. Not only did the labours of the week stop on the Sabbath, as farmers ceased ploughing and drovers, herding cattle to English markets, penned them mid journey, but so, in some cases, did activities that would not elsewhere be considered work – the winding of clocks, for example.

The first Welsh chapels, built following the Act of Toleration of 1689, were simple structures, like barns or cottages but with round-headed sash windows – 'little granaries of God' – but those of the nineteenth century swelled tremendously with architecture, as florid in their profusion of columns and pediments as the attitudes of the congregation were austere*. Often imposing, they were rarely delicate. The number of chapels – two or more in some villages – reflected the passionately held theological differences that divided the Calvinistic Methodists from Wesleyan Methodists† and the Baptists from the Independents and Congregationalists.

Sonorous names were chosen, not always from among the more obvious possibilities in the Holy Book – Berea, Salem, Beulah, Libanus, Pisgah, Caesarea, Hebron, Nebo, even, in despair at the world, Sodom and Babel: names that were too good to limit to a place of worship but came to designate and sanctify whole communities. In the twenty-first century, chapel going has fallen off; it is said that one chapel closes every week. But the names on the map are indelible.

*See Tremadoc, page 511. †See Devauden, page 471; Llangeitho, page 491*

# BORTH
## CEREDIGION                              *Public school invasion*

Drains: they were the nemesis of the Victorian ruling class, bringing even the Prince Consort to his deathbed. In 1875, the headmaster of Uppingham School in Rutland, the Rev. Edward Thring, was powerless to prevent typhoid from attacking his institution – the fault lay with the ratepayers of a backward country town, who were reluctant to spend money on improving the sewers. One outbreak was defeated (although a master's child died), but the fever returned. With superb generalship, Thring promptly mobilised the school and led it to temporary quarters at Borth on the Welsh coast.

'There is a comical side to most disasters,' Thring wrote bravely, having been asked to contribute an account of the upheaval to *The Times*, 'and the sudden uprooting of the school at Uppingham has been no exception to the rule.' The school property had been packed into a goods train: 'If anyone wishes for a new experience, let him try the unloading and rearranging of eighteen railway trucks, and the distribution of their contents among twelve or fourteen houses in a fierce match against time.'

An advance guard prepared a hotel to put up 150 boys; another 150 would go into the terrace beside it. Long dining tables were set up in passages. A large shed, hung with shingle, was rushed up as a great hall. The stables became the school carpentry shop; the coach house was turned into the gymnasium. Making the best of the educational possibilities, an aquarium was begun on the four-mile-long beach, with the prospect of botany rambles in the mountains inland. Cricket could be played on the sands. Sir Pryse Pryse of Gogerddan offered his field ('unfortunately four miles away') for matches.

Then the boys arrived, 'and Babel began'. Such an experienced educationalist as Thring knew that the first thing they needed was tea. After that they were turned out onto the beach, where they did 'what boys always do on the sea-shore', dodging waves, hurling pebbles at the sea, digging up shells or inspecting pieces of driftwood. 'The low talk of pensive strollers, the rattle of pebbles, the laughter of those who chase each other in merry vein, all mixed with the roar of the sea, and perchance some strains of music from the choir practice thrown in, give sights and sounds that may make the school, if not unfaithful to Uppingham it has left, yet more than half-reconciled to the new land.'

This account, as Thring admitted in a letter to his friend George Parkin, does not tell the full story. Thring had made the school his life's work, and the fever nearly destroyed it. In the event, his heroic response was regarded as 'quite Roman' by the headmaster of Wellington College, the future Archbishop Benson. Perhaps Thring, who would have done well in the army, rather enjoyed the excitement: the boys almost certainly did.

But what of the little village they had invaded? As the end of Uppingham's time drew near at Easter 1877, the villagers laid on a procession and some singing, and a farmer called Jones gave a speech. Having 'dreaded their coming', the villagers had been won over, seeming, according to Thring, 'particularly struck that [the boys] had never laughed at any one'. A West Country man, Thring himself was no snob, and his heart was touched: 'It has made me very proud, and happy, and strong within.'

In a last letter before leaving Borth, he wrote of his confusion of feelings, in which 'sorrow, however, predominates'. He did not relish the return to Uppingham, although the townspeople treated him as a hero when he appeared.

# BRITHDIR MAWR
PEMBROKESHIRE                              *Lost tribe discovered in Middle Earth*

A glint of sunlight on Perspex, a survey plane flying overhead – the secret of Brithdir Mawr was out. For five years, the environmentalists had enjoyed their simple, low-impact life in houses made of materials foraged from the surrounding woods. But in 1998, what newspapers described as a 'lost tribe' was discovered, following a pilot's sighting of a solar panel that ought not to have been there. Their homes had been built without planning permission in – of all places – a National Park. There began a decade-long battle to keep them.

The community was founded in 1993, when the architectural historian Julian Orbach and his wife, Emma, bought a 180-acre farm in the Preseli Mountains. At the time when they were spotted, the 'village' had grown to contain twenty-two people. Tony Wrench and his partner, Jane Faith, built a roundhouse: it was the solar panel set into its otherwise grass roof that would give them away. Wrench, who had been a council official, now made his living from woodturning and music. He and Faith wanted to live as sustainably as possible, growing their own food, composting waste and filtering sewage in a reed bed. The house, which they built themselves, cost three thousand pounds, and would decompose back into its natural surroundings if left uninhabited for long enough. They were joined by other couples and families; one built a geodesic dome, another constructed a dwelling from straw bales. Woodsmoke curled from the chimneys. It was, as *The Times* commented, a settlement in which the Hobbit Bilbo Baggins would have felt quite at home.

The planning battle, however, was a serious matter. In 2001, Wrench was ordered to demolish the roundhouse within a year. After a stay of execution, another order to demolish was issued in 2003. In 2004, squatters took direct action to prevent its being destroyed. The next year, a change in planning policy offered hope to self-built homes such as Wrench's, lying outside the usual 'settlement boundaries', providing that they are truly sustainable. A planning permission was sought in 2007. It was refused. Only in 2008 was the roundhouse given permission to remain, albeit for three years only.

It is perhaps too early to declare outright victory for the Hobbits, but the zeitgeist has moved in their direction. Houses built with their owners' hands, using local materials, absorb far less energy than conventional structures. Heating from wood that is grown nearby for the purpose is carbon neutral. In a world that is increasingly anxious about climate change, Brithdir Mawr offers an alternative way of building that could become increasingly mainstream.

# CAERWENT

MONMOUTHSHIRE *Village inside a Roman town*

The road to Caerwent is a Roman causeway. Most of the newer part of the village is organised around a large recreation ground. But the church, like all of the old village, lies within the square enclosed by the walls of the Roman town, Venta Silurum – 'sum tyme a fair and a large cyte', as John Leland described it in the 1540s. The very name of Caerwent preserves a memory of Venta (market) in the second syllable. This is a village that goes hand in hand with the past.

It is a past that we know something about. Other Roman towns have had the misfortune (for the archaeologist) of flourishing. They became modern towns and cities, such as London and Chester, whose residents would object to seeing their buildings demolished for the sake of an archaeological dig. Swathes of the forty-four acre Venta Silurum, by contrast, were left undisturbed after the Roman structures disappeared beneath the soil. It has therefore been possible to piece together an unusually complete picture of the town at its height.

Geometry was the ruling principle; the town was divided into squares like a simplified chessboard – twenty of them. There was everything to make people familiar with Roman culture feel at home: forum, basilica, public baths, and houses that would have looked more appropriate to the Mediterranean than to Monmouthshire. The Silures raised a pedestal in gratitude to Caerwent's patron, Tiberius Claudius Paulinus, who had done them a good turn as the legate of Legio II Augusta, which occupied the fortress at Caerleon ten miles away, and who had gone on to serve in Gaul. (He returned as governor of North Britain in AD220.) Now in the porch of St Stephen's church, it was a monument citizens would have passed on the way to the shops.

The town was bustling in the third century. Its foundation, however, is difficult to date. For years, the Silures tribe, whose territories included the counties of Brecknockshire, Glamorgan and Monmouthshire, bitterly resisted the Roman invasion, only being subdued in the mid 70s. Military roads were built to keep them under control. It is possible that Caerwent was founded soon after the Romans had the Silures under their thumb. Another theory has it that the town grew up as the area became more settled and Rome-minded inhabitants found it safe to live outside the Caerleon fortress. The seed for development would seem to have been an Iron Age crossing of the Severn. After the collapse of the Empire, Caerwent remained an important centre for the Kingdom of Gwent, until that also decayed and villagers plundered the remains to build cottages. *Sic transit gloria mundi.*

# CAREW

*The tide comes in, the tide goes out*

Carew possesses a piece of Tudor technology that would bear revisiting in the present age of sustainable energy: a tide mill. Water flowed into a pool as the tide came in; sluice gates were closed to impound it, and it drove a wheel as it went out again at low tide. It gave the miller some sleepless nights, since his working hours were determined by the tides. He therefore needed a house on site. In its present form, it is a gaunt, boxy, three-storey edifice, whose ability to command the eye is defeated by the presence of Carew Castle on the other side of the lake. The lake, all twenty-seven acres of it, contains the tidal water held back by a dam faced in stone.

Something of a grim structure, it was nevertheless imposing and strongly built, and perhaps that is why it still stands. Many tide mills were battered to destruction by storms. Carew is one of few that survive in working condition (the machinery has been restored, although it does not turn), the others being at Eling in Hampshire and Woodbridge in Suffolk.

There were many more watermills, powered by streams and rivers; the Domesday Book records six thousand, and that does not cover the whole country. They became a feature of many villages – not necessarily a greatly loved one, since villagers were obliged to use the mills provided by their lord. Millers were reviled for their trickery, with Chaucer's red-haired, furnace-mouthed miller being well up to stealing corn and taking three times the fee that he was owed. The mill at Carew was owned by the lords of the castle. In 1558, it was leased for ten sovereigns a year.

The mill is one of several interesting structures at Carew. An early Christian cross commemorates a prince's death in battle in 1035. The castle itself was built by Gerald de Windsor, husband of Nest and constable of Pembroke Castle, in the thirteenth century. It was later converted to an Elizabethan country house.

# CARNO

*Prettifying the nation*

The closing of a railway station is generally taken to reflect rural decline. But the availability of a redundant station building at Carno in 1966 was to bring the village its major industry. Laura and Bernard Ashley bought it for their young company. It was a brave move for a fashion brand, given that local women did not have experience of dressmaking beyond what they had done at home, and the only machinery the men knew was on farms.

Laura Ashley, however, was not any fashion designer. She created a world of flowers and charm, epitomised by the high-waisted print dresses that became instantly recognisable, and furnishing fabrics in delicate, perhaps fussy

patterns, which enabled the feminine-minded residents of Islington and Oxford, Clapham and Colchester to wrap themselves entirely in the visual world that Ashley created. It was essentially a village look, irresistibly suggesting Agas, water meadows, cats and straw bonnets. The inspiration was the childhood that Ashley spent in south Wales.

It was not an entirely romantic part of Wales. She was born at 31 Station Terrace, Dowlais, not far from the mining town of Merthyr Tydfil, in 1925; she remembered 'a terrace right at the very top of the hill on the south side of the Brecon Beacons, very exposed and bitterly cold'. Dowlais put on its best suits for Sunday chapel, and had little formal education after war broke out in 1939, being 'absolutely flooded with the Folkestone Grammar School'. The house at Dowlais belonged to her mother's parents, and although much of her childhood was spent in London, where her shell-shocked father worked as a Civil Service clerk, she often returned. Towards the end of the Second World War she became a Wren, being part of the first contingent to land on the Normandy beaches after D-Day. It was during the War that she met Bernard Ashley, the son of a grocer, whom she married. The company they formed started by printing tea towels in Pimlico.

The move to Carno was helped by government grants. It was also welcomed by local people, who turned out with their tractors to assist the move (later the Ashleys would return the compliment by lending cutters during sheep shear-ing – the cutters had been shearers in the first place). 'Until you've lived in Wales you don't know what cheerfulness is,' Ashley observed. As the business grew, new offices were required, built with impeccable sensitivity using random blocks of local granite.

As a look, Laura Ashley could best be described as floaty. This was in opposition to the sophisticated urban scene of the Swinging Sixties. When the rest of the fash-ion industry rejoiced in the mini skirt, Laura Ashley kept her hemlines low, creat-ing a prettier and more graceful image. It was not one that she designed herself: she outlined ideas to her team, or produced old prints or photographs to provide inspiration. As the *Oxford Dictionary of National Biography* puts it: 'She believed that most people yearned for a more natural lifestyle than had come to be accepted in modern industrial and urban society.'

Laura Ashley died in 1985, after falling down the stairs of her daughter's house in the Cotswolds. The company continued at Carno until 2004, but then consoli-dated its presence at Newport. But for forty years the village had thrived on Laura Ashley's gift for countrified nostalgia and romance.

# CARROG

*The ghost of Glyn Dŵr*

In Shakespeare's *Henry IV, Part One*, Owain Glyn Dŵr (or Owen Glendower) appears as a figure of supernatural powers, capable of calling 'spirits from the vasty deep': his birth was accompanied by portents in the heavens and a great shaking of the earth. Certainly he was a mysterious individual. Having led a revolt lasting a decade and a half against the authority of Henry IV and his son, Henry V, he vanished. Historians believe that he died around 1415; legend has it that he is still alive.

His presence is felt keenly around Carrog, at the centre of his family estates; the lordship of Glyndyfrdwy, after which he was called, is remembered in the village of the same name six miles away. Pools, stones bearing the impress of his knees, even tables are associated with him – it is almost as though he could walk back into the landscape without causing more than a raised eyebrow at his fifteenth-century dress. He was the last Prince, according to his own self-proclamation, of an independent Wales.

It was in 1400 that Glyn Dŵr unfurled his standard – a golden dragon on a white ground – against Henry IV. This was the year after Henry had deposed Richard II. Glyn Dŵr was not present at the Battle of Shrewsbury in 1403, at which Glyn Dŵr's ally Henry Percy, the fiery Hotspur, was killed. Instead, he pursued an effective guerrilla campaign, venturing as far as Worcestershire and capturing the King's baggage train when an expedition advanced to relieve Coity Castle. He held parliaments and sought to reorganise the church in Wales.

But these state-building initiatives brought little comfort to Carrog. He may have possessed a 'fine dwelling and park' here, one of several houses between which, in the manner of medieval grandees, he would have rotated. All the places belonging to Glyn Dŵr were destroyed by English raids, only the mound of Carrog's castle surviving as Glyn Dŵr's Mount, nibbled by sheep. Local people have been known to say that Glyn Dŵr's soldiers sleep beneath it. The house that Glyn Dŵr used as a prison was demolished, alas, by the council.

Carrog itself remained a hamlet, enjoying a lovely position beside the Dee but struggling to make much of a living from the valley's farmland, which soon gives way to the brushwood and rough ground of the hills. A flood of 1601 swept away the original church. So as not to be caught out again, the village moved itself uphill. Then, in the nineteenth century, the railway arrived. It has not quite left. Chuffa-chuff, chuffa-chuff: this is not Glyn Dŵr stirring, but the steam trains of the seven-and-a-half-mile Llangollen Railway, of which Carrog is the grand western terminus.

# CENARTH
## CEREDIGION

There is an oval, black boat hanging on the wall outside the White Hart pub at Cenarth. In outward appearance, it is a little like the upturned umbrella in which Winnie-the-Pooh rescued Piglet when he was Entirely Surrounded by Water. Shaped like half a walnut shell, the frame is made of basketwork – willow laths, woven together with hazel rods – with a plank to act as a seat. Calico has been stretched over the hull, then thickly coated with pitch to make it watertight.

This is a coracle. Until the early twentieth century, scores of these light craft would have been seen bobbing about on the river Teifi, their occupants paddling nimbly. 'They afford a specimen of the earliest British navigation,' Benjamin Malkin wrote in 1804, 'and are used at this day on many of the rivers in Wales, probably without any deviation from their original form.' Weighing around thirty pounds, they were tricky to balance on the water, particularly since the fisherman's hand that was not holding the paddle was likely to be grasping a net. But, as Malkin pointed out, their lightness was remarkably convenient: 'The fisherman, when his labour is over, slings his boat across his back, and marches homewards under the burden of his machine and booty.'

To some observers, the black coracle seemed to turn the man into a beetle, apparently walking, when seen from the back, on a pair of sea boots. 'There is scarcely a cottage in the neighbourhood of the Tivy, or the other rivers in these parts, abounding with fish, without its coracle hanging by the door.'

The chronicler Giraldus Cambrensis – Gerald of Wales – observed the abundance of salmon, 'more than any other river in Wales', when he visited Cenarth in the late twelfth century with the Archbishop of Canterbury, who was preaching the Crusade. The salmon could be seen leaping the great waterfalls. They still can, but there was already concern about salmon stocks when the Royal Commission into English and Welsh salmon fisheries reported in 1861. Three hundred or so coracles were fishing the Teifi – 'almost a legion', as one witness had it. Working in pairs, the coracle men set up nets across the river, leaving fish little chance of escape.

In the 1930s, the authorities decided that coracle fishing should be killed off. The licences issued to fishermen were not revoked, but neither were they renewed when those fishermen died. But coracles have not entirely disappeared. They can be used for things other than fishing – guiding sheep across the river when they are being washed, for instance. A dozen pairs (they are counted in pairs, from the old net-fishing days) still ply the river.

Traditionally, each of the villages on the river has a maker, the boats incorporating slight differences special to each place. They are explained in the National Coracle Centre, a museum that opened in 1991. In former centuries, the interior of the coracle was lined with hide, the outer covering being flannel from one of the forty mills that caused Dre-Fach, eight miles away, to be known as Little Huddersfield.

# COED DARCY
## WEST GLAMORGAN
*A village (urban) in the making*

Coed Darcy is a village in creation. It is called a village, although with the adjective 'urban' before it. Eventually, it will comprise four thousand houses, which will make it the size of a small town. But the essential 'villagey-ness' will remain, even when it is finished – and that will not happen for years. This is a major undertaking, being constructed on a former BP oil refinery near Neath – William Knox D'Arcy, who lends his surname to the development, was BP's founder.

A disused oil refinery is a classic brownfield site: one whose land has already been used for an industrial or military purpose. Since the late 1990s, successive governments have favoured such sites for house building, as they have seemed preferable to open countryside. Environmentalists are vociferous in their opposition to 'green-field' development, in places that were previously open countryside (often confused with the green belts that supposedly contain the expansion of certain cities*.) The trouble has been that preparing brownfield sites, which are often heavily polluted, for development is expensive. And since buyers are prepared to pay more to live next to fields than amid post-industrial dereliction, green-field sites represent an easier win.

Governments may exhort, but developers follow the market. They have seen opportunities in old airfields, lunatic asylums† and workhouses; on the whole they have shied away from redundant steelworks, petrochemical plants and the like. So Coed Darcy represents a rare, and brave, attempt to create an attractive place to live out of what was once the Dante's Inferno of an oil refinery. Masterplanned by Alan Baxter and Associates, work on the first of six areas, including nearly two hundred homes, began in 2009. Robert Adam, the architect whose office has designed this first phase of the scheme, claims Coed Darcy to be 'the largest brownfield redevelopment of its kind in Europe'.

With the Prince's Foundation for the Built Environment closely monitoring the project, Coed Darcy will embody some of the principles already established by the Duchy of Cornwall's model development at Poundbury on the edge of Dorchester**. The look of the buildings will be vernacular, based on careful observation of local traditions and materials. There will be a sense of architectural hierarchy, with civic and other important structures placed at key positions. It will be possible for inhabitants to walk to shops and workplaces, and the range of accommodation from apartments and modest houses to 'villas' will enable people to stay within the community all their lives. Terraces will be arranged around open community spaces – a radical notion when pioneered at Poundbury at the end of the twentieth century, but hardly different from that iconic British building type, the town square.

After a quarter of a century, it may be that Coed Darcy comes to seem more of a market town than a village, but with luck it will still have the essential village characteristics of neighbourliness, local identity and a sense of belonging.

*See Hunsdon, page 181. †See Charlton Down, page 25. **See Mawsley, page 338

# DEVAUDEN
## MONMOUTHSHIRE

*John Wesley targets Wales*

On Monday 15 October 1739, John Wesley 'set out for Wales'. At about four o'clock in the afternoon he reached the green at Devauden, at the foot of a hill a couple of miles from Chepstow, where three or four hundred 'plain people' had assembled. He preached on 'Christ our wisdom, righteousness, sanctification and redemption'. After preaching, he went to a private house: 'whither many following, I shewed them their need of a Saviour, from these words, "Blessed are the poor in spirit." In the morning I described more fully the way to salvation, "Believe in the Lord Jesus, and thou shalt be saved:" and then taking leave of my friendly host, before two came to Abergavenny.'

From Abergavenny, Wesley went on to make a tour of south Wales, finding that the people were 'ripe for the Gospel', meaning that 'they are earnestly desirous of being instructed in it; and as utterly ignorant of it they are as any Creek or Cherokee Indian. I do not mean they are ignorant of the name of Christ: many of them can say both the Lord's Prayer and the Belief; nay, and some all the Catechism: but take them out of the road of what they have learned by rote, and they know no more.'

As Wesley's nineteenth-century biographer Robert Southey remarked, these impressions were formed in a relatively developed area of south Wales. A deeper abyss existed in those parts of the Principality that were cut off by mountains and bad roads. It was a land of poor livings for clergymen, and the established Church had fallen into a bad way: what little influence it might have retained was lost by its refusal to appoint Welsh-speaking bishops. Methodism, the movement founded by Wesley (although he was never reconciled to the name), was the most prominent of the Nonconformist sects to fill the spiritual vacuum. By the end of the nineteenth century, the chapel – often classical in style, in contrast to the Church of England's Gothic – had become a defining feature of the Welsh village. Indeed, many villages had more than one.

But the brand of Methodism that became most successful was not Wesley's. His problem was that which confronted other clergymen from England – what he called 'the confusion of tongues ... All the birds of the air, all the beasts of the field, understand the language of their own species; man only is a barbarian to man, unintelligible to his own brethren!' Methodism in Wales was not principally a religion of the industrial towns, but of the Welsh-speaking rural areas, particularly Cardiganshire and Carmarthenshire. Through preachers such as Daniel Rowland* and Howel Harris, Calvinistic Methodism spoke to the small farmers and tradesmen of the countryside in words they could understand.

*See Llangeitho, page 491. See also Bethlehem, page 461

# DEVIL'S BRIDGE
CEREDIGION                                        *Awesomely Picturesque*

Thomas Johnes bought a farm next to Devil's Bridge in 1790, with the object of building a 'little public cottage', later to be rebuilt as an inn. It may be that the Devil's Bridge itself struck some observers as misnamed: now a curiosity because of the three spans built one above the other, the lowest and earliest arch did not 'require the skill of so excellent an architect', according to a Georgian tourist, given that the chasm at that point is only twenty feet wide. ('How art thou named?' Wordsworth asked, opening his sonnet 'To the Torrent at the Devil's Bridge, North Wales, 1824'.) Even so, the mountain scenery was spectacular, and Johnes had a motive in attracting visitors to it: the main activity of his life had become the development of his impoverished estate at Hafod into a showpiece of the Picturesque.

Johnes was born in 1748, into a family that owned several small estates throughout Wales. His parents established themselves at Croft Castle in Herefordshire, and foresaw a conventional career for their son, as a landed gentleman and MP. Johnes satisfied their ambition to the extent of entering Parliament, but by the early 1780s he had decided to make his main home at Hafod – a thoroughly unsuitable choice, being remote, boggy and unprofitable.

A new house by Thomas Baldwin – a strange choice for a Gothic mansion, being an elegantly classical architect from Bath – was finished by 1788; it did not satisfy, and the as-yet-undiscovered John Nash, who would soon show himself to be a master of the Picturesque*, was called in to soup it up. Nash also designed the guest cottage. (Architect and client, however, seem to have fallen out, to judge from a comment Johnes made after fire destroyed his mansion: 'all Nash's buildings are gone, & you will say, perhaps, no loss'. Baldwin did the rebuilding.)

In an attempt to transform a seeming wilderness into a profitable enterprise, Johnes began a programme of tree planting, seen as a patriotic activity at a time when Nelson's navy was built of wood. But it also had an aesthetic dimension. Johnes laid out two walks that showed the valley and glades to best effect.

At Devil's Bridge, the inn was intended to share more widely the benefits that Johnes brought to Hafod (just as the home farm that he established on model principles was intended to demonstrate best farming practice to backward

*Devil's Bridge: a destination for touring since the Regency.*

Cardiganshire farmers; he published a book of 'advice' in 1800). A tourism industry had begun to develop, as people who could not afford to undertake a Grand Tour, or were prevented from doing so by the wars with France, sought out the most beautiful landscapes in their own country. While the Wye Valley in south Wales and Snowdonia in the north had, in Johnes's day, been identified as beauty spots, the centre had been largely ignored. If visitors were to come they needed places to stay: the Hafod Arms at Devil's Bridge provided one. The hotel was rebuilt in a Swiss style in the 1830s; the Devil's Bridge falls are still a tourist attraction.

Johnes's championship of the area made at least one convert in his lifetime. The great Picturesque theorist Sir Uvedale Price was so taken with the scenery that he employed Nash to build him a castle-style villa at Aberystwyth.

*\*See Blaise Hamlet, page 302*

# EFAILWEN
## CARMARTHENSHIRE

*Farmers in petticoats fight tolls*

'And they blessed Rebekah, and said unto her, Thou art our sister, be thou the mother of thousands of millions, and let thy seed possess the gate of those which hate them.' These words from Genesis, chapter twenty-four, would have been known to the chapel-going people of Victorian Wales. Some of them would seem to have taken it as their text when taking direct action against the turnpike trusts.

Road tolls were deeply resented by country people, who found themselves having to pay for driving beasts to market. There were other resentments and hardships: tyrannical magistrates, absentee landlords, bad harvests and a new Poor Law condemning the needy to the hated workhouse*. In 1839, a gang of farmers attacked the toll house at Efailwen. Their leader, Twm Carnabwth, wore a bonnet and petticoats over his working clothes. It was the first of the Rebecca Riots.

During the next three years, the Rebeccaites visited dozens of toll houses in Wales. They did so according to ritual. The 'Rebecca' would get down from his horse and hobble up to the gate. 'What is this, my children?' he would ask his followers, also dressed as women. 'There is something in my way. I cannot go on.' They would ask what it was. 'I do not know, my children. I am old and cannot see well . . . Wait! It feels like a big gate put across the road to stop your old mother.' After some more lines of pantomime, the crowd would shout: 'It must be taken down, Mother. You and your children must be able to pass.' It sounds mild enough, nearly two centuries later. But at the time, the punishment for rioting was death. The rioters made no bones about frightening the toll keepers, who were threatened with being killed if they got in the way.

In sparsely populated west Wales, where Rebecca struck first, it proved impossible to catch the miscreants. After a lull, the Rebeccaites returned in 1843, and their disturbances spread towards Swansea. Only Glamorgan had a regular police force, and there ratepayers objected to the cost of employing special constables, particularly in parishes where they received little benefit from the turnpikes whose income was being protected.

It was a difficult time for Chief Constable Captain Napier of the Glamorgan Constabulary, particularly since he also had a strike at the copper works near Swansea to contend with. But he struck lucky with information from an informer. On the evening of 6 September 1843, he led half a dozen officers and two magistrates to the Pontardulais toll house, where they lay hidden until midnight. Then the rioters arrived, more than a hundred of them. Napier challenged the men, a gun went off, both sides shot at each other. The rioters thought they were outnumbered and fled. The 'Rebecca', a farm labourer called John Hughes, nicknamed Jac Ty-isha, was wounded, and finally captured. It was the first success for the police.

The riots continued, but when a seventy-five-year-old toll keeper called Sarah Williams was killed at Hendy, sympathy for the cause ebbed away. Jac Ty-isha was sentenced to twenty years' transportation to Tasmania. Other ringleaders got a similar stretch. They were relatively merciful sentences by the standards of the time, perhaps suggesting a degree of sympathy from the authorities. Dai'r Cantwr, expecting never to see his native land again, cast himself in Byronic guise, writing a threnody before leaving:

> They bound my hands with prison chains
> And yet my soul they could not bind . . .

It is probably a mistake to regard him as a folk hero: as well as destroying toll gates, he terrorised local people to get money. But the riots were not without their effect. For some time, the roads in west Wales were among the best in the country.
*See Abbey Dore, page 291

# ELAN VILLAGE
RADNORSHIRE                          *The romance of Edwardian engineering*

By the 1890s, Birmingham was thirsty. Its population had tripled to seventy-four thousand in the last half of the eighteenth century; by the end of the nineteenth century, it stood at six hundred and thirty thousand. Between 1876 and 1891, its water consumption had doubled. The strain on supplies meant that some people took their water from polluted wells, with terrible consequences for their health. But the city fathers proved equal to the challenge. They proposed the construction of a series of reservoirs over the Welsh border, in the Elan valley. In 1892, Joseph Chamberlain introduced the Bill into the House of Commons that would enable them to be created.

The scheme was, as Archibald Williams wrote in *The Romance of Modern Engineering* (1904), 'of course a very expensive one'. Six reservoirs would rise up the valley 'like a gigantic water ladder', providing a total storage of eighteen thousand million gallons, seventy-seven million of which could gush into Birmingham every day. When the works were completed, Williams wrote, water would 'flow copious from the wide glen in which the river rushes busily over its rocky bed on the way to the broad Severn . . . and over the Caban Coch dam will roar, in floodtime, "the finest waterfall in the kingdom," to use the words of Mr. Mansergh, the engineer of works'.

This miracle of water could not be achieved without sacrifice. Cwm Elan was a country house associated with the poet Percy Bysshe Shelley, who also stayed at Nantgwyllt. Around Nantgwyllt was a community with church, chapel, mill and schoolhouse. 'Beautiful lakes they will doubtless be,' reflected Eustace Tickell, a civil engineer involved in the project, who sketched the scenes that would soon be lost for his book *The Vale of Nantgwilt, A Submerged Valley* (1894), ' . . . but their construction dooms many a picturesque and interesting spot to destruction.'

But where one settlement was destroyed another sprang up. This was Elan Village, originally formed to house the thousand navvies building the dams. A few years before, Liverpool Corporation had constructed a similar village in connection with the Lake Vyrnwy reservoir; it was not, however, a model of good behaviour, falling prey to the common evils that afflict all-male encampments – drunkenness, fighting, venereal disease. At Elan, George Yourdi, the resident engineer, was determined to reduce the pitfalls by imposing a strict code of discipline. As Williams described: 'A bridge over the river is the only approach, and every one who would enter the village to seek employment is examined as to his physical condition, health, and capacities, before he is allowed to cross. A sort of octroi is established at the bridge end to keep out contraband articles, among which liquor is chief.'

As well as streets of houses, Elan Village contained a school, recreation rooms, hospitals and a pub with strictly limited opening hours, the profits of which were returned to the community to provide social welfare. The architecture of the dams was monumental, with walls and towers formed of ruggedly rusticated blocks of stone. Much of the village, by contrast, was built of wood, and has disappeared. Stone was reserved for the higher-grade houses, and these radiate the same air of Edwardian indestructibility as the dams. When the navvies moved out, commuters moved in. The landscape that they live among may be man-made, but it is also sublime.

# EWENNY
## MID GLAMORGAN                                    *Potted history*

The last ice age did Ewenny a favour, as far as its future industry was concerned. It left a deposit of clay: a humble yet wonder-working material, which – once shards of limestone have been removed and it has been suitably pugged into a smooth, workable lump – can be crafted and baked to form pottery. Coal to fire it could be found locally. The ore used in lead glazes could be dug in the parish. Potters have probably been working here since the Middle Ages, when a Benedictine priory at Ewenny, a Norman castle guarding the river crossing at Ogmore and the market town of Bridgend provided a market for their wares.

Certainly the craft had become established by the early seventeenth century. Caitlin Jenkins, who is a partner at Ewenny Pottery, one of two surviving potteries in the village, belongs to a family that were potting in 1610 (she belongs to the ninth generation in the business). Production peaked during the Industrial Revolution, when the coal mines, iron foundries and tinplate works brought thousands of new people to what had been an agricultural district. As many as fifteen potteries were in operation at different times.

The Ewenny potters made objects for which there was an everyday need: bowls for the farm dairy, jugs for the kitchen, chamber pots to go under the bed. Robustly made, such pieces were coated in a thick salt glaze that was decorated, if at all, with naively scratched motifs. The potters' wheels were made by the local blacksmith. Potting was not a full-time activity, but one that fitted in with keeping a farm or smallholding.

Their rustic wares went out of fashion in the second half of the nineteenth century, when white, mass-produced crockery undercut them in price. But the Arts and Crafts movement provided a new group of admirers. Boldly patterned brown or green slipware – country pieces that did not attempt to hide their hand-made character – sat well on the unpolished oak tables and dressers, themselves standing in white-painted rooms, favoured by William Morris's followers.

Ewenny itself might have remained in ignorance of such aesthetic developments: appreciation of old-fashioned crafts was keenest in those places where they had all but died out, such as London. But an emissary from that world arrived in the shape of Horace Elliot. He first came to Ewenny in 1883, and returned often during the next thirty years. A design man from London, he 'craved the simple joys of peasant life' (leaving his wife to run the home while he was enjoying them), and introduced Ewenny pottery to a wider public. Novelty wares went down well with the London market, a speciality being fantastically decorated, eighteen-handled wassail bowls for New Year.

After the First World War, tastes changed again: wassailing lost its appeal. But Ewenny Pottery and Claypits Pottery continue the village tradition.

# FELINFOEL
## CARMARTHENSHIRE
*First canned beer in Britain*

A brewery and a tinplate works: it was a suggestive combination, which produced the first canned beer in Britain. Felinfoel is a small village of terraced houses, more or less attached to Llanelli – although some of the larger houses try to break away from it, along the generously named Swiss Valley. In the 1830s, David John, a local ironmaster and tinplate manufacturer, bought the King's Head pub. With a toll house next door and the Rebecca Rioters on the warpath against road pricing*, he prudently abandoned the King in favour of a new name, the Union Inn.

The pub brewed its own beer. While this was common practice, John's commercial talent enabled him to expand operations, first by selling to other establishments, then, in 1878, by building a detached, stone-walled brewery in the orchard of his house, Pantglas, opposite the pub. Although far bigger than the old brew house, the new brewery was still an integral part of village life. It provided a useful source of hot water.

'Nearly every family kept a pig in their garden,' remembered a villager, whose reminiscences were captured by a brewery historian. 'When the butcher was booked to kill a pig in the back yard, large cans of hot water were carried from the brewery to scrape and clean the pig. Some people living in the vicinity even carried hot water for their weekly washing.' Animals were fed on the 'sog', or grains from the mash tun left over from brewing. Farm carts waited in the road outside to collect their load of sog; it became known as Farmers Row.

The process of preserving food in cans developed in the early nineteenth century. By 1900, it had been extended to liquids such as condensed milk and soup, but not beer. In the United States, the American Can Company began to direct efforts towards a can for beer in 1909, but the problems of pressurisation and lining the can with a material that did not affect taste were not solved until the early 1930s. British brewers were for the most part unconvinced by the technology. 'I cannot conceive the idea of a can ever replacing the half-pint, pint or quart bottle,' Sanders Watney of the London brewers Watney, Combe and Reid declared in 1934.

At Felinfoel, the proximity of the tinplaters of Llanelli gave a different perspective. The first canned beer was made in 1935. 'New Hope for Tinplate Industry,' the *Llanelli and County Guardian* trumpeted. While the Americans had to pasteurise their beer before canning, Felinfoel did without this process: superior linings enabled the Welsh beer to be canned in its natural state.

Where Felinfoel led, other brewers followed. It would be some time before the aesthetic challenge was mastered; in the early years, the cans had a conical top, causing comparisons to a tin of Brasso. Nor, initially, did the can have the importance it would later assume: before the Second World War, most drinking took place in pubs. But the future was mapped, the smell of malt still perfumes the village of Felinfoel, and the red Double Dragon on a dark green background is a welcome sight to beer drinkers throughout Wales.

*See Efailwen, page 474

# FERRYSIDE
CARMARTHENSHIRE                                        *On holiday with cockles*

In the twelfth century, the chronicler Giraldus Cambrensis – Gerald of Wales – mentioned Ferryside, a place, as its name suggests, with a ferry across the river Towy. It was not the ferry, however, that set the sands bustling at the beginning of the twentieth century, but two other water-related activities: holidaymaking and cockling. The holidaymakers have largely gone away now, but they set the cash tills ringing while they were there. 'You'd sell six to eight dozen walking sticks in one day,' remembered (perhaps with a blush of rose to his spectacles) the village barber Ocky Owen, who used to work from a wooden shed known, from its popularity and gossip, as the House of Commons. 'We might sell two dozen pairs of bathing trunks each day, cigarettes not by the thousand – by the ton.'

Those were the railway days, Brunel's South Wales line having arrived in 1852, its embankment making it possible for what had previously been a fishing village to expand. Holiday crowds arrived en masse and, having climbed down from the carriage, did not find it easy to leave again. Why should they want to? The pubs opened at six o'clock in the morning, ready for the rum and warm milk that would be served to day-tripping miners from the Rhondda, which they said would set them up for the coming year underground; the election of a mock mayor attracted a more prosperous sort to rattle in by pony and trap (the supposed honour would go to a popular visitor); and how better to spend a summer's afternoon than cockling?

'Very large quantities of cockles are taken on this coast,' Charles Frederick Cliffe observed in 1847, 'and hundreds of the country people go out far on the sands, and amongst brine pools, with donkeys, in search of them. The fish bury themselves in the sand, and are discovered by a small bubbling, occasioned by their breathing. On the day before the steamer sails for Bristol, eight hundred or one thousand people are often seen on these and the Laugharne sands seeking for cockles.'

While Tenby rejoiced in the prodigious quantities of whelks landed there, Ferryside was content with cockles – five hundred tons of the bivalves being landed annually, according to the Bristol Naturalists' Society in 1866. As an industry, it could only flourish when the cockles came – and since their movements could not be predicted, it was never mechanised. Speaking to the House of Commons (the one in Westminster) on 31 October 1994, Rod Richards, the Parliamentary Undersecretary of State for Wales, described an industry that remained 'precisely as it was in the 1700s, except that donkeys were replaced by horse and cart, which were in turn replaced by motor vehicles and trailers in 1987'.

That comment, however, came after the sands of the Towy became front-page news as the battleground for rival gangs of cockle pickers, fighting for the best catch (the shellfish had appeared in commercial quantities for only the third time in fifty years). It would be the public's first introduction to the brutality of an industry that, in 2004, could allow twenty-three Chinese gang workers to drown as they harvested cockles against a rising tide on Morecambe Bay. Since then cockle stocks have fallen and a harvest is allowed only occasionally at Ferryside. Oystercatchers and herons have been left to enjoy their lunch in peace.

# FURNACE
## CEREDIGION                                    *Its purpose is declared by its name*

The Industrial Revolution did not take place only in the English Midlands and Welsh Valleys. The little village of Furnace takes its name from the furnace that was built here in the mid eighteenth century; indeed the furnace explains why a settlement ever came to be in this remote woodland spot, six miles from Machynlleth.

The site was chosen for its trees. The need to burn wood and charcoal to smelt metals out of ores meant that the hills of the Lake District were growing bald (as they have remained ever since). The ironmasters Vernon, Kendall and Company found that it was cheaper to sail iron ore to a well-wooded place such as the Dyfi estuary, where there were quays at Glandyfi, than to transport timber from elsewhere to their mines. At Furnace, they identified a site that had been already developed, in some way, for industry, having been previously used by the Society of Mines Royal as a silver mill. The ironworks at Furnace was one of many that Vernon, Kendall owned around Britain.

The centre of the Elizabethan iron industry had been the Weald of Sussex and Kent*. It moved northwards when timber became scarce, and the advent of water-powered blast furnaces meant that new sites were needed. Fast-flowing streams were required to drive the waterwheels. There is plenty of water in mid Wales. Restored by Cadw, the Welsh historic environment service, the waterwheel at Furnace is the first thing you notice about the otherwise fortress-like structure, which is stone-built, with few windows and a massive chimney rising at one end.

A pair of huge bellows would have been located next to the wheel pit; kept open by a spring, they were pumped down by cams sticking out from an extension of the wheelhouse. The bellows blew air into the base of the furnace. When the ore – rocks containing iron oxide or, in the vernacular, rust – had been smelted, a flow of liquid iron ran sizzling into the casting house. Another process, to drive off excess carbon, re-melted this pig iron to make the more shock-resistant wrought iron.

Built around 1755, the furnace was abandoned around 1810. By then, however, the village had become established. The furnace later became a saw mill: it is the waterwheel of this period that has been restored.

*See Burwash, page 100. See also Taynuilt, page 629

# KILGWRRWG
## MONMOUTHSHIRE                              *The remotest church in Wales*

Two white heifers were yoked together and left to wander. They chose to lie down on a tump, signifying that this spot was divinely ordained for building a church. From a twenty-first-century perspective, one might have wished that the heifers had settled on somewhere nearer the village, because the church in question – Kilgwrrwg's little grey church of the Holy Cross – has been left by itself amid fields, and can be approached only when wearing stout walking shoes.

Many parish churches have founding legends, and it is not uncommon for cattle to be the instruments through which God's wishes were interpreted. The Greek cross plan of the church at Alfriston in Sussex was dictated by the discovery of four oxen, lying with their rumps touching and their bodies placed at right angles to one another. But at Kilgwrrwg and Alfriston the places indicated by the omens happened also to be ancient places of worship, perhaps used before the arrival of Christianity. The circular churchyard at Kilgwrrwg suggests that it may have developed from a very old enclosure, Celtic certainly, possibly pre-Christian. There are many such circular churchyards in Wales.

There are also many remote churches and chapels. Kilgwrrwg was fortunate in attracting the interest of James Davies, who would become the schoolmaster in nearby Devauden (see page 471). It was on Devauden green that John Wesley preached his first sermon in Wales; Davies was a figure of similarly evangelical stamp. 'Active benevolence, great humility, uncommon self-denial, and dread of a worldly mind and temper, were prominent features of his character,' wrote his biographer, Thomas Phillips, although he lacked some of the more conventional attributes of a teacher, since 'to the close of life he spelt many common words inaccurately'.

He had worked as a weaver and pedlar, selling rags to paper mills, before entering into his vocation as a schoolmaster in 1812. There being no church in the village of Devauden, Davies sacrificed his own schoolhouse, converting it into a place suitable for worship and raising the money, by forceful appeals to the parish, to build another schoolroom, where he not only taught but slept. Up to a hundred 'rude, ragged, and boisterous mountain children' would attend lessons, the fees that Davies obtained from them amounting to between fifteen and twenty pounds a year.

Kilgwrrwg church may have been, even in the nineteenth century, difficult to reach, but Davies nonetheless deplored the state into which it had fallen, with the roof open and sheep penned inside the walls (dung was shovelled out of the nave on the night before services were held, which was only twelve times a year). He kept on at the local community until it had restored the building to a condition of seemliness.

Happily, unlike many Victorian restorers, he was not able to do more than preserve the little structure, which survives as an example of rustic simplicity. There is no arch to divide the chancel and the nave. The sandstone of which the church is built comes from the place on which it stands. Davies seems to have been myopic in respect of a (possible) female fertility figure on the external west wall: a hint, like that of the circular graveyard, suggesting that the old paganism died hard.

# LEESWOOD
## FLINTSHIRE                    *Only so much a Welsh miner can take*

Life for Welsh miners was not always fair. At the small but productive Leeswood Green Colliery, they were paid by the amount of coal they dug. When they finished one seam and had to hack their way through to another, they got nothing. Similarly, no pay came if a tunnel flooded, or when, due to fluctuations in the market, no coal was required. Throughout Wales, mine owners belonged to families that may have originated in the Principality, but now lived in England. They brought in overseers with whom they could communicate in English. Most Welsh miners spoke English with difficulty.

There had been a Welsh manager at Leeswood Green in the early 1860s. He was popular with the men. Perhaps for that reason he was replaced by John Young, who came from Durham. Within five years, Young made himself hated. He was accused of favouring English speakers by putting them onto the best seams. On the grounds that it would be unsafe in an emergency if a miner called out in Welsh (not everyone would understand), an 'English only' policy was introduced underground.

In May 1869, Young placed a notice at the pithead stating that the price of coal was to be cut, triggering a reduction in miners' wages. A crowd of three hundred miners cornered him in the yard. Standing on a coal bank, Young addressed them, saying that he was merely a servant of the owners and shareholders. Unpacified, a few of them pushed him to the wet ground, kicking him as he lay in the grimy puddles. After forty-five minutes, they marched him to the railway station, and some policemen who happened to be there escorted him to Mold. Young was lucky to get away with his life. Afterwards, his house was broken into and his furniture taken out, dumped at the station as a strong hint that he might think of moving on.

Seven men were arrested and brought before the magistrates in Mold. All pleaded not guilty of the assault; all were found guilty as charged. The two ring-leaders were given a month's hard labour, the rest fined. By the standards of the day, they were not unduly harsh sentences. Nevertheless, a crowd gathered. By seven o'clock, it had grown to three thousand people. When the prisoners were marched towards the station to be taken to the county gaol at Flint, the police escort was blocked. Stones were thrown, then bricks. Slowly, prisoners and police-men inched towards the station, only to find that the frightened staff had shut the gates. By now, the missiles were falling so heavily that the train, which was in the station, could not leave.

Initially nobody could find a magistrate to take charge; then a passenger on the train announced that he was a magistrate, and authorised the Flintshire Yeomanry, whose presence had been summoned earlier in the day, to open fire. They were reluctant to do so, not least because the Riot Act had not been read or signed. But when the mob started to pull up the iron railings in front of the station, the soldiers fired over the heads of the rioters. With their blood up, they hardly noticed. The order was given to fire into the crowd.

Four people were killed. Edward Bellis, a young blacksmith, and Robert Hanaby, a nineteen-year-old collier, had been throwing stones; another victim, Elizabeth Jones, had been handing them out. Margaret Younghusband, a nineteen-year-old orphan from Chester, who had arrived that morning to take up a position as a housemaid, was an innocent bystander. So was Christopher Keane, manager of Mold Iron Foundry, who was shot through the shoulder but recovered.

The riot caused a national sensation. Afterwards, peace returned to the pits. John Young tried to carry on in Leeswood, but was forcibly put on a train and packed off. Soon, miners from the locality founded the Flintshire and Denbighshire Miners' Friendly Association, a forerunner of the National Union of Mineworkers.

# LLANAFAN
## CEREDIGION
*Social reform and jam-making*

A collection of photographs held by Ceredigion County Council shows the ladies of the Llanafan Women's Institute. In print dresses and cloche hats, they appear to be more than capable of keeping their hall, with its hurricane lamp over the bare table, spotless. Hall is perhaps a generous way to describe a little stone cottage, built in 1832. The 7th Earl of Lisburne gave it to the WI at the behest of his Chilean wife, Regina. The gift was made following the Armistice in 1918. There is now a neat iron gate with a WI monogram to go with it.

The Lisburnes used to live in an elegant Georgian house, encasing an earlier one, a couple of miles away at Trawsgoed. Along came the Edwardians with their shooting parties, and pumped iron, transforming a slip of a mansion into the sort of place that can be run only with an army of staff. The family was at that time rich from the Lisburne Mining Company, which dug into the hillsides for lead. It was

*Women's Institute Hall at Llanafan: a cottage given by the Earl of Lisburne after 1918. The WI came to Britain during the First World War.*

the 5th Earl who commissioned William Butterfield to build the little Victorian church in Llanafan, where the family is buried: a Gothic Revival counterpoise to the Georgian simplicity of the Calvinistic Methodists' chapel built earlier in the nineteenth century. There is, by contrast, no stylistic assertion about the Women's Institute Hall. With apple-green woodwork, it is a sweet building.

Wales has a long association with the Women's Institute. The organisation's first British branch was opened at Llanfairpwllgwyngyll on Anglesey (see page 489) in 1915. 'No existing body is so well fitted to further the general prosperity of a community as a Women's Institute,' the founders announced. It had taken some time for British women to embrace the WI, which was founded in Canada in 1897. The idea had been to give women training and education, and generally to combat the extreme provincialism of rural society in the nineteenth century.

'Educate a boy and you educate a man, but educate a girl and you educate a family,' co-founder Adelaide Hoodless told the British Columbia Women's Institute. Women's education in Britain was notoriously poor in the late nineteenth century. Matters in Wales were not improved for women by the sternly patriarchal character of the society. To some, an organisation that set out to challenge these embedded relationships seemed dangerously radical.

Indeed, the WI's appearance in Britain was part of the re-evaluation of women's roles that took place while so many men were serving in the armed forces, which was expressed, after the War, in women being given the vote. Because the British WI was founded in wartime, the emphasis was on strengthening rural communities, rather than, as in Canada, on the healing properties of the home. Nevertheless, the Llanafan cottage expresses the domestic tone of the organisation's first half century, during which the WI campaigned on issues such as rural education, school lunches and dental care, as well as the taboo subject of venereal disease. (During the Second World War it made a reputation for jam by preserving more than 5,300 tons of otherwise surplus fruit.)

This being Wales, a country that tends to fissiparousness, even the WI has its rival. During the 1960s, the WI, a global network of anglophones with eight million members, refused to adopt Welsh as an official language in the Principality. In protest, a group of Welsh-speaking women formed Merched y Wawr, or 'Women of the Dawn': more popular in some village circles than the lustily 'Jerusalem'-singing WI.

# LLANDDERFEL
## MERIONETHSHIRE                      *Queen Victoria visits Wales*

*The Illustrated London News* was in orbit: Queen Victoria was visiting Wales. In 1889, the plump, elderly monarch, swathed in black and leaning heavily on a stick, did not visit anywhere very much, except her beloved Scotland. The descent on

Wales was therefore an event, and merited more than thirty woodcut illustrations. The Queen proceeds through an arch of welcome at Bala; a royal address is presented; the Queen reaches Llandderfel railway station, which is *en fête*. From the station she goes to Palé Hall, the spanking Elizabethan mansion built for the railway promoter Henry Robertson, who had the misfortune to miss the occasion, having died the year before; Her Majesty knights his son, Henry Beyer Robertson, instead. She stays there for five days, visiting the banks of the Dee, 'scarcely less interesting than those of the Deeside in Scotland, where her favourite residence of Balmoral is situated'.

The Welsh Deeside had no Sir Walter Scott to bring out its romantic possibilities for the Victorian public. But supporters included the arbiter on all matters of landscape and aesthetic taste, John Ruskin: he compared the Valley of Llangollen favourably to his Lake District home, chosen because of the view over Coniston Water. 'The Dee itself is a quite perfect mountain stream,' he wrote. The poet Robert Browning was no less affected by the 'clear pre-eminence' of Llangollen: 'I received an impression of the beauty around me which continued ineffaceable during all subsequent experience of varied foreign scenery – mountain, valley and river.'

The village of Llandderfel lost its chief claim to fame in the sixteenth century. This had been a carving of the warrior Derfel Gadarn, son of Hywel, who was supposedly slain by King Arthur. A saint, his large wooden image was venerated until removed by Thomas Cromwell's agents and taken to London in 1538, despite a large bribe of forty pounds having been offered to leave it in place. It was said that the statue was capable of setting a whole forest on fire. In a grim piece of Tudor humour, it was placed beneath the Franciscan friar John Forest when he was burnt at the stake for his support of papal authority. A story, perhaps, worthy of Scott? Derfel Gadarn has a modern interpreter in Bernard Cornwell, who made him the hero of his Warlord Chronicles trilogy.

Presumably Queen Victoria saw the memory of Derfel Gadarn that is still in the porch of the church. During the Middle Ages, people would bring animals for the saint's blessing and cure, including horses and woodland creatures, such as deer. That at least is the explanation given for the primitive wooden sculpture of a sitting hart, rather age worn, which originally stood by the altar. Most of its head was removed in the 1730s.

# LLANDDEWI-BREFI
CEREDIGION                                              *Peace and love in west Wales, man*

Ceredigion is not California. Nevertheless, in the 1970s, it attracted people who wanted to drop out. Property was cheap, unexpected visitors rarely bumped down the muddy tracks leading to lonely cottages, and the sheep on the hillsides had nothing to say about alternative lifestyles and drug taking.

On 15 April 1975, a team of policemen, led by a drugs squad officer from Scotland Yard, assembled in Aberystwyth prior to raiding a suspicious address in Llanddewi-Brefi. One of them was the local bobby. When a colleague wanted to contact him about another matter, he phoned Aberystwyth police station, was told that the bobby was heading for Llanddewi-Brefi, and so phoned the bobby's wife. She said she would take a message, and went round to the house, to see if her husband had arrived. He had not, and, not surprisingly, by the time he and other policemen appeared, the substantial quantity of illicit drugs that had been on the premises had been hidden in a local quarry.

That time the drug dealers got away with it. Observant members of the community might have spotted that Llanddewi-Brefi was different. For one thing, pop stars such as John Lennon and Jimi Hendrix were said to visit 'an eccentric pop music adherent', who boasted an invitation card to Hendrix's funeral. As the writer Lyn Ebenezer told the BBC: 'Stuck on the card was a boiled sweet injected with a tab of LSD. I know, I saw it on his mantlepiece.' To most of the village, LSD meant pounds, shillings and pence.

But another trail had been started by a fatal road accident near Machynlleth, which killed the wife of a vicar. A Land Rover had been carrying slates. The police were suspicious of the driver, an energetic, hot-tempered, accident-prone man in his early thirties called Richard Kemp. When the slates were removed, twenty-six scraps of paper were found scattered among them. Carefully reassembled, they bore the words hydrazine hydrate: one of the ingredients in Lysergic acid diethylamide-25, better known as LSD.

Kemp shared a primitive stone cottage near Tregaron (see page 509) with Christine Bott, a qualified doctor, who liked gardening and showing her goats at the local agricultural show. The couple met at Liverpool University and were now running a factory making top-quality LSD. The quantities amazed the police. Previously it had been thought that twenty thousand tablets were taken each year in Britain. Kemp and Bott were producing eighteen million tablets a year. It was the hub of a multi-million-pound business that supplied half the world.

Fourteen-pound sledgehammers were used to smash down the cottage door when Operation Julie pounced on 26 March 1977. Simultaneous raids took place at Y Glynn in Llanddewi-Brefi, Birmingham and Périgueux in France. Like others of the flower-power generation, Bott believed that LSD produced a sense of oneness with the world, in which humble objects take on a wonderful beauty; she told the police that manufacturing it was her 'contribution to alter society'. The judge at Bristol Crown Court took a different view. Kemp was given a sentence of thirteen years, Bott ten years, and several co-defendants were similarly jailed. The police could not help noticing how smartly turned out and well-spoken they were.

Kemp and Bott were not the last hippies in west Wales. Others held a magic mushroom festival at Llanafan (see page 483) until police succeeded in stopping it. The last took place in 1982.

# LLANDDOWROR
CARMARTHENSHIRE                    *Teaching literacy, quick time*

Griffith Jones, rector of Llanddowror, could be a misery. Born in 1684, he had grown up as a sickly child in remote Pembrokeshire, his face marked by small-pox and his temper soured by asthma. For all that, he was a stirring preacher in the knee-trembling, wrathful style of the early Methodists, before Methodism had even been thought of (to some of his congregation, who might have walked miles to hear him, he seemed to be 'an angel of God'). And although it might not be thought that his morose temperament was well adapted to the instruction of the young, he had a galvanising effect on education in Wales, inventing an ingenious system for promoting it.

Preaching made Jones aware of the chronic state of literacy in Wales. His oratory from the pulpit, although delivered in Welsh, was apt to be lost on hearers who could not read the Bible. Besides, to a Protestant whose first years were lived under the reign of Catholic James II, it was especially important that the Bible should be read at first hand, rather than interpreted by 'popish locusts'. But conventional efforts, such as those by the Society for Promoting Christian Knowledge, had foundered on the lackadaisical attitude of pupils, who were needed on the farm, and the small number of schools.

In 1731, Jones devised a network of 'circulating schools'. They operated on the basis of a pyramid scheme. The first pupils were taught directly by Jones at Llanddowror; once able to read, they were sent out to schools in other parishes. Those schools instructed a cohort, which could then go out to yet more parishes, and so on. The schools were free and intentionally short-lived. As Jones wrote to his patron and lifelong friend Bridget Bevan: 'It is certainly much better to limit the time than if it was to continue long; for then most people would delay, think-ing they might have the opportunity some time hereafter, when they think they will be more at leisure.' Two-thirds of the people who came to the schools were adults, some of them weeping behind their spectacles that they had not had the opportunity to learn forty years earlier.

In his annual report, *The Welch Piety*, for 1741, Jones assessed progress: 'It is well attested by proper and credible witnesses, that by means of them, many parish churches, almost empty before, have been filled with large congregations, the number of communicants has much increased, very many householders have set up the worship of God in their families, a remarkable reformation is seen in many neighbourhoods, and many thousands of young and old people have been taught to read and to say the Church Catechism, and willingly repeat it before the congregation to their Parish Ministers.'

It is also possible that the pleasures of reading brought their own rewards to folk whose intellectual horizons did not extend beyond the valleys in which they lived.

# LLANDOGO
MONMOUTHSHIRE                      *Boat building in a Picturesque setting*

'Every elevated spot near the banks of the Wye, must from the nature of the ground, furnish either a Landscape or a Prospect, and enumeration would be endless,' Thomas Fosbroke opined in 1822. Fosbroke told of a man who had left the beaten track to climb a crag near Llandogo. While the 'extensive tract of country' that he could see was beautiful, the 'steepness of the precipice amazed and terrified him. Advancing a few paces, he looked over a tremendous chasm, overhung by trunks of trees, while water rushing over the rocks below, added much to the horror of the place.' Fosbroke was following in the steps of the Rev. William Gilpin, whose *Observations on the River Wye* had come out between 1782 and 1791. Polite travellers came to the Wye valley to be alternately charmed and awed by the scenery.

But the Wye valley meant something else to the people living there. Below Monmouth, the river flowed through several villages on its way to the Severn Estuary, often busy with industry. Only half a mile from the ruins of Tintern Abbey, celebrated by Wordsworth and Turner, was the Angidy Ironworks, which, Gilpin sniffed, 'introduce noise and bustle into these regions of tranquility'. The ironworks, however, had been going longer than Picturesque tourism, having been established during the reign of Henry VIII (the Dissolution of the Monasteries had opened up the area to new men). A few miles further up was Redbrook's iron and tin works. Archdeacon William Coxe, touring Monmouthshire in 1799, made the best of what he might secretly have thought to be a bad job, by writing that the metal bashers 'gave animation to the romantic scenery'. Wire and paper were manufactured at Whitebrook.

Llandogo was a centre of boat building, specifically flat-bottomed craft known as trows. The word derives from trough. There are many versions of boats with this name around Britain, from Tyneside to Norfolk. The kind preferred at Llandogo was rigged rather like a Thames barge. Once underway, even Gilpin must surely have agreed that they added to the charm of the river. In Bristol these boats of all work were so familiar that the Llandoger Trow pub was named after them. A contributor to *The Etonian* in 1822 took one as he left the village, describing his feelings on the occasion:

> Sweet spot! I leave thee with an aching heart,
> As down the stream my boat glides smoothly on,
> With thee, as if I were a swain, I part,
> And thou the maiden that I doated on.

Excruciating. But evidently he had had a good time.

# LLANFACHES
MONMOUTHSHIRE                                    *First of the Independents*

Llanfaches has the honour of being the first Nonconformist parish in Wales. During Elizabeth I's reign, Wales produced a martyr: John Penry, a Cambridge scholar who was hanged in 1593 for publishing a tract that, among other things, denounced Bishops as soul murderers for their neglect of the Welsh population. (He left behind four little daughters: Deliverance, Comfort, Safety and Sure Hope.) William Wroth, who became rector of Llanfaches in the 1610s, did not begin his career as such a firebrand. Probably born in Monmouthshire, he studied at Oxford and held more than one living in Wales. But around 1620 he seems to have undergone a conversion, becoming a zealous Puritan.

His church could not hold all the people who came to hear him preach, so in the summer he moved outside to the churchyard. When William Laud became Archbishop of Canterbury he quickly put a stop to schismatic activity within the Church of England. In what would later seem a typically Welsh manner, Wroth may have refused to read the Book of Sports, a declaration of James I's reign, which listed the sports that could be played on Sundays; Puritans such as Wroth could not reconcile their views of the Sabbath with entertainment of any kind. Ejected from the established Church in 1638, he immediately reformed his congregation as an Independent one, on the model of those in New England.

Wroth's creed was summed up in a verse that he taught to children:

> Thy sin, thy end, the death of Christ,
> The eternal pangs of hell;
> The day of doom, the joys of heaven:
> These six remember well.

Although a 'paedobaptist', who believed that infants should be baptised through the sprinkling of water, he remained on harmonious terms with Baptists, for whom the full-body immersion of adults was a cardinal principle – an example of toleration that was not always followed by later Welsh sects. He died in 1641, shortly before religious divisions were bitterly fought over during the Civil War.

# LLANFAIRPWLLGWYNGYLL
ANGLESEY                          *That will be 4d for a carriage with springs*

Toll houses come in a variety of architectural idioms – castle style, thatched, Gothick – but it is usually easy to spot them. They stand next to the road; they have segmental fronts (half a hexagon, for example) to allow the toll collector to look in both directions, and deep, overhanging eaves that gave him or her somewhere to stand in dirty weather. There are still scores left by roadsides across Britain, generally dating from the first half of the nineteenth century. They are a memory of the turnpike trust era of road maintenance, when private enterprise kept wagons, coaches and horses on the move.

The toll house at Llanfairpwllgwyngyll still has its list of tolls, displayed on a hand-painted board above the veranda. 'For every Horse, Mule, or other Cattle drawing any Coach or other Carriage with springs the sum of 4d . . . For every Drove of Oxen, Cows, or other neat Cattle per score, the sum of 10d.' It must have been exasperating for country people to pay charges for a service they may not have wanted (cattle drovers might have been just as happy going down a lane), but the Llanfair Gate stood on Thomas Telford's road to Holyhead, on the Anglesey side of the suspension bridge that he threw over the Menai Strait in 1818–26. Travellers who wanted to reach the crossing to Ireland without the discomfort of potholes or inconvenience of flooding ought to have been grateful.

Before the turnpike system, the burden of road repair fell on the parishes through which the road passed. This was unfair on parish ratepayers, who may not have benefited from the road. It was also unsatisfactory to the travelling public, because parishes had no incentive to make the roads better. In 1637, when John Taylor published *The Carriers Cosmographie*, there were just four coach routes to London. Indeed, wheeled transport of any kind remained unusual until the eighteenth century, most haulage being done by sledge.

The idea that road mending might be financed by a charge levied from the people using the road surfaced during the Civil War. It was first put into action in Hertfordshire, under Charles II. The idea spread. Travelling in Norfolk in 1698, Celia Fiennes found one road 'secured by a barr at which passengers pay a penny a horse in order to the mending of the way', albeit the road was still 'in many places full of holes'. By 1750, 146 turnpike trusts had been formed. By the end of the century, that number had increased by nearly six hundred.

In the eighteenth century, the surveyor John Metcalf – known as Blind Jack of Knaresborough, having gone blind after a childhood attack of smallpox – recognised the need for proper foundations and good drainage of roads; he would transverse marshy areas by building over a base of heather and gorse. But most road engineers were unskilled. Two colossi arose in the early nineteenth century. John McAdam built the Bristol turnpike after 1815 (with his brothers, William and James, he went on to act for twenty-five turnpike trusts, laying roads with angular stones that would be compacted by the wheels passing over them). Thomas Telford* was the more expensive, but he had the support of the Postmaster General.

Indignation against the tolls on country roads broke out as rioting in parts of Wales†. But the new roads opened up Britain, and villages experienced the benefit through greater trade.

*See Corpach, page 545; Craigellachie, page 547. †See Efailwen, page 474. See also Hindon, page 44.

# LLANGEITHO
## CEREDIGION
*'And Leap, Ye Lame, For Joy'*

People in Wales thought that Daniel Rowland was the greatest preacher of what Methodists call the Great Awakening. A tribute to his powers exists in the marble statue, showing Rowland in full flow, outside the chapel at Llangeitho, his own parish. When he refused to give up itinerant preaching and was forbidden from taking services in the church in 1763, he occupied a chapel built by his followers. His old congregation followed him to the new place of worship, and communion was not held in the church for fifty years. Not that Rowland preached only in churches and chapels. The power of his oratory drew thousands to hear him. His style may, to begin with, have been of the wrathful kind, which made vivid the terrors of damnation. As time went on, however, he evoked the joyous prospect of redemption – so much so that people felt moved to sing, dance and jump, for hours or even days on end. Although Rowland designated his sect as Calvinistic Methodists, they were more popularly known as Jumpers.

The conditions that Rowland faced at the beginning of his ministry were hardly propitious. Eighteenth-century Wales was a poor country, peopled almost entirely by peasants. Religion was at such a low ebb that, when he climbed the Aeron hills, he would look and exclaim sadly, 'Alas, alas, I can see not so much as one house where prayer is offered.' Most of the population could communicate freely only in Welsh, and struggled to understand the English-speaking clergy sent by the established Church. Rowland preached to them in their own language.

The first chapel at Llangeitho was not much more than a hut. In 1764, this was replaced by a singular building, in the form of a double house. The interior was plain, to allow the maximum number of people inside: seats were provided only for women and children. The communion table could be hoisted out of the way by means of pulleys. The pulpit was reached by a door from the outside, and to give communion Rowland had to walk round the building to get to the other part. The roof was half straw, half slate. Curious though it may have been, huge numbers of worshippers would make a pilgrimage to it, asking 'What must I do to be saved?' That building was replaced later in the Georgian age by the present structure, which retains the feature of a pulpit entered directly from outside.

It was in 1762 that the jumping started: 'as in the house of Cornelius long ago, great crowds magnified God without being able to cease, but sometimes leaping in jubilation as did David before the Ark', fellow exhorter Thomas Jones remembered. Perhaps not surprisingly, it attracted a degree of mockery, such as that expressed in this verse by Edward Williams:

Come, all ye true believers
Of Calvin's ranging sect;
Tho' deemed by some, deceivers,
We are sure the Lord's elect
And a-jumping we will go.

Rowland was not deterred. He went on preaching to crowds of thousands until his death in 1790.

# LLANGURIG
MONTGOMERYSHIRE                                    *The highest village in Wales*

'It is here that our longings for the beautiful are satisfied! It is here that the spirit drinks to repletion as nature's glorious fount!' So wrote an insect-hunting contributor to the *Entomological Magazine* in 1838, on visiting Llangurig, Wales's highest village. The roads, he reported, were good, but in the wrong light – and when a feeling for the sublime did not grip the soul – the scenery could be mistaken for 'vast and dreary mountains, that afford very little to catch the eye of the painter, the tourist, or the naturalist'.

Its fortunes might have been different if the railway had come. Or, rather, if the railways had stayed. The combined effort of the Mid-Wales Railway and the Manchester and Milford Railway Company in the 1860s, cooperating because Parliament had accidentally granted them both rights over the same terrain, did produce a result of sorts: the M and M completed its section of the work. But the expense of tunnelling west to the next station, Cwmystwyth, proved too much for the MWR, hit by the collapse of the Overend, Gurney and Company bank. A single train puffed up from Llanidloes; when it went back again, no others came.

In the 1890s, the local population tried to persuade Cambrian Railways to run a light railway from Llanidloes, but after a survey it was concluded that a village of two or three hundred souls would not generate more traffic than twenty-five people going to Llanidloes market each week. The Nantiago Lead Mine, four miles beyond the village, was lucky to produce a hundred tons a year. Otherwise, apart from lime for the fields, there would only be sheep. The projected revenue was £217; the estimated working expenses were £670. It cannot have taken the board long to reach a conclusion.

Another effort to interest the railway was made in 1917, with the prospect of POW labour held out as a cost-reducing inducement; but it was not to be moved. Llangurig was left with the unenviable record of being the station to have received the fewest number of scheduled trains anywhere in Britain.

When James Hissey wrote *The Charm of the Road* in 1910, he found the M and M rails still intact, although rusting; he admired the bridges and cuttings. 'An excellent scheme for the unprofitable investment of money,' he observed acidly. 'We were informed that the railway had . . . not even a name.' If the railway had been more successful, Llangurig would have been transformed, perhaps becoming another tourist destination such as Betws-y-coed in Caernarfonshire. As it was, Hissey was able to enjoy the Upper Wye, as yet 'little more than a frolicking mountain stream', in the solitude of the grand, if melancholy mountains.

# LLANOVER
## MONMOUTHSHIRE

*Making Wales more Welsh*

If you had gone to Llanover in the second half of the nineteenth century, it would have seemed extremely Welsh. The tenants of the Llanover estate would have been wearing tall pointed black hats and red cloaks, a demonstration of Welsh national dress. They had to. The workers on the estate would have been Welsh-speaking: it was a prerequisite of their employment. The contrast with nearby villages would have been striking, because Monmouthshire has not always regarded itself as part of Wales, and is by nature one of the least Welsh of the Welsh counties. But the lady of the big house, Augusta Hall, whose husband, Benjamin Hall, MP and iron-master – the Ben after whom Big Ben is named – was created Lord Llanover in 1859, was on a campaign to revive the intrinsic character of the Principality. Even now, some general ideas of Welshness are filtered through her eyes.

Since the eighteenth century, a view had been gathering that Wales had changed. Industrialism and coal mining were transforming the Valleys, bringing an influx of workers from other parts of the country, who were, naturally, ignorant of Welsh traditions. A people previously known for their jollity had come to live under the austere shadow of Calvinistic Methodism*. Having been ruled from Westminster since the Tudor period, its native language was not much cultivated by people who wanted to get on. These trends were deplored by Romantics, who rejoiced in local colour.

In 1834, Lady Llanover won first prize for an essay at the Cardiff Eisteddfod on the preservation of the Welsh language. Adopting the eisteddfodic title Gwenynen Gwent, 'the bee of Gwent', she became the leader of a movement to rescue the Welsh identity from homogenising Anglo-centricity. She collected books; she financed periodicals; she taught in schools (speaking Welsh, of course). The Anglican church that she and her husband had endowed was transferred to the Calvinistic Methodists after the vicar refused to conduct services in Welsh.

Welsh national dress was Lady Llanover's invention. It was adapted from a print she had discovered: perhaps mercifully, it showed only women, and the men in her household were spared from having to adopt anything similar. Like the kilts and tartans of Scotland, Lady Llanover's prescription bore only a loose relationship to anything that had been worn in past centuries. The new

Elizabethan-style house that the Llanovers commissioned Thomas Hopper to build for them in 1837 became a centre for music and poetry, in the spirit of the halls of the ancient past.

'We had more of the Welsh music in the evening,' recalled the indefatigable country-house visitor Augustus Hare. 'We went and sat in the armchairs in the hall, and the household filed in above, and filled the music-gallery, and sang most gloriously.' He was warned, before he visited, that 'I was not to be guided by her opinion on any subject, yet was never to contradict her.' By the end of it, 'her pertinacity in what she thinks right, whether she is right or not', won his admiration.

*See Llangeitho, page 491

# LLANSANTFFRAED
BRECKNOCKSHIRE                          *The mysterious Henry Vaughan*

In 1923, Siegfried Sassoon made a pilgrimage to Llansantffraed to visit Henry Vaughan's grave. It inspired his poem 'At the Grave of Henry Vaughan':

> Here sleeps the Silurist; the loved physician
> The face that left no portraiture behind;
> The skull that housed white angels and had vision
> Of daybreak through the gateways of the mind.

Vaughan was an important poet for Sassoon. The gravestone is one of the few concrete monuments from his life, which was spent almost entirely in the place where he was born. As Sassoon indicates, although Vaughan was sufficiently celebrated to become one of the subjects of John Aubrey's *Brief Lives*, there is no likeness of him. The established details of his life are frustratingly scant.

Vaughan was one of twins, his brother being Thomas, also a writer. Born in 1621, he seems to have gone to Oxford shortly before the Civil War, although he did not take a degree; later he fought briefly on the side of the King. Afterwards, Vaughan worked not only as a poet and translator but as a doctor – the letters MD are on his tombstone. It is not known where he qualified, if he did so; in a letter to Aubrey of 1673 he mentions that 'I have practised now for many years with good success (I thank god!) & a repute big enough for a person of greater parts than my selfe.' (Thomas was not only a doctor but an alchemist.) Clearly he had a strong sense of attachment to the area of his birth, calling himself a Silurist – after the Silures, the ancient British tribe that occupied the southern end of the Welsh Marches.

Most of Vaughan's poetry, inspired by George Herbert*, is devotional. It reveals an intense awareness of an unknowable God, who is yet present in all created things.

His imagery is often that of a keen-eyed countryman, noticing (in 'The Timber') the 'low violet' thriving at the roots of a grove of young trees. 'Resurrection and Immortality' opens with a description of a silkworm emerging from the chrysalis. Vaughan's direct observation of Nature later endeared him to the Romantic poets. Aubrey thought there was 'no man fitter' to consult about the natural history of Brecknockshire.

Vaughan's tombstone bears his coat-of-arms, identifying him as a gentleman. Below it, in Latin, is a cry of humility expressing the deep religious conviction that motivates his poetry: 'What he wished on his tomb: unprofitable servant, greatest of sinners, here I lie; glory to God; may He have mercy.'

*See Bemerton, page 12

# MANAFON
## MONTGOMERYSHIRE
*A poet's dreams – and reality*

The poet R. S. Thomas (he never published under his Christian names of Ronald Stuart) was sorry to have been born in Cardiff. It was a city, and he was not brought up to speak Welsh there. Later, he learnt Welsh and spoke it fluently, spending his life in close contact with Nature, which is one of the major themes of his poetry. Having been ordained as a priest and spending some years as a curate, he was appointed to be rector of Manafon in 1942. It brought his dreams into sharp collision with reality.

*The poet R. S. Thomas's church at Manafon: he cared deeply for the rural culture of Wales, however restricted it may have seemed in comparison with his own wide-ranging interests.*

'I was a little bourgeois, well-bred, with the mark of the church and library on me,' Thomas remembered. 'I now found myself amongst tough, materialistic, hard-working people, who measured one another by the acre and by the pound; Welshmen who had turned their backs on their cultural inheritance and gone to trade in Welshpool and Oswestry and Shrewsbury; farmers of the cold, bare slopes who dreamed of gathering enough money to move to a more fertile farm on the plains.'

Manafon was not a village in the English sense. Lying in a hollow, it had a church, a school and a pub, but the dwellings were scattered around the surrounding hills, some of them accessible only by grass tracks that might be waterlogged in winter. When he arrived, there was not a single tractor to be seen. Hoeing, shearing, hay gathering and hedge cutting were all done by hand. It was a toilsome existence, with little spiritual relief. 'Religion was a matter for Sundays.'

Thomas ministered to the community for twelve years. Its horizons must have seemed narrow for a man whose interests, in addition to birdwatching, included nuclear disarmament, Welsh politics, theology, philosophy and the arts. But he cared strongly for the culture that Manafon represented. It seemed deeply Welsh, even though the language was rarely used, except by 'the patrons of the public house [who] went home late at night bellowing Welsh hymns abroad'.

But the mountains were, like other upland areas in Europe, losing their population, as the children of farmers went away to factory jobs in the towns. 'These people must be helped,' Thomas pleaded in 1945. 'Oh, I know that they are not a hundred per cent efficient, as the contemporary world of scientific planning would have it, but they more than atone for this by their character and the native colouring of their lives. Besides they understand the land and the climate.'

It is a case that lovers of the countryside have been making for upland farmers ever since.

# NANTGARW
## MID GLAMORGAN                          *Most beautiful of British porcelain*

In 1813, William Billingsley arrived in Nantgarw, in the Welsh valleys. A painter of porcelain, he was a feckless, drifting individual, who may have travelled under the name of Beeley or Bailey, apparently to avoid being sued for breaking an agreement. Perhaps the same reason influenced his choice of such an out-of-the-way spot in which to settle and make porcelain. There was no china clay in the area, but plenty of coal for the firings, and rents would have been cheap. Furthermore, Nantgarw was on the Glamorganshire Canal, an important consideration, given that Josiah Wedgwood had been forced to dig one to serve his Etruria works in Staffordshire.

With his son-in-law Samuel Walker, another potter, Billingsley set up a factory, intent on making porcelain of the highest quality. He only partially succeeded, his business being a stop-go affair that did not last more than half a dozen years. But his ware came to be regarded as the loveliest porcelain ever made in Britain.

Billingsley aimed at porcelain of a delicate, glassy character. A flower painter called William Young was persuaded to back the scheme. They began experimenting with pastes and kilns. But with capital of only £250, little progress had been made before he petitioned the Board of Trade for a grant. A member of the Board was the botanist Joseph Banks, and he wrote for information to Lewis Dillwyn, a naturalist who was also proprietor of the Cambrian works at Swansea. Dillwyn was so impressed by the potential of the operation that he persuaded Billingsley to transfer to Swansea.

After three years, during which ninety per cent of production was broken or wasted, Dillwyn terminated the arrangement. Billingsley returned to Nantgarw, raised more capital, and began again. This time they had more success. As William H. Lewer observed in *The China Collector* (1922), 'The beautiful translucent body and delicate decoration brought the porcelain into temporary demand in London.' A dinner service painted with roses was made for the Prince Regent, and greatly admired.

But the factory was small, and such success as it had aroused the envy of Coalport. The partnership broke up in 1819, the improvident Billingsley and his son-in-law being assimilated into Coalport, with Young for a time soldiering on by himself. The doors finally closed in 1822. (This was not entirely the end of Nantgarw's association with pottery: later, a factory making red earthenware, such as tobacco pipes, was set up.)

Not all pieces stamped Nantgarw were decorated there or in Swansea. The London dealer John Mortlock would buy white blanks and have them decorated himself. But it was the body that, to W. Moore Binns, constituted 'the wonder of Nantgarw porcelain; it is difficult to conceive a china of greater beauty. It has the wonderful characteristic that, however thick it is, it is never quite opaque, and consequently, as specimens of it stand together, their shadows are never black, but soft-toned greys. This gives to a group, or even to a single piece, of Nantgarw, a charm which we do not remember to have found in any other porcelain.' Billingsley's financial difficulties meant that his porcelain would be rare as well as beautiful – an irresistible combination for the connoisseur. His whitewashed, slate-roofed Nantgarw House is now a museum.

# NANTYGLO
MONMOUTHSHIRE                              *Last private castle in Britain*

Nantyglo was a tough place in the early nineteenth century. The men who lived there worked down the pit or in the Nantyglo ironworks. No feelings of mutual kindness existed between them and their employers. Families struggled by on the wages the men received, and in times of downturn those wages were cut.

The ironworks was built in the early 1790s. Joseph Bailey and Matthew Wayne took the lease in 1811, Wayne selling his share to Bailey's brother Crawshay two years later. The Baileys were nephews of Richard Crawshay of the famous Cyfarthfa works. Under them, the Nantyglo works prospered, and in due course other furnaces were bought. By 1848, the ironworks could be described as 'now almost the greatest in the world'.

In 1816, Joseph Bailey made a statement of his wealth by building a handsome mansion at Nantyglo called Ty Mawr – something of an ill-timed gesture in the year after Waterloo, when the demand for iron fell and the Nantyglo Company threatened to reduce wages. The Nantyglo workers rioted, and on this occasion, wage levels were maintained. But the partners had been sufficiently alarmed for their own safety as to build what was, in effect, a castle. It lowered over the village, a visible demonstration of the bosses' power and a place of retreat if workers refused to be cowed. It was the last castle built for defensive purposes in Britain. (One might suppose that Joseph Bailey would have linked his mansion with his fortified farm by a tunnel, but, contrary to legend, no evidence of one has been found.)

The ruined structure of what used to be the farm can still be seen behind the foundations of Ty Mawr (all that now remain). The farm included stables for the horses at the ironworks, protected by a high wall and thick cast-iron gates; it is said that the workers who were brought in to break strikes were housed here, too. Above it arose two round towers – the Nantyglo Roundhouses –with four-foot-thick masonry walls and lancet windows. Each was more than thirty feet across. They were effectively keeps. They are still standing today.

Iron being the business, it was much used in the construction – for floor joists, windowsills, window frames, fire grates and roofs, the latter being made with iron sheets, on top of which were laid bricks and pitch. Iron doors were equipped with gun loops, oddly low down, from which the defenders could pepper their besiegers' legs.

Despite the dangers, the Baileys did nothing to soften their position. In 1822, they cut wages. About five years later, Crawshay Bailey built a terrace for his work-force on the opposite side of the valley. Characteristically, perhaps, the minute rooms provided meaner accommodation than any other workers' housing of the same date in Gwent.

The prospect of organised and violent unrest appalled the authorities. Among the Chartists taken down into the underground cells below Monmouth Shire Hall in 1839 was Zephaniah Williams, keeper of the Royal Oak inn at Nantyglo; he had been sentenced to be hanged, drawn and quartered for his part in organising the Chartist march on Newport during which twenty people died. By this date, Joseph Bailey had long retired from industry. An MP and future baronet, he resided at his seat at Glanusk Park near Crickhowell, a landed gentleman.

# NEWBOROUGH
## ANGLESEY
*A London shopkeeper remembers his home*

You might have thought, to judge from his moustaches, preserved in a bronze bust, that John Prichard Jones was an officer in the Blues. In fact he was a shopkeeper, one half of the emporium that was Dickens & Jones. The department store was a phenomenon of the late Victorian period. It was the commercial equivalent of an Aladdin's cave, splendid in its architecture and technology, apparently limitless in the goods it could supply. Prichard Jones, however, did not let the splendours of Regent Street, nor the waxed tips of his moustache, blind him to the homelier pleasures of his native village. He was born, one of seven children, at a small farm outside Newborough in Anglesey.

The new borough was founded by Edward I as part of his plan for the most perfect of his castles, Beaumaris. The place's golden age had, however, come before that, when it was a residence of Welsh royal princes and a seat of justice. Towards the end of Edward III's reign, Newborough had ninety-three houses, thirteen gardens, an orchard and twelve crofts. By 1832, however, it was 'a place greatly fallen away from its ancient consequence'. When Prichard Jones was growing up, it was no more than a village.

To this modest, if proud, settlement he gave an institute. Built in 1905, it was a work of Edwardian ebullience, with a clock tower, a black-and-white upper storey contrasting with dark rubble stone below, banks of windows set in pale limestone, and an air of swagger and bravado. It had a fully equipped library, meeting rooms and, this being Wales, a large concert hall. Two rows of cottages were built in front of it. It was endowed with property in London. But the property was bombed, and the income lost.

In recent years, the institute tottered. But thanks to £600,000 provided by the Welsh Assembly Government, Anglesey County Council, Heritage Lottery Fund, Anglesey Charitable Trust and the European Union, it is now fulfilling its historic role with as much vim as ever. A building of this quality cannot be swept away. The past passes its baton to the future, and if the present sometimes fumbles it, there are, thank goodness, too many concerned individuals, pressure groups and statutory bodies to let it slip. Bravo.

# NEW QUAY

CEREDIGION *The sloeblack, slow, black, crowblack, fishingboat-bobbing sea*

Dylan Thomas's radio play *Under Milk Wood* defined Welshness for the post-War generation. A prose poem for voices, it evokes the life of a seaside watering place, Llareggub, called a town but with a population of less than five hundred. Through the medium of Thomas's imagination we are invited to visit the dreams of the inhabitants before they are called from sleep by the ringing of the town hall bell, and then follow their emotions during the course of a day.

Mog Edwards, 'a draper mad with love', courts Myfanwy Price, dressmaker and sweetshop keeper; Polly Garter scandalises the neighbours by producing ever more babies out of wedlock; Mr Pugh the schoolmaster longs to poison his disagreeable wife; the retired, blind sea dog Captain Cat hears the voices of the children as they are 'shrilled' to school; Willy-Nilly the postman delivers letters previously steamed open by the hissing, spitting coven of kettles on his wife's range.

These are deftly drawn, unforgettable characters, humorous and yet tragic in being forever tied to a place of three decaying, pink-washed streets, beloved of the Rev. Eli Jenkins but populated as much by ghosts as by living people. Both are subsumed in the little town, 'breathing' as though it were an organism: a character in itself, which all the other characters seem to keep alive.

It is sometimes assumed that the town must be Laugharne, the village where Thomas lived with his family in a boathouse overlooking the Taf estuary and wrote in a garage, perched over the cliff. The boathouse was bought by Margaret Taylor, a patron, for the Thomases in 1949, although never given to them. Thomas himself, often drunk and permanently short of money, owned little beyond some cheap furniture and a couple of bicycles. Poverty is reflected in the still Victorian atmosphere of the houses in *Under Milk Wood*, with their ferns, harmoniums, Biblical texts, washstands and 'yellowing, dickybird-watching pictures of the dead'; that material culture could no doubt be glimpsed through the windows of Laugharne.

And yet Laugharne is not the setting evoked by Richard Burton, cast as the First Voice, one of the two narrators, when the play was first broadcast by the BBC's Third Programme in 1954, the year after Thomas's death in New York. Indeed, the germ of the idea came to Thomas in New Quay, where he arrived to live for nine months in 1944.

Laugharne, possessing both an imposing castle and a seventeenth-century town hall, is not the nondescript Llareggub – although neither of those architectural features is mentioned in Thomas's description of 'this timeless, mild, beguiling island of a town . . . there is nowhere like it anywhere at all.' New Quay, by contrast, is distinguished by its lack of distinction. Here, Thomas and his wife, Caitlin, lived in an asbestos bungalow called Majoda, overlooking Cardigan Bay. Some of the themes of *Under Milk Wood* were adumbrated in another piece for radio, *Quite Early One Morning*, a portrait of the town.

Thomas's sojurn at New Quay came to an abrupt end in March 1945, when he argued with an army captain, the husband of a family friend, who shot at Majoda with a machine gun. 'Caitlin and I go to bed under the bed,' Thomas wrote to his friend Vernon Watkins. The incident did not find its way into *Under Milk Wood*; real life villages can contain as much suppressed – or overtly demonstrated – passion as fictional ones.

# PENRHYS

## MID GLAMORGAN

*Our Lady, stuck in a tree*

The walk from the Abbey of Llantarnam to Penrhys shows the Rhondda Valley, indelibly associated with coal mining, in a new light. Or rather, an old light: this pilgrimage route goes along the high ground, from where it seems that the rooftops of the miners' terraces belong to a nether world. The pilgrims were seeking the shrine of Our Lady, with its statue and holy well. They hoped that statue or water would cure them of 'ague and fever', as they had the bard Gwilym Tew in 1460.

Another bard, Lewys Morgannwg, ramped up the site's reputation with tales of spectacular healing: the mad being baptised and becoming sane, the blind recovering sight, cripples being bathed in the waters and then running, the deaf being made to hear. The monks of Llantarnam ran the sheepwalks around Penrhys as a grange and built a hostel where pilgrims could rest. There was 'ever a host of them', according to Rhisiart ap Rhys, leaving offerings of wax figures.

On 14 September 1538, the statue was taken down and sent to Henry VIII's chief minister, Thomas Cromwell, in London. This was often done with images that attracted enthusiastic devotion: they were destroyed under the eyes of the highest authorities to be sure that the work was really done. Once in London, it was added to the grand bonfire of statues of Our Lady held on 26 September. But what was it that Cromwell consigned to the flames?

According to legend, the statue appeared miraculously, a gift of heaven, which was found embedded in the branches of a mighty oak tree in Penrhys. Try as they might, worshippers could not get it out of the tree until a chapel had been built to house it. If only we had the statue to study now. The likelihood is that it was an ancient Celtic carving, placed into one of the trees of a sacred grove beside a holy spring, the branches of which had grown around it. If so, the veneration of the pilgrims would have seemed to Henry VIII's servants even more idolatrous than prayers to a statue of Our Lady, for this one would have been pagan in origin.

Merely destroying the holy image was not enough to root out belief, among desperate people, in the curative properties of the shrine. In 1595, a large body of pilgrims was arrested and brought before the local magistrate, Morgan Jones of Tregib. Jones was a compassionate man: he saw that the prisoners were only sick people, hoping for a cure at the well, and let them off.

In 1966, Penrhys became part of that other world of the Rhondda, when the largest public sector housing project in Wales was opened. Since then, young people have been leaving the Rhondda, where the mines have now closed, and some of the houses are empty and vandalised. But the water continues to give hope: a modern pilgrimage takes place each Pentecost. A statue of Our Lady still looks out over the valley.

# PORTMEIRION
## MERIONETHSHIRE
*Cappuccino culture, avant la lettre*

For the first three-quarters of the twentieth century, Sir Clough Williams-Ellis – who died in 1978 at the age of ninety-four – was a conspicuous figure. Wearing breeches and long yellow socks, he was at the forefront of most battles about conservation, town planning and the countryside. He had a natural flair for drawing attention to his causes, and as an architect he was fully justified in playing the man of taste in a philistine world. His monument is Portmeirion, on the coast of Snowdonia. It is also a monument to his time.

Clough – he was universally known by his first name – denied the repeated allegation that his seaside caprice was inspired by Portofino. It hardly matters. The point of it was to offer a distillation of Mediterranean experience to an audience that had hardly been out of this country. The piazza and campanile and painted stucco and dome might have been transported on a magic carpet, from a hilltop in Italy to an unlikely but ravishing position on the Welsh coast, its beetling cliffs overlooking an estuary and endless sand.

*Portmeirion, the Mediterranean-style holiday village in Snowdonia built by the conservationist Sir Clough Williams-Ellis.*

As Clough himself wrote, the 'general improbability of Portmeirion's very existence' makes one ask the questions 'why?' and, to a lesser extent, 'how?' Naturally, he gave the answers himself. 'Why? Because the building of such a place to my own fancy on my own chosen site had been a dream at the back of my mind since the age of five, and never left me. Throughout the years of my war service abroad I had to dream of something other than the horror, destruction and savagery.'

There was a didactic streak: Clough wanted to demonstrate the joys of architecture to a nation that was not generally known for aesthetic sensitivity. There was also an economic imperative. Clough was not rich. Portmeirion arose out of his own earnings as an architect – and what the village could generate for itself. From the beginning, there was a hotel. It was a holiday village, a flavour of the warm South without the garlic. After the Second World War, day visitors began to arrive; there were as many as a hundred thousand a year in the 1960s.

Which leaves the question of 'how?' For Clough, Portmeirion stood on home turf. His uncle had owned the estate, although when he grew up it was tenanted by a recluse and could only be seen from the sea. The garden became 'utter wilderness'. Clough cleared it and made a plan, with strategic positions allocated to important buildings, such as watch house, campanile and chantry.

The shape that it ultimately took depended on unforeseen events, particularly related to Clough's passion for old buildings. On the point of building a small opera house, Clough noticed an advertisement in *Country Life* declaring that Emral Hall in Flintshire was to be demolished. He bought the ballroom, with its fine plasterwork ceiling showing the Labours of Hercules. (The ceiling cost thirteen pounds at auction; reassembling it in an architectural context cost several thousand pounds more.)

The 'Bristol Colonnade' was formed from columns that had stood in front of the Quaker copper smelter William Reeve's bath house at Arnos Court, until damaged by enemy bombing. Clough snaffled them up. His friend Sir Charles Reilly, head of Liverpool University's School of Architecture, persuaded him to buy the Ionic columns from Hooton Hall in Cheshire. He had no use for them at the time, and they gathered moss – or rather earth – for thirty years. Eventually they were dug up from under a garden to form the basis of the Gloriette.

# PUMPSAINT
## CARMARTHENSHIRE                                    *Gold in them hills*

Pumpsaint: five saints. Five is not a record for the number of saints to emerge from one family. St Teilo discovered a man plunging each of his newly delivered septu-plets into the river Taf; he brought them up and they in turn became saints, known collectively – their individual names being lost – as the Water Men (Dyfrwyr). The five after whom Pumpsaint, near Lampeter, is called were also of one birth. These were the five Sleepers: Gwyn, Gwyno, Gwynoro, Celynin and Ceitho, said to have lived in the sixth century.

Their legend probably resulted from the existence of a metre-high block of sandstone bearing scooped-out hollows, like the moulds for large jelly babies, on its sides (four, however, rather than five). The Sleepers are supposed to have laid their heads on a boulder during a storm brewed up by a wicked enchanter, and such was the force of the hail that their impression was left on the stone. They were then transported to the enchanter's cave, where they still sleep – to be awoken when King Arthur returns or (to quote S. Baring-Gould and John Fisher's *Lives of the British Saints*, 1908) 'the Diocese is blessed with a truly pious and apostolic prelate'.

There may, however, be an alternative explanation: the stone could have been shaped by miners in the Roman period, as part of the heavy equipment used to crush ore. If so, it would have been supplemented by a waterwheel – Vitruvius describes how they were made in the first century, and fragments of the wheel survive in the National Museum of Wales at Cardiff. The rafters that support stamping machinery, used to pulverise ore, used to be called sleepers, according to old dictionaries. Could carpentry have become involved in the saints' story?

The Dolaucothi mines produced gold. They could have been opened in the prehistoric period; the last attempt to extract the precious metal from them was made in the 1930s (they contributed to Princess Marina's wedding ring in 1934). The Roman army watched over them from a fort. Over time, the fort was halved in size, presumably because the district had been pacified, but they could not afford to leave entirely: convicts or slaves might have been used in the mines, or perhaps a contractor extracted the gold under military supervision. It is the only Welsh gold mine outside Snowdonia.

# RAGLAN
MONMOUTHSHIRE                                   *Last castle to hold out for the King*

When Puritans came to search Raglan Castle for weapons at the beginning of the Civil War, they were in for a shock. 'When the several engines and wheels were set a-going, much quantity of water, through the hollow conveyances of aqueducts, was to be let down from the top of the high tower', making a 'fearful and hideous noise'. It sounds like the sort of jape that Bertie Wooster might have perpetrated, but it had its effect in this case, because the unwelcome visitors ran away. Lord Herbert, later 2nd Marquess of Worcester, whose family seat this was, is thought to have invented a steam engine a century and a half before James Watt.

The village of Raglan's fortunes were tied to the castle and the noble family that kept it. The castle's strategic value lay in its position on the Great Road from Abergavenny into Wales. This was also of value to the village, which did well from serving travellers, particularly in the coaching days; a pilgrim's cross in the church-yard recalls an earlier form of passing trade. From 1354, the town of Raglan had been holding markets: the base of the market cross still stands at a crossroads near the Beaufort Arms Inn (the cross itself has been replaced by a lamp post). The road ran through the town.

Now the castle ruins form a landmark for motorists hurrying along the dual carriageway of the A40, not quite the statement of power and prestige intended by William ap Thomas, one of the many Monmouth men who had fought at Agincourt, when he began the Great Tower, or Yellow Tower of Gwent, in 1435. As successive generations inflated the scale and importance of the castle, the town occupied a subservient role. The lords of Raglan were carried forth from the gate-house for burial at St Cadoc's church. Their tombs, however, have been defaced: evidence that the castle could bring ill fortune as well as prosperity on the settle-ment beneath its walls.

The inventive Lord Herbert worked hard for Charles I, attempting to raise an army in Ireland. It was to Raglan that Charles came for two months after the disastrous battle of Naseby (see page 343) in 1645, in the hope of raising fresh troops from the Marches*. In 1646, this splendid edifice, bristling with battle-ments, the Yellow Tower of Gwent standing in a moat by itself, was infested by a Parliamentarian army. It was the last castle to defy Cromwell. Lord Herbert's father, the 1st Marquess, was still alive, aged sixty-eight, and held out from 3 June until 19 August.

The Parliamentarians under Fairfax destroyed 'every shelter or advantage the enemy might derive from the houses in the village, or its old church', levelling the church tower and burning the nearby streets, as well as defacing the Somerset family monuments in the church. When supplies had run out, the garrison capitu-lated, being allowed to leave with drums beating and bullets in their mouths, as a symbol of their undiminished warlike posture. But the 1st Marquess was taken to London and put under the custody of Black Rod; he was dead by the end of the year. The 2nd Marquess died in 1667 and was buried at Raglan, although not, as he had hoped, with a model of the steam engine in the tomb.

After the siege, the castle was partially blown up, its masonry being quarried by whoever needed stone to build with. The village became a charming backwater, through which reapers would walk carrying their scythes, and women in aprons would dig gardens, according to nineteenth-century engravings. The Somerset family, who became Dukes of Beaufort, did not rebuild the castle, relocating to Badminton (see page 298) instead. But they continued to take a protective interest in the village until selling it as part of the great divestment of aristocratic estates that took place during the 1920s.

*See Weobley, page 362

# SUDBROOK
## MONMOUTHSHIRE

*Village built for a tunnel*

It might have been fate. Just as the Great Western Railway was getting to grips with its tunnel under the Severn Estuary, the old jetty at Sudbrook – to be redundant when the work finished – burnt down. A helping hand might have been given to the fire by one of the navvies in the tunnel, because they had just called a strike. Perhaps generously, the contractor, Thomas Walker, denied it. The weather had been dry for some time, and any spark might have started the conflagration.

Walker was a confident man. The men had been striking for eight-hour, rather than ten-hour shifts, with a lunch break taken in dripping conditions underground. But he soon had them back to work, without having conceded – indeed, he used the excuse of the strike to clear out 'a number of bad characters' who had been impeding progress. Progress was what the Severn Tunnel was all about.

The funnel-shaped Severn Estuary has the highest tidal range in Europe. It had always been an inconvenience to people wanting to cross from Gloucestershire into Wales, the direct route being possible only by means of a ferry – uncertain because of the tides. That did not matter so much in the Georgian period, when few people made the journey. But in the Victorian age, south Wales was producing some of the best coal in the world. Demand for transport – both passenger and freight – increased.

After an Act of Parliament in 1872, Charles Richardson, who had worked on the Box Tunnel outside Bath, was given the job of building the Severn Tunnel. He was replaced as Chief Engineer by Sir John Hawkshaw in 1879, after the tunnel, having nosed its way from Gloucestershire to a point beneath the Monmouthshire shore, encountered the Great Spring and was heavily flooded.

The village of Sudbrook kept abreast of the work, growing in proportion to the labour involved. Initially, houses were built for foremen, the chief of whom was Joseph Talbot. Talbot ensured that a mission hall for two hundred and fifty people was built, together with a school and Sunday School: the tunnelling community was in for the long haul. More houses were built as pressure to complete the tunnel increased, and the workforce expanded to more than three thousand men. They were good cottages, too, built of local stone. One of them was made into a hospital to treat the diseases that miners acquired underground (congestion of the lungs, pneumonia); a purpose-built hospital was later constructed.

The families for whom Sudbrook was built lived in perpetual fear of disaster. It was easy for panics to start as men feared that the river had broken in, causing them to run – hundreds at a time – the mile or so back to the entrance. In October 1883, the worst happened, when gales coincided with an exceptionally high tide and the workings were engulfed in water. Eighty-three men spent an uncomfortable night on a wooden platform, pressed to the ceiling, until a boat could be got in to rescue them.

In 1886, fourteen years after work had started, the tunnel was opened. Trains still run its four-mile length. For more than a century it was the longest mainline railway tunnel in the UK, its record surpassed in 2007, when the High Speed 1 Tunnels under London were opened as part of the Channel Tunnel Rail Link.

# TAFF'S WELL
## SOUTH GLAMORGAN                    *The hill that became a mountain*

There is an artificial hillock on top of Garth mountain. Perhaps not a hillock exactly: an American correspondent to *Professional Surveyor* in November/December 1998 described it as a 'mound of dirt', noting that on top of it is a concrete marker that appears 'to be a surveyor's triangulation station'. This is the physical evidence to support the story, said to be a true one, on which Christopher Monger's screenplay and book *The Englishman Who Went Up a Hill But Came Down a Mountain* are based. Monger grew up in Taff's Well, outside Cardiff. He heard the tale from his grandfather.

The Taff is the local river; the well is formed by a spring that bubbles up – the bubbles formed, unusually, of nitrogen – from subterranean depths that are presumably volcanic, since the water is warm (hence its name in Welsh of Ffynnon Dwym, or tepid well). According to T. E. Clarke's *A Guide to Merthyr-Tydfil* (1848), the water has 'been applied to the cure of rheumatic affections with considerable success'. At the beginning of the nineteenth century, it gave its name to a village populated by farmers, publicans, milliners, shopkeepers, a butcher and a policeman, according to the 1841 census. The Glamorganshire Canal supported lock keepers and boatmen, carpenters and blacksmiths. By the 1880s, most of the population worked in the colliery and ironworks. There was a school and an inn, apparently built to accommodate visitors to the well. And there was the mountain.

The book and film turn on the visit of two British surveyors, detailed to measure the mountain in 1917. The project stimulates both curiosity and suspicion. How could they measure it? And what will they do with the measurements once they have them? 'By God, that's the worry of it,' one old farmer reflects, because it is generally recognised that 'the English only come when they want something'.

The English already had maps to help them get from place to place. But as Reverend Jones, the minister, speculates, 'maps, by and large, were made for less than altruistic purposes: maps were made to define the borders of property, more for reasons of exclusion than inclusion. Maps were to measure properties for taxation . . . Moreover, he had heard that these Englishmen were from His Majesty's Ordnance Survey . . . Wasn't that a synonym for bombs and ammunition?' To cap it all, the surveyors find that the hill falls short of the thousand feet that would confer mountain status. The village determines to do something about it – and, by a collective feat of will, the hill grows.

The story is only part of the book (if not, so much, the film). This is a nostalgic portrait of a Welsh village, considerably less tart in flavour than *Under Milk Wood**, distance having lent a degree of enchantment. England is a land of coordinated plans, wide horizons and material progress. The Wales of this imagined but believable village does not look further than Cardiff a few miles away, and only then when it cannot avoid doing otherwise.

Welshness is asserted not just through language, but names: 'Evans the Bottle, who was a notorious drunk, Williams the Petroleum, who owned the garage; and Williams the Telephone Box', a soubriquet denoting the place where he was born. Ambition either does not exist or seems doomed to be thwarted. Yet the villagers find, rather unexpectedly, a reservoir of local pride. By their Herculean effort in raising the 'mountain' by twenty feet, they seem instinctively to believe that they are striking a blow in the 'lifelong struggle with the invading English'.

*See New Quay, page 500


# TREFRIW
## CAERNARFONSHIRE
*A spa keeps its charm*

In the Edwardian period, when the King himself enjoyed baccarat at Marienbad and Baden-Baden, many previously unassuming spas grew in proportion to the girth of their plutocratic patrons. They needed casinos and winter gardens to attract the desired clientele. Not Trefriw. It must have been a pretty village on the river Conwy in the early nineteenth century. It remains one. The spa industry came, brought prosperity for a while, and – perhaps because of competition from the Marienbads and Baden-Badens – collapsed. Nobody who visits Trefriw will be sorry.

There is a mythology to Trefriw. Llywelyn the Great, Prince of Gwynedd, is supposed to have had a house here in the thirteenth century, a happy spot except that the church stood on a mountain. His wife, Joan, natural daughter of King John of England, had to scramble over a slope to reach it – and she and her ladies went at least once a day. Llywelyn therefore built the church at Trefriw, to be within convenient reach. It was a gallant act (although not one that secured marital harmony: Joan got into deep water with William de Braose, 10th Baron of Abergavenny, who was hanged as a result).

The chalybeate or iron-rich spring that was to found Trefriw's reputation as a spa has a less romantic story. Water in the area had long been used to treat cattle, who, it must be said, sometimes died from it. Around 1833, young William Owen, son of Lord Willoughby's mine agent, was detailed to clear the mouth of an old mine cutting, blocked by debris from a higher sulphur mine. When an opening was made, a torrent of water rushed out. By placing keys in it overnight, the agent concluded that it was similar to the water used to dose cattle. But marketing was all. It had commercial possibilities.

'This water has become celebrated, not only for the cure of skin diseases, but also for the cure of many other complaints; and is used not only externally but internally also,' wrote John W. Hayward in 1865. Sometimes as many as a hundred people a day would come and drink it. Its combination of minerals – alumina, magnesium, manganese, calcium and nickel, as well as iron – meant that it was good for practically any condition – nervous system, stomach, female troubles, not to mention the 'vast class of persons who, in these days of mental and bodily wear and tear, require "bracing-up"', having suffered the Results of Mental Fag ('one of the most prolific causes of derangement of digestion, sanguification, and assimilation' – one knows just what he means).

Sufferers had to be careful not to overdo it. No more than a couple of table-spoonfuls at a time were recommended. The elixir could be imbibed in a kind of rustic lodge – appropriate to somewhere that also traded on its pine-scented inland breezes and 'ozonised' sea air (particularly good for chest complaints).

A hotel opened. The village did a brisk trade in boarding houses, farmhouse apart-ments, tennis grounds, fishing, photography, carriages and brakes for hire, drapers and grocers, all advertised at the back of guidebooks in a stupefaction of different typefaces. Even so, it never became as racy as the places that attracted Edward VII. In fact, it was particularly popular with Nonconformist clergymen. As A. G. Bradley observed, 'It may seem strange that men who lead temperate, well-nourished, well-occupied, but not laborious lives, amid the fresh breezes of the Welsh hills, should be so fond of filling their insides with these nauseous fountains.'

The nauseous fountains have been recently reopened. The famous Fairy Falls in the village have not changed.

# TREGARON
## CEREDIGION

*The long and lonely road*

Tregaron was one of the assembly points for the great cattle droves that left mid Wales for the English markets, the best prices being found at London's Smithfield. Drovers and their herds were a familiar sight on tracks and roads between Wales and Scotland and the Midlands and Home Counties. Before the railways came, the only way to transport cattle was to walk them. Doing so was recognised to be so important in the Tudor period that drovers were licensed: they could not set up in the trade without a certificate of respectability, only available to honest men who were more than thirty years old and married.

They came to be regarded as responsible individuals, with a larger view of the world than the rest of the farming community. Charles I entrusted them with the transport of Ship Money. Oliver Cromwell required them to collect taxes. Dealing, of necessity, with large quantities of cash, they helped develop the banking system. The Bank of the Black Ox, established by David Jones in Llandovery in 1799, was one of a number of drovers' banks in mid Wales (it was absorbed by Lloyds during the First World War).

A drove might consist of five hundred cattle – stocky and black, when they came from Wales. Travellers on the turnpike roads often found themselves delayed by these congregations, driven by three or four men on horseback, shouting 'hoo, hoo' (or something in Welsh that sounded like it). The cry warned farmers to shut their gates, lest their own cattle be swept up into the general movement towards England. As often as not, drovers preferred to stay clear of the turnpikes, following the ancient trading tracks that had been beaten into the earth long before metalled roads came into existence. From Tregaron, the drovers would cross the mountains to Abergwesyn, west of Builth Wells, perhaps fattening some of their stock on the meadows beside the river Towy on their way east. If their destination was Kent, it might be a month before they got there.

The passage of a drove made a spectacular show, and also influenced the development of the stopping places en route. In Cilycwm, on the route from Tregaron, a stone conduit runs along the village street to water the hundreds of cattle passing through. (The drover Dafydd Jones of Caeo, a poet who translated hymns into Welsh, likened the waking of the dead on Judgement Day to the numbers of cattle that would converge on his home village.)

Droving gave the decayed market town of Tregaron its best days. The cattle could be corralled in the marketplace while the drovers entertained themselves at the Talbot Hotel. Behind the hotel was a smithy, where the cattle were shod, like horses, for the journey: a process that could be achieved only once the beasts had been 'felled', or wrestled to the ground, by two men, one of whom grabbed the horns, the other a front leg. (This field would also, in 1848, be the burial ground of an elephant from Batty's Menagerie, which died from poisoning after drinking from a stream near a lead mine.)

The droves left a legacy, most obviously seen in the number of inns called The Drovers' Arms. Halfpenny Lane and Halfpenny Pasture record the standard charge per head for keeping animals overnight.

# TRELLECH
## MONMOUTHSHIRE
*Once a major Welsh town*

Seen from a distance, Trellech looks like a flotilla of grey boats, bobbing in a sea of green. The church of St Nicholas is the mother ship, its spire reaching high above the surrounding slate roofs: a church here was endowed by the Kings of Gwent in the seventh and eighth centuries. But nothing suggests that this might once have been one of the most important towns in Wales.

There is antiquity here. The village may take its name from three standing stones in a meadow outside it: they came to be called Harold's stones, once – erroneously

– thought to have been erected by the Saxon King Harold to commemorate a victory over the Welsh (the legend is inscribed on a sundial at the church, dated 1689). In fact, they were hauled into position during the Bronze Age, the choice of site perhaps dictated by the presence of an iron-rich spring called St Anne's Well or the Virtuous Well (the virtue being the effect it could have in curing disease). Later, a castle may have been built on the mound known as Tump Turret – thought at one point to have been a tumulus beneath which the dead from a supposed Saxon battle were buried.

As part of the lordship of Usk, Trellech was in the hands of the de Clare Earls of Gloucester, a powerful family of marcher lords in the thirteenth century. They cut down trees, smouldered them into charcoal, and used the result to smelt iron ore. The town may have been only five miles from Monmouth – but five miles was a long way when the countryside was full of unruly Welshmen, watching for their chance to waylay travellers. It therefore developed independently. It had a manor house with two halls and a stout tower, recently uncovered by excavation. In 1288, the town may have contained 378 long, narrow burgage plots, each with a house on it. But, oh, those Welsh: they rebelled in 1294–5 and Trellech must have suffered badly, because afterwards 102 of the plots were declared vacant. Perhaps they were never reoccupied.

Then came the disaster of Bannockburn, when Edward II's army was shattered by Robert the Bruce. The Welsh Marches, held by men who were well used to fighting, traditionally supplied troops for English campaigns in Scotland. The last of the de Clares, the eighth Earl of Gloucester, then a young man of twenty-three who had already been active in court politics for several years, was among those who went north in 1314, but impetuously throwing himself into the battle without proper support from his knights – perhaps even without adequate armour – he was killed. With that some of the heart went out of the town.

It was finished off by plague. Plague was nothing unusual in Wales or anywhere else in the fourteenth century. But whereas other towns got back onto their feet, Trellech was left with forty-eight empty burgages after the plague of 1369, which struck twenty years after the Black Death; forty years later they were still vacant 'because of the Second Pestilence'.

# TREMADOC
CAERNARFONSHIRE                               *'The Wonder of Wales'*

In 1888, T. E. Lawrence, Lawrence of Arabia, was born at Tremadoc. His parents – an Anglo-Irish, drink-disposed landowner called Thomas Chapman, who had run off with Sarah Junner, an illegitimate Scottish nanny – sought out places where nobody was likely to know them, a criterion that remote, sleepy Tremadoc met admirably.

In 1798, its founder, William Alexander Madocks, had had quite different ideas for it. That year he bought a derelict estate on the Welsh coast, which included the salt marshes beside the Glaslyn estuary. Despite being elected MP for Boston – a town in the flat Lincolnshire fens – he set about huge engineering works, winning a thousand acres from the sea by means of embankments. On this land Tremadoc was built.

Madocks laid out a Market Square and two streets, High Street and Dublin Street, lined with ruggedly classical buildings against a backdrop of mountain. His own house – later to be occupied by the poet Percy Bysshe Shelley – was Tan-yr-allt, or Under the Wooded Cliff: a piece of studied Regency simplicity, created by adding a front with a veranda to an old cottage, but goodness, what a view.

The name of Dublin Street gives the clue to the development: the Act of Union with Ireland, passed in 1800, meant that it was likely more traffic would be coming this way. As yet, Telford's great road across Wales, which would culminate in a suspension bridge over the Menai Strait*, had not been planned. So many people preferred to leave for Ireland from Porth Dinllaen (on the Lleyn Peninsula) – or would have done, if it had not been for the business of crossing the Glaslyn. Another sea wall, the Cob, built in 1811, reclaimed more than three thousand acres for farming, as well as enabling Madocks to build his own port – Porthmadog. By diverting the course of the river, a passage was scoured for ships carrying slate from local mines.

These were epic undertakings, and Madocks was an impulsive tornado of energy, whose optimism swept all before it. It is thought that one of his literary friends, Thomas Love Peacock, who stayed in north Wales in 1811, took him as the model for Squire Headlong in *Headlong Hall* (1815): 'In all the thoughts, words, and actions of Squire Headlong, there was a remarkable alacrity of progression, which almost annihilated the interval between conception and execution. He was utterly regardless of obstacles, and seemed to have expunged their very name from his vocabulary.'

Alas, even tornados can blow themselves out. During the building of the wall, the Cob was breached by the sea. It was mended, but Madocks's finances were not. Always stretched, they were in a parlous condition when he left for the Continent in 1826. He was on the way home when he died suddenly in Paris.

Porthmadog prospered in the Victorian period, when the slate mines were busy; a railway line was built on the Cob. But having grown up without a man of taste to direct it, Porthmadog lacks form. Tremadoc, by contrast, stayed much as Madocks had envisaged it, never becoming larger than a village. There is the neat, Gothic church, a rather prim building, which ought perhaps to hold a memorial to Madocks but does not; the grandly classical chapel, modelled on Inigo Jones's St Paul's at Covent Garden, was the first of many Welsh chapels to have columns. It irritated the Bishop of Bangor, but expresses an important principle for Madocks: he believed passionately in free speech.

*See Llanfairpwllgwyngyll, page 489

# YSBYTY IFAN

CONWY                                                    *Defending the Faith*

Throughout southern France, the Iberian Peninsula and the Middle East, the powerful Knights Hospitaller, belonging to the Order of St John, built huge fortresses. From these they issued forth to defend pilgrims on their way to the holy city of Jerusalem. The little church at Ysbyty Ifan, in the mountains of Snowdonia, is at the other end of the architectural scale, a modest presence in a green immensity populated mostly by sheep. The Hospitallers were given the estate by a Welsh lord around 1190, and although nothing survives of their priory buildings (the church itself is Victorian), the name of the village perpetuates their presence (Ysbyty Ifan means St John's hospital).

In this remote and empty part of the country, pilgrims might have been relieved to be under the Knights' protection, as they made their way to Bardsey Island and the shrine of St Winifred at Holywell in Flintshire. The Knights also took an income from the land. The Hospitallers did not generally have the reputation of being generous landlords: the Order's overseas estates had to contribute towards the maintenance of the operation in the Middle East.

Nor did kings always welcome their presence. Having been created during the first Crusade, which ended with the capture of Jerusalem in 1099, the Hospitallers were an autonomous body, answering only to the Pope. By the middle of the twelfth century they had been endowed with land in several countries: they would eventually acquire their own powerbases of Rhodes and Malta on Christendom's front line against Islam. The Knights served a double function: dispensing hospitality and medicine on the one hand, they were also a fighting machine. Monarchs in the countries where they owned estates might take advantage of their knowledge and honesty – Hospitaller priors served as treasurers to English Kings, for example – but also feared the existence of such a mighty, independent body within their borders.

No doubt Ysbyty Ifan was beyond the reach of such political concerns. The priory was too small to threaten the status quo; on the contrary, the Knights seem to have fitted into the prevailing system to the extent of paying seneschals and officials to respect their privileges. Local people may have been glad of their presence, as they were at Llanrhidian on the Gower Peninsula, which was exposed to pirate raids: there the Knights built a church whose tower could double as a refuge in times of attack.

No complete example of a Hospitaller priory survives in Britain, although elements exist at different sites: for example, Quenington in Gloucestershire (see page 345) has a gatehouse and dovecote. The Hospitallers' Scottish headquarters was at Torphichen near the royal palace at Linlithgow. Part of their church survives, looking much like a castle keep.

The Knights Templar had, by the early fourteenth century, become so rich that they could finance France's wars against England: this led to brutal suppression by King

Philip, as a means of freeing himself of the debt. Pope Clement V, resident in France, was forced to follow his example. The Hospitallers fared rather better, surviving in England until the Order's property was confiscated by Henry VIII in 1540. In the nineteenth century, it was revived as The Most Venerable Order of the Hospital of St John of Jerusalem, whose most conspicuous activity is the St John Ambulance corps.

# YSTUMTUEN
## CEREDIGION                                          *Brought back to life*

Ystumtuen nearly died. It had boomed, uncertainly at times, during the seventeenth century, when Sir Hugh Myddelton – knighted by James I – was mining copper, gold, silver, and quicksilver. Myddelton, a Denbighshire man, had made a fortune as a goldsmith on London's Cheapside. This he invested in Cardiganshire, where at one point he rented all the mines royal, realising such a huge profit – two thousand pounds a month from one mine alone – that he could fund the New River Company, which he had ambitiously founded to supply London with drinking water. But the money ran out, and although not reduced to penury as some stories have it, he ended his life in difficulties.

After Myddelton's death in 1631, Thomas Bushell continued the mining operations. An ardent supporter of Charles I, he was allowed to start his own mint for silver coins, stamped with the Prince of Wales's feathers, at Aberystwyth. During the Civil War, he not only loaned the King forty thousand pounds but raised a regiment of Derbyshire miners and three other regiments that he maintained at stupendous cost, as well as supplying firearms and gunpowder. At the end of the War, he fled to Lundy Island, which he defended so successfully against the Parliamentarian forces that he was offered the chance to start mining again, although – his fortune depleted – he did not do so in Wales.

When George Borrow visited in 1854, the principle point of interest at Ystumtuen was the Parson's Bridge, a plank hung from chains over the deep Rheidol gorge. By the twentieth century, the village had been all but deserted – a 'ghost-settlement' in the words of the *Welsh Academy Encyclopaedia of Wales*, life having retreated to a Youth Hostel and post office. Miners' houses lay in ruins. To this nearly abandoned shell came new life in the 1970s, as the hippy generation sought out wild and remote places, which had the additional merit of being cheap. Cardiganshire, a county of green hills and tumbledown cottages, whose notoriously penurious sheep farmers used binder twine to fasten their old-fashioned overcoats, seemed a land of promise to adherents of alternative lifestyles. Some of them valued the privacy that existed at the end of muddy farm tracks: this was particularly the case for those associated with the drug culture*.

But others from those years remember the place as 'something of a paradise' for other reasons. You could buy a small farm for the price of a London flat. It was a laid-back and pastoral existence, of a kind only to be found now in the remotest parts of Scotland and Ireland. The university at Aberystwyth brought an influx of young people, who in some cases stayed on after their courses were finished. Books such as E. F. Schumacher's *Small is Beautiful* (1973), prepared a market for the vision of self-sufficiency promoted by John Seymour, whose *Complete Book of Self-Sufficiency* (1975) sold more than a million copies. Seymour, who settled in Pembrokeshire, celebrated mid Wales in a television programme following the path taken by George Borrow in *Wild Wales* (1862). By 1975, self-sufficiency had become so recognisable a phenomenon that it was parodied by the television series *The Good Life*. Ystumtuen flew the flag.

The new arrivals did not transform Ystumtuen completely: there are still some derelict houses to be seen. But their community gathered momentum. You would not know that the village had been on life support, or that hippy incomers were the people who saved it. There is, alas, no school, no pub, but the Ebenezer chapel, built by Cornish tin miners in the mid nineteenth century, holds services once a month.

*See Llanddewi-Brefi, page 485

# SCOTLAND

THERE IS a caveat to be made about Scotland. North of the Border, rural settlements are not always villages, as they would be understood in southern England. Much of the country did not acquire villages before the eighteenth century, when they were built by landowners wanting to improve their estates or promote fishing. Until that date, most country people lived in clachans or (as they were called in the Lowlands) fermtouns – developments built to house the two or three families who would share the tenancy of a piece of land and work it together. Buildings were scattered, and did not include the bustling butchers and bake shops, tailors and pubs that would have been found in an English village.

Change came after the Forty-Five. The Highlands were opened up. Landowners across Scotland saw the opportunity to develop their estates, in the expectation of obtaining higher rents. As the example of the 'enthusiastic agriculturalist' John Cockburn of Ormiston, near Edinburgh (see page 615), showed, the reality did not always live up to the dream. But by the time William Cobbett was writing in the early nineteenth century, Scottish farmers had come to be recognised as highly efficient. Villages such as Sir Archibald Grant's Monymusk (see page 608) and the Duke of Buccleuch's Newcastleton (see page 610) came as part of the process of modernisation.

People have lived in the Scottish landscape – if not in villages – since the end of the last ice age eight thousand years ago. Kilmartin (see page 592) celebrates in a museum scores of sites – rock carvings, standing stones, barrows, cists – that lie around it. At Callanish (see page 539), village dwellings crept up to the stone circle that stands beside the fretted coastline of Lewis, pursuing a humdrum life on the edge of a great mystery. But even in recent centuries, life could be hard. Boswell and Johnson found nothing to eat at Glenelg (see page 582). God's judgement was held to lie on Durness (see page 561), where the smallpox was likely to take off those who did not die through want of bread.

In the nineteenth century, Scottish rural life was shaped – in some cases, all but exterminated – by the Clearances. They were intended, if one looks charitably on the landowners, to replace a subsistence economy, prone to starvation when crops failed, with a more sustainable way of life, in fishing villages such as Helmsdale (see page 586), and to replace struggling tenants with sheep. Families were brutally turned out of their homes. At Crovie (see page 553), they could only shelter on a ledge of the cliff. Thousands emigrated. (Calgary in Canada, however, takes its name from the beautiful Calgary Bay, rather than the tiny village on Mull, see page 519.)

Canals came; railways came; sportsmen came. There was whisky and Aberdeen Angus, poetry, botany and golf. Scotland moved on. But it did not forget.

# Scotland

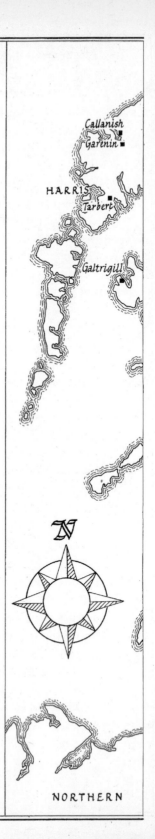

NORTHERN

ORKNEY
ISLANDS

Stromness

Port of Ness

LEWIS

Durness

Achfary

Kinbrace

Helmsdale

Croik

Lonemore • Gairloch

Dublin
(Ardross)

Cromarty

Burghead

Kingston
on Spey

Pennan

Crovie

Lonmay

Rosemarkie

Findhorn
Ecovillage

Fochabers

Old Deer

Applecross

Inverness

MORAY

Craigellachie

Fyvie

The
Braes

SKYE

Milltown of
Auchindoun

Alford

Aberdeen

Glenelg

Loch Ness

Tomintoul

Monymusk

Eilean Iarmain

HIGHLAND

ABERDEENSHIRE

Findon

Inverie

Drumlithie

Dunnottar

Glenfinnan

Corpach

Arbuthnott

Strontian

Fort William

PERTH and
KINROSS

Edzell

ANGUS

Ballachulish

Tobermory

Calgary

ARGYLL and

Fortingall

Aberfeldy

Meigle

Letham

Carmyllie

MULL

Taynuilt

Meikleour

Dundee

Tyndrum

Perth

Oban

BUTE

Innerpeffray

R. Tay

Abernethy

Ceres

Inveraray

Muthill

Crail

STIRLING

FIFE

St Monans

Auchindrain

Stirling

Crook of Devon

Lower
Largo

Kilmartin

Fintry

Larbert

Limekilns

Coulport

Kinneil

Edinburgh

Athelstaneford

Cockburnspath

Quarriers Village

1

Glasgow

Swanston

Ormiston

Oldhamstocks

2

West Calder

LOTHIAN

Humbie

Bowmore

Fenwick

LANARK-
SHIRE

West Linton

Ednam

Newstead

ISLAY

Dreghorn

Kilmarnock

Broughton

BORDERS

Mauchline

Sorn

Hawick

Denholm

Ayr

Catrine

Wanlockhead

Dunure

AYRSHIRE

Ettrick

Carlenrig

Turnberry

Penpont
Keir Mill

Beattock

Newcastleton

DUMFRIES and GALLOWAY

Dumfries

Beeswing

Palnackie

Gretna Green

IRELAND

Stranraer

Gatehouse
of Fleet

Eastriggs

1. Dunbartonshire
2. Renfrewshire

For a while, Field Marshal George Wade had the distinction of being the only individual to engross to himself a verse of the National Anthem (although by the time it was officially adopted as such, at the end of the eighteenth century, he had been dropped).

> Lord, grant that Marshal Wade
> May, by thy mighty aid,
> Victory bring.
> May he sedition hush
> And, like a torrent, rush
> Rebellious Scots to crush.
> God save the King.

By bad luck, this commemorates the least glorious episode of his military career, when, old and asthmatic, he commanded the British army's response to Bonnie Prince Charlie's invasion in 1745. The Jacobites outmanoeuvred Wade and his forces at Newcastle-upon-Tyne, by taking the western route and besieging Carlisle. Victory was eventually achieved by the brutal Duke of Cumberland, not Wade.

Wade had, however, done his best to further the rushing of the army around Scotland, by building Fort Augustus and other barracks, and the roads linking them. The bridge over the river Tay at Aberfeldy is the most magnificent of the forty bridges built during Wade's campaign; it was designed by William Adam, father of Robert and mason to the Board of Ordnance in North Britain.

Born in Co. Westmeath in Ireland, Wade was not a civil engineer; he joined the army at the age of seventeen in 1690 and fought in Flanders, Portugal and Spain. Before the 1715 rebellion he had been elected MP for the pocket borough of Hindon in Wiltshire (see page 44); Parliamentary duties did not prevent him from descending with two regiments of dragoons on Bath, where he rooted out Jacobite sedition. In 1724, he was sent to investigate the state of the Highlands, and having disarmed some of the clans, began to campaign for a programme of military roads. Slowly the government was prevailed upon to open its purse.

The difficulty of galvanising official enthusiasm for the roads can be seen from the accounts: only a thousand pounds was spent in the first four years. By 1734, however, nearly five thousand was spent in a single year. Wade's roads opened up the Gaelic-speaking Highlands. They began to change a way of life.

Built in 1733–5 out of greyish-green stone, the Tay Bridge cost four thousand pounds, more than half the total spending on bridges, and Wade probably saw it as his crowning glory. A note of pride gleams through the official words of his report, declaring that the 'best architect in Scotland was employed and master masons and carpenters sent from ye northern countys of England, who were accustomed to works of that nature'. A couple of hundred soldiers were also employed, preparing materials and driving in piles.

Adam ensured that the five-arched structure (the arches were ellipses, unusually at this date) was as handsome as it was functional, the central arch guarded by tall obelisks, the parapet concealing what might have otherwise seemed an inelegant hump. Wade ought to have known something about classical architecture: he was by now MP for Bath.

Was the new road network a success? London found that Wade's roads were just as useful to the rebellious Highlanders as they were to government forces. But they were essential to the systematic control and suppression of the Highlands after 1746, encouraging economic development and hastening the doom of the clans.

# ABERNETHY
## PERTH AND KINROSS                                  *A great Pictish centre*

Twenty-two metres tall and pencil slim, the eleventh-century round tower at Abernethy projects from the largely eighteenth-century village like a spear shaft, left as the marker of another time. It is supposed to be where King Malcolm Canmore did homage to William the Conqueror in 1072, agreeing the Treaty of Abernethy, which set the northern bounds to William's territorial ambition. At the base of the tower is an even older fragment: a Pictish symbol stone, as mysterious as everything about a people who left no written documents behind. Somebody used it as part of the foundations of his house, and somebody else later – we do not know when – dug it out again; fortunately it was recognised as being of importance and displayed on the round tower. There is a similar symbol stone built into the wall of a house nearby. The iconography of both is the same: a hammer (clearly), an anvil (possibly) and an emblem that is generally described as a tuning fork – clearly important because it is placed in the centre of the composition, but as to its meaning, who knows?

The stones hint at Abernethy's importance to the Picts. It was their southern capital in Scotland. (There is a view that the round tower was begun earlier than the eleventh century, and was Pictish, too.) The name Abernethy means 'mouth of the Ethy', presumably the ancient name for the river Earn, since it stands at the confluence of the Earn and the Tay. According to the Pictish Chronicle, the place was dedicated by King Nechtan the Great to the Irish abbess St Brigit, whose spiritual help he had sought before succeeding to the kingdom, and whom he remembered in gratitude afterwards.

Some scholars think that St Brigit was never a person, but evolved as a means of incorporating the cult of the pagan goddess Brigid into the early church. (Just as pagan deities were reworked as saints, so Pictish stones can incorporate pagan

*The eleventh-century round tower at Abernethy.*

symbols alongside the Christian cross.) Even the identity of Nectonius magnus is confusing: did he rule in the fifth century or the seventh century, and may he have been the same ruler as Neithon, King of Strathclyde? Abernethy grew into an important religious centre, conveniently near the royal power base at Scone.

The best place from which to view the burgh, as Abernethy became in the fifteenth century, is from the top of the round tower. From here you look down on the kirk and kirkyard, and the roofs of the village. As *Nelson's Hand-book to Scotland* observed in 1860, it 'stands amid pleasant environs, with much extent of gardens and orchards, but is poorly edificed, and has no regular street alignments'. By poorly edificed, the author perhaps meant that it has no Victorian town hall or other monument of civic pretension. There can be few visitors who would feel their lack today.

*See also Meigle, page 604*

# ACHFARY

Cream on the stucco, black on the doors – those colours are the livery of the Duke of Westminster's Belgravia estate. The family evidently liked them so much that they used them as the theme of the two-hundred-thousand-acre Reay Forest estate, which the Grosvenor family bought for stalking and fishing in the remote north-east of Scotland. Achfary is the capital of this kingdom of pine trees and solitude. The solid stone construction of the houses, neatly presented, gives a cosiness to the place, in defiance of the immensity of the Scottish landscape around it. Even the telephone box is, uniquely, in the estate colours of black and cream.

By the time of his death in 1899, at the age of seventy-four, Hugh Lupus Grosvenor, 1st Duke of Westminster, was the richest commoner in Britain. A tablet to him was erected 'by the people of Edderachillis and its vicinity including his Grace's foresters and servants' on the wall of the estate office (recently restored). It expresses their gratitude for 'his character as a philanthropist at home and abroad, and for the courtesy and generosity exercised by him during his tenancy for about fifty years of the forests of Stack, Badnabay, Reay, Cobernuiscach, Ben Hee, Corrie, Kinloch and Glendhu with the angling attached. He built lodgings and dwellings, erected fences, made roads and paths to and through these forests, thus giving employment to tradesmen and labourers and adding to the comfort of many.'

Sport, by the late nineteenth century, had become a more profitable activity (for the local economy, not the landowner) than sheep farming. Sir Walter Scott had made Scotland romantic, Queen Victoria and Prince Albert's love of Balmoral had made it fashionable, and the railways made it possible for a Duke to regard even the far north as accessible. Brewers and bankers, ship owners and steel magnates spent huge amounts of money equipping sporting estates such as Achfary, creating architecture of a solidity sometimes never seen in those areas before.

Stalking was regarded as a supreme challenge by men who prided themselves on their powers of endurance and love of the outdoors. They despised the practice of driving deer towards guns; the very difficulty of tracking a stag across open country was the point. As James G. Bertram, writing as Ellangowan, observed in *Out of Door Sports in Scotland* (1889): 'It is, perhaps, because there is no royal road to deer-stalking that many sportsmen have praised it so highly, looking upon it as the very poetry of sport . . . Men will tramp long miles of uneven ground, crawl in damp moss, climb rugged rocks, wade breast high through foaming streams and placid lochs, or tear along with determined face for miles in the rough furze or underbush, and, after enduring six or seven hours of such hard pedestrian work, may yet be disappointed in their search.'

By 1900, more than two and a half million acres in Scotland had been given over to sporting use. Now that deer numbers have multiplied to unsustainable levels, the management provided by controlled shooting is a necessity as well as a sport.

Not that this is taken as an excuse to modernise stalking methods at Achfary; quite the reverse. Ponies are increasingly used to carry dead stags back from the hill.

# ALFORD
## ABERDEENSHIRE

*The Aberdeen Angus is born*

Queen Elizabeth The Queen Mother's final public engagement in Scotland took place in 2001. It was to accompany Prince Charles when he unveiled a life-size statue of a bull outside Alford. The bull, sculpted by David Annand, is an Aberdeen Angus, the breed created by William McCombie of Tillyfourie and other grizzle-bearded Scottish farmers in the Victorian age. For sixty-four years, The Queen Mother was patron of the Aberdeen Angus Cattle Society, as well as being a successful livestock farmer herself.

Cattle had been driven through Aberdeenshire to markets at Falkirk and elsewhere in the Lowlands since the fourteenth century. From 1828, this trade was supplemented by the paddle steamers that chugged into Aberdeen harbour, taking cattle straight to London and other cities. Another transportation route came with the railways. Better access to markets stimulated farmers such as McCombie to improve their cattle.

The McCombies had been living near or at Tillyfourie since 1714, and had become the largest cattle breeders in Aberdeenshire. William started his herd in 1832. To the astonishment of conventional wisdom, which held that a Scottish animal would never become a champion at the Smithfield Show, he took a gold medal there in 1866 with Black Prince, a bull that weighed more than a tonne and had a girth of nearly ten feet. Queen Victoria was impressed. She asked for

*The sculpted Aberdeen Angus bull, which is the symbol of Alford.*

Black Prince to be taken to Windsor for a private audience, and next summer she visited Tillyfourie from Balmoral. In 1878, another McCombie beast won at the Paris Universal Exhibition, a show of shows.

The next year, McCombie retired, the sale of his stock being attended, it was said, by the largest gathering of agriculturalists ever seen around a sale ring. He died in 1880. The tablet raised to him in Tough church records, in measured terms, his life's achievement: 'For several years Member of Parliament for West Aberdeenshire . . . he attained a distinguished position as an agriculturalist; and in rearing and improving the black polled Aberdeenshire cattle he earned for himself a high and wide spread reputation.' (After McCombie's time, cattle were sold, together with sheep and pigs, in the Alford livestock market – the 'aul' mart': a corrugated-iron building which has been smartened up as the Heritage Centre.)

McCombie would have been the last person to deny credit to the other farmers who contributed towards shaping the Aberdeen Angus, notably Hugh Watson of Keillor in Angus and Sir George Macpherson-Grant of Ballindalloch in Banffshire. No doubt he would also have respected the contribution of American and Canadian breeders in saving the Aberdeen Angus during the black years of the 1960s, when 'growthier' breeds were in favour for providing beef that could be sold cheaply through supermarkets. Canadian bloodlines were used to reinvigorate native stock, developed with artificial insemination and embryo transplant as well as the selective breeding practised in McCombie's day.

# APPLECROSS
HIGHLAND                                    *St Maelrubha comes to Wester Ross*

There used to be a stone circle at Applecross, a remote fishing village in Wester Ross. In the centre of it was a stone with a hole, serving as a meeting place and focus of ritual; villagers would put their heads through the hole to bring them luck. It was also associated with prophecy. The Presbytery of 1656 was forced to take a dim view, linking the custom with quasi-pagan practices, such as the sacrifice of bulls, the adorning of wells and marching around ruined chapels. Perhaps the Applecross circle was deliberately dismantled, because it no longer stands – in fact archaeologists are not sure what form it took. But its previous existence – and former use – shows that this remote village, reached by a spectacular, tortuous, cloud-shrouded single-track mountain road, has always had a vigorous, if possibly wayward, spiritual life. It was here that the missionary St Maelrubha arrived from Ireland in 673, continuing the work that St Columba had begun on Iona in the previous century.

St Maelrubha landed initially on Saint Island, perhaps being wary of the reception he would receive from the Picts on the mainland. Applecross derives from the Gaelic A'Chomraich, meaning a sanctuary: a reference to the monastery that

St Maelrubha founded here. The only remains of the monastery are a primitively carved stone that marks the burial place of an abbot: the paucity of evidence possibly reflecting the raids that this vulnerable community suffered from the Vikings.

St Maelrubha's influence survives in a variety of place names, such as Loch Maree; a regime of drinking holy water from the well on an island there, combined with being towed three times round an island behind a rowing boat, was thought to benefit the mentally ill. ('The awful shock and the fear of having it repeated did, I believe, occasionally subdue some of the most violent cases,' the garden-maker Osgood MacKenzie remembered in 1921, 'but it was a cruel ordeal, and quite an example of "kill or cure".') There are churches dedicated to St Maelrubha throughout the Highlands.

Wester Ross was relatively populous after the last ice age. The remains of a broch – a kind of circular fortification with drystone walls, resembling a tower house – have been discovered next to the campsite, showing that Applecross was a centre of some importance during the Iron Age. The village could be reached by boat, although old people still remember a time when it was unwise to depend on the ferry services.

It remained, however, more or less inaccessible by land, at least to government troops. The Bealach nam Bo – pass of the cattle – was the last of the Parliamentary roads to be constructed after the 1745 rebellion, and was not finished until 1822. Snow often blocked it in winter. The coast road was not opened until 1975. By then, the population of the Applecross peninsula had dwindled from the three thousand who lived here in the mid nineteenth century. The present figure is two hundred.

# ARBUTHNOTT
## ABERDEENSHIRE                               *A terrifying Scottish curse*

In 1491, the vicar of Arbuthnott, James Sibbald, wrote a missal for use in his church. It is remarkable in being the only complete service book in Latin to have survived the Reformation in Scotland. Through it we can glimpse what going to kirk, such an important activity in every village and town, would have been like in the fifteenth century. Clearly Sibbald put a high value on beauty because, unusually for a missal, the book is beautifully illuminated with floral borders, decorated initials and a full-length picture of St Ternan, the patron saint of the church.

The book contains the chants, prayers and readings necessary for saying mass, as well as a calendar of saints' days. The form of the mass was a variation of the Sarum Rite (so-called from its origin at Salisbury Cathedral), which, having become standard in England, penetrated Scotland before the Reformation. But the missal also has some specifically Scottish characteristics: for example, the feasts of Scottish saints, such as St Columba, who brought Christianity to Scotland, and St Ternan himself, the first bishop to the Picts, are made red-letter days. Devotion to Scottish saints had been increasing since the fourteenth century, a sign of growing national self-confidence. St Ternan's picture shows him standing beneath a canopy, wearing a costly blue robe, while, in the Renaissance manner, a landscape can be glimpsed through the windows behind him. His head is supposed to have been based on that of the Bishop of St Andrews.

The most strikingly Scottish dimension of the missal, however, is the service of excommunication. The importance that this held for Sibbald can be seen from its position near the front of the book and the fact that it appears in both Scots and Latin. Evidently he wanted the miscreants to be in no doubt about the awfulness of their misdeeds and the dire extremity of their punishment. 'Cursit be thai syttand, standand, rydand, gangand, slepand, waikand, etand, and drinkand: In hows and owt of hows: Cursit be thai fra the crowne af the hede to the soile of the fute.'

In other words, they were to be cursed sitting, standing, riding, walking, sleeping, awake, eating and drinking; indoors and outside; from the crowns of their heads to the soles of their feet. They were to be cast out and shunned; their days would be few. They would be taken out of the book of life. And in case there was any doubt about the priest's meaning, the service concluded with a candle being thrown to the ground, symbolising the condemned soul being cast 'into the depast pot of hel, ever to remaine with cursit Nero the wikkyt emperor and his cursit falowschip'. The congregation must have trembled to hear it. Fear of damnation (and of the power of blood-chilling rhetoric from Scottish pulpits) did not start with John Knox.

The missal is now in Paisley Museum.

# ATHELSTANEFORD
## LOTHIAN
*Origin of the saltire, supposedly*

The saltire flutters over countless Scottish steeples, towers, private houses and village halls. We thank the monks of St Andrews, writing around 1140, for giving an account of its adoption as the national flag, an event which, they said, took place at Athelstaneford in the tenth century. The village takes its name from Athelstane, a Saxon leader (certainly not the Saxon king), who found himself at the head of a Northumbrian army. He led his force into Scotland, pillaging territory belonging to Unust, King of the Picts. Unust applied for help to Achaius, King of Scotland. Achaius, already outraged by the English, lent Unust ten thousand men, commanded by his son Alpin, who was also Unust's nephew. The Scots invaded Northumberland, looted what they could, and were pursued back over the border by Athelstane. Both parties prepared for battle by a stream called the Lug Down burn.

Unust's army being heavily outnumbered, the Pict prudently sought divine assistance. After his prayers, he fell into a deep sleep, during which St Andrew the Apostle appeared to him in a vision, promising a glorious victory. As a good commander, Unust lost no time in communicating this vision to his troops, who were duly inspired. When the battle was fought, the St Andrew's cross appeared magnificently irradiated in the sky. This miracle overawed the Northumbrians, who were quickly defeated.

Athelstane was slain on the banks of the burn, his head put up on a pole over the bridge. Athelstaneford must be the only example of a village whose name honours a defeated enemy. Or so that story goes. It may be that Athelstane lived to fight another day, winning the Battle of Brunanburh in 937. It could equally be that he had nothing to do with Athelstaneford, which could be derived from the Gaelic for stone ford (although, if it does, it involves a tautology, ath-ail-stane meaning stone ford, making the final syllable redundant). The origins of the saltire are, however, celebrated in a Flag Heritage Centre, housed in a restored dovecote.

The monks may not have troubled to tax their inventive powers unduly; their account of the flag in the sky is strangely similar to that of the conversion of Constantine the Great, who saw a cross of light before the Battle of Milvian Bridge.

Did any of this make much difference to the East Lothian village? Probably not. The inhabitants seem to have been happy and well-balanced, according to the report that their minister, the Rev. George Goldie, gave in the *Statistical Account of Scotland* (1792): he considered that 'upon the whole, there are few parishes in Scotland that enjoy greater advantages than the parish of Athelstaneford, and none in which the people, in general, are more comfortable, contented, and happy'.

# AUCHINDRAIN
## ARGYLL AND BUTE                              *One of the last of the clachans*

Until lairds began to improve their agriculture in the eighteenth century, the basic unit of settlement in the Highlands was the clachan (sometimes called a fermtoun*, a term that has come to be associated more with the Lowlands, although the two words seem to have been more or less interchangeable). The clachan was a huddled cluster of habitations and barns. Most clachans were cleared to make way for the new sheep-farming economy, organised around large farmsteads and estate villages in the eighteenth and nineteenth centuries. At Auchindrain, however, the old ways persisted, and the last of the multiple tenants did not die until 1963. Auchindrain is now a museum.

The buildings date from the late eighteenth and early nineteenth centuries, a time when lairds generally preferred more structured developments. Indeed, the Argyll Estate did propose to replace the apparently random scattering of homes and outbuildings with a neatly planned village around a central court, but it never happened. Families lived with their animals immediately next to their cottages, under the same thatched roof. It would have been a muddy, pungent but thermally efficient system. Conserving heat was important. A close look at the planning of the clachan shows that it was not as haphazard as it might appear: doorways and windows were placed to face away from the rain.

The clachan would have been a winter town, a main base of operations to which families retreated during the harsh, dark Highland winters. There may have been shieling huts in the hills, where shepherds could camp out in summertime as the movement of flocks demanded. Around Auchindrain there would have been an infield, cultivated in rounded strips, separated by furrows, and an outfield – a pattern of fields that changed between arable and pasture on rotation. It could be hard land to work. In the Highlands, cultivation by plough on machair (or low-lying) ground had to be supplemented by hard digging by spade where the ground was stony or peaty. Potatoes came to replace oats and rye in the eighteenth century, although this left less winter fodder and straw for the cattle.

The object of clachan life was not to produce a surplus that could be sold, but to survive. Lairds preferred to generate tangible profits through farming sheep. Tenant families themselves increasingly came to think that there were easier ways to get by. Their sons and daughters drifted to the industrial towns, or overseas, leaving only the toughest, stubbornest but least enterprising behind them.

*See Swanston, page 626

# BALLACHULISH
HIGHLAND                                                    *The Appin Murder*

For eighteen months, the decomposing body of James Stewart – James of the Glen – was left to swing on the gibbet at Ballachulish, erected prominently near the ferry across Loch Leven. In May 1752, he had been found guilty of a murder that it is generally accepted he did not commit, the victim being Colin Campbell of Glenure. In writing *Kidnapped*, Robert Louis Stevenson called Campbell the Red Fox. That is unkind to his memory: he was a red-haired man in his mid forties, known as Red Colin.

Six years earlier, ninety-one men from Appin, the area around Ballachulish, had been buried in a trench at Culloden. Since then, the Hanoverian government had done what it could to repress the lawless Highlands by force, although only weeks before Red Colin's death Westminster tried a new course. Under the Forfeited Estates Act, the profits from the lands that had been confiscated from lairds involved in the uprising would be used to establish schools to teach English (rather than Gaelic) and Protestantism (most Highlanders were Roman Catholics), as well as 'several branches of agriculture and manufactures'. The hope was to bring a measure of prosperity to a desperate region, and make the wild Highlanders more like the rest of the population.

Thomas Pennant approved of the results when he toured Scotland in 1769. Girls were being shown how to spin, spinning wheels were being given to poor families, bridges were being built over mountain torrents and disbanded soldiers were being settled on the land. Good works, no doubt. But the factors, such as Red Colin, who were charged with collecting rents and – on the day he arrived at Ballachulish – ensuring that proper arrangements were made for the ferry, were generally hated. And this one, furthermore, was a Campbell. The Campbells had not supported Bonnie Prince Charlie. Loyalty had paid off. They were richer than clans who had risen in support of the doomed Stuart cause, as could be seen from the ostentatious rebuilding of Inveraray Castle (see page 589), seat of the Campbell Duke of Argyll.

Red Colin crossed the loch. He was one of a group of horsemen making their way along a track through the woods when a musket shot rang out. It was, in the Highland way, double charged, and the bullets entered his back on either side of his spine. 'Oh, I am dead,' he cried out – and he was. The assassin made off undetected.

Within a couple of days, Stewart had been arrested as an accessory. Taken to Inveraray, he was tried by the Duke of Argyll, supported by a jury packed with Campbells. It is said that the community knew the identity of the real killer but kept it secret.

The story has been taken to symbolise the solidarity of rural life in Scotland, capable of closing ranks against outside interference, even, in the case of poor Stewart, at the expense of one of their own. The ghastly spectacle made by his body eventually drove a halfwit called Daft Macphee to tear up the gallows. Thrown into Loch Linnhe, the remains floated into Loch Etive before washing up near Bonawe. The bones of the dead man were then gathered up and buried.

But even Ballachulish was tamed. As the politicians who passed the Forfeited Estates Act had predicted, it was industry that did it. The hill behind Ballachulish was developed as a quarry to supply most of the slate roofs in Scotland. It employed 322 people in 1791, when the *Statistical Account of Scotland* was published. The only purpose to which gunpowder was put was blasting.

# BEATTOCK
## DUMFRIES AND GALLOWAY
*A railway village*

After a modest dinner in the old spa town of Moffat, Richard Hannay, hero of John Buchan's *The Thirty-Nine Steps\**, walked two miles to the railway junction. 'The night express from the south was not due till near midnight and to fill up the time, I went up on to the hillside and fell asleep, for the walk had tired me. I all but slept too long and had to run to the station to catch the train with two minutes to spare. The feel of the hard third-class cushions and the smell of stale tobacco cheered me up wonderfully.'

The station was Beattock, then in its inter-war heyday. Beattock Bank, famous in railway circles as the steepest gradient on any British mainline, demanded that as many as eight auxiliary engines, or 'pilot pugs', were on hand to help trains to the top. Two hundred people worked in the locomotive depot – drivers, firemen, coalmen, lengthmen, supervisors, foremen, signalmen, porters, porter guards, shunters, transhippers, lampmen, signal linesmen and wheel tappers. Their combined efforts were recognised in W. H. Auden's *Night Mail*:

> Pulling up Beattock, a steady climb,
> The gradient's against her, but she's on time.

Beattock was a railway village. It had previously been a coaching village. A carved stone set into the old stone bridge records that it was built by Thomas Telford† in 1819. It served a road cut, with formidable difficulty, across boggy land, which put Beattock on the route from Carlisle to Glasgow. Telford thought this was an ideal place to build a coaching inn, and one arose. The place flourished; the population of 932 recorded in the 1841 census for the parish of Kirkpatrick Juxta, of which Beattock is part, included five blacksmiths, six masons, five joiners, five handloom weavers, six shoemakers, five tailors, four dressmakers, a stocking maker, two millers, two gardeners, two road surface-men, a cooper, a forester and a piano tuner. Most earthly needs could be served locally.

The Caledonian railway arrived in 1843; a single-track branch line to Moffat opened in 1883. Exactly a century later, Beattock's role as a transport hub ended. Moffat station closed in 1954; the locomotive depot was not needed once more powerful diesel engines had replaced steam, and Beattock's own station closed to passengers in 1972, and ceased operation completely eleven years later. If you want to find Beattock now, you have to look for it. Traffic now speeds past on the M74; Telford's bridge was replaced with a new structure, seventy-eight metres downstream, in 1951.

*See Broughton, page 536. †See Craigellachie, page 547*

# BEESWING
## DUMFRIES AND GALLOWAY                    *'A! what a mare she was'*

R. S. Surtees's novel *Handley Cross* introduces Mr Jorrocks, the cockney grocer, in the character of a Master of Foxhounds; we also meet his huntsman, Pigg – outwardly unpromising, often drunk and generally disrespectful, he turns out to know as much as there is to know about horses. 'A! what a mare she was,' he says of the racehorse Beeswing, in his pantomime Geordie accent, 'won ninety gold coops. Squire Ord had been forced to build a granary to keep them in.' A remark that could only be followed by drinking off a tumbler to Beeswing's health.

She was, indeed, a remarkable horse, still remembered in the Beeswing Ladies' Day at Newcastle. Her owner, the MP William Orde, had become a barrister in London, but returned to his home in the North when his elder brother John died and he inherited the family estates in Northumberland (he employed the architect John Dobson to remodel Nunnykirk, the Ordes' country house). Respected as 'an honest and an honourable sportsman', he owned a string of successful racehorses, including Tomboy, but none could match Beeswing.

On 15 September 1842, she 'closed her wonderful career on the turf by winning the Doncaster cup', *The Gentleman's Magazine* recalled fifteen years later. 'This was Bee's-wing's fifty-first victory, and the twenty-fourth gold cup which she had won – a number quite unprecedented.'

If Pigg overstated the number of cups, he may be forgiven; Beeswing had a tremendous local following in the North. One of her triumphs was to win the special trophy given by the colliery owner George Baker of Elemore in the shape of a silver coal wagon made from three hundred and fifty pieces of silver at Newcastle in 1838.

The village of Beeswing is named after her – surely the only case of a settlement taking the name of a racehorse, even in a country such as Britain, devoted to racing since the first recorded horse race was run at Chester in 1539. The name was originally given to the pub in Lochend, whose owner was William Orde's brother, Robert. Lochend is a factual but prosaic description, given the village's position at one end of the modest Loch Arthur. Beeswing seemed altogether more dashing. The church remained firmly in Lochend.

But *O tempora! O mores!* An old caravan has been parked outside the church: it is being converted to flats. And, Beeswing, Beeswing, where is your pub? Gone the way of the racehorse itself, leaving only a name and a legend behind.

# BOWMORE
## ISLAY                                   *The joy of Islay malt*

Alfred Barnard, author of *The Whiskey Distilleries of the United Kingdom* (1887), was not a man to mince words. When he visited Islay, he found 'the coach drive from Port Ellen to Bowmore one of the most uninteresting that we had ever experienced'. It took four hours, and as he looked gloomily out of the window he saw little to beguile his eye: 'but two or three habitations, and scarcely any trees; in all our wanderings we have never travelled by such a dismal and lonely road.' But the scenery improved as he approached 'the aristocratic village of Bridgend', and if his heart did not expand as he drove the final three miles along the shore of Lochindaal to Bowmore, it should have done.

Bowmore, Islay's capital, is as charming a white-harled village, its harbour jaunty with fishing boats, as the Hebrides have to offer, having been laid out by Daniel Campbell II in 1768. It replaced the old settlement of Kilarrow, which was

*The distillery at Bowmore on Islay.*

demolished as part of improvements around Islay House. The grid plan provides an orderly setting for the architectural monument that is Kilarrow parish church, a boldly circular building with a tower over the entrance. Inside, the roof is held up by a single massive column in the centre of the round nave.

By 1779, an agreeable industry had been established in the shape of a distillery, the oldest to be licensed on Islay (although some illicit stills operated before, and no doubt after, that date). At the time when Barnard visited, the Bowmore distillery still occupied the original building, low and white-harled. The key to the product was the island's water, brown from the peat through which it had drained. It was brought from the Laggan river by a lade, or watercourse, nine miles in length – 'the longest to any Distillery in Scotland, though, as the crow flies, the distance is not more than five miles, but the engineering difficulties met with were so great, owing to want of fall, that a very tortuous course had to be made'. The barley came from Inverness-shire and Moray. The mash tun in the mash house was seventeen feet wide and six feet deep, 'said to be the largest in Islay', with a capacity of nearly eight and a half thousand gallons.

With employment from the distillery as well as fishing, Bowmore prospered better than many of the new communities built in the Highlands during the late eighteenth and early nineteenth centuries. In the 1830s, a practical step was taken to encourage better farming, by instituting competitions for proficiency in using what, to some parts of the Highlands, was a novel implement – the spade. According to Mr Campbell of Islay, the prizes were 'all very keenly contested', and at Bowmore, 'men were carried off the ground fainting from over-exertion'.

# BROUGHTON

*John Buchan roams the hills*

John Buchan spent his childhood holidays at Broughton, and it shaped his life and writing. Later, he would say that 'Since ever I was a very little boy I have liked Broughton better than any other place in the world.' His sister, Anna, also a writer, who used the pseudonym O. Douglas, felt a similar bond. 'In our early childhood it was the quietest of villages,' she remembered in *Farewell to Priorsford* (1950). 'An infrequent carriage and pair, some gigs and slow-moving farm carts, a baker's van or two, and – great excitement – the pigman's cart. The "pigman", let it be explained, had no connection with swine, but gave "pigs" or dishes in exchange for old clothes.' It was all quite a contrast with the surroundings amid which they spent the rest of the year, the Buchans' father, also John, being a Free Church minister in the notorious Gorbals area of Glasgow.

At Broughton, John and Anna stayed with their grandparents, the Mastertons, at Broughton Green farm, once an inn, at the end of the village. They provided a warm home life that veered between idiosyncratic and severe. The house and farm at Broughton were comfortingly well-ordered, and gave John the chance to roam the countryside with an independence that would later be reflected in novels such as *The Thirty-Nine Steps.* He would walk the hills looking for burns to fish, then return to the farmhouse with the catch in his pockets for a tea of newly baked scones and apple-and-rowanberry jelly.

It was a religious household, with two church services on Sundays, but one that was also steeped in the romance of the Borders, with tales of Covenanters hiding from government forces among the peat hags. Buchan drew on his memories of Broughton for his novel *Witch Wood*, published in 1927. It was his favourite of the huge number of novels that he wrote. Richard Hannay, hero of *The Thirty-Nine Steps, Greenmantle, Mr Standfast* and other books, takes his surname from the area; a window dedicated to a local Hannay can be found in the Broughton Free Church (now the John Buchan Centre).

'Publishing is my business, writing my amusement and politics my duty,' Buchan was apt to remark. His political work bore fruit when he was appointed Governor General of Canada in 1935, an appointment that came to seem crucial as war approached and Buchan had the task of ensuring active support from the Dominion. The same year he was created Baron Tweedsmuir of Elsfield: the Tweedsmuir part of the title taken from a village near Broughton, the Elsfield from Elsfield Manor near Oxford, which had been his family home since 1919.

# BURGHEAD
## MORAY

'Any Hogmanay afternoon, a small group of seamen and coopers, dressed in blue overfrocks, and followed by numbers of noisy youngsters, may be seen rapidly wending their way to the south-western extremity of the village, where it is customary to build the Clavie.' So observed the *Banffshire Journal* in the 1860s, and things have not changed greatly since. Burghead, on a headland of the Moray Firth, once probably a detached island or long promontory, could be described as resistant to change.

Hogmanay, for this purpose, takes place on 11 January: the village has remained true to the Julian calendar, replaced elsewhere by the Gregorian calendar in 1752, causing riots by country folk who thought that the government had lopped off eleven days of their life. The Clavie is a half barrel, filled with combustible material. Like many things about Burghead, its origins are ancient but obscure. Some say that it derives from the Gaelic *cliabh*, a basket, others from the Latin *clavus*, a nail.

The nail is a ritual object: the same one is used each year to nail the barrel onto a pole, which is then shouldered, set alight and carried blazing through the village by a relay of fishermen (in glorious defiance of health and safety). To return to the *Banffshire Journal*: 'As fast as his heavy load will permit him, the bearer hurries along the well-known route, followed by the shouting Burgheadians, the boiling tar meanwhile trickling down in dark sluggish streams all over his back . . . the least stumble is sufficient to destroy his equilibrium.'

Fire and New Year go together in many places in Scotland. Elsewhere in the Highlands, they used to burn juniper, bitterly aromatic, in front of their cattle and in their houses. Shetlanders called the practice of carrying burning peat through their byres 'saining', a protection against the powers of darkness. Other Scottish communities light bonfires or parade with torches. A vestige of such fire rituals survives in the common practice of carrying a lump of coal into houses after the last stroke of midnight, to bring luck for the coming year.

Nobody, however, can say when the tradition of Clavie started. It has been associated variously with the Picts, the Celts, the Vikings and the Romans. The Picts had a large fort at Burghead, covering three hectares; the walls on the cliff edge were eight metres thick. It was probably built in the fourth century and burnt down five hundred years later. Carved plaques, presumably from a shrine, show bulls in different states of temperament, from aggressive to docile. The Romans were in the area briefly, forming a camp at Bellie, near Fochabers (see page 573). Agricola regarded Burghead as the key to the north of Scotland.

Further mystery surrounds the well that was discovered in 1809. Underground, it is cut out of solid rock: not so much a well in the conventional sense as a chamber with a tank sunk into the floor. The worn condition of the twenty-six descending steps shows that a lot of feet went down to it – but whose?

# CALGARY
## MULL                                    *A name that means more in Canada*

Calgary, the city of a million people in Alberta, Canada, famous for the Calgary Stampede, takes its name from the quiet, green island of Mull in the Inner Hebrides. Near the little village of Calgary are the ruins of Inivea, a settlement depopulated by the Clearances that first came to Mull in the 1830s, when a Moray improver bought the Isle of Ulva and reduced its population from six hundred to a hundred and fifty. (Among those who were forced to leave the island was David Livingstone's father, Neil, who made a new home at Blantyre, a cotton-spinning town near Glasgow.)

On the promontory known as the Ross of Mull, and on Mull's satellite of Iona, the 7th Duke of Argyll considered that his family's policy of maintaining the population through the reduction of smallpox, the introduction of potatoes and the development of a kelp-burning industry had been too successful, particularly after the potato blight of 1846 and the collapse in kelp prices due to the advent of guano as a fertiliser*. His 'object', he told the Select Committee on Emigration, was 'to get the farms divided into large proportions and have proper tenants on them, and the rest of the tenants to be provided for by emigration or induced to go to the low country'.

Rent arrears were no longer tolerated by his successor, the 8th Duke, at a time when crofting had become economically unviable. As the Duke's hated factor John Campbell wrote to him in 1850, 'The small crofters are generally in debt, otherwise than rents, to a larger amount than the value of their effects, even could they get a market for them.' The Duke of Argyll was not as brutal in his methods as the Duke of Sutherland – in fact crofts were allowed to remain on the really unworkable land – but hundreds of islanders emigrated. It was the same all over Mull, including at Calgary.

But the Canada connection has nothing to do with the Clearances. At the highest point of Union Cemetery, in Alberta's Calgary, rests the body of Colonel James Macleod, who named the city. He was born on Skye in 1836. The previous generation of Macleods had taken one of the obvious routes for a Scottish family unable to support itself at home by joining the army; but no fewer than seven of James's uncles had died of tropical diseases in far-flung places, and his own father, Martin, had been seriously ill while on service in Demerara. To avoid a similar fate for his children, Martin emigrated with his family to Canada, where he bought a farm.

The Macleods were comfortably off, and James graduated with a degree in classics and philosophy from Queen's College, Kingston. He subsequently became a barrister, but after a decade he was unable to suppress his love of the outdoors, and he joined Colonel Garnet Wolseley's expedition against the Red River uprising in 1870. His reputation for probity among the native chiefs with whom he negotiated helped him to bring peace to Alberta.

Fort Calgary, out of which the city grew, was built in 1875. Macleod chose the name of Calgary after Calgary House on Mull, where he had stayed; the memory of the beautiful sands of Calgary Bay had stayed in his memory as an image of Nature at its most poetic.

*See Wraxall, page 82

# CALLANISH
LEWIS                                                         *Living with a mystery*

The great stone circle at Callanish stands in a landscape of mystery: a stretch of coast so low-lying and fretted that it is difficult to know what is sea and what is land – particularly as the surface of the latter has been stripped away by peat digging. The stones add to the sense of puzzlement. What are they doing here, on this remote island, and what do they mean?

The first question is easier to answer than the second. Six thousand years ago, Lewis had not been so nibbled away by the sea. The land was higher, and relatively fertile, farmed for a primitive form of barley that was sown in banks heaped up to make the best use of the limited sun in this northern latitude. Men used antlers to dig a ditch, separating a patch of ground off from the rest; it was hard work, but they were dedicating this place to ritual.

About 3000BC, the first stones were hauled into position. As it happens, they were shards from an ancient rock formation: what geologists call the Lewisian gneiss, formed three thousand million years ago. Eventually the stones would peg out the shape of a frying pan. The handle, projecting north, forms an avenue, along which one can suppose that processions approached the main ring of thirteen standing stones. In the centre of it stands a monolith nearly five metres in height. Erecting the stones must have been a cooperative effort, since each would have taken thirty or forty men to haul upright.

Perhaps the structure was designed to celebrate an astronomical phenomenon, which takes place every eighteen and a half years or so, when the moon is so low in the sky that it seems to dance along the southern hills. We live in an age that explores the moon and probes the stars: it could be that we are projecting a preoccupation to match our own onto this early site. But they may have felt that the moment when the moon seems to kiss the earth deserved special recognition.

Men and women have always lived among and around the stones. There was a burial chamber here, used for several centuries, which might later have become a house. Then it was cleared away and the site was farmed. In the Bronze Age, farming stopped and peat built up around the stones – to a depth of a metre and a half by the time archaeologists took an interest in the nineteenth century. By then the legend had grown up, as a visitor wrote at the end of the seventeenth century, that the stones 'were a sort of men converted into stone by ane Inchanter', although by the time Martin Martin wrote *A Description of the Western Islands of Scotland* in 1703 the idea that this was 'a Place appointed for Worship in the time of Heathenism' had taken hold. A settlement of black houses* crept up to the hem of the circle. The ones closest to the stones were swept away, but the community still has a sense of ownership of the site, running the visitor centre provided by Historic Scotland and keeping it open for chance visitors, even in the bleakest months of winter.

*See Garenin, page 579

# CARLENRIG
BORDERS                                                      *Death of a gangster*

Nothing became Johnnie Armstrong of Gilnockie so well as his death, evoked in the Border ballad 'Johnie Armstrang':

> 'Farewell! my bonny Gilnock Hall
> Where on Esk side thou standest stout!
> Gif I had lived but seven yeirs mair
> I wad a gilt thee round about.
> John murdered was at Carlinrigg
> And all his gallant companie;
> But Scotland's heart was ne'er sae wae
> To see sae mony brave men die.'

The younger brother of Thomas Armstrong, laird of Mangerton, Armstrong built the stronghold of Gilnockie Tower around 1520. He needed it. Gilnockie was then in the thirty square miles whose nationality was so insecure that, until 1552, it was known as the Debatable Land. Armstrong led one of the most notorious of the bands that terrified the Border country with thefts, house burning, extortion rackets and other lawlessness. He was outlawed and possibly excommunicated in 1528.

In 1530, King James V of Scotland determined to suppress some of this activity. Although heading an army of eight thousand men, he gave orders for the gentlemen attending him to bring their best dogs, as though it were only a hunting expedition. Border noblemen who were known to protect reiving families, in return for political support, were imprisoned in their castles. Once this had been done, the King captured a couple of the worst offenders (one of them as he prepared a great royal entertainment) and had them hanged in front of their towers.

Johnnie Armstrong was due to meet the King at Carlenrig church, and duly rode up to the rendezvous with the large body of retainers that usually accompanied him. James, however, was so infuriated by the brazen display that he ordered him and more than twenty of his followers to be hanged. They were strung up from the trees of a grove beside the church. Afterwards the dead were supposedly buried in the churchyard.

It is one of the quirks of romance that Johnnie Armstrong should be remembered as a hero, rather than a vicious gangster. Sir Walter Scott's *Minstrelsy of the Scottish Border* (1802) is largely to blame.

# CARMYLLIE
ANGUS                                                              *Origins of a great scientist*

Robert Burns* was not the only eminent Scot to grow up as a plough boy. So did James Bowman Lindsay, a scientist who was thought something of a crank in the second quarter of the nineteenth century, but whose vision is now recognised as prophetic. He is representative of a Scottish type, rising above unpromising beginnings to conquer, in his case, an extraordinary number of subjects – although so 'indifferent to fame', as his biographer, A. H. Millar put it in 1925, that 'he sank, almost unnoticed, into an undistinguished grave'.

Windyedge is an evocative name for a Scottish turf-roofed farmhouse; Carmyllie, the village near Arbroath where it was situated, is indeed windy enough. In 1799, Lindsay was born here, a delicate child who would have grown up to follow his family into farming if he had been stronger. Instead he developed his skills as a weaver. Like John Duncan of Drumlithie (see page 556), he combined weaving with intellectual pursuits, and would be seen on the way to Arbroath with a length of cloth tied to his back, reading an open book as he walked. In 1821, his parents sent him to St Andrews University.

After four years of mathematics and science, Lindsay turned to theology, with the idea of becoming a minister. In the end, he became science and mathematical lecturer at the Watt Institution in Dundee. 'Had he been more practical, less diffident, and possessed of greater worldly wisdom,' remembered one of his pupils, Alexander Maxwell, historian of Dundee, he 'would have gained for himself a good place amongst distinguished men. As it was, he remained little more than a mere abstraction, a cyclopaedia out of order, and went through life a poor and modest schoolmaster.'

Electricity was one of his passions. In 1834, an advertisement in the *Dundee Advertiser* announced that his forthcoming lectures would include the demonstration of an electric battery, already powerful and 'undergoing daily augmentation'. This was a big step from Humphry Davy's observations of 1800. At a time when voltaic electric light was nothing more than a laboratory experiment, Lindsay made the bold prediction that 'Houses and towns will in a short time be lighted by electricity instead of gas, and heated by it instead of coal; and machinery will be worked by it instead of steam – all at a trifling expense.'

Electricity could also be used to communicate between Britain and the United States, he predicted, and if his own system (using water rather than air as a medium) did not go anywhere, he was saluted by Marconi as 'the first man who thoroughly believed in the possibility and utility of long-distance wireless telegraphy'. Lindsay had also succeeded in using electricity to 'obtain a constant stream of light on 25th July 1835', according to an autobiographical note.

That note was found in a mass of papers, which found their way to the Dundee Free Library in 1893. They were the chaotic fruits of a massive labour, which was to have formed a *Pentecontaglossal Dictionary*, compiled in more than fifty languages, with notes. The task, which occupied every spare moment for twenty-five years, was intended to discover, by a comparison of languages, when and where mankind originated.

A bachelor, Lindsay was offered a post at the British Museum, but would not leave his aged mother to go south. Instead, he took a job as a teacher at the prison in Dundee, until he was granted a government pension of a hundred pounds a year in 1858, four years before his death.

*See Mauchline, page 603

# CATRINE
AYRSHIRE                                    *A village to attract the workers*

The Big Wheel at Catrine mill was the biggest and most powerful waterwheel in Scotland when it was built in the 1820s. Turning at three revolutions a minute, the falling water scattering rainbows though the wheelhouse on a sunny day, it powered what a guide of 1903 described as 'the gigantic works' that was Catrine's *raison d'être*. Catrine was a mill village, planned as logically as the Big Wheel itself.

There had been nothing much to the place before the 1780s: a mere eleven buildings, including the corn mill and smithy. The name was derived, unpromisingly, from cateran, originally a Gaelic word for fighting man, which had come to mean marauder or cattle rustler – an indication of the principle employment. But, in 1786, Sir Claud Alexander, a Scotsman who had, like other of his countrymen, made a fortune in India, returned to his homeland and Ballochmyle, a mansion designed by Robert Adam, which his friends had acquired for him *in absentia*. (Sir Claud's sister Wilhelmina was walking one evening in the grounds of the house when she was startled to see a man dressed in country clothes, leaning against the trunk of a tree. It was Robert Burns*, who was inspired to write 'The Lass of Ballochmyle' in tribute. Alas, when he wrote to request permission to publish the poem, she did not reply.)

Sir Claud knew David Dale, Richard Arkwright's partner in the early years of the New Lanark cotton-spinning mills: a model employer as well as a dynamic businessman, with a grasp of engineering. They formed a partnership, initially to spin the warp and weft yarn for handloom weavers. Within ten years, the twist mill and 'Jeanie house' (for spinning jennies) were employing thirteen hundred people, working at more than five thousand spindles.

Catrine had the fast-flowing river Ayr, whose waters were diverted into a series of 'voes' or reservoirs to provide a head for the mill wheels. But to attract a workforce it needed houses. They were built around what became Mill Square, dominated by the five-storey mill, with streets neatly intersecting at right angles. The architecture was simple: the two-storey buildings had stone window and door surrounds, and plainly harled walls. (Where the harling has come off, you can see that the material underneath is red sandstone.) A brewery was constructed in the 1790s, a school was opened on the top floor of the mill, and an elegant red sandstone church with Gothic windows and classical cupola was built on a rise above the village. Every effort was made to keep workers in this otherwise remote location; nevertheless, Catrine's population fell by three hundred between 1793 and 1796.

For the mill, a new phase of development opened in 1801, when it was acquired by James Finlay and Co. They put in gas lighting, as well as the Big Wheel. With the creation of a bleach works, Catrine had ballooned to a place of three thousand inhabitants by the time Queen Victoria came to the throne. The Big Wheel kept turning until 1947: a delight for romantics, but evidence that British textiles had not moved with the times. When fire ravaged what had become the Old Mill in 1963, it was demolished, leaving Catrine as a Hamlet without the Prince.

*See Mauchline, page 603

# CERES
FIFE                                              *Plack and Penny Day*

In the days when Ceres had a fair, it was held on 24 June, the anniversary of Bannockburn. The next day the games were held, and the tradition continues. Plack and Penny Day, as the event used to be called, is now the Ceres Games, having been fixed as the last Saturday in June. The right to hold a fair is said to have been granted in recognition of the role played by the men of Ceres at the Battle, while the Games celebrate the contingent's safe return.

The more famous Braemar Gathering in Aberdeenshire may have older roots, originating in the reign of Malcolm III, who came to the throne in 1058 and was killed in 1093. The first sword dance supposedly took place at Dunsinane when Malcolm slew one of Macbeth's followers, threw his own sword on top of that of his foe, and danced in triumph over them. There are various other ways in which Malcolm is supposed to have influenced the form of the games, such as the institution of a competitive hill race to select a gille-ruith (messenger).

Braemar cannot, however, claim the continuous history of the Ceres Games, which, despite the disapproval of the sixteenth-century Kirk, have continued without interruption since 1314, except during the periods of the Act of Proscription

(1746–1782), which followed Bonnie Prince Charlie's rebellion, and the two World Wars.

The men of Ceres may well have been conspicuous at Bannockburn. The barony of Struthers, of which Craighall (to which Ceres belonged) is part, was held by Sir Robert Keith, great marischal of Scotland. He commanded Bruce's cavalry. Keith is supposed to have encouraged archery practice on the Bow Butts at Ceres. A games would have been an appropriate celebration. Like the sports of the Olympics itself, most of the elements of a Highland Games had an obvious benefit in warfare: they involve feats of strength and endurance, and even the bagpipes were regarded as an instrument of war (if only to the ears).

It is fortunate that Ceres is one of the few villages in Scotland with a green, because this forms the arena. The centre is used for sword dancing and tossing the caber and sheaf. Racing cyclists whirl around the perimeter, giving way to a horse race in the afternoon. A pipe band starts the day.

The name of Ceres has nothing to do with the Roman goddess; the church is dedicated to the seventh-century saint St Cyras or St Seres, a daughter of Eugenius IV of Scotland. Besides, in the Roman pantheon, Bacchus might have been a more appropriate deity: there were about twenty-five houses in the parish licensed to sell 'spirituous liquors' in 1840.

# COCKBURNSPATH
BORDERS *This is how the world was made*

In June 1788, the Scottish geologist James Hutton set off in a small sailing boat from Dunglass, near Cockburnspath, with his friends Sir James Hall and John Playfair. It was a fine day, suitable for observing the Berwickshire cliffs. They crept down the coast, keeping close to the land. After about a mile, they were rewarded by finding what Hutton had been looking for – Siccar Point, a headland that displayed a geological formation, which confirmed the ideas that Hutton had been forming, to be published in his *Theory of the Earth* later that year.

The action of the waves had laid bare vertical beds of glittering sedimentary rock, called schistus, above which had been deposited a cliff of red horizontal sandstone. Hutton deduced that the juxtaposition could only have occurred if the schistus had been laid down horizontally, then forced through ninety degrees by some tumultuous upheaval of the earth's crust; it had then sunk down again into the seabed, upon which the red sandstone formed, making jagged peaks at a later era.

Playfair described the excitement of the moment in his biography of Hutton: 'On landing at this point, we found that we actually trode on the primeval rock, which forms alternately the base and the summit of the present land . . . Dr Hutton was highly pleased with appearances that set in so clear a light the different formations of the parts which compose the exterior crust of the earth, and where all the circumstances were combined that could render the observation satisfactory and precise.'

They then listened with 'earnestness and admiration' as Hutton expounded his interpretation of the rocks before them. 'The palpable evidence presented to us, of one of the most extraordinary and important facts in the natural history of the earth, gave a reality and substance to those theoretical speculations, which, however probable, had never till now been directly authenticated by the testimony of the senses. We often said to ourselves, What clearer evidence could we have had of the different formation of these rocks, and of the long interval which separated their formation, had we actually seen them emerging from the bosom of the deep . . . The mind seemed to grow giddy by looking so far into the abyss of time.'

Their wonder is understandable. Although Hutton emphasised his belief that the processes by which the earth had been shaped were the work of a beneficent Creator, his observations contradicted the Biblical account of the origins of the world, seventy years before Darwin's *On the Origin of Species*. Needless to say, it took many years for his theory to be accepted.

Meanwhile, in Berwickshire, he enjoyed a different kind of renown, as the landowner who introduced the Norfolk two-horse plough into the Borders, on his family estate at Slighhouses.

# CORPACH
## HIGHLAND                                   *Neptune's Staircase*

Corpach is a canal village. It was dismissed by *The New Statistical Account of Scotland* of 1845 as having 'no houses of any value'. By contrast, the Caledonian Canal, rising from a basin outside it, was a 'stupendous work'. Its first steps on its way north-east towards the North Sea were taken up Neptune's Staircase, a series of eight huge locks enabling ships to navigate the twenty-seven-metre difference in level between Loch Eil and Loch Lochy, separated by a distance of eight miles.

The canal cut a waterway along the Great Glen from one coast of Scotland to the other. Ships leaving Newcastle, for example, could now reach Liverpool without battling their way through the Pentland Firth, which separates the mainland from Orkney, and round Cape Wrath, on Scotland's north-western tip. It saved five hundred miles of dangerous sailing.

James Watt, inventor of the steam engine, had surveyed the ground as early as 1773; he pronounced the project practicable. Another great engineer, John Rennie, prepared a scheme in 1791, but nothing happened. There was a flurry of activity during the Napoleonic Wars, when canals were wanted as a means to allow ships to move around Britain without being attacked. Thomas Telford* was called in. Writing to Watt to seek his advice, he observed: 'The object appears to me so great

*Corpach basin, the western terminus of Telford's Caledonian Canal.*

and so desirable, that I am convinced you will feel a pleasure in bringing it again under investigation.' The basin at Corpach was begun in 1804. It took years to hew it out of the adamantine rock beside Loch Eil.

Twenty years later, the canal was complete. Everyone agreed that it provided a spectacular journey. 'All admire the magnificent scenery along its banks for sixty miles,' *The New Statistical Account* observed, 'particularly at the southern entrance', which was made under the awesome, white-browed bulk of Ben Nevis. But that optimistic author was cautious about its practical value. 'No one can yet say how useful it may prove,' he wrote – with good reason. With so many cast-iron locks to build, so many mountain streams (swelling to torrents in winter) to put into culverts, so many sluices (required to let off excess water running down from the mountains) to construct, it is not surprising that the works ran late and massively over budget.

Worse, Telford was not able to provide the draught that he had envisaged; by the time the canal was opened, it was inadequate for the larger ships that were in use. Besides, in the age of steam they could negotiate Scotland's north coast more easily. The Caledonian Canal was Telford's only white elephant.

But what a splendid one. Corpach, putting forth a lighthouse that seems little bigger than a Roman candle, shelters in the lee of two of Britain's greatest landscape features: a mountain that is the work of Nature, a canal that is the work of man.

*See Craigellachie, page 547

# COULPORT

*The summer resort that produced the Kibble Palace*

Coulport grew up around a ferry across Loch Long. Ferries were important at a time when it was easier to get around Argyll by ship than by road. People would gather around the old ferry house when the sea was too rough to cross. The Victorian ferryman, Archibald Marquis, would lead a team, headed by a piper, to play shinty on New Year's Day.

In the second half of the nineteenth century, Rosneath developed as a summer resort for rich Glasgow families, arriving by steamer. Coulport House was owned by the inventor and engineer John Kibble. Not all his ideas took off: his floating bicycle, on which he claimed to have cycled across Loch Long, came to nothing, as did the enormous camera that he created, with a lens diameter of thirteen inches (the apparatus had to be mounted on a horse-drawn cart). In 1851, Kibble built the enormous conservatory that, dismantled and moved in 1872, was eventually re-erected as the Kibble Palace in Glasgow's Botanic Gardens.

A monkey puzzle tree from Coulport House survived into the twenty-first century, but now even that has gone: both Coulport House and the adjacent Swiss Cottage were demolished to make way for a different kind of construction: nuclear bunkers. Since the 1960s, the village has been taken over by the Royal Naval Armaments Depot (RNAD), which stores nuclear weapons for the naval base at Faslane on the other side of Rosneath, home to Britain's fleet of Trident submarines. Sentry posts are operated when weapons are on site.

The light and airy curves of Kibble's conservatories have been replaced by the crude, angular silhouettes of military structures, and an untold volume of concrete. Under cover of darkness, a submarine will occasionally creep round the tip of the peninsula, slipping into the RNAD for rearming. Coulport lives a double life. But just as in the days of the ferry, its present existence is a consequence of geography and the sea.

# CRAIGELLACHIE

*Laughing Tam opens up the Highlands*

Samuel Smiles, Victorian author of *Self-Help*, wrote the engineer Thomas Telford's biography. He was a good choice. Telford, who was born in a hamlet near Langholm in Dumfriesshire, managed not only to pull himself up by his bootstraps (while remaining so good-humoured he was known as Laughing Tam), but through his industry also enabled others to flourish.

Nowhere was this more evident than in his native Scotland. In the middle of the eighteenth century, it had been, according to Smiles, 'a country without roads, fields lying uncultivated, mines unexplored, and all branches of industry languishing in the midst of an idle, miserable, and haggard population'. Even after 1800, the only practicable roads through the Highlands were those built by the military after the Jacobite rebellions, which were not particularly convenient for the ordinary population.

An Argyllshire minister, the Rev. Mr Macdougall, described the condition of the people around 1760: 'Indolence was almost the only comfort they enjoyed. There was scarcely any variety of wretchedness with which they were not obliged to struggle, or rather to which they were not obliged to submit.' Food was so short that they would bleed their cattle in order to boil up their blood and drink it. Without ploughs, the cultivation of the land had not improved much on medieval practices. There were no roads west of the Great Glen, and travellers between Perth and Inverness usually made their wills before they set out, for fear of the bands of robbers who roamed the country after the Forty-Five. The journey from Inverness to Edinburgh took eight days. Enter Telford.

The government called upon him to make a survey of Scotland in 1802. One of the deficiencies that he found was an absence of bridges. Lord Cockburn, who travelled the northern circuit as a barrister, remembered without affectation the 'wretched pierless ferries, let to poor cottars, who rowed, or hauled, or pushed a crazy boat across, or more commonly got their wives to do it'. Even the river Tay on the main road to Inverness could be crossed only by boat.

With government support, Telford proceeded, during the next eighteen years, to build 920 miles of 'capital roads', connected by twelve hundred bridges. The first stagecoaches left Perth for Inverness in 1806. The use of wheeled carts became practicable, so that women no longer had to carry manure to the fields on their backs. As Smiles rejoiced, 'Sloth and idleness gradually disappeared before the energy, activity, and industry which were called into life by the improved communications.' To quote Telford himself: 'About two hundred thousand pounds has been granted in fifteen years. It has been the means of advancing the country at least a century.'

Craigellachie first grew up around a ferry. Telford's bridge over the Spey, built in 1812–14, spans a gorge using a cast-iron structure brought by boat from an iron foundry in Denbighshire. On its completion, William Marshall* was moved to write a strathspey on it. And Smiles was right: improved communications inspired industry, in the shape, at Craigellachie, of a hotel, a whisky distillery and a cooperage to supply the distillery with barrels.

*See Milltown of Auchindoun, page 607

# CRAIL

*The Glasgow Boys out of Glasgow*

One might have expected the group of painters known as the Glasgow Boys to have produced a vision of Glasgow. They were realists, wanting to explore grittier subject matter than would have been welcomed by the Royal Scottish Academy in Edinburgh, using a technique influenced by the Impressionism that some of them had encountered first-hand in Paris. But the industrial city did not constitute their principal theme, because every summer they would migrate to fishing villages in Berwickshire, the East Neuk of Fife and the Trossachs, finding material among the tough, salty communities that lived there.

In 1883, William MacGregor, sometimes called the Father of the School (perhaps because of his air of gravitas), favoured Crail. MacGregor's father was a partner in a Glasgow shipbuilding firm, who died when his son was only three, leaving him well off. Affluence allowed him to withdraw from the city, which he had to do: badly asthmatic, he needed the pure air of the coast or hills. In Crail, MacGregor painted *en plein air* a large scene of the main street, its architecture still preserving some of the dignity of a burgh founded in the Middle Ages, when the fishermen supplied herring to the royal household, but which, by the late nineteenth century, had become a backwater, where its inhabitants could stop and gossip in groups of twos and threes without interrupting the traffic (as MacGregor shows it, there was none). *The Shore at Crail* shows some of the boats, successors to those of the medieval period, pulled up on the beach; *A Cottage Garden* makes a humble scene of vegetables growing in their natural state into a drama of heavy shadows and sculptural forms. MacGregor settled at Bridge of Allan in Stirlingshire in 1886.

James Guthrie, who vied with MacGregor for artistic leadership, preferred Cockburnspath (see page 544) in Berwickshire, which he first visited with the watercolourist Arthur Melville in 1883. Melville was older than Guthrie and more cosmopolitan. His travels had taken him to the Middle East, where he had been robbed by bandits, stripped naked and left for dead. He developed a style in which subjects were often painted in bright sunlight. Northern light and the influence of the Glasgow Boys made his palette more sombre.

Guthrie's Impressionism had come via the works of Jules Bastien-Lepage, who had exhibited at Glasgow. His influence can be seen in 'A Hind's Daughter', which Guthrie painted at Cockburnspath during the first summer that he spent there. It shows a peasant's daughter cutting cabbages in a garden. She is sturdy and ruddy cheeked, seen against the light; the muted colours evoke a world of hard toil under cloudy skies.

Scratched onto the diamond-shaped windowpanes of Croik church are the memorials of a community's tragedy. 'Glen Calvie people was in the churchyard May 24th 1845', one reads; another declares 'Glen Calvie people the wicked generation', and 'This place needs cleaning'. The people who wrote these words had been driven from their crofts to the churchyard, where they erected a lean-to shelter. Their fate was not uncommon at a time when landowners and farmers found it more profitable to run sheep than sublet their land to agriculturally inefficient, Gaelic-speaking crofting folk, who were lucky if they could produce enough food for their basic needs. The dispossessed of Glen Calvie were, however, unusual; not only did they etch a message to posterity on the church windows, but their plight was reported as a scandal in the London press.

The landowners and factors responsible for the Clearances were powerful local figures, who could silence criticism in the newspapers of their area. But word of events at Glen Calvie had reached the ear of *The Times*, which sent what it grandly called a 'commissioner' (we would now call him a journalist) to report the proceedings. He found about two hundred and fifty members of the Free Church assembled on a hillside, listening to one of their elders read psalms as they witnessed the tragedy. They formed a circle, the women in scarlet or plaid shawls, the men wearing blue bonnets, and with shepherd's plaids wrapped about them – 'their only covering'.

By contrast, only a 'miserably thin' congregation had gathered at the Church of Scotland. It was here that a shelter of tarpaulin stretched over poles had been erected, with rugs and horse blankets on the floor. Notice to quit had been given to the crofters a year earlier, but twelve of the eighteen families had been unable to find alternative homes. The harshness of the treatment still retains its power to shock. Eighty people spend the night in the churchyard.

'The whole countryside was up on the hills watching them as they silently took possession of their tent. A fire was kindled in the churchyard, round which the poor children clustered. Two cradles, with infants in them, were placed close to the fire, and sheltered round by the dejected-looking mothers.'

The newly dispossessed had been far from destitute previously, owing no rent and owning their own stock. Sale of the beasts provided each family with eighteen pounds, on top of which seventy-two pounds and ten shillings was given to the group for leaving quietly. The *British Farmer's Magazine* was among those disgusted by such treatment. On one farm of thirty thousand acres, only eleven shepherds were employed, 'so that it will be seen that no other branch of agriculture could furnish less employment to the rural labourers than this sort of sheep-farming, if farming it can be called'.

We do not know what became of the Glen Calvie families; if they did not emigrate, they would have soon got through their money and been made paupers.

Letters from others who had been cleared from the Highlands and made new lives overseas suggest they became considerably happier in their new circumstances than they had been in the old.

# CROMARTY
HIGHLAND                                            *Fishing and fossil hunting*

'The herring is one of the most eccentric little fishes that frequents our seas,' wrote Hugh Miller (1802–56), a native of Cromarty. 'For many years together it visits regularly in its season some particular firth or bay; – fishing villages spring up on the shores, harbours are built for the reception of vessels; and the fisherman and merchant calculate on their usual quantum of fish, with as much confidence as the farmer on his average quantum of grain.' Then comes a year when the herring stays away. The good times are over. The village becomes 'a heap of green mounds'.

So it happened with Cromarty. In one legendary season during the reign of Queen Anne, fish came in such numbers that the curers ran out of barrels and salt. So many herrings were left over that, spread on the fields, their smell was appalling and people feared they would catch something. Just as unexpectedly as the glut had appeared, the herring deserted the coast. The market dwindled in importance to the point where only children went, to be served by old folk selling toys and sweetmeats.

But Cromarty continued to look to the sea. It could hardly avoid doing so, given its position at the neck of a deep natural harbour. These days a chain ferry clanks across, when a gale does not blow, to the naval port of Invergordon. In the early twentieth century, the firth was used by the navy – Invergordon gave its name to the last mutiny, which took place after budget cuts in 1931 – and became a flying boat base during the Second World War. More recently, it has made its money from the North Sea oil rigs that light up like vast, year-round Christmas trees, sparkling through the grey dawn. There is a squat lighthouse, raised in the 1840s, beside the little harbour, but the place is so sleepy that it need not open more than half an eye.

Hugh Miller did not go to sea. Having been thrown out of school for brawling with a teacher at the age of sixteen, he became a stonemason. For an intelligent man, it was a fine trade to pursue at a time when fossils were capturing the imagination of educated society. Two fossils of fish were named after Miller, and his collection of more than six thousand specimens forms the core of the collection in the National Museum of Scotland in Edinburgh. He was also a writer, a polemicist and an evangelical Christian. But Miller's house – thatched, like most vernacular buildings before the twentieth century, although with six rooms, and therefore considerably grander than Robert Burns's birthplace at Alloway in Ayrshire – had salty connections, having been built by a sea captain in 1711.

# CROOK OF DEVON

*Satan wears a bonnet*

James VI and I took a special interest in witches, going so far as to write a book on the subject, *Daemonologie*, in 1597. They were outlawed by the Witchcraft Act of 1563, which remained in force until 1736. During that period it has been estimated that nearly four thousand people were accused under it, most of them from country areas. Superstition survived longer in the wilds than it did in towns and cities.

The inhabitants of Crook of Devon, surrounded by 'bleak dreary moor, flat and extensive', according to an account of 1802, the river Devon being remarkable for waterfalls with names such as the Devil's Mill, seem to have been specially vulnerable. Twelve women and a man from there were tried by His Majesty's Justice-General Depute for Scotland, Alexander Colville of Blair, in 1662; all but one pregnant woman, who was granted a temporary stay of execution, suffered death, being either strangled and burnt or, in the case of the seventy-nine-year-old Margaret Hoggin, apparently dying during the course of the trial.

It was normal for so-called confessions to be extracted from supposed witches by torture, sleep deprivation possibly inducing hallucinogenic descriptions of flying and metamorphosis into animals. But the Crook of Devon thirteen seem genuinely to have been a coven. Beyond forming the right number, the evidence that they gave to their interrogators was unexpectedly consistent.

One feature common to all of their accounts was the presence of Satan. He was described in everyday language as a bearded figure in 'ane blue bonnet and grey clothes', who made them forswear their baptism by placing one hand on the crown of their heads, the other on a sole of their feet, and declaring that everything between belonged to him. He gave them new names and had sex with the women, including Hoggin. The warlock seems to have fared particularly badly. He was promised 'silver and gold, whilk he never got', and given food that disagreed with him. They met together after midnight, although the orgies, as described in the confessions, seem to have been fairly tame. 'They all did dance, and ane piper played' was about the sum of it.

R. Burns Begg, who published the Minutes of the Assize in the *Proceedings of the Society of Antiquaries of Scotland*, suggested that Satan was probably an impostor, perhaps one of the disbanded and desperate soldiers who roamed the countryside. To have a body of willing servants would have been gratifying, and – if he existed – he was never caught. On the other hand, some of the devilry inflicted on neighbours cannot have benefited him: Bessie Henderson confessed that, with Janet Paton, she had 'trampit down Thos. White's rie in the beginning of harvest 1661'. It may have been that the local gentry and ministers were just as prone to believe as the supposed witches. Certainly they were zealous in their pursuit of the accused, and the jury's verdicts against the thirteen were unanimous.

# CROVIE

## ABERDEENSHIRE

*Clinging to the cliff face*

Crovie is as near to a seagull's nest as it is possible for a human community to build. It clings to the cliff face, having squeezed a row of cottages onto a narrow ledge. Gable ends point outwards to the bay, making the same cheek-by-jowl, repeating pattern as the houses on a Monopoly board. It is one of the least hospitable sites on which it is possible to imagine building a village. Even on a sunny day you have to hold onto your hat.

Scenically, the view beyond the narrow strip of shingle beach and rock pools, across the sea towards the bay holding the larger settlement of Gardenstown, is splendid. This stretch of coast presents, in the words of the geologist Sir Archibald Geikie, 'the noblest sea-cliffs in the north of the mainland of Scotland'. But scientific interest fades during the darkness of a winter afternoon with the wind picking up. On 31 January 1953, a storm, bad even by the standards of the Aberdeenshire coast, pounded Crovie, and huge waves swallowed a couple of houses. It also ate up the coastal path between Crovie and Gardenstown. Many residents left.

Crovie (pronounced Crivvy, a sound that seems to imitate a seagull's cry) is a living witness to the desperation of Highland families after the Clearances of the nineteenth century. Driven off their crofts to make way for sheep farming, some

*Families dispossessed by the Clearances built homes on a ledge of cliff at Crovie.*

of them settled here, on a platform of rock just the length of a cottage – hardly an ideal site on which to found their new lives. A small community already existed, first recorded in 1297. But Crovie contained only a hundred souls, according to *The Statistical Account of Scotland* of 1791; by 1900, the population had grown sixfold. The newcomers were farming people. Now the men had to learn to fish. This they did in boats belonging to the laird, who also took most of the profit. The population eked out a meagre existence, only one step above starvation, as before, but at considerably more risk.

Such an exposed location was to have one benefit, although the fishermen would not have been aware of it. Crovie's inaccessibility – it is impossible to drive a car there – means that it has been preserved. There has been no room on the ledge to add anything beyond the red telephone box that shelters behind one of the dwellings. The main industry is now holiday lets. What arose out of misery has been transformed into the twenty-first-century equivalent of a holy site, healing the spirits of the soul-weary city folk who make the pilgrimage.

# DENHOLM
## BORDERS                                          *Wellspring of talent*

Denholm is only sixteen miles from the border with England – a fact of which former inhabitants must have been painfully aware, since the settlement was destroyed by English raiders in the sixteenth century. When the village rebuilt itself in the seventeenth century, it did so in an organised fashion, with well-ordered streets grouping round an English-style village green. Today, there are three hundred and fifty houses.

In the nineteenth century, the big industry for Denholm was knitting stockings: eighty-seven knitting frames were rattling away beside cottage windows in 1844, and the money they brought in enabled many of the dwellings to be rebuilt. Perhaps fortunately for Denholm, however, it never acquired more than a couple of large mills: stockings turned nearby Hawick into a Victorian stone-turreted town, a sort of 'Glasgow in miniature', as the publisher Robert Chambers called it in the 1820s.

So the monument on the Green at Denholm – a crocketed Gothic affair – does not commemorate the knitting trade, but industry of a different kind: scholarship. Denholm fostered brains as well as commerce, and produced no fewer than four learned sons – an achievement that no English village can match, yet does not seem completely exceptional in Scotland, given the erudition that bubbled up in the apparently parched intellectual landscape of the countryside.

John Leyden was born on the north side of the Green in 1775. (Typically, his family's cottage later became the scouring house for a knitting firm). He grew up on an uncle's farm three miles away at Henlawshiel, where his father moved to become a shepherd. At Edinburgh University, fun would be poked at Leyden for his 'rustic appearance and strong Teviotdale accent'. But he wrote poetry, a book about European settlements in Africa, and helped Sir Walter Scott with the earlier volumes of *Minstrelsy of the Scottish Border* (1802), contributing poems and a learned disquisition about fairies.

Fired by what Scott called the 'ardent and unutterable longing for information of every description', as well as the need for an income, he went to Madras (a qualified doctor, he took charge of Madras general hospital), later becoming a judge, as well as assay-master of the mint at Calcutta. In 1811, he accompanied Lord Minto, a fellow Roxburghshire man, to Java, where he was to help settle the country and act as 'interpreter for the Malay language'. After studying in an airless native library, he caught a fever and died, aged thirty-five. The monument at Denholm is to him, erected by public subscription in 1861.

At Denholm, the minister of the Cameronian* chapel, the Rev. James Duncan, tutored Leyden in classics. Duncan's son, James, in due course became a naturalist, specialising in insects; he wrote several books on entomology. John Scott, known in Denholm as the boy who collected all the prizes in the annual flower show, went to Edinburgh, where he worked at the Botanical Gardens and corresponded with Darwin. James Murray, distinguished in later years by a snowy beard of marvellous length, was born in Denholm's Main Street in 1837, the son of the village tailor; having worked as a schoolteacher and (in London) a bank clerk, he became editor of the *Oxford English Dictionary*, to which he dedicated thirty-five years. He received nine honorary degrees and was knighted in 1908. His birthplace is marked by a plaque.

*See Dunnottar, page 559

# DREGHORN
AYRSHIRE                                    *John Dunlop pumps it up*

John Boyd Dunlop was the inventor of the pneumatic tyre. Anyone who doubts it should go to his birthplace of Dreghorn: there is a plaque that says so. Dreghorn was an unlikely crucible for such talent. It was a small farming village when Dunlop was born in 1840 – in fact it had probably been so for an enormously long time. A dig in 2004 uncovered the remains of a Neolithic well dating from 3500BC, which would have supplied water to a community like that of Skara Brae on Orkney; but whereas Skara Brae was abandoned, Dreghorn may have been continuously occupied for five and a half millennia, making it the oldest still-functioning village in the country.

Rather more recently, the village acquired an octagonal church, sometimes known, by people who can remember the pre-decimal threepenny piece, as the Thrup'ny Bit. It was built in 1780 by the Montgomeries of Eglinton, one of a select number of octagonal churches in Britain, the geometry perhaps echoing Masonic principles. Into this slow-moving, well-ordered community Dunlop was born, the son of a farmer but too delicate for farm work. He became a vet and practised in Edinburgh and Northern Ireland.

It was his son's experience that suggested the pneumatic tyre. Aged nine, the child found himself being jarred by riding his tricycle, with its solid rubber tyres, over granite paving stones. Dunlop applied his mind to the problem, bent an air tube round a wooden frame, covered it in linen and found that it bounced. In 1888, he obtained his first patent. Tricycles and bicycles followed. Retiring from veterinary practice, Dunlop sold his patent to Harvey Du Cros, president of the Irish Cyclists' Association, and invested in the company formed to exploit it.

It emerged that Dunlop's patent was not the first for a pneumatic tyre: Robert William Thompson got there before Dunlop in 1846 (perhaps the Dreghorn plaque should be amended). But the subsidiary patents that had been obtained were valuable, and there would be a great future for the Dunlop Rubber Company Ltd. Dunlop himself did not profit greatly from it; the company in which he had been interested was sold in 1896. He died comfortably off, but not rich. The invention he championed paved the way for the motor car.

# DRUMLITHIE
## ABERDEENSHIRE                    *Botanical contribution of a weaver*

It was said that the people of Drumlithie were so proud of the circular, stone steeple on their church that they would rush out, when rain threatened, to take it indoors, with the washing. The steeple was part of their daily lives, having a bell that rang to regulate their mealtimes.

Drumlithie, a village of three hundred inhabitants, was a weaving village. Fathers and sons worked at the looms, whose clatter could be heard from open windows; women and daughters spun. It was a noisy place for six days a week, the day beginning and ending with the horn of the village cowherd (from the tooting, cowherds across Scotland were invariably known as Tootie). On the seventh day, Drumlithie fell silent. People went about, if they had to, speaking in subdued tones, before crowding into the several places of worship.

To this thatched village, with its comfortable inn and neat gardens, came John Duncan, the illegitimate son of a weaver turned soldier who had been brought up at Stonehaven, seven miles away. Born in 1794, he had been tending cattle since he was ten, lodging with his employers and often the butt of cruel jokes. At the age of fifteen, he entered into an apprenticeship with a Drumlithie weaver, a violent man who was a gin smuggler and illicit distiller; his wife, however, taught Duncan to read, which enabled him to pursue the love of botany that he had already formed in the fields.

In *The Life of John Duncan* (1883), William Jolly presented a picture of Drumlithie's inhabitants in the years before Waterloo: 'Weavers then formed, as a whole, a remarkable class of men – intelligent, and observant of the progress of events at home and abroad; devoted to politics, strongly or wildly radical, if not tainted with revolutionary sentiments, after the intoxication of the first French Revolution; great talkers when they gathered together in the street or public house, during the intervals of work, intensely theological, often religious, well versed in all the intricacies of Calvinism . . . in a word, general guardians of the Church, reformers of the state, and proud patrons of learning and the schoolmaster . . .'.

They wove green or unbleached linen mostly, with some woollen fabric called 'wincey'. Among the cloth that Duncan himself produced was the blue material that went into his own singular suits – two of them for best, which he dignified with a top hat, preferring a tam-o'-shanter bonnet for everyday wear. By dint of rolling his trousers up, he was able to preserve the same clothes for fifty years. A shy, stooping, short-sighted man, he was, perhaps not surprisingly, a subject of comment, not least by the children in the areas where he worked.

All Duncan's spare time was spent searching for plants, inspired by the medicinal uses revealed in Culpeper's *Herbal*. Aged twenty, he moved to Aberdeen to get on in weaving. He married, had two daughters, but left his wife forever when he discovered her adultery. For most of the rest of his life he moved from village to village, to progress his collecting activities. He never achieved riches – far from it: in old age he was a pauper, until rescued by a public subscription raised by Jolly – but before his death he presented his herbarium of native plants to Aberdeen University. His grave at Droughsburn is marked, as he asked, by a volcanic boulder.

# DUBLIN
### HIGHLAND                                     *A landowner does the right thing*

Even the leviathan of wealth that was the Duke of Sutherland's estate could not digest the smaller estate of Ardross in Ross-shire. Having snapped up its sixty thousand acres in the late eighteenth century, it was forced to disgorge it in 1846. The sale netted the Duke ninety thousand pounds; the purchaser was Sir Alexander Matheson, promoter of the Highland Railway, which (through the Duke's influence) promised to bring a measure of prosperity to the North.

Matheson, who soon became an MP, undertook a campaign of improvement, which, unlike the infamous Sutherland Clearances, actually increased the number of people supported by the land. An account of how this was achieved has been left by his factor, the engineer William Mackenzie, in a report to the Highland and Agricultural Society of Scotland.

The centre of the estate was the Scots Baronial castle, a composition of towers and turrets that dwarfed the saplings that had recently been planted, raised by

Matheson on the site of a shooting box built by the Duke of Sutherland. Matheson not only let the public wander through seven hundred acres of pleasure grounds beside the Alness river, but allowed the poor to graze their horses, cows or pigs in the new plantations, 'and the young trees are as carefully preserved . . . as if done under the eye of a forester'.

Enclosed by mountains, Ardross is surrounded by spectacular views of snow-capped peaks and red sandstone cliffs. But it was not an easy place to find love. As Mackenzie observed, 'Among other things for which Ardross had a local reputation was its number of bachelors, for no fewer than eleven of the nineteen tenants lived in single blessedness.' They were too poor to marry. Certainly their homes would not have been an inviting prospect for potential brides. 'To spend the long winter nights beside a peat fire, enveloped in smoke, thickly issuing from every crevice, window, and door, is the fate of the majority of our Highland crofters,' Mackenzie wrote.

Worse than the smell of the peat was the moral consideration of having whole families huddled into a single bedroom, horrifying the Victorian imagination with the all too likely possibility of incest. As Mackenzie concluded, fortified with the confidence that his employer did not derive his main income from his estate: 'It must be the aim of every landlord who is anxious to raise the condition of his crofters, morally and physically, to repair such of their houses as will repair, giving them light, and making them dry by drainage, and to erect plain but airy cottages where they are necessary.'

The state of the barns was equally shocking to Mackenzie's engineer's eye. No arrangements had been made for collecting liquid manure from the fields, so it collected in green dank ponds, often in front of the houses, for ducks and children to paddle in. Investment swept these nuisances away. Fences were erected, roads laid, fields cleared of stones and drained, farms and outbuildings replaced. To do this required far more than the local labour force could supply. Barracks were therefore put up for two hundred extra men.

The old tenants were kept on their farms. 'Indeed,' Mackenzie observed, with a swipe at the Dukes of Sutherland, 'there has been no clearing of the old inhabitants to make room for improvements or sheepwalks.' The population rose from 109 to 429. The number of bachelors fell to three. Four rows of stone cottages were built. The settlement is called Dublin, apparently after the Irish workmen who laboured on Matheson's great works of improvements, liked what they did, and stayed.

# DUNNOTTAR
ABERDEENSHIRE                                    *A meeting with Old Mortality*

It was in the churchyard of Dunnottar that Sir Walter Scott met Robert Paterson in 1793. Born in 1715, Paterson kept alive the memory of the Killing Time of the seventeenth century, when hundreds of Scottish Covenanters* were killed, in battle or cold blood, during the Stuart persecutions. The Covenanters wanted the freedom to pursue their own fearsome brand of Calvinism, as opposed to what they regarded as the papist liturgy (including the *Book of Common Prayer*) imposed by Charles I and his line.

Scattered across the Lowlands of Scotland, with the occasional outlier such as Dunnottar, are memorials to those who perished. Paterson, brought up near Hawick in the Borders, belonged to the religious sect called Hillmen, or Cameronians, who followed the teachings of a Covenanting preacher called Richard Cameron, who had died in 1680. Trained as a stonemason, Paterson made it his mission to tend the memorials to the dead, recutting the letters where necessary. It occupied the last forty years of his life, during which he lived as a kind of mendicant. His self-imposed task earned him the name of Old Mortality. Scott wrote him into his novel of the same title, published in 1816.

Paterson had come to Dunnottar churchyard to tend the memorial to the 167 Covenanters who were imprisoned in Dunnottar Castle during James II's reign. The castle had a glamorous Royalist history; it was from one of its windows that, after the Civil War, the coronation regalia known as the Honours of Scotland had been lowered onto the seashore, where a serving woman pretending to collect seaweed gathered them up. They were then hidden beneath the floor of Kinneff church until they could be unearthed when Charles II was crowned.

It was also an inaccessible, windswept location, the castle so tempest-tossed that even now it is closed to the public during bad weather. The Covenanters, who had been rounded up in the Lowlands and herded like cattle to Dunnottar, were locked into a dark, airless cellar, and held there, with little water, less food and no sanitation, from 24 May until the end of July. Nine of them died during that time. The rest were transported to the West Indies.

The church at Dunnottar descends from one established by St Ninian of Whithorn in the fifth century. Rebuilt in the thirteenth century, it was Georgianised and Victorianised, before being given its present, rather barn-like shape in 1903. Many of the memorials that Old Mortality would have tended throughout his travels are to single deaths, such as that of the shepherd Arthur Inglis, shot at Cambusnethan in Lanarkshire when surprised in the fields reading his Bible; or at Tynron, Dumfriesshire, where nineteen-year-old William Smith, having been executed without trial, was apparently buried under the threshold of his parents' house as a mark of disrespect, before being moved to the graveyard. The monument now at Dunnottar is a reproduction of the original; the words, in boldly cut capital letters, run together, the dignified, somewhat untutored simplicity of the style reflecting that of the text itself:

Here lyes John Stot, James Atchison, James Russell & William Broun and one whose name wee have not gotten and two women whose names also wee know not and two who perished comeing doune the rock one whose name was James Watson the other not known who all died prisoners in Dunnottar Castle Anno 1685 for their adherence to the word of God and Scotlands Covenanted work of Reformation. Rev 11. Ch 12 Verse

*See Sorn, page 623

# DUNURE
## AYRSHIRE
*Surly but brave – a fishing community shows its colours*

In the winter of 1883, Peter Maersk Møller was in command of his father-in-law H. N. Jeppesen's sailing barque *Valkyrien* off the west coast of Scotland. One reason that Jeppesen these days stayed ashore might have been that three of his brothers had drowned. It was difficult being a ship's captain before twentieth-century communications equipment arrived. Møller had often shepherded the ship across the Atlantic; on this occasion, it had left Virginia with a cargo of walnut and was headed for Glasgow.

The voyage had gone well, until, on 11 December, the moderate gale increased to hurricane force and the sails of the ship were blown away. The wind was blowing from the west, driving the *Valkyrien* onto the rocky shore. Møller did all that he could. He called the men into his cabin, explained what had happened, read from the Bible and prayed with them. He may well have thought that he would not see his ten children again. By three o'clock the next morning, the ship was held fast by the rocks, while the huge waves smashed her masts and yards into splinters. Fortunately for the crew, the fishermen of Dunure had seen the plight of the ship, and mounted a rescue. The Rev. William Murdoch commemorated the event in verse:

> William Munro the brave and strong
> Breast deep within the wave,
> Now seized two shipwrecked mariners
> Determined them to save
> But all at once a mighty sea
> Swept him and them away
> Whose fate was sealed but for the pluck
> Of fearless Johnnie May.

And so on. Of the dozen sailors on board, all but the ship's boy were brought ashore.

When Møller went home early in the New Year, he may have taken with him a different impression of this fishing village from that given by Robert Louis Stevenson. Stevenson had arrived there thirteen years before, again in the winter. 'Everything was grey and white in a cold and dolorous sort of shepherd's plaid.' The profound silence was broken only by 'the noise of oars at sea'. Behind the breakwater, which was in a state of 'consummate disrepair', stood twenty or so fishermen's houses. Dabs of snow lay on the castle ruins, roosting in the 'crannies of the rock like white sea-birds'. The people in the pub were not welcoming, but sent him to the chilly guest room.

The harbour had been completed in 1811, costing the landowner Thomas Kennedy £50,000. It was built to serve local coal mines, and when they failed, development ceased. Until the 1960s, fishermen such as those who gave Stevenson a surly reception in the pub, but rescued the crew of the *Valkyrien*, kept a fleet of up to thirty boats there. The lighthouse was built on a curious pattern: not guiding sailors by the visibility of its light, but the reverse. To quote the information board that explains operations, 'a fire within the Lighthouse itself would be occluded by an external wall if the correct angle of approach was being used'.

In summer, with forty or so pleasure craft and a few brightly coloured lobster boats bobbing in the harbour, Dunure is a-sparkle. Just remember the Victorian winters.

# DURNESS
HIGHLAND                                    *God's judgement on a Sutherland parish*

'The Small Pox are on their march towards us, making execution as they travel through the country,' wrote the eighteenth-century minister of Durness, Murdoch MacDonald; 'there are three of my Children yet unvisited by that formidable Emissary of an offended God.' Windy, scattered Durness is the most northwesterly village in Scotland, a place where, centuries later, John Lennon would share boyhood holidays with his cousin Stan Parkes, who lived there, running happily over the seven acres of the Parkeses' croft. But when MacDonald was there, it managed to keep only one step ahead of starvation.

God's judgement against the little community, as MacDonald viewed it, could be unremittingly severe, when the perennial scarcity of food was compounded by exceptionally bad weather or disease. As he noted in his diary on 1 August 1741, during a famine that had lasted many months, 'Within the Compass of 2 months, there are upwards of 40 persons dead on this Side of the Parish! . . . it is little less than one in ten!' Durness struggled through to harvest, after which there was, at last, 'plenty of Bread'.

Another man of the cloth, Richard Pococke, Bishop of Ossory in Ireland, visited in 1760, leaving another account of the 'very hard' way of life at Durness. The people lived mostly off 'milk, curds, whey, and a little oatmeal', particularly when they were at their mountain shielings or cabins in the summer months, tending their cattle. The best they could hope for was oatmeal or barley; a piece of salted meat was a rarity. Although fish abounded round the coast, it seems to have been despised: 'they will hardly be at the pains of catching it but in very fine weather'. Though lean, the population was active, the men going 'the Highland trot with wonderful expedition'.

The fortunes of the settlement seemed to look up in the early nineteenth century. In 1818, an entrepreneur called James Anderson leased the coast around Durness from Lord Reay, to fish for cod. For the first decade or so, trade went well, and Anderson was able to employ many local people. By 1839, however, it had declined, the fishermen were falling into debt, and he decided that sheep farming would be more profitable. With brutal suddenness, he gave thirty-two families – a hundred and ninety people – two days' notice to quit.

Another expulsion took place in 1841. Ironically perhaps, the Durness people appealed to the 2nd Duke of Sutherland – whose parents were to become satanic figures in the mythology of the Clearances – for protection. For once, the Duke was on the side of the crofters. But Anderson was within his legal rights, and the evicting party set off from Dornoch, bagpipes playing, giving out the word that they were off to a wedding. 'It was,' the stonemason Donald Macleod commented, 'rather a divorce, to tear the native people away from their dearly loved – though barren – hills.'

# EASTRIGGS
## DUMFRIES AND GALLOWAY                    *Stirring the Devil's Porridge*

H. M. Factory was the name for the munitions works at Gretna Green (see page 585). It was developed during the First World War on the west coast of Scotland, to put it beyond the reach of Zeppelins. The scale of the place reflected the quantity of high explosive shells that was turning the Western Front into a mudscape of craters, shattered trees and stumps of buildings. It was nine miles long, stretching from Eastriggs, on the Scottish side of the Solway Firth, across the river Sark to Longtown in England.

Thirty thousand people worked there, kneading nitroglycerine and guncotton into an explosive paste; when Sir Arthur Conan Doyle*came to visit the factory in 1918, he called this paste the 'Devil's Porridge'. Dried, it became cordite, wads of which were used to fill shells and bullets. More cordite was made at Gretna than at all the other works in Britain put together – a thousand tonnes of it. Gretna was vital to the war effort.

This meant that special consideration had to be given to the people who worked there. Their numbers had increased rapidly after the outbreak of war. To provide accommodation, the government turned to the chief housing architect to the Ministry of Munitions. This was Raymond Unwin, high-minded architect of the Garden City movement, who, with Barry Parker, had already planned New Earswick outside York (see page 429), Letchworth Garden City in Hertfordshire and Hampstead Garden Suburb in North London.

In another vivid turn of phrase, Conan Doyle called Eastriggs and Gretna Garden Village the Miracle Towns. So they must have seemed to their new inhabitants, many of whom came from the cramped, airless, soot-blackened terraces of industrial towns. Thirty-six per cent of the women – and, with men away at the Front, many of the workers were women – had been in domestic service before the War, with little personal freedom or privacy. The Miracle Towns gave them light and greenery, orderly planning and solid building.

There was not time or money to build with the Arts and Crafts sensitivity of the pre-War period, but Eastriggs and Gretna showed what could be done by government effort. They became the model for the Homes for Heroes built after the Armistice, inspiring Unwin with the idea that the problem of poor housing could be solved only through municipal action. He was able to progress the idea through membership of the influential Tudor Walters committee. Its report of 1918 gave rise to the council house.

Gretna and Eastriggs would leave another mark on national policy. New houses did not eliminate old habits, one of which was an inclination to spend any spare money on drink. The money in the munitions factory was good; it led to appalling scenes of drunkenness, which contemporary descriptions painted in Hogarthian colours. Worried that productivity would fall off as its workforce fell over, Lloyd George introduced the 1916 Defence of the Realm Act (with the inappropriately cosy acronym of DORA). The state took control of alcohol sales. Pubs and breweries around the Factory, as well as naval bases and elsewhere, were nationalised. Licensing laws limited the hours during which alcohol could be sold. Gretna pubs remained nationalised until the 1970s. The licensing laws were not relaxed until 2003.

*See Ipplepen, page 49; Great Wyrley, page 326

# EDNAM
BORDERS                                    *Remembering James Thomson*

The idea of a monument to James Thomson outside his native village of Ednam had been floated in 1790, forty-two years after his death. Thomson, born in 1700, was the great nature poet of Augustan Britain, having written *The Seasons* in more than five thousand lines of blank verse.

Wide o'er the brim, with many a torrent swelled,
And the mixed ruin of its banks o'erspread,
At last the roused-up river pours along:
Resistless, roaring, dreadful, down it comes,
From the rude mountain and the mossy wild,
Tumbling through rocks abrupt, and sounding far;
Then o'er the sanded valley floating spreads,
Calm, sluggish, silent; till again, constrained
Between two meeting hills, it bursts a way
Where rocks and woods o'erhang the turbid stream;
There, gathering triple force, rapid and deep,
It boils, and wheels, and foams, and thunders through.

Thomson's writing can be as powerful as Wordsworth's, as in this description of a rushing mountain stream from 'Winter', a reflection of the closer interest that was being taken in landscape as the Picturesque movement developed in parallel with natural science. Until the appearance of Robert Burns* and Sir Walter Scott, Thomson could be regarded as Scotland's national bard.

This was the role in which he captured the imagination of David Steuart Erskine, the 11th Earl of Buchan. In 1790, Buchan organised a Thomson Festival at Ednam on the poet's birthday. It was a jovial, if not bibulous gathering, whose merriment was distinctly at odds with the funeral then taking place of one of Thomson's sisters, who had died a few days earlier. Then the carriage taking Buchan and his friends to his nearby estate at Dryburgh overturned. But despite this misfortune, the plan for a Thomson monument was laid, and sketches of what it might look like commissioned.

Despite sending letters to everyone in Scotland worth writing to, Buchan was unable to raise any money for it. Not everyone would have liked the political subtext, Buchan promoting greater Scottishness in the context of political reform that to many contemporaries seemed too radical by half at the time of the French Revolution. Besides, Buchan himself, a penniless aristocrat, might not have been deemed a safe recipient of funds: he had a fondness for neoclassical ceremonies in which he himself took a leading role (one, in which nine young ladies of rank were dressed as the Muses, dissolved when a naked boy appeared as Cupid, carrying the tea kettle).

As an interim measure, Buchan procured a plaster cast of the bust of Thomson that forms part of Robert Adam's monument to him in Westminster Abbey. It was intended that this should be crowned with laurels in a ceremony during the second Thomson Festival of 1791. Unfortunately, the bust was smashed during some roistering at Dryburgh before it could be installed at Ednam. Buchan laid the laurels on an edition of *The Seasons* instead. But he did not give up. Thirty years after the first Thomson Festival, a monument in the form of a tall obelisk was erected on

Ferny Hill, outside Ednam, overlooking Kelso racecourse. Burns wrote 'Address to the Shade of Thomson' for the opening.

As the son of a Presbyterian minister, however, Thomson cannot be supposed to have gained his impressions of Nature from around Ednam. His father was called to serve as minister of Southdean, near Jedburgh, twenty-six miles away, the year after James was born.

*See Mauchline, page 603

# EDZELL
ANGUS                                                      *A scene worthy of Balzac*

Towards the end of the nineteenth century, Edzell, with a bustling population of eight hundred or so, was 'a pleasant little place', as F. H. Groome, author of the *Ordnance Gazetteer of Scotland* (1884-5), noted. With its 'neat stone houses, flower-plots, and pretty environs' it was elegant and self-possessed, and presumably happy with its laird, the 13th Lord Dalhousie, since his tenants would erect an arch over the single broad street in his honour in 1887. To visitors, the arch serves as a gateway to the wild Angus glens.

It had not always been like this. Previous lairds had been the subject of considerable moralising, on the part not only of Victorian clergymen but of their successor, the Earl of Crawford. In his *Lives of the Lindsays* (1849), he wrote about the 'proud lady of Edzell', Margaret Lindsay, who, although married to Alexander Watson of Aithernie, still managed to keep her easy-going brother David in subjugation, contributing to the loss of all his estates through extravagance in 1714.

'Years passed away, and the castle fell to ruin. The banner rotted on the keep – the roofs fell in – the plesaunce became a wilderness – the summerhouse fell to decay – the woods grew wild and tangled – the dogs died about the place, and the name of the old proprietors was seldom mentioned, when a lady one day arrived at Edzell in her own coach. She was tall and beautiful, and dressed in deep mourning. When she came near the ancient burying-place, she alighted and went into the chapel, for it was then open; the doors had been driven down, the stone figures and carved work were all broken, and bones lay scattered about. The poor lady went in, and sat down among it a' and wept sore at the ruin of the house, and the fall of her family, for no one doubted her being one of them, though no one knew who she was or where she came from . . . She stayed a long while weeping sadly.' That was Margaret of Aithernie, the now not-so-proud Lady of Edzell. The scene is worthy of Balzac.

True it was that the castle fell into ruin. So did the old parish church; most of it was eventually demolished, leaving only the Lindsay burial aisle to stand alone and forlorn in the churchyard. The present village of Edzell began its life as Slateford. Old Edzell, a couple of miles away, had a reputation for making steel pistols, but the demise of the castle put its own existence in jeopardy. By 1818, it had passed out of existence. That was the year in which most of the church was dismantled, the materials being reused in a new one at Slateford. Slateford was given the more ancient and romantic name of Edzell. The railway brought golf, visitors and the decorous prosperity that expressed itself in flowerplots. Self-destructing rakes such as Lord Lindsay were put firmly into the realm of novelettish family history.

# EILEAN IARMAIN
## SKYE

*What was that you said?*

After Robert Burns*, tartan and haggis, Scottish identity must surely be defined by its language, Gaelic. Actually, no: Burns himself never spoke it. His language was Scots (although he made an effort to master parts of the Gaelic wedding ceremony when chasing his 'Highland lassie', the pretty servant girl Mary Campbell). Gaelic is only one of the traditional languages of Scotland, which include Doric in Aberdeenshire – a variant of Scots mixed with a smattering of French words – and Norn, derived from Old Norse and spoken in the Shetlands until the eighteenth century, although subsequently replaced by Shetlandic. (Pictish disappeared with the Picts).

Gaelic was the Highland and Hebridean tongue, spoken by most of the clans who followed Bonnie Prince Charlie's standard in 1745, or who huddled into the holds of ships bound for the New World and Australia in the next century. It is part of the romance of a downtrodden culture, as evocative of its origins as a lament on the bagpipes.

But as early as the late eighteenth century, Gaelic was in retreat. In the 1790s, many of the church ministers whose observations make up the *Statistical Account of Scotland* would have agreed with the report from Strathdon in Aberdeenshire: 'The language spoken is English', Gaelic being confined to the remoter parts of the district and even there 'much on the decline'. It limped into the twentieth century as a language of the poor and unenterprising, that stay-at-home rump of population that had not left to better itself elsewhere. But even in the *Statistical Account*, Gaelic had its admirers, such as Alexander MacGibbon of Doune in Perthshire, who found it 'a noble language, worthy of the fire of Ossian, and wonderfully adapted to the genius of a warlike nation'.

What had been lonely voices swelled into a chorus when Gaelic seemed to be at its last gasp. An important contribution to the change in attitude was the establishment of a college for Gaelic studies, Sabhal Mòr Ostaig, on Skye in 1973. It began on the twenty-one thousand acres around Eilean Iarmain, which the banker Sir Iain Noble had bought the year before. He had developed a passion for Gaelic after teaching himself the language. One of the properties included in the purchase was a steading, which was 'really too good for agriculture'. This became the college's first campus. In 2000, it was joined by a suave, vernacular-inspired structure, with an accommodation tower and teaching block and a viewing platform overlooking the Sound of Sleat.

This is a land steeped in legend: it was here that the third-century hero Cuchulain leapt ashore, to pursue his alarming courtship of the warrior princess Scathaich (having slaughtered all her retinue, he fought her into submission). Romance was not the only reason that Sir Iain wanted Gaelic to survive; he thought that reviving the language would invigorate the community.

Experience has proved him right. The college has brought opportunity and hope; there is no unemployment in the parish. What might have seemed a hopeless cause after the Second World War has now, like Cuchulain, triumphed against the odds. The next edition of the Ordnance Survey will print Hebridean place names in their Gaelic, not English, forms. Goodbye Stornoway, welcome Steòrnabhagh. The once-dying language has been put, literally, back onto the map.

*See Mauchline, page 603*

# ETTRICK
BORDERS                                  *Jamie the Poeter, a.k.a. the Ettrick Shepherd*

When the shepherd poet James Hogg was told he would be introduced to Mr Wordsworth, then visiting Edinburgh, he assumed he was the 'celebrated horse-dealer of the same name'. But the pair formed such a bond when they travelled through the Yarrow valley together that Wordsworth would later write his 'Extempore Effusion upon the Death of James Hogg' in 1835:

> When first, descending from the moorlands,
> I saw the stream of Yarrow glide
> Along a bare and open valley,
> The Ettrick Shepherd was my guide.

Like Robert Burns*, Hogg was the literary equivalent of rough trade. Ettrick Forest, once a royal hunting preserve, had, by the time of Hogg's birth in 1770, sunk to being a backward sheep-rearing district. Hogg's parents were doing well when he came into the world; his father had taken a lease on the farms of Ettrick Hall and Ettrick House. But the price of sheep fell, one of their debtors absconded and they were ruined. He later remembered 'well the distressed and destitute condition that we were in'. From the age of seven he was sent out to herd cows, 'the worst and lowest known [employment] in our country'.

In his *Memoir*, Hogg recalled the hardship of his early years, a period when he was 'exceedingly bare of shirts'. His 'extensive education' lasted no more than two or three months, during which time he learnt to read the Bible and form letters. By

*Verses by James Hogg, the Ettrick Shepherd, incorporated into a stone wall in his native village.*

the age of eighteen, he had lost the skill of reading, but re-mastered it with encouragement from a kind-hearted farmer, James Laidlaw of Blackhouse Farm, who lent him books. It was then that he began to write poetry. Laidlaw's son, William, later companion and steward to Sir Walter Scott, became a lifelong friend, 'the only person who, for many years, ever pretended to discover the least merit in my essays, either in verse or prose'.

It was through William that Hogg first met Scott in 1802; Scott was delighted to hear Hogg's mother singing old ballads. 'There are not above five people in the world, who I think, know Sir Walter better, or understand his character better than I do,' Hogg would write.

Locally, Hogg became known as Jamie the Poeter. His farming ventures did not prosper, and he went bankrupt in 1810. Financial crisis caused him to move to Edinburgh, where he started a newspaper. With the publication of a long narrative poem about Mary, Queen of Scots, *The Queen's Wake*, he was lionised by a public entranced by his untutored origins. The Duke of Buccleuch gave him the farm of Altrive Lake in Yarrow rent-free for the rest of his life.

But success did not last. Educated opinion in Edinburgh found him too raw; it detected a want of 'delicacy' in his treatment of extra-marital sex. It shuddered at his radicalism. Famous in his persona of the Ettrick Shepherd, and enthusiastically received when he visited London in 1832, he nevertheless suffered another bankruptcy, that of his publisher, which ruined his plans to make money from a collected edition of his works. He died at Altrive in 1835. He had predicted that he would outlast Sir Walter Scott (another bankrupt), 'as I am five months and ten days younger', and he had.

At Ettrick, Hogg was remembered by the Victorians with an anthemion-capped obelisk, bearing a portrait medallion. More recently, some of his verses have been carved on slate and propped against the mossy stones of the field walls that separate the country lane from the hill.

*See Mauchline, page 603

# FENWICK
AYRSHIRE                                    *Self-help among the weavers*

In Elizabethan times, the guild* system had sought to protect members from some of the most pressing hardships of life, such as unemployment and the cost of falling sick. But the guilds did not survive the upheavals of the seventeenth century, causing some imaginative communities to invent new ways of clubbing together to keep adversity at bay. One was pioneered at Fenwick.

In 1769, a group of local people formed the Fenwick Weavers Society. Its name suggests that it may have been a trade organisation, intended to keep non-members out of the magic circle of village weavers, but the object was in fact to provide food. The Society bought oatmeal at wholesale prices, and sold it to its members without the markup that would normally be imposed by a middleman. The Fenwick Weavers Society has been called the first cooperative society, seventy-five years before the Rochdale Pioneers came into being in Lancashire.

But even the Fenwick Weavers were not wholly original. There were in fact many bread societies in Georgian Britain – at least forty-six. They were established, in the words of one set of articles, 'for the Purpose of Reducing the Unexampled Prices of Bread and Flour, and to Prevent the Adulteration of these Articles with Materials of Inferior and Pernicious Qualities'. Prominent in the movement were shipwrights working in the naval ports in southern England, who found that their flour had been mixed with china clay.

The Fenwick Weavers showed that country people were just as concerned about the quality of essential foodstuffs. They never grew to the size of owning their own corn mills, like some of the urban friendly societies, but they kept going until 1800, when they were spending forty pounds a year. The Govan Old Victualling Society in Glasgow, which came into being in 1777, lasted until 1909. There may have been many other village oatmeal and bread societies which, leaving no written evidence behind them, are now forgotten.

The Fenwick Weavers were at the beginning of a tradition of cooperation that was developed by Robert Owen, the successful mill owner who wanted to reorganise society. Whole communities were founded on cooperative principles, the most comprehensive in Scotland being Orbiston near Motherwell, which was founded by an Edinburgh tanner, Abram Combe. On a site of nearly three hundred acres, they ran an iron foundry, seeking to integrate agriculture and industry: waste was disposed on cooperative principles, the product of the community sewage works being spread on the land. The utopians who settled there called it Babylon.

The settlement that can be seen there now is, alas, very different from the one Combe conceived. After his death, the cooperators fell out and the land was sold; the new owner ordered that all trace of the settlement should be removed. It is now covered by a housing estate, Orbiston being remembered only in street names such as Babylon Avenue.

At Fenwick, the aims of the Weavers were not only material; in 1808 they founded the Fenwick Library. But the decline of hand-weaving was reflected by the institution of an Emigration Society in 1839, and as the village population fell, the Weavers Society was wound up in 1873. In 2008, the Fenwick Weavers Society was reconvened, in order to research the possibility of establishing a heritage facility on the Weavers' role in the cooperative movement.

*See Lavenham, page 251

# FINDHORN ECOVILLAGE
MORAY                                     *Alternative, but becoming mainstream*

Mention the Findhorn community to some people in Scotland and they respond as though you had invoked a religious cult. The impression is not dispelled by Jonathan Dawson, executive secretary of the Global Ecovillage Network, who likens the place to 'a medieval monastery with a village around it'. The Findhorn Foundation's website declares it 'a spiritual community, ecovillage and an international centre for holistic education'. All of which may be a bit much for some tastes.

But what might have been described as a hippy commune when it started in 1962 (one of the founders, Dorothy Maclean, 'discovered she was able to intuitively contact the overlighting spirits of plants – which she called angels, and then devas') has come to seem increasingly relevant to the sustainability agenda. There are more than forty houses on the Field of Dreams, in different variants of wood cladding, brightly painted or stained – the effect being a jolly seaside jumble that is reminiscent of Cape Cod. There is a hexagonal home, built by a beekeeper, and one roofed in corrugated iron, a memory of its owner's homeland of Australia.

But architectural style is hardly the point of this settlement. It is about spiritual fulfilment. Some of that is derived from a sense of community, in which families look out for the safety of one another's children, and neighbours can always pop round to borrow a cup of sugar. It may sound like a Ladybird book from the 1950s, but enthusiasts say that it works.

Harmony with nature is another guiding light. The houses may be built from old whisky barrels or straw bales. They are double- and triple-glazed, so that the minimum of energy is required to heat them. What heating is needed comes from a boiler fuelled by wood pellets. Electricity is generated by four wind turbines, the surplus being sold back to the National Grid. There is also the Living Machine – a system of reed beds for filtering sewage.

Residents work for the community. But many are professionals who work elsewhere, too. A marina, a pebble beach and a couple of convivial pubs complement gardens that sweep down to the shore. The Gulf Stream ensures a temperate climate. Findhorn is onto something. Having visited, I would have been happy to stay.

# FINDON
## ABERDEENSHIRE
*A great delicacy from the sea*

The king of the Scottish fisheries is haddock. More of this species, *Melanogrammus aeglefinus*, is landed than any other – a hundred and ten thousand tonnes in 2005, a third of the world's catch. Findon, south of Aberdeen, is famous for its tribute to a fish of sweet-tasting flesh, less flaky than cod, less bony than herring – the finnan haddie. Finnan haddies were already 'well known' when Walter Thom wrote *The History of Aberdeen* in 1811, being 'esteemed a great delicacy for their delicious taste and flavour'. Hung over smouldering peat turfs, they were on sale twelve hours after being hauled from the sea. 'Many hundred dozens are annually sent to Edinburgh and London, and not a few to America.'

Smoking has been used to preserve food since ancient times. It is a method particularly applicable to fish, because of its high water content (remove as much water as possible, and the fish will last longer). Often the fish is salted before being dried over a smoky fire. James Boswell recalled that Dr Johnson was served 'dried haddocks broiled, alone with our tea' when visiting Scotland in 1773. Boswell ate one, but Johnson called for them to be removed. 'A protest may be entered on the part of most Scotsmen against the Doctor's taste in this particular,' Sir Walter Scott observed. 'A Finnan haddock dried over the smoke of the sea-weed, and sprinkled with salt water during the process, acquires a relish of a very peculiar and delicate flavour, inimitable on any other coast than that of Aberdeenshire.'

The difference was not purely one of opinion, gastronomic or patriotic. Johnson's fish had probably been smoked so that it would keep; it would therefore have been tough and strong in flavour. Scott appears to have had in mind the finnan haddie as we know it today: a delicacy whose light smoking is designed to add a subtle note to its palatability, not preserve it. By common consent, the plumper the fish that is brought to the smokehouse, the better the result on the plate. These days, peat has been replaced by oak, hickory, cherry and other hardwoods to provide the smoke.

Haddock that were split on being landed, laid out on the stony beach and left to dry in the sun were known as spelding. They were also highly regarded. I have sought for them in vain. Do not confuse either finnan haddies or speldings with Arbroath smokies, first produced in Auchmithie, three miles from Arbroath. The smokie is 'hot smoked', traditionally in a half whisky barrel covered with dampened hessian sacking; it is therefore cooked and can be eaten on purchase. It will keep for about a week.

*See also Craster, page 418*

# FINTRY
## STIRLING
*In our back yard, please*

One thing you can say about Britain is that it is windy. Until recently, this may have seemed a doubtful benefit, as holidaymakers packed their bags for sunnier climes to avoid the gales that famously blow around our coastal resorts. But as fossil fuel prices rise, and the EU imposes ever-stiffer targets for reducing carbon dioxide emissions, wind is increasingly being seen, in some quarters, as an asset. According to RenewableUK, Britain possesses as much as forty per cent of the 'wind resource' in Europe. How best to exploit it, however, remains the subject of heated debate, particularly if a wind farm is proposed near a village. Fintry, however, has found a modus vivendi.

Just before he left office in 2007, Tony Blair committed Britain to producing twenty per cent of our energy (not just electricity, as he may have thought) from renewables by 2020. His government had always favoured wind power as the green technology of choice, not least because it cost the Treasury far less than major infrastructure projects such as the Severn Barrage would have done, and it avoided a decision about a new generation of nuclear power stations. Now, with the deadline approaching, wind is the only form of renewable energy that can be provided in time.

In the countryside, there is usually a strong body of opinion against the visual intrusion and noise of wind turbines, not to mention the supposed propensity of the blades to mince up birdlife, and alleged dangers to mental health; quite apart from doubt about their contribution to the greening of Britain's energy supplies, given that the wind does not always blow, and coal-fired power stations are kept on standby to take up the slack when it does not.

But not everybody is against it. Britain's first wind farm, built at Delabole in Cornwall (see page 31) in 1991, has become something of a tourist attraction. In recent years, communities from Somerset to Berkshire have teamed together to erect their own turbines, excited by the prospect of producing green electricity that can be sold to the National Grid. The number of small projects – anything from a windmill erected on the roof of a house to a fifty-megawatt turbine capable of powering a factory or village – is increasing at a fast rate. RenewableUK expects numbers to rise from the present few thousand to hundreds of thousands, perhaps millions, during the next twenty years.

At Fintry, the developer West Coast Energy was astonished when the community asked for an extra turbine to be added to the fourteen-turbine wind farm that it had proposed for the hills above the village: local people wanted to buy the turbine, operate it as a community resource and turn Fintry into one of the greenest settlements in Britain. The blades started turning in 2008. Electricity will be sold to the National Grid, with profits being retained by the community, once mortgage and maintenance payments have been met. Initially, the surplus will be spent on making Fintry energy efficient.

# FOCHABERS
## MORAY
*Elegance is all*

By 1764, when the first plan for Fochabers was made, the Hanoverian government had changed its attitude towards the Highlands. After the 1745 rebellion, it wreaked vengeance, attempting to eradicate Jacobite sentiment by slash and burn. During the 1750s, it tried a softer approach, with a policy designed to improve and civilise Highland life. A fillip was given to this way of thinking by the contribution of Highland soldiers – brave but expendable – made to the British army during the Seven Years War.

There began one of many campaigns, by both government agencies and estate owners, to stem depopulation. The Annexed and Forfeited Estates Commission, formed in 1752, was charged with administering thirteen estates that had been confiscated from rebel leaders*. The income was to be spent on development projects, such as the 'enlargement, or new erection of towns and villages'. A new town at Fochabers was part of this agenda.

But as is the way with government agencies, the Commission was ineffective. Its new settlements did not flourish. No start was made at Fochabers. The elegant village that now stands beside the Moray Firth – somewhat disfigured, alas, by the busy Aberdeen–Inverness road that runs through the centre – is the creation of the 4th Duke of Gordon, the Cock of the North (as Gordon chieftains are called), who inherited his estates at the age of nine in 1752.

Gordon had a different motive from the commissioners. The old town of Fochabers lay next to Gordon Castle. This might not have mattered in the 1660s, when it was nothing more than a hamlet. But a century later it was a bustling burgh, with a grammar school, 'several good lodgins & inns', a weekly market and a courthouse. It had been expanded as recently as 1754, when the Duke's mother sold some leases, or feus. But the Duke came of age, went on a Grand Tour and rebuilt the castle 'in all the elegant magnificence of modern architecture', remodelling the park, laying out drives and planting woods. He made no bones about being 'desirous to remove the present town or village of Fochabers upon account of inconvenient nearness to Gordon Castle'.

Accordingly, a lawyer was instructed to buy up the old feus and issue new ones. As often happened, however, the townspeople did not care to be improved, preferring the homes and businesses that they already had. Having begun in 1775, the project was not finished until 1802, when the old Fochabers was flattened. The new Fochabers was designed by John Baxter, the Edinburgh architect who had refashioned the castle. Its centrepiece is a square, dominated by a splendid Athens-of-the-North style church flanked by solid, well-proportioned houses.

Yet the Duke never intended it to be more than a village, a grand architectural statement en route to his palatial castle. Rather than enterprising business people, it was filled with retainers and other dependents, being as Lord Cockburn sourly called it, 'a kennel for the retired lacqueys and ladies'-maids of the castle, and the natural children and pensioned mistresses of the noble family, with a due proportion of factors, gamekeepers and all the other adherents of such establishments'. One of the adherents was the butler and composer William Marshall†.

*See Ballachulish, page 531. †See Milltown of Auchindoun, page 607

# FORTINGALL
## PERTH AND KINROSS                    *Arts and Crafts, by a forgotten master*

Fortingall, set in a pastoral valley leading to Loch Tay, is a place of pilgrimage for tree lovers: in the churchyard grows a yew tree, its centre so long-ago decayed that life now continues in a ligneous wall surrounding the original site, which could be a thousand, or even five thousand years old. This ancient organism is extraordinary, as – in a more modest way – is the architecture of the village.

Behind the loops of the black-painted iron railings on the village street are to be seen rows of neatly thatched houses, the line of the eaves rising like an interrogative eyebrow over each of the dormer windows in the roofs. The walls are white, the woodwork green. The upper floor of the terraces steps forward slightly over the lower one. The hotel – strange, perhaps, to find a hotel in such an out-of-the-way spot – has crow-stepped gables and a central bay that projects forward over the bold, square, red sandstone pillars that flank the entrance. The lettering on the entablature is Arts and Crafts. Ah, that is the clue to the care that has been taken over Fortingall, as well as its vernacular yet not wholly Scottish architecture. It is the masterwork of James MacLaren.

MacLaren died in 1890, at the age of thirty-seven. For an architect, he was but a youth, and had he lived longer, his name would surely be better known. He might have given Charles Rennie Mackintosh a run for his money. Instead, he claims the interest of connoisseurs, who have founded the James M. MacLaren Society to pursue MacLaren studies (the M., incidentally, which might seem superfluous in terms of distinguishing this James MacLaren from others in the architectural sphere, stands for Marjoribanks).

The sixth child of a farmer, MacLaren was educated at Stirling High School, to which he and his brothers walked barefoot, their boots under their arms, to save the soles from wear. Afterwards, he worked in an architects' office in Glasgow, before moving to London, initially to join fellow Scot John James Stevenson. In the mid 1880s, he was able to launch his own firm, having won a competition to rebuild his old school and acquired a rich private client, Sir Donald Currie (the Liberal MP for Perthshire, who had been supported by MacLaren's father in the previous two elections).

Currie was a ship owner, hence the apparently unlikely commission to design a hotel in Las Palmas in the Canary Islands, to receive passengers from Currie's Castle Line. Currie also wanted his Glenlyon estate to be rebuilt: mansion house, farmhouses and Fortingall.

MacLaren combined the native Scots tradition with West Country elements, such as the eyebrow thatch, observed during his time restoring Lanhydrock House in Cornwall. The style was absorbed by his assistant Robert Lorimer, who had the drive, not to say pushiness, to become Scotland's premier architect in the early twentieth century.

In 1887, MacLaren showed the first symptoms of the tuberculosis that would kill him. He left Fortingall incomplete. The church was rebuilt by his partners Dunn and Watson in 1901–2, with a screen added by Lorimer in 1913. Currie had died in 1909, but architectural standards were maintained: the suave London architect William Curtis Green built the village hall in 1936.

# FYVIE
## ABERDEENSHIRE                              *A millionaire comes home*

By the beginning of the twentieth century, the name of Louis Comfort Tiffany had become an American byword for opulent yet aesthetic stained glass: rich in colour, often organic in inspiration. Few of his works, however, had penetrated the British countryside. So the presence of a full-length Tiffany window at the east end of Fyvie church suggests that a degree of cosmopolitanism once descended on this Highland village. It did. Sir Alexander Forbes-Leith, laird of Fyvie Castle, was one of the many Scots who had left their home country to prosper in the United States. And in his case he came back.

Forbes-Leith made his fortune from steel, the Illinois steel company that he managed becoming part of Andrew Carnegie's United States Steel Corporation; Forbes-Leith was one of Carnegie's fellow directors, as well as a partner in a merchant bank. Like Forbes-Leith, Carnegie had been an emigrant from Scotland;

he returned to build a pumped-up version of a baronial castle at Skibo on the Dornoch Firth, as well as scattering Carnegie libraries across Britain and the Empire to encourage poor children to get on, as he had, through self-help.

But whereas Carnegie was the son of an impoverished handloom weaver, Forbes-Leith's beginnings were rather different. He was the son of a rear admiral, John James Leith; he took the additional surname of Forbes from his mother's family, which, in the distant past, had owned Fyvie Castle. When he bought the castle in 1889, it was sadly dilapidated. He restored it, built a new tower and installed all the transatlantic comforts to which he had become used, including a bowling alley. The new world had ridden to the rescue of the old.

American money had a transforming effect on country houses at the turn of the century. William Waldorf Astor was one of the men who settled here, building a wing in the form of a Tudor village at Hever Castle in Kent (too 'bijou', as he put it, to contain a plutocratic lifestyle), where the association with Anne Boleyn strongly appealed to his sense of romance. More numerous, however, were the 'dollar princesses': daughters of the rough diamonds who made millions out of the expansion of the United States after the Civil War, and were now acquiring ancient titles through marriage. Houses such as Blenheim Palace in Oxfordshire and Floors Castle in the Borders were revitalised by the dowries that they brought with them – although as Consuelo Vanderbilt found when she became Duchess of Marlborough, marriage into a grand, self-important and still, to her mind, bafflingly feudal family, in which the women were uneducated, was anything but a blessing: she ran away from the frigid splendours of Blenheim to live with a new husband in a cosy half-timbered manor house in Surrey.

Fyvie Castle was, in a different way, cursed. Thomas the Rhymer, a thirteenth-century laird and prophet, is supposed to have placed the malediction, and throughout history the owners of Fyvie have been unlucky enough to lose their heirs. The Tiffany window in the church commemorates Sir Alexander Forbes-Leith's own son, Percy, who died while serving in the Boer War.

# GAIRLOCH
## HIGHLAND
*A big audience for the preachers of wrath*

Leabaidh na Ba Baine means Bed of the White Cow in Gaelic. At Gairloch, it refers to an oval turf hollow in the landscape, where, by tradition, Fingal's white cow calved. Now it is part of the golf course, but in the second half of the nineteenth century it served a different purpose: the natural amphitheatre was used for services by the Free Church, which had parted from the Church of Scotland during what is known as the Disruption of 1843. Thousands came. The parish church was deserted, even by the parents of Osgood MacKenzie, author of *A Hundred Years in the Highlands*, and they were lairds.

Because of the dire state of the roads, combined with a dearth of wheeled vehicles to travel over them, communion was given only once every three years, and then it was a five-day festival. 'No one should miss attending if he be anywhere in the neighbourhood,' Alexander Polson urged in a guidebook of 1920. MacKenzie, an old man looking back to his childhood, remembered it as always having taken place in fine midsummer weather.

The events were also something of an ordeal. To quote the account given by his uncle: 'In Gairloch every hold or corner with a roof over it was got ready by strewing it with straw for the visitors' beds during the six nights of their stay . . . Our barns and stables were all scrubbed out and ready for visitors, and for days before the feast there was much killing and cooking of cattle, sheep, and salmon, for all the hungry visitors who were expected. Such really hard labour for the house ser-vants all through the five days would, if I were to detail it truly, hardly be believed as occurring in a Christian land in connection with religion. It was simply fearful.'

The attraction was not just the communion celebration, but the joy of hearing the preachers. At Shieldaig near Torridon, these men of God would stand in a wooden booth or preaching box, somewhat on the pattern of an unadorned Punch and Judy theatre, which kept off the sun and such rain as might fall on Wester Ross in June (it can be seen in the Gairloch Heritage Museum). The travelling pulpit used at Gairloch had no roof, leaving the minister and precentor (who led the singing of the psalms) as uncovered as the congregation. From this elevation, MacKenzie reported, their words could be heard clearly all around Leabaidh na Ba Baine.

They preached in Gaelic. Theirs could be a hard message, denying communion to dance- and even concert-goers. 'I see Satan seated on some of your backs,' one cried as the congregation knelt at the altar. But they spoke the language of the people, and that is the issue that had caused the Disruption in the first place. Just as the seventeenth-century Covenanters* had fought for freedom to worship as they chose, the Free Church broke away from the Church of Scotland on the issue of ministers; too often patrons had appointed individuals who were not Gaelic speakers, and in a culture that saw God, above all, as the Word, it was a fatal deficiency.

Having split once, the Frees themselves proved fissiparous, dividing into the Wee Frees (as the Free Church is affectionately known) and the Free Presbyterians in 1893, to the confusion of many people outside its Highland heartlands.

*See Sorn, page 623

# GALTRIGILL

SKYE                                                    *Kings of pipers*

On a windy day – and windy days have been known on Skye – you may be pleased
of the cairn at Galtrigill. The land falls away abruptly at the edge of a cliff, and it
is comforting to have something solid and stone-built to guard against the wind
catching your jacket, turning it into a sail and carrying you off into the sea. No
wind, however, is strong enough to blow away the spirits that belong to this place.
Some of them are commemorated by the cairn.

Since the inscription is in Gaelic, many visitors may be none the wiser as to what
it commemorates, and assume that it marks the spot of the pre-Clearance township. But the shells of those dwellings survive elsewhere, remarkably complete, in
a grove of aspens and alders above a ravine. The cairn remembers the family that
once held Galtrigill and neighbouring Borreraig, the MacCrimmons. If you think
you can hear the wail of the bagpipe amid the buffet of the rushing air, it is theirs.

Like so much else in the Hebrides, there is something of myth about the
MacCrimmons. Some say that they came from northern Italy; their name, according to this idea, was originally Mac Cremona – son of Cremona. Another story
has them descending from Irish kings. They were famous musicians. The earliest
that we know by name is Iain Odhar MacCrimmon (Odhar 'the Dun', probably
referring to his sallow complexion), who lived at the beginning of the sixteenth
century. He would have played for the great MacLeod chief Alasdair Crotach, who
gave the MacCrimmons Borreraig, free of all feudal dues, on condition that the
family trained up at least one son per generation to act as piper to the chief. They
were later given Galtrigill, too.

At Borreraig, the MacCrimmons established an informal college of piping, to
which chiefs throughout the Highlands sent their young pipers. They developed
a unique system of notation, described in Alexander Nicolson's *History of Skye*
(1930). They were also composers, and it has been claimed that the classical canon
of bagpipe music, known as Ceòl Mòr (Grand Music) or Piobaireachd, began with
Donald Mòr MacCrimmon (*c.*1570–*c.*1640) – although musicologists suspect that
Donald Mòr's compositions were too conventional for him to have invented the
genre. Not surprisingly, the MacCrimmon name features in the titles of many
bagpipe airs.

In 1745, the MacLeods, having nursed a century-old disgruntlement with the
Stuarts, came out for the Hanoverian establishment. Domhnall Bàn ('fair-haired')
MacCrimmon was captured by the Jacobites, whose pipers went on strike in
protest at this treatment of the King of Pipers. The lament that he wrote in captiv-
ity, 'MacCrimmon Returns no More', proved prophetic when, standing beside
Norman, the MacLeod chief – the Red Man, who would perpetrate some of the
worst Highland atrocities after Culloden – he was killed by a stray bullet.

# GARENIN
LEWIS

*The black house*

Garenin is a hamlet composed of the most distinctive type of vernacular dwelling to have emerged in the Highlands and Islands: the black house. Keeping low to the ground, their rounded thatched roofs giving the impression that these houses have pulled up their collars and turned their shoulders to the wind, the Garenin habitations do not look hugely sophisticated. Nor were they. But the fact they have survived at all indicates a degree of solidity not possessed by most homes of the modest kind in Scotland, nearly all of which have disappeared without trace. The few that have come down to us have generally been preserved through being associated with great people or events – a cluster linked to Robert Burns* and his poetry; Leanach Cottage on the Culloden battlefield. By contrast, Garenin was inhabited until 1974.

For much of history, rural Scottish homes seemed primitive in comparison to those in England. When Martin Frobisher visited Orkney on the way to search for the north-west passage in 1577, his secretary was shocked. The pebble-built dwellings had no chimney, and the family had to share their roof with their cattle. In the mid seventeenth century, a Cromwellian soldier found 'low thatcht cottages full of smoke and noisome smells' – and that was in the relatively developed Lowlands.

*Black houses at Garenin: keeping low to the ground to avoid the wind,*
*these thatched dwellings always had a peat fire smouldering within.*

The black house is a variant on the long house, or more accurately byre house, which was the standard dwelling type of rural Scotland. Half of the accommodation was given over to the animals. A sloping site was preferred, so that liquid manure would drain away down the hill rather than seep into the family's living quarters. The term 'black house' is something of a mystery. It was probably adopted to distinguish traditional dwellings, with their drystone walls, from the new style that arrived in the nineteenth century, whose mortar-filled walls were hurled and limewashed; these were the white houses.

Some people assume that the blackness was that of their smoky interiors. There were no openings to let out the smoke from the peat fires, which smouldered most of the year round; everything that came out of a black house – clothes, hair, faces – would have been coloured by it. This may seem almost painfully backward, chimneys having become commonplace in England during the sixteenth century. In fact, it seems to have been a deliberate development.

Earlier black houses did possess smoke holes; it is likely that they were done away with when pressure of population made it necessary for the Hebrides to produce more food. When impregnated with soot, thatch was a good fertiliser, so conscious efforts were made to trap the smoke. New thatch was applied every year, the old being spread on the fields.

Nineteenth-century black houses were built with a double thickness of wall, which had a combined width of more than two metres. The space in the middle was filled with peat or earth. Rather than overlapping the walls to form eaves, the straw thatch came to an end over this central filling. The outer part of the wall formed a convenient ledge when rethatching. Rain fell on the earth core, keeping it moist and windproof. It would, however, have been damp, and the inner face of the stone would have had to be carefully laid to stop water trickling through.

Externally, these dwellings seem supremely well adapted to the prevailing conditions. But Victorian health campaigners disapproved, thinking that the dark, airless interiors bred disease – sunshine and fresh air were antidotes to tuberculosis, a national scourge. The thatch, hastily reapplied, was not of the best; the water that oozed through it took on the colour of the precious soot, being known as the 'black drip'.

Garenin was restored in 1999–2001, and the houses became holiday lets, a bunkhouse, youth hostel, cafe, office and resource centre. One house has been kept as it was when last occupied in 1972. But without the black drip.

*See Mauchline, page 603*

# GATEHOUSE OF FLEET
## DUMFRIES AND GALLOWAY

*A would-be cotton town,*
*defeated by transport*

Sir Joshua Reynolds used plenty of red in his portrait of James Murray of Broughton; the laird's red coat with its splayed tails takes centre stage. Legs planted firmly apart, one hand on hip, a walking stick in the other, Murray looks the embodiment of self-confidence, and he was. Having inherited the Kirkudbrightshire estate of Cally in 1751, he continued the improvements begun by his father and rebuilt the modest mansion house on palatial lines, to the design of Robert Mylne.

Meeting him in 1762, James Boswell, biographer of Samuel Johnson, found him a 'most amiable man', with 'very good sense, great knowledge of the world, and easy politeness of manners'; his wife, Lady Catherine Stewart, a cousin he married the year after inheriting, was 'very beautiful' and no less engaging. They were a couple with flair. When Robert Heron visited Cally in 1792, he declared that the grounds were 'laid out and decorated with great taste', fully in line with the 'stately elegance of the house'. But it was clear that the affable Murray needed to repair the hole that so much elegant living had left in his fortunes. His answer was to found Gatehouse of Fleet.

On the road from Ireland, recently improved by the military, a small settlement already existed at Gatehouse, with a cattle market. Murray wanted cotton mills. To that end he laid out two parallel streets, to be built in terraces, each house of which would possess a long garden. The first recorded plot was taken in 1763, by Samuel Ramsay; the lease specifically forbade Ramsay from selling drink, presumably because Murray already intended to open his own hotel: the Murray Arms (where Burns would write 'Scots Wha Hae' in 1793).

By 1777, Murray was using the local press to advertise his new town, trumpeting the 'remarkable good houses' that were to be found there. By the end of the century, the population had risen to more than a thousand. The key to success was the fast-flowing water for the mills. There are two local burns, supplemented by a dam at Loch Whinyeon three miles away (water from it came via a series of lades). By the time of Murray's death in 1799, Gatehouse of Fleet possessed four textile mills and looked set fair to prosper.

But even the fairest winds sometimes blow contrary. Murray's marriage, which looked so promising in the 1750s, collapsed spectacularly when this otherwise level-headed man ran off with a local girl, Grace Johnston, in 1787. It was a mid-life crisis that lasted: the couple lived together as man and wife and had four children together.

After a vigorous youth, Gatehouse of Fleet also suffered a reversal, if not such a public one. It simply found itself in the wrong place. A port was built in 1824, connected to the sea by a canal. But this was not enough to overcome Gatehouse's geographical remoteness from the major centres of production. Textile mills were turned over to sawing timber. The cattle market continued. But when the Irish artist Robert George Kelly painted a panorama of the place in 1852, Gatehouse was little bigger than it had been half a century earlier. And so it remains: not, perhaps, everything that had once been hoped for it, but Murray's whitewashed streets are as charming as ever.

# GLENELG
## HIGHLAND
*'No meat, no milk, no bread, no eggs, no wine'*

In 1722, government soldiers came to Glenelg. They built the Bernera Barracks, the roofless, stone ruins of which still look out over the bay, and constructed houses in the village for officers. Having come they meant to stay, and well they might – the journey, if made overland, had been difficult enough. There was nothing but a track over the Mam Ratagan pass, its top, even on a fine day, lost in cloud.

The soldiers built bridges and a road, but it still provided Dr Johnson with the one moment of real anxiety, when his horse stumbled, during his Journey to the Western Isles. He and Boswell descended into Glenelg only to find an inn, provisioned copiously with negatives but little else – 'No meat, no milk, no bread, no eggs, no wine'. Knowing the penury of the place, a gentleman, who had heard of their arrival, sent his servant on a two-hour journey to fortify them with rum and sugar. Straw was found with difficulty, and Johnson lay down on it in his riding coat to sleep. Conditions in the barracks can have been little better.

The place was, however, strategic. Here the crossing to the Isle of Skye is at its narrowest. Drovers in flat-bottomed boats led cattle, tied nose to tail, across it to the mainland – a swim that not all the animals were able to complete. There is still a little ferry, the successor of many others, uniquely constructed with a turntable on deck; the swivel is necessary to allow cars to drive sideways off the jetty.

The barracks was constructed beside what was then one of many townships, which, having the church, grew into the principal village (although generally called Glenelg by outsiders, it ought properly to be known as Kirktoun or its Gaelic equivalent). The minister, since 1707, had been Murdoch Macleod, a hard man who was rebuked by the Presbytery for beating one of his congregation after communion 'to the effusion of his blood, upon which his wife coming to assist him and crying "Murder," the said Master Murdo used her likewise barbarously and inhumanly . . . and put his foot upon her neck to stop her vociferation'.

Improvements to the Mam Ratagan pass were considered by General Wade* in the 1740s, but rejected. It was left to Thomas Telford† to construct new bridges, some of which remain visible. By this date, Bernera Barracks had fallen out of use, although one instrument of war remained in the glen: the 'Great Highland Bagpipe', upon which Lieutenant Donald MacCrimmon**, living in retirement at his farm outside Kirktoun, was a famous performer.

*The resonant Glenelg war memorial, sculpted by Louis Reid*
*Deuchars on Robert Lorimer's plinth, a grand vision of Highlander*
*and winged figure of Peace against the Sound of Sleat.*

After the First World War, two further memorials were created. One takes the form of a sculptural group by Louis Deuchars, in which a Highland soldier is garlanded by Victory while another female, somewhat incautiously dressed for the climate, makes a supplicating gesture at Victory's feet; it stands on a pedestal by Sir Robert Lorimer, architect of the Scottish national war memorial in Edinburgh Castle. At the head of the roll of honour is the name of Major Valentine Fleming, father of James Bond's creator, Ian. The second memorial is the crofts, settled by returning soldiers on land given to them by the government.

*See Aberfeldy, page 522. †See Craigellachie, page 547. **See Galtrigill, page 578

# GLENFINNAN
HIGHLAND *On the way to Hogwarts*

When Malcolm McAlpine, barely out of his teens, was injured by a flying rock during blasting at Lochailort during the construction of the railway line to Mallaig, which was opened in 1901, his father, Sir Robert McAlpine, commissioned a special engine to rush the surgeon Sir William Macewen from Glasgow to Fort William. Having changed into a carriage, Macewen arrived at Lochailort five hours later, and performed an operation. A detail of twelve navvies was organised to carry the wounded man on a stretcher, in relays of four at a time, to the head of Loch Eil, where a steamer was waiting. He was rushed to Glasgow – and survived to live into his eighties.

Some of the ordinary navvies at work on the Mallaig extension were not so lucky. They rest in Glenfinnan churchyard, their graves marked, sometimes, by headstones of concrete. It was not for nothing that Sir Robert acquired the nickname of Concrete Bob.

Their real memorial, perhaps, can be seen in the glen: a great crescent-curved viaduct of twenty-one thirty-metre-tall arches, a hundred metres in length, whose appearance is so magical that it was used to depict the journey to Hogwarts in one of the *Harry Potter* films. It was built for fish. The catch landed at Mallaig could then be rushed to London and other markets, the revenue at last providing a *raison d'être* for the West Highland Railway line already laid from Glasgow to Fort William, which was struggling to achieve profitability.

Mallaig had been built in the 1840s, when Lord Lovat, like other Highland landowners, was encouraging his tenants to become fishermen*. In this case the policy worked. The Glasgow firm of Sir Robert McAlpine and Sons won the contract to build the extension, using concrete wherever possible: it was thirty per cent cheaper than stone. The Glenfinnan viaduct was the largest concrete structure in the world when it went up. Sir Robert's eldest son, Robert, was appointed construction manager, with young Malcolm consigned to assist him. Robert devised a method of harnessing water to power turbines that provided compressed air to work the drills needed to cut through the exceptionally hard rock that was one of the challenges of the route. Originally it was envisaged that two tunnels would be needed; in the end, they built eleven.

The spectacular form of the viaduct seems appropriate to the glen where Bonnie Prince Charlie raised his standard in the doomed adventure of 1745. An army of three and a half thousand navvies was assembled to construct the line – not an easy task, given the workers' objection to the dismal weather, which made many desert; bonus payments had to be offered. Inevitably the glen took on a Wild West appearance for a time. There were so many fights that the extension built onto the taproom of the Corpach Hotel, a favoured venue, became known as the slaughterhouse.

When the line was completed, Mallaig flourished: fishermen, fish curers and coopers moved in from the Aberdeenshire and Berwickshire coasts. Teams of herring girls appeared during the season to gut and pack the fish. But ultimately, the greatest benefit would be to tourism. This railway journey remains one of the most beautiful in the world. There may be precious little romance about the carriage in which you sit, but for the duration it is converted into a viewing platform on wheels. A ride on the Mallaig extension has become a tourist destination in its own right.

*See Helmsdale, page 586

# GRETNA GREEN
## DUMFRIES AND GALLOWAY

*Harmonious blacksmiths*

Until the First World War, every village had its blacksmith's shop. Its most important function was to shoe the horses that provided transport and haulage (there were so many of them that a third of Britain's farmland was given over to growing hay and oats). This was also where broken ploughs were mended, blades sharpened and railings made.

The blacksmith himself was a stock type of the countryside. He had a reputation for wisdom and experience, and could recognise the nature of the shoes of a horse, and who had put them there, from the ring that they made on the road. He may have been a free thinker. His shop was likely to stand in the centre of the village, and because the blacksmith was generally in it, it became an informal meeting place; the gossip passed there meant that the blacksmith was unusually well-informed about village life. While others watched, he would continue to hammer out a piece of red-hot iron held in his pincers, which he might point at the assembled company for emphasis. You did not want to cross the blacksmith.

Outside, there had to be enough space for horses to stand while awaiting their turn to be shod. Cartwheels would be laid here to have hot iron hoops hammered onto them, before being cooled with water from the pond. In the dark interior of the shop stood the anvil, mounted on a block of elm, and forge. A great pair of leather bellows would blow the fire into life. All around would be tongs, chisels, files, punches for stamping the holes into horseshoes, a mandrel around which hoops could be shaped, an assortment of hammers, and – as any reader of *David Copperfield* will know – files.

Buchanan Smithy, a hamlet at the gates of the Duke of Montrose's Buchanan Castle in Stirlingshire, took its name from the three blacksmiths who worked there. The most famous blacksmith's shop in Britain, however, was at Gretna Green – although not for any skill in workmanship. It was the first village north of the Scottish border, and therefore a favourite destination of eloping couples after the 1754 Marriage Act outlawed clandestine marriages in England.

It was popularly supposed that runaways would be married 'over the anvil' by the blacksmith. In fact, as Peter Hutchinson declared in *Chronicles of Gretna Green* (1844), 'in spite of all our inquiries, and searching, and scrutiny, we could not discover that a blacksmith had of late years performed the ceremony, nor indeed, that a blacksmith had ever done it at any period whatever'. Since a marriage was binding if declared in front of two witnesses, an inn was a more convenient place for the ceremony. Consummation, without which it could be annulled, might then take place in one of the bedrooms.

# HELMSDALE
*The answer to the Clearances: fishing*

The problem was that Elizabeth, Countess of Sutherland got married. She might have accepted the condition of the enormous estates in north-eastern Scotland that she inherited, but her cultivated, well-travelled husband, the Marquess of Stafford, 'a Leviathan of wealth', as Charles Greville called him, 'brought a new set of eyes upon it, eyes accustomed to quite a different face of things'. So wrote Hugh Miller, in a book of 1843, graphically entitled *Sutherland as it Was and is; or, How a country may be Ruined.*

'It seemed a wild, rude county where all was wrong and all had to be set right – a sort of Russia on a small scale, that had just got another Peter the Great to civilize it . . . Even the vast wealth and great liberality of the Stafford family militated against this hapless county! It enabled them to treat it as a mere subject of an interesting experiment, in which gain to themselves was really no object – nearly as little as if they had resolved on dissecting a dog alive for the benefit of science.'

In this far quarter of Britain, the Sutherland tenants eked a living that hovered just above the level of subsistence – sometimes falling below it – in conditions that seemed horribly primitive compared to those of the English Midlands. The 'experiment' was to eject families from their remote crofts, encourage them to live in neat villages by the sea and set the men fishing; the land that had been vacated could be let to sheep farmers, at greater profit to the estate. As a theory, it did not seem unreasonable, but it failed to take account of the fact that many of the crofters did not want to leave the communities in which they had grown up.

In 1807, the Sutherland Clearances began. Families who were compelled to leave their homes could at least take the cattle, goods and timber from their old dwellings; from the last they were able to build new ones, even if, for a while, they had to sleep under the stars. But the clearing parties found that if the old hovels were left standing, some families would sneak back to them. So the severity of the operation increased. Huts were burnt, in one notorious case over the head of a bedridden woman of nearly a hundred, who had to be snatched from the flames and died shortly afterwards.

Helmsdale was everything that a crofting township was not: regularly planned, solidly built, sanitary and well-provided with shops, inns and employment. It was laid out in 1818, with a harbour, cooperages and distillery, the roads and bridges constructed by Thomas Telford*. It delighted the eye of the landowner, Lady Sutherland, writing enthusiastically that August: 'The going out of the boats was one of the most cheering sights I ever saw – the manner they dispersed themselves along the coast having the most picturesque effect.'

The Sutherlands' intentions are expressed in an ice house of adamantine construction, where ice from winter lakes could be stored to provide refrigeration for fish being transported south. Alas, by this date, the brutality of the minions on the estate had made the Sutherlands figures of hate, their motives mistrusted by the tenants, whom they were, after their fashion, wanting to help. The experiment did not turn out as the Sutherlands had supposed. There was not a sufficient living to be made from fishing to support families by itself. They reverted to being crofters, supplementing their income from external sources, as Highland people had always done.

*See Craigellachie, page 547

# HUMBIE
## LOTHIAN
*Country air for the young*

The Children's Village was charming. Begun in the first years of the twentieth century, it provided holiday accommodation for disadvantaged and disabled children. It had been recognised that fresh air and sunshine were beneficial to development, particularly in preventing harmful diseases, such as the dreaded tuberculosis. So a series of Voysey-esque cottages were scattered across a grassy bank outside Humbie. The project was founded by a doctor's wife, Mrs Stirling Boyd, and the cottages often bore the names of the friends whom she persuaded to act as sponsors. (A plaque by the doorway of Pettie Cottage declares that it was 'gifted by Miss Elizabeth Pettie Edin in 1920' and intended specifically for the children from Canongate Parish, Edinburgh.)

The grandest of them is called Sharon, distinguished by a loggia, polygonal tower and nursery-rhyme weathervane. At least one has a balcony at bedroom level, probably to provide an outdoor sleeping area, to maximise the health-giving benefits of country air. Presiding over all was a matron, while mothers could stay with their children in the cottages. Harled walls and sweeping, red-tiled roofs were the keynote; the architect appears often to have been J. H. Cooper. He did a good job. The cottages are simple, but no two are alike. Building continued into the 1920s.

The heart of the development was the school, built in 1903 with a bell tower added later. Around 1923 came the village hall or dining hall, its entrance porch surmounted by a bell cote with a pyramid roof. Architecturally the Children's Village was a success; too little has been written about it to know if it worked for the children. By the end of the century, Humbie was being run by a fundamentalist Christian group as a care home for people with learning difficulties; allegations of abuse and neglect were raised in Parliament in 1996. But even without the scandal, this piece of private philanthropy would have come to seem dated, the funds insufficient to maintain the property to the standard required. It has now been sold, and the cottages that once existed for poor children are being turned into conventional homes.

# INNERPEFFRAY
## PERTH AND KINROSS
*The first public library*

Who would have thought that the little building next to the church at Innerpeffray housed Scotland's first public library? There is not much more to Innerpeffray than the church, the library and the adjacent schoolhouse. The reason the library finds itself here is that David Drummond, 3rd Lord Madertie, was a bibliophile. Under his will of 1680, four hundred books were made available for reading in the loft of the church. The present library building dates from 1758–62, having been designed by Charles Freebairn. It is a charming structure, appropriately white-harled and rustic, yet with a handsome Palladian window on the first floor to light the reading room.

Lending libraries first enter recorded history with John Shirley, a fifteenth-century London publisher, who ran a circulating department. Nothing more is heard of them for two centuries, the next chance references coming in obscure Restoration plays. By the Georgian period, they had become established institutions – although not particularly high-minded ones, the books available reflecting the tastes of paying subscribers, who wanted popular reading material. Instead of philosophy, history and poetry, the works most in demand were romantic novels. No wonder it could seem, according to a verse of 1781, that:

> Our Sages, Historians, and Heroes, intreat
> You'd give us the run of a snug window-seat:
> Our Poets request you would honour their fables,
> By letting them lie on your Ladyship's tables …

The Innerpeffray library was different. Uniquely for the time, it was free. Without the need for subscriptions (the library building had been commissioned by Robert Hay Drummond, then Archbishop of York), the tone could be faultlessly austere. Works of fiction were out; astrology, demonology, chiromancy, spiritualism, war, politics, law, agriculture, horticulture, natural history, history and the Classics were in. Lord Madertie had it in mind to help 'particularly the young students' rather than the population at large.

The first entry in the borrowers ledger, kept from 1747, records that on 5 June that year James Sharp took out 'The Life and Death of the Twelve Apostles which I oblige me to deliver in three months after this date under the penalty of ten shilling': the enormous fine presumably reflected the cost of books. We do not know what Sharp did for a living, but no fewer than twenty-seven vocations – including barbers, farmers, millers, surgeons – are recorded, showing that even a scholarly collection of books could have an unexpectedly wide appeal in the literate Scottish countryside.

# INVERARAY

## ARGYLL AND BUTE

*Dr Johnson: 'a stately place'*

'This place will in time be very magnificent,' wrote Thomas Pennant of Inveraray in 1769. He did not care much for the castle, recently built by the 3rd Duke of Argyll: 'from without' it made 'a most disagreeable effect'. Nevertheless, the works at both the castle and town showed Argyll's determination to establish his position in the Highlands, while demonstrating the benefits of the Union, at the time of the Forty-Five.

Argyll, a long-standing politician who had drawn his income from various lucrative government appointments before inheriting from his brother, had come out on the right side. Inveraray was partly rebuilt using government money: compensation for the 'heritable jurisdictions' (the right of trial enjoyed by some great landowners), which Argyll had helped persuade Parliament to abolish, even though they had nothing to do with the rebellion.

When Pennant visited, the 'old town . . . composed of the most wretched hovels that can be imagined', still 'disgraced' the waterfront of Loch Fyne. The Argylls had been attempting to improve Inveraray for a century, before pulling down the old castle, too rotten to repair, in the 1740s, but had not got beyond planting trees. Some of them shaded The Mall, a long line of beech trees separating the town and the castle, which are mutually out of sight.

Although the 3rd Duke was able to complete the new castle by his death in 1761, the town had not progressed beyond 'a few houses, a custom-house, and an excellent inn'. While the Duke's plans for granaries, warehouses, tannery, brewery and stocking manufactory were never realised, Pennant found that the herring boats made a 'busy scene . . . Every evening some hundreds of boats in a manner covered the surface of Loch-Fine, an arm of the sea, which, from its narrowness and from the winding of its shores, has all the beauties of a fresh water lake.'

It was characteristically shrewd of the Duke, a distinguished lawyer, to ensure that the 'excellent inn' was built early. As Pennant predicted, Inveraray was destined to be a showplace. He may have not liked the castle, revealed like a conjuring trick from the bridge over the river Aray, but others did, and both it and the accompanying town became places that no Highland itinerary could miss out.

Dr Johnson came, finding it 'a stately place'. (According to Boswell, he liked the inn and, although generally abstemious, drank whisky there.) Keats came, so appalled by the 'horrors of a solo on the Bag-pipe' and an execrable play, that he wrote a (poor) sonnet about them. Dorothy Wordsworth came, finding that the neat, black-and-white street, 'so little like an ordinary town, from the mixture of regularity and irregularity in the buildings . . . had a truly festive appearance'. Dickens* came, and let us hope that he was cheered by what he found, because he had suffered a terrible 'adventure' at the hands of the mountain weather the day before. Burns† came, to discover that no room was to be had at either the castle or the inn, and wrote a sour epigram 'On Incivility Shewn him at Inveraray':

Whoe're he be that sojourns here,
I pity much his case,
Unless he come to wait upon
The Lord their God – his Grace.

Tourists have, since his time, failed to take the warning – they come in coach loads.
*See Bowes, page 413. †See Mauchline, page 603

# INVERIE
## HIGHLAND
*Place of myth*

On the remote and wild 'rough bounds' of the Knoydart peninsula, still inaccessible by motor vehicle, a wound that was opened in the eighteenth century has been healed. In 1999, ownership of the land was vested in the local community.

The inhabitants of Knoydart, whose largest village is Inverie, had a bad time of it after the 1745 rebellion. Troops arrived to punish the estate for its support of Bonnie Prince Charlie, carrying off cattle and laying waste the land. Most Highland habitations had, before the rebellion, been scattered settlements, known as townships, rather than tightly composed villages; on Knoydart, Inverie was promoted as part of the programme of modernisation that was supposed to bring this wayward, Gaelic-speaking land within the Hanoverian fold. Such centres would, it was believed, increase settled industries and reduce Highland 'idleness'.

Accordingly, a small group of disbanded soldiers and sailors was settled here after the Seven Years War. They had houses, three acres of land, a sum of money, and it was expected that they would become fishermen, presumably to set an example to the rest of the area. A few local people occupied cottages in the village as 'King's Cottagers', on condition they practised a trade. Predictably, the former servicemen did not behave impeccably; John Macdonald, given charge of the changehouse (or pub), squandered the money that was meant to fit it out. Three years later, the fishing nets were still unused.

The policy succeeded, however, to the extent that Inverie became established as the area's only village. It had a school, the purpose of which was to 'civilise' the rude Highland population by teaching English and commercial subjects. Yet from the mid 1780s, the district lost many of its most enterprising families during a wave of emigration to Canada. More than three hundred people left in 1786, causing one observer to worry about the loss of 'our gallant Highlanders' as troops for the army, fearing that the sheep replacing them would provide 'but a sorry defence against our enemies'.

Forced emigration took place during the Clearances. Passages were promised to Australia, the destination subsequently revised to Canada. Those who could not immediately depart had their houses levelled. 'In two instances, aged females who refused to quit, were dragged out by force, and thrown to the ground,' a correspondent to the Quaker magazine *The British Friend* fumed. Visiting the peninsula, he was shocked by the devastation: 'For a long stretch of seven or eight miles, once sudden with houses, all was ruins, and the people burrowing in holes, beside ditches and rocks, as if they had been a lot of savages.'

The policy of suppressing the population continued until after the Second World War. The efforts of several ex-servicemen to obtain smallholdings under Acts intended to encourage resettlement were rebuffed by the Ministry of Agriculture and Fisheries in 1947. Knoydart was by now a sporting estate*, owned by an absentee landlord. Deer were more valuable – and less troublesome – than humans.

Since the government-assisted buyout of 1999, brought about by the Knoydart Foundation, the peninsula's future is in the hands of its own small community. It is a brave venture, and on the face of it successful: the population has risen from sixty to a hundred and twenty; there is a school, a pub, a shop. Nearly everyone has a qualification, some several degrees. While the community used to depend on grants, several enterprises are now self-sufficient – the forestry, for example – and summer visitors find it difficult to get a room without booking. There is, however, one anomaly. None of the people now living on Knoydart is descended from families who were there in the eighteenth century. That is part of the Highland romance: myth is more powerful than fact.

*See Achfary, page 525

# KEIR MILL
DUMFRIES AND GALLOWAY     *Kirkpatrick Macmillan goes before the beak*

In 1842, Kirkpatrick Macmillan was fined five shillings at the Gorbals Police Court for having injured a small girl. Not a bad accident, it was, nevertheless, a remarkable one: Macmillan had been riding the world's first bicycle. His journey had started at the white-walled blacksmith's forge outside Keir Mill, where he had grown up. It must have taken considerable effort to pedal the seventy miles to Glasgow (with overnight stop), although he was adept at the fourteen-mile cycle into Dumfries. The machine weighed half a hundredweight, and moved on wooden wheels rimmed with iron. The collision that landed him in court no doubt reflected its lack of manoeuvrability.

Macmillan had been baptised in the month that Napoleon entered Moscow, September 1812, his Christian name paying compliment to the local sheriff and landowner Sir Thomas Kirkpatrick. His father was the village blacksmith, and Kirkpatrick Macmillan went to work at a young age on a nearby farm. From this he progressed to being a coachman, but smithing was in his blood, and aged twenty-two he became assistant to the Duke of Buccleuch's blacksmith at Drumlanrig.

The riding of hobby horses was a popular fashion – the hobby horse being a frame with two wheels, which the rider drove along with his or her feet. Macmillan realised that it would be better to balance the machine, and keep the momentum going, without feet touching the ground. This could be achieved if the wheels were kept turning by means of cranks. The cranks, attached to the rear axle, were driven by rods connected to two swinging arms, connected to foot treadles. The frame, except for the forks holding the wheels, was made of wood. It was cumbersome, but Macmillan quickly mastered the technique of riding it, although the bumpy, rutted country roads must have made it tough going.

Unlike many Scots, Macmillan did not leave to make his reputation elsewhere; he was happy to stay at Keir Mill. Shortly before his father's death in 1854, he married and had six children, only two of whom survived into adulthood. He continued to work at the smithy where he had grown up. He did not patent his invention, although its potential had been noticed by others. Copies of Macmillan's bicycle were soon selling for high prices – and for half a century it was forgotten that Macmillan had been their progenitor. 'With all these developments,' the *Oxford Dictionary of National Biography* observed, 'Macmillan was quite unconcerned, preferring to enjoy the quiet country life he was used to.' He died in 1878, a true philosopher.

# KILMARTIN
## ARGYLL AND BUTE                    *An archaeological landscape*

People have lived in Kilmartin valley, on the watery seaboard of lochs and islands of Scotland's west coast, for millennia. Or rather, they have been in the valley: the first hunters who came to this boggy landscape, then wooded, ten thousand years ago may only have passed through. Perhaps they spent part of the year here, fishing with sharpened flints attached to spears or tiny flint hooks, using the meanders of the river and the sea as their highways.

We do not know where they lived. In time, however, they left their mark, felling trees and domesticating the land as far as they could – which was not perhaps that far, considering how wild the remote, fretted coastline of Argyllshire feels, even today. They also left evidence of their presence in an astonishing number of monuments: cairns and rock carvings, barrows and cists, standing stones and a henge, used and reused over the centuries: a kind of extended necropolis, since the dominant purpose appears to have been honouring the dead.

This heritage is interpreted in the remarkable Kilmartin House Museum, which displays scholarship and understanding of the surrounding area with a flair that seems doubly unusual in a village. It is a well shaft sunk into the deep, hidden aquifers of the remote past. As well as artefacts displayed in cases – polished stone axes and flutes made out of eagle bones – it contains more intimate items left by the people of the glen as witness to their existence. They include the pollen of cereals preserved in the peat, lying dormant as though waiting for the right conditions to sprout; charred hazelnuts from a midden on Colonsay, which some prehistoric cook left too long in the fire. The museum shows blackened cereal grains and the shells of cockles, of which the loch would have provided an ample harvest.

These are objects from the remote past. In the first centuries after Christ, priorities changed. The inhabitants of the valley thought less about commemorating the dead and more about preserving themselves. A landscape of spirits gave way to one of competing families, led, one imagines, by petty tyrants living in strongholds on top of hills. Monks came: the first syllable of Kilmartin derives from the Gaelic for church, itself associated with the Latin *cella*, or cell. The holy people, coming from Ireland, built stone beehives near springs, in which to contemplate death. Another layer of the palimpsest was added in the nineteenth century: the broken walls of ruined farmhouses record the lives that were played out here before tenants were forced off the land to make way for sheep.

If the little village of Kilmartin looks rather sprucer and better equipped than many of the settlements on the west coast, that might also be due to the long continuity. In a modest way, it has become a heritage destination, which worships and broods over the past, just as the post-glacial settlers may have done.

# KINBRACE
## HIGHLAND                                    *On the railway to nowhere*

There is something of the Australian Outback about Kinbrace. It sits in a wide open landscape, green and peaty and cloudswept rather than arid, with scarcely a tree other than an unfortunate conifer plantation which has – as it deserved to, in this unsuitable place – partly blown over. The mountains that roll along the horizon are far away. On a fine day, it makes a peaceful but empty scene, where nothing moves more quickly than the Strath Beg, a sluggish burn that dawdles the last of its looping way before meeting, which it soon does, the Helmsdale river. Any sound seems to carry preternaturally far, unless, as well there might be, a wind is blowing; then you have to raise your voice to make yourself heard.

Trailing through the immensity of the plain is a railway line: just one track. Kinbrace clusters around the station. A motor repair garage has been made out of one of the sheds, and somebody is fixing a car. Nothing else stirs. To complete the Australian analogy, a few of the cottages have been made from corrugated-iron sheets*. The cemetery is a walled rectangle that seems to have been dropped down, with no attempt to make it relate to the settlement, on the grass of the sheepwalk. This is frontier territory. Victorian railwaymen who ran into snowdrifts risked death from hunger and cold.

But prehistoric tribes appear to have coped with this tundra. Evidence of their existence can be seen in the vaults that they made in the ground, then covered with big roofing slabs. These chambered cairns, as they are called, were used for burial rites, and the oldest are said to date from around 2800BC. There are a number of them around Kinbrace, particularly in the area known as Ach-na-h'uaidh, or field of the graves. They are found with the 'hut circles' that survive from Bronze Age dwellings: Alexander O. Curle, Secretary to the Royal Commission on the Ancient and Historical Monuments of Scotland, was 'much impressed by the extraordinary number' of them when he surveyed Sutherland in 1909. They are to be found by the side of straths, or valleys, along which it was easy to travel. (Do not confuse them with the grouse butts that are next to them.)

The early inhabitants of Sutherland shared the landscape with wolves, bears and wild pigs, but they would not have gone as hungry as we might, if we tried to live off the same land today. The pigs rotavated the banks of the rivers in their search for edible roots. This prepared the soil to take seeds, some of which would have grown up to be bushes and trees, bearing their own seeds and berries. The wolves kept deer numbers under control. There are now no wolves to do this. As a result, deer numbers have exploded, and they nibble or root up saplings that would otherwise grow into trees. The view from Kinbrace may be eerily beautiful, to eyes attuned to the spare, bald character of the modern Sutherland landscape; our prehistoric forebears would have seen it as an ecological desert.

*See Babingley, page 211

# KINGSTON ON SPEY
MORAY                                                      *Village founded on logs*

Kingston on Spey, usually called Kingston, was one of the more successful planned villages of the eighteenth century. There came to be something of a vogue for founding model villages after the Jacobite rebellion passed into memory, and lairds – some of whose confiscated estates had been returned to them – attempted to wring money out of the Highlands. Unlike the dispersed crofting townships that had preceded them, they provided a focus for industry; industry generated money, which stimulated commerce; both were a source of profit to the laird.

They were also part of the process of agricultural improvement, which sought to replace subsistence farming with a more efficient system: responsible landowners recognised that alternative work had to be found for the crofters who were being deprived of their livelihoods. There were too many people in the Highlands for them to prosper; villages such as Kingston were needed to siphon some of them away. But, unlike Kingston, many of them disappointed expectations. Either the people or the industry would not come.

Kingston was founded on logs. They were sent down from the Duke of Gordon's Rothiemurchus Forest. Originally, they were exported from Garmouth, a port a mile inland from Kingston, where Charles II landed in 1650 in his attempt to recover the Crown after his father's execution. Its harbour was already becoming inaccessible by the time of the Muckle Spate in 1829, when the river Spey burst its banks, carrying away houses and changing the course of the river.

The process of sending logs down the river was described in a history of Moray published in 1882: 'The logs and spars belonging to the English company are at times floated down in single pieces, to the number of perhaps 20,000 at a time, conducted by 50 or 80 men going along the sides of the river to push them off by poles as they stick to the banks, hired at ½d per day and a competent allowance of spirituous liquor.' Rafts might also be made, requiring skill and daring on the part of those who rode on them.

In 1784, William Osborne and Ralph Dodsworth contracted to buy all the Duke's timber. They intended not only to sell it on in its native state but to turn it into ships. Coming from Kingston upon Hull, they named their new settlement on the Spey after it. During the first decade they built twenty-five vessels, from twenty-five-ton sloops to ships of five hundred tons; another thirty were constructed before 1815, at least one being a man-of-war. At its height of activity, Kingston had seven shipyards and a flourishing population (more than 2,300 people lived in Urquhart parish, of which Kingston is part, in 1861). Tea clippers, such as the *Chieftain* built by James Geddie, which could sail from Shanghai to London in a hundred days, were a speciality.

Born out of wood, Kingston died by it: the shipyards did not convert to the production of metal-hulled ships, and the last of them died in the early twentieth century. Now the shipbuilding docks have been reduced to indecipherable creeks in the riverbank, and the only busy people seem to be birdwatchers.

# KINNEIL
## LOTHIAN

*On the Antonine Wall*

Britannia was in mourning. Roman bronze coins minted in 154–5 for circulation in Britain show her lamenting an insurrection against the occupying force, pitying the foolishness of the tribesmen whom Rome found it necessary to suppress. The trouble came from Scotland. An indication that uprisings of this kind had been foreseen was the construction of the Antonine Wall, which had recently been completed. A turf rampart, it formed a necklace of forts and fortlets – perhaps also watchtowers, although no archaeological evidence for these has been found – across the throat of Scotland, between the Clyde and the Forth. The site of one of the fortlets is now occupied by Kinneil House, tucked in among the smoking oil refineries and dismal housing estates of the Firth of Forth.

The Antonine Wall marked the northernmost limit ever reached by the Roman Empire. Hadrian's Wall, built in AD122, had been almost theatrically impressive, as though to declare that it represented Rome's final boundary. It was not enough, however, for Emperor Hadrian's successor, Antoninus Pius. A single sentence in his biography notes that he carried on many wars, including the defeat of the tribes north of Hadrian's Wall. This must have happened at the start of his reign, because work on the Antonine Wall began four years after he came to power in AD138.

The new dispensation seems to have caused something of a life change for the Lowland Scots. They started to come down from the hill forts and built farmsteads

– a sign that they were managing to live at peace with one another, as part of the settlement with Rome. Harmony was encouraged by the Roman policy of conscripting young tribesmen and sending them off to the German frontier. But the rebellion of the mid 150s showed that old habits died hard. Peace was restored: it had to be as a matter of prestige for the Emperor, given his investment in the wall. But the project of pacifying the Lowlands did not outlast his death in 161. The wall was probably abandoned when the fortifications of northern Britannia were rethought in 163.

Kinneil House began life as a tower house – evidence that the area was still unsettled a millennium after the Romans' departure. In time, this residence of the Dukes of Hamilton developed a level of comfort that would have been unimaginable to the legionaries manning the Antonine fortification. History took another turn here, when James Watt came to build an improved steam engine to reduce flooding in the Hamilton coal mines, then leased by John Roebuck of the Carron Iron Works. This was the dawn of the modern age.

The rural township, still represented by an ancient, rusty iron sign pointing to Upper and Lower Kinneil, has, for most practical purposes, been overpowered by the grey expanse of Bo'ness. Nevertheless, a memory of Antoninus Pius's military works remains indelibly printed on the place: the name of Kinneil derives from the Gaelic for turf wall.

# LARBERT
## STIRLING                         *Iron monument to a colourful Georgian explorer*

In a car park of Larbert church stands a tall, red, cast-iron obelisk commemorating James Bruce Esq., of Kinnaird. According to the inscription, 'His life was spent in performing useful and splendid actions. He explored many distant regions. He discovered the sources of the Nile. He traversed the deserts of Nubia . . . By the unanimous voice of mankind his name is enrolled with those who were conspicuous for genius, for valour, and for virtue.'

All of which, particularly the last line, must be taken with a pinch of salt. But there is no denying that Bruce's achievements, although not everything he claimed for them, were remarkable, like the man himself.

Bruce was born at Kinnaird House, in the central Highlands of Scotland, in 1730. In order to protect him from the risk of Jacobitism, his father arranged for him to be brought up as an English gentleman, educated at Harrow School. His first inclination had been to become a parson. Instead, he was made to study law at Edinburgh University, did not take to it, and married the daughter of a wine merchant, which seemed to open up the prospect of an agreeable career.

Visiting Paris, his wife died of tuberculosis, and Bruce was devastated. But a stroke of good fortune made it unnecessary for him to pursue the wine trade or any other profession: the family owned land near the Carron Iron Works, where John Roebuck had developed an improved method of smelting, using coke (made from coal) rather than charcoal. Bruce owned the nearest coal mine; the income freed him to do what he wanted.

What he wanted to do was to travel. An inspiration was Robert Wood, author of *The Ruins of Palmyra* (1753) and *The Ruins of Balbec* (1757), who combined the role of archaeologist with that of courtier and politician. Bruce cut his teeth on the Iberian Peninsula, where, under the pretence of inspecting the grape harvest, he acted as an amateur spy. He then made for Algiers, serving as consul general – a post for which his volcanic temper made him plainly unsuitable. He was soon replaced. Slighted, he set off on the epic journey to Abyssinia and Egypt, which would become the subject of his *Travels to Discover the Source of the Nile*, sumptuously published in five volumes.

Bruce was away so long that his return was a sensation. Equally sensational were his tales. A red-haired giant of a man, he travelled under the guise of an itinerant fakir or dervish. With him went his voluminous baggage, which at one point he was forced to abandon, when reduced to eating his last camel. Having picked up some medical knowledge, he was able to cure the entire court of Ras Michael, de facto ruler of Abyssinia, of smallpox; among the saved were the favourite child of Ras Michael's beautiful wife Princess Esther, one of the many women who found him irresistible. Eventually, he stood 'in that spot which had baffled the genius, industry, and inquiry, of both ancients and moderns, for the course of nearly three thousand years'. Bruce did not mention that a Jesuit priest had got there in 1630, nor that he had reached only the source of the Blue Nile, not the much longer White Nile.

That, however, was the least of the criticisms made by contemporaries, many of whom refused to believe him. Boastful and disingenuous, Bruce gave them some reason for scepticism. Having married again, he delayed writing his books for sixteen years, and did not trouble himself to look at his notes. But history has shown his account to be broadly true. Immensely corpulent by the age of sixty-four, Bruce died when he toppled over on the stairs, while escorting a woman to her carriage.

# LETHAM
ANGUS                                                    *Village of improvement*

'I am persuaded in a free Country all Towns have a tendency to swell and increase, and when we see any stunted miserable Place in such a Country it could be traced to some vice or defect retarding the operations of freedom.' So wrote George Dempster of Dunnichen, MP. He hoped to demonstrate his confidence at Letham, on his Angus estate.

Dempster was not only a laird; he spent much of his life at Westminster, and his energy could be felt in many schemes of improvement. Every month during the fishing season he received the gift of a fine Tay salmon from a grateful friend, to whom he had introduced the idea of using ice as a means of refrigeration, allowing him better access to the London market. He was also a moving force behind the British Fisheries Society\*, which sought to establish would-be fishing towns and stem emigration by providing employment.

At Dunnichen, Dempster sought to revolutionise farming – but not at the expense of the people who worked there. Indeed, in a nation whose memory has been seared by the Highland Clearances, Dempster stands out as a figure of affability and benevolence. When he inherited the family estates, acquired by a merchant grandfather, in 1754, they were run on the medieval runrig (ridge and furrow) system. As he later described: 'The farmers having no leases, or short ones, were extremely poor . . . They were also bound to grind their corn at the mill of the barony, and to employ the proprietor's blacksmith. They paid double price for their work at the mill and the blacksmith's shop and were besides saucily and ill served.'

Dempster introduced leases for life, giving the tenants greater security and a reason to invest in their land, and abolished the requirement to use only the land-owner's mill and tradesmen. He was the only laird in the area to introduce such measures: 'There was never a less successful apostle than I have been. In a mission of forty years, I cannot boast of one convert.' Trees were planted, fields were richly marled – and Dempster campaigned for another development to improve the countryside: reforming the number of people who could vote, to allow what he called the 'industrious farmer and manufacturer' a say in politics.

He believed that settlements such as Letham would serve as markets and commercial centres, attracting specialised craftsmen and providing a base for industries that might generate money. At the end of 1788 he advertised: 'To Weavers and other Industrious Tradesmen. At the Village of Letham . . . Land for Houses and Gardens, and little Fields, may be had.' Dempster promised moderate rents, good soil, a warm situation, plenty of water, a convenient kirk, stone quarries, quantities of peat and marl and the prospect of employment for masons, slaters, blacksmiths and wrights in the village itself. By 1790, twenty families had arrived; six years later, the population had grown to more than two hundred.

One of the guiding principles was democratic self-government, development being guided by a committee of nine members, elected by an ingenious method of secret ballot (voting sticks with a sliding grooved tongue, which could be moved to indicate either a Yes or No vote). Letham may not have grown into the town that Dempster had hoped, but it remains an attractive village, in which George Dempster is remembered with pride.

\*See Tobermory, page 631

# LIMEKILNS

*Burning limestone: perilous trade*

Limekilns, as its name suggests, made its living from burning lime. It had not always done so. In the fourteenth century, what is now a little village served as the port for Dunfermline. A sixteenth-century warehouse, fancifully known as the King's Cellar, survives from the old harbour. It was then known as Galletts. But as the port declined, lime rose in importance and the place changed its name.

Lime was a crucial commodity until the twentieth century. It served two functions. In agriculture, farmers spread it on the fields. Like marl, which was routinely dug out of pits, lime was regarded as a fertiliser, giving calcium oxide and other minerals to the soil. There have since been two views on its efficacy, some writers regarding it as little better than a superstition. It was, however, widely used from the seventeenth century until guano – fossilised or fresh bird droppings – began to arrive from Peru in the 1830s*.

In building, quicklime was the active ingredient in mortar, joining courses of brick together. It was also used as a protective wash over plaster, to keep it sealed against the rain. It is still used in this way in Romania, where every house in some country villages still has a tub of slaked lime – a kind of putty made by mixing quicklime with water – in the cellar.

The first step towards making quicklime was to burn limestone. There were plenty of quarries around Limekilns, supplying limestone that was rich in fossils. To begin with, they used charcoal and then coal to fuel the kilns; the region abounded in both woods and mines. In the nineteenth century, the centre of production transferred to the neighbouring village of Charleston, which, according to *The New Statistical Account of Scotland*, was selling fifteen thousand tons of limestone annually in 1845, as well as four hundred thousand bushels of shells. The kilns at Charleston survived into the 1950s. Once the quicklime had arrived at its final destination, it would be slaked in pits, perhaps being left for several months.

These days, lime burning is regarded as a perilous activity because of the fumes that are emitted, and cannot be undertaken without full-length protective suiting in some parts of the European Union. In Romania, lime burning is a normal part of village life, which causes no fuss or comment – much as it would have been at Limekilns two centuries ago.

*See Wraxall, page 82. See also Barrow upon Soar, page 299

# LONEMORE

*Big Damp Meadow – a crofting settlement*

Sir Francis Mackenzie, fifth baronet, who inherited the Gairloch estate in 1826, had strong views about houses. In 1838, he shared them with the public by writing a book: *Hints for the Use of Highland Tenants and Cottagers. By a Proprietor.* Many of the dwellings around Gairloch were rented by cottars. They were primitive structures – 'dens', as he called them – with only a hole in the roof to let out the smoke from the hearth (sometimes improved by a fishing creel to do service as a chimney).

'The houses of the people in general,' the minister of Gairloch, the Rev. James Russell, observed in *The New Statistical Account of Scotland* in 1836, 'have but one outer door', used by both people and cattle, the bipeds taking 'possession of one end of the house, and the quadrupeds of the other'. While most of their inhabitants seemed generally content, so long as they had a small parcel of land, two or three cows, and a salmon cobble to fish with, the minister urged that grants should be made available to encourage emigration. Gairloch would be better off if a third of the population left for Upper Canada.

Sir Francis took matters in hand, replacing the insanitary dens with more generously built crofts. The bones of one of his crofting townships can be seen at Lonemore, outside Gairloch, on the road to the lighthouse. Visitors to the Gairloch Heritage Museum will be able to piece together its nineteenth-century form from the wall footings of vanished houses and survivals that exist beneath modern disguises.

Crofting came to Scotland in the eighteenth century. It was a system of land tenure that allowed the tenant a smallholding to farm on his own account, combined with rights of common grazing shared with the rest of the township. Lonemore, laid out as crofts in the 1840s, came late in the story. With Victorian method, Sir Francis and his brother John, a doctor (who managed the estate after Sir Francis's death in 1843), organised the crofts on a regular pattern, replacing earlier habitations or retaining them for use as byres.

From the name, it might not have seemed a propitious location: Lonemore derives from the Gaelic for big damp meadow. Nor would the reddish-brown colour of the water, caused by the presence of bog iron, have seemed more promising. But the *Inverness Courier* approved of the land holdings of four or five acres, which 'a man and his family, if industrious, can properly cultivate with the spade alone without aid from a horse'.

By the time John Mackenzie handed over the estate to Sir Francis's son, Sir Kenneth, on the latter's coming of age in 1856, Gairloch as a whole, and Lonemore in particular, had been transformed. Bridges and mills, schools and Sunday Schools, paddle steamers and postal services, proper tools (in place of the 'wretched Celtic crooked spade') and decent houses – all had sprung up where there had been none before. Cattle no longer died of starvation before the winter was out. Boggy land had been drained. These things had happened at a time when other Highland landlords were clearing their estates of people and replacing them with sheep.

# LONMAY
## ABERDEENSHIRE
*Are You Lonesome Tonight?*

The year 1745 was memorable for Scotland. In August, Bonnie Prince Charlie, the Young Pretender, raised his standard at Glenfinnan (see page 584), rallying the Highlands to the adventure that would end on Culloden Moor. The same year, a young man from Lonmay, an obscure village near Fraserburgh, left for the New World, stepping onto a quayside in North Carolina and probably counting himself lucky to have avoided all the disturbance at home. His name was Andrew Presley. It was the beginning of a long journey that would end, two hundred years later, at Graceland – according to convincing research by Allan Morrison, Andrew Presley was the ancestor of Elvis Presley, born in East Tupelo, Mississippi, in 1935. Elvis would be hailed as The King in a way that, it is safe to say, Bonnie Prince Charlie could never have imagined.

Lonmay was a scattered settlement, with sandy beaches and fishermen on the coast, a harvest to be taken from the quantity of wreckage that was washed up from ships, air that was 'rather moist, but not unhealthy' (according to *The Statistical Account of Scotland*), no navigable rivers, no coal, little useful stone, but several bogs or mosses, and a surfeit of moles. This was a staunchly Episcopalian area, and as late as 1770 an upset would be caused by the appointment of a Jacobite, who refused to swear allegiance to George III, as minister of Lonmay. A stork was spotted during the winter of 1837–8; it was shot and nailed to the door of a barn. In 1713, an Andrew Presley married Elspeth Leg. Their son, Andrew, may have felt there was little to keep him at home.

The Scottish diaspora has been vast. Not only did many of the most enterprising Scots make their careers in London, but they were famous for their intrepidity and efficiency, becoming a core element of the British armed forces and of the administration of Empire. It has been estimated that as many as seventy thousand emigrated after the Highland Clearances of the nineteenth century.

Once they were settled in their new countries, the Scots adopted local ways; they did not on the whole keep alive a spirit of Scottish Zionism, expecting that they or their descendants would permanently return to their homeland (although some did\*). Rather in the way that Roman Catholics think of Rome, they remembered it as a place of pilgrimage. This has led to the phenomenon of roots tourism, as people of Scots ancestry return to the place of their family's origin, generally leaving again before the first snows of winter have fallen. Genealogy has turned from being an unusual amateur hobby into a consuming and increasingly professionalised passion.

The Presleys kept alive the memory of their Scottish beginnings, although they had lost the details. The King himself put his feet only once on the ground trod by his ancestors, and that was to change planes at Prestwick Airport in 1960. But since Mr Morrison made his discovery in 2004, a Presley tartan has been produced.

*See Fyvie, page 575

# LOWER LARGO
FIFE                                                    *Robinson Crusoe at home*

Alexander Selkirk, born at Lower Largo in 1676, was the seventh son of his parents. He ought therefore to have been a lucky lad, according to the superstition of the time. His fate, however, was to prove quite different. His father, John Selcraig – Alexander later changed the spelling – was a shoemaker and tanner. He is supposed to have been a disciplinarian, but Selkirk's mother, Euphan, was indulgent, and Selkirk grew up to be headstrong.

He was not the only one in the family with this disposition. In 1689, his brother John led an armed mob that stopped the minister, who had sworn allegiance to William and Mary after the overthrow of James II, from entering the church. (The minister took the course of discretion by distributing the contents of the poor box among the needy and retiring from the parish.) Alexander, then aged thirteen, was at his brother's side.

During the next six years, Alexander must have been a worry. On 25 August 1695, he was summoned to appear before the congregation for 'indecent conduct in church'. Before the time of his appearance, he had – against his father's wishes – gone to sea. After six years, he returned. Again, he was called to appear in church, this time as the result of a domestic 'tumult'.

Before long, he had sailed for England, en route to the South Seas. The expedition that he joined as sailing master appears to have been manned by hotheads such as himself, who were at loggerheads with the captains. Rashly, he announced that he would rather leave his ship, the *Cinque Ports*, than sail in her, and taking him at his word, the captain disembarked him on the island of Juan Fernandez, with only 'his Clothes and Bedding, with a Firelock, some Powder, Bullets, and Tobacco, a Hatchet, a Knife, a Kettle, a Bible, some practical Pieces, and his Mathematical Instruments and Books'. Seeing the *Cinque Ports* sail away, he had a profound change of heart; but by then it was too late.

No doubt his friends in Largo would have been surprised by the fist that he made of his stay on Juan Fernandez. He mastered the art of hunting goats, whose kids he domesticated to provide a source of food. (On one occasion, he fell over a precipice in pursuit of a goat, which left him unconscious; he awoke to find the goat dead beneath him.) But he also followed a devout regime of Bible study and psalm singing, reading the holy texts aloud to retain his use of speech.

After four years and four months, two Bristol privateers landed for water. There Selkirk was found, 'a Man cloth'd in Goat-skins', barely able to understand language or to speak, according to the captain who found him. He became mate of one of the ships, returning to Britain in 1711.

In 1713, Selkirk was in trouble for assaulting a shipwright in Bristol. But when he returned to Lower Largo, he was a changed man, living as a recluse in a cave specially constructed in his father's garden. 'O, my beloved island!' he is credited as crying. 'I wish I had never left thee!' He ran away with a local girl, and finally went back to sea. He died off the Guinea coast in 1721. A statue of him was erected in 1885 on the site of his birthplace in Lower Largo.

# MAUCHLINE
## AYRSHIRE                                                          *Burnsland*

A twenty-metre red sandstone tower, of fantastic silhouette, announces Mauchline – a monument as only the Victorians knew how to make them. It is to the national poet, Robert Burns. Although the 'auld clay biggin' at Alloway, where Burns was born, has been preserved as a literary shrine, he spent relatively little time there, being only seven when his father moved the family to a larger home at Mount Oliphant farm, Doonholm.

As a man, Burns moved around Ayrshire and Dumfriesshire, with visits to Edinburgh and a foray to London, generally leaving a trail of illegitimate children in his wake. But Mauchline has more right to honour him than most places. It was here that he found Jean Armour, the love who not only bore him children (nothing new there) but eventually became his wife.

In 1784, twenty-five-year-old Robert and his brother Gilbert had set up as farmers, renting Mossgiel Farm outside Mauchline from Burns's friend Gavin Hamilton. It was hard graft, and Burns may have suffered from one of the bouts of depression that seem to have been hidden behind his outwardly exuberant personality. To begin with, Burns viewed Jean as only one of a cluster of 'Mauchline Belles', whom he serenaded (more than serenading had already taken place with Elizabeth Paton, an illiterate servant girl, who gave birth to his daughter 'Dear-bought Bess'), and to whom he would go on paying court after the relationship with Jean had begun.

Burns met Jean at a dance. Merriment was caused by Burns's dog, which skipped around his master's heels. How he 'wished he could get any of the lasses to like him as well as his dog did', he remarked. Not long after, he passed through the washing green at Mauchline, where Jean was bleaching clothes. The dog ran through the clothes; conversation started; Burns was away. In 1786, Jean gave birth to twins.

The daughter of a stonemason, Jean had obtained a letter from Burns offering marriage. In Scottish law, this was enough to constitute marriage. When Burns, without option, came forward to regularise matters, Jean's father held that marrying an impoverished, perhaps incompetent farmer, who had thoughts of emigration, was worse than continuing as a single mother. The lovers were summoned to Mauchline church to admit their behaviour and do penance. But afterwards, Jean chose to stay with her father rather than Burns, greatly to his mortification. 'It is not the losing her that makes me so unhappy, but for her sake I feel most severely,' he wrote in a letter. 'I foresee she is in the road to, I am afraid, eternal ruin.'

Two years later, however, Burns's affair with Jean resumed. Another set of twins was on the way. Mr Armour threw her out of the house. Burns was in London, pursuing an epistolary romance with a woman in Edinburgh, and had to ask friends to take her in. He seems to have had no intention of formally marrying her until, suddenly and in secret, he did.

The Burns family moved to Ellisland Farm in Dumfriesshire. Burns later took a job as a revenue man, attempting to suppress smuggling. The eye that Sir Walter Scott thought 'indicated the poetical character and temperament', which was large, dark and would glow '(I say literally glowed) when he spoke with feeling or interest', now scoured the hiding places around Sanquhar during long and punishing days on horseback.

Jean and Burns would have nine children together. Four of the infant daughters are buried in Mauchline churchyard, together with Gavin Hamilton and several of Burns's other friends.

# MEIGLE
## PERTH AND KINROSS                                   *Tale of the stones*

It is easy to get things muddled. Legend had it that the north entrance to Meigle churchyard was the grave of Queen Guinevere, known locally as Vanora. The Queen had been seized by the Pictish King Mordred and kept as a prisoner near Meigle. Arthur, when she managed to return to him, was unforgiving: regarding her absence as infidelity, he had her torn to death by wild beasts.

The mound that represented Vanora's grave was given a wide berth by young women wanting to bear children: poor Vanora had been barren, and it was thought her influence would blight the prospects of the living. A cross slab carved in the ninth century stood on the spot; another, rather earlier one faced it across the pathway.

Actually, it was probably the cross slab that attached the legend to Meigle, if it did not give rise to it in the first place. On the front of the slab is a cross on the Northumbrian model, carved after the pattern of a metal cross studded with jewels, small enough to be carried. In the centre of the back is a weathered scene, which could represent a woman being pawed by lions (the best lions, incidentally, carved in the Dark or Middle Ages). In fact, the central figure is not Vanora, but

*Ninth-century prayer cross, which used to stand near the entrance to Meigle churchyard. The story of Daniel in the lions' den is carved on the back.*

the Old Testament Daniel, whom Darius the Mede threw into the lions' den (not to be devoured like Queen Vanora, which is why the lions are shown behaving like pussycats). The confusion is understandable: Daniel is wearing a kilt.

Meigle is a village wrapped in mystery and symbolism, the royal estate of a ninth-century Pictish king, which was also the site of a monastery. The churchyard became the resting place for the greatest collection of Pictish stones in existence – more than twenty of them. We do not know why; but then we do not know many things about the Picts.

The Picts are thought to have emerged from the tribal societies of the late Iron Age. They ruled northern Scotland from the fourth to the ninth centuries, and then disappeared. Their culture ceased to exist. Their language was lost. They left no literature behind them. The lists of their kings that have come down to us were compiled centuries later. Virtually the only record of how they lived and thought is provided by their carvings. These are often as cryptic as everything else to do with the Picts. The hieroglyphs on them have not been decoded. But they make the Meigle collection, now in a museum formed out of the old schoolhouse, exceptionally important. Through them we can glimpse something of the Picts' most pressing anxieties and concerns.

The story of Daniel spoke to them. They converted to Christianity around AD700. While lions were unknown in Scotland, they seem to have felt that Daniel's struggles in the den reflected something in their own lives. They were beset by wild and threatening forces, most obviously death. Daniel's defeat of the lions seemed to foreshadow Christ's triumph over death. But his prowess also seemed pressingly relevant to a warrior people. On one stone a huntsman and his hounds follow an angel. But the world of ninth-century Scotland merges with that of Biblical times, and of myth. While a wild beast devours an ox, a centaur takes an axe to a tree.

To judge from tenons on its side, which would have fitted into a wall, this slab may once have been incorporated into the church, which was rebuilt several times on the same site. The early church was itself handsomely decorated. Only part of a carved frieze now survives from it: reposing between two fearsomely clawed beasts is a mermaid with an elaborately knotted tail.

*See also Abernethy, page 523*

# MEIKLEOUR
## PERTH AND KINROSS
*A truly splendid hedge*

'We wish the hedges and they who made them in the ditches,' some Oxfordshire rioters spluttered in 1596. They were attempting to halt the destruction of the open medieval landscape of communally farmed fields, pastureland and commons. It was not a countryside entirely devoid of hedges: great ones were used to mark parish boundaries in many parts of the country. But the England over which Prince Rupert made cavalry charges in the Civil War, or the Scotland in which Bonnie Prince Charlie's Highlanders were destroyed at Culloden, offered few obstacles to the wind other than trees.

In the fateful year of 1745, a beech hedge was planted at Meikleour, ten miles north of Perth. For nearly six hundred yards it has defined the bounds of Meikleour House, which had been built twenty-five years earlier by Robert Murray Nairne. Nairne intended to create a feature that was both practical and decorative. Hedges have many benefits to the farmer: they provide a shelter against the wind, which prevents soil erosion and protects crops; the trees in them, if allowed to grow up, give shade to animals; if properly laid they will present an effective barrier to cattle and other stock. (They also presented an irresistible sporting challenge to foxhunters, who liked jumping their horses.)

The choice of beech suggests that Nairne was interested as much in the look of the thing as its agricultural benefits. The aesthetic possibilities of hedges had long been realised. Topiary, generally made out of yew, had been a feature of Elizabethan gardens. Hedges that articulated gardens into architectural shapes became de rigueur in the seventeenth century. The geometry of these classical gardens was swept away in favour of naturalistic parkland in the era of the Picturesque; no doubt the Meikleour hedge was planted as part of a landscaping project for the park.

Since 1745 the hedge has become an essential feature of British life. Villages teem with them. The quick-growing privet hedge became an essential element of suburbia in the twentieth century. By the end of that century, the even quicker- and taller-growing leylandii was causing problems: those who value the privacy that their dark foliage walls provide are pitted against the detractors, who object to the blocking effect that they have on views and light. Neighbours have murdered one another over them.

But no leylandii hedge can compete with the glory of Meikleour. During the past two and a half centuries, it has grown into what the *Guinness Book of Records* recognises as the biggest hedge in the world, with an average height of one hundred feet. It is the pride of the village, whose approach it lines. How could it have grown to this size? Tragedy played a part. Nairne supported the Stuart cause, followed his prince and was killed at Culloden. Once laid, the hedge had no one to make sure it was trimmed.

# MILLTOWN OF AUCHINDOUN
MORAY                                              *Better than Jeeves?*

The Duke of Gordon had an extraordinary butler. William Marshall spent all his life in and around Fochabers (see page 573), where he was born in 1748. His parents were modestly situated, and William did not receive more education than that which his father could give him, plus six months at the grammar school. And yet he emerged as a significant musical talent, whose Scottish dances, composed for the fiddle, have become part of the canon of Scottish music.

Well-built and handsome in his youth (portly, although carefully dressed, in later life), he was himself a fine dancer. That, however, was only one of his accomplishments. 'He understood the craft of falconry, was an excellent angler, could throw the hammer, leap, and run with dexterity, agility, and speed, against which few could successfully cope,' the *Inverness Courier* noted after his death. A clock that he made, given to the Duke of Gordon, is in the Fochabers Museum: it shows the months and days of the year, the age of the moon, the sun's rising and setting, and various other astronomical phenomena. All these skills had to be acquired, or polished, during the hours for which he was not employed by the Duke, whose service he entered at the age of twelve. Later, he would accompany the family wherever they went.

Some of the titles of Marshall's airs curried favour with his employer: for example, 'The Duke of Gordon's Birthday' and 'Miss Admiral Gordon's Strathspey'.

To the latter, 'one of the sweetest in the whole range of Scottish melody', Robert Burns* wrote the words 'Of a' the airts the wind can blaw', the combination becoming a general favourite. Not having the confidence of a professional musician, Marshall would try his airs on his wife, Jane Giles. Those that she disliked were rejected, the rest – about 270 – committed to paper. He was a famous fiddle player in the area. 'When Marshall played strathspeys, the inclination to dance was as irresistible as if the listener had been inoculated by the Tarantula,' *Chambers's Edinburgh Journal* wrote. Several of his tunes became popular at Covent Garden.

The Duke of Gordon appears to have prized him. Although there may have been a *froideur* after Marshall was robbed of more than a hundred pounds of the Duke's money while in London, he was given the tenancy of a farm called Keithmore outside Milltown of Auchindoun, and eventually became the Duke's factor. As such, his capabilities showed no diminution: as well as serving as a Justice of the Peace, he built roads and bridges – contributing to the 'improvement' of an estate that had already transformed Fochabers (the old settlement had been demolished as being too near Gordon Castle and replaced with a model village in the cool neoclassical style that makes Moray such an epitome of civilisation).

On the farm of Keithac, near Keithmore, Marshall found a friend in Priest George Gordon, who helped him write out his music; he composed 'Chapel Keithac' for him. His own retirement in 1823 was marked by the slow melody 'Farewell to Keithmore'. Marshall was buried at Bellie parish church in Fochabers in 1833.

*See Mauchline, page 603. See also Galtrigill, page 578*

# MONYMUSK
## ABERDEENSHIRE
*Thricely remarkable*

There are three reasons why Monymusk is an exceptional place in the history of Scotland. First, it seems to have had a magnetic attraction for remarkable objects. The earliest evidence of human creativity here is a group of standing stones beneath some beech trees, half a mile to the north of the village. From a later period, the church contains the Monymusk Stone, a two-metre-high granite slab decorated with a Celtic cross and knotwork in the Pictish manner.

It has been suggested, doubtfully, that a step motif in the carving makes reference to the celebrated Monymusk Reliquary. This is the most important work of art to survive from the first millennium of Scottish history. Shaped like a miniature house, it is thought to have been made on Iona in the eighth century. The top and sides are covered with silver or copper alloy, decorated with interlacing animals. Large discs and squares on the surface would have accommodated precious stones. It is believed that this could have been the holy Breccbennach (in English: embossed thing with peak), which Robert the Bruce carried before his army at Bannockburn. One school of thought has it that the reliquary was guarded by the monks of Monymusk Priory, to be produced as a potent battle talisman when required. An alternative theory believes that it was kept at Arbroath Abbey, not arriving at Monymusk until the late Middle Ages.

The second reason for Monymusk's significance is that we know an unusual amount about the place in the early Middle Ages, an otherwise obscure time for the Scottish countryside. The settlement of Pitmunie, in the parish of Monymusk, was extensively studied by the archaeologist Henry Hamilton in the 1930s. Like an English village, its size was dictated by the trudging of the eight-ox ploughs, which were able to till an infield of forty to ninety acres. On this land were grown oats and barley. Beyond it, sheep, cattle and pigs wandered through fallows and sheepfolds. Husbandmen cultivated their own rigs, or strips, while four families possessed their own crofts or smallholdings. Unlike in England, Pitmunie did not gather itself around a green or other focal point; it remained a scattered township – the usual Scottish pattern – until the time of the Grants.

Sir Francis Grant bought Monymusk House and its estates in 1713. When he arrived to take possession of his property, he found that it was practically derelict. In 1716, he handed the problem to his son Archibald, who became factor; the estate was given to him on his marriage the following year.

Archibald's life was not without colour: in 1732, he was expelled from the House of Commons for a huge number of speculative activities, some of a suspect nature. Afterwards, he made Monymusk his main home, and here – reason number three – he is remembered as a great agriculturalist. One of his first acts was to clear the fields of stones, which were built into walls. Turnips were introduced, providing feed for stock over winter.

It could be uphill work to persuade tenants to adopt his innovations: 'Your misfortune is not the want of good soil but your mismanagement of it,' he told one of them in exasperation. Nor was he a universally caring landlord, as can be seen from the order to nineteen tenants to 'flitt and remove themselves, their wives, bairns, family, servants, cotters, dependents, goods and gear whatsoever' when the land that they had previously worked was required to make more efficient, larger units.

Nevertheless, he replanned Monymusk to create a centre for the estate. In the middle is a large square, which allowed cattle drovers en route to Aberdeen to keep their beasts somewhere safe overnight. Perhaps it says something for the quality of Grant's work that most of his cottages were rebuilt attractively – and substantially – in granite a century later. They form a strikingly well-ordered ensemble, the woodwork of their porches and gables painted maroon, the lattice between the diamond panes of their dormer windows being white.

# MUTHILL

*Burnt by the Old Pretender*

Muthill was one of half a dozen villages that suffered from the 'Burning Order' perpetrated by James Stuart, the Old Pretender, in 1715. Stuart's cause had been going badly. There had been initial elation when his army, without Stuart, invaded England, but by the time the would-be King arrived in person, his troops had been beaten back by battles at Preston and Sheriffmuir. Pursued by the Duke of Argyll, he unwisely ordered that six villages in his path – Auchterarder, Blackford, Crieff, Dalreoch, Dunning and Muthill – should be laid waste. Accordingly, in late January 1716, in the freezing cold of a Highland winter, the inhabitants were turned out of their homes to see them burnt.

Brutality on that scale might have been an acceptable tool of war on the Continent, but it hardly won him friends in Scotland. Besides, Argyll's men were amply provisioned; they marched onwards, the Jacobites withdrew to Dundee, and on 3 February Stuart returned, ignominiously, to France, somewhat less welcome there than when he had left. It took the devastated villages sixty-five years to obtain compensation from the government, the award being nearly five thousand pounds.

But the disaster was not entirely to Muthill's disadvantage. It was rebuilt on more handsome lines than before. Most of the buildings date from the late eighteenth century: well-proportioned, two-storey structures with sash windows. Gillespie Graham built the parish church in 1828.

No more suffering would be inflicted by Jacobites pursuing a scorched earth policy after 1716. The next campaign of terror, when Highland settlements were destroyed, winter stores burnt and cattle driven away, was visited by the Hanoverian government after the Battle of Culloden in 1746. But the event that made the village's blood run cold in 1749 had nothing to do with war. A dog was seen running about with part of a human leg in its mouth. A stocking and shoe were on the leg, which belonged to an unfortunate young woman, whose other remains were found scattered about. She had been murdered on her way to help with the harvest, by her children's father, who wanted to marry another woman.

# NEWCASTLETON

*The Duke of Buccleuch thinks big*

The most ambitious Georgian estate village in the Border country is Newcastleton, established by the 3rd Duke of Buccleuch in 1793. Scottish landowners were great founders of villages; they not only wanted to develop their estates by creating centres of trade and commerce*, but, in some cases, to give dispossessed crofters somewhere to go after their land had been cleared for sheep. They often saw fishing as an alternative source of employment†.

Plenty of these developments exist in the Highlands and north of Scotland, places where settlements had traditionally, because of crofting, been scattered, and nucleated villages were unknown. Newcastleton is unusual. Situated just a few miles north of the border with England, it lies in an area that already possessed good towns and compact villages on the English model.

The Duke fulfilled everything that was expected of an aristocrat. After Eton, he and his brother went on a Grand Tour with no less a tutor than Adam Smith, the economist who would write *The Wealth of Nations* (1776). They got on well. Shortly before Smith's death in 1790, Buccleuch wrote to him: 'We have long lived in friendship, uninterrupted for one single moment since we first were acquainted.'

Back home, he put the ideas he had learnt from Smith to good use, giving leadership to a nation whose prominent figures were keen to catch up with England. He promoted manufactures, championed a canal to link the Forth and Clyde, and used his estates to underwrite the Ayr bank – and although that failed, he served as governor of the Royal Bank of Scotland from 1777 until his death in 1812. Newcastleton was part of his vision for improvement. It was intended to house handloom weavers and miners.

When Isaac Slater, compiling a commercial directory in 1852, visited, he found 'two long streets of neat houses' occupying a haugh on the right bank of the river Liddle. It seems not to have prospered as much as Buccleuch might have hoped, however, since Slater continued ominously: 'Except that a few of the inhabitants are employed by the cotton manufacturers of Carlisle, there is no other business worth mentioning.'

Of the ten weavers listed in the 1851 census, only two were described as handloom weavers. The industry had changed, which might have pleased the shade of Adam Smith, but it seems that Buccleuch came to doubt some of his precepts at the end of his life. Rather too much industry had developed in Britain for his taste. The textile mills that had grown up around Langholm, near Newcastleton, may have increased the value of his land, but they made it unattractive, 'if not disgusting', to live there. (And, after all, he did not have to. Having married the heiress of the Duke of Montagu, from whom he inherited Boughton House in Northamptonshire, he also inherited the title and estates of his cousin the Duke of Queensbury in 1810.) Newcastleton itself remained what it had been when he first built it: neat, orderly, unruffled and conservatively attached to the name it used before Newcastleton had been thought of: Copshaw Holm.

*See Letham, page 597. †See Helmsdale, page 586*

# NEWSTEAD

BORDERS                    *The Romans leave, the settlement continues*

The name of Newstead does not sound old, and is not recorded before the sixteenth century. But the settlement, unusually, can trace it roots to the Roman period, when the Ninth Legion built a camp here in AD80, protecting the crossing of the Tweed. A few years later it was strengthened. The fort took the name of Trimontium from the three peaks of the Eildon Hills, a landmark to transports in the mouth of the Tweed.

A native settlement emerged to service Trimontium. It was the sort of place that usually grew up around barracks, providing food and brothels as well as stabling, smithies and places where local tribesmen could put up when coming to pay tribute money. After twenty years, Trimontium was decommissioned, but it was brought back into use after 120, before the building of the Antonine Wall*. This time construction was on a grand scale, with a massive rampart made up of three ditches, above which was raised a two-metre-thick wall of red sandstone, probably brought by boat along the loops and meanders of the river Tweed from Dryburgh, two and a half miles away.

The new fort could house fifteen hundred men in seventeen barrack blocks. Entertainment must have been a priority in this farthest outpost of Empire, because an amphitheatre was built – the most northerly that the Romans constructed. Sometimes the soldiers seem to have buried precious objects, such as helmets, rings or pieces of horse armour, perhaps as religious offerings that would protect them in this northern clime.

The Romans left in 185; the remains of the fort were lost beneath the earth, until navvies digging the railway line between Edinburgh and Hawick rediscovered them. But the native settlement that evolved into Newstead continued. It put up the stonemasons who built Melrose Abbey in the Middle Ages. In the seventeenth century, Newstead was full of stonemasons, many of whom worked their own patches of land, acquired after the Abbey lands had been broken up. It became the site of one of Scotland's first Masonic lodges in the 1670s, admitting malt men, weavers and ostlers (innkeepers) as well as practising stonemasons. (This was officially the Melrose lodge; there was a tradition that lodges should not meet within towns.) So the village ought to be solidly built, and it is. Trimontium lasted a century; Newstead has done rather better.

*See Kinneil, page 595

# OLD DEER

*First words in Gaelic*

William Comyn, earl of Buchan, chose well when he founded the Abbey of Deer in 1219; the Cistercian monks were able to enjoy a sunny position on a south-facing slope next to South Ugie Water. The monks would in turn found the village of Old Deer, now chiefly distinguished by the beautiful arboretum that formerly belonged to the Aden estate. However, the importance of this place does not reside in the ruins of William Comyn's monastery, but in a little book, which has resided at Cambridge University since 1715, annotated by the monks of an earlier monastery. It dates from the mid tenth century. It contains the earliest written words in Gaelic.

The Celtic monastery had been founded in the sixth century. The Book of Deer was an aid to devotion, written in Latin. Passages from the Gospels are accompanied by an office for the Visitation of the Sick and the Apostles' Creed. It is not known where the book was made, but by 1100 it had come into the possession of Deer Abbey. Parchment being precious, later monks filled up odd spaces with notes of the lands granted to the Abbey, using their native Gaelic.

From the central text, the marginalia and the illustrations, we can construct a picture of life in rural Scotland before and after the first Millennium. Land holdings were enormously important: they were the basis of prestige, power and wealth. The monks, however, could not have had much contact with their rich patrons; instead, they shared the common concerns of the countryside, dominated, to judge from the illuminations, by the care of animals. The very parchment from which the book was made came from goat skin. Not that the surroundings enjoyed by the monks resembled the smoky, poorly made hovels that ordinary people shared with domestic animals, complete with unsavoury, flyblown middens near the doors. The vaulted halls, towering church and advanced hygiene arrangements must have been a source of wonder to the local population. Operating like the board of directors of a modern company, the monks ran their estates, but did not descend to manual work.

With only half a million people living in the whole of Scotland in 1000, the countryside would not have been crowded. Life expectancy was low. No wonder, then, that the Book of Deer puts an emphasis on prayers for the sick; the promise of healing had been influential in converting the Picts* to Christianity. Monasteries were centres of medicine, although medical knowledge at Deer was probably primitive in comparison to the great hospital at Soutra in Lothian (where surgery was practised, a cocktail of opium and deadly nightshade administered as anaesthetic, and watercress dispensed to counteract scurvy and loss of teeth – large quantities of human teeth have been recovered through archaeology).

Nothing of the monastic period survives, however. The present kirk was built in 1788. New Deer was founded by James Ferguson of Pitfour in 1805. Ferguson was a great founder of villages, having three others to his credit. The existence of the earlier settlement combined with the topography persuaded him to forgo a centralised plan around a square in favour of a single long street, which is nearly half a mile long.

*See Meigle, page 604

# OLDHAMSTOCKS
## LOTHIAN

*Carpenter turns piano maker*

'Sir, the noblest prospect that a Scotchman ever sees, is the high road that leads him to London.' Dr Johnson's sarcasm was insensitive to the feelings of the Scots, but it was undoubtedly true that, for many people living north of the border in the Hanoverian period, Scotland offered limited opportunities for doing well. One person who took the road to London was John Broadwood. He was born at Oldhamstocks, the son of the village wright or carpenter, in 1732.

These days, Oldhamstocks is an ambling hamlet in the beautiful Lammermuir Hills, made up of a single street and many gaps that open directly onto fields of grazing sheep. Doughy pink walls are punctuated with blocks of the dark purple stone, like currants in a bun. The name means, in Saxon, old dwelling place, and there are signs of antiquity in the white-harled kirk, a simple, late-medieval box to which the minister Thomas Hepburn added a low-built stone burial aisle, projecting from the east end, in 1581. The rest of the kirk dates from the eighteenth century, but it has never been more than a modest structure.

Oldhamstocks was bigger in the 1880s, when Francis Groome's *Ordnance Gazetteer of Scotland* was published; the village school had more than sixty pupils. For a time, coal was mined, but it was not a big seam. In 1793, the minister John Cochran noted approvingly that the farmers had started to make something of their land, clearing it of stones and rotating their crops. One of them had put up a threshing machine. Keeping pigs had greatly improved the way of life, even among poorer folk. But much of the land, particularly on the hills, was still unenclosed, giving 'the country a bleak appearance'. This was more than thirty years after Broadwood had left. In his day it must have been bleaker still.

It is said that Broadwood walked to London with only a half crown in his pocket. Probably he also took a letter of introduction from Sir John Hall of Douglass, the local laird, which enabled him to become apprentice to the harpsichord maker Burkat Shudi. Shudi, who had come to London from Switzerland at the age of sixteen, built a harpsichord for Frederick, the Prince of Wales, as well as his father George II; when Mozart visited London as a child prodigy in 1765, he played a Shudi instrument.

After eight years with Shudi, Broadwood married one of his daughters, Barbara, and jointly inherited the workshop with Shudi's son, also Burkat, on Shudi's death in 1773, running it alone from 1782. It was the age when the piano was being developed.

The earliest that came to London were square pianos; Broadwood succeeded in fitting one to a harpsichord case, in anticipation of the grand. The firm stopped making harpsichords in 1793, and became John Broadwood and Son two years later. (When another son joined it took its present name of John Broadwood and Sons in 1808.) Broadwood was a rich man when he died, after suffering a stroke when dining with his son Thomas in Great Pulteney Street, London, in 1812.

The piano's gain was Oldhamstocks's loss. But visiting this out-of-the-way settlement today, with its kirkyard watch house (built in 1824, to prevent body-snatching), you wonder how he could have left.

# ORMISTON
LOTHIAN                    *'Unfortunately he was an enthusiastic agriculturalist'*

In 1735, a farmer called Alexander Wright exhibited a turnip weighing 34¾ lb in a coffee house in Edinburgh, as a demonstration of what Scottish agriculture could do. It was evidence of the revolution being wrought by his landlord, John Cockburn of Ormiston, 'the father of Scottish husbandry' as he was called by Robert Chambers's *Biographical Dictionary of Eminent Scotsmen* (1835).

Agriculture before Cockburn's time had been at a low ebb in Scotland. Money for investment was short. Tenants were so poor that they could not buy enough animals to stock their land. Andrew Fletcher of Saltoun, writing a discourse on the affairs of Scotland in 1698, described contemporary methods of farming as being so backward that a gentleman trying to improve his estate would waste his effort. It was difficult for landowners to let farms, which they did only on short leases. But Cockburn had other ideas. As a member of the Westminster Parliament from the Act of Union in 1707 until 1741, he was often in England, and saw what was happening there. He imported some of these practices to Scotland.

The greatest innovation was to extend the length of the leases he offered to good tenants. This gave them an incentive to invest in the land. They began to enclose. Cockburn's father, the lawyer Lord Ormiston, had made people sit up by giving leases of eleven years. Cockburn gave leases of thirty-eight years. Agriculturalists from England were brought down to teach the latest thinking about turnips and the rotation of crops. The seed drill was introduced.

As Cockburn wrote in 1725, 'No person can have more satisfaction in the pros-perity of his children, than I have in the welfare of persons situated on my estate. I hate tyranny in every shape; and shall always show greater pleasure in seeing my tenants making something under me, which they can call their own, than in getting a little more money myself, by squeezing a hundred poor families, till their necessities make them slaves.' Part of his vision was to transform Ormiston from a 'mean and squalid hamlet', as Chambers described it, to a 'neat and well built street'.

Further employment was provided by a linen works. Workers in the linen business could help on the land at busy times, such as harvest. They would also provide a market for the food being produced. Accordingly, Cockburn brought over an experienced man from Ireland to establish a bleach field, the first in East Lothian; before 1730, fine linens were sent to Haarlem in Holland to be whitened and dressed. Potatoes were grown from 1734. In 1736, Cockburn instituted the Ormiston Society, where noblemen, gentlemen and farmers could discuss the latest farming developments.

Alas, Cockburn's avidity to improve agriculture ran ahead of the income he took from it. It took patience to wait for the rewards of investment to be reaped; Cockburn did not have it. In 1747, he was forced to sell the Ormiston estate to the Earl of Hopetoun. As the Victorian historian of the family wrote, 'for the interests of the family, it would have been well had he been satisfied with a political life; but unfortunately he was an enthusiastic agriculturalist'.

# PALNACKIE
## DUMFRIES AND GALLOWAY　　　　　*Celebrating the humble flounder*

'The flounder is generally the least esteemed of our flat fish,' Thomas Webster observed in *An Encyclopaedia of Domestic Economy* (1844). 'It is very abundant on our coasts . . . Great quantities of them are brought to the London market, and are sold at a cheap rate.' Whatever London may have thought of the flounder, the view was different around the coasts of Scotland, where they formed an important part of the diet. White flounder, sole flounder, spotted flounder, dab flounder, Craig flounder, maiden flounder . . . it took many shapes, all of them flat.

Other names for it were fluke or butt. Flounder, however, is suggestive: it reflects its manner of flapping along the mud at the bottom of the sea and rivers (it comes into river estuaries to breed). When not swimming, it lies on the sea-bed, its brown, mottled skin making a perfect camouflage. The coves and estuaries of Kirkcudbrightshire provide an ideal habitat, the mud rich in insects and worms.

At low tide, the Urr Water shrinks to a thin stream between elephant-backed walls of mud, but at high tide the long meander is navigable, and Palnackie, four miles from the sea, still has a harbour, used by cockle boats. It used to celebrate the traditional method of catching the fish in a Flounder Tramping championship every August. Contestants would wade, as quietly as possible, through low water, feeling the mud with their toes. If they found a flounder, they kept it under their foot, before bringing it to the surface with their hands. Elsewhere, the technique is known as flounder gigging. The championship has now become an irregular event. Locals blame lack of enthusiasm among the young, combined with a decline in the number and size of the flounders.

Thomas Webster might have thought more highly of the flounder had he known its life cycle. When juvenile, it looks like an ordinary fish, with an eye on either side of its head. As it grows, one of the eyes migrates to join the other, so that both of them can keep watch for predators – and possibly feet – when lying on the mud.

# PENNAN
## ABERDEENSHIRE
*Reflected in the silver screen*

There was no red telephone box in Pennan before the film *Local Hero* was filmed there in 1983. The telephone box is a key device in the story; the film ends with a shot of it, ringing unanswered. It had been brought in by the film-makers especially. But so many fans arrived wanting to see the original that the village installed one – just a shell at first, it was later supplied with a working telephone, at the very time when British Telecom was ripping out thousands of the familiar red boxes as part of a modernisation programme. The tale is rich in irony, but then so is the film. Written and directed by Bill Forsyth, it comes from a land where the edge of irony has been sharpened since the Enlightenment.

The film tells the story of Mac's journey from Houston, Texas, to a remote Scottish village, which his company wants to replace with an oil refinery. Mac has been chosen for the mission because his name – Macintyre – sounds Scottish, although in fact his parents were Hungarian. Arriving at the village, he opens negotiations with the local solicitor, who also runs the hotel. It is kept from Mac that the villagers would be delighted to take the *Silver Dollar*, as one of them has renamed his boat. The price goes up. The villagers discuss the merits of Rolls-Royce over Maserati.

Meanwhile, Mac falls in love with the village, stops shaving and offers to swap his highly paid job and Porsche for a position at the warm heart of this community. An obstacle to the villagers' hopes of wealth appears in the shape of Ben, an old, shack-dwelling beachcomber, who, it turns out, owns the foreshore. He has no interest in selling. The locals are about to visit Ben en masse, with no good intentions towards him, when the boss of the company, Felix Happer, arrives in a helicopter. More interested in astronomy than the oil business, he is excited by reports of the Aurora Borealis, which is displaying to spectacular effect. He hits it off with Ben. Instead of an oil refinery, he proposes to build a research establishment to study the sky and the sea. Mac goes home to the United States. It is he who makes the call to the lonely telephone box, still ringing as the credits start to roll.

The dilemma facing the villagers in *Local Hero* echoes that which has confronted many small communities in the age of globalisation. How far should the old ways – cosy but deprived, human in scale but limited in mental horizon – be kept, when joining the modern world will bring prosperity? It is the stuff of parish council debates about new housing and road improvements across Britain.

Do not look on the beach at Pennan for a real-life version of the philosophical Ben. The beach scenes were shot at Camusdarach, near Fort William on the west coast. It is, after all, only a film.

# PENPONT
DUMFRIES AND GALLOWAY

*To the Central African Lakes . . .*
*but not always back*

Joseph Thomson spent the first twenty years of his life around Penpont, where he was born in 1858. When he was ten, his father, a stonemason, moved the family to Gatelawbridge four miles away, where he had acquired a quarry. It is an area of placid water and gentle hills. Beyond the pinkish stone, which gives some of the character to Victorian Glasgow, the Gatelawbridge quarry had another interest – Robert Paterson*, the mason known familiarly as Old Mortality, who preserved the memory of Covenanters by tending and recutting their memorials, had worked there. Thomson could not wait to get away.

It was natural for a Scot to think of exploration: David Livingstone, the mission-ary who opened up the heart of Africa, had come from Blantyre, south of Glasgow. Thomson, who left school at fifteen, developed a passion for geology; he was encouraged by a local doctor, who loved science. It was when fossil hunting in the ravine of Crichope Linn that he met Professor Archibald Geikie, who persuaded him to leave the stone quarry where he was working to further his studies.

This he did at Edinburgh University, studying chemistry, botany and natural history. On leaving in 1878, he applied for a post with the Royal Geographical Society's Tanganyika expedition. To his surprise, he was appointed geologist and naturalist under Alexander Johnston. The object was to open a road between Dar es Salaam and lakes Nyasa and Tanganyika. With a hundred and twenty-five porters, the expedition duly left for the interior in 1879. After not much more than a month, Johnston died from dysentery, leaving Thomson in charge. He felt compelled to follow his destiny by going forward.

There ensued a truly epic journey, which took him, while suffering from fever, to places that were unknown to Europeans, often through hostile country. In four-teen months he covered three thousand miles. A gazelle that he shot was named after him. An even greater achievement, perhaps, was that he had not fallen out with his fellow travellers, discovering that one of the secrets of successful explora-tion was to go 'gently' and therefore 'safely'. The adventure is recounted in *To the Central African Lakes and Back*, published in two volumes in 1881, which amazed the Victorian public.

This was the start of a life dedicated to Africa. He was, he said in 1888, 'thor-oughly tired and disgusted with life in England'. But already he had suffered from serious illness, and his health would be broken irreparably on his last trip, made at the behest of Cecil Rhodes in 1890. Five years later he died aged thirty-seven, having been, in the words of his biographer Robert I. Rotberg, 'a man of action, not a student of the little known'.

*See Dunnottar, page 559

# PORT OF NESS
## LEWIS
*Hunting the guga*

'This ile is full of wild fowls,' wrote Donald Monro, High Dean of the Isles, of the island of Sula Sgeir. When the chicks of these birds were 'ripe', men from Ness on the northernmost point of Lewis would descend on them, staying there a week or so 'to fetche with thame hame their boatful of dry wild fowls with wild fowl fedderis'. This account dates from 1549, and the fearsome men of Ness still go to Sula Sgeir once a year. Their haul is guga, the young of gannets, one of the few kinds of seabird that it is possible to eat. Animal rights campaigners have expressed disapproval.

There are astonishing numbers of gulls on the islands round Britain. While farmland birds, such as the corncrake, have been pushed to the edge of extinction by changes in agriculture, seabirds have benefited from the Common Fisheries Policy of the EU, which compels fishing boats to return their by-catch (fish of non-target species) to the water, often dead. For gulls, this represents an unprecedented bonanza, and numbers have boomed.

Human ingenuity has never found much to do with them. Most cultures regard gulls as inedible (too much salt). The trade in their feathers had declined by the First World War, hastened to extinction by their ineradicable smell. On St Kilda, oil from fulmars was used in childbirth to anoint the newborn's umbilical cord. An appalling rate of infant mortality ensued. A sound of sawing and tapping accompanied a lying-in; the husband was making the coffin.

The guga, however, were worth having. Or so the Nessmen thought. They went after them with wild bravado, according to *The Statistical Account of Scotland* in 1797. 'There is in Ness a most venturous set of people who for a few years back, at the hazard of their lives, went there in an open six-oared boat without even the aid of a compass,' wrote the minister of Barvas parish, the Rev. Donald Macdonald. They could not land the boat, so some of the party stayed in it, while the others leapt onto the rock, knocking down birds with their sticks.

More recently, the pursuit has been described in *The Guga Hunters* (2008) by Donald S. Murray, a Ness native. 'To many, even in the other traditional seabird-hunting communities of the British Isles, the Nessmen and their guga hunt must seem to belong to the age of Odysseus, a throw-back to those long, hard centuries when it wasn't possible to take the car down to Tesco's, ASDA or the Co-op to fill up the boot with foodstuffs and other goods.' A special clause inserted into the Protection of Birds Act 1954 allows it to continue – at Ness and nowhere else.

# QUARRIERS VILLAGE

RENFREWSHIRE                    *Orphans get the childhood they never had*

At the age of six, William Quarrier, born in 1829, went to work in a pin factory, working ten hours a day for a shilling a week. His father, a ship's carpenter, had died three years earlier in Quebec. His mother was very poor. They lived in a part of Glasgow, off the High Street, which a government inspector described in 1835 as 'revolting' on the outside, filthy and destitute within. Later, he remembered standing, 'barefooted, bareheaded, cold and hungry, having tasted no food for a day and a half', puzzled that no passer-by should show compassion.

At eight, Quarrier was apprenticed to a shoemaker; it was a trade that he would eventually thrive in, having married the daughter of one of his bosses. He established one of the first chains of shoe shops in Glasgow. A pillar of the Baptist church, he took in the children of his sister when she died, caring for them as part of his family. Prospering, he might have put his early years behind him, but the sight of a little match-seller crying over the stock that had been stolen by an older boy touched his pity.

He started a self-help group for shoeblacks; the boys wore a uniform and put some of their earnings into a common fund. They had to attend night school and Sunday School. This was followed by other 'brigades', also with education included. In 1871, he opened a home for orphaned children in Glasgow. Five years later this beginning had matured into a village, built on forty acres of land at Bridge of Weir, outside the city.

It was planned as a series of cottage homes, each household under the eye of a 'father' and 'mother', with playgrounds attached. The fathers would teach in the school and workshop that all shared; the mothers would cook. All would go to Mount Zion church, marching there along avenues called Faith, Hope, Love, Praise and Peace. This structure was to replicate, as far as it could, that of the families that the children did not have. The village grew to have fifty cottages, each in an individual style reflecting the different donors who had helped Quarrier to realise his vision. They fitted into an overall design by Robert Bryden of the Glasgow firm Clarke and Bell, who gave his services for free.

This being Scotland, Quarrier arranged an emigration scheme to help his boys and girls start new lives. They passed through his own distribution centre in Ontario, Canada. Later the Orphan Homes were joined by a tuberculosis sanitarium and, after Quarrier's death in 1903, a centre for epileptics. The village continued in operation, much as Quarrier conceived, until the late twentieth century, when it was sold. Its buildings, including Mount Zion church, have now been converted to flats, creating a village of a different kind. But the charity itself continues, providing help for young and old with disabilities, epilepsy or housing needs through more than a hundred projects in Scotland and beyond.

# ROSEMARKIE
## HIGHLAND

*Ups and downs of a royal burgh*

Rosemarkie, aglow in pink sandstone, has the appearance of being a decent little village, with more architectural presence about it than most (there are columns to one of the nineteenth-century buildings in the main street, and the Plough Inn is striking). Actually, it is a royal burgh. There are many royal burghs, together with their lesser relations, burghs of barony, in Scotland; some grew up into flourishing towns, whereas others decayed, or never grew up at all.

The plan of a burgh of barony was laid out at Penkill in Ayrshire; a pole was stuck into the ground to mark the position of the mercat cross, but no settlers could be tempted to move there, and not a single house was built. By founding burghs, with their rights to hold markets and courts of justice, charge tolls and (in the case of royal burghs) trade overseas, it was hoped to stimulate trade. It says something for Scotland's impoverished condition that attempts were being made to establish burghs into the seventeenth century, after England and the rest of Europe were already well provided with prosperous centres. Like Rosemarkie, many are now villages, having failed.

Rosemarkie's case was unusual; immediately next door was another royal burgh, Fortrose. Already described as 'a very ancient town' by Bishop Leslie in 1578, Rosemarkie may date from the sixth century, and at least fifteen Pictish stones have been found in the vicinity. In the early twelfth century it became the seat of the Bishop of Ross. At one point it possessed a school of law.

*Rosemarkie lighthouse: from this rocky headland you
can spot porpoises, dolphins and whales.*

By 1590, however, both Rosemarkie and Fortrose were struggling, with the result that they merged. The union was confirmed by an Act of Parliament in 1661, which suggested that Rosemarkie was the under partner, 'now totallie decayed'. Nothing by way of trade had happened 'this many yeires agoe', no tolls collected, no justice dispensed. Fortrose had also had its misfortunes: Cromwell's troops had ruined the cathedral, transferred there from Rosemarkie, using the stone to build a fort at Inverness – just one aisle and the chapter house remains.

Neither got much of a write-up from Robert Chambers's *The Picture of Scotland* (1827), Rosemarkie having sunk to the condition of a 'miserable' village, while Fortrose, once a seat of learning, now possessed only a 'very inconsiderable' grammar school. Like distinguished but decrepit old ladies, they awaited the smelling salts of golf and a branch line of the Highland Railway to revive them.

The story of Rosemarkie has a parallel in many old Scottish villages. There were few of the kind familiar in England – cottages clustered around church or green, with a few gentry residences to keep an eye on the rest – before Scottish landowners replanned their estates in the eighteenth century. North of the Border, what seem to be ancient villages are for the most part technically burghs.

# ST MONANS
FIFE                                     *Fresh from the games of English school life, he fell*

There is only one memorial in the great, cliff-top church of St Monans, built by King David II as a thanks offering in the 1360s (his prayers to St Monan, an Irish missionary killed by the Danes in the ninth century, had either helped extract an arrow from a wound or saved him from a storm at sea). The memorial is a poignant composition, made of a military standard, a soldier's hat and a sabre, set in a Gothic frame and surmounting an inscription describing the 'early but glorious death' of 2nd Lieutenant Henry Anstruther of the Royal Welsh Fusiliers.

Anstruther fell at the Battle of Alma in the Crimea in 1854. His company had been attacking a Russian gun emplacement, when the young man – not much older than a boy – ran forward with the regimental colours in his hand. As A. W. Kinglake described in his history of the Crimean War, 'Fresh from the games of English school-life, he ran fast; for, heading all who strove to keep up with him, he gained the redoubt, and dug the butt-end of the flagstaff into the parapet; and there for a moment he stood, holding it tight, and taking breath. Then he was shot dead; but his small hands, still clasping the flagstaff, drew it down along with him, and the crimson silk lay covering the boy with its folds.'

A memorial that might have stood in the churchyard is instead in King's Lynn, Norfolk. By 1875, thirty boats from St Monans and scores from other ports on the East Neuk of Fife were going south to fish for herring off Great Yarmouth and Lowestoft. The men who sailed in them were a hardy breed, because the wooden boats had little covering. That November, a storm blew up just as the fleet was returning home. The St Monans boat *Quest* foundered off the Suffolk coast, with the loss of all seven crew. The *Beautiful Star*, also from St Monans, was found, swamped, by a steamer and towed to King's Lynn; five of the crew were drowned, two missing and the skipper had a fractured skull. The mast of the *Thane*, a third St Monans boat, was spotted by a Trinity House cutter: it must have collided with a steamer, which cut through the hull. The crew had been lost to the sea.

In addition, two boats from nearby Cellardyke, the *Vigilant* and the *Janet Anderson*, also foundered, all hands being drowned. Altogether the villages had lost thirty-five men. The toll may not have been quite as great as those recorded on the memorials erected after the First World War, but coming as a single blow, the effect on these little communities must have been terrible.

War and fishing: traditional Scottish pursuits followed by country people in preference to emigration. Both required bravery on the part of those who took them up, and resignation in those left behind.

# SORN
## AYRSHIRE
*Last of the Covenant martyrs*

Sorn is, in its older part, an unexpectedly comely village to find in the Ayrshire coalfields. With its high-arched bridge and stone pointing the way to local villages, it is leafy and tranquil. But a crudely lettered tablet in the graveyard shows that it was not always peaceful:

> HeRE LYeS GORG
> WOOD WHO WAS SHOT
> AT TINKHORNHILL BY BL
> OODY JOHN ReiD TRVPeR
> FOR HIS ADHeRANCE TO
> THE WORD OF GOD AND
> THE COVeNANTeD VORK
> OF ReFORMATION 1688.

George Wood was only sixteen when he was 'martyred' during the Killing Time, when covenanting was mercilessly suppressed by the Stuart monarchy. The boy was the last of the Covenanters to be killed before the Protestant William III claimed the throne from James II, putting an end to religious persecution with the Act of Toleration in 1689.

The Scottish National Covenant had been drawn up in 1638 to protect the purity of the Kirk from state interference. The year before, Charles I had outraged Calvinist opinion by imposing an Episcopal Book of Common Prayer on Scotland, in an attempt to bring the Scottish and English churches closer together. Although the Covenant emphasised Scotland's loyalty to the King, it rejected him as the religious head of the kingdom. The clash resulted in the Bishops' Wars of 1638 and 1639, during which the King personally led his badly prepared troops north of the Border. The outcome was inconclusive, but the league that Scottish Covenanters subsequently made with Parliamentary forces contributed to the King's defeat during the Civil War.

After the Restoration of Charles II in 1660, the Stuart monarch (although he had signed the Covenant to obtain Scots' support in 1651) avenged his father through an even more bitter campaign of persecution. It has been estimated that eighteen thousand Covenanters died. Some were slaughtered when their ramshackle forces were confronted by a professional army at Rullion Green and elsewhere. Others were shot simply for attending services, or being suspected of the wrong sympathies. One of them was George Wood.

Sorn was likely to be a flashpoint. It had been the birthplace of the revered orator Alexander Peden, who travelled Scotland preaching in fields after being denied a pulpit, until his death, harried for his faith, in 1686. For some time before his death he had been living near Sorn, in a cave on the banks of the Ayr. The curate imposed on Sorn kirk was not popular. A mile outside Sorn is Daldilling, home of 'bloody Reid of Daldilling', a fanatical local gentleman; according to James Gibson's *Inscriptions on the Tombstones and Monuments Erected in Memory of the Covenanters* (1881), 'The site of his castle is still pointed out to the curious, as also the spot where his victims were hanged.'

Wood was shot by a trooper, without so much as being accused. 'The murderer, on being challenged for what he had done, replied he knew him "to be one of the Whigs, and they ought to be shot wherever they were found".'

*See also Dunnottar, page 559*

# STROMNESS
## ORKNEY
*A poet's world*

Apologies to Stromness. It is the second town in Orkney, and although the population numbers little more than two thousand – barely that of a large village in southern England – I acknowledge its urbanity and hope that it will forgive its inclusion this book. For its intimacy is that of a village. 'I heard somebody had arrived,' said the Orkney poet George Mackay Brown when fellow writer Ronald Blythe appeared completely unannounced. A stranger had been spotted reading a book in the pub. Word had got round by the time Blythe met him the next day.

Sir Walter Scott did not care for 'little dirty straggling' Stromness in 1814, he and his friends parading the mile-long principal street 'like turkeys in a string', inconvenienced by the stairs (now gone) that prevented carts, or even horses, from getting along it. But he recognised it as a place of legend, to judge from his visit

to 'an old hag', who lived in an upper part of the town, and subsisted 'by selling winds'. Given sixpence, this wrinkled crone, 'dried up like a mummy', would boil her kettle and procure favourable breezes for ship's captains.

Brown went further. The place became its own world of sound and myth: Hamnavoe, as he called it, beyond conventional time. Brown's Stromness is to be found partly in a fishing port overlooking Hoy Sound, partly, like James Joyce's Dublin and Thomas Hardy's Wessex, in the geography of the imagination.

Brown had been, as he wrote in his autobiography, 'the last child of a poor family'. By trade, his father, John Brown, was a tailor; but in an age of mass-produced clothing there was little demand for his needle, and so he became a postman, setting off on his round after sorting the mail, which arrived each after-noon by the mail steamer *St Ola*. 'I have one image of him, on what must have been a night of winter storm, coming into our kitchen-living room at Clouston's pier, the rain streaming off him. He had possibly come in to trim the lantern that every postman had, pinned to the lapel of the overcoat, to read the names and addresses on winter nights. Then he went once more into the tempest.' In his poem 'Hamnavoe', Brown described the 'gay poverty that kept / My seapink innocence / From the worm and black wind.'

Famously, Brown rarely left Orkney. A shy but funny man, who was a brilliant mimic, he lived modestly, in a council flat. There he would 'interrogate silence', as the coal fire burnt, winter and summer, in the grate, a ballpoint waiting beside a writing pad for when the words came. The horizons were narrow enough physi-cally. But he was more than an Orkney poet; he gave Orkney, strained through the filter of his imagination, rendered timeless and universal, to the world.

# STRONTIAN
## ARGYLL AND BUTE

*Discovering strontium*

Since the eighteenth century, Strontian has spun a living out of its guts – those contained in the great maw that takes the form of a hill behind the village, on the shores of Loch Stuart. Minerals abound in this outcrop: galena, sphalerite, pyrite, quartz, calcite and the rare harmotome and heulandite, some of them in the form of pretty crystals, formed when the earth's magma – later cooling to form granite – burst into layers of other rock millions of years ago. Brewsterite was discovered here. Strontian gave its name to strontianite. Half a dozen chemists, from William Cruikshank in 1787 to Humphry Davy in 1808 claim the credit for discovering the element strontium, which exists in it. We have strontium to thank for some of the most impres-sive flashes in firework displays, as well as the picture tubes for colour television sets.

None of this would have meant much to the speculators who brought industry to Strontian in the eighteenth century. They were only interested in the metal that could be extracted from the galena: lead.

Lead mines were opened in 1722. Among the (English) investors who hoped to make a profit from them were the Duke of Norfolk and General Wade*. The latter, born in Ireland, spent his summers in the Highlands, supervising the military roads of which he had charge. His involvement was providential: he was able to detail off a detachment of twenty soldiers to guard the mineworkers, who were experiencing that particular form of Highland hospitality that consists of stealing cattle, throwing sheep over cliffs and torching buildings.

It was in the lead mines that strontianite appeared, a fibrous lump of a yellowish, whitish or greenish colour. Although the element conferred a degree of fame on Strontian, at least among chemists, the mine workings also left their mark. Behind the village lies a kind of post-industrial moonscape in contrast to anything else in this land of spongy greenness and forests.

By the nineteenth century, lead's heyday was over. But the miners returned during the 1980s to extract barite from opencast mines. It was needed for lubricants used on North Sea oil rigs. Now the mountains yield only stone for road building, but who knows what will be dragged out of them in the future. Brewsterite is one of a group of minerals used as an environmentally friendly ingredient in washing powder: the miners could well be back.

*See Aberfeldy, page 522

# SWANSTON
LOTHIAN                      *Robert Louis Stevenson gets his sense of adventure*

Robert Louis Stevenson spent his late teenage summers at Swanston, five miles from Edinburgh, where his father, Thomas, took a lease on Swanston Cottage from 1867 until 1880. Swanston was – and, as a rare survival, remains – a fermtoun.

The fermtoun was the characteristic form of settlement in the Lowlands before landowners built planned villages in the eighteenth century, an equivalent of the Highland clachan*. Land in Scotland was on the whole too poor to support the kind of centralised villages that developed in England. Instead, the rural population lived in scattered hamlets, all the families of which – between six and a dozen – would generally share in the common tenancy by which they had clubbed together to rent a farm.

Outwardly, there appears to be little rhyme or reason to the planning of a fermtoun; the Swanston houses are a jumble. Randomness was compounded by the habit of rebuilding houses at frequent intervals, often on adjacent sites: early structures, made of wood, were too flimsy to last long, there being little financial incentive for the farmers to make much of them. The Swanston houses seen now, perhaps dating from the seventeenth century, have stone walls; what would have been thatched roofs have been replaced with slate.

This settlement pattern has its parallel in other poor areas of Europe, such as the South-West of England, Ireland and Brittany. In Scotland, one of the fermtouns

would be dignified by possessing the kirk (it might then become the kirktoun). But this did not suggest that it was necessarily more important than its neighbours. Sometimes the kirk stood in an isolated position, away from any one settlement but convenient for all. Poor cottars, who could not afford to keep animals but hired out their labour, might scratch a living in a fermtoun; otherwise they banded together in their own communities, providing services to farmers: these settlements are commemorated in the place name 'Cottoun'.

Stevenson, whose imagination transposed Swanston Cottage into his novel *St Ives*, where it became the home of the heroine, described Swanston in *Edinburgh: Picturesque Notes* (1878): 'Upon the main slope of the Pentlands . . . a bouquet of old trees stands round a white farmhouse; and from a neighbouring dell you can see smoke rising and leaves rustling in the breeze. Straight above the hills climb a thousand feet into the air. The neighbourhood, about the time of the lambs, is clamorous with the bleating of flocks; and you will be awakened in the grey of early summer mornings by the barking of a dog, or the voice of a shepherd shouting to the echoes. This, with the hamlet lying behind unseen, is Swanston.'

Springs rose there, and the Edinburgh authorities bought the land around them, building a water house and pipes. They then turned the dell into a pleasure garden. Swanston Cottage stood in its midst, 'a little quaint place of many roughcast gables, and grey roofs', as Stevenson recreated it in *St Ives*, with 'something of the air of a rambling infinitesimal cathedral . . . grotesquely decorated with crockets and gargoyles, ravished from some medieval church'. (In fact, the crockets and gargoyles came from St Giles's Cathedral when it was being restored.)

When renovated around 1960, the hamlet's original ten cottages were made into seven.

*See Auchindrain, page 530

# TARBERT
## HARRIS                                    *Lady Dunmore likes tweed*

Tarbert is one of the chief villages on Harris and Lewis where Harris Tweed is woven. Famously, the cloth is so hard wearing that it lasts forever, and the story of its production is one of similar endurance. The industry today is a rare survival of hand-weaving on cottage looms, an echo of a past before factories came to dominate production in the nineteenth century – and long before most textile production moved to the Far East in the twentieth. Two philanthropists saw the importance of weaving to the island economy. Their legacy teeters occasionally, yet steadfastly refuses to collapse.

The word 'tweed' was coined in the 1830s, apparently as the result of a London tailor misreading the word tweel, meaning a type of cloth. It was therefore on hand in time for the discovery of Scotland as a sporting destination, its popularity boosted by Queen Victoria and the Prince Consort's devotion to Balmoral. Rough, weatherproof clothing was required by men who spent most of their days fishing and stalking and the remaining hours knocking about poorly heated country houses.

Harris and Lewis (one island, but two names) was owned by the 6th Earl of Dunmore's estate. On his death in 1845, his widow, Catherine, daughter of the 11th Earl of Pembroke, inherited it. The next year saw the potato famine that brought as much suffering to the Highlands of Scotland as it did to Ireland. Like other landowners, she initially saw emigration as a way to relieve distress, and offered to help anyone who took this route. The islanders chose not to.

Nothing daunted, Lady Dunmore set about boosting the economy by supporting weaving. She admired the high quality of the cloth, having ordered a quantity in the Murray tartan to be worn by her gamekeepers and ghillies. Now she set about promoting it to her friends. Being entirely home produced, the cloth was uneven in quality. This was overcome by sending some Harris women to train in Alloa near Stirling, and developing new dyes. By the time of Lady Dunmore's death in 1886, Harris tweed had an established reputation and market.

After the Trades Mark Act was passed in 1905, Harris Tweed was registered as a trademark. The Harris Tweed Association Ltd was formed to authenticate the product. Towards the end of the First World War, the redoubtable and compulsive acquirer of property Lord Leverhulme* bought Lewis, then Harris. Although now in his late sixties, he could not help reorganising his fiefdom – or trying to. The people of Lewis were resistant; Harris, however, was more receptive, and one settlement went so far as to change its name to Leverburgh. He established Mac Fisheries to market fish; he also caused controversy among the weavers by introducing a new loom, the Hattersley.

Hattersleys, as well as the more traditional wooden looms, remained in use, although at the end of the twentieth century it was realised that few garment makers could cope with the eccentrically narrow widths of cloth that they produced. From 1996, the double-width Bonas-Griffith loom was introduced. It makes softer, lighter cloth, which helps to combat Harris Tweed's reputation for hairy indestructibility.

One of the virtues of weaving to the island community is that it can be combined with crofting; the cottage weaver can adjust his hours to suit himself (because of the weight of the old looms, it is generally done by men). Tarbert, founded for fishing in 1779, also has a dual identity, being both the main port and the capital of Harris; its population, however, remains at five hundred.

*See Thornton Hough, page 397

# TAYNUILT

*A Scottish tribute to Nelson*

As Admiral Lord Nelson lay dying on the orlop deck of HMS *Victory* in 1805, he was tended by the ship's surgeon, William Beatty. Beatty was a Scot. In this he was typical of the military and naval doctors of the time, most of whom came from villages and small towns in Scotland and Ireland – situations where it would have been difficult to build up a conventional practice. While the contribution that Scotland made to Wellington's army cannot be easily overlooked – think of the charge of the Scots Greys at Waterloo – the Scottish component of Nelson's navy is not always so obvious. But there were plenty of Scots in the service. Sixty-four were listed as being on *Victory* four days before Trafalgar.

Scots were even more substantially represented among high-ranking officers, with Admiral Lord Duncan, the hero of Camperdown, and Admiral Lord Keith, at one point Nelson's commander-in-chief, being among them. The words of Rule, Britannia were written by a Scot, James Thomson*. These links no doubt explain why Scotland was quick off the mark in commemorating the victory at Trafalgar. Glasgow erected a monument in the shape of a 44-metre-tall obelisk in 1806 (the top section crashed to the ground when it was struck by lightning in 1810 – an event depicted in a watercolour by John Knox, which is in the Burrell Collection in Glasgow). The remote village of Taynuilt, near Oban, moved even more quickly. A granite monolith was raised here in 1805.

There was a direct connection between this area and the battle that had taken place. In 1753, a group of ironmasters from the Lake District had established an ironworks at Bonawe. The trees in the Lakes had already been cut down to make charcoal for smelting; it made economic sense to ship haematite ore to Argyll to smelt it using locally made charcoal, then transport the iron back again. The Bonawe works supplied forty-two thousand cannonballs to the ordnance at Woolwich, some of them being fired at Trafalgar. You can still see the lade that brought water to the waterwheel, the charcoal and ore sheds, as well as the cottages that housed some of the six hundred workers.

The Scottish scholar John Stuart Blackie wrote a sonnet to Taynuilt's Nelson monument:

> . . . but this rude stone,
> Perched in his unhewn ruggedness alone,
> Stands, a stout witness of heroic will

Rude it may have been: it was formerly a standing stone – possibly one of a circle – that was lying prone a mile away. The workmen of Bonawe hauled it into position.

*See Ednam, page 563. See also Furnace, page 479

# THE BRAES

ISLE OF SKYE                    *Saving a way of life – by force*

A cairn beside a quiet road on the misty east coast of Skye marks the spot at which the Battle of the Braes was fought in April 1882. It was not much of a battle. Nobody was killed, and the opposing forces were armed only with batons on one side, projectiles and farm implements on the other. But it would lead to a new dispensation for crofters, giving them the security of tenure that their predecessors had so woefully lacked during the Clearances four decades earlier.

A croft was not enough to support a family by itself. It was left to the wives to look after the sheep, the pig, the cow and the potato patch. During the summer months, the men worked with the fishing fleet that followed the herring around Scotland. Hardship drove these families to make a stand. Without being pushed to the brink of starvation, they would not have dared to oppose the awesome factors, who had the power to turn them out of their crofts and make them homeless with little notice. But 1881 was a harsh year for the Hebrides: the harvest failed, the fishing season was a disaster and the agricultural depression meant that little work was to be had in the Lowlands. At the same time, Lord MacDonald, their landlord, was pushing to increase rents. Hostilities opened over the right to graze sheep on Ben Lee, removed from the crofters during the Clearances.

It may have been that some of the men on Skye had absorbed ideas from Ireland while fishing along the coast. Agitation there had caused Gladstone to pass the second Irish Land Act in 1881. They may also have been inflamed by the campaign for land reform mounted by urban radicals. As in Ireland, they began to withhold rent. When a force of fifty policemen arrived to evict the ringleaders, hundreds of crofters from the area set off in pursuit, hurling stones from the cliffs onto the roadway that the policemen had taken. Lurid newspaper coverage made the blood of the establishment run cold. More trouble flared up on Lewis, then elsewhere on Skye. Fences were pulled down, hayricks set ablaze. The rent strike spread across the island.

The government responded by setting up a commission under Lord Napier. If it had expected a whitewash, it was wrong. The Highlanders faced, the report said, 'a state of misery, of wrong-doing, and of patient long-suffering, without parallel in the history of our country'. That in itself did not quell the unrest, which, by the autumn of 1884, had spread throughout the Highlands. The laird-favouring organ *The Scotsman* thundered against men who were 'taking what does not belong to them . . . setting law at defiance, and . . . instituting a terrorism which the poor people are unable to resist'.

For the first time since the Jacobite rebellions, the government dispatched an expeditionary force to the Highlands and Islands, in the shape of four hundred marines. But in Parliament, the weakness of the Liberal majority gave pro land-reform MPs the power to bargain. A Crofters Act was passed in 1886, setting up a Land Court to fix fair rents and establishing security of tenure. A way of life had been saved.

# TOBERMORY

MULL                                                    *One of the best of the new fishing villages*

Let us give thanks to the British Society for Extending the Fisheries and Improving the Sea Coasts of the Kingdom. It gave us Tobermory, that most charming of harbours, nestled among a village of brightly painted houses. The village was planned in 1787 as part of a semi-philanthropic drive to encourage the development of fishing in the Highlands. In other ventures, the Society was not a success; it had hoped to attract as many as two hundred thousand settlers to thirty or forty settlements, but those plans were quickly abandoned. Of those villages that were built, Lochbay on Skye languished, not least because the rents asked for cottages were too much for ordinary Highlanders to afford. Ullapool, now a town, only got going after the Society had been forgotten.

Tobermory, however, survives as the cheerful proof that the Society's optimism was not entirely unfounded. It may have been far from the fishing grounds, and lacking in a sufficient hinterland to make it thrive as a commercial centre, but as a village – the largest on Mull – it became quickly established and continues to work well, even though the fishing industry has largely departed.

Tobermory sits on a gently curving bay; Dr Johnson noted that it 'appears to an unexperienced eye formed for the security of ships'. Until the British Fisheries Society arrived, Tobermory's fishermen had used the stern of an Armada galleon, the *Florida*, which sank in 1588, as a romantic, if not wholly practical staircase to the landing place. In 1788, however, the British Fisheries Society built a pier. A street of shops was run up alongside the bay, another street of houses behind it. By 1793, the population had risen to three hundred.

When the committee of the British Fisheries Society came to inspect in 1786, Mull could offer little more than it had in 1688: a 'Change-House (so they call a House of Entertainment) if a place that had neither Bed, Victuals or Drink, may be allow'd that name'. The author of that account, William Sacheverell, had spent a night on a bed of fern. Fifteen years after Dr Johnson's visit, the architect and engineer Robert Mylne built an inn, as well as a Custom House in 1789–90.

'Romantic is the term we would apply to the appearance of this town,' William Craig Maxwell observed in *Iona and the Ionians* (1857), 'the houses rising in a succession of terraces from the margin of the sea. Its bay may be said to be unequalled in Scotland, and by many it has even been compared to the world-renowned Bay of Naples.'

# TOMINTOUL

*Highest village in the Highlands*

A ballard called 'The Lass o' the Lecht' commemorates the night in 1860 when Margaret Cruikshank, a 'blooming lass in her eighteenth year', failed to find her way home to Corgarff. She had been in domestic service. The son of the house took her a mile or two on her way, and when he left her, the weather was fair. But a sudden storm blew up. Blinded by snow, the lass missed her turning, stumbled onto the moor, and – despite a search that lasted several months and six stanzas – her body was not found until a shepherd boy came on it in the spring. Corgarff lies on the road to Tomintoul, where snowdrifts are still a common feature of winter. Tomintoul is the highest village in the Highlands.

The place owes its existence to the 4th Duke of Gordon. Before 1776, the inhabitants of Kirkmichael, the parish within which Tomintoul was created, had been scattered, on the traditional Highland pattern. This seemed inefficient to the improving mentality of the age. If the population could be concentrated, there was more chance that industry would develop, and with it, commerce; both developments stood to increase the Duke's revenues.

In 1754, a military road had been built as part of the Hanoverian policy of opening up the Highlands following the 1745 rebellion. The surveyor Thomas Milne inspected the site and found it to be promising, noting on a plan of the clachan, which preceded the village: 'Dry Moor Ground of a hazley soil lying level having a gentle rising, a fit subject for Improvement and a proper Stead for a Stagehouse or Village.'

Plots were accordingly laid out, on a grid plan focused on a central square. School and kirk were relocated. Villagers were given land to work, some of it on the muir, or moor, which they could bring under cultivation. The settlement was intended to thrive on growing flax and spinning linen yarn, the principles of which had been introduced some time before. A lint mill, where the woody outer casing of the flax would be removed, was built; a bleach field, for whitening linen, was made; a spinning school established.

The Duke himself lent his substantial weight to the proceedings, by lodging at one of the Tomintoul inns during the shooting season. But the village never became what he had hoped for it. Skills were scarce in the Highlands; so were raw materials. Besides, transport was an extra cost, which tended to prevent industry from developing.

So Tomintoul had to rely on agriculture, not industry, for its livelihood. It did, however, develop with time. It succeeded in making a second living from the scenery. The Duke of Gordon's instincts had been right when he stayed at the inn. Tourism, fortified with a little Glenlivet whisky, would be the future.

# TURNBERRY

## AYRSHIRE

*Wonder-working powers of golf*

To the Hanoverians, Scotland meant Jacobites. To the Victorians, it spoke of tartan. To the Edwardians, it was golf. The Scots had been playing golf since the fifteenth century. Only in the late Victorian period was it taken up widely south of the Border, where the booming middle class welcomed a gentle game that could be played without dangerous horses or rough teams. The principal Edwardian prime ministers, Arthur Balfour and Herbert Henry Asquith, were both golfers. Turnberry was one of a number of Scottish courses made over for the railway age.

Or, to be more specific, the railway hotel age. Grand luxury hotels, often built by railway companies, appeared throughout Scotland in the years around 1900. Many were in cities, such as the first of the breed, the Station Hotel in Inverness, opened in 1878 and owned by the Highland Railway. Edinburgh acquired the cliff-like North British Hotel in 1902 and the flamboyant Caledonian Hotel in 1903. But watering holes of this stamp also appeared in would-be tourist destinations, offering a range of sporting possibilities (fishing and hunting, as well as golf), together with electric lights, lifts and opulent cuisine (hotel restaurants were one of the few places where men and women could dine together respectably in public).

The Turnberry Station Hotel opened in 1906. Designed by the architect James Miller, who created a number of railway stations, it is spread out along a terrace as though it were a super-sized country house, its red roof broken by pediments, gables and chimney stacks. Rail travel to Turnberry had been made possible in 1905, when a special railway line was built between Alloway and Girvan. (The line closed in 1942 and the station roof went to cover a terrace at Dunbarton Football Club's old Boghead Park ground.)

There were two courses at Turnberry when it opened, one of them a specially designed links course in which the sea itself formed a hazard. This was a new definition of the outdoors for prosperous visitors to Scotland. Sportsmen had always gathered on northbound London railway platforms around 12 August (the start of the grouse-shooting season). But Scotland's great draw for the Victorian tourist was its scenery and historic sites.

Health and recreation came to the fore towards the end of the nineteenth century, the trend being personified by Peggy, a modern young woman in *The Epistles of Peggy*, published by the North British Railway in 1910. After playing golf and tennis, fishing, swimming and going for mountain walks, she could report – to what would have been the horror of any well-brought-up Victorian young lady – that she was as brown as a fillet. In the 1830s, Beriah Botfield had considered it necessary to explain the rules of golf in *Journal of a Tour Through the Highlands of Scotland*. There was no such necessity in 1906.

Not that the Station Hotel's progress through the twentieth century would be untroubled. In the First World War it became an officers' mess, for Canadians who were training as pilots. During the Second World War, even the hallowed courses were sacrificed to the great national need, when they became airfields. By 1977, when the Ailsa course hosted its first Open Championship, it had been restored.

The hotel has spawned a community where one did not exist before, with a market in luxury apartments (within the hotel) and more modest bungalows outside.

# TYNDRUM

## PERTH AND KINROSS

*Up, hardy Mountaineer!*

'Descended upon the whole, I believe very considerably, in our way to Tyndrum,' wrote Dorothy Wordsworth in her journal, making a walking tour of Scotland with her brother in 1803; 'but it was a road of long ups and downs, over hill and through hollows of uncultivated ground; a chance farm perhaps once in three miles . . .'. It was, in addition, raining. This inspired William Wordsworth to write his sonnet 'Suggested at Tyndrum in a Storm', comparing British swains with their Arcadian equivalent: rugged crags and mountain torrents had shaped the sensibility of the former, putting them in communion with the superhuman forces of Nature.

> Up, hardy Mountaineer!
> And guide the Bard, ambitious to be One
> Of Nature's privy council, as thou art,
> On cloud-sequestered heights, that see and hear
> To what dread Powers He delegates his part
> On earth, who works in the heaven of heavens, alone.

More prosaically, they found the inn at Tyndrum to be better than the reports they had had of it. 'We had a moorfowl and mutton-chops for dinner, well cooked, and a reasonable charge. The house was clean for a Scotch inn, and the people about the doors were well dressed.' Which goes some way to dispel the impression given by another traveller, who wrote of the inn's 'unspeakable badness and dirt'.

Tyndrum was used to catering. It was a crossroads. What is now the A82 from Glasgow carries on northwards to Fort William, while the A85 branches off to Oban and Inveraray (see page 589). The Wordsworths had come on foot, but it could also be reached by coach. Later, it acquired the distinction of two railway stations, reflecting its status, once again, as a crossing point. One station served the West Highland Railway heading to Fort William, the other the Callander and Oban Railway. Physically they are separated by only a few hundred yards, but the route would take ten miles by rail. On some maps, Tyndrum was marked in bigger letters than Edinburgh.

'At Tyndrum the first pulse of human life is felt,' Hugh MacMillan wrote in a guidebook of 1901. No doubt he sank with gratitude into the 'large hotel', which rose above the cottages, mean and thatched, built to house the lead miners (later, gold prospectors) that had been the settlement's original inhabitants. It was still an awesome spot. MacMillan noted the 'little church standing by itself', presumably the one to St Fillan, survivor of a monastery established by Robert the Bruce out of gratitude for St Fillan's arm, one of the relics carried before him into battle at Bannockburn. (Even in 1901, two hundred lunatics would come every year to be immersed in St Fillan's pool. It had previously been the practice to tie them up afterwards and leave them overnight on the site of a former church; others would have the bell of St Fillan placed on their heads.)

'But these human features only accentuate the loneliness,' MacMillan continued. 'The gigantic scenery around, and the universal stillness, seem to swallow them up and to make them parts of the great overwhelming realm of nature.' You can bet he had read Wordsworth.

# WANLOCKHEAD
## DUMFRIES AND GALLOWAY       *Wild West? Those men could read*

Even today Wanlockhead gives the impression of being a shanty town, the kind that might have emerged from the Californian gold rush if that had taken place amid the Duke of Buccleuch's grouse moors in the windy Lowther Hills. At 467 metres, it is the highest village in Scotland, and grew up from the pursuit of minerals. Terraces, stone-built to stop them being thrown away, have been scattered about the hilly site. The reason why men created this place is indicated by the name of the neighbouring village: Leadhills. There are so many minerals in the Lowther Hills that the area was known as God's Treasure House, but lead was the most fully exploited.

*The Leadhills and Wanlockhead Railway: the two-foot-gauge track, laid in the 1980s, replaces a line that was built to serve the lead mines.*

Wanlockhead and Leadhills were established by different companies – the Quaker Company (as the London Lead Company was generally known here)* at the former, the Scotch Mining Company at the latter – to develop different parts of the same lead field. It was arduous work. 'The labour of the miners is severe and unremitting. Through night and day it is continued; one class relieving another by turns,' the traveller Robert Heron commented in 1793. The miners were famously a tough lot, prone to militancy when not mollified by the paternalism of their employers.

This being Scotland, even these hard men were literate. In 1842, the Royal Commission on the Employment of Children found that even the poorest of the Leadhills miners, who slept on heather mattresses, owned a few books. Libraries were highly valued. An English sportsman who visited a mine on Ben Cruachan, Argyll, in 1784 found that the men spent half their wages on books for the library 'for their amusement in this sequestered situation'. During the Victorian period, the miners at Leadhills and Wanlockhead were thought of as intelligent and sober individuals. They tended smallholdings, while their wives could embroider muslin.

The air was clear at this altitude. But it was nevertheless an unhealthy occupation. When the natural historian Thomas Pennant visited in 1769, he noticed that a dire form of lead poisoning known as 'lead-brash' was common; miners and smelters would suffer 'palsies and sometimes madness, terminating in death in about ten days'. This was eliminated during the nineteenth century, but pulmonary disease was still rife. Miners worked in a cloud of particles from blasted rock and lead ore, their feet up to the ankles in water, their clothes damp from dripping roofs. 'Few of the miners live long,' a visitor to Wanlockhead observed in 1845.

They rested in cottages that were deplored by the investigator for the Children's Commission in 1841: 'The principal apartment serves both as bedroom, sitting room and kitchen, an arrangement inimical to cleanliness and only of advantage bearing in mind the wretched climate and the cost of fuel.' Often cottages were built into hillsides for greater insulation. It was somewhat different from the accommodation of the Hope family, which owned the land. They built Hopetoun House on the profits.

*See Nenthead, page 393

# WEST CALDER
## LOTHIAN
*Paraffin Young makes a mess of West Lothian*

Born in 1811, James Young was the son of a Glasgow carpenter. The next few decades would see his home city reinvent itself, as cotton stalled and Scotland began to produce large volumes of pig iron; this would be converted into the railway locomotives, rolling stock, ships' engines and shipping that made Glasgow the industrial capital of the Empire.

Young's story was different. It was based on science, his knowledge of which was acquired when he started to attend evening lectures at Anderson's University, aged nineteen. By the age of twenty-six, he had left with his professor, Thomas Graham, to work at University College in London, but he did not stay long in academe. Having married, he needed more money. This led him to work for various chemical businesses, producing ammonia, making the vivid dyes that Victorian women loved for their clothes, and extracting valuable minerals from stone.

In 1847, he started a small refinery in Derbyshire to process the petroleum that had started to bubble out of some mine workings. It seemed to him, wrongly, that this oil was a product of the coal surrounding it, and he therefore started to see what would come out of coal if it was heated in a retort. He investigated various types of coal and coal-like substances, taking out a patent on the process he evolved in 1850.

Torbanite was the most promising material. Unlike coal, formed from vegetable matter decomposing in swamps, torbanite, or boghead coal as it was popularly known, seems to have been made from the algae and fungi in lakes. A source was found in the Bathgate coalfields between Glasgow and Edinburgh. When distilled, it yielded naphtha, used as a solvent, and different lubricating oils – the residue became black tar for sealing roads.

But the most profitable oil to emerge was paraffin. Paraffin was valuable for lighting – an improvement on colza oil, similar to rapeseed oil, which had lit early Victorian drawing rooms, because it burnt cleanly and without smell. Even more welcome was paraffin wax. Until it appeared, candles were made either from beeswax (expensive) or tallow (smelly, dirty and fast burning). Paraffin made Young's fortune, and gave him a nickname: Paraffin Young. When the torbanite gave out, the same process was applied to the oil shales around the village of West Calder.

By 1870, Darwinianly bald and long-bearded, Young withdrew from business to spend the last thirteen years of his life pursuing his scientific interests, both theoretical (the velocity of light) and practical (electric light, the telephone, the Channel tunnel). He endowed a chair of chemistry and built a laboratory at Anderson's University. Honours rolled in. He helped finance his friend David Livingstone's expeditions and acted as guardian to his children.

While bings, or waste tips, of used oil shale were transforming the landscape around West Calder, Young chose to live on the west coast, in the new suburb of Wemyss Bay. His home, Kelly House, burnt down in 1913 and is now the site of a caravan park. He is commemorated by a Gothic Revival monument in Inverkip churchyard.

# WEST LINTON
*Bettering themselves and their children*

By the middle of the nineteenth century, an estimated twenty-five thousand benevolent or friendly societies existed across Britain. They were a practical embodiment of the spirit of self-help that was encouraged by the laissez-faire economy – the alternative, should people without provision fall on hard times, was the workhouse. By paying a weekly fee of a few pence into a fund, members could draw some shillings a week if they were sick, or their families would receive a lump sum to provide a respectable burial.

Evangelicals had been promoting them since the late eighteenth century, as part of their campaign to isolate and destroy the moral and social evils – drunkenness, illiteracy, bad housing, lack of thrift – that they saw as besetting the poor. In West Linton, the Whipmen, or carters, of the village formed themselves into a benevolent society called the Whipmen of Linton, with the object of 'bettering themselves and their children'. They took advantage of a local horse fair to promote their fund-raising work, visiting the houses of the gentry to solicit subscriptions and providing games and sports for the populace. From 1803, the celebrations became known as the Whipman Play; the Play is now a festival lasting nine days, having been revived in 1931.

Transport was once important to Linton (the name was changed after the introduction of postal services, to distinguish it from East Linton in Lothian). Armies are said to have passed through it: Edward I of England on his way to Ayr in 1298; Sir John Comyn and Sir Simon Fraser of Neidpath en route to the Battle of Roslin four years later. The exiled Charles X of France, living at Holyrood, stayed at the Brig House Inn. Another visitor was Robert Burns*, a friend of the innkeeper. Finding him away on two occasions he inscribed a window with the words: 'Honest Graeme, aye the same, never to be found at hame!'

Drove roads going north/south and east/west cross at the village. Linton sheep, with their black faces and black legs, were hardy creatures, short of body and coarse of wool, but prized for the sweetness of their meat.

The Whipmen of Linton can be compared to the Incorporated Society of Whiplickers in St Andrews, Fife, although the latter was a later foundation (1872) and no longer exists. The elaborate designation of such institutions, together with the composition of long and largely bogus histories, was part of the game. There was a memory of the Elizabethan guild system here, and, like the old guilds, friendly societies were often based on real or imagined trades. They rarely succeeded in becoming incorporations, which would have allowed them to impose a closed shop and force everyone engaged in the trade in that area to become members. Instead, they had to compete on the benefits they offered, allowing members to come from other walks of life.

The Ancient Order of Free Gardeners, particularly popular in Lothian and Fife, emerged in the late seventeenth century. The Ancient Order of Foresters originated in Yorkshire in the early nineteenth century, as did The Loyal Order of Ancient Shepherds. They were joined by the Independent Order of Odd Fellows, the Druids Friendly Society (still in existence) and the Royal Antediluvian Order of Buffaloes, all marching beneath banners, accoutred with sashes, aprons, ribbons, cuffs and collars, and likely to impose initiation rituals on newcomers, in the tradition of the most successful self-help group of all – the Freemasons.

*See Mauchline, page 603*

# FURTHER READING

Anstey, Sandra (ed.), *R. S. Thomas, Selected Prose* (Seren, 1993).

Bailey, Brian, *The English Village Green* (Hale, 1985).

Barker, Katherine (ed.), *The Cerne Abbey Millennium Lectures* (Cerne Abbey Millennium Committee, 1988).

Beazley, E., *Madocks and the Wonder of Wales* (Faber, 1967).

Beckett, J. V., *A History of Laxton* (Basil Blackwell, 1989).

Beresford, Maurice and Hurst, John (eds.), *Deserted Medieval Villages* (Sutton, 1989).

Beresford, M. W. and Hurst, John, *English Heritage Book of Wharram Percy: Deserted Medieval Village* (Batsford, 1990).

Biddell, Barbara, *The Jolly Farmer? William Cobbett in Hampshire, 1804–1820* (Hampshire County Council, 1999).

Birrell, Jean, 'The Medieval English Forest', *Journal of Forest History 24, No. 2* (April 1980).

Blythe, Ronald, *Going to Meet George, and Other Outings* (Long Barn Books, 1999).

Brassley, Paul, Burchardt, Jeremy and Thompson, Lynne (eds.), *The English Countryside Between the Wars* (Boydell Press, 2006).

Brittain-Catlin, Timothy, *The English Parsonage in the Early Nineteenth Century* (Spire Books, 2008).

Brown, R. J., *English Village Architecture* (Robert Hale, 2004).

Cantor, Leonard, *The English Medieval Landscape* (Croom Helm, 1982).

Clifton-Taylor, Alec, *The Pattern of English Building* (Faber, 1972).

Cousins, Rodney, *Lincolnshire Building in the Mud and Stud Tradition* (Heritage Trust of Lincolnshire, 2000).

Crowther, Janice and Crowther, Peter (eds.), *The Diary of Robert Sharp of South Cave: Life in a Yorkshire Village 1812–1837* (Oxford University Press, 1997).

Darley, Gillian, *Villages of Vision* (Five Leaves, 2007).

Devine, T. M., *Clanship to Crofters' War* (Manchester University Press, 1994).

Dunlop, Jean, *The British Fisheries Society 1786–1893* (John Donald, 1977).

Dunmore, Richard, *This Noble Foundation* (Sir John Moore Foundation, 1992).

Evans, Eifion, *Daniel Rowland and the Great Evangelical Awakening in Wales* (The Banner of Truth Trust, 1985).

Fellows Jensen, Gillian, *The Vikings and their Victims: The Verdict of the Names* (Viking Society for Northern Research, 1995).

Fido, Martin and Skinner, Keith, *The Peasenhall Mystery* (Stroud, 1990).

Fitzpatrick, Kathleen, *Lady Henry Somerset* (Jonathan Cape, 1923).

Fletcher, Ronald, *The Akenham Burial Case* (Wildwood House, 1974).

Garnett, Edward, *The Story of the Calverley Murders: 23rd April 1605* (Calverley, 1991).

Garnett, Ronald, *Cooperation and the Owenite Socialist Communities in Britain, 1824–45* (Manchester University Press, 1972).

Gilbert, Edward, 'Brixworth and the English Basilica', *The Art Bulletin 47, No. 1* (March 1965).

Gloag, John, *Mr Loudon's England* (Oriel Press, 1970).

Gough, Richard, *The History of Myddle* (Caliban Books, 1979).

Gregory, D. L., *John Abel of Sarnesfield, Carpenter* (Caradoc and Severn Valley Field Club, 1980).

Grenier, Katherine, *Tourism and Identity in Scotland, 1770–1914: Creating Caledonia* (Ashgate, 2005).

Griffin, Emma, *England's Revelry* (Oxford University Press, 2005).

Griffiths, Clare, *Labour and the Countryside: the Politics Of Rural Britain, 1918–1939* (Oxford University Press, 2007).

Griffiths, Jenny and Griffiths, Mike, *The Mold Tragedy of 1869* (Gwasg Carreg Gwalch, 2001).

Hadfield, Alice, *The Chartist Land Company* (Square Edge Books, 2000).

Hanson, Harry, *The Coaching Life* (Manchester University Press, 1983).

Havinden, Michael, 'The Model Village' in Mingay, G. E. (ed.), *The Victorian Countryside* (Routledge and Kegan Paul, 1981).

Hobsbawm, Eric and Ranger, Terence (eds.), *The Invention of Tradition* (Cambridge University Press, 1992).

Hobsbawm, Eric and Rudé, George, *Captain Swing* (Pantheon Books, 1968).

Hoskins, W. G., *Devon* (David and Charles, 1972).

Howson, Brian, *Houses of Noble Poverty* (Bellevue Books, 1993).

Ingrams, Richard, *The Life and Adventures of William Cobbett* (HarperCollins, 2005).

Jewson, Norman, *By Chance I did Rove* (Earle and Ludlow, 1952).

Lambert, Richard, *The Universal Provider* (George G. Harrap and Co. Ltd, 1958).

MacKenzie, Osgood, *A Hundred Years in the Highlands* (London, 1921).

Macve, Jennifer, *The Hafod Landscape: An Illustrated History and Guide* (Hafod Trust, 2004).

Miers, Mary, *The Western Seaboard* (Rutland Press, 2008).

Podmore, Colin, *The Moravian Church in England, 1728–1760* (Clarendon Press, 1998).

Prince, Alison, *Kenneth Grahame: An Innocent in the Wild Wood* (Allison and Busby, 1994).

Pritchard, J. L., *Sir George Cayley* (Parrish, 1961).

Rowley, Trevor and Wood, John, *Deserted Villages* (Shire, 2000).

Rowley, Trevor, *The English Landscape in the Twentieth Century* (Hambledon Continuum, 2006).

Scott, S. H., *A Westmorland Village* (Archibald Constable and Co., 1904).

Shaw, Nellie, *Whiteway: A Colony in the Cotswolds* (1935).

Spufford, Margaret, *A Cambridgeshire Community: Chippenham from Settlement to Enclosure* (Leicester University Press, 1965).

Temple, Nigel, *John Nash and the Village Picturesque* (Alan Sutton, 1979).

Thacker, Joy, *Whiteway Colony: The Social History of a Tolstoyan Community* (Stroud, 1993).

Thirsk, Joan (ed.), *Agricultural Change: Policy and Practice 1500–1750* (Cambridge University Press, 1990).

Thirsk, Joan (ed.), *Rural England: an Illustrated History of the Landscape* (Oxford University Press, 2000).

Thurgood, Graham, 'Silver End Garden Village, 1926–32', *Thirties Society Journal 3* (1982).

Uglow, Jennifer, *Nature's Engraver: a Life of Thomas Bewick* (Faber, 2006).

Underdown, David, *Revel, Riot and Rebellion* (Clarendon, 1985).

Wailes, Rex, *The English Windmill* (Routledge and Kegan Paul, 1967).

Watkins, Alfred, *Early British Trackways, Moats, Mounds, Camps and Sites* (Simpkin, Marshall and Co., 1922).

Watts, Kenneth, *Snap: The History, Depopulation and Destruction of a Wiltshire Village* (Wiltshire County Council, 1989).

Waugh, W. T., 'Sir John Oldcastle', *The English Historical Review 20* (1905).

Weller, Philip, *The Hound of the Baskervilles: Hunting the Dartmoor Legend* (Devon Books, 2001).

Whitehead, John, *Sunk Island: The Land that Rose from the Humber* (Highgate, 1991).

Whyte, Ian and Whyte, Kathleen, *The Changing Scottish Landscape 1500–1800* (Routledge, 1991).

Wild, M. T., *Village England* (Tauris, 2004).

Williams, David, *The Rebecca Riots: A Study in Agrarian Discontent* (University of Wales Press, 1955).

Williams, Richard, *Limekilns and Limeburning* (Shire, 2004).

Williams-Ellis, Clough, *Cottage Building in Cob, Pisé, Chalk and Clay: A Renaissance* (Country Life, 1919).

Williams-Ellis, Clough, *Portmeirion* (C. Williams-Ellis, 1982).

# INDEX

Illustrations are in italics

Bainbridge (N. Yorks) 409–410
Baker, Thomas (Peasants' Revolt) 230, 231
Baldwin, Stanley, 1st Earl Baldwin of Bewdley 140, 366
Bale fire 445
Bale, John, Bishop of Ossory 225
Balfour, Lady Eve 240–241
Ballachulish (Highland) 531–532
balloon flights 194–195
Bamford, Lady Carole 316
bankers 52, 61, 62, 190, 509–510, 566, 611
Bannister, Roger 30
Bannockburn, battle of 543, 544
Banwell (Somerset) 10
Baptists 156, 210, 462
Bardwell (Suffolk) 212–214
bare-knuckle fighters 324
Bargate stone 146
Barings Bank 61, 62
Barnsley, Ernest and Sidney 350–351
barracks 582
Barrow upon Soar (Leics) 299–300
Barton Turf (Norfolk) 214–215
Barwick in Elmet (W. Yorks) 410
bats 182
Battle of Britain 132, 215
Bawden, Edward 90, 238
Bawdeswell (Norfolk) 215–216
Bayeux Tapestry 96, 97
beach huts 250, 275
Beattock (Dumfries & Galloway) 532–533
Beatty, William (surgeon) 629
Beaufort, Lady Margaret 312
Beaulieu (Hants) 93–94
*Beauties of England and Wales, The* (John Britton) 231, 459
beavers 123
Becket, Thomas à 111
Bede 97
Bedford, Francis Russell, 5th Duke of 119, 202, 203
Bedford Levels 259–260
beech hedges 606–607
Beer (Devon) 11
Beeswing (Dumfries & Galloway) 533–534
Bell, Adrian 265, 266
bell-ringing 75–76
Bemerton (Wilts) 12–13
Bentham, Jeremy 270
Bernera Barracks 582
Bersham (Denbighshire) 460–461
Berwick (E. Sussex) 94–95
Bethlehem (Carmarthenshire) 461–462
Betjeman, John 16, 69, 278, 357
Bewick, Thomas 419–420
Bible, The (Welsh translation) 459, 461
Biblical place names 461–462
Bibury (Glos) 300–301, *301*
bicycles 388, 547, 556, 591–592 *see also* cycling
Big Ben 493
Billingsley, William 496, 497
Birch, Colonel John 363
Birdsedge (W. Yorks) 411–412
bishop's palace (Abergwili) 458, 459
Black Death 171, 223, 360
black houses 579–580
Black, Joy 92
black poplars (tree) 295–296
Blackie, John Stuart 629
blacksmiths 585, 591
Blagdon (Somerset) 13–15
Blair, Robert (poet) 199

Blaise Hamlet (Glos) 302
Blanchland (Northd) 412–413
Blisland (Cornwall) 15–16, *15*
Bloomsbury Group 94, 95
Blue John 308, 309–310, *309*
Blunden, Edmund 155
boat building 469–470, 488 *see also* ship building
Bolster Festival 67–68, *67*
Bonchurch (I. of Wight) 95–96
Bonomi, Ignatius 393
Book of Deer 613
booksellers 90, 164
Boorde, Dr Andrew 128
Booth, William 216–217
Border shows 406
Borrow, George Henry 457, 514, 515
Borth (Ceredigion) 462–463
Bosham (W. Sussex) 96–97, *97*
Bossenden Wood, battle of 109
Boston, Lucy M. 244, 245
Boswell, James 571, 581, 582, 589
botanists 241, 246–247, 488, 555, 556, 557
Botley (Hants) 97–98
bottle-kicking 328–329
Bourne, George *see* Sturt, George
Bourne, Hilary and Joanna 108
Bowes (Co. Durham) 413–414
Bowmore (Islay) 534–535, *535*
Boxted (Essex) 216–217
boy scouts 425–426
Brabin, John 381
Braes, battle of 630–631
Braishfield (Hants) 98–99
Bramfield (Suffolk) 217–219
Brangwyn, Frank 105, 108
brass bands 306–307
bread societies 569
Breakspear, Nicholas (Pope Adrian IV) 164
Bredwardine (Herefordshire) 303
Brenan, Gerald 351, 364
Brent Knoll (Somerset) 17–18
breweries 390, 391, 477, 478, 563
Brewster, Colonel Humphrey 277
Briantspuddle (Dorset) 18–19
brickworks 196–197
bridges
    concrete 248–249
    medieval 178–180, *179*, 226–227, *226*, 429
    Roman 178, 434
    Tay 522–523
    Thomas Telford 548
    Thomas Telford's 490, 533, 582, 586
    toll 391, 392
Briggs, Raymond 108
Brithdir Mawr (Pembrokeshire) 464
Brixworth (Northants) 304–305
Broad Chalke (Wilts) 19–20
broadcloth 251, 252, 310
Broadway (Worcs) 305–306
Broadwood, John 614, 615
Brockley (Somerset) 20–21
Brompton (N. Yorks) 414–415
Bronze Age *see* prehistoric sites
Brooke, John & Sons 408
Broughton (Borders) 536
Broughton (Hants) 99–100
Brown, George Mackay 624, 625
Brown, Lancelot (Capability) 427–428
Browne, William (poet) 54
brownfield sites 470

Fiennes, Celia 78, 89
Filly Loo 8
film locations 584, 617 *see also* television and radio
    series
film making 172–174
Findhorn Ecovillage (Moray) 570–571
Findon (Aberdeenshire) 571–572
Findon (W. Sussex) 114–115
finnan haddie 571–572
Fintry (Stirling) 572–573
Finzi, Gerald 92–93
fire brigades 324–325, 325
First World War 56, 167–168, 562–563, 583, 583
fish 278–279, 418–419, 469, 571–572
fishing industry 63–64, 551, 584–585, 598, 616, 631 *see also*
    fly-fishing
Flash (Staffs) 323–324
Fleming, Robert 190
Flemish communities 252, 283
Flemming, Ian 139–140, 583
Fletcher-Watson, James 216
flint 148
floods 320 *see also* coastal erosion
flounder 616–617
fly-fishing 99–100, 300, 311, 427
Fobbing (Essex) 230–231
Fochabers (Moray) 573–574
folk music 272, 351, 379, 395–396, 411–412 *see also* Scottish
    dance music
Folkingham (Lincs) 231–232
folklore 131–132, 242 *see also* festivals
foot-and-mouth disease 423–424
football 120, 144, 236, 328–329, 375, 406
Forbes-Leith, Sir Alexander 575, 576
Ford (Northd) 421–422
Fordingbridge (Hants) 124
Fordwich (Kent) 115–116, 115
Forest of Arden 339
foresters 339, 409, 409, 638–639
forests and woodlands 20–21, 333–334, 347, 409
forgery 324
Forncett (Norfolk) 232–233
Forster, E. M. 311
Forster family 412
Forsyth, Bill 617
fortified villages 392
Fortingall (Perth & Kinross) 574–575
fossils 10, 81, 299, 551
Fothergill, Matt 311
Fox, George 393
fox hunting 35, 298, 380
Framsden (Suffolk) 233–234
Free Church 576–577
Freemasons 612, 639
Fressingfield (Suffolk) 234–235
friendly societies 638, 639
Frosse, Ulrich 456
Fulneck (W. Yorks) 422–423
fund raising 73–75, 113–114, 325, 334, 335
Furnace (Ceredigion) 479–480
furniture makers 350–351
Fyvie (Aberdeenshire) 575–576

Gaelic language 566, 567, 577, 613
Gairloch, Francis MacKenzie, 5th Baron of 600
Gairloch (Highland) 576–577
Galtrigill (Skye) 578
gang crimes 315, 342, 540–541
gaols 231 *see also* lock-ups
garages and petrol stations 166–167

garden villages 267, 563
Gardiner, William 262, 263
Garenin (Lewis) 579–580, 579
Garth mountain 507
Gascoigne, George 35
Gatehouse of Fleet (Dumfries & Galloway) 581–582
Gatsonides, Maurice 26
Gatton (Surrey) 116–117
Gatwick (W. Sussex) 117–118
gavelkind 102–103
Geddington (Northants) 324–325
Gedney (Lincs) 235–236
gentrification 43, 71–72
geologists 544–545, 553, 618
Georgeham (Devon) 37–38
Gerrards Cross (Bucks) 176–177
Giant Hill 22
giants 67, 68, 389–390
Gibbs, George 82
Gibbs, J. Arthur 345
Gilbert, Thomas (reformer) 66
Gildeborne, William 231
Gill, Eric 19, 56, 107
Gilpin, Rev. William 488
Gimson, Ernest 33, 350, 351
Glasgow Boys 549
Glastonbury, Abbot of 18, 62
Glastonbury Festival 62–63
Glen Calvie (Highland) 550
Glendower, Owen 468
Glenelg (Highland) 582–583
Glenfinnan (Highland) 584–585
Glyn Dŵr, Owain 468
Glynde (E. Sussex) 118–120
Godolphin Cross (Cornwall) 38–39
Godolphin family 38–39
Godstone (Surrey) 120
Godwick (Norfolk) 237–238, 237
Golby, Rupert 316
gold mines 504, 514
Golden Valley 310
Goldsmith, Oliver 191, 282, 313
golf 633, 634
gooseberries 374–375
Gordon, Alexander Gordon, 4th Duke of 573–574, 607,
    608, 632
Gosse, Edmund 95
gossips 255
Goudhurst (Kent) 121
Gough Map 221, 439
Gough, Richard 226, 342
Grahame, Kenneth 169–170
granite 60–61
Grant, Duncan 94
Grant, Sir Archibald 609
graveyards 199, 423
Gray, Thomas 75, 198, 199
Great Bardfield (Essex) 238–239
Great Bentley (Essex) 239–240
Great Bookham (Surrey) 121–122
Great Explosion (Faversham) 147
Great Ouse, River 178, 179, 244
Great Tew (Oxon) 177–178
Great Work (tin mine) 38
Great Wyrley (Staffs) 326–327
green villages 376–377, 404, 570–571
greenbelts 181–182
Greene, Graham 173
Greg, Samuel 396, 397
Gregor, William 30–31

piano makers 615
Pictish stones 605, *605*, 608, 622
Picts 523, 537, 604, 613
Picturesque 188, 189, 223, 302, 322, 472–473, 488, 564, 607
Piercebridge (Co. Durham) 433–434
pilchards 63–64
pilgrimages 80, 150, 491, 501, 502, 513, 601
Pilton (Somerset) 62–63
pinfolds 292–293
pisé de terre 32, 33, 203
pit disasters 314, 457–458
Pitfour, James Ferguson, 3d Laird of 613
Pitt-Rivers, Augustus Henry Lane-Fox 36–37
Place, Francis 112
Plack and Penny Day 543
planning laws 57, 181–182, 250, 338, 464
plastic bags 58
Plot, Robert 136
ploughs 77, 144, 203, 262, 545, 609
Plush (Dorset) 411
pneumatic tyres 555, 556
Polish migrants 228, 236
ponds 7–8, 131
Pooley Bridge (Cumbria) 394–395
Poor Laws 66, 129, 257, 291
poorhouses *see* workhouses
Pope Adrian IV (Nicholas Breakspear) 164
Pope, Alexander 300
poplar, black (tree) 295–296
porcelain *see* potteries
Port of Ness (Lewis) 619
Port Sunlight (Merseyside) 398
Portmeirion (Merionethshire) 502–503, *502*
Portscatho (Cornwall) 63–64
Posidonius 69
post boxes 46, 47
Post Office 48, 234
potteries 476–477, 496–497
Poundbury (Dorset) 338
pounds, animal 292–293
poverty 171–172, 183, 185–186, 193–194, 355
Prayer Book Rebellion 70–71
Pre-Raphaelites 140, 153, 193
prehistoric bones 10
prehistoric sites 8–9, 99, 434–435, 510–511, 527, 528, 539, 592–593, 593–594, 629
Premonstratensians 412 *see also* Cistercians
Presley, Elvis 601, 602
prisons 232 *see also* lock-ups
public houses 36–37, 186–187, 390, 391
Puddletown (Dorset) 64–65
Pugin, A. W. N. 66
Pulk, Jim 131
pumps *150*, 151
Pumpsaint (Carmarthenshire) 503–504
Purbeck stone 81
Puritans 34, 276, 458, 489, 504, 505
Puttenham (Surrey) 138–139

Quakers 53, 70, 128, 184, 302, 344, 393, 411, 429–431, 636
Quarles, John 313
Quarriers Village (Renfrewshire) 620
Quarry Bank Mill 396, 397
Queen's Head (Newton) 187
Queenwood (Hants) 112–113
Quenington (Glos) 345–346
Quennell, Charles Henry Bourne 266, 267
quintains 135–136, *135*
Quintinshill rail disaster 109

rabbit farming 73
race relations 326
Radwinter (Essex) 264–265
Raglan (Monmouthshire) 504–505
Raikes, Robert 344
railways
    construction 506, 584
    electric 127
    impact on village development 176, 375, 379, 492, 533, 584–585
    industrial 635, *635*
    model 91–92
    Quintinshill rail disaster 109
    stations 68, 105, 533, 633–634, *634*
    and tourism 68–69, 187, 478–479, 633, *634*
rambling 180
Rampisham (Dorset) 66–67
Ravilious, Eric 90, 238
Rayner, Horace 149
Rebecca riots 474–475
rectories 66–67, 142
Reculver (Kent) 139–140
Red Baron 83
Red Colin 531, 532
Redisham (Suffolk) 265–266
Religious Society of Friends *see* Quakers
remotest villages 590–591, 593–594
renewable energy 456, 572–573
Revelstoke, Edward Baring, 1st Lord 61, 62
Ricardo, Halsey 18
Richmond Park 106
Ring, The (dairy farm) 18, 19
riots
    Battle of The Braes 630–631
    Chartist 498–499
    enclosure 232–233, 313
    Mold 482–483
    Nantyglo ironworks 498
    Peasants' Revolt (1381) 230–231
    Prayer Book Rebellion 70–71
    Rebecca 474–475
    Swing 50, 51, 129
Ritchie, Lady Anne Isabella Thackeray 200
RNLI 53
road markings 387–388 *see also* speed cameras
roads
    Roman 111, 221–222, 434, 465
    Scottish 522, 528, 632
    turnpike 222, 391, 474, 490
Robert, Count of Mortain 164
Robert, the Bruce 377, 511, 609, 635
Robertson Scott, J. W. 182–183
Robinson, Fletcher 49
Rockingham (Northants) 347–348
Rogers, Thorold 170
Roman
    amphitheatres 612
    cemeteries 137
    concrete 248
    forts 137, 140, 410, 433, 434, 504, 595–596, 612
    mines 308, 375, 504
    roads 111, 221–222, 434, 465
    towns 465
    villas 45–46, 99, 133, 435
Rosemarkie (Highland) 621–622, *621*
Rossetti, Dante Gabriel 154
Rottingdean (E. Sussex) 140–141
Rowland, Daniel 472, 491–492
Rowntree, Frederick 184
Rowntree, Joseph 429, 430, 431

# ACKNOWLEDGEMENTS

I have had such a happy time visiting the villages in this book that I ought to begin by thanking their residents. I don't know the name of the man who was walking his dog on the evening that I tried to get into Ilmington church to inspect the Apple Map, but his recommendation to pick some of the plums from the trees hanging over the churchyard wall was inspired; at the end of a long day, plums – in that wonderful year for soft fruit – were exactly what I needed to fortify myself for the journey home. Equally, I am grateful to the individual who approached me in Sampford Courtenay and suggested I should see Honeychurch, down the road. The motorboat onto which I leapt from the pier at Mallaig, before I slithered onto the seaweedy rocks of the Knoydart peninsula and waited for a Land Rover to take me to Inverie, had really been chartered to whisk a gentleman celebrating his fiftieth birthday with his friends to dinner, along the coast at Glenelg: thank you for diverting to carry me across the mouth of Loch Nevis, as well as your company and the beer while we were crossing. People who I did not previously know have given me their time and lent me their books. If any member of a Neighbourhood Watch was disconcerted to see an unfamiliar man taking a close interest in the surroundings, I apologise for my nosiness; I was casing the architecture, not the antiques.

I have discussed villages with many friends, to the point, no doubt, that they have dreaded the subject coming up. I am particularly grateful for the help and advice given to me by Stephen Davies in Kent and Richard and Bridget Sudworth in Herefordshire, as well as Roy Strong in the same county. Mary Miers provided the key to much of Scotland, her knowledge of ferry crossings being almost as encyclopaedic as that of topography. Kylie O'Brien and Fiona Temple have expertly edited some of the journalism I wrote along the way.

I am grateful to *Country Life* for releasing me into the environment as Editor at Large, and to the present Editor, Mark Hedges, for encouragement to roam at will.

At Bloomsbury, sense has been made of the loose, baggy monster I have brought back by my editor Richard Atkinson, abetted by Rachael Oakden, Natalie Hunt and Xa Shaw Stewart. I would also like to thank Jude Drake. My agent Zoe Pagnamenta has boosted morale, while lending a critical eye.

Inevitably, a book about villages throughout Britain has meant that an amount of time – increasing towards the deadline – has been spent visiting them. Sometimes I was lucky enough to do this with my wife Naomi and three boys, William, Johnny and Charlie, but more often than not the demands of the timetable have meant that, in horsey parlance, I had to kick on; and then there were the hours when I was stabled in various libraries. Throughout it all, their support and encouragement have kept me going: without them, this book – nay, this author – could hardly exist.